THE HEBREW
SCRIPTURES

BOOKS BY SAMUEL SANDMEL

A JEWISH UNDERSTANDING OF THE NEW TESTAMENT
PHILO'S PLACE IN JUDAISM
THE GENIUS OF PAUL
WE JEWS AND JESUS
HEROD: PROFILE OF A TYRANT
WE JEWS AND YOU CHRISTIANS: AN INQUIRY INTO ATTITUDES
THE FIRST CHRISTIAN CENTURY IN JUDAISM AND CHRISTIANITY
THE SEVERAL ISRAELS
TWO LIVING TRADITIONS
THE ENJOYMENT OF SCRIPTURE
ALONE ATOP THE MOUNTAIN (*A NOVEL*)
CO-AUTHOR: ECUMENICAL INTRODUCTIONS TO THE BOOKS OF
     THE BIBLE
A LITTLE BOOK ON RELIGION (FOR PEOPLE WHO ARE NOT RELIGIOUS)
WHEN A JEW AND CHRISTIAN MARRY
JUDAISM AND CHRISTIAN BEGINNINGS
EDITOR: OLD TESTAMENT ISSUES
GENERAL EDITOR: THE NEW ENGLISH BIBLE WITH THE
     APOCRYPHA: OXFORD STUDY EDITION

THE HEBREW SCRIPTURES

AN

INTRODUCTION
TO THEIR LITERATURE AND
RELIGIOUS IDEAS

BY

SAMUEL SANDMEL

PROVOST, HEBREW UNION COLLEGE
JEWISH INSTITUTE OF RELIGION

NEW YORK · *OXFORD UNIVERSITY PRESS* · *1978*

Grateful acknowledgment is made to the publisher
for permission to reprint the poem on page 237
from H. H. Rowley, *The Relevance of Apocalyptic*,
London: Lutterworth Press, 1944, and Harper &
Row, Publishers.

Library of Congress Cataloging in Publication Data

Sandmel, Samuel.
  The Hebrew Scriptures.

  First published in 1963.
  Bibliography: p.
  Includes index.
    1.   Bible. O.T.—Introductions.   I.   Title.
BS1140.2.S2   1978   221.6   77-25830
ISBN 0-19-502369-2

Printed in the United States of America

TO MY TEACHER

Dr. Julian Morgenstern

Preface

THIS book is addressed to the beginner, not the scholar. It is a nontechnical introduction, nontechnical in the sense that when words or terms in the biblical Hebrew are used, they are invariably explained, and an introduction in the sense that it assumes little or no previous knowledge on the part of the reader. Yet I have tried not to write down, nor to set before the reader, a mere array of superficialities. Perhaps the aim of the book might be put in this way: to acquaint the reader who goes on to become a biblical scholar in the fullest technical sense with basic material that he will not have to unlearn. In no sense is this book a substitute for the Bible, and the student who has read only this book has scarcely read Scripture. This is a tool, and only a tool. The serious study of Scripture necessarily involves the use of a biblical atlas, a biblical encyclopedia, and commentaries on each of the component books. Indeed, the use of these is ultimately inescapable; for the beginning stage, this book must include aspects of all of these, but obviously without completeness.

I have read articles and books that have tantalized me by referring to a biblical passage by the book, chapter, and verse (e.g. Ex. 35.15) without reproducing the content. When I have been on a train or a bus and not had Scripture with me, many such allusions and references have been lost on me. To spare the reader this annoyance, I have deliberately designed this book so that the text (as distinct from the footnotes) is clear without immediate recourse to Scripture. This seems to me a sensible procedure, so long as the reader does not mistakenly believe that my paraphrase of a passage makes it either unnecessary or undesirable to consult Scripture itself. To repeat, this book is in no sense a substitute for the Bible.

Of the good translations that exist, the Revised Standard Version (1946) is more reliable than the King James for two reasons. First, the English words, terms, and usages in the King James (a translation made between 1604 and 1611) have undergone changes of meaning, with the result that the Revised Standard Version English conforms to the English of our day, as the King James does not. Second, through the accumulation of some 340 years of scholarship, a greater and more accurate store of information was available to the men who made the Revised Standard Version. Yet while the R.S.V. is more reliable, its neutral, flat language makes it less appealing in majesty and poetic expression than the King James. Indeed, one must attribute to the King James the quality of being a classic in *English* literature, even though it is deficient as a translation suitable for our day. The New English Bible (1970) is a much more fluent translation than the Revised Standard Version, being marked by the effort to translate ideas rather than words or phrases. One who knows Hebrew and who tries to retranslate could readily reconstruct the Hebrew original from the Revised Standard Version, but so relatively free is the New English Bible that such reconstruction would not so readily follow. For the student, the R.S.V. is excellent; for the reader wishing to grasp the sense and the tone, the New English Bible is to be commended. The Oxford Annotated Bible is an edition of the R.S.V. with explanatory footnotes, maps, and useful essays; the Oxford Study Edition of the New English Bible is a quite similar work. Both these editions can be exceedingly useful to the student. A sensible procedure is for the student to use the R.S.V. or N.E.B. for the sense, but the King James for an exalted though less reliable, translation.

My task would have been easier if I had used one of these or other extant translations, rather than supplying my own, as I have done. In reality, my renderings are not translations as much as they are paraphrases. A translation inevitably hews so close to a word-for-word correspondence that idioms, the life-blood of language, are used all too seldom. The intent of my paraphrases is to be clearer than any translation can hope to be. Where textual problems occur in the Hebrew, the translator is bound to render the original without correction; he must also translate the untranslatable passages. I have felt free to confess that I cannot translate certain passages and I have left them untranslated—R.S.V. or K.J. at these points are elaborate or ingenious guesses. I have also translated the text after altering it, in those cases where alteration is indicated.

In illustration of the differences between translation and para-

phrase, a well-known verse can be useful. Psalm 23.1 runs as follows
in the K.J. and R.S.V.: "The Lord is my shepherd, I shall not want."
I paraphrase it: "Yahve is my shepherd; I lack nothing."

The attention of the reader is invited first to the tenses. K.J.
and R.S.V. use the future; I use the present. The fact is that in
biblical Hebrew a verb form lacks a time factor in itself, being
limited to asserting whether the action is complete (perfect) or
incomplete (imperfect). The translator into English frequently has
the problem of having to decide what tense to choose for transmitting
the biblical intent. Often the best rendering of an imperfect is by
the English future, but often an English present conveys the intent
more precisely. Here, the intent is best expressed in the English
present. The Hebrew says simply, *I do not lack.* Three centuries ago
want was a direct synonym for *lack*; today it means *wish.* Thus, I
want money no longer means, I *lack* money; it means I *wish* it. But
direct translation, *I do not lack,* seems to me wooden by comparison
with, *I lack nothing.* This last word is not stated in the Hebrew. A
translator would be wrong to resort to paraphrase; a clarifier would
be wrong not to.

As to my use of Yahve, the issue is a complicated one. If Yahve
is a *name*, then The Lord is wrong; if Yahve is, rather, a *title*, then
The Lord is correct, and the rendering Yahve ill-advised. The fact
is that Yahve was originally the name of Israel's special deity. In
time Yahve was conceived of as the one and only Deity of the
universe, and hence, to complicate matters further, the tradition
arose among Jews of never pronouncing the name Yahve; *adonoi*
is its substitute. Indeed some very traditional Jews carry the tradition into English by spelling God "G-d." I have usually employed the
form Yahve rather than Lord because I feel that the true biblical
tone is reproduced better thereby. I would find it repugnant to use
the form Yahve in modern religious worship, but I find its usage
inescapable in a book designed to help in the *study* of Scripture.

When I first began to write this book, the basic objective was to
set before the reader the richness of the biblical materials. Yet,
another objective was to draw on those insights of modern critical
scholarship which seemed to me capable of enhancing that richness.
As I proceeded, there were the usual problems of inclusion and
omission and of proportion and emphasis. These were more acute
respecting the critical scholarship than of the biblical literature
itself, for many reasons but chiefly because of the great proliferation
of biblical studies in recent decades. An endless flow of new theories
and imaginative treatments of quite minor matters has made, and
makes, its way into the professional journals. The quantity of

biblical scholarship, then, has constituted a problem: how much should an author convey to his reader?

Again, whenever there is a striking archeological discovery, as recently at Ebla, in due course there may, or may not, emerge new materials which may affect the understanding of the Bible. An unhappy by-product in biblical archeology has been that of premature judgment, which the public press disseminates even before scholars have sifted the materials with good care and responsibility. A key question, often difficult to answer, is this: does a particular archeological discovery enlighten the Bible itself, or only the backgrounds or setting of the Bible? That is, an archeological discovery can be exciting in its own terms but not significantly relevant to the Bible itself. The scholarly study of the Bible has by now been going on for at least two hundred years; in the past one hundred the purely literary studies, as distinct from the contributions of archeology, has had little that is new in the sense that archeology produces something strikingly new. Rather, scholars have refined older theories or suggested some new modes of study, and some of these new modes have become something of a "fad" for a few years, before giving way to some other innovative fad. For example, there have been two emphases in biblical scholarship in the past two decades, very little of which is directly reflected in this book. One is called "Form Criticism." The footnote on p. 243 mentions Hermann Günkel, a very great scholar. I did not there mention one aspect of his contribution to biblical scholarship, namely, his adaptation of techniques used in studies in folklore to the study of the Bible. This technique is Form Criticism. In brief, when in folklore or in the Bible there are different versions of the same tale, or episode, or law, a comparison of the form as it appears in the different versions can lead to some reasonable inferences. In Genesis 27.42-43 it is related that the patriarch Jacob fled from home out of fear of vengeance on the part of his brother Esau; in Genesis 26.34-35; 27.46, the patriarch leaves home at the behest of his mother lest he, like his brother Esau, marry a local girl outside the fold. The deliberate change of motivation would appear to have a certain immediate significance; that the patriarch Jacob must not marry outside the clan is possibly related to materials found in Nehemiah 13.23-27, where such marriages are thoroughly opposed. The first account of Jacob's flight seems much, much older and free of direct relationship to known specific events or periods in biblical history, the second much younger and able to be related to other biblical materials. In Gunkel's study of Genesis he approached the question of the historical backgrounds of the differences which the study of forms disclosed by raising the question, "Under what historical circumstances do these differing versions appear to be written?" (He used the phrase *Sitz im Leben*, "real-life situation," as the clue to the historical setting or settings which the study of the forms presumably disclosed.) Form Criticism had come to dominate New Testament scholarship in the late twenties; it dominated for about thirty-five years. As Form Criticism was beginning to recede from New Testament scholarship, it became a strong force, quite dominant, in Old Testament scholarship, and seems still to dominate it.

But all too often so-called "form critical" studies have lacked the requisite controls, with the by-product that Form Criticism all too often becomes a quite subjective approach. Indeed, from time to time studies have been published which deal not with different versions of the same or a similar item, but just one single item— Form Criticism by axiom demands that there be a minimum of two examples!—and become merely a speculation on the background of that item.

But beyond the deficit of often being sheerest speculation, form critical studies can represent desperate efforts to explain the unexplainable. For all that biblical scholars can and do know about the Bible, the fact is that more is unknown than is known. What is better, to admit that we do not know, or to speculate as if the unknowable can be known? Moreover, the question that is always of the essence is this, what contribution is being made to understand the Bible itself?

Related to Form Criticism is a younger approach which is often called Tradition History. It is an inquiry into the manner in which biblical traditions, or complexes of tradition, were transmitted. In such studies, when restraint exists, Tradition History can illuminate many things; but when there is no restraint, then sheer subjectivity enters in. Some such published endeavors trespass far beyond the convincing evidence. A view often encountered, for example, is that the Sinai episode comes from a body of tradition quite different from the Exodus experience. Possibly this is so; probably it is wrong. But whether right or wrong, the Bible presents the Sinai episode as deeply and fully related to the Exodus.

Were I persuaded that recent scholarship greatly impinges on what I wrote here some twenty years ago, then I would have wanted to re-cast substantial portions of it. I have not found that need, though I have tried carefully to consider it. Perhaps for other books on the Bible, Form Criticism and Tradition History would be more significant than they seem to me to be for this book. In a word, this book is primarily about the Bible and not primarily about biblical scholarship.

The thrust of modern critical scholarship, especially that on the historical books, might be more fully set forth than what appears on pages 332-33. In those pages I describe how the great scholar Julius Wellhausen tried to give a basic solution to the historical problems presented in the biblical matters. Perhaps, though, an amplified statement might here be helpful. To that end, we begin here with the biblical view of biblical history. According to the Bible, prior to the emergence of the Hebrews, in the person of Abraham, there took place the creation of the world, and of mankind. Ten generations after Adam there emerged Noah, during whose time a world flood wiped out all but Noah and his family. From Noah's children the world was repopulated. The inhabitants of Africa were descended from the second son, Ham, and of the Grecian islands from the youngest, Japheth. From the oldest son Shem were descended the inhabitants of Asia, eastward of Palestine. Abraham, a descendant of Shem, was the tenth generation from Noah. Abraham had several children. From Hagar there was born Ishmael; from Keturah (Gen. 25) there were born six sons, progenitors of peoples kindred to the Hebrews. From Sarah there was born Isaac, who, in the biblical perspective, is the significant child, for he is the second of a direct line of three ancestral patriarchs. To Isaac were born two sons, Esau and Jacob; the direct line of descent of the Hebrews was through Jacob, the third of the ancestral patriarchs. That is, there were peoples kindred to the Hebrews who were descended from Abraham and Isaac, and, indeed, there were descended from the nephew of Abraham, Lot, even more kindred peoples, namely the Ammonites and the Moabites. There were, then, direct descendants and related collateral peoples.

To Jacob were born twelve sons, through whose birth we end the line of the three single patriarchs; the sons of Jacob are the ancestors of the twelve tribes who instituted the "Children of Israel." In due course, in connection with Jacob's son Joseph, Jacob/Israel and his family, at that time numbering seventy souls, settled in Egypt.

The Israelites increased in numbers, and underwent slavery in Egypt, to be released by the Deity through Moses, who was to lead them through the Wilderness to Canaan. That land had been divinely promised to Abraham, but it was to become the property of his preferred descendants only after the Wilderness period. At Sinai the Deity revealed Himself and concluded a collective covenant with the people. He revealed Laws to Moses pertaining to many

matters, including the construction of a portable sanctuary and of
sacred vessels for use in it. Instructions were then given for a
sacrificial system, to be administered by priests, whose ancestor was
Aaron, the brother of Moses; Moses installed Aaron in the hereditary
office of High Priest. Other laws were recorded, and it was now time
to move on from Sinai. Twelve spies were sent to scout out the land
of Canaan; on their return two reported favorably, but ten were
fearful that an Israelite invasion could not succeed. The people
sided with the ten. As a consequence, the generation of the Wilderness was not to enter the Holy Land, but had to continue wandering
to fill out the period of forty years; by that time a new generation,
worthy of entering the land, would have been born and grown to
maturity.

At the end of the period, Moses handed the leadership on to
Joshua and then passed away. Under Joshua the land of Canaan
was conquered and the tribes given the areas allotted to them. Next
came the age of the Judges, the leaders who freed certain of the
tribes from foreign domination, this prior to the emergence of
monarchy in Israel in the person of Saul and thereafter in David.
Such, in greatest brevity, is the biblical view of early biblical history.

In the eighteenth century, rationalists and deists challenged
the historical correctness of the claims of Christendom as expressed
in Scripture. The Christian reply was to try to demonstrate the
correctness of Christian claims, this through scholarly rather than
doctrinal demonstration. As a part of this Christian response, the
Pentateuch was analyzed with respect to its component sources,
since the historian must always begin with sources. In this context
there arose the view of Astruc (p. 329), who wrote of two sources,
Yahwist and Elohist, that Moses seemed to him to have utilized.
What for a time persisted of Astruc was his theory of the two
sources; in due course this theory, that it was Moses who had made
use of these two sources, was progressively abandoned; someone
other than and later than Moses had used the two sources. In time
a third source, Deuteronomy, was set forth, and then the Elohist
source was divided by scholars into a younger source, P, and the
older source, the Elohist. Scholars then assigned probable dates to
the sources. From the chronological sequence of these sources, once
dates were allotted to them, and from literature outside the
Pentateuch, such as the Prophets and Psalms, there arose the effort
of Wellhausen to set forth an unassailable history of the Hebrews
designed to supplant the fallible biblical view of its history. For
example, as mentioned in the text, the institution of priesthood and
of systematic cult worship were not truly to be ascribed to the very

early Wilderness period, but instead to the very late post-exilic period. In general, the events related in the Pentateuch were to become viewed in modern scholarship as "pre-history," with actual history beginning only in the period of the Judges. The conquest under Joshua too was ascribed to legend; indeed, the view came to arise that a collective Israel arose only after monarchy developed, and not in pre-Exodus Egypt. A loose confederation, called an amphyctyony (p. 370), bound the related tribes to each other in the period of the Judges. The point is that modern scholarship had tried to provide a supposedly tenable reconstruction of Hebrew history, to correct or supplant the supposedly untenable presentation in and by the Bible.

A rather generous measure of such scholarly reconstruction of Hebrew history is reflected in various parts of the book. I have not, however, conceived my task to be that of the historian, and for that reason, history as such is not emphasized in this book, as I explain on p. 8. I must say, however, that I grow increasingly skeptical of the success of the scholarly effort, exemplified in the peerless Julius Wellhausen, to supplant the untenable history in the Bible with a supposedly tenable history. I should record that it is only the general pattern of Wellhausen's reconstruction that appeals to me, but this is not the case with innumerable efforts in recent times in matters of detail. Hence, I am still content with my focus, deliberately chosen, on religious ideas and on literary values as the thrust of this volume.

In the years since writing this book, I have discovered to my dismay an increasing neglect of the Bible as worthy literature on the part of professional scholars. In an essay, "The Bible as Literature," I stated that modern scholarship has approached the Bible from almost every standpoint except that it is literature. My book, *The Enjoyment of Scripture* (Oxford University Press, 1972, 1974), sets forth in compass much briefer than here the aspects of Scripture that seem to me to have high literary quality. To my intense gratification, there has been in recent years a rising interest among biblical scholars in "Rhetoric and Scripture," and the literary qualities are now being inquired into by competent scholars with gratifying emphasis and worthy results.

The priorities I have chosen, and adhere to, seem to me to need some clear statement. In the matter of priority, the question of history, whether traditional or modern critical, is not better than third. The issue of the understanding of the religious ideas is clearly a higher priority than that of history, but it too is not the first priority. The first priority is the knowledge of the contents, and an assimilation of the great literary heritage. Devoted as I am to modern biblical scholarship, and insistent as I am on its importance, I should want to state as emphatically as I can that biblical scholarship is not nearly as important as the Bible itself.

And, finally, I have not considered it to be my task in this book to appraise the value or significance of the Hebrew Scriptures for our own day. That is properly the task of the theologian rather than the historian.

SAMUEL SANDMEL
Cincinnati, Ohio
January 1978

Acknowledgments

THE STEPS which include the assembly of material, the handwritten manuscript, the typed script, and the printed book involve the author but also those who assist him. The staffs of the Hebrew Union College Libraries, Cincinnati and New York, have been courteously helpful. Mrs. Helen Lederer has patiently transformed a penned script into a typed version, and the greatly emended typescripts into a final typescript. My secretary, Mrs. Sam November, has helped me, with her rare skills, in countless ways.

Three students, Rabbi Joseph Karasick, the Rev. Mr. Hugh Haggard, and Mr. Allen Kaplan, have helped me check the references to Scripture; they are not, however, responsible for any errors that may remain. For the preparation of the Subject Index I am grateful to Mr. Michael Abraham, and for the preparation of the Index of Scriptural Citations, to the Reverend Hugh E. Haggard.

Dr. Nelson Glueck, the President of the Hebrew Union College–Jewish Institute of Religion, has graciously made available to me, as to other faculty members, the assistance mentioned above. Mrs. Charles (Terry) Kroloff won my gratitude and admiration for her editorial assistance in matters of style and clarity.

Miss Bridget Gellert and Miss Judith Hillery of Alfred A. Knopf, Inc., have both been unfailingly co-operative, sympathetic, and gracious.

A new printing makes it possible to correct certain errors to which scholars have invited my attention. I here express my gratitude to them, and principally to Professor William F. Stinespring of Duke University. In any book where chapter and verse entail Arabic numerals, the opportunities for inadvertent mistake are abundant, as are uncaught typographical errors. I would welcome having my notice drawn to any residual errors.

Contents

CONTENTS

Maps

BY THEODORE R. MILLER

A Brief Chronological Chart

The Wilderness period	
The Patriarchal Age	Prehistory
The Exodus	

Moses and Joshua	±1325—1250
Conquest and Settlement	±1250—1002

The Monarchy

David (Hebron period)	1002—995
(Jerusalem period)	995—962
Solomon	962—922

The Divided Kingdom

Israel		Judah	
Jeroboam	922—901	Rehoboam	922—915
		Abijam	915—913
		Asa	913—873
Nadab	901—900		
Baasha	900—877		
Elah	877—876		
Zimri	876		
Omri	876—869	Jehosaphat	873—849
Ahab	869—850		
Ahaziah	850—849		
Joram	849—842	Joram	849—842
		Ahaziah	842
Jehu	842—815	Athaliah	842—837
Joahaz	815—801	Jehoash	837—800

Israel		Judah	
Joash	801—786	Amaziah	800—783
Jeroboam	786—746		
Zechariah	746	Uzziah	783—742
Shallum	746	Jotham	742—735
Menahem	745—738		
Pekahiah	738—737	Ahaz	735—715
Pekah	737—732		
Hoshea	732—724		
Final Assyrian			
Conquest	722/721	Hezekiah	715—687
		Manasseh	687—642
		Amon	642—640
		Josiah	640—608
		Jehoahaz II	608
		Jehoiakim	608—597
		Jehoiachin	597
		Zedekiah	596—586
		Final Babylonian	
		Conquest	586

Babylonian Exile	586—520±
Haggai and Zechariah	520—516
Fall of Jerusalem	485
Nehemiah	445—433
Ezra	398
Final Greek Conquest	320
Maccabean Revolt	168—165

Abbreviations

Amos	AMOS	Hag.	HAGGAI	Nah.	NAHUM
Chron.	CHRONICLES	Hos.	HOSEA	Neh.	NEHEMIAH
Dan.	DANIEL	Isa.	ISAIAH	Num.	NUMBERS
Deut.	DEUTERONOMY	Jer.	JEREMIAH	Obad.	OBADIAH
Eccles.	ECCLESIASTES	Josh.	JOSHUA	Prov.	PROVERBS
Exod.	EXODUS	Judg.	JUDGES	Ps.	PSALMS
Ezra	EZRA	Lam.	LAMENTATIONS	Sam.	SAMUEL
Ezek.	EZEKIEL	Lev.	LEVITICUS	Zech.	ZECHARIAH
Gen.	GENESIS	Mal.	MALACHI	Zeph.	ZEPHANIAH
Hab.	HABAKKUK	Mic.	MICAH		

NOTE: Where biblical passages are reproduced, an asterisk (*) indicates that the English translation given is based on an emended Hebrew text, rather than on the traditional text. The general bases of such emendations are given on pages 16–17. A dash, or series of dashes indicates an untranslatable word or verse.

THE TRANSLITERATION of Hebrew words into the English alphabet has been simplified. The person who knows no Hebrew would find scientific transliteration mystifying. I have tried to avoid presenting strange spellings of well-known words or names, and hence I have been deliberately inconsistent. Two consonants might be noted: the sign ʻ represents the *ʻayyin* and the ḥ the heth. The ʻayyin is usually left unpronounced; the ḥ is like the german ch.

THE HEBREW
SCRIPTURES

INTRODUCTION

MORE PEOPLE praise the Bible than read it. More read it than understand it, and more understand it than conscientiously follow it.

The Bible, of course, is not one book, but a collection, a library.
The individual volumes were written by diverse men at diverse times,
and, indeed, some single volumes, such as the Book of Isaiah with its
sixty-six chapters, are themselves the products of men living at
different times. The Bible, as it is commonly understood by Christians, consists of two major divisions. The Old Testament, reckoned
by them as the first division, is that earlier collection of books made
by Jews, while the New Testament, the second division, was made
later by Christians, the Old and New Testaments constituting for
Christians one single Bible. Jews, on the other hand, do not regard
the New Testament as part of their Bible; when Jews speak of *Bible*
they mean what Christians mean by Old Testament; the term that
Jews customarily use is *Tanak* (tah-náhk).[1]

Our concern is with the Tanak. There are some clear marks of
distinction between it and the New Testament. The Tanak was
written in Hebrew. (A few chapters in Daniel and in Ezra and a verse

---

[1] The term is formed from the first letters of the names of the three divisions.
Torah ("Revelation"), Neviim ("Prophets"), and Kesuvim ("Writings"). Jews
actually pronounce the word Tana*ch,* ending with the German ch, not k.

in Jeremiah are exceptions, for they are in Aramaic, a language akin to Hebrew.) The New Testament was written in Greek. The Tanak represents literary productivity dating from approximately 1300 B.C. to 150 B.C.; the New Testament writings come from A.D. 50 to A.D. 150. The difference in the ages is underlined by the notable fact that the New Testament in page after page quotes passages from the Tanak. This not only demonstrates that the Tanak is much older but also that the New Testament regards the Tanak as already sacred.

The Tanak, a library in itself, is something to study. Well-intentioned and pious people urge the reading of the Bible as though this were an easy task, with attendant rewards lying near at hand. These rewards are spoken of as inner serenity or inspiration, or similar profound benefits. All too often, however, those who follow the advice to read Scripture encounter bitter frustration, finding not inspiration but perplexity, and not clarity but a jumble of words. The Tanak is a very difficult book.

In synagogue and church worship, excerpts from some books, such as the Prophets or Psalms, are arranged for alternate reading by the congregation and the rabbi or minister. For purposes of convenience, long verses are broken into seemingly appropriate segments, even though coherence and sense are thereby sometimes lost. Allusions recognizable only by the research scholar punctuate the readings, which have often been wrenched out of the context that alone could give communicable meaning. Perhaps such alternate readings contribute affirmatively to the mood of worship, especially if the austere and magnificent (and obscure) King James translation is used. Badly understood lines or speeches in a Shakespearean play can contribute to the mood of the theatergoer, for there is a sense in which mood is quite independent of understanding. Yet the question of simple understanding is an elementary necessity in any approach to the Tanak. One often wonders if the mood produced by the readings is truly that which the passage meant to elicit. I have known people who have found themselves unable to enter into a worshipful mood, not despite the biblical readings but rather because of them. Random excerpts are sometimes so inappropriate, or so inappropriately placed, that they disrupt the development of a continuous or deepening tone or feeling. Since a mood of worship is probably more important than the ideas expressed, it is lamentable when biblical readings designed to further the mood actually obstruct or break it.

To regard the Tanak as sacred is reasonable, but its sanctity ought to be impressed on us by study, rather than assumed beforehand. Too easily the vocabulary of religion—words like righteous-ness and sin—tends to become mere slogans, devoid of meaning. To call the biblical writings Sacred Scripture is to put over them a curtain which can conceal their form and meaning. Such unthink-ing attribution of sanctity compounds the obscurity of the Tanak. Any ancient library is hard to read and understand. Because the contents of biblical life and thought are already blurred through antiquity and distance, an unconsidered attitude that the writings are "sacred" can move the onlooker even beyond haziness into blindness itself.

The Bible has been sacred for at least twenty centuries to very many people in very many lands. As a result there have arisen dif-ferent modes of interpretation, some of which have survived into our own time. Interpretations complicate any understanding of the Tanak, and caprice has characterized many of the interpreters. Only in the past two centuries has the primary focus of interpretation been on what the Bible meant at the time when each of the individual portions was written. Before that time, "literal" interpretation in its strict sense was only sporadic. The fanciful, on the other hand, was the rule; it resulted when religionists in some specific cultural milieu, on an unquestioning assumption of the sanctity of the Bible, made it applicable to their own age by reading into it the transitory concerns of their own age.

Naturally, subsequent ages have considered such transitory "meanings" far-fetched and even grotesque. For example, a Greek Jew named Philo (20 B.C.–A.D. 40), nurtured on Plato and Stoicism, read Plato and the Stoics into the Bible through a device known as allegory ("to say another thing"). Allegory supposes that when the Bible says something, it is saying not what it is saying, but rather something different. In Philo's allegory, for example, Abraham was not so much the ancestor of the Hebrews as a type of mind, able to progress through learning. The same allegory held that Sarah, Abraham's wife, represented true wisdom, while Hagar, her Egyptian maid, was interpreted as "college education." When Genesis tells us that the childless Sarah bade Abraham marry Hagar so as to beget offspring, Philo's allegory means the following: Abraham's marriage to Hagar represents the "progressing mind" at the stage of the college boy. At that period the mind can beget only sophistry, symbolized by Ishmael, the son of Hagar and Abraham. Only when the mind goes beyond college subjects (Hagar) can it mate with true wisdom (Sarah); and out of this latter union comes Isaac, representing spiritual joy.

The literal meaning of Scripture is the exact opposite of allegory. It is the precise sense of its passages at the time, or times, when they were written. We are readily able to recognize the unliteral character of far-fetched allegory; but there have appeared various types of unliteral interpretations not so promptly to be identified as far-fetched. While Philo's allegorizing of the Bible is now known only to researchers, allegory, like the phoenix, is constantly reborn, but without retaining its proper label. Every generation has numbered those who have read whimsical meanings into Scripture and then proclaimed that what was read in was there all the time. I shall later modify this harsh judgment on non-literal interpretation, but our concern will be with the purely literal meaning of Scripture.

In addition to centuries of ingenious interpretation, there is yet another obstacle to understanding the Bible. This is and has been a desperate effort to justify Scripture rather than understand it. For example, the Bible relates miracles, which may or may not be true. A recurrent form of understanding such passages distorts the intent of the Bible (which did not disdain to narrate miracles) by merely obliterating the miraculous! Thus, we are told, in such interpretation, that the parting of the Red Sea was a quite natural occurrence, for a convenient earthquake separated the waters and provided a raised ledge for the Hebrews to walk across. According to this view the seven days of creation of Genesis represent time divisions (epochs, aeons, or centuries) different from our measurement of twenty-four-hour days. Or we are told, respecting the New Testament, that Jesus walked not on the water but on a sandbar visible to him but hidden from the sight of his disciples. It is intellectually more honest to say that one does not believe in a certain miracle than to imply that one believes in it, having transformed the miracle into a mere fortuitous coincidence of commonplace events. There was a period (around 1810) when such rationalization was prominent; the miracles related in Scripture were handled by asserting that they were not miraculous.

Again, violence could be and was done to Scripture by refusing to concede that certain passages express viewpoints lacking in nobility and elevation. Certain of the Psalms show an unseemly vengeful attitude; certain parts in Judges exhibit cruelty; some passages portray protagonists in blameworthy conduct. Many of the interpretive manipulations underline the negative aspect of the passages being interpreted. Some traditional interpreters have shrunk from admitting or even seeing that infelicities are present at all. Often they decry vengeance in general, but applaud it as meritorious in

Scripture; they can abhor cruelty, but vindicate it in Scripture; and they condone the conduct of certain protagonists, even at the cost of damaging the intent to portray an unadmirable facet in an admirable character. The pitfall in devices such as allegory, rationalization, or artificial vindication is that the clear intent of Scripture is blunted or destroyed. We shall have to cast aside, in the present effort, all allegory, all rationalizing, and all tendencies that attempt to vindicate Scripture artificially.

To understand the intent of the Bible we must put ourselves back into a period in history and a geographical region, far removed from us. This implies a sturdy refusal to read our age and our ideas into Scripture. We must be especially cautious about the terms in the vocabulary of religion; in our day they are often no more than generalities, but in biblical times they had specific meaning.

This array of obstacles, however, can be partly if not completely overcome. The Bible that emerges thereafter is more rather than less valuable than the allegorical or rationalized version.

The complexities inherent in the technical study of the Bible are such that the ordinary reader is well advised to steer clear of many details, in particular those bits and pieces that need concern only the specialist. A host of deterrents to comprehension exist, but the common reader is not under the same compulsion as the scholar to deal with minutiae. What the common reader must be ready to do is to put some good measure of reliance on some scholar, and be prepared to let him provide the essence of important matters. For the ordinary reader, the professional scholar must provide a distillation of what is essential, rather than an overburdened and overburdening totality. Thus, for example, the scholar needs to have first-hand knowledge of Hebrew and other Semitic languages, but the reader can be content with English alone. The scholar needs to study closely each of the thirty-nine books of the Tanak. He must try to answer such questions as these: Who wrote this piece? When? For what purpose? Is it a unity, or are different hands represented in it? Moreover, he needs to be able to adduce the evidence that supports his answers.

Such questions are known in Bible study as questions of "Introduction." "Introduction" is an inescapable discipline for the student seeking exact knowledge. In an "Introduction" an author usually devotes one chapter to each Scriptural book. The nature of his purpose impels him to proceed in unimaginative sequence from one book to the next in the order in which the books are now found in Scripture. There is the danger in the study of "Introduction," that each of the thirty-nine books may seem the peer of all the others and all the accumulated problems assume an equal value. This absence of accentuation and subordination makes study of the Bible tedious; the trite example of not seeing the forest for the trees is applicable. Excellent "Introductions" have been written, two in English [2] are indispensable to the scholar, though too complex for the general reader.

I have shunned writing an "Introduction," for I am concerned with giving a distillation of what is in the Tanak rather than a full, undigested report on it. I have two main interests. One is to focus on the eminent passages. My purpose in doing so is to acquaint the student with them. It is not my deliberate aim to assess the literary eminence of the Tanak. I scarcely know how to praise the Psalms adequately; their authors were more gifted at expression than I am, nor do I write as well as the remarkable author of the narrative of King David's court, in II Samuel 9–20. My second interest involves a focus, different from that of many university courses called "The Bible as Literature," on the religious ideas found in the Tanak, even those that are expressed with no great literary skill. Some of these ancient ideas will seem relevant today, *but some may not*. But these ideas, whether they are majestic or less exalted, are worth knowing. Where an understanding of the literary values and the religious ideas are made clearer by "Introduction" material, I give it summarily, and often I present conclusions without supplying their basis.

Accordingly my purpose is not to narrate the *history* of the biblical period; I shall pass over without discussion many of the kings of Israel and of Judah, the learning of whose names continues to plague some Sunday School children even today. Yet I must include some history. The words of the Emancipation Proclamation carry their own message; but knowing the occasion of its utterance, seeing it as a document that was composed at a moment of stirring human crisis, rather than in a vacuum, completes our understanding of it.

The date of the Emancipation Proclamation is January 1, 1863. Suppose we did not know the exact date, but only that it came after 1860 and before 1865. We would be a little poorer in appreciation, but not perceptibly so. Rarely can we date biblical utterances exactly; for the most part we shall have to be content to mention periods or epochs or eras. We shall deal mostly with general aspects of biblical history, seldom with specific dates. The general reader, unlike the

---

[2] S. R. Driver, *An Introduction to the Literature of the Old Testament*, New York, 1897 (often reprinted, and now available in paperback); Robert H. Pfeiffer, *Introduction to the Old Testament*, New York, 1941.

professional historian, can be content with such an imprecise procedure. He will have to learn that Assyria destroyed the northern kingdom around 725, but he need not care whether the correct date is 722 or 721. Although he will lose some perspective if he puts the event into the sixth century when it belongs in the eighth, he need not be distracted by some marked discrepancies in Scripture as to the precise dates of certain kings.

History as the mere record of events is of limited importance in the present quest. In one sense, it is valuable primarily for enabling the reader to acquire a tolerably good orientation to those ideas that events called forth. But in quite another sense, history tends to become the most acute problem to the student of the Tanak. He often falls into the error of many modern readers of telling himself that events are true only if they are correct as history. He asks, Did Moses really get the Ten Commandments on Mount Sinai? Did Abraham really beget Isaac long after Sarah had lost her fertility? Did God really create the world in seven days? Did Jonah really spend three days in the belly of the whale?

The extraordinary conclusion of many readers, and of college students especially, is that if these matters are not historically accurate the Tanak is false and therefore worthless. I shall give my opinion of the historical reliability of such questions in the proper place. Here, however, the reader must begin to understand that the biblical authors were not research historians who frequented archives and libraries. He must not shrink from concluding that they could be, and were, wrong on many points in history. Quibbles about these matters of "history" are analogous to the situation in which a man begins to relate a funny incident that occurred on his way downtown the previous Thursday. His wife promptly intervenes to insist that it happened on Wednesday. The usual outcome is that the anecdote is never told, and the assembly is titillated, if at all, only by the Thursday-Wednesday exchange.

Even if one conceded that the "historical" data provided by the Bible were all inaccurate, its religious ideas would not be decisively affected. If one dated the Emancipation Proclamation in Washington's time rather than in Lincoln's, the history would be wrong, but a formidable idea would still remain to be explored. Nineteenth-century biblical scholarship doubted the reliability of virtually every historical statement in the Tanak. The pendulum has now swung away from skepticism. The reader might be cautioned that a book by Werner Keller, *The Bible as History: A Confirmation of the Book of Books* (New York: William Morrow & Co., Inc.; 1956), goes to the other, and equally improper, extreme. Instead of stressing the need for greater respect for biblical data, Keller ascribes an absurd degree of accuracy of virtually all the data.

Scholars doubted the biblical statement about King Solomon's copper mines; it has been healthful that a celebrated archaeologist confuted these scholars by finding the mines, which the State of Israel is now modernizing. But Solomon's thousand wives have not been found by archaeologists, nor have all his proverbs been uncovered. We can be certain that the Book of Proverbs attributed to him is not entirely by him; we can, indeed, doubt that any of it is.

Archaeology, a tool of tremendous importance in biblical study, does not solve all the problems of biblical accuracy. Archaeology has justly moved modern scholars from doubt about many biblical statements to a mood of relative trust in them. Yet the archaeologist who finds the Rappahannock River does not by this alone prove conclusively that George Washington threw a dollar across it. Verifying that cherry trees grew in Virginia in Washington's youth does not establish the reliability of "Father, I cannot tell a lie." Much archaeological "confirmation" is distorted in the public press. Archaeology falls short of touching the particular biblical narratives, especially in Genesis, in the form in which they are couched.[3] To find Mount Sinai (it has not yet been found) would not prove that God descended on it and gave Moses the Decalogue there. To discover the site of Bethel does not verify that Jacob saw angels ascending and descending a ladder or ramp there.

To generalize, when the Tanak alludes in passing to certain natural, human events (the reigns of kings, the wars, or the period of exile), it is, despite some Thursday-Wednesday questions, reliable. But what of Moses on Mount Sinai? What of God appearing to Abraham and bidding him to leave home and go to the land which God would show him? What of Isaiah's account of having seen the Lord God on his high and exalted throne? Surely there is all the difference in the world between the petty questions of the accuracy of dates of human events, and the accuracy of events of a supernatural character.

It is not objective historical research but subjective faith that relates to questions of supernatural events; or, more precisely, historical research does not penetrate beyond the external or peripheral facts. The Bible contends that the Hebrews were in slavery in Egypt and that God redeemed them. Historical research can confirm or deny the bare facts, assuming that adequate evidence for decision exists; that is, records could conceivably be recovered either by archaeology or from historical works, which would substantiate a period of slav-

[3] See pages 507ff., "Archaeology and the Tanak."

ery and a release into freedom. But whether the act of release was literally performed by God falls outside the domain of the historical researcher.

Indeed, it must be said plainly that it is an error to appeal to the historian to verify supernatural events, for historical method is more apt to arrive at negative conclusions than affirmative ones. This is true partly because the biblical authors were not modern historians, and hence the modern historian may be trying to get at something the ancient writer did not even remotely have in his mind; precision and accuracy in details could not possibly have the same weight with ancient as with modern writers. Moreover, the ancient writers, being of the folk, did not avoid myth and legend, and to use such terms in considering biblical material is to suggest the absence of historical validity. Thus, I am personally persuaded that the enslavement in Egypt is basically historical, but, in being retold, ventured into the legendary. I consider the enslavement historical because I do not believe that an ancient people would deliberately select slaves as their ancestors, but as yet neither inscription nor ancient document outside the Tanak has confirmed the enslavement in Egypt. This absence of confirmation tends in itself to be a negation rather than a confirmation. If, on the one hand, research were to have to conclude that the enslavement is not historical, then there would scarcely be any point in asking whether or not it was God who effected the release. On the other hand, if research were to confirm the fact of enslavement and release, this confirmation would extend only to the externality of the events. Whether God was or was not the active redeemer is a matter of subjective faith. Accordingly, historical research only impinges on faith, and is not faith itself; it can clarify or refine aspects of faith, but never substitute for it.

The Tanak asserts that it was God who effected the release from slavery in Egypt. This conviction is more important to the Tanak than questions of historic fact. The issue for the student in the first stage is not so much whether he personally shares the biblical faith, but whether he understands it.

If the difference is clear between the faith of a modern person respecting the Tanak, and that person's comprehension of the biblical faith, then we can proceed to delineate some aspects of the literature with which we will be dealing. These are best understood through example. Among the narratives about Adam and Eve we read of a serpent that speaks; the Gentile prophet Balaam rode an ass that conversed with him. Or take the appealing passage which relates that the boy David slew Goliath. In its own terms it need not arouse great skepticism. But a summary of the achievements of David's lieutenants, in II Samuel 21:19, tells us plainly that it was a certain Elhanan who slew Goliath.[4] Did David slay Goliath? Is it an important question in the history of ideas whether he or someone else did?

The different kinds of materials in the Tanak can elicit various kinds and measures of skepticism. There is, to be sure, biblical material that contains reliable history. There are legends, material with a historical kernel but with fanciful expansions. There are myths, or anecdotes devoid of any genuine historical basis; usually these are "etiological," that is, they explain the reason for something. The serpent crawls on the ground because the serpent of Eden enticed Eve to eat forbidden fruit. Women undergo pain at childbirth because Eve let herself be enticed by the serpent. Men must toil with the sweat of the brow to earn a livelihood because Adam lost Paradise by succumbing to Eve's blandishments. Folk-tale, folk-wisdom, legend, myth, and reliable history are the warp and woof of much of the Tanak. One decides how to classify a segment by examining its form and content, in the light of one's presuppositions. If the reader is of a skeptical bent, he will arrive at an abundance of doubts and denials. If as a result of his rearing he is unquestioningly loyal to some historic religious tradition, he will have no inclination to deny or doubt. Should he be momentarily troubled, doubt will soon vanish, for the mind determined to gloss over problems or harmonize contradictions invariably succeeds.

But the residual question looms much larger than whether the human materials are historical, legendary, or mythical. Did God truly disclose himself to the ancient worthies? This is a more profound question.

And it must not be dodged. The Bible asserts unmistakably that in the act of revelation, God acts on His own initiative; man is the passive recipient of God's gracious act. The term "revelation" means that God did disclose Himself. I stress this because the word "revelation" in particular has undergone a great deal of interpretation. Some modern reinterpreters seem to suggest that the initiative is with man while God is passive. The idea was often expressed in the nineteenth century, and is still echoed today, that "revelation is progressive." According to this view, man in the successive generations learns more and more about the nature of the universe and God. His progress in this learning (so it is alleged) gives him a constantly unfolding knowledge about God.

The question of whether or not "progressive revelation" is a rea-

[4] Much later, the author of the Book of Chronicles, apparently bothered by the discrepancy, gets out of the difficulty by assuring us (I Chron. 20:5) that Elhanan slew Lahmi the *brother* of Goliath.

sonable and attractive opinion for a modern man is quite different from the question of whether or not it is what the Tanak has in mind. The Tanak does not mince words; by revelation, it means revelation. This is not altered by the circumstance that modern scholarship is able to show, or sometimes even trace, aspects of the development of views about God in the Tanak. Though we can see developments, the biblical authors never for one moment embraced progressive revelation, nor did they ever ascribe the initiative in revelation to man.

Revelation in the biblical sense is an article of faith. One chooses to believe or to disbelieve. My own purpose in the ensuing pages is not to prescribe what is today believable, but rather to portray what was once believed. Although, as I have said, the historical reliability of revelation is the crux of the problem in the Bible, the believer and the skeptic can both come to understand what the Bible meant.

Since my personal biases are bound to influence this book, the reader is entitled to know something about me. I am a rabbi, a teacher in a school for rabbis, and an administrative official of that school. I espouse organized religion, despite its inherent weaknesses. A Reform Jew, I acknowledge that I have simultaneously a deep regard for orthodox Judaism (and for orthodox Christianity as well); my private beliefs and practices are in many ways quite distant from traditional Judaism. I do not distinguish between those of my attitudes that result from my being a rabbi and those that result from my being a professional scholar; I am not able to separate the two. What I set forth in the ensuing pages as a specialist in the Bible reflects quite as fully what makes me a rabbi. I have no reluctance in avowing that I believe in God. At the same time, I acknowledge that I know much less about Him than about man.[5]

As to the reliability of the judgments expressed in the following pages, biblical scholarship is not all of a piece, and I hold views that others reject, just as others hold views that I reject. Yet the reader perhaps should be assured that the views I express belong for the most part to the usual assumptions of modern free Jewish and Christian scholars.

The Tanak is a library, as we have said. It is a selected library, because far more books were written than found their way into it. Scholars call the list of selected and admitted writings the *canon* of the Bible. Canon means "measuring rod"; it refers to the standards the

---

[5] Though I have opinions on religion today, I am not a theologian, I am a historian of theological views.

selectors presumably used in admitting or denying admission to books.

The canon of the Hebrew Bible is a list of thirty-nine books. Because certain books are divided into two parts (I and II Samuel and I and II Kings), and because twelve short prophetic books ("the minor prophets") formerly were counted as one book, the number was usually given in ancient times as twenty-four rather than thirty-nine. The reader may ask when and how the list of the twenty-four was completed and stabilized. We do not know the answer in precise terms. Evidence from the writings of the rabbis of old leads to a frequent conclusion that the time was A.D. 90, and the place a small town in Palestine, which the Jews called Yavne and the Greeks Jamnia.⁶ Twenty years earlier the Temple in Jerusalem had been destroyed, ending a system of worship (predominantly animal sacrifice) prescribed in the Tanak. The Tanak became subtly changed from a prescription for how people should worship into almost an object of worship. By 90 some of the twenty-four books were already acknowledged as sacred, but disputes centered around others. What took place in 90 was predominantly a settlement about the disputed books, those belonging to a grouping Jews call *kesuvim* ⁷ ("Writings") and Christians call Hagiographa ("sacred writings").

The Tanak contains three divisions, much like a work published in three volumes. The *kesuvim* represent one of these three. The *kesuvim* contain Psalms, Proverbs, Job, Ruth, Lamentations, Song of Songs, Ecclesiastes, Esther, Daniel and Chronicles-Ezra-Nehemiah. A most heterogeneous collection, the *kesuvim* came to be "canonized" long after the first two divisions had already been fairly firmly settled. Some of the *kesuvim* (for example, Esther and Song of Songs) were challenged but accepted. Others were challenged and rejected. Acceptance led to the veneration of a book and to its being copied and preserved. Rejection led to neglect and either total disappearance or fragmentary preservation. By fragmentary preservation we allude to the citation of passages in later works, or to actual fragments, which turn

⁶ The interested reader can find fuller information under "Canon" in an encyclopedia. Jamnia and 90 represent a convenience, not an irrefutable conclusion. Many objections to Jamnia and 90 exist. Two are worth mentioning here. First, disputes over some books are known to have continued beyond 90, so that to speak of a settlement in 90 is an exaggeration. Second, to speak of Jamnia 90 creates the false impression that some convention along modern lines was held, with delegates debating over the agenda and then coming to a vote and decision. Canon, however, was a matter of the evolution of opinions which converged over a period of decades, 90 being a likely terminal date, but far from a definitive one.
⁷ *Kesuvim* represents the usual way in which most American Jews pronounce the word. A precise transliteration would be *kethubhim*.

up from time to time in the storeroom of some remote synagogue or Christian monastery, or through an archaeological discovery.

Some of the books that failed of acceptance in Palestine were accepted into the Greek canon at about that same time (± A.D. 100) by Jews in the far-flung Mediterranean lands. Therefore the Greek Tanak includes some books not found in the Hebrew (First and Second Maccabees, Jesus ben Sirach, and the like). Most Protestants, following the sixteenth-century bent, regard only the Hebrew collection as authoritative; those books to be found in the Greek Tanak, but not in the Hebrew, they have termed Apocrypha. The Latin Bible of Roman Catholics, the Vulgate, is based on the Greek, so that Catholics call canonical certain books which Protestants call Apocrypha.

By no means all the books rejected in Palestine were accepted by Greek Jews. Many writings were rejected by both groups. Such books include several whose titles falsely suggest that they were written by ancient worthies; *The Testament of Abraham* and *The Book of Enoch* are among them. These books have been collected only in modern times, and they are known collectively as the Pseudepigrapha ("false titles"). The term Pseudepigrapha is thus used broadly to classify those quasi-biblical books that failed to be admitted into the Hebrew or the Greek version, while the Apocrypha are those that got into the Greek, but not into the Hebrew. Most of the Pseudepigrapha were written prior to the canonization of the Kesuvim and were at hand for possible inclusion. Their absence from the canon implies deliberate rejection.

Until the Kesuvim were assembled, the Tanak as we now know it was incomplete. The canonization of the Kesuvim, perhaps in 90 at Jamnia, was the final step in the creation of the Tanak.

Jews call the first part of the Bible the Torah; they use this term in other and broader senses, too, but pre-eminently they mean by Torah the first Five Books. Tradition attributes their authorship to Moses; the Torah, consisting of Genesis, Exodus, Leviticus, Numbers, and Deuteronomy is therefore often called *The Five Books of Moses.* A Hebrew word meaning *five* leads Jews to speak of these books also as Ḥumash; scholars use a Greek term, Pentateuch, meaning five books, for Ḥumash.

The Hagiographa, we may say, were canonized about A.D. 90. We have said that the Ḥumash or Torah was canonized earlier. But when? We do not really know. The evidence is rather good that the Torah was translated into Greek around 250 B.C. The translation was made, according to an unreliable legend, by seventy-two men and is known as the Septuagint, the Greek word for seventy. The translation of the

Hebrew Humash into Greek makes it certain that it was in a rather fixed form by 250 B.C.; otherwise it would not have been fit for translation. Since the Humash merited the signal honor, almost without parallel in the ancient world, of being translated, it must have had some generations of veneration behind it well before 250.

At any rate, we have a terminal date of 250 B.C. for the canonization of Part One, and a convenient date, A.D. 90, for Part Three, the Kesuvim. For the date of Part Two, Neviim [8] ("Prophets"), we have scarcely more than reasonable guesses, and the period around 100 B.C. can be offered.

Collection and canonization occurred, naturally, later than the time of the writing of the individual books. The lapse of time, in some instances centuries, between composition and canonization provided ample opportunity for manuscripts to be torn and worn and for tiny pieces to be lost—time, indeed, for whole sections of the parchment to become disarranged before being resewn together. As yet the so-called codex form (pages piled up and sewn together on one edge) had not been used by Jews; they used a scroll form, sewing the right edge of page two to the left edge of page one, and the right edge of page three to the left edge of page two, and so forth, forming a long, continuous writing. This was rolled up for convenience into a scroll, for which the Hebrew word is *megillah*.[9]

The normal vicissitudes of copying come to light especially in the rigid scroll form. Thus, the man copying a section might skip a word or a line, or the copyist might add his own comment as a marginal note and a later copyist incorporate the note into the body of the text. The comparison of written manuscripts has enabled a classification of the most frequent types of scribal errors. Moreover, the ancient Hebrew alphabet was one of consonants (written vowels, now found in printed Hebrew Bibles, are early medieval in origin). The letters KBD can be read *kibed* [1] to mean "he honored"; or *kabed*,[2] the imperative "honor"; as *kavod*, "glory," or *kaved*, "liver." The passage in Psalm 16:9, "my heart is glad, my *glory* rejoiceth," should read "my liver rejoiceth," for how can glory rejoice? The ancient Hebrew thought that the emotions were centered in the inner organs, as did medieval man, who attributed the mood of depression, for example, to *melancholia*, "black bile." The consonantal text made it easy for major errors such as a change from *liver* to *glory* to be introduced.

[8] A more scientific transliteration is *Nebhi'im*.
[9] When applied to non-biblical writing by Jews the word comes to mean a synonym for something overlong; a lengthy letter, for example, can be called a "whole megillah."
[1] More precisely, *kibbed*.
[2] More precisely, *kabbed*.

Around the 6th century B.C., Hebrew began to give way to Aramaic as the spoken language. As a result, a copyist with some limitation in his knowledge could err because he was dealing with a literary, not a living language. "Scribal errors" are found throughout the Tanak. They occur to a limited extent even in the Ḥumash, which was the most often copied and hence the best known part. In such books as Ezekiel, Job, and Psalms, the problems raised by scribal errors are enormous.

But still another problem, beyond that of inadvertent slips, will confront us. It is that of the unity of a book. Imagine a writing which for eight and a half chapters says in unreserved fashion that the people are going to undergo devastating punishment, and then, in the last half chapter, promises wonderful happiness. If the same writer wrote both, he certainly changed his mind. But perhaps two different writers are represented. Perhaps a copyist, having recorded the dire eight and a half chapters, shunned ending on a negative note and added a happy section from some short manuscript. Often, in the prophetic writings, long sections on doom are followed by brief assurances of a glowing future. Modern scholars believe that the ancient texts underwent such deliberate interpolation in the age previous to canonization. Or imagine a copyist who has prepared more parchment than he needs. Finishing one job, he goes on to another on the same piece of parchment. He needs one more piece to finish the second task and then finds he has space to begin even a third. The Book of Isaiah, sixty-six chapters long, shows signs of interpolation in its first portion; writings by others than Isaiah were appended to the same scroll. The Book of Isaiah consists of at least the original Isaiah (and interpolations); a writer, unknown by name, but called Second Isaiah (and interpolations); and a third writer, or group of writers, often called Third or Trito-Isaiah.

Between the time of original composition and the much later time of canonization, a writing underwent such vicissitudes. Copying involved attendant errors, possible displacement or dislocation of parts, interpolations and additions, or the incorporation of writings by several different hands in one and the same scroll. On canonization it was the scroll with all these vicissitudes that was accepted.

A counterbalance to the difficulties arising before canonization is the noteworthy fidelity with which the works were copied once they were canonized. All the perfections and imperfections, all the accuracies and inaccuracies were then transmitted with scrupulous fidelity. In the course of time, Jews developed an extensive literature of notations, designed to transmit the canonized books with undeviating accuracy. These notations and the text they support are known as *Ma-*

sora ("tradition"); scholars usually allude to the Hebrew text as the "Masoretic" text.

Error-laden through the vicissitudes of pre-canonic times, but faithfully copied with the anomalies and mistakes, the Masoretic text was the object of suspicion and even scorn among nineteenth-century scholars. They argued that the Masoretes were unreliable and that conscious and deliberate changes, as well as inadvertent slips, were discernible. No original compositions ("holographs") of biblical writings have survived to our day. The oldest Hebrew manuscript of the Bible could be dated around A.D. 900. It was therefore argued that between canonization and A.D. 900, the Masoretes had consciously or unconsciously tampered with the text. Septuagint manuscripts are older than the Hebrew; one, the Vaticanus, comes from the fourth century. Scholars, especially in Germany, often argued that the Greek translation of the Hebrew Bible represented a Hebrew version, since lost, which was more reliable than the Hebrew version preserved by the Jews. The Septuagint was overvalued, the Masoretic text scorned.

Biblical fragments and two versions (one partial, one complete) of the Book of Isaiah were found among the Dead Sea Scrolls. They are important because they vindicate the high reliability of the Masoretic text. Assuming that the Scrolls come from about 100 B.C.–A.D. 100, they represent manuscript authority in Hebrew almost a thousand years older than what we previously had. Although there are countless minor differences, mostly orthographic, between the Scrolls and the Masoretic text, there is not one variation significant for either biblical history or biblical religion.

Although the relatively high reliability of the Hebrew text subsequent to its canonization is now established, the problems arising from the lapse of time between composition and canonization remain. Thus, we have now a manuscript of the Book of Isaiah a thousand years older than what we had before the Dead Sea Scrolls were found; but Isaiah flourished around 725 B.C., at least 600 years before the Dead Sea Scrolls. Much could happen to a writing over a period of 600 years. For example, in that time the work of three authors (plus interpolations) was assembled into a long book, incorrectly attributed to one man.

The study of the manuscripts and of their readings is known technically as "lower criticism." "Higher criticism" is the study of the meaning, significance, origin, and purpose of the writings. Higher Criticism needs to use Lower Criticism. Anyone who asks about the origin or meaning of a biblical book or passage has trespassed into Higher Criticism. Some representatives of conservative denominations, aghast at the iconoclasm of some Higher Critics, try to limit the term to a contemptuous epithet for a type of scholarship they cannot accept. One Jewish scholar (whose field was not the Bible) said that "the Higher Criticism is higher anti-Semitism." Similarly, "fundamentalist" Christians have regarded Higher Criticism as anti-Christian.

This book is unabashedly a book of Higher Criticism. The Jewish scholar whom I have quoted was right to a limited extent—certain German Higher Critics were psychotic Jew-haters, but they were few. Higher Criticism is a process, not a conclusion. The discipline itself stands or falls on its rightness or wrongness, not on the personal foibles of its practitioners. Each generation of scholars is obligated by the requirements of scholarship to scrutinize and assess the work of earlier generations. Some of the heritage is found to be sound and acceptable, some unsound and in need of rejection. To label the Higher Critics anti-Semites is silly. Indeed, a more devastating judgment can be passed on the nineteenth-century Higher Critics by demonstrating that their scholarship, however laborious and vaunted, was often shabby, and that they were seldom able to rise above their own presuppositions and intellectual biases. Modern biblical scholarship, however, inevitably uses nineteenth-century scholarship as a point of departure. To ignore it is as grievous an error in judgment as never to depart from it.

How much history shall we need to use for our purpose? Although we should know as much as possible, let us consider the bare outline here.

The Hebrews were a nomad people in the desert. As a group of associated tribes (traditionally numbering twelve), they left the desert, where their leader had been Moses, and entered into Canaan under Joshua, who, according to tradition, quickly conquered the resident peoples. This conquest was followed by a period in which tribal independence, under tribal leaders known as Judges, led to federation and ultimately to nationhood under a king.

Saul was the first monarch, but he did not found a dynasty. Kingship passed to David, and from David to Solomon. After the death of Solomon the national unity came to an end, and the kingdom became divided into two parts, Judah to the south and Israel to the north. In Judah the dynasty of David retained the kingship for almost three centuries, but in Israel a series of usurpers reigned, sometimes briefly, but sometimes long enough to fashion a short-lived dynasty. Thus, Jeroboam II, of Israel, during whose reign (786–746) flourished Amos, the first of the literary prophets, was the great-grandson of

Jehu who had seized the kingship from Joram in 842; that seizure
ended the dynasty of Omri, Ahab, Ahaziah, and Joram, which had
lasted from 876–842.

The somewhat greater stability of the monarchy in Judah may
well have been due to geographic and therefore economic conditions.
The southern kingdom was pastoral and somewhat isolated, especially in comparison with the agricultural north, across which lay the
great highway from Egypt in the west and Assyria in the east. Urbanization and cosmopolitanism characterized the northern kingdom, and the resultant greater complexities in society, with upper,
middle, and poor classes, may have increased the frequency of inner
political upheaval.

Involvements with foreign nations were inescapable, whether
in the north or the south, and whether through efforts at conquest beyond the borders or through the need to repel invaders. In the middle
of the eighth century, Assyria was pressing westward in its world empire. Israel fell to Assyria in 722–721. The people were transported
eastward, and a new population was brought in westward. The transported Israelites became the "ten lost tribes"; in reality these were absorbed by the people of the lands to which they were transported and
they disappeared.

The southern kingdom survived for another century and a half.
When the Assyrians were overthrown by the Babylonians toward the
end of the seventh century, the new conquerors were soon to overwhelm the southern kingdom. The international intrigues, in which
Egypt was almost continuously involved, made it inevitable that tiny
Judah would be overrun. The Babylonians conquered Judah in
597–586. Again transportation of the population took place, this time
of the Judeans to Babylonia.

The foregoing events can be divided into three periods, all before
the time of the Babylonian exile. First is the Wilderness period; next,
the Conquest of and the Settlement in Canaan; third, the Monarchy.
Were our study primarily political and social, we would need to sub-
divide the pre-exilic period further; but for our purposes, this division
can suffice.

Whereas the deportees from the northern kingdom a century
and a half earlier lost their sense of community and identity and
thus were swallowed up, the deportees of the southern kingdom to
Babylonia retained their identity and remained a community. Moreover, they cherished a deep longing to return to their fatherland, and
ultimately they succeeded—between 539 and 520, when the Persian
conquest of the Babylonians made the return possible. Tradition
gives the period of sojourn in Babylonia as seventy years, an accept-

able number, for the period can be reasonably considered to have lasted from 586 to 516. Significant changes occurred during the exilic period, not only in the daily economic and political spheres, but also in religious thinking. Hence there is justification for distinguishing between the pre-exilic period and the exilic period.

The return to Palestine brought, in turn, a number of very important changes in religious thought and practice. Though these were quite varied, it is useful to allude to them as belonging to the post-exilic period. From 539 to 331 we can speak of the Persian period, for Palestine belonged to them. After 331, we identify the period as Greek, recalling thereby the new conquerors.

To sum up, then, the periods are these: the Wilderness, the Conquest and Settlement, and the Monarchy in pre-exilic times; the exilic period; and the postexilic period, divided into a Persian and then a Greek era.

In considering the Tanak, we might reasonably proceed in the order in which the books are found, beginning with Genesis, but, this method as I have said, tends to be monotonous. Since we will emphasize the religious ideas, it is more useful to have some kind of chronological arrangement. Thereby we can have some sense of how and when and why certain religious ideas arose. Yet a danger lurks in such an exposition, for it seems to imply falsely that when once some new doctrine or idea was expressed, it promptly obliterated everything that went before it. Moreover, it suggests that each and every segment of the population held to one and the same opinion on some matter. Many nineteenth-century treatises on Hebrew religious thought fell victim to a tacit assumption of "rectilinear"—straight-line—development of religion. It is more realistic and more accurate to recognize that some ideas gained acceptance only slowly and partially; some struggled in vain against the old and lost out; and at times the populace entertained different and contradictory opinions. A new religious idea generally stems not from a group of people, but from one man. He conceives the idea and utters it or writes it. His hearers or readers respond, by rejecting it, by partly accepting it, or by wholly embracing it.

Several considerations impel us to begin with the prophetic writings, rather than with the Ḥumash. In the first place, the prophetic writings can be regarded as the framework of Hebrew thought. Secondly, the Prophets lend themselves to a quasi-chronological arrangement more readily than does the other literature, and in addition provide us with milestones in the growth of religious ideas. Thirdly, though it is harder to read the Prophets, since they are abstract, than the narratives, which open the Tanak, in point of fact a proper understanding of the narrative books includes a recognition of their complexity. There is indeed a sense in which the narratives of the Pentateuch, easier to read than the Prophets, are yet more difficult to understand. Proper understanding of the Pentateuch comes more easily, as I have learned from my teaching, when the Pentateuch is reserved for the last.

After considering the Prophets then, in whom we shall find a remarkable blend of religious ideas and poetry, we shall study the Hagiographa, and finally the Torah and the other narrative books.[3]

---

[3] Some repetition is inevitable, and some is deliberate. Where it seems easiest to repeat briefly, I do so, rather than subject the reader to an overabundance of cross references.

CHAPTER

I

The Historical

ANTECEDENTS

SCRIPTURE preserves for us a host of recollections of a Wilderness period, but no literature from the period. The recollections found in the later writings comprise a large variety of materials, which we could classify today in various categories. Thus, we can notice, respecting the economic life, that water was of crucial importance; in the realm of anthropology, we can discern traces of a society that was matriarchal ("centered in the mother") rather than patriarchal ("centered in the father"). The folklorist can assemble materials, ranging from direct statements to tantalizingly vague clues, on primitive customs and usages. Obviously, a well-rounded approach to the biblical period would involve all these disciplines, and indeed several more.

We shall have to bypass much that is related, but only indirectly so, to our purpose for two reasons. First, space does not permit the inclusion of too many details, and we must simplify even at the risk of oversimplification.

The second reason for passing over some details is a little more complicated. It involves a distinction between the origin of some custom or practice and the meaning that developed beyond the primitive origin. In our day, the handshake is a social convention symbolizing friendship and trust between two people; the custom is presumed to have come from an age when men went around armed, so that the extension of the bare hand disclosed that he who extended it had no weapon in it. Not everybody today who shakes hands knows the origin of the custom. If we were writing a commentary to a book, which said simply that John shook hands with Tom, we might explain briefly, for the benefit of a man from Mars, that "handshaking was one of the amenities of common courtesy," or we might write a longer note, appending the information about the remote origin of handshaking.

The Bible preserves customs that had undergone development long before the time a given passage recorded them in writing. Often an understanding of such a passage is clear from a brief explanation of what the custom had come to mean; occasionally, however, understanding is further aided by an account of the origin and background. To explain the background of everything, however, would throw up too many obstacles to the reader's progress. Although consistency might demand that one should give the origin either of everything or of nothing, I shall be inconsistent, indicating the origin of certain customs and not of others. The focus will not be on origins, but on the meaning of the developed custom.

The word "wilderness" means something a little different from what the word "desert" implies. Although the Hebrew term *midbar* [1] is translated by either word, each presents a different picture, especially to us Americans. "Desert" usually connotes the trackless sands, familiar to us from the movies, of the Sahara, a place that must occasionally be traversed, but in which one scarcely dwells. Although the Wilderness seems to have contained such an area (*Debbet er-Ramleh*), it was a place with vegetation that cattle could eat, dotted with tiny fertile places where a few people might settle. Because the vegetation was poor, people had to move from place to place in search of better pasturage. Some writers speak of the Hebrews of the Wilderness period as nomads, while others prefer to speak of them as semi-nomads.

The Wilderness area is roughly the region south and southwest of Palestine. Its eastern border is formed by a line running from the Dead Sea to the Gulf of Aqaba, where the city of Elath is now located. West of this line the Wilderness stretched even further southward

[1] Other Hebrew terms are *ye'shimon, 'araba, sia, tohu, shamma, sharab;* Sinai and Shur are place names.

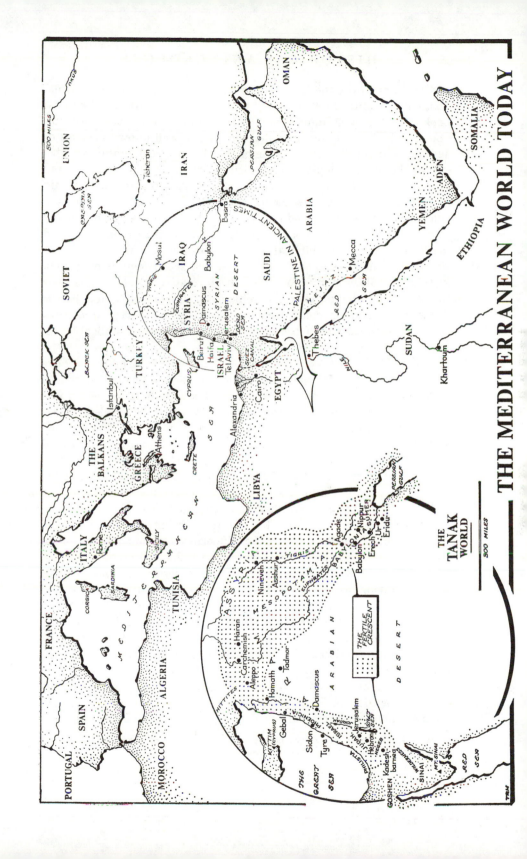

THE MEDITERRANEAN WORLD TODAY

and westward over the land that is now called the Sinai Peninsula. Today it is bounded on the west by the Suez canal and the Red Sea. Looking at the geography in another way, the extreme southern portion of Palestine is a region called the Negeb, well known because of developments in the modern state of Israel. Until reclamation was begun by the Israelis, most tourists assumed that the land, desolate into modern times, had always been so. However, both archaeology and literary sources furnish evidence that the Negeb at one time provided sustenance for a good many tiny settlements and a good many people. The Negeb is probably a little too far north to be considered the Wilderness of the biblical account; for our purposes let us consider the Wilderness to be the area west and southwest of the Negeb. In this infertile, mountainous area the formative facets of the early Hebrews took shape. That the religion of Israel originated in the Wilderness must be considered an established historical fact; evidence for it appears with great frequency in all types of biblical literature.[2]

The Wilderness period is reported, almost invariably, to have lasted forty years. Virtually all biblical students accept forty as a round number rather than a precise one. The length of the period was probably fixed in this way because centuries after the Wilderness period people who looked back to it, without having done modern research in archives, were content to summarize its duration in a round number. They told many legends about the period; indeed, a mention of the Wilderness period is often accompanied by the assertion that this period occurred immediately after the miraculous Exodus of the Hebrews from Egypt where they had been enslaved. The student interested primarily in history has many puzzling questions to play with regarding the Exodus and the Wilderness. In due course, I shall speak of the Exodus and its relation to the Wilderness period; but for the moment all we need to know is that a period of nomadism or seminomadism preceded the Hebrews' entrance into Palestine and that the Wilderness period was formative. The nomadic Hebrews were a group of related tribes; their actual units were relatively small and could probably be called clans rather than tribes. Perhaps a tribe was a group of related clans, while a clan was a group of related families.

Three matters command our attention, for they were consistently influential in later times, even though they went through change and reinterpretation.

2 The following passages might be consulted: Amos 2:10, 5:25; Hos. 2:16–17; 13:5; Jer. 2:2; Deut. 2:10; Ezek. 20:10–11; Ps. 107:4.

First, there is the question of the dwelling place of the God of the Hebrews. In the Wilderness, the tribes had a Deity whom modern scholars are accustomed to speak of as Yahve.[3] The modern person who believes in God usually thinks of Him as dwelling in heaven. In the Wilderness period, and occasionally later, Yahve was believed to dwell in or on a sacred mountain in the Wilderness, or perhaps in a cave on that mountain. We do not know today which mountain that was. In some biblical accounts the mountain is called Sinai, and in others Horeb. Did these two names refer to one and the same mountain? Or was one name that of a mountain range and the other that of a particular peak? We do not know.

When the Hebrews wandered into Palestine, it was believed that Yahve accompanied them. Nevertheless, inconsistent as this may seem, He was thought of as still maintaining His authentic or permanent dwelling in the cave on the sacred mountain. Although the time between the Hebrew migration into Palestine (perhaps about 1300 B.C.) and the time of Elijah (about 900) was an interval of at least 400 years, a narrative about the later period (I Kings 19) vividly depicts the motif of the mountain cave. Elijah, according to the narrative,[4] had aroused the wrathful enmity of Ahab and Jezebel, the king and queen. Fearfully, he went southward to Beer-Sheba. Then he journeyed for a day in the Wilderness. When he became faint from discouragement and lack of food, a benevolent angel gave him food and drink. Once refreshed, he journeyed for forty days and forty nights (again forty is a round number) until he came to Horeb, the mountain of the Deity. "He came there to the cave"—notice that the text says *the* cave—"and spent the night there." To be more precise, the cave was not considered as the dwelling of the Deity, but as the place where He appeared to people. If someone wanted to commune with the Deity, he could not do so simply anywhere, but he had to go to that mountain cave and there await the "theophany"—the appearance of God.

[3] In German the name is spelled Jahweh. Many generations after the Exodus the custom arose (still observed by Orthodox Jews) of not pronouncing the divine name. Hebrew is a language of consonants (written vowels were added in medieval times). Jews read the consonants as *adonoi*. Out of medieval Latin there has been bequeathed to us the form *Jehovah*. Perhaps the name Yahve means something akin to "he who causes things to be"; scholars debate about this, and with good reason, because there is no clear certainty about it.

[4] Elijah flourished in the days of King Ahab, 869–850 B.C. I and II Kings came into literary form, though using older sources, in two stages, the first "version" emerging about 600 and the second perhaps a century later. That is to say that three hundred years after Elijah's time the narrative of his trip to the cave did not undergo suppression by those who produced the Book of Kings.

Still another narrative relates to the cave on the mountain. We read in Exodus 33:17ff., in an account not free from some confusion, that Moses, after ascending Mount Sinai to receive the Ten Commandments, wanted the assurance that the Deity would accompany him and the Hebrews on the remainder of their journey through the Wilderness and into Palestine. Moreover, Moses desired to see what the text calls the divine "glory." The Deity replies to him, "A man cannot see My face and live." Yet there was a rock nearby, and Moses was told to stand in its cleft; the Deity proposed to cover him "with My hand until I have passed by. And I will take away My hand, and you will see My back, but My face will not be seen." The cleft in the rock and the cave are markedly synonymous.

The second matter influential in later biblical times was the persistent view that during the Wilderness period the Hebrews and their Deity had entered into a relationship with each other which bound them together and prescribed some mutual obligations. A bond with mutual obligations sounds much like the modern contract; the Hebrew term for this bond is b'rith, customarily translated as "covenant." The obligations are not completely clear, but they can be stated in general ways. The Hebrews obligated themselves to serve Yahve, and to abide by what they could learn about His will and wishes. In return, the Deity was to keep at least a benevolent eye on the Hebrews; possibly He would go further and provide them the best possible protection. Protection might mean succor from danger, or, in a positive sense, waging war on behalf of the Hebrews.

By its nature a contract can be broken. The breach can occur through mutual assent; or one party, convinced that the other has already broken the contract, can proceed on that assumption. Naturally, only fallible human beings would capriciously or arbitrarily break a contract; the Deity would never do so. Yet the Deity, thinking that the people had already broken the contract, might thereupon act as though it were null and void. The obligation of the Deity to defend or to do battle would be nullified.

According to a persistent tradition, a covenant in the Wilderness between the Hebrews and Yahve was fundamental in their relationship. The accounts of that covenant in the Tanak are idealized. Tradition holds that after the Hebrews had left Egypt and were wandering in the Wilderness they entered into the covenant at the foot of Mount Sinai. Exodus 19 relates that in the third month after the Hebrews left Egypt they encamped opposite Mount Sinai; Moses ascended to God, where according to the narrative he was enjoined by Yahve to say to the Hebrews: "If you hearken to My voice and keep My covenant, then you will be My treasure from among all peoples" (19:5). In this passage the covenant is only alluded to, as if the author of the passage felt that mere allusion would be sufficient.

Between this reference to the covenant and one that follows, the narrative relates that Moses was enjoined to prepare the people for an occasion that was to occur on the third day following. The giving of the Ten Commandments and then a rather long series of laws follow. In Exodus 24 Moses returns to the people to relate to them the regulations he has heard. Then,

> Moses wrote all the words of Yahve; he arose early in the morning, and built an altar at the foot of the mount, and twelve pillars, corresponding to the twelve tribes of Israel. He sent the young men of the children of Israel and they offered holocausts and peace offerings [5] of oxen to Yahve. Moses took half of the blood and put it into basins; the [other] half of the blood he sprinkled on the altar. He took the Book of the Covenant [*my capitals*] and read it in the hearing of the people. These said, "All which Yahve has spoken we will do and obey." Moses took the blood [from the basins] and sprinkled it on the people and said, "Here is the blood of the covenant which Yahve has made with you concerning all these commandments." [24:4–8]

While this story is idealized and not necessarily historically accurate, its form shows that the author and his audience were so keenly aware of the tradition of a covenant in the Wilderness that a lengthy dissertation on it was not needed.

The Hebrews, then, were a seminomadic people, bound by a covenant to their Deity, who was associated with a sacred mountain in the Wilderness. When they came to migrate into Palestine, they believed that their Deity accompanied them.

The third matter we must consider is the character of the religious rites and ceremonies the Hebrews brought with them to Palestine. The most significant religious object they possessed was a box known as the Ark of the Covenant. According to tradition (Exod. 25 and 37; Deut. 10:1–5) the Ark had been made at Yahve's command to contain two tablets on which the Ten Commandments had been inscribed.[6] One of its functions was to accompany the Hebrews into battle to ensure their victory (Num. 10:33–6). On one occasion,

[5] Portions of the animal serving as a "peace offering" were reserved to be eaten; the holocaust, however, was completely burned up.

[6] This was the second set of tablets. The first set had been broken, according to the narrative in Exodus 32:19, by Moses when he descended from Sinai and beheld the Golden Calf.

when neither Moses nor the Ark accompanied the Hebrews, defeat ensued (Num. 14:44). The term "Ark of the Covenant" [7] implies that the tablets inside it were in some way connected with the document of the contractual relationship established in the Wilderness. The Ark was housed in a tent, sometimes called the "Tabernacle" and sometimes the "Tent of Meeting." While biblical accounts relate what happened to the Ark after the immigration into Palestine, there are no comparable accounts of the Tabernacle.[8]

The reader may recall from his Sunday School days that King Solomon, who reigned from about 962–922, built an elaborate Temple. If we assume that the immigration into Palestine was at its height around 1200, then a little over two hundred years elapsed between the introduction into Palestine of the desert paraphernalia and the housing of the surviving items in Solomon's Temple. Yet we do not know how important such equipment was in the period of the Settlement. Once the Temple was built, the Wilderness connotation of the various implements receded but was never totally lost.

Much more significant than any equipment, however, was a series of ceremonial acts. One of these, circumcision, was a rite widely practiced among Hebrews, other Semites, and even non-Semitic peoples. The tradition that circumcision was a sign of the "Covenant of Abraham" (Gen. 17:10–11) is a rather late (indeed, postexilic) account, explaining the supposed origin of the custom.[9] Another institution, the Sabbath, may date back to the Wilderness period, since the seven-day week was used by the Assyrians even before that time. The significance of the ancient Sabbath, and that of circumcision, was heightened in the exilic period. Since it is this heightened significance that appears in the Tanak, the question of the origin is not too vital for us.

The one institution that we are certain was important in the Wilderness is the Passover. In our day it is customary (and has been so for two thousand years) to regard Passover and the Festival of Matzoth as one and the same holiday, ostensibly commemorating

---

[7] There are many puzzles connected with the Ark; these must not here detain us.
[8] See pages 385, 478.
[9] An interesting tradition is found in Joshua 5:2–9. The children of Israel are represented as being at a place named *Gibeathha-araloth*, which means "hill of the foreskins." It is said that Joshua, cognizant that in the period of forty years in the Wilderness no circumcisions had taken place, obeyed a divine injunction to circumcise all the Hebrews. Next in the text comes a pun: the place is to be called Gilgal, for by Joshua's action the Deity has gilgalled ("rolled away": Heb. *galothi*) the reproach of uncircumcision.

the release of the Hebrews from slavery in Egypt. While such an enslavement may have some small historical kernel to it, Passover-Matzoth is connected with it only artificially, in accordance with a practice in late biblical times of seeking some historical basis for religious observances. (In the same way, Christmas, a very old holiday, was artificially connected in the fourth Christian century with the unknown date of the birth of Jesus.) Passover and Matzoth were once two separate and distinct holidays. The Festival of Matzoth was not a Wilderness observance, but Passover was.[1]

Since in the late biblical period the two occasions, Passover and the Feast of Matzoth, became blended into one holiday commemorating the Exodus from Egypt, it is clear that considerable history and development attach to these sacred days. The varied accounts in different portions of Scripture strengthen this impression. Thus, with regard to the date, some passages (Deut. 16:1ff.; Exod. 34:18) prescribe Passover merely for the *Abib* (the name either of a month or of a season). In other passages (Lev. 23:5–6) the month and day are enumerated precisely. Sometimes this designated month is called "First Month"; sometimes it is called Nisan, the name still used in the Jewish calendar. Ultimately the Passover-Matzoth festival was one of the three occasions for which a pilgrimage to the Temple was enjoined. A specific prohibition (Deut. 16:5) against an observance at home (the text says, "in one of your gates") suggests that there were those who clung to a tradition of the Passover as a home ceremonial, just as it has survived in the home *Seder* of modern times.

That Passover preceded the immigration to Palestine is not important in itself but is a major key to our knowledge of Wilderness practices. Once these practices were transplanted into Palestine, they were necessarily transformed. Passover-Matzoth, important in itself, is even more important as an indication of broader and more significant changes.

During the immigration, a seminomadic people became sedentary and a pastoral people became in part farmers. Farm communities developed into cities, especially in the north, and these cities, some of them on the great land route between Egypt to the west and Assyria to the east, became complex urban civilizations, as we have said. The immigrants brought with them the recollection of a special covenant with their Deity, who, though He accompanied them, was

[1] The passage most clearly indicating that these are different festivals is Leviticus 23:5–6: "In the first month, on the fourteenth day of the month at dusk is the Lord's Passover. And on the fifteenth day of this month is the feast of unleavened bread for the Lord . . ."

associated with a sacred mountain in the Wilderness. The obligations in the covenant, originally specified for Wilderness life, were to remain in some sense normative for ensuing generations and even centuries.

Once the Hebrew religion was firmly established in Palestine, its development and growth were largely a reflection of the events of Palestinian history. Thus, in the eighth pre-Christian century, the judgments and opinions of an Isaiah reflect the conflicts between Egypt and Assyria; and, similarly, the religious ideas of the period from 586 to 516 reflect the circumstances of the Babylonian exile.

The epoch preceding kingship and the rise of "national" sentiment is known in Scripture as the age of the "Judges." The Hebrew term means both judges and rulers—perhaps the flavor of the period is contained in the word "chieftains."

According to tradition, after Israel, under its leader Joshua, had entered and conquered Palestine, his death was followed by the period of chieftains, under whom the land was settled. The years of Conquest and Settlement were crucial to the molding of the Hebrew religion. The relation of the Hebrews to the population already resident in Palestine would determine its future shape, indeed its very survival as the religion that had emerged in the Wilderness.

How reliable is the tradition that under Joshua there was a complete, orderly, and easy conquest, marred by only one setback? Unhappily, this tradition is an idealization, which was formulated many, many centuries after the invasion. Indeed, when people looked back in the late biblical period some felt that no war of invasion should have been necessary (Exod. 23:27–30): "I will send my terror before you and will confuse all the peoples among whom you come, and I will make all your enemies turn their backs before you. I shall send the hornet [2] before you, and it will drive out the [resident] Hivite, Canaanite, and Hittite before you." In still another account, conquest would be easy, for Yahve would accompany Israel (Deut. 9:3): "Yahve your God . . . is a consuming fire. He will destroy them before you, and bring them prostrate before you, and you will drive them out and destroy them quickly." This easy conquest was to have provided Israel with a "land of milk and honey." Moreover, Yahve was to bestow upon them not a rude frontier land or a desolate area: the Deity will "give you great and fine cities which you did not

[2] The hornet is similarly promised for easy conquest in Deut. 7:20. No narrative about the hornet is found in connection with the Conquest, but it is hearkened back to at the close of Joshua's career (Josh. 24:12).

build, and houses full of all good things which you did not fill, and hewn-out cisterns which you did not hew, and olive trees which you did not plant . . ." (Deut. 6:*10–11*).

We may conclude that these accounts and traditions are the product of meditative piety rather than accurate historical reminiscence. This conclusion is substantiated not only by the unrealistic character of these passages (for such felicitous invasions are scarcely to be encountered in human experience), but also by some flat contradictions in the Bible. At the beginning of the Book of Judges (*1:1–2:5*), there is a rather ancient document from which a totally different picture of the immigration emerges. The document tells in some detail, without reference to Joshua, about conquests by certain individual tribes after Joshua has presumably already died. Yet in the Book of Joshua, these same conquests are related as occurring in Joshua's own lifetime.[3]

Accordingly, the traditions of an easy conquest under a single leader must give way to the more likely conclusion that the process of invasion was slow and sporadic, accomplished by individual tribes acting unilaterally or with some confederate tribes.

Who were the conquered residents? Scripture often refers to them as six[4] nations; some of these have been accurately identified, though others have not. Frequently, and perhaps carelessly, the term *Canaanite* is used as a collective term. I shall follow this custom, though only for the purpose of simplifying matters—by *Canaanites* I shall mean the people resident in Palestine when Israel wandered in. We cannot pause in a work of this kind to ask how the Canaanites chanced to be in Palestine, nor the fascinating pre-biblical history of that area; similarly, I shall not go into the various theories concerning the identification of the Hebrews with the *Habiru*.[5] I must not linger over such worthy theories as the one that Joshua preceded Moses (the Bible makes Joshua the successor of Moses), or that Joshua led an invasion into Palestine across the Jordan while Moses led one into Palestine from the south. For our purposes it must suffice that when the Hebrews filtered in, slowly and sporadically, they found a resident population whom we shall allude to as the Canaanites.

The Canaanites were well rooted in the land when the Hebrews

---

[3] Compare Judges 1:*10–15*, 20 with Josh. 15:*13–19*; Judges 1:*21* with Josh. 15:63; Judges 1:*27–8* with Josh. 17:*11–13* and Judges 1:29 with Josh. 16:*10*. See pages 422ff.

[4] Six is the most frequent, but not the invariable number. Exodus 3:8 and *17*, each gives six names; Gen. 15:*1–21* gives ten. The six usual names are these: Canaanites, Amorites, Hittites, Perizites, Hivites, and Jebusites.

[5] See page 356.

entered it. Moreover, they were not exterminated, though in the Five Books of Moses the injunction that they should be is frequent,[6] but abided side by side with the Hebrews for centuries. While the religious differences between the Hebrews and the Canaanites were sharp at some points, the notion that the Canaanites and the Hebrews were people totally different in language, race, and other attributes is a misconception. The Canaanites, like the Hebrews, were a Semitic people. Their language, therefore, was akin to Hebrew; indeed, one theory holds that the Hebrews gave up their kindred dialect and absorbed that of the Canaanites—in other words, they absorbed Hebrew from the Canaanites.

When peoples who have nothing in common encounter one another, little mutual interpenetration can occur; when peoples meet who have something in common, they can naturally borrow from each other. Since the Canaanites preceded the Hebrews into Palestine, they were settled there in walled cities and in developed farm lands, with their temples already quite ancient. When the military conquest was over, how much would the Hebrews borrow, consciously or unconsciously, from the Canaanites? The most important factor that inhibited borrowing was the view of the Hebrews that they had their own Deity, Yahve, with whom they had made a compact in the Wilderness. Had this conviction been dormant or weak, it would unquestionably have been overwhelmed in the new environment. Yet it not only survived but was recurrently strengthened. The Settlement experience did somewhat blunt the Yahvism of the Wilderness, and forms of religious syncretism (that is, the blending of diverse strands) developed, but Yahvism was destined to survive.

A decisive event, the battle of Taanach, made a notable contribution to this survival. This battle is a landmark in the history of the religion of Israel. The circumstances of this battle between the Hebrews and the Canaanites became the subject of the Song of Deborah, the oldest piece of writing in the Tanak. This Song (Judges 5) describes a situation in which such chaos existed that "the highways ceased, and travellers walked through the byways" (5:6). We see the Hebrews in a military crisis. To the urgent call to battle,

---

[6] The Book of Joshua, which accepts the axiom that the Canaanites should have been exterminated, relates (9:3–27) that the residents of Gibeon, fearing extermination, had recourse to a ruse; they donned torn and worn clothes, and represented themselves to the Hebrews as distant, non-Canaanite people who asked for a covenant which would preserve them, and received it. The purpose of this fictitious narrative is to point out how it was that Canaanites continued to reside in the land.

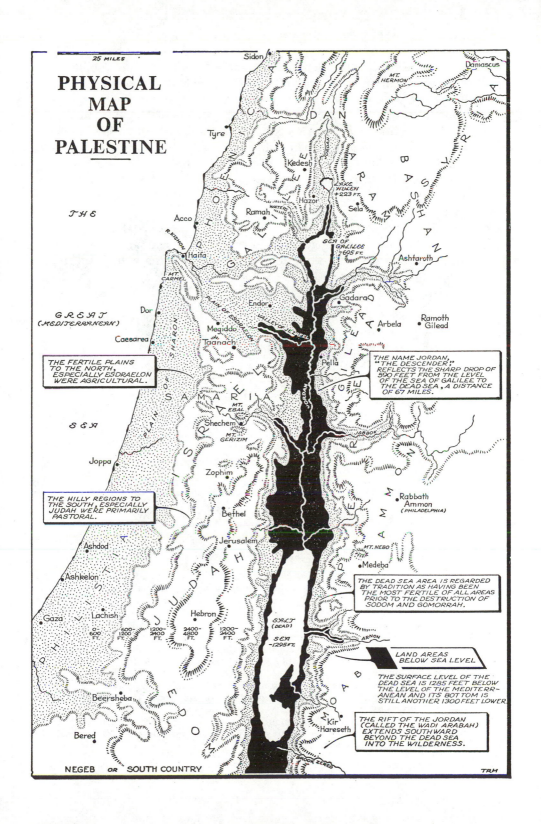

PHYSICAL MAP OF PALESTINE

25 MILES

Sidon

Damascus

MT. HERMON

Tyre

Kedesh

LAKE HULEH +223 FT.

Hazor

Sela

Ramah

Ashtaroth

Acco

R. KISHON

Haifa

MT. CARMEL

THE

SEA OF GALILEE 695 FT.

Gadara

Ramoth Gilead

Arbela

Endor

Dor

GREAT (MEDITERRANEAN)

Megiddo

Taanach

Caesarea

VALLEY OF JEZREEL

PLAIN OF ESDRAELON

Pella

THE FERTILE PLAINS TO THE NORTH, ESPECIALLY ESDRAELON WERE AGRICULTURAL.

THE NAME JORDAN, "THE DESCENDER," REFLECTS THE SHARP DROP OF 590 FEET FROM THE LEVEL OF THE SEA OF GALILEE TO THE DEAD SEA, A DISTANCE OF 67 MILES.

SEA

SAMARIA

MT. EBAL

Shechem

MT. GERIZIM

JABBOK

Joppa

Zophim

THE HILLY REGIONS TO THE SOUTH, ESPECIALLY JUDAH WERE PRIMARILY PASTORAL.

Rabbath Ammon (PHILADELPHIA)

Bethel

Jerusalem

MT. NEBO

Ashdod

Medeba

Ashkelon

THE DEAD SEA AREA IS REGARDED BY TRADITION AS HAVING BEEN THE MOST FERTILE OF ALL AREAS PRIOR TO THE DESTRUCTION OF SODOM AND GOMORRAH.

Gaza

Lachish

Hebron

SALT (DEAD)

0-600 FT.

600-1200 FT.

1200-2400 FT.

2400-4800 FT.

1200-2400 FT.

SEA -1295 FT.

ARNON

LAND AREAS BELOW SEA LEVEL

THE SURFACE LEVEL OF THE DEAD SEA IS 1285 FEET BELOW THE LEVEL OF THE MEDITERRANEAN AND ITS BOTTOM IS STILL ANOTHER 1300 FEET LOWER.

Beersheba

Kir Hareseth

THE RIFT OF THE JORDAN (CALLED THE WADI ARABAH) EXTENDS SOUTHWARD BEYOND THE DEAD SEA INTO THE WILDERNESS.

Bered

BROOK EZRED

NEGEB OR SOUTH COUNTRY

TRM

some tribes (Ephraim, Benjamin, Machir,[7] Naphtali, and Zebulun) responded affirmatively, while others (Gad, Reuben, and Dan) did not. The Hebrew tribes met the foe (called in the text the Kings of Canaan), led by Sisera at Taanach, near the waters of Megiddo. In the battle the Canaanites were routed. The stream Kishon, swollen by a sudden flood, completed their ruin, and Sisera had to abandon his chariot to flee on foot. He stopped to ask for food at the home of a woman named Jael. This he received, as well as a bed. While he slept, Jael slew him by driving a tent peg into his head; some of these details are found in the prose version in Judges 4.

The leader of the Hebrews was a woman named Deborah, to whom the poem in Judges 5 is attributed. (Poem and song are synonymous in biblical literature.) The poem begins with a call to people to praise Yahve:

> When locks of hair hung loose [8] in Israel
> And when people willingly offered themselves—
>   Praise Yahve!
> Hear, O kings; give ear, O rulers!
> I unto Yahve, I [9] shall sing
> I shall make melody to Yahve, the God of Israel.

The next lines are addressed to Yahve:

> Yahve, when you came out of Seir, in your march from the
>   fields of Edom,
> The earth quaked, and the heavens dripped, indeed the
>   clouds dripped water.
> The mountains melted before Yahve, the God of Israel.[1]

The invocation over, the narrative of triumph now follows:

> In the days of Shamgar son of Anath, in the days of Jael,
> Highways ceased to exist; travelers went on crooked ways.

[7] The usual number of the tribes is given as twelve, named after the sons of Jacob: Reuben, Simeon, Levi, Judah, Gad, Asher, Zebulun, Issachar, Naphtali, Dan and Benjamin; Levi's name was to be subtracted since his tribe became ecclesiastic and without land, thus leaving ten; the other two tribes were named for Jacob's grandchildren, Ephraim and Manasseh, the sons of Joseph. This is romance, not history. Machir and Gilead make the tribes number at least fourteen; tradition relates that Machir's father was Manasseh and Gilead was Machir's son. Any composite list of the twelve tribes, like the twelve disciples of Jesus, gets to fourteen or even higher.

[8] Possibly a symbol of a vow, taken to promise military aid.

[9] The "I" occurs twice in the Hebrew, possibly for emphasis. The English can scarcely convey this intent.

[1] A note by a scribe identified the mountains as Sinai; this note was thereafter copied into the text, giving the reading: "The mountains melted before Yahve, **This is Sinai**, before Yahve the God of Israel."

*Dwelling [2] outside [2] fortresses [2] ceased in Israel—how they
ceased!*
Until you arose, O Deborah, arose as a Mother in Israel.

The next verses, 5:8–9 are quite beyond understanding:

New leaders were chosen,[3] and there was war in the gates.
Was a shield or spear seen among the 40,000 in Israel?
*My heart goes out to the rulers of Israel, who offer them-
selves among the people willingly.*
Bless Yahve![4]

Wake up, wake up, O Deborah! Utter a song!
*Rise up, O Barak, the son of Abinoam, and lead away your
captives!*

The poem gives next, 5:13–18, a résumé, here omitted, of the tribes
that answered, or failed to answer, Deborah's call.

*The kings came, they fought—it was the kings of Canaan
who fought—*
*At Taanach near the waters of Megiddo—a profitless
venture!*
*From heaven the stars did battle, they did battle against
Sisera.*
*The stream Kishon swept them away, the stream Kishon
grappled with them.[5]*

Then the horses' hoofs beat the ground [as they fled][6]
From the galloping, galloping of the steeds.

Next comes a verse, 5:23, proclaiming a curse upon Meroz, an
allusion completely dark, and often taken to be a town which was
hospitable to the fleeing Sisera. By contrast with Meroz, the action
of Jael emerges more sharply:

[2] The Hebrew word rendered by three in English is unknown. I have given a guess,
neither better nor worse than that of others: "Inhabitants of villages ceased";
"The peasantry ceased."
[3] The phrase is not so much a translation as a guess.
[4] The succeeding verse, 5:10–11, cannot be understood. A typical translation
reads: "You who ride on red asses, who sit on rich cloths, and walk by the way—
tell of it, louder than the voices of musicians among the watering troughs. There
they will rehearse the triumphs of Yahve, the triumphs of his ——(?) in Israel;
then the people of Israel went down the gates."
[5] A guess about an obscure word; the phrase is often translated "that ancient
river."
[6] Another obscure passage, often rendered "O my soul, you have trodden down
strength."

*Jael, the wife of Heber the Kenite, is blessed above all
women,*
Blessed more than all women who dwell in tents.
He [Sisera] asked for water—she gave him milk!
She brought him curds in a bowl fit for a nobleman!
*She put her [left] hand to the tent-peg, her right hand to
the laborer's mallet,*
She struck Sisera a blow; she shattered his head,
She struck and pierced his temple.
*At her feet he went to his knees, he fell [to the ground and]
lay there!*
*At her feet he went to his knees; there where he went to
his knees, he fell, slain!*

The mother of Sisera looked out of the window,
She peered through the lattice, [wondering]:
   "Why is his chariot so long in coming?
   Why do the hoofbeats of his chariots tarry?"
Her wisest noble companions answer—
Indeed, she answers herself:
   "Are they not finding spoil and dividing it?
   A wench, or two wenches for every man?
   For Sisera, a prize of dyed materials,
   *A prize of embroidered materials—[not one,[7]] but
      two embroidered, dyed garments for
      the neck!"*

So may all your enemies perish, O Yahve!
May His friends be like the sun when it rises in its might.[8]

The warlike character of much of the Song of Deborah presents
us with the paradox of a poem whose strong and vivid power elicit
our admiration, even though its vindictive spirit may bother us.

The first and last lines of the poem attribute the victory to
Yahve. It is clear that at Taanach a heavy downpour of rain made
a raging torrent of the stream Kishon, which often dried up in
summer. This sudden storm offset the advantage the chariot gave
to the Canaanites, permitting the Hebrew foot soldiers to win a
decisive victory. That Yahve was a warrior Deity is stated specifically
in another victory poem, Exodus 15:3–6: "Yahve is a man of
war . . . Your right hand, O Yahve, has glorious power, your right

[7] My addition, designed to clarify the intent of the verse.
[8] The passage is obscure.

hand dashes the enemy into pieces." Psalm 18:8–16 (repeated in II Samuel 22:8–17) and Psalm 68:8ff. give descriptions of how Yahve utilized what we would call natural phenomena against His enemies.

With Yahve taking part in the battle, Taanach was a victory not only of the Hebrews over the Canaanites, but of Yahve over the Canaanite deities. After accompanying the Hebrews into Palestine, He bested the gods of the inhabitants. The great victory ascribed to Yahve strengthened the Hebrews in their belief that they owed an allegiance to the Deity with whom they had made a covenant in the Wilderness. Having won a victory over the local gods, Yahve was without question the God of the land. From the standpoint of the adherents of Yahve, He possessed full legitimacy, while the Canaanite deities were poachers or intruders. The outcome, reflected in page after page of Scripture, was that in Hebrew thought the Canaanite deities were illegitimate, helpless—indeed no deities at all. Fidelity to Yahve implied obligations on the Hebrews to abstain from any favorable recognition of the Canaanite deities and especially to desist from those practices that marked the worship of them. These obligations were interpreted as emanating from the covenant in the Wilderness.

Yet the Canaanites, though subdued, continued to dwell in Palestine and to worship their own gods. One deity was male, Baal, a word meaning master or husband. Baal's consort is known in both biblical and extra-biblical literature under various names: Baalat, Ashera, Anat, and Astarte. Throughout Palestine there were small temples or shrines sacred to the Baal. Certain trees, upright stones, or springs were considered to be places at which one could appease the Baal, or elicit his approval, or come to know his will. To a Yahvist, these temples or trees were objectionable. Since much of northern Palestine was a rich agricultural land, Baal can be considered an agricultural deity. The fate of the crop depended on his benevolence. As animals and men reproduced through sexual union, so too, it was believed, the earth produced through sexual union. The ground became *Mother* Earth. When impregnated by its husband, it too produced. Perhaps Astarte was a symbol of the earth, for she was a goddess of fertility. Her place was taken at festivals by sacred prostitutes who were available to worshipers. Perhaps the act of sexual union with the prostitute was a rite urging sexual union between Baal and Astarte, whereby Astarte, and thus the earth, could be impregnated.

Since Baal and his consorts were agricultural deities, they could be petitioned in advance for their benevolence, or thanked in retrospect for it. There were three harvest festivals, timed to the peculiarities of the semitropical climate of Palestine. The first of these, in spring, marked the beginning of the barley harvest; the second, in early summer, coincided with the wheat harvest; the fall festival celebrated the harvest of fruit and vegetables.

The festivals, in principle, were objectionable to the Yahvist. Moreover, as the villages and towns grew and were touched by cosmopolitan influences, they harbored a society more complex than the simple one of the Wilderness. The rugged standards of morality and ethics, well suited to the Wilderness, were too elemental for transfer to and observance in the cities. To a strict Yahvist, city life was wicked.

Several reflections of hostility to the settled agricultural or urban life can be seen in biblical literature, for example, in the narrative of Cain and Abel (Gen. 4:1–12). Abel was a shepherd and Cain was a tiller of the soil. After a time Cain brought fruits of the ground as an offering to Yahve, and Abel brought firstlings of his flock. Yahve found Abel's offering desirable but not Cain's. Nothing in the narrative explains why one offering was acceptable while the other was not. A conventional explanation, completely unsubstantiated by the text, attributes to Abel a character better than that of Cain, who, a few verses later, murders Abel. The only reasonable explanation is that the story represents a feeling, found elsewhere in the Bible, that the pastoral nomadic life is preferable to the settled agricultural one. The literary prophets, as we shall see, draw a contrast between the virtues of the recollected life in the Wilderness and the evils inherent in urbanization.

The term syncretism, as we have said, means religious borrowing or the confluence of different religious streams. Some traditional interpreters like to believe that Judaism developed without ever borrowing from any other civilization, without undergoing any syncretism. This viewpoint is an antecedent conclusion, a state of mind existing before the evidence is scrutinized. Throughout history Jews have borrowed concepts, infusing them with their own creativity. They borrowed, as we shall see, from the Canaanites, from the Babylonians, and from the Greeks. The Christians syncretized too, from the Greeks and the Romans. Significantly, Jews and Christians took only those ideas and practices that seemed consistent with their own; nothing palpably alien was borrowed. In the very process of being taken over, new material was Judaized or Christianized.

It was inevitable that the Hebrews would annex part of the Canaanites' culture. They dwelt in the civilization the Canaanites had created. Much of their borrowing was done unconsciously. Sometimes individuals became alert to the fact and arose to denounce it, but the borrowing went on. The Hebrews borrowed the three agricultural festivals from the Canaanites. They did not leave them unchanged; indeed, we deal in a special appendix with the Sacred Calendar [9] and its history and changes.

Part of the essence of the pre-exilic religion of the Hebrews is the interaction between the Canaanite sedentary civilization and the Hebrew belief that its past period of nomadism in the Wilderness was the normative age. Perhaps the problem might be put in this way: how could the Hebrews, with their tradition of a covenant with Yahve in the Wilderness, come to terms with their life in Canaanite Palestine? This new life included not only a developing agriculture and increasing urbanization, but also, when the tribes moved from a federation into a monarchy, an involvement in international power politics. Such questions as how the demands of fidelity to Yahve conformed to alliances with Egypt or with Assyria, or the nature of Yahve's relationship to Egypt and Assyria became important after the establishment of the kingdom. What was Yahve's power, and what was its extent?

The Wilderness formed the outlines of the religion of Israel. The pre-exilic period, from the conquest and through the divided kingdom, and the devastation of the surviving southern kingdom, gave it substance and shape.

[9] See pages 518ff.

PRELIMINARIES

IN THE MIDDLE of the eighth pre-Christian century, an incident of considerable dramatic intensity took place. The worship at a royal sanctuary of Jeroboam II of Israel was interrupted by an obscure man; the resident priest scolded him and ordered him from the sanctuary. The words spoken by that obscure man, Amos, were recorded, and with this writing literary prophecy begins. Before Amos prophecy was oral; at least no previous prophetic message survives in its own scroll.

To jump, as it were, from the Song of Deborah to the Book of Amos is from some standpoints an exercise in leapfrog. A strictly chronological treatment would demand that we notice the literature from the intervening period. However, we shall here bypass an extended consideration of some of this literature, not because it is unimportant, but because we are at this stage not yet prepared for the perplexities involved. This literature is prose in form, and in content a narration of history. The early prose histories survive as portions of late compilations. Thus, for example, an ancient account of events in the court of King David who reigned from 1002–962 B.C. appears in II Samuel 9–20. The Book of Samuel—two books in the present arrangement—was re-edited around 510 B.C. My experience in teaching leads me to think it wiser to defer considering even the early sources imbedded in the Book of Samuel until we consider why and when an author wrote, or compiled, the total book. Although portions of the Five Books of Moses were recorded before the time of Amos, we shall defer scrutinizing any of this material for the same reason until we consider the relatively late compilation of the Five Books.

The book of Amos is not only in poetry, but in poetry of an extremely high order. It is necessary, therefore, to consider what biblical poetry consists of. In the first place, as we saw in the Song of Deborah, poetry is found quoted in books of prose. In such quotations the poetry is more ancient than the prose, for it needed to exist before it could be quoted. Some scholars have gone so far as to suggest that poetry is a form of composition older than prose. A more reasonable suggestion is that poetry lent itself more readily to fixed preservation in oral form; the folk songs of the mountains of Carolina and Tennessee are an example. The oldest biblical writings survive in poetry because prose could be, and was, more changeable with oral transmissions.

Secondly, poetry was almost invariably metrical. It consisted of a series of lines, each of which adhered to a number of beats. Usually each word was a beat, though such particles as "not," "in," or "on" could be joined to a word to equal a single beat.[1] The most frequent pattern is that of a line consisting of two closely related ideas, totalling six beats, but unmistakably divided into two units of three beats: ———— ———— ———— / ———— ———— ————. Less often, we find other patterns, still usually in two units, but sometimes consisting of four beats in each unit, or sometimes a unit of three beats balanced by one of two. The importance of emphasizing that a line or verse consists of two parts (rather than being two separate lines)

---

[1] Certain technicalities of Hebrew are worth noting. 1) The indefinite article, "a" or "an," is left unexpressed; *sus* is "*a* horse." The definite article is joined to the word; *ha-sus*, telescoped into the single word *hassus*, is "the horse." 2) Possession is shown in English by adding an apostrophe and s to the possessor: the *man's* dog. In Hebrew, though, the thing possessed undergoes a change of form. A possessive pronoun (his, her, my) can be added to the "possessed" form, still one word. Dog is *keleb;* his dog—and here dog is possessed—is *kalb-o*, telescoped into the single word *kalbo*. 3) a verb form implies its subject; in English it takes two words to say "he went"; Hebrew says it in one word, *halakh*. 4) Prepositions are often joined to a word. Nahal is "river"; *ke-nahal* is "like a river."

As a consequence, Hebrew meter is able to retain its regularity, yet express in a brief number of beats or words ideas or sentences which in English would require many. The six English words "Let justice flow like the waters" require only three in Hebrew: *yiggal kammayim mishpat*. The metrical regularity of Hebrew can seldom be duplicated in an English translation, so that a strictly metrical poem unhappily turns into free verse whether the translator is slavishly faithful to the original, or reckless.

lies in the close, often inseparable connection between the two segments. The second part supplements, or refines, or enforces the
first part and often makes no sense without it:

> *Let justice flow like the waters*
> *And righteousness like a perennial stream.*

Notice that the verb "let . . . flow" (Amos 5:24) occurs only in the
first part, but its effect must carry over to the second part. "Let justice
flow like the waters" expresses a complete thought, but the second
part by itself ("righteousness like a perennial stream") is clearly
incomplete. "Parallelism" is the technical term for the literary device
by which the two parts are joined together in this way.

Metrical poetry, when it is fortified by parallelism, is not unduly
difficult to remember. As a result, centuries could elapse between
the first appearance of a poem, in oral or written form, and its
inclusion in some larger prose work.

At least two ancient poems, or perhaps collections of poems,
are known because they are cited in later works. One such poem,
or anthology, bore the title "The Book of the Wars of Yahve"; only
two lines of it are quoted, and in only one passage, Num. 21:*14–15*. In
context the passage, touching on a question of geography, deals
with an aspect of the journey of the Hebrews during the sojourn
in the Wilderness. The prose line (21:*13*) preceding reads: "From
there they journeyed and camped beyond the [River] Arnon, which
is in the Wilderness [and] which comes out of the border of the
Amorite, for Arnon is the border between Moab and the Amorites."
The verse is contending that this movement by the Hebrews did not
violate the territory of Moab. To substantiate this assertion the following obscure lines from "The Book of the Wars of Yahve" are
cited:

> *Waheb* [2] *in Suphah* [2] *and the valleys of Arnon*
> *And the slope of the valleys*
> *Which inclines to the seat of Ar* [2]
> *And leans towards the border of Moab.*

In sum, the contention in a prose passage is buttressed by a quotation from an old poetic work. Since this is the only quotation from
that work, and it is hazy, one can only speculate on what kind of a
poem, or possibly anthology, "The Book of the Wars of Yahve" was.

---

[2] Waheb and Suphah are place names, now quite unknown; Ar is mentioned elsewhere in the Tanak (Numbers 21:28, if the Hebrew text is not in error, for *Ar*
may be the true reading); *Ar* is apparently another version of *Ir* of Moab. The
student who is interested might consult a good Bible lexicon under *Ar*.

The other ancient poem or collection is cited in three places. In the Hebrew text the work is called "The Book of the Yashar." *Yashar* means "upright," but we do not know whether the "upright" is the Deity or some hero. Indeed, to make matters more complicated and uncertain, one of the three citations occurs in the Hebrew text in I Kings 8:12 without mention of the source. The Greek translation does mention it,[3] but calls it "The Book of the Song." If we translate "song" into Hebrew we get the three consonants *sh-y-r*. An error by a copyist could have altered *sh-y-r* into *y-sh-r*, the Hebrew word for "upright." Some scholars therefore believe that we should emend "upright" into "song" in the two passages where it occurs; others believe that the Greek "song" should be emended to read "upright."

The first of the three citations from "The Book of the Upright/ Song" is in Joshua 10:12–13. It concerns the well-known myth about the sun's standing still:

Then Joshua spoke to Yahve on the day when Yahve gave the Amorites over to the children of Israel, and he spoke in the presence of Israel:

> *O sun, stand still at Gibeon* [4]
> *O moon, stand still in the valley of Ajalon.*[4]

The sun stood still and the moon paused until the nation took vengeance on its enemies. This is written [5] in the Book of Yashar . . .

The second citation (II Sam. 1:17–27) is the lament by David over the death of Saul and Jonathan:

Then David sobbed [6] this lament over Saul and over Jonathan his son. And he said—so as to teach children of Israel onerous [7] things—behold, it is written in the Book of Yashar:

> *O Israel, your glory is a corpse on your hills!*
> *How came it that the mighty fell?*

[3] In the Greek, the verse is I Kings 8:53.
[4] The place names have been identified, Gibeon definitely and Ajalon probably. The latter is the Wadi Selman, the former slightly eastward, both of them ten to twelve miles west, or slightly northwest of Jerusalem.
[5] Literally: "Is it not written in the Book of Yashar?" The sense is affirmative and declarative, even though the sentence is couched in the interrogative and negative.
[6] The Hebrew reads "lamented this lament."
[7] "Onerous things" comes from emending the Hebrew from *qesheth* (bow) to *qashoth*. Without this or some comparable emendation, this part of the verse is meaningless. The Greek translation either omitted *qesheth*, or else had a Hebrew text which lacked the word.

Do not relate this in Gath,
Nor proclaim it in the streets of Ashkelon,
Lest the Philistine women rejoice,
Lest the women of the uncircumcised exult.
O mountains in Gilboa, let there be no dew nor rain on
*   you, O deceiving hills.*[8]
For there the shield of heroism was defiled,
The shield of Saul, the weapon of the anointed [king].

The bow of Jonathan did not turn back,
Nor did the sword of Saul return empty
From [consuming] the blood of men slain,
And the fat of the mighty.

Saul and Jonathan, in their life
Loving each other and amiable—
Even in their death they were not separated.
They had been swifter than eagles,
They had been stronger than lions!
O daughters of Israel, weep over Saul
Who clothed you [in spoils of] scarlet and linen,*
Who put on your apparel ornaments of gold.

How came it about that the mighty fell in battle—
That Jonathan lay wounded unto de*ath?
I grieve over you, Jonathan my brother—
You have been a joy to me.
My love of you has been to me [something]
More wondrous than the loving of women.
How came the mighty to fall?
How came the very weapons [9] *of war to perish?*

The third citation is both brief and obscure. As we have said, it is reconstructed by blending the Greek translation with the Hebrew. In context (I Kings 8:12–13), it occurs in the midst of the occasion on which Solomon is dedicating the Temple built at his direction. Then Solomon said:

---

[8] This is an emendation into *Sadoth merammoth.* The Hebrew reads "fields of offerings."
[9] That is, Saul and Jonathan in this line have become figuratively more than wielders of weapons, the weapons themselves.

Yahve had set the sun in the heavens,
But He Himself determined to dwell in deep darkness.

------------------------------------- [1]

This is written in The Book of Yashar/Song.

The significance of these citations is that they provide some clue to time factors. Since David and Solomon are mentioned, we know that this poetry was written after the time of Solomon. This date, which is the earliest reasonable time, is technically called the *terminus a quo,* the date after which the writing must have occurred. The latest limit is called the *terminus ad quem,* the time to which we could extend the date of the writing.

One more instance throws a little more light on ancient poetry. The Hebrews had captured a city, Heshbon, wresting it from Sihon, King of the Amorites. But Sihon, according to the passage, had himself taken the city from the Moabites. Here is the poem (Num. 21:27–30):

Come to Heshbon, let it be rebuilt,
Let the city of Sihon be re-established.
When fire came out of the Heshbon
Flame from the city of Sihon,
It consumed the cities of Moab,
It swallowed the banks of the [River] Arnon.

Woe unto you, Moab!
You have perished, people [of the god] Kemosh!

He [who?] made his [Moab's] sons fugitives,
His daughters captives . . .

The source of the poem, according to the text, is the *moshlim,* a word meaning, literally, "those who make parables." The Revised Standard Version renders the word as "ballad singers." One need not quarrel with this translation, though I know of no evidence to support it, nor any proof that these "ballad singers" were a professional class. Yet the *moshlim* were obviously people who were accustomed to recite poems of triumph and of taunt such as this, and "ballad singers" is surely a translation superior to the King James' "they that speak in proverbs."

---

[1] Although the verse is beyond translation, let me make an attempt: "I have built a lofty dwelling for you, a site of your eternal residency." My translation is not to be taken seriously; its content, implying that Yahve had taken up residency in the Temple, is at variance with an abundance of conflicting data. Here and elsewhere the dashes indicate that the Hebrew is untranslatable.

The samples of poetry we have looked at are heroic, but a more homely sample is also worthy of attention. A man, Lamech, is named in the genealogy of the primitive generations between Adam and Noah. The text pauses to tell us about him and his two wives, relating to us what a great man he was (Gen. 4:23).

Lamech said to his wives Adah and Zillah:

> *Hearken to my voice, O wives of Lamech,*
> *Hear what I have to say!*
> *I killed a man for [merely] a wound to me,*
> *A youth for an injury to me.*
> *Cain reaps a seven fold vengeance,*
> *But Lamech seventy-seven fold!*

Unquestionably the good ladies were greatly impressed.

Even though we have not noticed other types of poems—blessings, curses, charms, incantations, liturgical bits, and, indeed, psalms—we have seen that poetry was ancient and widespread. We need not be surprised, therefore, that the earliest of the literary prophets bequeathed his message to us in poetry rather than in prose.

What exactly was a prophet? And what course had prophecy run prior to Amos? A prophet, simply stated, was someone deemed close to the Deity who through special revelation was able to predict the future. The remarkably elevated content of the literary prophecy in the Tanak led scholars toward the end of the nineteenth century to minimize the element of prediction in prophecy. From that generation we have inherited the misleading epigram that the prophets were not "foretellers" but "forth-tellers." In fact they were both.

The interpretive literature makes a distinction, valid except when it is carried too far, between prophet and priest. In general, the priest was the trained, appointed functionary at a permanent religious site such as a temple. He presided over it, and, through the devices or paraphernalia in his charge, was able to disclose answers to questions about the will of the Deity. The priest could also predict the future. He might use the entrails (usually the liver) or the flight of a bird, or cast lots or throw a stick into the air (rhabdomancy). "Divination" was one of a priest's several functions.

A prophet, by contrast, was not usually the functionary of an institution. He was, we may say, a layman who was believed, or believed himself, to be close to the Deity. He might be of a priestly family, like Jeremiah, but his prophetic activity was not connected with a sanctuary or a temple. The conception of the prophet as a solitary individual near to God and therefore respected is rather well advanced. Behind it lay a development which is so thoroughly entangled that it is almost impossible to write a consecutive history of it. I use the word "entangled" because the Tanak confronts us with two semantic problems worthy of notice. First, at least four different terms are used to describe the individual for whom today we would use the one word "prophet." One term is "man of God," a second *ro'e* ("seer"), a third *hoze* ("gazer"), and the fourth *nabi*. The last is the usual term. The exact differences in these terms cannot be deduced from Scripture. However, and this is the second problem, in some passages *nabi* is a term with an overtone of contempt, while in others it is the highest term of approbation. How shall we account for this difference in attitude?

Possibly the explanation lies in the humble origin of the *nabi*. The word seems to mean "to bubble over." It may describe a person who in a state of ecstasy or seizure frothed at the mouth. The *nebiim* (the Hebrew plural of *nabi*) are often described as a "band" [2] of prophets. We can well conceive of such a band of *nebiim* as a group of whirling dervishes. They were ecstatics who used external paraphernalia, such as incantations or musical instruments, to put themselves into trances. Two related passages clarify the contrast between the respected personage and the men treated with contempt —the characters include Samuel, Saul, and a "band of prophets." In the longer of the two passages (I Sam. 9:*1*–10:*13*), Samuel is called both "man of God" and "seer." The narrative relates that the asses of Saul's father Kish were lost. After Saul and a servant had sought them in vain, they had recourse to Samuel who gave these instructions: " 'You will meet a band of *prophets* descending from the high place, and before them will be a harp, a drum, a fife, and a lyre, and they will be *prophesying*. A divine spirit will possess you, and you will prophesy along with them, having been turned into another man.' " When Saul became possessed, "everyone who had known him previously, seeing that he was prophesying with the prophets, said one to the other, 'What has happened to the son of Kish? Is Saul also among the prophets?' " [3]

In this long passage one verse, 9:9, provides the clarifying information that terminology has changed, and that at the time when

---

[2] A band is often alluded to as the "sons of the prophets."
[3] 10:*12* is uncertain as to its meaning.

the narrator was writing—four to five hundred years after Saul's time—that individual who had earlier been called a "seer" had come to be called a "prophet." Samuel, a highly respected person, is termed either "a man of God" or a "seer"; the experience of Saul, which led to his being called a "prophet," is deemed a lamentable one. In Saul's time, "seer" was a favorable term, "prophet" an unfavorable one. Centuries later, when the Books of Samuel were being re-edited, "prophet" had become a favorable term.

The second passage (I Sam. 19:23–4) describes Saul in a subsequent scene near Naioth in Ramah: "A divine spirit came upon him too and he went about prophesying until he came to Naioth in Ramah. He too took off his clothes, and he too prophesied before Samuel, and he fell naked all that day and night. Therefore people say, 'Is Saul also among the prophets?' " The latter phrase, we are told, became proverbial. Let us paraphrase it in the language of our day. "Is a youth from a fine family also to be found among the holy rollers?" The title was not a compliment, but exactly the reverse.

We saw that in addition to the title *nabi*, there were three other terms signifying an office of similar import. "Man of God" was highly favorable; *ro'e* was favorable. The term *hoze* was probably not quite as complimentary as *ro'e* nor quite as uncomplimentary as *nabi*.

It is important to recognize that mankind has had mixed feelings towards individuals thought to have some special relation to God. On the one hand, the assertion that God reveals His will or Himself to men has prompted some men to be deceived, or to become deceivers, and to make false claims that they have received revelation. On the other hand, the repudiation of each and every claim by men of divine revelation is equivalent to the contention that God does not reveal Himself. A religious tradition normally asserts that God has indeed revealed Himself in particular ways at particular times to particular men—religions born or matured in Palestine make such assertions. Consequently, such traditions must confront some claims that demand rejection. If we abandon for the moment the technical distinctions among *nabi*, *hoze*, and *ro'e*, we can state the proposition in the following way: a religious tradition which asserts that prophecy occurs finds it necessary to proceed with the assertion that some would-be prophets are true prophets, while some are mistaken or even false. Deut. 18:14–22 describes Moses giving his judgment on the distinction between true and false prophets. (The passage does not stem authentically from Moses, but was composed much later, perhaps about 510 B.C.) It runs as follows:

These [Canaanite] nations whom you will dispossess hearken to soothsayers and diviners. But as for you, Yahve has not permitted you to do so . . . Yahve has said, "I will raise up from your midst a prophet like you [Moses]. I will put My word in his mouth and he will speak to you in accordance with what I have commanded. The man who does not obey the word which [the prophet] will speak in My name—I will exact [punishment] from him. However, a [so-called] prophet who presumes to speak in My name something which I have not commanded him to say, or who speaks in the name of false gods— that prophet will die. And if you ponder, "How can we recognize a word which Yahve has not spoken?" [the answer is that] a word which the prophet speaks in Yahve's name and does not happen and does not come about, is a word Yahve did not speak. The prophet spoke it presumptuously, and you need not be afraid of him.

This passage evades, of course, prescribing how hearers who believe in prophecy can distinguish between the false and the true at the moment a would-be prophet speaks.

In early days, then, the *nabi* was essentially someone who was not believed in, while the *ro'e* was accepted. Accounts of certain prophets prior to Amos illuminate a distinction that ultimately arose between the *nabi* as an admirable figure and as a man held in contempt. Since these accounts contain legendary material, it is unsafe to rely too strongly on their historical validity. Yet if we read them for their general sense, we can gain a great deal of insight.

The earliest of these prophets was Nathan, whom we might call the "court prophet" of David. We first encounter Nathan (II Sam. 7) in connection with an avowal by David of an intention to build a Temple to Yahve. However, Yahve has revealed to Nathan that Solomon rather than David is to have this great privilege. Our second encounter with Nathan is in a celebrated story. David was standing towards evening on the flat roof of his house, when he saw a beautiful woman, Bathsheba, bathing herself. Sending for her, he took her to bed. When she became pregnant he had her husband, Uriah, drafted into the army, and put into the forefront of the battle zone, where he died. Then David married Bathsheba. At this point Nathan enters the story (II Sam. 12:1–7):

Yahve sent to David Nathan who said to him: "Two men lived in the same city, one rich and one poor. The rich man had an abundance of sheep and cattle, while the poor man had nothing but one ewe which he had bought. He reared it, and it grew up with him and his sons. It ate of his morsel, and drank of his cup, and it slept in his bosom, and was like a brother to him.

"There came a visitor to the rich man. The latter, reluctant to take of his own sheep or cattle to provide for the guest who had come, took instead the ewe of the poor man, and prepared it for the guest who had come."

David was greatly furious at the [rich] man and he said to Nathan, "As Yahve lives, the man who did this is to be put to death, and he shall make a four-fold recompense for the ewe . . ."

Nathan said to David, "You are the man!"

In its present form this magnificent anecdote is often judged as legend rather than history.[4] What concerns us, however, is not the historical accuracy of the story, but the unique role assigned to the prophet in it. Why should a ruler—we may describe him as an oriental despot—listen to a prophet without summarily sending him to execution? Did not Nathan take his life in his hands in daring to speak so sharply to the king? Or did he assume that his role as prophet provided some protection? And why should the text declare that the Deity sent Nathan to David? Did Yahve care about which woman or women David added to his harem?

The two narratives—about the Temple and about Bathsheba—are clearly not on the same plane, nor does the same type of concern motivate the prophet in each case. If in the matter of the building of the Temple Nathan is little different from the whirling dervish, certainly in the Bathsheba incident he is a staunch spokesman for morality and equity.

It is reported, in several passages, moreover, that David, before embarking on certain military campaigns, consulted Yahve for sanction (I Sam. 23:2; 30:8; II Sam. 5:19–23). Saul, David's predecessor, did the same (I Sam. 28:6): "Saul inquired of Yahve, but Yahve did not answer him, not in dreams, not by lots,[5] nor by prophets."

---

[4] As the story concludes, a reluctance to find unreserved fault with David results in added verses some of which denounce him and some of which soften the denunciation.

[5] The Hebrew for "lots" is *Urim*. "Lots" is a guess, though not a bad one. *Urim* and *Tumim* are often paired together (Exod. 28:30; Lev. 8:8). Their meaning is unknown. The Latin guess yields "Light and Truth" (*Lux et Veritas*). The seal of Yale University carries both the Hebrew and the Latin. We can be certain that "Light" and "Truth" is not correct; the *Urim* and the *Tumim* were part of the priestly paraphernalia, and hence my rendering of "lots." Scholarly explanations of the phrase are multitudinous, and the reasonable conclusion is that all of them are wrong.

The late Frank Porter of Yale, a great scholar, confided to the secretary of

In the incident of Bathsheba, David did not consult Yahve—indeed, he would scarcely have wanted to. The action of Nathan is no less than an intrusion in this case, for through Nathan David receives the answer to a question he has not asked.[6] Whether it is history or legend, or history overlaid with legend, this narrative about Nathan shows us the level on which the later literary prophets were to work. It enables us almost to anticipate the types of pronouncements they would make.

Nathan was not the only prophet in David's court; a second prophet was called Gad. He is mentioned in two contexts, but in the first (I Sam. 22:5) only to the extent of advising David on a military maneuver. The second action involving Gad is a curious narrative (II Sam. 24; see I Chr. 21:9ff.). David had displeased the Deity by taking a census. According to the narrative, Yahve sent Gad to David to let the monarch select one of three possible punishments: some years of famine, or three months in flight from enemies, or three days of pestilence in the land. David chose the third.

The court, then, had a prophet, or even two prophets. Gad does not rise above the stature of a mere diviner;[7] Nathan, in the Bathsheba incident, is a prophet in the later noble sense of the word. This is not the place to recount what the Books of Samuel and Kings, with their inseparable mixture of history and legend, tell both about a succession of prophets and about bands or groups of prophets.[8] We can only mention certain anomalies: in one incident, bands of prophets were loyal to Baal,[9] and in another, four hundred prophets loyal to Yahve could seemingly be wrong through Yahve's design.[1]

Yale that he had finally succeeded, after canvassing all the theories on the phrase, in finding the true meaning. Shortly thereafter Porter passed away. Unhappily, he wrote his explanation in the shorthand he had himself devised, and no one can read that shorthand.

[6] Psalm 51, a confession of sins, bears a superscription that it is by David and that its occasion is Nathan's intrusion in the Bathsheba incident. The superscription cannot be taken seriously; the content of the psalm discloses not one allusion to Uriah or Bathsheba. It is a great psalm, especially verses 18–19:

> "You do not desire [animal] sacrifices, or else I would give them,
> You do not look favorably on a holocaust.
> My sacrifice . . . is a broken spirit. A heart brought low, God will not despise." (Emended slightly.)

I Chronicles 29:29 mentions Nathan as a chronicler of events in Solomon's life.
[7] II Sam. 24:11 terms him "the nabi, the ḥoze of David."
[8] See, for example, Ahijah of Shiloh, I Kings 11:29–40, and 14:1–11; Shemaiah, I Kings 12:22–4; two unnamed prophets, I Kings 13:1–32; Elijah and Elisha, I Kings 16:29–II Kings 13:21; Micaiah the son of Imlah, I Kings 22:8–23. See below, pages 468–469.
[9] In reality, the Phoenician Melkart, I Kings 16:31–2.
[1] I Kings 22:6ff.

What should rather command our attention is that the prophets were invariably brought into contact with kings. (This generalization needs only one modification: the prophets about whom the most is related, Elijah and Elisha, also dealt in part with commoners.) Of course, since the focus of Samuel and Kings is on royalty, we may be seeing the prophets as part of this focus. When a king consulted one or more prophets about the best time to wage war, the prophet was involved in political affairs. Certainly, in many instances, the role of prophet in such consultation was passive. On the other hand, we read that just prior to the death of Solomon a prophet, Ahijah of Shiloh, wearing a new garment, encountered a warrior named Jeroboam the son of Nebat. Ahijah took off the garment, tore it into twelve pieces, and invited Jeroboam to take ten of them. This symbolized Jeroboam's receiving from Yahve ten of the twelve tribes to reign over (I Kings 11:29ff.). Again II Kings 9:1ff. relates that Elisha the prophet dispatched "one of the sons of the prophets" to anoint one Jehu as the new king in place of Jehoram (843 B.C.). From several such passages we can conclude that prophets often played an active role in political affairs. Some scholars seem to exaggerate the amount of such intervention, but assuredly prophets were occasionally makers and breakers of kings. Such intervention could not be limited to internal affairs. The prophet who felt that a monarch was inept in domestic matters could proceed to counsel him on foreign affairs as well.

To sum up, then, the prophet could, at one extreme, give advice concerning the whereabouts of some wandering donkeys, and, at the other extreme, anoint a man as king. He might provide a widow with unending food, as the legend of Elijah and the widow of Zarpheth relates; he might rebuke a David as Nathan did; or, like Elijah, he might chide a Jezebel. The prophet who was not merely a court functionary, or a whirling dervish strolling about in a band of dervishes, set his own high level of activity. He left to the priest the care of sanctuaries and to the usual court prophet the mumbo jumbo of mere fortunetelling. The prophet in the highest sense of that word was a man of noble thought and courage.

AMOS

NINE AVERAGE-SIZE CHAPTERS comprise this earliest of the writings of the pre-exilic prophets. The whole book does not stem from Amos. We must subtract from it, initially, eight verses (7:*10–17*) which relate an incident about Amos, and were not composed by Amos. Next, there are five "visions" which we shall consider and which explain how Amos came to speak out. Finally, the original Book of Amos, being of a very early date, has been altered and added to in the process of transmission. Many of the additions serve to soften the book's prevailing tone of denunciation. Other additions were appended to apply to the southern kingdom the message addressed originally to the northern kingdom. Modern liberal scholars are agreed that such additions have been made, and they are generally agreed in identifying certain passages as additions; other passages remain the subject of controversy. Of course, religious conservatives reject entirely any supposition that there are such additions. Their usual argument rests on the premise that the initial words of a biblical book (in this case, "The Words of Amos") are a complete guarantee of its authorship.

· Scholars cannot really *prove* that a section such as the latter half of Chapter 9 is an addition; it must be conceded that a subjective element enters in. Yet let us look at two different sections in Amos;

then let each person determine, as his own judgment persuades him, whether one and the same man could *reasonably* have uttered both statements:

> *Only you have I known of all the families of the earth,*
> *Therefore I shall visit upon you all your iniquities.* [3:2]

> *Behold, days will come when the man plowing will overtake*
>   *the man reaping [for crop will be abundant],*
> *And the treader on grapes [will overtake] him that sows*
>   *seed.*
> *The mountains will drip with sweet wine,*
> *And all the hills will be liquid.* [9:13]

Or, to take what is found in one single verse:

> *The eyes of Yahve are fixed against the sinful kingdom*
>   *[saying:]*
> *"I shall destroy it off the face of the earth,*
>   *Even though I shall not totally destroy the House of*
>   *Jacob."* [9:8]

Is the last clause integral, or added by a later hand to soften the harsh judgment of the preceding words?

Those of us who believe that there are additions and alterations in the prophetic books by no means insist, as conservatives allege we do, that the prophets must exhibit some superhuman consistency. We simply note how frequently comforting passages, usually in prose, follow fierce poetic denunciations. We question why a prophet should utter an unrelenting denunciation in one half of a verse, and then take it back in the second half. As others have long ago amply demonstrated the phenomenon I am describing, I shall present to the reader the end result of the study as it has come to be accepted among free biblical scholars.[1]

We have said that a prophet was a lone figure, not connected with an established sanctuary. What could prompt such an individual

---

[1] See C. F. Kent: *Student's Old Testament* "The Sermons, Epistles and Apocalypses of Israel's Prophets." New York: 1910, p. 52. Kent lists seven important evidences of addition: (1) variations from the prophet's characteristic vocabulary and literary style; (2) words or clauses that interrupt the logical sequence or else are very loosely connected with the context; (3) words that destroy the regular metrical structure of the verse; (4) wide variations in thought and teaching from those contained in the unquestionably genuine sections; (5) allusions to events of a time later than that of the original prophet; (6) reflections of the ideas and interests of a later age; and (7) obvious products of the scribal tendency to repeat, expand, or explain words or phrases found in the original text.

to feel that the Deity had selected him to serve some such specific purpose? What gave him the sense of having received a "call"? The answer, in the case of Amos, is contained in the five visions spoken of above. Happily, the first of these is in fairly good form:

> *Yahve caused me to see that—*
> *Behold—He was preparing locusts*
> *At the time [in spring] of the sprouting of the late growth.*
> *They were intended to consume the herbage completely.*
> *I said, "O my lord Yahve, be forgiving.*
> *How shall Jacob survive, being so small?"*
> *Yahve repented about this. "It will not be," said Yahve.*
> *[7:1–3]*

The vision is clear from the standpoint of time. The locust is a symbol for some agent of destruction, while "small Jacob" is a symbol for the Hebrew people. The vision discloses Amos' belief that the Deity had prepared some agent of destruction, but had responded to Amos' plea and changed His purpose. The second vision is as follows:

> *Yahve caused me to see that He was summoning fire*
> *To destroy the whole earth.*
> *It had consumed the great ocean,*
> *And was devouring the dry land.*
> *I said, "O my lord Yahve, desist! How shall Jacob survive,*
> *   being so small?"*
> *Yahve repented about this. "It will not be," said Yahve.*
> *[7:4–6]*

The time is no longer spring, but the beginning heat of the summer. Whereas the first vision uses a locust as a symbol, the second vision employs not symbol but hyperbole ("extreme exaggeration") in the suggestion that the ocean has dried up. The vision closes with the refrain of Amos' plea and the Deity's altered plans.

The third vision [2] is not as well preserved:

> *Yahve caused me to see*
> *That in his hand was a* qayyitz (*summer*)-*basket.*
> *Yahve said to me,*
> *The* qaytz (*end*) *has come for Israel,*
> *I shall not continue to pardon him . . . [8:1–3].*

[2] Various considerations make it reasonable that the vision in 8:1–3 be placed as previous to that in 7:7–8, and hence I term 8:1–3 the third, and 7:7–8 the fourth.

The remainder of the vision cannot be restored. The pun of *qayyitz* and *qaytz* is typical of the literary prophets. We have moved in point of time from early summer to midsummer.

The fourth vision is as follows:

> *Yahve caused me to see*
> *That He was standing on a wall.*
> *In His hand was a plumbline. He said,*
> *"I am about to put a plumbline*
> *On the toppling walls of the cities of Israel—*
> *I shall not continue to pardon him."* [7:7–8]

The falling of city walls is the symbol of such destruction as an invading army would occasion.

The fifth vision is the most vivid:

> *I saw Yahve standing on the altar.*
> *He said, "Smite the top and let the thresholds quake . . .*
> *I shall split it all at the top,*
> *And their followers I shall slay,*
> *Not one of them will survive, even as a fugitive. . . ."*
> [9:1]

These visions move us to a climax with a growing intensity, progressing from the fields and locusts, through the heat of the summer fruit, to the city and its supposedly secure walls, and finally to the altar, the central place in the sanctuary. Moreover, in a narrative quite separate from the visions, we are told that while Amos was a shepherd, his message, or at least one of his messages, was spoken within a royal sanctuary. The arrangement of the visions conforms to our knowledge of the man who moved from the southern fields to the royal temple of Jeroboam II in the northern city of Bethel, where he spoke.

Amos was interrupting some solemn occasion on which people were gathered at the royal shrine, and the occasion must have been a festival day. The text does not give the time or name of this festival, but most likely it was the fall festival of the New Year. This account of the succession of visions was rendered after, probably long after, the expulsion of Amos from the temple in Bethel. The series of visions is probably his reply to a question put to him, "How did you happen to go to Bethel for the fall festival, and why did you speak up there and interrupt the service?" Amos, we may conjecture, replied, "I saw a series of visions. After three of them I was prompted to visit Bethel to see for myself what went on. I knew that our evil conduct condemned us to destruction by foreign invasion. In the temple, I saw Yahve Himself in the act of causing our destruction. Therefore I spoke up."

The modern reader may ask which one of three possibilities *really* occurred. Did Amos have "hallucinations"? Did he *really* see these things? Or, did he simply relate usual and ordinary convictions in striking symbols and melodramatic form? We cannot know. I personally do not favor the second possibility, and I also doubt the third possibility, because I prefer to think that Amos truly believed he had seen what he reported. We must understand that in Amos' time his audience was startled not by the report of such visions, but startled because they threatened punishment. The term hallucination would be more applicable to visions reported in an age that disbelieves in them.

What infuriated the priest Amaziah at the sanctuary to such an extent that he ordered Amos out? Was Amos expelled merely for a crude interruption, much as the modern minister or rabbi might dismiss someone who broke the decorum of worship by speaking out from the pews, or was it rather the content of Amos' statement that aroused Amaziah? Here is the account:

> Amaziah the priest of Bethel sent a message to Jeroboam [II] the king of Israel, reporting, "Amos has plotted against you in the midst of the house of Israel. The land cannot contain all the things which he has said. For Amos has said, 'Jeroboam will die by the sword and Israel will go into exile from its native soil.'" To Amos Amaziah said, "Gazer! Go, take yourself away to the land of Judah and prophesy to earn your living there. But do not come back again to Bethel to prophesy; this is a royal temple and the seat of the royal residence."
>
> Amos spoke up to Amaziah saying, "I am not a prophet. I am not a member of a prophetic band. I am a shepherd and a picker of sycamore figs. But Yahve has taken me away from the sheep, and Yahve has said to me, 'Go, prophesy to My people Israel.' Now listen to Yahve's word. You tell me not to prophesy to Israel, and not to foam against Isaac [i.e., Israel]. Because of this [incident], your wife is going to be ravaged in this city; your sons and daughters will die by the sword. Your piece of land is going to be divided by lot, and you yourself are going to die on impure soil, when Israel goes into exile." [7:10–17]

Amos was not simply being a nuisance; rather, he had interrupted the divine worship to say something so momentous that Amaziah interpreted his words as subversive. We will turn to these words later.

According to most scholars the Book of Amos, that is, those parts of it that are Amos' words, constitutes a collection of short excerpts from as many as thirty-four addresses. I favor a minority view that Amos gave only one address, on the occasion of the fall festival. Right or wrong, from this viewpoint the Book of Amos has more intensity and significance than if it is seen as a tabulation of thirty-four fragments. When we subtract the visions, the account of the conflict with Amaziah, and the added portions such as the last part of the last chapter, we have a message short enough to have been delivered in perhaps ten to twelve minutes. It was extemporaneous, and was written down or even dictated only later, perhaps when events bore out the general tenor of Amos' prediction. The way in which the Amaziah narrative and the visions intervene in the body of the message reflects the vicissitudes involved in the copying of manuscripts. The message stands out in the greatest relief if we connect the portions closely related in thought.

To go back to the beginning, then, a shepherd from Tekoa (twelve miles south of Jerusalem) wandered north and saw conditions that appalled him. A sense of outrage induced in him visions of a divine punishment, which, since it was merited, was sure to come. At the royal sanctuary he attended a service of worship—possibly to be identified as an equinoctial [3] day. If so, it was just before dawn, at the climax of the service, that Amos spoke up.

The message would be considered "radical" in any age. There are people in our own day who would denounce it as subversive and who would be shocked to recognize it in the Bible. It is a biting commentary on current events made by a man from a rural district who wanders into a metropolitan area. Social class distinctions and enormous disparities between rich and poor confront him. The Book of Amos is a tract on the evil inherent in the economic life of a city—evils compounded by greed, injustice, cruelty, and the oppression of the poor.

Amos begins with a preamble. He invites his hearers to listen to denunciations, probably agreeable to them, of neighboring peoples:

> *This is what Yahve says:*
> *"For repeated transgressions [4] by Damascus*
> *I do not revoke [punishment].*
> *They threshed [the Hebrews] in Gilead with instruments*
> *of iron.*

[3] See "The Sacred Calendar," pages 517ff.
[4] Literally, "for three transgressions, yea for four."

Therefore I will send fire into the [royal] house of Hazael,
And it will consume the palaces of [King] Ben-hadad.
I will break the bar [locking the gate] of Damascus.
And cut off the inhabitants of Aven.
And the scepter-wielder of Beth Aden.
The people of [the kingdom of] Aram shall go in captivity
    [eastward] to Kir," says Yahve. [1:3–5]

Amos inveighs in turn against the Philistine city of Gaza, against the Ammonites, and the Moabites.[5] Then he proceeds:

For the repeated transgressions by Israel,
I do not revoke [punishment].
They sell the righteous for money
And the needy for a pair of shoes.
They trample on the head of the poor,
And they turn justice away from the lowly . . .
They loll, near every altar, on garments taken in pledge.[6]
The wine of those [unjustly] fined they drink in their
    temples. [2:6–7A, 8]

These brief verses are the keynote to a message that annually elicits gasps of surprise from my Bible students; somehow, modern people seem to feel that they alone have the insight to notice that men can be guilty of reprehensible acts to their fellow men and yet be punctilious members of a church or synagogue. Amos adds a special note of irony, for the target of his attack is not simply the familiar evil of the disparity between daily conduct and public worship; rather it is the more heinous sin of bringing the gains from improper conduct into the sanctuary. We might paraphrase him in this way: "You cheat and steal from the poor and helpless, and thereby are able to put a stained glass window into the sanctuary."

This charge, the substance of his message, is also present in much of the remaining passages. Amos goes on to describe further examples of injustice and to raise, unflinchingly, the crucial question of the validity of worship by those who are unjust. He describes the idle wives of the wealthy as "cows of Bashan on Mount Samaria, who oppress the poor and crush the needy, while saying to their husbands, 'Provide, so we can drink!'" (4:1). The husbands are "at

[5] Later editors added comparable denunciations of Tyre, a Phoenician city, of Edom, a country to the south of Judah, and of Judah.
[6] These were outer garments, needed by the poor for warmth at night. Exod. 22:25–26 reads: If you take your neighbor's garment in pledge, by sunset you must return it to him . . . In what else shall he lie down?

ease in Zion, and reliant on [the temple on] Mount Samaria!" (6:1).
They are eminent men, the leaders of the people; it is they whom the
less highly placed come to consult. Is this evil in Israel, Amos asks,
any different from that in the despised foreign countries, whose
leaders also are unconcerned about the poor? In Israel, people in
high places, "lying on beds of ivory, stretched out on couches, eat fat
lambs from the flock of sheep, and calves from the barns; they im-
provise on the harp like David, they try to compose a song. They
drink wine out of a mixing-pitcher; they spread on ointments made
of the finest oils—yet they are not sickened over the sickness of the
populace." [7] (6:4–6)

If we would appreciate the uniqueness of the thought of the
literary prophets, we must notice that Amos is not issuing a personal
protest against what is going on, but is certain that it is Yahve who is
the critic and whose will has been thwarted. It is not mere human
social standards or requirements that have been violated, but divine
ones. In Amos' view there was no distinction between "religion" and
"social conduct"; unlike some people today, he did not restrict
"religion" to its narrow "essential" meaning of man's relationship to
the Deity. Indeed, what made the Hebrew religion different from
kindred Semitic religions was its fusion of religion and ethics.

What place does ritual worship occupy in a religion? Amos says:

"Come to [the sanctuary] Bethel—and you will be sinning!
To [that at] Gilgal, and you will be multiplying your sin.
[Similarly,] bring on the sacrifice due at morning,
And the payment of your tithes!
Offer up a thanksgiving offering of fancy [leavened] cakes.
Call out your contributions; proclaim them!
This is what you like, O house of Israel," says Yahve.
          [4:4–5]

If all that Amos said was true, what would the consequence be?
The answer, from Amos' standpoint, was that the accumulation of
social injustices had finally amounted to the rupture of Israel's long-
standing covenant with Yahve. As the covenant was now broken, the
obligations incumbent on the Deity were null and void, and His
benevolent protection over the land of Israel was gone. A foreign
nation, if it cared to, could invade successfully—Assyria was at that
moment fashioning its growing world empire.

In Amos' view, it was not one single act or period of evil that
had broken the covenant. Rather, evil had accumulated over the

---

[7] The text reads, "the sickness of Joseph." Joseph, as the ancestor, often symbolizes the northern kingdom.

years to a point of climax, and though Yahve had tried, by punishment, to reform Israel, His divine efforts were in vain:

"*I, Myself sent [a famine, resulting in] cleanness of teeth
    on all your cities,
And lack of bread in all your settlements,
But you did not return unto me," says Yahve . . .
"I smote you with a withering and a mildewing of your
    many gardens and vineyards;
The grasshoppers ate your figs and dates,
But you did not return to me," says Yahve.
"I sent a plague on you; ***
*I let an army of youths be killed by the sword and the horses
    be captured.
The stench of the camp I brought to your very noses,
But you did not return to me.
I brought upheavals [8] upon you, and you were a brand
    pulled out of a fire,
But you did not return to me," says Yahve.
"Therefore, this is what I will do, O Israel:
Prepare to meet your God!"* [4:6–12]

We must keep in mind that the scene is still the sanctuary at Bethel. The words that follow are most pointed:

*Thus says Yahve to the house of Israel:
"Seek me in order to survive!
Do not seek out Bethel, and do not go to Gilgal,
And do not wander over to Beer-Sheba.
Gilgal will disappear,[9] and Bethel ('God's house') will pass to
    the demons!"* [1]

*Seek out Yahve to survive,
Lest fire [military conquest] fall upon the house of Joseph,
    and consume it,
And no one be able to put it out.*[2] [5:4–7]

*You are people who turn justice into wormwood,
And put righteousness on the ground,
Hating someone who publicly rebukes you
And despising him who speaks true things.*

[8] A gloss mistakenly identifies these military upheavals with the "overturning" of Sodom and Gomorrah, Gen. 19.
[9] The Hebrew has a pun: Gilgal will go into exile (Gilgal will *yiggale*).
[1] A paraphrase suggested by Julius Wellhausen
[2] Omitting "to Bethel."

Since you have crushed the poor, and have taken from him
    the grain that he has,
Though you have built fine houses of hewn logs,
You will not get to live in them.
You have planted delightful vineyards,
But you will not drink wine from them.
For I know that your sins are many, and your transgres-
    sions mighty ones.
You are foes of the righteous, you are takers of bribes.
You have pushed aside the needy. [5:10–12]

Seek good and not evil, so that you may survive,
So that Yahve, the Lord of the hosts [of heaven] may be
    with you,
As you have thought.
Hate evil, and love good!
Establish justice in the courts; perhaps Yahve may be gra-
    cious to Joseph.

"But," Yahve says, "in all streets there will be mourning,
And in all courtyards people will say, alas!
The farmer too will be called to lament;
There will be genuine mourning even for the professional
    mourners.
In all the vineyards there will be lamenting when I cross
    through your midst." [5:16–17]

Amos believed that Yahve would come into the midst of the land, for the equinoctial festival was focused on just that notion. The festival had been borrowed from the Canaanites. The sun was believed to represent the Deity. The temples were built in an east-west alignment, and at the east end of the temple there were gates. (Psalm 118:19 calls the eastern gates of the Jerusalem temple the "Gates of Righteousness.") On the equinoctial day, the rays of the rising sun would shine through the temple without casting any shadow because of the east-west orientation. The entrance of the rays was the equivalent to the entrance of fire; and the descent of the "sacred fire" meant that the Deity had come into the temple. Although the term for the descending sacred fire is not found in the Book of Amos, it is elsewhere called "the glory of Yahve." [3]

[3] See Leviticus 9:23–4: "Moses and Aaron went into the Tent of Meeting, and then came out and blessed the people. Then the fiery radiance (*kabod*, glory) of Yahve appeared to all the people. Then fire came out from before Yahve and consumed the holocaust on the altar." One verse later we read (Lev. 10:1–2): "Nadab and Abihu, the sons of Aaron, took each his fire-pan for carrying hot coals

The occasion of Amos' address, that is to say this fall festival, was what Jews came to call "New Year." [4] The term Amos uses is "Day of Yahve." Centuries later, "Day of Yahve" was interpreted not as the annually recurring occasion when Yahve judged the world, but rather as a single event in the future, when Yahve would bring all the world to a climax of final and terrifying judgment. In Amos' mind the judgment is neither future nor remote; it is taking place on that same day on which he is speaking. He mentions first the day itself, and then the activities connected with it:

Woe unto those who are fond of the Day of Yahve.[5]
What is the Day of Yahve for you?
It is darkness, and not light,
Thick darkness, with no brightness to it!
I hate, I despise your festivals,
I get no pleasure from your solemn assemblies.
If you offer me burnt animal and meal sacrifices,
I do not accept them.
I do not look favorably at what you pay me in your fat ani-
    mals.
Remove from me the host of your songs!
I do not listen to the song of your flute!
Rather, let justice flow as water,
And righteousness as a perennial stream. [5:18, 20–24]

Amaziah's sharp command to Amos to leave the temple was the result of the priest's personal involvement in Amos' criticism— Bethel was worthless, the Day of Yahve a mistake, the ritual unnecessary. How else could Amaziah have responded?

Did Amos oppose all ritual, or did he oppose it only if it was accompanied by social injustice? The question has often been

---

and put in them fire and on it incense; they brought before Yahve alien fire which He had not commanded them. Then fire came out before Yahve and consumed them, and they died, before Yahve."

See also Ezekiel 43:1–4; it states that the eastern gate is to be closed permanently, for Yahve is forsaking the sky as His residence and now dwelling permanently in the Temple. Four dwelling-places were ascribed in succession to Yahve. First, the sacred mountain at Horeb-Sinai. Next, the sky (this belief dominated from the Settlement until the end of the sixth century), third, for a short time, the Temple in Jerusalem, fourth, in the sky again. When I say that a belief "dominated," I do not want to imply that the conception of one period gave way completely and immediately to the conception of a later period; rather, vestiges remained from one period into another.

[4] The term New Year is rare in Scripture. See page 522.

[5] A glossator, tampering with the passage in Amos, as he did with other "Day of Yahve" passages in the Tanak, read futurity into this phrase. The version I give omits the gloss.

debated, and eminent scholars can be cited to support either opinion. The question under consideration is not whether ritual is useful or necessary to religion *today*, but rather to what extent Amos opposed it in *his* day. The opinions of modern scholars about Amos have often been colored by their own view of ritual, those in ritualistic churches contending that Amos denounced only empty ritual, while scholars in nonritualistic churches hold the opinion that he opposed all ritual. I personally maintain that though ritual is a necessity for religion, Amos (and Micah and Isaiah and Jeremiah) was dead against it.

Amaziah attributes to Amos (7:11) some words—a violent death for King Jeroboam—not plainly to be found in any of the preserved texts. If we are charitable to Amaziah, we can say that he is paraphrasing rather than quoting. Amos then predicts (5:27) that Israel will go into exile. He says, in the Deity's name:

"A foe will go all through the land;
Your very strength will be taken away from you; your palaces will be plundered.
On the day when I visit Israel's sin upon her,
Then I will visit Bethel, And the horns of the altar will be knocked off and fall to the ground.
I will smite the winter home as well as the summer home; The houses of ivory will be destroyed; many houses will come to an end." [3:11, 14–15]

Amos gives an elegy over Israel likening her to a dead virgin:

Fallen, the virgin of Israel cannot again rise;
She is thrust down to her soil, there is no one to raise her.
    [5:2]

The prediction of destruction, permitted by Yahve because of the breach of the covenant, is unmistakable. Amos gives us to understand that the punishment will be two-pronged—in part it will come directly from Yahve; in part it will come from a foreign nation. When Yahve was still conceived of as dwelling on a sacred mountain, it could be assumed that His power was limited and that only one people, Israel, could be His people. Later, when He was thought to have accompanied Israel into Canaan and overcome Baal, it stood to reason that His power transcended the mountain. If His dwelling was now rather the sky, was there not one sky and therefore one God for all the world? If Yahve was the only God, did He favor one people, Israel, or was He equally concerned for all peoples? The view that there is one God for all the world is called "universalism," and in a large sense Amos was a universalist. He attributed to Yahve a benevolence toward other nations quite equal to His solicitude toward Israel:

> *Are you not [exactly] like the sons of Kush [Ethiopia] to
>   me, O children of Israel?*
> *Yes, I brought Israel out of Egypt,*
> *But [also] I brought the Philistines out of Crete,*
> *And the Arameans out of Kir.* [9:7]

For Amos, there was only one God in the world. Scholars debate as to whether Amos or Moses was the first monotheist and universalist in Hebrew history. Two arguments are advanced against attributing monotheism and universalism to Moses. One line of argument states that if these doctrines had been formulated and promulgated as early as Moses, we should have got some reflection of them before the time of Amos. The second argument is simply that the figure of Moses is so shrouded in legend, and the accounts of him so late and hence relatively unreliable, that we cannot know very much about him. This first argument seems to me specious, since it "argues from silence." The second argument is reasonable, but dodges the question. It cannot be "proved" that Moses was a monotheist, but it can be proved that Amos was. Here we must promptly digress to raise a point of fundamental concern: Was Amos as a universalist at variance with the thought of his time, or was he reflecting well-established views? Was Amos' universalism his own personal creation or was universalism in the air? Perhaps Amos' great, though limited contribution, was to draw new implications from the prevailing thought of the day. While many scholars are inclined to see the prophets as originators of doctrines, as to some extent they were, my own disposition is to see them primarily as men who applied to real situations the consequences of ideas already in some currency. I see Amos as a universalist but not as the originator of universalism. He does not argue that universalism exists, but rather assumes it, and then proceeds from the abstract to the concrete assertion that the Ethiopians, the Philistines, and the Aramaeans are Yahve's concern as much as Israel is. The specific application of universalism is Amos' contribution.

The logic of abstract universal monotheism would lead to the conclusion that Yahve has no special place in His scheme of things for a particular people such as Israel. In the view of Amos and of his successors, indeed in the view of Judaism and Christianity, such a conclusion would be carrying logic to an absurdity. Amos, as well as subsequent prophets, always maintained some sense of Israel's special role in relation to Yahve, the one universal Deity.

Outside the prophetic writings, this special role is often described as resulting from a choice made by Yahve—made, it would seem, arbitrarily or capriciously—after which the "chosen people" are specially privileged. Such passages occur frequently in the Tanak and New Testament. But other, non-prophetic passages, as well as some prophetic utterances, assert that the special position Yahve has accorded to Israel brings about not privilege but obligation. Amos portrays Yahve as saying:

> *Only you have I known of all the families of the earth;*
> *Therefore I shall visit your iniquities upon you.* [3:2]

In Amos' view, special punishment is the consequence of a special position!

We can now review the dramatic scene at Bethel in the light of our understanding of the man and his thought. On the most sacred day of the year,[6] the services at the royal sanctuary were interrupted by Amos, a stranger to the region. He asserted that the services were not only useless, but contrary to the Deity's wishes; as a result, punishment lay in the immediate future. Israel's conduct had effected a breach in her covenant with Yahve, and therefore she lacked Yahve's protection. A foreign nation would successfully invade, ravage the land, and take the population, royalty and commoner alike, into exile. Amos insisted that worship at a sanctuary was out of keeping with Israel's earliest past and distasteful to Yahve. What Yahve wanted, indeed demanded, was social justice.

How did Amos' words come to be gathered into a "book" and thereby preserved? If he spoke spontaneously at Bethel, when was his message written down? Did Amos himself write it, or was this done by some unknown disciple? We can give only tentative answers to these questions, for Scripture provides almost no information. We are given relatively full information about the recording of Jeremiah's message, a century and a half after Amos, but we have only a few random clues to put together in Amos' case.

Three pieces of evidence may point to the answer to our questions: the conquest by Assyria in 722 or 721, the earthquake of 749, and the significance of the five visions. When Assyria invaded in 722/21, some people would remember hearing or hearing about an obscure prophet who had interrupted the services at a royal sanctuary to predict the event. The Assyrian invasion would appear to have borne out Amos' judgment, which would then seem worth preserving.

[6] Yom Kippur, the Day of Atonement, regarded today as the most sacred day, did not yet exist in the time of Amos.

Secondly, the superscription to the Book of Amos laconically tells us that his prophetic activity was "two years before the earthquake." Zechariah (14:5), written several centuries after Amos, alludes to this earthquake; he helps to date it, for he promises an upheaval necessitating a flight, "as you fled before the earthquake in the days of Uzziah the king of Israel." The Jewish historian Josephus (who flourished in the second half of the first Christian century and supplied material additional to Scripture) tells about the terrible destruction caused by this earthquake. If we trust him, Josephus enables us to understand why the event was called *the* earthquake in the Book of Amos, rather than *an* earthquake; it may have served as the occasion for writing down Amos' message. If the temple was destroyed by earthquake two years after Amos' appearance there (and here we have gone beyond the evidence), then the material recorded two years after the earthquake became destined for preservation when the Assyrians invaded a quarter of a century or so later.

Finally, Amos' five visions seem not so much part of a public preachment as an explanation to a circle of followers of why he spoke at Bethel. Once we begin to conjecture about disciples, further horizons open up to us. Suppose that upon returning to his native Tekoa Amos related his experience, and that when he reconstructed from memory what he had said, some disciple wrote it down. It is possible that another disciple recorded the visions of Amos, the incident of Amaziah, and the superscription about the earthquake. A tentative theory about disciples, together with what we know of the earthquake and the Assyrian invasion, suggests how Amos' words might have come to be the Book of Amos.

Few incidents in religious history were to become more influential than the transmutation of Amos' verbal message into a written book. Perhaps Amos' predecessors, Elijah for example, were equally meritorious, but their messages, if they were written down, were lost. In the Book of Amos we have the oldest book devoted completely to the utterances of a prophet. Even if Amos had had nothing of importance to say, the recording of his words would have been significant. But for people who regard social ethics as important, literary prophecy begins at a remarkably high point with Amos. As a written record, the Book of Amos helped turn the monotheism of Israel into ethical monotheism.

Amos denied (7:14) that he was a prophet—to him the term was one of contempt. The high status reached by prophecy later on is indicated by the shift in the sense of the term. When subsequent generations called Amos a prophet, the term had become an accolade. Men like Amos made it so.

CHAPTER

4

HOSEA

WE HAVE SEEN that according to the view of Amos, Yahve had tried by a series of punishments to deflect Israel from its wickedness, but in vain. Consequently, Amos declared, the die was cast; Israel was to be punished, and hence events were moving inexorably to that outcome. There is a somewhat mechanical pattern in Amos' view that cumulative guilt must lead straight to disaster. The fourteen chapters that make up the Book of Hosea are often interpreted as an admirable contrast to the mechanical pattern of Amos. In general, this contrast seems correct. Often, however, the Book of Hosea is described as if it were sticky with sentimentality. We shall see that it is not.

It is rather difficult to present a lengthy citation from Hosea because the text is in very bad shape. A rough private count leads me to conclude that about one third of the individual verses in Hosea defy easy translation, unless the translator resorts to drastic conjectural emendations. In chapter after chapter, two or three intelligible verses are followed by passages beyond comprehension. The extant translations of Hosea owe a greater debt to the ingenuity of translators than to the original Hebrew. Although it is therefore impossible to quote extensive passages from Hosea, the intelligible portions do enable us to grasp his thought.

Before considering the historical times in which Hosea lived, we must take note of a related problem. The Book of Hosea contains some verses that deal with the southern kingdom, Judah. Scholars consider these passages [1] to be secondary, that is, additions by a later scribe. As a result of these additions the message, originally meant for the north, became applicable in later times to the south as well. The principal basis for the scholarly view that Hosea's message was addressed only to the northern kingdom is that he mentions by name a good many places in the northern kingdom, but not one place in the southern kingdom. Moreover, in 7:5, where the context is unquestionably the northern kingdom, Hosea speaks of its monarch as "*our king.*" It is generally held that Hosea is the only literary prophet who was a northerner, and that his background was the growing crisis faced by the northern kingdom shortly after 750 B.C. We are able to fill in the backgrounds by correlating the chronological statements in the superscription,[2] Hosea 1, with data provided in II Kings 15–20, pointing to a period encompassing 745 B.C. through possibly 725. Hosea accordingly would appear to have flourished shortly after the time of Amos (roughly 750), yet before the Assyrian conquest of Palestine in 722/21. In 737 the power of Assyria first began to be felt by the northern kingdom; in that year Israel, under King Menahem, paid tribute to Assyria (II Kings 15:*19*–20). Three years later, nearby Damascus fell to this eastern empire. Under King Pekah (737–732) the Assyrians had stripped the northern kingdom of its outlying possessions (II .Kings 15:29) but had left the main body of the kingdom intact. Under King Hoshea (733–724) Israel sought the assistance of the Egyptians to the west (II Kings 17:4). The payment of tribute to Assyria was suspended, an act that was to seal the doom of the northern kingdom in 722–21.

The history of Hosea's period, then, is known in some detail. Some historians fancy that two opposing factions existed in Samaria, the capital of the northern kingdom, one pro-Assyrian and the other one pro-Egyptian. This suggestion goes beyond the evidence. A more reliable statement would be that the harassed monarchs, faced by possible conquest from east or west, could elect to call in assistance from the one direction against the menace from the other. Hosea alludes to such desperate appeals by the northern kingdom for help (7:*11*–*12* and 12:2 Heb., 12:2 Eng.) and scorns them as futile and even sinful, for to appeal to a foreign nation was in Hosea's mind the equivalent of apostasy from Yahve.

[1] The principal "Judahite" additions are 1:7; 2:2; 4:*15*; 5:5; 6:*11*; 8:*14*; *12*, *1* and *3*. In 5:*10*, *12*–*14* "Israel" is to be read in place of "Judah"; so too 6:4.

[2] Some problems are inherent in the laconic superscription. Four Judean kings are mentioned, but only one king of Israel, Jeroboam; the reign of the four Judeans was longer than the reign of Jeroboam.

His message is a repeated denunciation of infidelity to Yahve. Hosea seems to have felt that evil actions stem from an improper basic attitude, for unlike Amos, he abstains from elaborate lists of specific misdeeds. Accordingly, he is not the stirring preacher of social justice that Amos is. Infidelity is not limited, in Hosea's view, to political maneuvering; it manifests itself more obviously in ritual worship of Baal in place of Yahve. II Kings 11 relates that a generation earlier than the time of Hosea, between 800 and 785, a religious "reformation" led by a priest, Yehoiada, had occurred in the southern kingdom. One result was the destruction of a temple of Baal [3] and the killing of its priest, one Mattan.

Perhaps that "reformation" was one of several, each with the principal aim of eliminating overt Baal worship. Eventually, though long after the time of Hosea, Baal worship was eliminated, or partly absorbed and adapted. But in Hosea's time, Baal worship appears to have reached a new eminence—indeed, Hosea provides enough details to be a very rich source of information about Baal worship.

Amos had said nothing directly about Israel's worship of Baal. Indeed, so unconcerned was he with ritual worship that he seemed to consider it futile, when the worshipers are guilty of ethical transgression, even when it was addressed to Yahve. Hosea says very little about ethical transgressions, lamenting, rather, that it is Baal and not Yahve whom Israel is worshiping. Hosea repeatedly laments that unfaithful Israel is worshiping Baal, not Yahve. Hosea sees Yahve looking forward (2:18 Heb., 2:16–17 Eng.) to a time when Israel will address its Deity as "my man" (Heb. *ishi*) and not as "my Baal" (*baal* means "husband"):

> *And I shall remove the names of the Baals from her mouth*
> *And their names will no longer be mentioned.*

He presently adds:

> *I will betroth you to Me forever,*
> *I will betroth you to Me in righteousness and justice, in re-*
> *   liability and love.*
> *I will betroth you to Me with confidence,*
> *And you will know Yahve.* [2:21–2 Heb., 2:19–20 Eng.]

A description of the Baal worship is found in Hosea 4:9–14. People and priest alike sin, so that

> *I shall visit upon him [Israel] his sins,*
> *And his deeds I will requite to him.*

[3] In this account, as elsewhere, the Baal is probably more properly to be identified as the Phoenician deity Melkart.

They shall eat, but they will not be satisfied.
They shall commit adultery with temple prostitutes [4] *but*
find no satisfaction.
They have left Yahve, to be heedful of adultery.

Old wine and new wine have captured the heart of my peo-
ple.
They ask counsel of a tree,
Or one's tree image [5] *declares [counsel] to him.*
The disposition to lust has led him astray—
They [all] indulge in sex, this in faithlessness to their God.
They offer sacrifices on hilltops [6]
And on promontories they make offerings,
Under an oak, or a poplar, or a terebinth
Whose shade is favorable.
Accordingly, your daughters go in for sexual orgies
And your young men for copulation;
Indeed, they retire, along with the harlots, to private
places; [7]
They make their offering with the temple prostitutes!

A long chapter follows (6, with possibly the last verse of 5 as its prelude) which is not entirely clear. It appears to be mocking at the insincere repentance of Israelites, who say:

Come, let us return to Yahve—
He has torn us—He will heal!
He has smitten—He will bind up [the wound] for us . . .
[6:1].

But, in Hosea's mind, this is of no avail:

Your reliability [8] *is like a morning cloud—*
It is like dew which is dissipated in the earliest part of the
morning. [6:4B]

---

[4] The temple prostitute, for whom there exists the technical name *hierodule* ("temple slave") was commonly found in near eastern sanctuaries. She was available to communicants for intercourse. Possibly the folklore of the custom lay in the belief that when the worshiper impregnated the hierodule, he was acting out his wish for the Deity—Baal the husband—to impregnate the earth, so that it might become *Mother* Earth. Such prostitution is prohibited by Deut. 23:18–19, Heb., 17–18 Eng.

[5] Scholars disagree as to whether or not the tree image was a symbol of a phallus.

[6] Hills or artificial mounds (Heb. *bamoth*) are spoken of as places where the despised Baal worship was practiced.

[7] That is, outside the temple, so as to consummate the deed.

[8] The Hebrew *ḥesed* is too often rendered "love." See below, page 80.

Hosea's manner, so unlike that of Amos, can mislead the unwary reader. The misinterpretation of Hosea as saccharine or sentimental arises primarily from the first three chapters, where Yahve's relations with Israel are compared to Hosea's sad experience with his own wife. Hosea, it appears, had married a woman incapable of marital fidelity, and after forgiving her a succession of adulteries he finally divorced her. Israel was to Yahve what the adulterous wife was to Hosea. Because of the instances where Hosea forgives his wayward wife, views of divine mercy and solicitude, at variance with Amos' stern and uncompromising severity, are attributed to him. Certainly, there are clear statements of Yahve's love for Israel in Hosea:

> *When Israel was a boy, I loved him;*
> *Out of Egypt I called his sons.*
> *Despite My calling them, they went far away from Me.*
> *They sacrifice to the Baals,*
> *They make offering to images*
> *It was I [Yahve] Who reared Ephraim [the northern king-*
>   *dom];*
> *I used to take them up in My arms.*
> *They never understood that it was I Who healed them*
>   *[from their boyhood bruises].*
> *I drew them [to Me] with a halter for men [not an ani-*
>   *mal],*
> *[I drew them to Me] with bands of love.*
> *I was for them like someone who takes the bit out of their*
>   *mouths.[9]*
> *I used to bend to them and to feed them.* [11:1–4]

> *How, Ephraim, can I give you over,—*
>   *Give you up, O Israel?*
> *How can I give you over to be like Admah,[1]*
>   *How can I make you like Zeboim!*
> *My intention has changed within Me,*
> *My sympathies have reached their acme,*
> *[So that] I shall not put My anger into effect,*
> *I shall not revert to [a plan to] destroy Ephraim,*
> *For God am I—not man.*
> *Sacred am I—I shall not come furious.* [11:8–9]

---

[9] The text says "yoke from off their cheeks."
[1] In Deuteronomy 29:23, Admah and Zeboim, otherwise unknown, are coupled with Sodom and Gomorrah of Gen. 19 as proverbial places which underwent destruction, probably through earthquake, at Yahve's hands.

This passage, clearly enunciating Yahve's intention to withhold merited punishment, does not, however, represent Hosea's final view. He goes on to describe the nature of Israel's transgression:

Ephraim [Israel] surrounded Me with falsehood,
The House of Israel with deception.
Ephraim shepherds the wind,
And he pursues the east wind;
All day long he multiplies lies and frauds.
He makes a covenant with Assyria,
Or despatches a [treaty] gift to Egypt. [12:1–2 Heb.,
    11:12–12:1 Eng.]

Hosea here portrays Yahve as indignant and incensed that Israel is flirting with political alliances, now with Assyria in the east, now with Egypt to the west. The potential practical benefits from these political efforts do not move Hosea; in his view, they are inherently evil, equivalent to apostasy, because they show a reliance on man rather than on Yahve. The passage continues:

Yahve has a quarrel with Israel,
With the result that he will repay Jacob for his deeds.
From the [mother's] womb, he cheated his brother[2] *. . .*
A tricky merchant! In his hands are deceptive balances,
He enjoys defrauding.
For he says, "How did I become rich? I found a treasure for
    myself!"
Yet all his gains will not last,
Because of the transgression which he has incurred.
    [12:3–4A, 8–9 Heb., 2–3A, 7–8 Eng.]

Such infidelity is sure to bring punishment, especially in view of Yahve's past solicitude:

For I, Yahve, your God since Egypt,
Will make you dwell in tents[3] *as in olden days . . .*
[You] Ephraim have given a bitter provocation. [12:10,
    15A Heb., 9, 14A Eng.]

The prophet promptly comments:

God will push on to him the guilt for bloodshed,
And will bring to him his shameful act. [12:15B Heb., 14B
    Eng.]

[2] The allusion is clarified in Gen. 27:35. Two brothers, Esau and Jacob, were born to Isaac. Jacob, in an early source, is depicted as the cheater who deprives his brother of the *bekora* ("rights of the first-born") and of the *beraka* ("blessing"). See pages 361ff.
[3] That is, the luxury of urban life will disappear.

The passages we have just looked at can be taken as the epitome
of the Book of Hosea: Israel, though deeply loved by Yahve, has been
faithless, and now its deserved punishment is at hand.

The first three chapters of Hosea are the source of the frequent misinterpretation of this important but difficult book. In them it is set
forth that Hosea was married to a loose woman, whose infidelities he
forgave again and again, *until he divorced her.* If we simply overlooked the telling matter of the divorce, we could agree with the
interpretation of Hosea as the man who typifies forgiveness. Yet the
point in Hosea is that forgiveness is now a thing of the past; the
divorce has finally come. Hosea has cut off his faithless wife, just
as Yahve has cut off Israel. The text bears out this view:

> Yahve said to Hosea, "Go, marry a wife who will prove prone
> to infidelity, and bear children adulterously, just as the land has
> committed adultery away from Yahve." Hosea married Gomer,
> the daughter of Diblaim. She conceived and bore him a son.
> Yahve said to [Hosea]: "Call him Jezreel; shortly I shall visit
> the blood [4] of Jezreel on the [royal] house of Jehu, and bring to
> an end the monarchy in Israel. . . .
>
> Again she [Gomer] conceived and bore a daughter. Yahve
> said to him, "Call her name Unloved, for the house of Israel is
> unloved to Me." Unloved was weaned, and Gomer then bore a
> son. Yahve said, "Call his name Not-My-People, for you are not
> My people and I am not your God." [1:2–4, 6–9].

Now the prophet speaks: [5]

> *Find fault with your mother, find fault with her,*
> *For she is no longer my wife, and I am no longer her hus-*
> * band.*
> *Let her remove her harlotry from her [brazen] counte-*
> * nance,*

---

[4] In I Kings 21, it is related that King Ahab desired a vineyard at Jezreel owned
by one Naboth. Queen Jezebel arranged for Naboth to be accused by false
witnesses of blasphemy and to be executed, whereupon Ahab confiscated the
vineyard. Elijah, according to this account, predicted that Jezebel would die at
Jezreel. Blood (literally, "bloods") means "murder." King Jehu had come to the
throne (II Kings 9–10) after slaying Ahab's son King Joram. Then he murdered
the Queen Mother at Jezreel; next he slew the seventy sons of Ahab and Jezebel
and had their heads brought to Jezreel.

[5] There intrude some verses (2:1–3 Heb., 1:10–11 Eng.) designed by a later
hand to soften the harshness of the preceding.

*Let her cease to expose the cleavage between her breasts to
    entice to adultery*
*Lest I strip her naked, and have her pose as on the day of
    her birth,*
And make her [unclothed] like a wilderness,
And set her [naked] like an arid land.[6]

I shall kill her by thirst,
And show no love to her children,
For they are offspring of adultery.
She who conceived them behaved shamefully.
She had decided: "I shall go after my lovers,
*Who give me bread and water, wool and flax, oil and
    liquids."*

Again the prophet speaks:

*Therefore I shall imprison her in a place surrounded by
    thorns*
And make escape-proof a wall around her
And she will find no way out.
After pursuing her lovers and not reaching them,
After seeking for them and not finding, then she will say,
"I will return to my first man,
For then it was better for me than now!"—
*Not knowing that it was I who had given her the corn, and
    wine, and oil. . . .*
*But I shall reclaim my corn at its season, my wine at its oc-
    casion;*
I shall snatch my wool and flax
With which she had covered her nakedness.
Now I shall lay open her shame. . . .
And no one will snatch her from me.
Her happiness will terminate,
Her festivals, her new moon holidays, her sabbaths . . . !
*I shall visit on her payment for the day when she sacrificed
    to the Baals*
And adorned herself with her ring and jewelry
And pursued her paramours
But forget me, says Yahve.[7] [2:8–15 Heb., 6–13 Eng.]

---

[6] There is evidence in Ezekiel 16:38–9 that the punishment of an adulterous
mother included being stripped naked.
[7] The remainder of the chapter, namely 2:16–25 Heb., 14–23 Eng., is regarded
by many as a later addition, or a composite of additions. Verses 20–5 (18–23
Eng.) are undoubtedly an addition, but 16–19 (14–17 Eng.) may not be.

This passage scarcely reflects tenderness; it shows bitterness in a man once tender. The message of Hosea in its final import is just as stern as that of Amos, and the only difference is in the process which led each to his conclusion.

Chapter 3 still remains to be considered. Whereas in Chapter 1 the narrative of Hosea's marriage with a loose woman is told in the third person, it is told in the first person in Chapter 3. I agree with the many interpreters who regard these two chapters as different accounts of one and the same incident, although the word "again" in 3:1 must be deleted to support this view. "Yahve said to me [Hosea], '*Again* go love a woman who loves someone else, and who is adulterous.'" The passage continues with the injunction to Hosea to love the woman ". . . with a love like that of Yahve for Israel, though they turn to false gods and they love raisin cookies.[8] I bought [the woman] for fifteen silver pieces, a homer and a half of barley. I said to her, 'You will dwell with me many days. You will not commit adultery, nor have sex relations with any man; I too will have no sex relations with you . . .'" (3:1–3). This is all that Chapter 3 tells about Hosea's marriage. Perhaps 3 was once longer, and its ending has been lost or suppressed. This puzzling chapter is so short that it is scarcely prudent to build any theories on it. Least of all should one suppose, as many have, that Hosea experienced two successive divine injunctions to marry two different loose women. It is just as unlikely that the wife Gomer, who was divorced in Chapter 1, was brought back from a house of adultery in Chapter 3. A jigsaw puzzle can scarcely be solved when too many pieces are missing, but it is impossible not to speculate whether Hosea and his loose wife are to be taken in a historical or merely in a symbolic sense. There is some human fascination in wondering if Hosea came to recognize Yahve's relation to Israel through a bitter marital experience.

Some scholars deny that the adulterous wife is historical. They contend that with Hosea began the prophetic practice, followed increasingly by later prophets, of dealing in symbols. According to this view the names of the children, Unloved and Not-My-People, are proof that we are dealing with symbols, not history. A weakness in this argument is often pointed out: Gomer, the name of the wife, has so far defied recognition as a mere symbol. The argument between the "historicizers" and the "symbolists" is destined to continue, since final demonstration is impossible. Yet significantly even the historicizers conclude that the purpose of the children and the adulterous wife is to *serve as a symbol*. Accordingly, historicizers and

[8] These delicacies were part of Baal worship, and in this passage they epitomize that worship.

symbolists agree on the symbolic significance of the episode and disagree only on the reality of the events depicted.

As I have indicated, the message of Hosea is not soft and sentimental. The apparent softness is limited to attributing reluctance to the Deity in reaching His decision to punish. Where Amos would say, "Your sins have obligated Yahve to punish you," Hosea says, "Yahve has wanted not to punish you, but you have forced Him to."

A dispute exists among scholars over a truly striking passage, Chapter 14, which deals with repentance. Some scholars believe that the verses are not by Hosea, since a call to repentance is useless if it is too late to avert a divine decree of punishment. Others hold that the passage contains Hosea's authentic words, at a stage when he still believed punishment might be averted. Some scholars contend that the basis for denying the words to Hosea rests on considerations of logic which are irrelevant. Modern western man worships consistency; but is consistency necessarily to be attributed to an oriental and poetic mind? Could not Hosea, in the midst of his castigations, have changed momentarily and spoken passionately of repentance, even if it was too late? I myself do not know the solution and change my mind from week to week.

The passage is notable for being read in the Synagogue on the Sabbath of Repentance, the Sabbath that comes between Rosh Hashona and Yom Kippur. The issue of its authorship is picayune, for it is a superlative piece of religious poetry:

> *Come back, O Israel, to Yahve your God,*
> *For in your iniquity you have stumbled.*
> *Bring with you [proper] words, and come to Yahve.*
> *All of you, say to Him:*
> *"Take away our iniquity*
> *And receive what is good.*
> *We will render, as our [sacrificial] cattle, our lives.*
> *Assyria cannot save us;*
> *We shall not trust in Egypt's power.*[9] *[14:2–4A Heb.,*
> *1–3A Eng.]*
> *We shall not call things we have made our God.*
> *In You does the helpless one find solicitude."*

The Deity is portrayed as replying:

> *I will heal their sickly apostasy,*
> *As an act of free will I will love them,*
> *For My anger against them has dissolved itself.*

[9] Literally, "We shall not ride upon horses"; my paraphrase is true to the meaning.

I shall refresh Israel as does the dew,
He will blossom profusely, like the lily,
Yet strike deep roots like the poplar.[1]
The shoots will spread out
To make him as glorious as the olive tree,
And he will be as aromatic as the [cedars of] Lebanon.

Again will those who dwell under [My] protection
Abide like a garden and blossom like a vine.
The report of them will be favorable like the wine of Leba-
            non. [14:2–8 Heb., 1–7 Eng.]

In a short passage Hosea shows a scorn for animal sacrifice. The
Hebrew word *ḥesed* must be left untranslated for the moment:

    . . . I desired ḥesed *and not a sacrifice,*
    And knowledge of God, more than burnt offerings. [6:6]

In the King James Version *ḥesed*, following Greek and Latin versions,
is translated "mercy"; in the Revised Standard Version it is "steadfast love." Hosea is not speaking of man's love of God, which is
enjoined in Scripture.[2] He portrays Yahve as loving; what he wants
of man is reliability, dependability. The best rendering of the verse
is this: "I desire steadfastness, and not a sacrifice."

It seems to me that if Amos is a judge dealing severely with a
mature man, Hosea is more like a judge in a juvenile court, dealing
sternly, despite his compassion, with the wayward young.

[1] This is a guess; the verse makes no sense in the Hebrew.
[2] As in Deut. 6:5 ("You shall love your God Yahve with all your heart, soul, and
substance") the Hebrew here uses *ahab*, not *ḥesed*.

ISAIAH

THERE IS no great harm in speaking interchangeably of Amos and the Book of Amos, or Hosea and the Book of Hosea, for although both books underwent minor interpolation, the author can in each case be identified with his work. But in the case of Isaiah we must distinguish sharply between the man and the book. By the Isaiah of the present chapter we shall mean an eighth-century prophet whose writings form the initial portion of the very long Book of Isaiah. By the Book of Isaiah we shall mean an anthology of prophetic and poetic writings numbering sixty-six chapters and representing many authors and many ages. Moreover, Chapters 36–9 simply repeat without important alteration II Kings 18–20.

The book is a peculiar kind of anthology. Its lack of structure might be likened to a student's notebook devoted to different courses, whose pages were scattered and then gathered together without being set in order. The Book of Isaiah is a similar hodgepodge, which defies intelligible consecutive reading more than any other book of Scripture. Although modern scholars are somewhat agreed on how to restore the parts to their proper places, the area of disagreement is still quite extensive. We shall need to be rigidly selective, and to

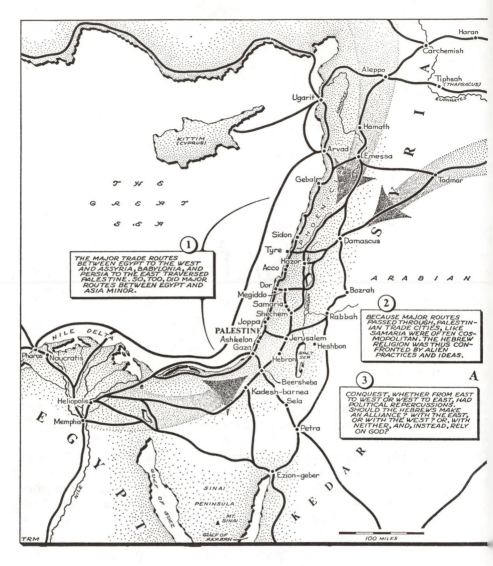

THE MAJOR TRADE ROUTES
BETWEEN EGYPT TO THE WEST
AND ASSYRIA, BABYLONIA, AND
PERSIA TO THE EAST TRAVERSED
PALESTINE. SO, TOO, DID MAJOR
ROUTES BETWEEN EGYPT AND
ASIA MINOR.

BECAUSE MAJOR ROUTES
PASSED THROUGH, PALESTIN-
IAN TRADE CITIES, LIKE
SAMARIA WERE OFTEN COS-
MOPOLITAN. THE HEBREW
RELIGION WAS THUS CON-
FRONTED BY ALIEN
PRACTICES AND IDEAS.

CONQUEST, WHETHER FROM EAST
TO WEST OR WEST TO EAST, HAD
POLITICAL REPERCUSSIONS.
SHOULD THE HEBREWS MAKE
AN ALLIANCE? WITH THE EAST,
OR WITH THE WEST? OR, WITH
NEITHER, AND, INSTEAD, RELY
ON GOD?

limit ourselves to the leading ideas.[1] Isaiah himself is found only in
Chapters 1–31, but even in these chapters many later additions intrude, representing numerous authors and ages.[2]

[1] An outline of the contents will help in the consecutive reading of Isaiah: A,
Chapters 1–12, prophecies dealing with Judah and Jerusalem; B, 13–23 (mostly
not by Isaiah) denunciations of foreign nations; C, 24–7, an appendix from a
very late period; D, 28–33, the "woe" oracles; E, 34–5, two separate late additions, with the likelihood that 35 is to be linked with 40–55. 36–39 repeat
II Kings 18–20.

[2] The principal "secondary" passages may be listed as 2:2–4; 4:2–6; 9:1–16;
11:1 – 14:23; 15:1 – 16:14; 19; 21:1–17; 23–27; 30:18–26; 32:1–8; 34–35.

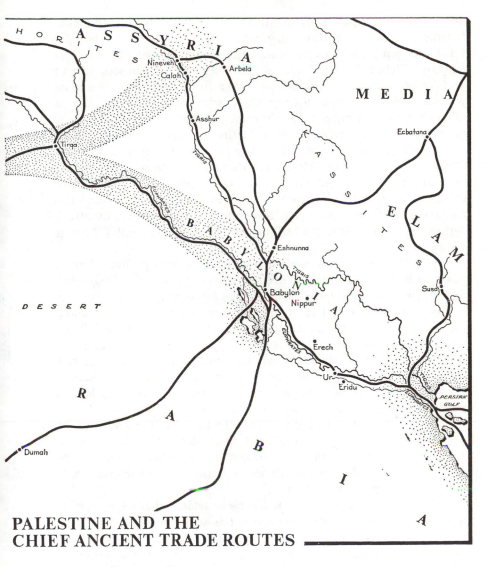

PALESTINE AND THE
CHIEF ANCIENT TRADE ROUTES

Isaiah was active during the reigns of four Judean kings. The period can be represented by the dates 742–695. During this time, the eastern empire, Assyria, was expanding westward, aiming apparently at absorbing even Egypt. Since the route of conquest lay through Palestine, the two kingdoms of Israel and Judah were menaced. The agricultural northern kingdom was in graver danger than the somewhat isolated pastoral south. As we saw above (p. 71), Assyria invaded Israel's territory about 738 but Israel bought off Assyria by paying tribute. Some three years later Israel joined with Damascus, under King Rezin, in an attempt to form a confederacy against Assyria. Ahaz, King of Judah, was invited to join this confederacy and was even threatened with force if he refused. Ahaz did refuse to join, and instead bought Assyrian protection from its emperor, Tiglath Pileser. The Assyrians destroyed Damascus in 734 and Israel in 722/21. Ahaz reigned over Judah until 715, when he was succeeded by Hezekiah (715–687), who continued the policy of alliance with Assyria. But in 711 some rebelliousness, known to us only vaguely, was promoted in Palestine by Egypt. The Philistine city of Ashdod was destroyed in reprisal by the Assyrians under Sargon. In 705, when Merodach Baladan succeeded Sargon as emperor, there was general unrest, with Egypt instigating more rebellion. Hezekiah apparently joined in the newest revolt. The Assyrians then sent a strong force under Sennacherib to attack Jerusalem, but Hezekiah paid tribute to buy off Sennacherib (II Kings 18:13–16).

Isaiah's words were spoken against this background. Certain passages in the Book of Isaiah are sometimes spoken of as "memoirs" and others as "biography." These are misleading labels, for the reality is that we do not know much more about Isaiah than about Amos and Hosea. The text mentions a wife ("the prophetess," 8:3), but does not name her, and two sons (7:3 and 8:3) whose names are symbolic, but we do not know whether they are the names of real sons, or simply figures of speech. It is frequently said that Isaiah's knowledge of Jerusalem indicates that he was a native or at least a resident of long standing. Perhaps he was of a priestly family.

Some of the passages clearly reflect the time encompassed by our brief historical review and lend themselves to a chronological arrangement. We can only guess about the occasion of other parts. A thorough consideration of all the chronological elements would require a book, not a mere chapter.

Two preliminary matters should be considered before we turn to Isaiah's message. The first concerns the social level at which he worked. In terms of modern times, we might say that Hosea's career revolved around the people he found in the small outlying churches, while Isaiah was conversant with and critical of kings. Hosea was the village gadfly; Isaiah was well known in the highest circles of the capital. The second matter concerns a practice that began with Isaiah —the use of symbolic action as well as symbolic words. Thus, Isaiah describes himself as walking naked and barefoot (20) to portray or underline the fate awaiting Egypt and Assyria; in one pronouncement (5) he likens Israel to a vineyard. One of his sons was named Shear-Yashub, "a remnant abides"; the other was Maher-Shalel-Hash-Baz, "booty hastens, prey speeds." Although Isaiah's use of symbol is still restrained enough for clarity, he gave an impetus to later prophets whose words can no longer be understood because their symbols obscure their meaning.

Isaiah informs us of the beginning of his prophetic career:

> In the year that King Uzziah died, I saw Lord [Yahve] seated on a high and lofty throne; the skirts of His robe filled the temple; [3] fiery creatures stood above Him, each with six wings, two to cover the face, two to cover the feet, and two to fly with. They called, one to the others: "Most holy is Yahve [God] of Hosts [of Heaven]. The whole earth is filled with His radiance!" The threshold foundations shook at the sound, and the temple was filled with smoke [so that the vision was quickly obscured]. Then I thought, "Horrors! I am as good as destroyed, for I am a man of impure speech who dwells among people equally impure, yet my eyes have beheld the royal Yahve of the Hosts."

> But one of the fiery creatures flew to me. In his hand was a hot coal which he had taken off the altar with tongs. He touched it to my mouth, saying, "See! This has touched your lips; your guilt is gone, your sinful state is atoned for."

> Then I heard Yahve's voice saying, "Whom shall I send? Who will go on our behalf?"

> I said, "Here am I! Send me."

> He said, "Go and say to this people: 'Be sure to hear—but don't understand! Be sure to see—but don't perceive! The mind [heart] of this people is grown too fat, its ears too heavy, its eyes turned away—this in order that they just might see or hear or understand, and [then] be healed."

> I said, "How long [is it to be this way]?"

> He said, "Until cities are so wasted that they have no inhabitants, and houses have no dwellers, and the land is thoroughly desolate." [4] (6:*1–11*)

The "call" of Isaiah is without question one of the very vivid passages of Scripture—poets and artists throughout the ages have felt its fascination. As the phrase "in the year of the death of King Uzziah" indicates, Isaiah related this event long after it took place. This was unquestionably a real experience of ecstasy for Isaiah. Strangely, no other passage in the book refers back to this vision of Yahve. Why is it in the book? Possibly because Amos had established,

---

[3] Some scholars hold that the "vision" was of a heavenly "temple." I do not agree. This was the Jerusalem temple into which Yahve was believed to enter on the equinoctial day. Cf. Psalms 18:7–8; 97:2–5; Ezek. 10:4; Lev. 16:13.

[4] The next verse, which concludes the chapter, is an addition. It modifies and eases the foregoing by suggesting that a "tenth" will survive.

or continued, the practice of describing the prophet's divine call. Certainly the clarity of this chapter in Isaiah enables us to understand why subsequent prophets almost invariably included an account of their call.

The prophet spoke of himself as being quite as impure as those among whom he dwelt, not out of modesty, but rather in order to intensify the indictment soon to come. All are evil, including him. Some divine election, rather than personal merit, had vouchsafed for him the unexpected boon of the vision of Yahve—by all rights he should have perished there and then. As he was spared, he responded to the commission, which he took to be divine. The lapse of time between the call and the time when he let it be recorded in writing enabled him to set down the frustration of being ignored during his ministry. This frustration is described as something preordained. According to the prophet, Yahve completely controls history; therefore, with Him and not with obdurate man lay the decision of what would happen to His people. The people were wicked; yet to make Yahve responsible for what men did could amount to making the blameworthy innocent. But to ascribe to men a full freedom of choice between doing good or doing evil implies that Yahve's control of history was not complete. Isaiah, like other biblical writers, touches here on the age-old question of providence and free will. In much the same way, Exodus 10 relates that when Yahve sent Moses to Pharaoh to obtain the release of the Hebrews from slavery, Yahve so hardened Pharaoh's heart that he would not release them; even Pharaoh's disobedience was a result of Yahve's will. Neither Isaiah nor other biblical writers "solved" the problem of providence and free will, though Isaiah was very much concerned with it. He therefore attributed to Yahve the decision that His words were to be ignored, implying that the stage had now been reached when punishment was completely inevitable, completely foreordained.

Isaiah counseled kings—and was ignored by them. During the unsuccessful assault of Rezin of Aram and Pekah of Israel upon Judah, and especially Jerusalem, Isaiah spoke directly to the King, Ahaz:

> Yahve said to Isaiah: "Go out toward Ahaz . . . towards the
> the end of the aqueduct of the upper reservoir, to the road near
> the field of the launderer.[5] Say to him:
> " 'Be on guard, yet keep calm; do not be afraid nor alarmed [6]
> because of these two ends of firebrands [which are not burning

[5] We cannot identify the place.
[6] Literally, "let not your heart be faint."

but merely] smoldering, namely because of the anger of Rezin
of Syria and [Pekah] ben Remaliah. Indeed, Aram has planned
evil against you, along with Ephraim (the kingdom of Israel) and
ben Remaliah, thinking, Let us go up against Judea, worry it,
and split it into segments for us, and install as king ben
Tabeel. . . .'[7]

"If you Judeans do not trust, you will not endure"[8] (7:3–9).

The last two lines are of key importance. Faith in Yahve, according to
Isaiah, is the most practical weapon in dealing with foreign nations.
Isaiah was not saying, "Praise the Lord and pass the ammunition!"
Such a thought would have horrified him. He meant simply and
literally, "Rely only on your faith in Yahve." The passage continues:

Isaiah[9] said further, "Ask [any] sign of Yahve, as deep as the
netherworld or as high as heaven."

Ahaz said, "I shall not ask. I shall not put Yahve to a test."
Isaiah said, "[In your stalling,] as if you do not want a sign, you
are wearying me, a mere mortal. Are you intent also on wearying
our God? Yahve will give you a sign. See, a young woman, being
pregnant, will bear a son, and call his name Immanuel[1] (God is
with Us). Before the boy [is old enough to] know to reject evil
and choose good, the land of the two kings whom you fear will be
desolated . . . Yahve will whistle summoning the bee in the
land of Assyria.[2] They will come all and settle in the steep
valleys and in the clefts of rocks, and on thornhedges and pastures.

"On that day Yahve will hire a razor from beyond the Euphrates River, namely, the king of Assyria, [who] will shave off
the hair of the head, and of the legs! And [the razor] will make
an end even to the beard." [7:10–20]

Curiously, despite its clarity, this passage has provided centuries of
interpreters with an unnecessary but inevitable problem. In early
Christian times, at least seven hundred years after Isaiah, Jews (and
early Christianity was a form of Judaism) often followed the practice

---

[7] This proposed puppet is not mentioned anywhere else.

[8] The Hebrew is a pun: If you ta'aminu not, then you will te-amenu not! Literally,
"If you do not have faith, you will not abide."

[9] The text in error says "Yahve"; at one stage only the first letter "Y," common to
Yahve and Yeshayahu (Isaiah), stood in the text; a later scribe expanded the
abbreviation wrongly.

[1] A later scribe embellished the text by adding that the child "would eat butter and
honey, until such time as he learned to reject evil and choose good."

[2] The verse is expanded in later times as though Egypt, in addition to Assyria,
was going to invade.

of "proving" contentions by citing passages from Scripture, in or out of context. When this passage was translated into Greek, the Hebrew "young woman" was rendered as *parthenos,* which means virgin. The Gospel According to Matthew (1 : 22–33) contends that Jesus was born of a virgin and that this virgin birth was predicted in Isaiah. The argument about the "true" reading has gone on for centuries. Most recently—in the past decades—the argument has been waged within Christendom. Modern Christians, aware that "proof-texting" scarcely preserves the original sense of Scripture, notice that when the passage is taken as a whole, the question of the young woman's virginity is irrelevant; the point is rather that punishment will come on Israel and Damascus in the number of months that pregnancy, birth, and weaning require. Had Isaiah chosen to say, "Punishment will come in three years," the passage would be unchanged in meaning. The sense of the passage is not affected by the question of the young woman's virginity. The "child," according to the passage, is to be called Immanuel. We do not know if this refers to a real child or is just a symbolic name; nothing in Isaiah justifies associating it with a Messiah, for Isaiah in authentic passages does not mention this doctrine, which arose after his time. The name "God is with us" is fitting in Isaiah's context, for he is consistently arguing that faith in Yahve is man's only reliable weapon. God—not Assyria, not Egypt—is with us, says Isaiah.

Moreover, Isaiah makes an inference that goes beyond Amos. The latter said that in view of the rupture of the covenant and the resultant loss of Yahve's protection, some foreign nation would invade. Isaiah specifies that the foreign nation is Assyria. He tells us that Yahve "will whistle" to it; in other words, Assyria will not provide its own initiative to conquest, but will be summoned by Yahve.

When the Deity is thought to have universal power, the belief that He manipulates nations in accordance with His will is but a short step away. We shall elaborate on this theme, which is central to Isaiah, but first the passage under discussion calls for further clarification.

In citing the passage I have omitted some words found in the Hebrew (7 : 3) : "Go out toward King Ahaz, you and *Shear Yashub* your son," because I feel that they serve only to confuse matters. Evidence throughout the passage suggests that at one stage in the transmission of the Book of Isaiah, some scribe wrote explanatory glosses, probably in the margin. A later scribe incorporated these glosses into the text. That is why "King of Assyria" intrudes so often and so needlessly into the narrative. I take the mention of the child, Shear Yashub, to be one of these explanatory glosses, too. The tiny question of whether the mention of this child belongs in this passage is the only matter at stake here, and, were it not that an undue amount of attention has been paid to the name and to its implication, we could pass over this question as we must pass over other aspects of Isaiah's thought. It is likely that there once existed a narrative whose central theme was the birth of Shear Yashub. Like other substantial portions of Isaiah's message, it was not preserved, but it may well have been akin to the story of the birth of another "son," "Speedy Spoil, Hasty Booty" in 8:3.

The name *Shear Yashub* is sometimes incorrectly paraphrased as meaning a "saving remnant," and this phrase is so well known that we must inquire into the matter. *Shear* means "remnant"; *yashub* means "will return" or "will repent." The difficulty is not in translating the name, but rather in making some sense of the translation. While Amos and Hosea maintained that the whole nation, as a single entity, was destined for catastrophe, passages in Isaiah indicate that the catastrophe he expected was not a total one, for a remnant would survive. Some scholars want to change the vowels, though retaining the consonants, and read *yesheb*, "will abide." In any case, *yashub* does not mean "saving," though it may mean "survive." Later thinkers than Isaiah contemplated a saving remnant, that is, a portion of the populace so meritorious that the whole nation might be saved on their account. A narrative in Genesis 18–19 depicts Abraham bargaining with Yahve over the quantity of righteous men needed in Sodom and Gomorrah for those cities to be spared; at Abraham's behest Yahve progressively reduced the number from fifty to ten, but as the cities lacked even ten, they were necessarily destroyed. Although Isaiah thought of a saved remnant, he himself did not envisage a "saving" group.

A brief passage (10:22–3) sets forth more clearly the symbolic meaning of this "son," Shear Yashub:

> Though your people Israel is as numerous as the sand of the sea, [only] a remnant will abide of them; destruction, overflowing with justice, is decreed. For Yahve, Lord of Hosts, has decreed a destruction in the land, and will execute it.[3]

So far we have noted Isaiah's conviction that faith in Yahve is the only reliable weapon, his prediction of great destruction by an invader summoned by Yahve, and his belief that a remnant would escape the catastrophe. Isaiah's conviction of some imminent destruction is portrayed in another passage:

---

[3] A comforting word is interpolated (10:20–1): "It will come to pass that the remnant of Israel, and the escaped portion of the house of Jacob will no longer rely on such as have smitten them, but in truth on Yahve, Israel's Holy One. The remnant of Jacob, a returning remnant, will return to the Mighty God."

Yahve said to me, "Take a long piece of paper and write on it in large letters, 'Speedy Spoil, Hasty Booty.' "

I summoned reliable witnesses, Uriah the priest and Zecharia ben Berachiah. I went into my wife and she conceived and bore a son. Yahve said to me, "Call his name Speedy Spoil, Hasty Booty, for before the boy can say Father and Mother, the wealth of Damascus and the booty of Samaria will be carried away to the King of Assyria. . . ."

Inasmuch as this people (Judah) has refused the slow driblet of the waters of Shiloah,[4] yet melts in terror before Rezin and ben Remaliah, Yahve is bringing on them the strong and abundant waters of the River, [namely,] the King of Assyria and all his possessions; he shall rise over all his channels and overflow all his banks. He will press into Judah, overflowing and reaching as high as the neck. The stretching of its outshoots will encompass the full breadth of your land. . . . [8:1–8]

To paraphrase: because Israel rejected Yahve, a beneficial though seemingly weak source of refreshing water, it would be destroyed along with Damascus by malevolent water, Assyria. Israel's faithlessness consisted, partly, in empty ritual:

Hear the word of Yahve, you rulers of Sodom,
Hearken to the revelation of our God, O nation of Gomor-
rah; [5]
"What do I care about the abundance of your sacrifices?"
says Yahve.
"I am overfilled with burnt offerings of ram
And the fat of well-fed beasts
I have no wish for the blood of bullocks, lambs, or goats,
Nor that you come to see My face.
Who asked of you that you should trample in My court
[in the Temple]?

"Do not bring any more useless offerings!
Incense is to Me an abomination!
The new moon [festival], the sabbath, the proclamation of
an assembly—
I will not abide iniquity and solemn assembly!
I hate your new moons and your appointed festivals,

---

[4] A canal connected a spring, Gihon, to the pool of Shiloah, known in the New Testament as Siloam. Shiloah-Siloam was a water reservoir for Jerusalem.
[5] Sodom and Gomorrah are the proverbial quintessence of evil.

They have become a burden upon Me, I am tired of bearing
*   them.*
And when you spread out your hands [in prayer],
I will cover My eyes from you.
Even if you multiply prayer, I will not hear,
For your hands are full of blood!" [1:10–15]

Again, faithlessness is manifest in what Isaiah calls rebellion:

Hear, O heavens, and hearken, O earth, for Yahve has
*   spoken:*
"Sons have I reared and raised up, but they have trans-
*   gressed against Me.*
An ox knows its owner, an ass [knows] its master's stable;
Israel does not know,
My people does not understand!

"Woe unto a sinful people,
A nation heavy in iniquity,
The scions of evildoers,
Offspring who are corrupt.
Yahve they have abandoned,
They have despised Israel's Holy One . . . !

"Why do you continue to be smitten,
Why do you continue to rebel?
Every head is sick, every heart faint,
From the sole of the foot unto the head, there is no un-
*   bruised place:*
[But] wound, and sore, and bleeding bruise,
Unattended, unbandaged, unsmeared with ointment.

"Your land is desolate, your cities consumed by fire.
In your very presence, strangers devour your land.
It is desolated, like [a land] overturned by invaders."
*   [1:2–7]*

According to Isaiah, punishment was distinctly contrary to Yahve's affectionate expectation for Israel and could have been averted.
In His love for Israel, Yahve wanted Israel to have the benefit of His
solicitous affection, as the covenant implied. But faithfulness brings
reward, infidelity disaster:

I shall sing to my beloved a [troubadour's] love song to his
*   vineyard.*

My beloved had a vineyard in a lush corner of land.
He put a fence around it, removed the stones,
*   planted it with excellent vines,*
*   built a watch tower,⁶ and hewed out a wine vat.⁷*
He hoped it would yield grapes—
It yielded stinking fruit!

Now, O inhabitants of Jerusalem, and men of Judah,
Judge between me and my vineyard.
What else was there to do for my vineyard which I did
*   not do?*
Why did it come about that I hoped for grapes and it yielded
*   putrid fruit?*
Now I will tell you what I will do with my vineyard,
I will remove its hedge, and it will be consumed;
I will break down its wall, and it will be trampled over.
I will make it waste—it will not be pruned or hoed;
Briar and thistle will spring up.
I will command the clouds not to drip rain on it.

For the vineyard of Yahve is the house of Israel,
The men of Judah are the plant of his enjoyment.
He hoped for justice, but there was bloodshed,
For righteousness, [but there was] outraged cry. [5:1–7]

The Tanak has no disdain for puns, and the last two lines contain
two, which come as a gripping climax of denunciation at the end of
this love song:

> *He hoped for* mishpat *but there was* mispah,
> *For* tzedaqa, *but there was* tze-ʿaqa.

From the mention of bloodshed and violence, the text proceeds
to enumerate categories of sinful people, among them the luxury-
loving rich:

Woe to those who annex house after house
And make field after field adjacent. . . .
Woe to those who arise early in the morning to pursue
*   alcohol,*
And tarry beyond twilight for wine to inflame them . . .
Woe to those who pull iniquity like a bull on a rope,

---

⁶ Guards were sometimes stationed in towers to frustrate thieves.
⁷ This, then, was no ordinary vineyard, but one which had received special, and
costly care.

Who drag sin as with cart ropes . . .
Woe to those who are mighty—at guzzling wine,
And men of valor—at shaking up a drink.
They acquit a guilty person for a bribe,
And deprive the innocent of his innocence. [5:8–23]

Although the picture is not so clear as what we have seen above in Amos 2:6–8 and 5:10–12, it is a similar portrayal of widespread social injustice.

The evils of empty ritual, social iniquity, or reliance on a foreign nation, no matter which, are all equated with infidelity to Yahve. If we are to grasp the full import of Isaiah's thought, we must carefully consider several of its consequences. In the first place, Yahve was the one and only Deity, the universal Deity. Therefore, He could not be unaware of Assyria's future plans, and, indeed, her present actions. If so, what was Yahve's attitude towards Assyria's brash expansion westward? He could not merely have been tolerating her passively, for that would have compromised what was axiomatic for the prophet, namely Yahve's omnipotence. But if Yahve was omnipotent and not passively tolerant, how could He permit Assyria to roam about and conquer? Isaiah's answer to this question is tremendously significant to biblical thought. According to Isaiah, Yahve was manipulating Assyria; her conquests were no accident, but part of Yahve's plan and providence. Yahve had deliberately stirred up Assyria to embark on conquests, especially the conquest of Israel.

At this point Isaiah goes significantly beyond Amos. The latter had said that because Israel had broken the covenant, Yahve was withdrawing his protection, with the result that a foe would find it possible to invade. Isaiah contends that because Israel broke the covenant, Yahve has reached out to summon Assyria westward, in order to punish Israel.

Though the Assyrians did not know it, their march was not a result of free choice:

Woe unto Assyria! He is the rod of My anger;
He is the staff in My hand of My fury.
I am sending him against an impious people [Israel]
And commanding him against the people of My wrath,
To seize spoil, and grab plunder,
To tread them down in the streets like clay.

But he [Assyria] does not reckon it this way,
And in his heart he does not so consider things!
Rather, it is in his heart to destroy,

And to annihilate many nations.
For he says, "My local commanders were all once kings!
Calno [8] *is now [conquered] like Carchemish,*
Hamath is like Arpad,
Samaria is like Damascus.
As my hand subdued these kingdoms [9] . . .
Shall I not do likewise with Jerusalem?" [10:5–11]

But Yahve will punish the vaunted arrogance of Assyria, for he says:

"By the strength of My hand I have done this
And by My cunning, for I am skillful.
I have removed the boundaries of nations,
I have pillaged their treasuries,
And, powerfully, have laid low the inhabitants.
My hand has reached in to the wealth of nations as into a
        bird's nest,
As one gathers abandoned eggs
So have I gathered all the earth!
There was no one who flapped a wing
No one who opened his beak and chirped!" [10:13–14]

Promptly, Isaiah portrays Yahve's comment on Assyria:

"Does the axe elevate itself over him who hews with it?
Does the saw possess ascendancy over him that plies it?
Does a rod wield him who raises it?
Can a staff raise something as if it is not wood?
Therefore the Lord Yahve of Hosts will send a shrivelling to
        Assyria's fat ones
And a burning in his innards like the burning of fire. . . ."
        [10:15–16]

If the actions of nations are part of Yahve's plan and providence, then history at its profoundest level is not merely the ebb and flow of events, but the external record of Yahve's will and deed. For Isaiah, events themselves can never be more than secondary manifestations of Yahve's eternal and unlimited might.

Isaiah gives us the clue to the biblical understanding of history. Historical events merely represent milestones; history is the account of Yahve's will and deeds as disclosed by these markers. The highest reality—to borrow a Grecian phrase—is the Deity. The Greeks tried

[8] Calno, Carchemish, Hannath, and Arpad were in northern Syria.
[9] A conjectural translation of a corrupt passage.

to penetrate to reality by analyzing the static nature of things. The Hebrews possessed no such interest or scientific skill. For them the highest reality was to be discerned in history; they saw God in the parade and succession of events.

This conception is concrete, not abstract. In the Hebrew view, Yahve was not a metaphysical entity whose existence was to be discovered by dialectic; He was not the god of philosophers and theologians. Rather, He was the force behind those events that truly happened. Assyria's conquest was a reality; hence Yahve, Who caused the conquest, was real. This emphasis on history has marked Judaism and central elements in Christianity. In the early Christian centuries, there were some Christians who, lacking this sense of history, saw symbol rather than reality in the Incarnation, Death, and Resurrection. They contended that God had not really become incarnate in Jesus; He only *seemed* to have. The exponents of "seemingness" are called "Docetists," and the Church came to view them as heretics. In Christian creeds, the assertion that Jesus "suffered under Pontius Pilate" contradicts the philosophy of the Docetists by giving a historical basis to the events. The Church remained true to its Hebrew legacy when it insisted on the historical character of its contentions.

Isaiah was the first man to insist that Yahve is discerned in history and controls history; his message, therefore, represents a milestone in Hebrew thought. Since Yahve controls history, the pious should have recourse to Him rather than to Assyria or Egypt—this was Isaiah's message. Although decency and honesty were also required of Israel, the only policy that could and would prevail was faith in Yahve.

Isaiah does not draw the corollaries for us. He never tells us what actions should follow from faith in Yahve and perhaps he never raised the question. Like many who stir men to reach fundamentals, he probably had no sense of the practical consequences. He says simply that God is omnipotent and universal, and Israel must rely on Him alone. Isaiah's injunctions to have faith led inevitably to further questions about God's justice. If Israel was so faithless that she needed punishment, was she worse than Assyria or Egypt? Was it just that Israel was to be singled out for special punishment? In biblical literature after Isaiah's time, we find examples of the kind of theological problem that is called by the technical name of "theodicy." The word means "God's justice." Anyone who begins with the axiom that God is just encounters incidents in his experience that raise the question, "How can a just god permit these things to happen?" Although no questions of theodicy arise in Isaiah, they inevitably came up later, as a result of his exalted conception of Yahve's omnipotence and justice.

Another consequence of Isaiah's insistence on faith concerns the covenant. In Isaiah's thought Israel was bound to break the covenant, and because it was destined to be broken, doom awaited Israel. Later writings such as Jeremiah and Second Isaiah confront the question of the status of the covenant, once the predicted doom had arrived.

Curiously, the happiest, most lyrical, most optimistic passages in the Tanak have found their way into the Book of Isaiah. The beating of swords into plowshares (2:4) and the lying down of the wolf and the lamb (11:6) are both from this book. In the view of many traditional interpreters, Isaiah emerges as a man of happy expectations for the future. These joyful passages, however, are not from Isaiah, the eighth-century prophet. The recognition that these parts are late insertions reveals Isaiah as even more of a prophet of doom than Amos and Hosea. In all three, but especially in Isaiah, the early Hebrew religion expresses a basic hopelessness. Israel's doom, synonymous with mankind's doom, was regarded as inevitable. Isaiah proffered his age a gripping, stirring faith but man's inability to achieve that faith or abide in it spelled only disaster.

We have seen that Isaiah hints of a "saved remnant." Since these intimations are not fully articulated or developed passages, we must beware of reading too much into them. A conjecture, however, seems reasonable: perhaps Isaiah's recognition that his basic doctrine was one of doom led him to mitigate it with the idea of the "saved remnant." Could the righteous escape the coming doom? Not until almost a century and a half after Isaiah does a prophet declare that the fate of the righteous individual is different from that of the unrighteous. Amos certainly gives us no sense of such a distinction. Scholars have concluded that Amos and Hosea conceived of the Deity as dealing with Israel collectively, rather than with individuals. A righteous man could be lost in the total destruction of his people.

Perhaps Isaiah's "saved remnant" [1] is the beginning of the individualism that becomes pronounced only in later biblical thought.

In Isaiah's lifetime the northern kingdom was conquered; the ten tribes comprising it were transported eastward, there to be absorbed and to disappear. They were later regarded as "lost," as pursuing their existence beyond a miraculous river, which flowed six days a week and piously stopped on the Sabbath. Later ages "found" them in a number of fanciful places; the Indians, the Eskimos, the Chinese,

[1] See note 3 on page 88.

even the Britons, have been at various times identified as their descendants. The territory of the northern kingdom was repopulated by importing peoples from the east (see II Kings, 17:24ff.). The northern kingdom had met its doom, and doom was predicted for the southern kingdom also.

MICAH

THE SUPERSCRIPTION of the Book of Micah reveals that this eminent prophet lived in the same period as Isaiah and was active in the days of the kings who reigned during the last part of Isaiah's career. Unhappily, there are no clear indications of the dates of any of the passages. Indeed, while the superscription allocates the activity of Micah to the reigns of Jothan, Ahaz, and Hezekiah—reigns that would encompass the period from 742–687—a good many scholars argue from the content of the book that the superscription is in error and that Micah was active a generation later, during the times of Hezekiah and his successor Manasseh. Others would confine him to the early years of Hezekiah (715–687). The student who is caught between the superscription and the scholarly reservations can simply say that Micah was a younger contemporary of Isaiah's. The book is short, numbering only seven chapters, but even so, it contains passages that are later additions.

We know very little about Micah. He was a native of an unidentified village probably known as Moresheth,[1] and hence he is called "the Morashtite." Even though he is obscure to us, he was at least well enough known to be spoken of by Jeremiah, in 26:*18*.

[1] Some scholars identify the village as the modern Marissa, between the coastal plain and the central highlands of southwestern Palestine.

Two passages in the Book of Micah have a striking literary quality, and Micah's abiding eminence is literary, for his religious ideas,
though remarkably elevated, are not strikingly original.

In the first three chapters, we are in territory already familiar to
us after reading Amos and Isaiah. Micah inveighs here against social
injustice, especially the oppression of the poor by the rich:

> *Woe to those who devise wickedness,*
> *Planning evil while in their beds,*
> *And practicing it when the morning is light,*
> *Because they have the power to do so.*
> *They covet fields, and seize them,*
> *Houses, and acquire them.*
> *They oppress a man and his house, a human being and his*
>   *possession.*
>
> *Therefore thus says Yahve:*
> *"Behold I devise, against this family, evil*
> *From which you cannot remove your necks*
> *So that you will no longer walk haughtily."*
>
> *On that day someone will use you as a bad example,*
> *And wail about you with wailing lamentation, and say,*
> *"We are utterly destroyed!*
> *He [Yahve] makes changes in people's portions—*
> *There is no one to restore the fields which have been di-*
>   *vided up." [2:1–4]*

The rich object to such a message:

> *"Do not prophesy"—thus they prophesy—*
> *"People should not prophesy such things!*
> *Shameful things will not overtake us!" [2:6]*

The prophet answers:

> *Should such things be said, O house of Jacob?*
> *Is the spirit of Yahve too short [to reach you]?*
> *Are the [misdeeds] His deeds?*
> *Are not His words good for His people Israel*?" [2:7]*

Now Micah resumes his thread:

> *You [wealthy] rise up against my people * as a foe,*
> *You strip * them of the robe, you take off the mantle,*
> *You bring war-like destruction on those who go about*
>   *peaceably.*

You drive the women among my people out of her pleasant
    home;
From her children you take away their * beautiful things
    forever,
Commanding them "Arise! Go! This is no place to rest!"
For a tiny nothing * you acquire that which deals out
    pain.*

A prophet for this people would be a man, going about utter-
    ing wind and lies, and saying,
"I will prophesy for you about wine and liquor." [2:8–11]

Or again, Micah condemns those

Who eat the flesh of my people,
And strip their skin from off them,
Who break their bones into pieces,
Who chop them into a kettle like meat,*
Like flesh in a pot.
They then call out to Yahve,
But He does not answer them.
He will hide His face from them . . .
As they themselves have done evil deeds. [3:3–4]

Micah is the first literary prophet to be concerned with those
who, from the standpoint of the canonical prophets, merit being
called false prophets:

Thus says Yahve about the prophets who lead my people
    astray,
Who having some [food] to sink their teeth into, call out,
    "Peace."
Yet against someone who does not put food into their
    mouths, they proclaim woe. [3:5]

He then addresses the prophets directly:

"To you [false prophets] there will be night [too dark] for
    visions,
And utter darkness, without chance for divination." [3:6A]

He reverts to the third person:

The sun will set on the "prophets"
And the day become black upon them,
The "seers" will be disgraced,
And the diviners be put to shame.

They will all cover their lips,
For no reply comes from God.

Yet I [on the other hand] am filled with power,
With the spirit of Yahve,
With judgment and strength,
So as to declare to Jacob his transgression
And to Israel his sin. [3:6B–8]

This mention of false prophets is brief but illuminating. Since the ancient Hebrews enjoyed censure no more than we do, prophets who scolded and promised catastrophe could have little reason to expect a popular following. When we come to Jeremiah, we shall see that the opposition to a prophet with an unpleasant message could be most severe.

It is all the more amazing that Israel, in preserving the message of the prophets, preserved wholesale and categorical denunciation of herself. Such a procedure is unusual for any nation, ancient or modern, for most people tend to preserve only that which glorifies them. The prophetic literature, especially that of the pre-exilic period, reveals the least glorious aspects of Israel; but, perhaps paradoxically, the courage to preserve and remember these aspects reflects a grandeur far exceeding that of false glorification.

As we have said above, the religious doctrines of Micah provide no new profundity. Chapters 4 and 5 are uniformly regarded as late additions. We shall revert to Chapter 4 (see below, pages 204–205), in order to deal with the age of that remarkable section, but all that is relevant to our present discussion is its duplication of the passage in Isaiah 2; indeed, the initial three verses of the two passages are virtually identical.

It shall come about in the latter days
That the mountain of Yahve's house will be ready as the
*   chief of the mountains;*
It will be loftier than the hills,
And nations will stream to it.
Many peoples will come and say,
"Come, let us ascend to Yahve's mountain,
And to the Temple of Jacob's God.
Let Him teach us some of His ways,
So that we can walk in His paths"

For it is from [Mount] Zion that revelation goes out
And from Jerusalem that Yahve's word [comes].

He [Yahve] will judge among mighty nations,
And make decisions for distant powerful nations,
So that they will beat their swords into plows
And their spears into pruning hooks,
And they will no longer study warfare. [4:1–3]

There are a good many deuterographs ("repeated portions") in the Tanak. Thus, Psalm 18 and II Sam. 22 are virtually the same. Probably two versions were preserved because they appeared in collections made by different people. The passage under consideration comes from a time later than Isaiah and Micah; the contents reveal an age later than the eighth or seventh century. The mere fact that it appears in duplicate form is often cited as evidence against its being the product of either Micah or Isaiah. The passage is important in our context because we see that the ancients thought so much of it that two recensions of it exist in the Tanak. The conclusion does not need laboring: the value of a passage lies in what it says, not in who said it. Moreover—and here I am deliberately repeating—when a scholar says that a prophetic passage is "interpolated" or "secondary," he is not passing a value judgment on it, but only describing its relationship to the book in which it occurs.

Another passage in Micah (6:6–8) is universally acknowledged to be a peak in biblical literature. Almost all scholars consider it to be a later addition. To my mind this conclusion is not only unnecessary but mistaken, for the passage seems to me to be in harmony with Amos, Hosea, Isaiah, and Micah. The prophet, thinking aloud, tries to answer the question, What is true religion?

With what shall I visit Yahve,
And bow before God on high?
Shall I visit Him with animal sacrifices,
With year-old calves?
Does Yahve want countless rams,
With untabulated streams of oil?

Shall I give my first-born child in place of my transgression,
The fruit of my body as a sin offering for me?

He [Yahve] has already told you, O man, what is good,
And what He seeks of you:
    Merely to do justice,
    To love righteousness,
    To walk humbly before your God. [6:6–8]

Chapter 7 contains many allusions, which we are regrettably unable to understand. Since despair dominates its beginning, and hope its conclusion, this chapter has provoked a variety of theories. Most scholars believe that the chapter consists of two separate compositions (verses *1–6*, and *7–20*), and that these compositions are psalms or poems rather than prophecies. They are generally considered to be products of a time several centuries after Micah. This opinion does not convince me, especially with regard to the second part of the chapter. One senses here that the writer has been engaged in some kind of physical or spiritual struggle from which he has emerged with some sense of triumph. That this half-chapter is hopeful scarcely points to a late date of composition. In the first part of this chapter, the author laments the absence of honest and worthy men. The second part deals with the vindication of the speaker and the downfall of his enemies ; the section is neither clear nor exalted. In the last three verses (*18–20*), words of adoration are spoken to Yahve who pardons iniquity; the next to last verse speaks, of Yahve's "casting our sins into the deep." From this verse a quaint custom arose among Jews, a custom so nearly obsolete in the United States that American Jews scarcely know about it. According to this practice, Jews gathered at a river or a lake on the afternoon of the New Year and cast bread crumbs into the water, as if symbolically casting sins into it. The custom is called *Tashlich* ("you will cast").

Although Micah's social message is quite the equal of Isaiah's, if not of Amos', in vigor, it is not quite as vividly specific as his predecessors'. The sturdy defense of the poor against exploitation by the rich, however, reflects Micah's sympathies and his moral earnestness. The absence of novel religious doctrines should not lead us to underestimate him. He was a prophet of the highest stature, and the Book of Micah is one of the gems of Scripture.

CHAPTER

7

ZEPHANIAH

ONE SINGLE VERSE (1:15) from the Book of Zephaniah is cited more often than the rest of the brief set of three chapters:

> *A day of wrath is that day,*
> *A day of trouble and distress . . .*

The expressed and implied significance of the verse, and not any poetic value, earned for it its large measure of attention. Apart from this verse and its immediate context, Zephaniah contains little that is sharply distinctive, for prophets like Amos and Isaiah speak more eloquently the worthy message of Zephaniah.

Zephaniah's message is clear, although its background is not entirely so. The superscription (1:1) dates him more positively than does the content of the book; according to this verse, he seems to have been active during the time of Josiah, whose reign stretched from 640–608. Assyria, which had destroyed the northern kingdom in 722/721, was still in its ascendancy in the early days of Josiah's reign; its decline began in 626. In the decades before Josiah, she had extended her conquest westward to include the subjection of Egypt. Josiah's predecessors had been the notorious Manasseh (687–642) and his son Amon, who reigned briefly from 642–640. II Kings depicts Manasseh as a complete scoundrel, who promoted the revival of Baal practices.

Indeed, the great Reformation [1] of Josiah in 621, recorded in II Kings 22–3, was directed against the Baal worship. If Zephaniah's activity was in Josiah's reign, as the superscription indicates, then it was probably in the early years of that reign, between 638 and 626. In short, Zephaniah was active at a time when Assyrian influence was still dominant, and when Baal syncretism had reached a new high point.

However, our knowledge of the period can possibly be amplified, at least in the view of some scholars. The Greek historian Herodotus (*History*, Book I, 104–5) relates some events connected with the end of the Assyrian empire in 612. Two eastern peoples, the Medes and the Babylonians, had arisen to challenge the Assyrians. The Medes attacked the Assyrians, but at this juncture a third eastern people appeared on the scene. These were the Scythians, who, according to Herodotus, became "masters of Asia. . . . They marched ahead designing to invade Egypt," but were bought off in Palestine by emissaries of the Egyptians. The Scythian domination lasted for twenty-eight years.

The hazy Scythian period partially overlaps the time of Zephaniah, and it is therefore reasonable for scholars to search each syllable of Zephaniah (and Jeremiah, too) for allusions to these obscure people. An allusion in Jeremiah 4:5ff. is commonly believed to be to the Scythians, and it has been thought that Zephaniah 2 traces the progress of the Scythians on their southward march along the Palestine coast. On the other hand, it seems much more reasonable to see Zephaniah 2 as a series of denunciations of foreign nations in general, and not of the Scythians in particular. Hence, the rejection of the Scythian explanation changes the background of the Book of Zephaniah

---

[1] This religious Reformation took place in 621; the account of it is given in II Kings 22–3. King Josiah had undertaken to refurbish the Temple at Jerusalem. The workmen found a scroll, a Book of Torah, which contained regulations that were obviously being ignored. The Reformation consisted in carrying out the provisions found in the scroll. Accordingly, the Baal practices and vessels, which had made their way even into the Temple, were done away with; the priests of the sanctuaries outside Jerusalem were deposed and their sanctuaries destroyed; the priests were brought to Jerusalem to join the priests resident there. Before this Reformation, sanctuaries outside Jerusalem and priests of whatever origin were deemed legitimate; after it, only the Jerusalem Temple and only priests of the tribe of Levi were so deemed.

The Book of Deuteronomy contains provisions that limit priesthood to Levite Priests and prescribe that there should be only one sanctuary in the land. Modern scholars have believed for almost a hundred and fifty years that there is some direct connection between the Book of Deuteronomy and the Reformation of Josiah; see my discussion below on Deuteronomy, pp. 412–413. The scroll found in the Temple has often been identified as Deuteronomy or some portion of it. Consequently the great Reformation is spoken of both as the Reformation of Josiah and as the Deuteronomic Reformation.

from a specific moment into a vague period. Indeed, were it not for the superscription we should be hard put to find some historical setting for the book from the contents alone, except one passage, 2:13–15, that pronounces a doom soon to fall on Assyria and its capital Nineveh. Perhaps this passage can be dated about 612, when Nineveh fell.

While Zephaniah shows the same hatred of syncretism and of Baal worship that marked his predecessors, especially Hosea, he does not leave a clear stamp of his personality on the content or the style of his book. So bereft is the book of individuality that some scholars have been almost desperate to find some personal trait of the prophet. The mention in 1:1 of a Hezekiah as Zephaniah's grandfather has led some scholars to conclude that this Hezekiah was the king who reigned from 715–687, just before the wicked Manasseh. Such an attribution of royal ancestry may be correct, but is uncertain; the uncertainty underscores our ignorance about Zephaniah.

The great Reformation of Josiah in 621 (as a result of which all sanctuaries except that in Jerusalem were closed and destroyed and only the Jerusalem priests retained the full franchise to officiate) was an event of major importance. Since Zephaniah shows no awareness of it, scholars place his activity four to five years before the Reformation. But an equally good explanation of his silence on this topic lies in his general vagueness.

The third of the three chapters is considered to be a psalm from the period a century after Zephaniah. The first two chapters contain traces of additions from later times. Chapter 2 has fifteen verses, but only half of the chapter is really from Zephaniah:

> *Be greatly ashamed, O nation that has no shame;*
> *Before you are forced away like passing chaff,*
> *Before the fierce anger of Yahve comes on you . . .*
> *Gaza will be deserted,[2] and Ashkelon a desolation,*
> *Ashdod, at noon its populace will be expelled,*
> *And Ekron [3] will be uprooted.*
> *Woe to you who dwell on the coast of the sea,*
> *You people who are Cretans [4] . . .*
> *"I will bring you low, land of the Philistines,*
> *And destroy you until no inhabitant remains . . .*

[2] These are two puns. In Hebrew we read Aza (i.e., Gaza) is azuba ("deserted"), and Eqron will te-aqer. Ashkelon and Ashdod are not punned on.
[3] These four were Philistine cities.
[4] The Philistines originated from Crete.

[*Animals*] *will graze in the houses of Ashkelon,*
And lie down for the night in Ekron . . .
You too, O Ethiopians, will be victims of my sword."

He will stretch His hand northward [*from Ethiopia*]
And destroy Assyria.
He will make Nineveh[5] *a desolation,*
Dry like the desert.
Then will crouch down in her, herds of all the beasts of the
     field:
The vulture and the porcupine (?) *will lodge in the lintels,*
The owl will hoot in the window, the raven on the thresh-
     old . . . [2:1–2A, 4–5, 7B, and 12–14]

This is neither exalted religion nor exalted literature. It is denunciation unaccompanied by any comment on its justification or its relation to Yahve's purpose. Possibly, when it was originally spoken it came in a worthy context, which failed to survive.

The significant single verse mentioned at the beginning of this chapter is from a context equally uninspiring. In Chapter 1, the verses regarded as authentically by Zephaniah are: *4–5, 8B–11, 13, 12, 7–8A,* and *14–18.* This rearrangement is found desirable by many scholars. Zephaniah depicts Yahve as speaking:

"I shall stretch forth My hand against Judah and all of Jeru-
     salem's inhabitants;
I shall cut out from this place the remnant of Baal worship
     and its priests *
And those who on the roofs [6] *bow down to the host of*
     heavens,
*Those who, bowing down and swearing to Yahve,**
Yet swear by Milcom; [7]
Those who don foreign clothes.

[5] Assyria's capital.
[6] This is typical of the worship of the Baal; see II Kings 23:5 and 12 and Jeremiah 19:13 and 32:29.
[7] *Milcom* represents a change in the vowels of the word in text, not in the consonants. The Hebrew wrongly reads *malkam,* "their king." Milcom—also known as Moloch—was the god of the Ammonites, but Milcom appears to be a generic term for alien deities whose worship was imported into Palestine. Baal, on the other hand, was a native deity. See I Kings 11:5 and 7 and II Kings 23:13 for an account of Solomon's regard for Milcom. A prominent feature of Moloch worship was making children "pass through fire"; see II Kings 23:10. Such worship—child sacrifice on a burning altar—is expressly prohibited in Leviticus 20:2–5.

I shall punish everyone who leaps over the threshold,[8]
Who fill their lord's house [9] *with wrongdoing and fraud.*

"There will be on that day," says Yahve, "an outcry from the
    Fish Gate [1]
And wailing from the Second,[2]
And a great shattering from the hills,[3]
And wailing from the Machtesh [4]
The whole tribe of tradesmen is destroyed,
The weighers of silver [5] *are cut off.*
All their goods will be plundered, their houses made
    waste . . .

"I shall search throughout Jerusalem with candles
And punish men who think they are secure,
Who have become solidified like wine lees [6]
Who say in their heart, 'Yahve does neither good nor evil.' "

Now the prophet speaks in his own words:

Be silent before the Lord Yahve, for the Day of Yahve is
    near.
For Yahve has prepared an offering,
He has sanctified His invited guests.
For on the day of Yahve's offering,
He will punish the officials and the princes.
The great day of Yahve is near,
It is greatly speeding.
Swifter [7] *is the day of Yahve than a runner,*
And faster than a warrior.

---

[8] There was apparently a Philistine custom (see I Sam. 5) of not stepping on the threshold when entering a temple. Therefore, to "leap over the threshold" meant to enter a pagan temple.

[9] Perhaps the meaning is Temple of the Lord, not the house, or palace, of the ruler.

[1] This was an entrance on the north of the city of Jerusalem, possibly near a fish market; see Neh. 12:39.

[2] In II Kings 22:14 a prophetess, Hulda, is spoken of as residing in "The Second"; presumably, this was a quarter in the northern section of the city.

[3] The allusion is lost. Perhaps a section of the city was called "the hills."

[4] The allusion is not clear. The word may mean "low-land"; some translate it "Mortar."

[5] In the absence of coinage, the weighing of precious metal was necessary.

[6] A colorful figure of speech for a sense of security. The idea is that lees are too thick for pouring.

[7] The verse is emended.

A day of wrath is that day,
A day of trouble and distress,
A day of ruin and destruction,
A day of darkness and gloom,
A day of cloud and thick darkness,
A day of trumpet blast and signal against the fortified cities
and the high battlements.

He will bring distress upon man, and they will walk like
the blind . . .
Their blood will be poured out as if dust,
Their flesh as if dung.

Neither their silver nor their gold will be able to save them
On the day of Yahve's wrath
And in the fire of His zealous anger
All the earth will be consumed,
For He will make an end, a sudden one, of all the dwellers
on earth.

This prophecy has a basic unity. The Deity proposes to visit punishment on Judah and Jerusalem, whose citizens are worshiping alien deities and, apparently, pursuing business as usual instead of feeling concern for the divine will. This punishment is scheduled to occur on the Day of Yahve, an occasion that is said to be speedily approaching. While Amos saw the Day of Yahve as the annually recurring New Year day, Zephaniah does not envision a recurring occasion, but rather a single climactic event.

How shall we account for the changed conception of the Day of Yahve? First, the change reflects the lapse of time between the two prophets. As we saw in the case of Amos, both a devastating earthquake and also the Assyrian invasion invested Amos' prediction with the character of a doom which came after the passing of considerable time. Therefore, when people looked back at his prediction, it seemed to refer to a remote occasion rather than to a recurring one. The result was that the Day of Yahve began to connote some disaster in the relatively distant future, rather than merely judgment on the annual New Year day.

The New Year did not entirely lose its character of a judgment day. The Day of Yahve, as if quite distinct from the New Year, came to connote some special future time free from a calendar's schedule. Zephaniah could therefore proclaim that the Day, popularly held to be in some distant future, was now speeding to arrive.

Second, the Day of Yahve as the annual New Year was bound up with persistent vestiges of solar worship; the transformation of the Day of Yahve from the scheduled equinox to the uncertain remote future was connected with the rejection of such worship. Third, a view that God controls history and shapes its events raises the question of why He permits evil to exist, and evildoers to escape punishment. The person believing in divine providence, omnipotence, and justice must at times take refuge in the belief that the evildoer's merited punishment is only being delayed. In this view, therefore, the true judgment day is not here and now but in the future, and it is a short step from the conviction that the future day will come, to the conviction that it will come soon.

When we question what lies in the future, we have come into the domain of *eschatology*. This word means simply "the study of what happens at the end of time." Eschatology makes its first vivid entrance into recorded Hebrew thought with Zephaniah; he is the literary father of Hebrew eschatology.

The traditional idea of the covenant was too mechanical to allow a place for eschatology. Its implication was that if, or when, Israel broke the covenant, punishment would come relatively soon, and not in the distant future. In this sense, the traditional covenant and eschatology were mutually exclusive. The entrance of eschatology into prophetic thought meant that the older conception of the covenant would have to be revised.

Zephaniah's view of the future could scarcely be darker. The medieval poem *Dies Irae* is based on the first words of 1 : 15:

> *Day of wrath, O day of mourning,*
> *See fulfilled the prophets' warning*
> *Heav'n and earth in ashes burning.*

The Hebrew language is not rich in adjectives and the relatively few that connote gloom and darkness, anger and wrath are all utilized by Zephaniah. Moreover, when Zephaniah becomes specific about the events on the coming Day of Yahve, he opens the door to eschatology's twin brother, *Apocalypse*. This word comes from the Greek; it is a noun meaning "revelation." Scholars usually narrow and restrict the term *"apocalyptic"* to those passages that "reveal" exactly what will happen at the eschatological moment.

The danger for an author of being specific was twofold. First, the day might never come. Zephaniah, Jesus, and Paul are among those who wrongly predicted the early arrival of the End. Second, the more specific a prophet became, the more he could arouse incredulity. It was better for him to couch his predictions of specific events as ambiguously as possible, and symbol therefore became more congenial to the apocalyptist than simple statement. Biblical apocalypses tended to become cryptic; we can translate passages in Daniel and in Revelation without really knowing what is being discussed. Zephaniah is not the father of apocalypse; he is its grandfather. The father of apocalypse is eschatology.

The passage in Zephaniah we have concentrated on is a milestone in biblical thought. Without the concept that Yahve controls history, there would have been no eschatology. Without eschatology the idea of the Messiah would scarcely have arisen. Without eschatology, there would have been no Christianity.

Indeed, without Zephaniah's implicit criticism of the covenant, those changes that mark off the Hebrew religion from Judaism would not have arisen. The older idea led to doom. When covenant, partly through the rise of eschatology, changed finally from inevitable doom to a new view of an unbroken and unbreakable relation between Yahve and His people, Hebrew thought developed into Judaism. This significant development occurred not long after Zephaniah's time.

Zephaniah's legacy of eschatology and its offspring, apocalypse, were destined to grow in significance and in rich and elaborate formulations, sometimes without restraint, as is the case in surviving writings that were never accepted into the Tanak or the New Testament. But Zephaniah himself belongs rather with Hosea, Isaiah, and Micah, than with the later figures whose spiritual ancestor he was.

8

NAHUM

NEITHER the Book of Nahum itself nor outside sources give us any information about this prophet. He is identified as being from Elkosh, but that place is unknown. Perhaps it is fitting that this least religious of all the prophetic writings should be the work of an unknown author.

The first chapter is a large fragment of a poem written centuries after the main poem, which is found in the second and the last chapters. This main poem is a bloodcurdling song of rejoicing that Nineveh, Assyria's capital, has fallen, a victim of Yahve's just and merited vengeance. The taunt at a nation's disaster unhappily does not stir us to disapproval. We are too civilized to gloat when a man is destroyed, but we do not feel the same squeamishness when a whole people suffers annihilation.

Originally the introductory chapter was an alphabetical acrostic, that is, the first line began with A(aleph), the second B (beth), and so on. Towards the middle of the alphabet, however, the acrostic and the poem fade away because the text is not well preserved. The nature of the Hebrew language is such that an acrostic poem is not as artificial as it is in English. Indeed, English acrostics seldom rise above the level of "M is for the many things she taught me." A Hebrew acrostic can be a fine piece of literature.

The paradox of the Book of Nahum, both in the initial acrostic and, especially, in the long poem, is that the literature is as good as the religion is bad. The Book of Jonah (see below, pages 494ff.), which deals with God's concern even for the wicked city Nineveh, is not great literature but is religiously exalted. The Book of Nahum, on the other hand, expresses unedifying ideas with supreme poetic skill; Nahum jumps for joy when Nineveh is destroyed by military conquest. Commentators seem loath to speak plainly about the unexalted character of the religion in Nahum. The nearest to plain speech is that of Taylor in the *Interpreter's Bible* (VI, page 954); yet even he is able to find some affirmative religious sentiment in Nahum by supposing that Nahum, who was stirred to great moral indignation by the evil deeds of Nineveh, is expressing a "concern over entrenched wrong." I do not find such sentiments in Nahum, and I do not believe they are there. Nahum belongs in a national literature, such as the Tanak is. One can question, however, if it belongs in prophetic literature and if Nahum merits the high title of prophet.

There are those who believe the author must have witnessed personally the siege and capture of Nineveh in 612 in order to have described the scene so vividly. Provided that this opinion is valid, and I consider it to be highly reasonable, the long poem can be dated shortly after 612. There are, on the other hand, those who regard the poem as a prediction of what is to come, rather than a description of what has taken place. Even if this is the case, the poem so clearly assumes the inevitability of Nineveh's fall that its date must be placed very near to 612; whether we date it 614, before the fall, or 610, after the fall, is really inconsequential.

Before considering the long poem, let us turn to a portion of the late introductory acrostic, in order to note its character. The names of the letters of the Hebrew alphabet are given in parentheses, but are, of course, absent from Scripture:

(ALEPH)   *Yahve is a jealous and vengeful God,*
           The master of wrath,

(BETH)   *In storm and tempest lies His road,*
           A cloud serves as dust to His feet.

(GIMMEL)   *He scolds the sea, and makes it dry,*
           He parches every stream of water.

(DALETH)   *Crushed are Bashan and Carmel,*[1]
           The bloom of Lebanon.[2]

[1] Bashan is in the fertile northeast of Palestine; Carmel, a coastal mountain, is a place of mist and moisture.
[2] Lebanon, now an independent country, is in the extreme north. It was famous for its cedars which yielded fine lumber.

(HE)   *Mountains tremble before Him,*
                    The hills quake,

(VAV)   *And the earth is waste before Him,*
                    The world and all its inhabitants.

(ZAYIN)   *Before His wrath, who can stand?*
                    Who can endure His anger?

(HETH)   *His fury is poured out like a fire,*
                    Rocks are shattered by Him.

(TETH)   *Good is Yahve to those who rely upon Him,*
                    A stronghold in the day of trouble.

(YAD)   *He knows those who trust in Him . . .*

(KOF)   *Destruction He works on His adversaries,*
                    Darkness overwhelms His foes.

(LAMED)   *His enemies do not rise a second time,*
                    ----------------------------------.

(MEM)   *What will you devise against Yahve?*
                    He works total destruction.

(NUN)   *Revenge Yahve takes on his foes,*
                    He stores up [vengeance] against his
        enemies. [1:2–9] [3]

The above can be accepted or dismissed as competent poetry. The longer poem is of a higher order. It is addressed to Nineveh:

Out of you came he who planned evil against Yahve,
A scoundrel of a plotter! . . .
Yahve has commanded concerning you
That your name shall no more be perpetuated. [4]
From the house of your god I shall cut off statue and molten
        image;
Your grave I will make a stench. [1:11 and 14]

After this denunciation, there is a description of the attack on Nineveh.

He who puts to rout has come against you!
Let the defense be manned,

---

[3] The verse order is rearranged to conform to the Hebrew alphabet. Since only half the alphabet is represented, some scholars believe that the second half of the poem has been lost.
[4] Literally, the word is "sown" like seed.

The road be watched,
Loins be girded,
Full strength be mustered! . . .
The shields of his warriors are red,
The soldiers are garbed in scarlet.

Like flames of fire are the chariots. . . .

The horsemen are posting,
In the streets the chariots (?) shimmer,
In the boulevards they dance,
Their appearance is like flames,
They dart about like lightning. [2:2, 4A, 5 Heb., 1, 3A, 4
 Eng.]

Now comes the capture of the city:

He summons his officers—
They stumble on their way.
They rush to the city wall—
The cover [*of the foe's battering ram*] *is ready.*
The floodgates of the river are opened,[5]
The palace is in dismay.
The queen (?) is led out, carried off,
Her maidens are driven away.
They moan like doves;
They beat their breasts.
Nineveh is like a conduit of water—

The water flees away—
"Halt, halt, [*O water*]*!"*
None turns back.
Take spoil of silver; take spoil of gold.
No end is there of treasure. . . .
Desolation . . . *and plunder!*
The heart faints; the knees collapse,
Shivering is in all loins;
All faces have become flushed. [2:5–10]

Now, sarcastically, the poem asks:

What has become of the lion's den—
The cave of the young lions
Where the [*lion*] *returned,*
Where the cubs, unfrightened, were [*waiting*]?

[5] That is, the foe has made this good progress.

The lion used to tear enough for his cubs,
And strangled [enough] for his lionesses.
He used to fill his caves with prey,
His dens with torn flesh. [2:11–12]

Yahve of hosts says:

"I am against you!
I shall burn your multitude in smoke (?).
The sword will devour your whelps.
I will bring an end to your cruel raids,
And the voice of your emissaries will not be heard."

Woe unto the city guilty of murder,
Completely deceiving,
Full of ill gotten gains,
Where rape never ceased!
Crack of whip,
Loud sound of wheels.
Horse gallops,
Chariot bounces,
Cavalry charges,
Sword flashes,
Spear shines,
Hosts fall!
Abundance of corpses,
No end of cadavers,
A stumbling over bodies!
For the abundance of her whorelike whorings,
Though she has a graceful fine appearance,
She is mistress of witchcraft,
Selling nations in her whoredom
And families in her witchery.
"I am against you," says Yahve of Hosts,
"I will roll your skirts up, over your face,
And show your private parts to the nations,
And your shame to kingdoms.
I will throw upon you filth. . . .
I will make you a sight to look at!" [2:13–3:6]

Nahum is rich in imagery, bright in colors, agile in the use of words. But it is a hymn of hate. It is possible and even likely that the hatred was justified by the events. In our day such hatred is all too frequent; we may therefore be unjust in lamenting that a prophet succumbed to it. Nahum's may well have been an immediate emotional response; for a reflective, considered judgment we must turn to Jonah. Animosity towards foreign nations does appear, though not as strongly, in the Books of Isaiah, Jeremiah, and Ezekiel; Nahum is therefore not alone in expressing such sentiments. But here the animosity is the major, indeed the sole theme of the prophet's message. For this reason Nahum is unusual, and scarcely to be considered on the same high level as most of the prophets.

CHAPTER

9

HABAKKUK

ONE TURNS from Nahum to Habakkuk with a sense of relief, for here one encounters a sensitive heart and a profound spirit. Habakkuk is one of the great books of Scripture.

It is lamentable that some pedestrian problems arise in the Book. The third of the three chapters, although as lofty as the first two, represents a different author from the author of the first two chapters. Even in the first chapters a problem intrudes, but as the majesty and depth of the book are not greatly affected by the problem, it is sufficient for our purposes simply to state it and then proceed as if it did not exist. When did Habakkuk flourish, and against what background? 1:6 reads:

> *I am raising up the Chaldeans,*
> *A bitter and hasty nation*
> *Which travels the breadth of the earth*
> *To seize dwellings that are not his.*

The Chaldeans established their independence from Assyria in 625 and conquered Babylonia in 614. We usually speak of the Chaldeans as the Babylonians. In concert with the Medes, they conquered Nineveh in 612; they conquered Jerusalem in 597. Some verses in Habakkuk seem to assume that the Chaldeans have already completely overrun Palestine, while other verses seem to envisage this as a future event. There are scholars who feel that the messages of Habakkuk must be assigned to an age much later than the end of the seventh century.[1]

The second aspect of the problem concerns the relationship of the section about the Chaldeans to the chapter in which it is imbedded. There is some evidence that the section does not belong here, that it was originally quite independent. Nevertheless, I shall interpret and translate as if the passage were in its proper place. Such a procedure will in no way distort the basic significance of Habakkuk.

One more word about history is needed. Josiah (640–608), who was regarded as a great and noble king, fell in battle at the hands of the Egyptians. Some disunity and wide disorder may have followed. Against such a possible background, we hear Habakkuk speak to Yahve:

For how long, O Yahve, shall I cry and You will not hear?
[For how long] shall I call out, "Violence is done!"—
But You will not help.
Why do You permit me to experience evil, and encounter
*   ordeal?*
Destruction and violence are at hand,
Dissension is my lot, and I undergo strife. [1:2-3]

Obviously, in this address the prophet is not speaking to people, as were the earlier prophets, but directly to the Deity. The passage is not a record of some spoken address, therefore, but a poem or a meditative essay in dialogue—a studied composition.

The complaint to the Deity continues for one more verse:

In light of this [silence on Yahve's part], revelation has
*   come to a standstill*
And true justice cannot emerge;
For the wicked circumvent the righteous,
So that justice stands forth as distortion. [1:4]

To the prophet's challenge that Yahve has permitted such affairs to exist, Yahve is portrayed as replying:

[1] Some of the solutions offered by scholars have been fantastic. One such involved changing the text, so that it deals not with Chaldeans but with Kittites, and supposedly refers to Alexander the Great (around 331). I shall assume that the text, since it says Chaldeans, means Chaldeans.

Look, you traitorous people, and be greatly astounded
For I am doing a deed which, if it were only told, you would
not believe.
I am raising up the Chaldeans, a bitter and hasty nation
Which travels the breadth of the earth to seize dwellings
that are not his.
Fearsome and terrifying is he, and from him emerge de-
crees.
His horses are swifter than leopards, and sharper than
wolves at evening-time,
His cavalry come dancingly from this distance, flying like
an eagle rushing for food.

His people are bent entirely on violence, terror of their wan-
tonness precedes them,
And they gather prisoners like sand.

[Their king] scoffs at kings, and rulers are a joke to him,
He laughs at every fortified place; he heaps up mounds of
earth and captures it.
He passes like the wind [to another place], and becomes
guilty, [ascribing] this strength to his false god.

Yahve has raised the Chaldeans, whose conquest is the substance of the prophet's lament. Although the Chaldeans are to pay a price for not recognizing that they are Yahve's tool, the prophet is not comforted by this assurance, for it seems to imply that only later will this price be exacted. The prophet asks:

Are You not more ancient than he (Chaldea), O Yahve,
My holy God, not subject to death? [2] *[1:12A]*

This all has happened, then, for the following reason:

You appointed him as an instrument of justice,
Established him as a means of chastisement.
Your eyes [O Yahve] are too pure to see evil,
And You are unable to look at wrongdoing.

Yet why do You countenance treacherous people,
Keep silent while he swallows the wicked,
Who are, nevertheless, more righteous than he? *[1:12B–13]*

[2] Ancient rabbinic sources record that this verse was deliberately altered to read "*we* are not subject to death," because it was believed impious even to suggest Yahve's mortality by mentioning His immortality. The change is one of "the emendations of the scribes" (*tiqqune soferim*).

That is, those whom the Chaldeans destroy are less wicked than their destroyers. Nevertheless Yahve tolerates the Chaldean conquest.

> You make man [weak] like fish of the sea, like crawling
>   things without a ruler [to protect them].

> All of them he (Chaldea) pulls up with a hook, or drags
>   together in net,
> Or collects them in his sieve—and consequently is happy
>   and rejoicing.
> He offers sacrifices to his sieve, and incense to his nets,[3]
> For through them what he has to eat is cream,
> And his food is rich. [1:14–16]

The prophet inquires:

> Is it right that he should constantly wield the sword
> Pitilessly to slay peoples? [1:17].

Now the prophet turns to speak a personal thought:

> I take my stand on my place of watch and station myself on
>   my tower,
> And look forward to see what He will say to me,
> And what He will reply to my complaint.
> Yahve answered me,
> "Record a vision, make it plain on tablet,
> So that even one who runs by will be able to read it.
> The vision will still abide to the appointed time,
> It will speak out at the end, and not lie,
> If it tarries, wait for it; for it will surely come and not too
>   late:
> 'Behold, the wicked; for him I have no uprightness.[4]
> But let the righteous person abide in his faith.'" [2:1–4]

The prophet now speaks out:

> Woe unto him who piles up what is not his,
> And loads himself up with debts [owed to him]. . . .
> Woe unto him who acquires gain evilly for his house,
> So as to set his nest high, so as to be safe from evil. . . .
> Woe unto him who builds a city with blood,

---

[3] That is, he treats his instruments as deities. This is a figure of speech, with sieves and nets representing sword or spear.
[4] The Hebrew of the first half of 2:4 is not intelligible; I have given here only a guess.

And founds a town on iniquity. . . .
Woe unto him who makes his neighbor drink,
Blending anger and liquor. . . .
Woe unto him who says to a tree, "Wake up!"
To a silent stone, "Rouse up!"

Yahve is in His holy Temple, let all the earth be silent before
   Him. [2:6, 9, 12, 15, 19–20]

Habakkuk starts with the premise that Yahve controls the
events of history. What is happening now is disconcerting, for why
should He allow the more wicked to conquer and destroy the less
wicked?

The prophet is telling us that in the face of evil, which logically
God should not cause or tolerate, the pious man, though incapable
of understanding, must abide in his righteousness. He must be
confident that although he does not understand now, the evils will
ultimately disappear and will prove to have had some purpose.

Although this conclusion was probably ancient even in the days
of Habakkuk, its inevitable logic is of essential importance. The
person with strong faith in an omnipotent God has no attractive
alternative when evil strikes, except to abide in that faith. He might
rebel against God—but what good is rebellion against omnipotence?
He might simply submit, but submission might imply that man
should passively and discontentedly put up with God's capricious
conduct, and the ascription of capricious conduct to God amounts
both to denying His goodness and to repudiating His justice.
Theodicy ("God's justice") presents this religious problem: on the
one hand, a man must maintain the conviction that God is just,
while at the same time the events of his experience—even the
unlikely ones—must seem to conform to that justice. If one asserts
that God is not just, one no longer has a problem in theodicy.

Habakkuk cannot see why things are as they are, so he makes
bold to question God about them. Instead of an answer to his question, he receives the instruction, which he is to disseminate, that in
due time all will be rectified. In the meantime, in the face of the
incomprehensible and in the face of delay in his vindication, the
righteous person must abide in an undiminished faith. If man remains strong by virtue of such faith, he can be certain that evil will
be ended and the evildoers punished. Therefore, Habakkuk can proceed to express his feelings against the Chaldeans. The counsel to
abide in faith represents man's only affirmative possibility when
the problem of theodicy arises. With faith, there is a prospect that

events and experiences will become meaningful; without some faith all experience and all life are meaningless.

Although Habakkuk's statement is not new, his admirable profundity lies in his daring. He does not shrink from throwing his complaint, as it were, directly in the teeth of the Deity. He does not talk behind God's back, but directly to Him; he argues with Yahve as though they were peers. Moreover, his statement that the righteous must abide in faith is not the premise with which he begins but the conclusion to which he is ultimately led. His words are not an expression of nimble piety; they arise from one who has experienced evil, who has questioned Yahve's way, and who finds himself drawn to an irresistible affirmation. Habakkuk is a man who through stresses, disappointments, and griefs sees what for him is the only answer.

The psalm in the third chapter, like many passages in the Book of Psalms, reflects some primitive folklore in its description of the upheavals in nature at Yahve's theophany. Similar materials are found in Judges 5, Psalm 18, and Deuteronomy 33. Scholars have noticed that there are in these materials affinities to the Babylonian myth of the god Marduk's conquest of the ocean (Tiamat; in Hebrew *tehom*, the deep).

It is a worthy bit of poetry, a product of either an age or a segment of the population which, unlike the prophets, conceived of deity in the light of natural phenomena, such as earthquakes and lightning and thunder, rather than in the light of history.

JEREMIAH

JEREMIAH is the only prophet about whom we get almost enough information from Scripture for a well-rounded study of the man. Since he had a striking and profound personality the abundance of material about him gives us a unique opportunity for studying a prophet.

It is too much to ask of a Scriptural book that it be totally free of problems, but the few that are to be found in the Book of Jeremiah are relatively minor. For example, the Greek translation of the book is about an eighth shorter than the Hebrew, and certain materials are differently placed. Is this the result of accidental omissions from the Greek, or additions made to the Hebrew? Again, some passages in the text are not by Jeremiah; a comparison of Jeremiah 49:7–22 and Obadiah 1–9 discloses that they are two versions of a single writing, neither of them by Jeremiah. Fortunately, such problems are not of great consequence in understanding Jeremiah.

From the standpoint of Jeremiah's development, scholars are prone to emphasize that the span of time in which Jeremiah lived was long and significant, and that his writings reflect his spiritual growth. His earliest addresses are regarded as having been delivered during the reign of Josiah (640–608), and during the years before Josiah's great Reformation of 621. In Jeremiah's lifetime the Babylonians destroyed Nineveh (612); Josiah died in battle against the Egyptians in 608; and, in 605, the Babylonians defeated the Egyptians. In 605, or possibly in 601, Judah became a vassal of Babylonia; in 598 a refusal to pay tribute aroused Babylonia's anger; and a year later, in 597, the Babylonians under Nebuchadnezzar obtained the surrender of besieged Jerusalem. Thereupon the great exile began.

The period of the exile is reckoned by some as beginning in 586, rather than 597. Either date can be defended, so long as it is clear what happened. In 597, as a result of the initial Babylonian conquest, King Jehoiachin and the upper classes were transported to Babylonia. The Temple remained standing in Jerusalem, and a new king, Zedekiah, was crowned. When disorders in Jerusalem flared into open rebellion about 588, the Babylonians made a new siege of Jerusalem (lasting a year and a half). This time the Temple and the palace were conquered and burned to the ground, and Zedekiah and others were taken to Babylonia. No new king was designated for Judah; rather, Judah became a province of the Babylonians.

The character of the religion of Israel changed decisively during and because of the Babylonian exile. Jeremiah, surviving briefly into those momentous days, nevertheless provided an important sense of direction for the new times. As a consequence the closing years of Jeremiah's life mark the transition from the Hebrew religion to its offspring, Judaism.

The Book of Jeremiah supplies some striking information about the manner in which prophetic books came to be written down. We are told in Chapter 36 that the divine word came to Jeremiah to record on a scroll all that Yahve had spoken to him. Thereupon Jeremiah summoned a certain Baruch ben Neriah, whom we may describe as a stenographer or secretary, and Jeremiah dictated while Baruch wrote. Then Jeremiah sent Baruch to the Temple to read the scroll. A fast having been coincidentally proclaimed for that day, the Temple was crowded, with many of the nobility in attendance. A certain Micaiah ben Gemariah ben Shafan reported to the nobles at the palace what Baruch had read; they called Baruch to the Palace to read the scroll to them, and he did so. They said to Baruch, "Tell us, how was it that you wrote these things from his [Jeremiah's] mouth?" Baruch replied, "From his own mouth Jeremiah spoke these things to me, and I recorded them in ink on the book" (36:*17–18*).

The nobles advised Baruch and Jeremiah to hide, and pro-

ceeded to inform the king about the scroll. The monarch had the
scroll brought to him to be read. After the reader had completed
three or four columns he (either the king or the reader) cut it up
with a pen knife and threw it into the fire, so that the entire book
was consumed. No attention was paid to Jeremiah's words. Instead,
the order went out for both Baruch and Jeremiah to be seized, but
they were able to hide. "Then Jeremiah took another scroll, and
gave it to Baruch ben Neriah; the latter recorded from Jeremiah's
mouth all the words of the book which Jehoiakim,[1] King of Judah,
had burned; moreover, many similar things were added" (36:32).

Inasmuch as that chapter is in the third person, it is not by
Jeremiah but about Jeremiah, and we cannot be sure just who wrote
it. Many scholars have concluded that Baruch was the author, and
this may be the case, though one wonders why Baruch would be
writing about himself in the third person. The author of the chapter
is not interested in telling us how prophetic books came to be
written, but in the vicissitudes through which Jeremiah passed. The
information about the writing of this book, therefore, is adventitious.
It seems clear, at least, though it may be foreign to the presuppositions of many readers of the Bible that the books of the prophets
did not just happen. A prophet lived as other people lived and wrote
as other writers wrote. The narrative is completely simple and
natural in its description of how the Book of Jeremiah, or a large
portion of it, came into existence. A prophet wrote or dictated;
this writing was copied and put into circulation. The wish to
suppress the book is quite understandable, for such an impulse
exists in society in almost every age.

While Jeremiah did his most significant teaching at the end of his
career, the early prophecies are important for the manner in which
he expresses himself. In the usual descriptions of the prophet Jeremiah it is assumed that his early activity began in the days of the
king Josiah, who came to the throne in the year 626. There is nothing
within the poems to support this assumption, which arises from the
circumstance that some enemies, who are mentioned in 4:5–31,
are described as men "from the North." As in the case of the prophet
Zephaniah,[2] biblical scholars have assumed from a passage in
Herodotus that an obscure group called the Scythians were active
and on the verge of invading at this time. If we were to conclude that

[1] The two kings, Jehoiakim and Jehoiachin must not be confused. They were
father and son, Jehoiachin succeeding to the throne in 597.
[2] See pages 105–106.

Jer. 4 alludes to the Scythians then we should say that the chapter comes from the year 626. In recent times, scholars have challenged the assumption that the chapter deals with the Scythians, and indeed, the account in Herodotus has come to be regarded as totally unreliable. If the folk from the North were not the Scythians of 626, who were they and when did they flourish? A likely alternative has been suggested: namely, that these were the Chaldeans, who were active around the year 605.

The choice lies before us, then, of dating Jeremiah's early prophecies from the year 626 or the year 605. If we accept the date 605, we are reducing his period of prophetic activity by twenty-two years, although his career would still be a long one. For sentimental reasons some scholars wish to portray Jeremiah as an old man in the year 597; therefore there is a great inclination to persist in the theory that his activity began in Josiah's time. The meaning of Jeremiah is much the same, whether we use the date of 626 for his early career or 605.

The later date appears more probable to me for the following important reason. In the year 621, during Josiah's reign, there took place the great Reformation already mentioned. This Reformation is described in II Kings, 22–3. Bible scholars have been puzzled that these chapters of Kings, which deal with an event of paramount importance to the religion of Israel, not only do not mention Jeremiah but name instead a woman called Hulda as a prophet whom King Josiah consulted. Since we do not possess a full history of the days of Josiah, and are therefore free to speculate, scholars have wondered how there could have been a great Reformation with which the great Jeremiah apparently had no contact. Some have held that Jeremiah did know about the Reformation and was in favor of it; others have maintained that he knew about it, but was uninterested or even opposed to it. To my mind, the most likely explanation is that his prophetic ministry had not begun as early as 621.

The Reformation of Josiah was far-reaching, especially with respect to the Temple in Jerusalem. Before Josiah's drastic action, temples had existed throughout the land, presided over by priests of varying backgrounds and qualifications. Josiah destroyed all the temples in the land but the one in Jerusalem, and in effect he disqualified all the priests but the priests in Jerusalem. Some of the priests of the outlying temples were slain; some of them were moved to Jerusalem to become minor auxiliary priests to the Jerusalem group. Along with this highly significant change was the thorough endeavor to extirpate the Baal worship. In the years immediately following 621, Baalism was probably on the way to complete destruction; however, Jeremiah leads us to believe that by 605 Baal worship, if not as common as before 621, again existed side by side with Yahve worship. Certainly in Jeremiah's early days there was enough Baal worship to invite his condemnation.

Josiah was killed in battle by the Egyptians around 608. Nineveh, the capital of Assyria, had fallen to the Medes and the Babylonians in 612. Egypt, now able to hold sway over Palestine, set on the throne in Jerusalem Josiah's son Jehoahaz, who reigned only three months, and thereafter another son of Josiah, Jehoiakim, who reigned from 607 to 597. In 604 the Egyptians were routed by the Babylonians at the city of Carchemish. Thereafter Babylonia [3] became the virtual master of the West. Against this background of Babylonian activity in the East and Jehoiakim on the tottering throne in the West, Jeremiah spoke out.

As we turn to the words of Jeremiah, we shall be struck by the importance of his own personal feeling in his prophetic career. In a sense, the words of Amos and Isaiah do not seem so directly to reflect the men who spoke them. In the case of Jeremiah, however, the man is so much in evidence that he comes to be as important as his message. Here is how the substance of the book begins:

The word of the Lord came to me saying,
"Before I formed you in the womb I predestined you,
And before you came forth from the womb I sanctified you;
I made you a prophet to deal with the concern of nations."

I said "My Lord Yahve, I have no knowledge of how to speak
    for I am but a boy."
Yahve said to me: "Do not say, 'I am a boy,'
For wherever I send you, you will go, and whatever I command you, you will speak
Do not fear them,[4] for I am with you to deliver you," says
    Yahve.

Then Yahve stretched forth His hand and He put it on my
    mouth
And Yahve said to me: "See, I have put My words in your
    mouth.
See, I have set you over nations and over kingdoms

---

[3] In the time of Jeremiah Babylonia and Chaldea are interchangeable names for the same eastern kingdom which was the successor to Assyria.
[4] The text does not identify the "them."

To uproot and to pull down and to destroy,
And to throw down and to build and to plant." [1:4–10]

This divine call is something Jeremiah has heard rather than seen, but two visions immediately follow. The description of the first involves a play on words quite impossible to reproduce in English.

The word of Yahve came to me saying: "What do you see,
Jeremiah?"
I said: "I see the rod of an almond tree."
Yahve said to me: "You have seen well. For I am carefully
watching over
My word to perform it." [1:11–12]

In the Hebrew, "to watch carefully over" has the same three letters as the word "almond." The vision seems to signify the Deity's assurance that He will support Jeremiah's message to the people.

The second vision concerns a pot of boiling water. Although the ancient pot did not have a spout we can think of it as a modern teakettle:

The word of Yahve came unto me a second time saying, "What do you see?" I said, "A boiling teakettle do I see, and its spout is toward the north."

Yahve said to me: "From the north will the evil open up upon the dwellers of the land. For I am sending all the families of the kingdoms of the north, and they will come and each [king] will put his throne at the opening of the gates of Jerusalem and round about all its walls and all the hills of Judah. I will speak My condemnation of them [the Judeans] for all their evil, in that they have forsaken Me, and they have offered sacrifice to false gods, and they have bowed down to that which their own hands have made. But you [Jeremiah], gird up your loins, and rise and speak to them all that which I command you. Do not fear them lest I should take occasion to frighten you [for fearing them].

"See, I am making you into an impregnable city with brazen walls [5] against the whole land, against the kings of Judah and the princes and the priests and the people of the land. They will struggle against you but will not prevail over you, for I am with you to deliver you," says Yahve. [1:13–19]

This is Jeremiah's "call." As in the case of Isaiah (see page 85), the description of call is composed in the light of the prophet's

[5] This is a slight emendation. The usual translation is "a column of brass."

subsequent experiences. The call forms a sort of prologue to the
entire book. On the one hand, it sets forth those elements in Jeremiah's personality that made him simultaneously aware of his
mission and of his own weakness. On the other hand, it foreshadows
the vicissitudes he will have to endure, for if ever a man was exposed
to the terror of having his life threatened by those whom he was
earnestly seeking to help, that man was Jeremiah.

In Chapter 2, Jeremiah points to Israel's loyalty to Yahve in
the ancient times, thus underscoring the defection of recent times.
Jeremiah's message here resembles that of the prophet Hosea, rather
than the stern social message of Amos. The softness and sensitivity
of Jeremiah are nowhere more clearly discernible than in this second
chapter.

> *The word of Yahve came to me:*
> *"Go and proclaim in the ears of Jerusalem as follows:*
> *Thus says Yahve:*
> *'I remember on your behalf the reliability of your youth,*
> *The love of your bridal days, when you went after Me in the*
> *   wilderness*
> *In an unsown land.'*
> *Holy then was Israel to Yahve,*
> *The first fruits of his increase;* [6]
> *Anyone who eats him will undergo guilt;*
> *Evil will come upon him," says Yahve.* [2:1–3]

Despite this special relationship to Yahve Israel did not remain firm:

> *Yahve says this, "What defect did your fathers find in Me*
> *That they have moved far from Me?*
> *They went after vanity and they became vain.* [7]
> *They did not ask, 'Where was Yahve Who brought us out of*
> *   Egypt,*
> *Who led us in the wilderness,*
> *In the land of the desert and the pits,*
> *In the land of dryness and darkness,*
> *In the land which no man has passed through*
> *And where no man dwelt?'*
>
> *"Indeed, I brought you to a fertile land,*
> *To eat its fruit and its goodly yield.*

[6] See Exod. 23:19 and Lev. 22:10 and 16. Israel is compared to first fruits, set
aside as sacred.
[7] There is a pun which the English cannot quite reproduce. The word which is
translated "became vain" should really be translated "they became nothing."

And you came and you contaminated My land
And you made My possession into an abomination.
The priests did not say, 'Where is Yahve?'
And the guardians of revelation did not know Me.
The leaders transgressed against Me;
The prophets prophesied in the name of the Baal,
And they walked after things which did not profit them.

"Accordingly, I must still carry on a litigation against you,"
  says Yahve,
"And with the sons of your sons will I dispute.
For pass over to the island of Cyprus and look,
And send to Kedar [8] and consider diligently,
And see if there ever was anything like this.
Did any other people exchange their god—
And those gods are not gods!
But My people exchanged its glory
For something which yields nothing.

"O heavens, be astonished at this,
Shudder and tremble exceedingly!" [9]
Says Yahve,
"For two evils has My people done:
Me have they forsaken,
A fountain of living water—
To hew out for themselves broken cisterns
Which cannot contain water." [2:5-13]

The chapter continues to set forth Israel's infidelity to Yahve and the attendant punishments that have come upon her. It is too much to say that the chapter contains allusions to Egypt's conquest of Palestine in 608; yet this seems to be the intent of verses 2:16–18, which accuse the children of Noph, which is Memphis, and the children of Tahpanes, a fortified city on the northeast frontier of Egypt, of having "broken the crown of Judah's head." With irony Jeremiah makes the following prediction:

In the time of trouble you will say to Yahve: "Arise and
  save us!"
But where are your gods that have made you?
Let them arise and save you, if they can, in the time of
  trouble.

[8] This was a Bedouin tribe residing in the Arabian desert.
[9] This translation follows the reading in the Syriac.

For your gods are as numerous as your cities, O Judah.
  [2:27B–28]

In the light of such infidelity, can Israel be restored to good favor? In the early days, Jeremiah sees no possibility of it. He expresses this through the figure of a divorced wife:

"If a man sends away his wife, and she goes away from him and becomes someone else's wife, can he return to her again? [1] Will not that land be greatly polluted? You have played the harlot with many friends, and shall you return to Me?" says Yahve.

"Lift up your eyes to the high places,
And see if there is anywhere you have not committed
  adultery.
You have sat on the roads [waiting for lovers]
Like an Arab in the wilderness [waiting for passers-by];
In your whoring and your wickedness you have polluted the
  whole land." [3:1–2]

Later in the chapter the mood of the prophet changes:

A voice is heard on the high places,
The weeping supplications of the children of Israel.
They have distorted their way,
They have forgotten Yahve, their God—.
Return, O wayward sons, and I will heal your waywardness.
  [3:21–2A]

They reply:

"Here we are come before You,
For You are Yahve our God.
In truth only from Yahve our God is there salvation for
  Israel.
It is false that it can come from the high places [2] or from the
  abundance of hills. [3]

"The shame [of Baalism] has consumed, since our youth, the gains of our fathers, [namely,] their sheep and their cattle, their sons and their daughters. We lie down in our shame, and

---

[1] According to Deuteronomy 24:1–4 a man could not remarry his divorced wife.
[2] Baal orgies took place on hills; hence hills and high places signify Baalism.
[3] The parts of this verse, 3:23, are rearranged.

our disgrace covers us, for against Yahve our God have we sinned, we and our fathers, from our youth unto this day; we have not hearkened to the voice of Yahve our God."

"If you will return, Israel," says Yahve, "If you return to Me, and if you remove your abominations from Me and not wander away, and if you will swear: 'As Yahve lives,' in truth and in justice and in righteousness, then nations will bless themselves by you [4] and in you [4] will they glory." [3:22B–4:2]

In Chapter 7 and in part of Chapter 8 a terse account in the third person reflects Jeremiah's negative attitude toward the Temple of Jerusalem. As the words will reveal, Jeremiah had no great confidence in the institution. We do not know the date of the incident described, but if it comes from the period after the great Reformation of 621, the passage amounts to a denunciation of the Reformation. Jeremiah says that even though the Reformation exalted the Temple and resulted in its refurbishing, nothing was really accomplished:

The word that came to Jeremiah from Yahve saying: "Stand in the gate of the Temple and proclaim there this thing, saying: Hear the word of Yahve, all of Judah, who come in these gates to bow down to Yahve. This is what Yahve of Hosts, the God of Israel says: Improve your ways in your deeds and I will dwell [5] with you in this place. Do not rely upon the lying words that say, The Temple of Yahve, the Temple of Yahve, the Temple of Yahve, is this place! [6] But if, instead, you will truly improve your ways and your deeds and if you will truly execute justice between a man and his neighbor, and if you will not oppress the stranger, the orphan and the widow, and not . . . go after false gods to your harm, then I will dwell with you in this place in the land which I have given to your fathers from eternity to eternity.

"Behold, you rely on words of falsehood which cannot profit. Is it to be that you will steal and murder, commit adultery, swear falsely, offer sacrifices to the Baal and go after false gods whom you have not known, and then come and stand before this house upon which My name is called and then say: It is to do these abominations that we have been spared! Is this Temple, upon which My name is called, to be a den of thieves in your eyes? Behold I have seen [what goes on]," says Yahve.

[4] The point is that nations will say: "We wish we were blessed as Israel." The text is emended from by *him* and in *him*.
[5] A slight emendation has been made.
[6] What Jeremiah is saying is that those who believe in simply calling upon or relying upon the Temple are misguided, and certain to be astonished.

"But now go to the temple in Shiloh [7] where I had let My name rest in the beginning, and see what I did to it on account of the evil of My people Israel. Now, inasmuch as you have [too] done all these things, though I spoke to you and you did not hear, and I called to you and you did not respond, then I shall do to this Temple, upon which My name is called and upon which you rely, and to the place which I have given to you and to your fathers, what I did to Shiloh. And I will cast you out of My sight, just as I cast off all your brothers,[8] all the seed of Ephraim." [7:1–15]

A similar passage in Chapter 26 also declares that the fate of Shiloh is to overtake the Temple in Jerusalem. There we are given what Chapter 7 lacks, namely the reaction of those who heard Jeremiah. We must therefore interrupt the account in Chapter 7 to see what this reaction was.

The priests and the prophets and all the people heard Jeremiah say these things in the Temple. When Jeremiah finished all that Yahve had commanded him to speak to the people, the priests and the prophets and the people seized him, saying: "You shall die! Why have you prophesied in the name of Yahve saying, this Temple will be like Shiloh and this city will be destroyed beyond possessing a single inhabitant?" And all the people gathered around Jeremiah in the Temple. The princes of Judah heard this matter, and they went up from the palace to the Temple of Yahve, and they sat down in the opening of the new gate of the Temple. The priests and the prophets said to the princes and the people, "This man is worthy of death, for he prophesied concerning this city just as you have heard with your own ears."

Jeremiah said to the princes and to all the people: "Yahve sent me to prophesy, about the Temple and about this city, all the words which you have heard. But you should mend your ways and your deeds and obey the voice of Yahve your God; then Yahve will change His mind about the evil which He has devised against you. As for me, I am in your hands; do to me what is good and proper in your eyes. But you must be sure to know that if you kill me, you are putting the guilt for the blood of an innocent person upon yourselves, upon the city, and upon all its in-

---

[7] Shiloh had been destroyed by the Philistines; see I Sam. 4:10–11.
[8] This is a reference to the destruction of North Israel which was exiled in 722/721.

habitants. For in truth, Yahve sent me against you to speak in your ears all these words."

The princes and all the people said to the priests and the prophets: "This man is not worthy of death, for he spoke to us in the name of Yahve our God." Then some of the elders of the land arose and they said to the assembly of the people, "Micah the Morashite prophesied in the days of Hezekiah, the King of Judah, and he said to all the people of Judah: Thus says Yahve of Hosts: '[Mount] Zion will be plowed like a field, and Jerusalem will be no more than heaps, and the mount of the Temple will be turned over to the beasts [9] of the forest.' Did Hezekiah, the King of Judah, and all Judah put him to death? Did not Hezekiah hear Yahve, and entreat Yahve's favor so that Yahve repented of the evil which He had spoken against him? We are doing a tremendous evil against ourselves."

Moreover, there was another man who prophesied in the name of Yahve, namely Uriah the son of Shemaiah, of Kirjath-jearim. He prophesied against this city and against this land words similar to the words of Jeremiah. When King Jehoiakim and all the princes heard his words the King thought to slay him. Uriah learned about this and fearfully fled to Egypt. Thereupon King Jehoiakim sent men to Egypt, namely Elnathan ben Achbor and men with him. They brought Uriah from Egypt and led him to King Jehoiakim, and he slew him with the sword, and threw his corpse into the graves of the common people.

However, the protection of Ahikam ben Shafan came to Jeremiah, so that he was not given into the hands of the people to be put to death. [26:7–24]

We can see from this passage that great personal danger could attend the prophet for speaking words that went against the grain cr attacked the illusions of those who heard him. The account in Chapter 7 continues with Yahve's words to Jeremiah:

"But you should not pray to Me on behalf of this people and you are not to raise song and prayer on their behalf, nor entreat Me, for I will not hearken to you. Do you not see what they are doing in the cities of Judah and in the streets of Jerusalem? The sons are gathering wood and the fathers are kindling the fire and the women are kneading the dough to make cakes [1] to the Queen of Heaven and they pour out drink offerings to false

[9] This is a slight emendation.
[1] These cakes were probably shaped like a star and used to worship the Babylonian goddess Ishtar, the Queen of Heaven. See also Jer. 44:17–25.

gods to provoke Me. Is it I whom they provoke to anger? Do
they not provoke themselves, for the confusion of their own
faces? Therefore," says Lord Yahve, "My wrath and anger are
poured out on this place on man and beast, on the tree in the
field and on the fruit on the ground. They will burn and they
will not be quenched." [7:16–20]

The next section is, in all probability, an address from a different
time, possibly also given at the Temple. Jeremiah first represents
Yahve as speaking in a sarcastic vein:

"Add burned offerings to your sacrifices and eat meat! I did
not speak to your fathers and I did not command them on the
day that I brought them out of the land of Egypt concerning
burnt offerings or sacrifices. Rather the word I commanded
them was this, 'Hearken to My voice and I shall be your God and
you shall be My people, and you shall walk in the way which I
shall command you in order that things shall be well with you.'
But they did not hear, and they did not incline their ear, and they
went in the counsels, in the stubbornness of their evil heart, so
that they have gone backwards and not forward. Since the day
when their fathers came out of the land of Egypt until this day,
I have sent my servants, the prophets, ceaselessly. But they did
not hearken to Me and did not incline their ear and they increased their stubbornness. They have been more evil than
their fathers.

"Now you shall speak all these things to them, but they will
not listen to you. You shall proclaim to them, and they will not
answer you, and you shall say to them: 'This is the people
which did not hearken to the voice of Yahve their God, and did
not accept chastisement. Truth has perished and is cut off from
their lips.'" [7:21–8]

There ensue further denunciations of the worship Jeremiah
regarded as unsuitable to Yahve—worship we would describe as
pagan. The Deity's attitude is summed up in a well-known verse:

"I shall cause to disappear from the cities of Judah and from
the streets of Jerusalem the sound of joy and the sound of
rejoicing; the sound of the bridegroom and the sound of the
bride. For the land shall become desolate." [7:34]

In our experience a man who makes public denunciations is
often characterized by a "holier than thou" attitude. Such a person
often appears to derive great satisfaction from his words of con-

demnation. How different is Jeremiah's response to the hostility of the people and to the manner in which he is ignored:

> *Sorrow* [2] *is upon me. My heart is sick within me.*
> *Hear the sound of the cry of the daughter of my people,* [3]
>   *throughout the land:*
> *Is Yahve not in Zion? Is her King not in the land?*

Yahve speaks:

> "Why have they provoked me with their images, with foreign statues?"

The people say:

> "The harvest is over and the summer is gone
> And as yet we have not been saved."

Now it is Jeremiah who speaks:

> *For the hurt of the daughter of my people I have been made*
>   *to be hurt.*
> *I am clothed in mourning; dismay has taken hold of me.*
> *Is there no balm* [4] *in Gilead, is there no physician there?*
> *Why is the health of the daughter of my people not recovered?*
>
> *Oh that my head were waters and my eyes a spring of tears,*
> *Then I would weep day and night for the destroyed of the*
>   *daughter of my people!*
> *Would that I had in the wilderness a lodging place for wayfarers!*
> *Then I would leave my people and go away from them.*

His next words are both his own and the Deity's:

> *For all of them are adulterers,*
> *They are an assembly of treacherous people.*
> *They bend their tongues like a bow for falsehood and not*
>   *for truth.*
> *They have grown mighty in the land, for they have gone out*
>   *from one evil to another,*
> *But Me they have not known, says Yahve.* [8:18–9:2 Heb.,
>   8:18–9:3 Eng.]

[2] The opening words in verse 8:18 really belong in verse 17. I omit these words in the translation.
[3] The people are personified as a young girl.
[4] The balm is a medication derived from the gum of the mastic tree.

Jeremiah felt the pain of being rejected and ignored. Having begun his career believing that Yahve had elected him to bring the divine word to the people, he turns in his distress to Yahve to complain about his fate.

> O Yahve, You have led me astray and I have succumbed.
> You are stronger than I and you have overcome me.
> All day I am a laughing stock,
> Everyone mocks at me.
> As often as I speak, I cry out
> And I shout: "Violence, Spoil!"
>
> For the word of Yahve has meant for me reproach and deri-
>   sion all the day.
> And if I say: I will not make mention of Him,
> Nor will I again speak in His name,
> Then there is in my heart, as it were, a burning fire
> Shut up in my bones.
> I become weary trying to restrain it,
> And I am not able to.
> I have heard the defaming by many.
> Terror is all about.[5]
>
> "Denounce him and we [too] will denounce him,"
> Say all my acquaintances who watch for my stumbling.
> "Perhaps he will be led astray and we will prevail against
>   him,
> And take our revenge upon him."
>
> Yahve is with me like a dreaded warrior;
> Therefore those who persecute me will stumble and not pre-
>   vail.
> They shall be greatly ashamed, for they shall not succeed;
> Their everlasting shame will never be forgotten . . .
> Cursed is the day on which I was born,
> The day on which my mother bore me—may it never be
>   blessed!
> Cursed is the man who brought the tidings to my father,
>   saying
> "A male child has been born to you"—making him glad.
> May that man be like the cities which Yahve has overturned
>   without regret,

[5] The same line is to be found in Psalm 31:14 Heb., 31:13 Eng.

Let him hear the cry of violence in the morning and the
alarm at the noontime,
For not having slain me from the womb,
That my mother was not my grave.[6]

Why is it that I came out of the womb
To see toil and pain,
And for my days to be consumed in shame? [20:7–18]

The above lines are pervaded by the strong personal emotion and sensitivity that distinguish Jeremiah's early message from those of his predecessors.

Scholars have arranged a number of passages into a collection that some have called a "biography."[7] These are indeed biographical notations, though they do not add up to a concerted biography. Most of them tell of a period previous to the fall of Jerusalem. We read, for example, that Jeremiah came before King Zedekiah when the Babylonians were besieging Jerusalem and informed him that the city would fall. The prophet informed Zedekiah that there would be no rescue by the Egyptians. In his anxiety over the siege Zedekiah made a promise to release all slaves, but afterward broke his promise. Thereupon Jeremiah issued a denunciation. When the Babylonians temporarily raised the siege to meet a threat from the Egyptians, Jeremiah predicted that the Babylonians would return. Accordingly, when the Babylonians went away Jeremiah was imprisoned. The King visited him in the dungeon, asking "Has there been any word from Yahve?" Jeremiah replied that the king would be delivered into the hands of the Babylonians. Zedekiah removed Jeremiah from the first prison, in the house of a certain scribe, and put him into the courtyard of the regular prison. Next Jeremiah was removed from the courtyard and put into a muddy cistern, from which an Ethiopian eunuch, Ebed-melech, rescued him and restored him to the courtyard. Again King Zedekiah came to visit Jeremiah. This time Jeremiah asked for assurance that he would not be put to death if he spoke. So assured, Jeremiah proposed that Zedekiah should submit to the Babylonians so as to avert the ruin and burning of the city. The King did not comply with Jeremiah's advice, so Jeremiah remained in prison until the conquest of Jerusalem. The Babylonian captain of the guard sent men to release Jeremiah, and he was committed to the care of one Gedaliah, who was later appointed the governor of

---

[6] The usual rendering, which makes no sense, is: "her womb was always great."
[7] The passages are the following: 34:1–7, 37:1–10, 34:8–22, 37:11–15, 37:16–21, 32:1–15, 38:1–13, 38:14–28, 39:1–46.

Jerusalem. When Gedaliah was murdered, many wished to flee to Egypt, and though Jeremiah warned against flight to that country, he and Baruch were taken there. Jeremiah predicted that the Babylonians would conquer that land too. He denounced his fellow Jews who were in Egypt and predicted that a small number of them would return to Palestine.

How much of this story is history and how much is legend it is difficult to say. There is, however, no reason to doubt that the account is basically correct.

So far we have seen the message of Jeremiah's early days and we have glimpsed something of his career. A series of passages,[8] which are called the "confessions" of Jeremiah, also merit attention. In these passages the prophet addresses the Deity in a form reminiscent of a legal trial in which the condemned pleads his case before a judge. Jeremiah first speaks of the treachery of his adversaries and then makes his own plea for mercy and assistance. We shall select for presentation here only some of the verses which typify what is expressed at greater length in the whole series of passages.

> I know, O Yahve, that man's path is not his own.
> It is not possible for man to direct his steps as he goes.
> O Yahve, correct me, but do so justly.
> Do not in Your anger reduce me to insignificance. [10:23–4]

> Righteous are You, O Yahve,
> Therefore I dispute with You.
> Yet it is matters of justice about which I shall speak to You.
> Why has the way of the wicked prospered,
> Why are they who deal treacherously happy?
> You have planted them and they have taken root,
> They grow and they even produce fruit.
> You are frequent in their mouths, but You are far from
>   their innards.
> But You, O Yahve have known me, You have seen me,
> You have examined my heart with respect to You.
> Pull them away like sheep for slaughter,
> And prepare them for the day when they will be slain
>   [12:1–3]

> Woe unto me, O my mother, that you bore me,
> A man of contention, a man of contention to the whole
>   earth.

[8] These passages are: 10:23–4; 11:18–12:6; 15:10–21; 17: 9–10, 14–18, 18–23; 20:7–12, 14–18.

I have neither lent money nor have men lent money to me—
Yet all of them curse me. [15:10]

Heal me, O Lord, and I shall be healed.
Rescue me and I shall be safe.
For You are the object of my praise.
Behold, they say to me: "Where is the word of Yahve?"
Let it come now!
Yet I have not hastened after You urging evil,*
Nor have I desired a day of punishment—
This You have known.
That which came out of my lips has been clearly said be-
fore You.
Do not be a source of terror unto me;
You are my hope on the day of evil.
May those who persecute me be put to shame.
Let them be dismayed and let me not be dismayed.
Bring upon them the day of evil,
And destroy them with a double destruction. [17:14–18]

Hearken unto me, O Yahve, and hear the substance of my
argument.
Is evil to be repaid for good?
They have dug a pit for me.
Remember how I stood before You to speak good for them,
Urging You to nullify Your anger against them.

Therefore deliver their sons to famine,
Turn them over to be destroyed by the sword.
Let their wives be bereft of children and become widows,
Let the men meet death in battle,
And the young men be smitten by the sword in warfare.
        [18:19–21]

The picture of a defendant pleading for mercy for himself and asking for punishment for his persecutors emerges clearly from these lines. We are so wont to idealize the prophets of Israel that it is hard for us to admit that Jeremiah is scarcely at his best when we find him in such a human situation. We become sentimentally prone to wish that he spoke only well of his foes.

It is essential to recall, however, that Jeremiah's life was always an unhappy one. His dedication to being a prophet brought him not rewards, but distress, pain, and anguish. If we do not grasp this we cannot grasp the true greatness of the man. Jeremiah has the conviction that God will vindicate him and will punish his foes. In a number of passages, especially in *17:10*, there is a clear statement:

> I, the Lord, search the hearts, I try the inner feelings of men to give to every man according to his ways and according to the effect of his deed.

Yet Jeremiah says that God wants him to remain steadfast despite his adversaries:

> "I will make you respecting these people a fortified wall of bronze . . . Though they contend against you they will not prevail, for I shall be with you to save and deliver you," says Yahve. [*1:18–19*]

It becomes clear, then, that the message of Jeremiah is conditioned to a great degree not only by external political events but also by Jeremiah's personal vicissitudes.

After predicting doom for at least two decades (longer, if his ministry began in the early days of Josiah), Jeremiah had earned the full right to say, "I told you so," when disaster came. Destruction did arrive and exile did become the lot of the people. It would have been quite understandable for Jeremiah, who had pleaded for his foes to be punished, to have said, "This is deserved; this is good." But Jeremiah said exactly the opposite. He uttered no syllable of self-satisfaction. Rather, out of the destruction he spoke unexpected words of hope.

The first glimpse of this hopeful message is found in one of the narratives of the biographical passages we omitted above. In *32:1–15* we read that Jeremiah had bought a field in his native Anathoth. The symbolic purpose of the purchase is expressed in the words: "Houses and fields and vineyards shall be possessed again in this land" (*32:15*). That is to say, even in the misery, almost at the moment of the destruction, Jeremiah did not lose confidence about the future. In Chapter 33 he predicts, especially in verses *6–11*, that the exiled of Judah will some day return and that Jerusalem will be rebuilt as it first stood. The exiles will be cleansed from their iniquity, for Yahve will pardon them. Moreover, as Chapter 33 continues, there is a prophecy of a restoration of a permanent Davidic dynasty, and of a permanent priesthood.

It is not possible to discover from any passage the source of this hope, or the reason for another of Jeremiah's beliefs. He draws a distinction between the Judeans who remain in the land after the destruction by the Babylonians and those who go eastward into captivity. He presents this distinction in a parable.

Yahve showed me two baskets of figs brought before the Temple of Yahve, after Nebuchadnezzar, the king of Babylon, had exiled Jeconiah, the son of Jehoiakim, the king of Judah and the princes of Judah and the carpenters and the smiths to Babylon. One basket had very good figs like the first figs to ripen; the other had bad figs which were too poor to eat. Yahve said to me: "What do you see, Jeremiah?" I said: "Figs. The good figs are very good and the poor ones are very poor so that they cannot be eaten, on account of their rottenness."

The word of Yahve came to me saying: "Thus says Yahve the God of Israel: I regard the exiles of Judah whom I sent from this place to the land of the Chaldeans like these good figs. I shall pay attention to them for good, and I shall bring them back to this land, and I shall build them up and not tear them down, and I shall plant them and not pluck them up. I shall give them a heart of understanding that I am Yahve and they shall be My people and I shall be a deity to them, for they shall return to Me with all their heart.

"Like the poor figs which cannot be eaten because they are so bad, so I shall make Zedekiah the King of Judah and his princes and all the remnant of Jerusalem who remain in this land, and those who dwell in the land of Egypt. I shall make them the laughingstock of all the kings of the earth, a shame and a parable, a taunt and a curse in all the places where I shall drive them. And I shall send against them sword and famine and pestilence till they will be consumed from off the land which I gave to them and to their fathers." [24:*1–10*]

Why were the Babylonian exiles regarded favorably, while those who remained in Palestine and those who went to Egypt were considered as sinful and capable of being written off? The only explanation that seems available is that Jeremiah saw the experience of the Babylonian exile as a means of regeneration. Jeremiah uses the Hebrew word *musar* six times, apparently meaning by it, "punishment for the purpose of *discipline*." A passage in which there occurs an inflected form of this word seems to contain Jeremiah's basic thought:

"It shall come to pass," says the Lord of Hosts,
"That I shall break the yoke from off your neck
And the chains that bind you will I break.

No longer will foreigners oppress you.
They (the Judeans) will then serve Yahve their God,
And David, their king, whom I shall raise for them.
But do not be afraid, O My son Jacob," says Yahve,
"And do not fear, O Israel,
For behold, I shall deliver you from the distance
And your children from the land of their captivity.
Jacob shall return and be at ease,
And he shall find peace and no one will make him afraid.
For I am with you to rescue you," says Yahve.
"For I shall make an end of all the nations among whom I
    have scattered you,
But of you I will not make an end.
I shall discipline *you to the point of justice*
For I will not hold you entirely guiltless." [30:8–11]

The words to note are "discipline you." Jeremiah seems to believe that the deserved punishment, in the form of exile, is to be followed by healing:

Behold, I shall change the fortune of the houses of Jacob
    and upon his dwellings I will have mercy,
And a city will be built anew on his own rubble heap and
    the place will be restored to what it once was.
And from them shall come thanksgiving and the voices of
    those who are making merry.
I shall multiply them, they shall not be few
I will glorify them and they will not be considered insignifi-
    cant.
Your children shall be what they once were,
And their community will be established before Me,
And I will punish all those who oppressed them. [30:18–
    20]

This confidence in the distant future is matched by sagacity in the immediate present. Jeremiah wrote a significant letter from Jerusalem to the elders and the priests and the people who were exiles in Babylonia:

Build houses and dwell in them and plant gardens and eat their fruit. Marry women and beget children and take daughters for wives for your sons, and give your daughters to husbands. Let them bear sons and daughters and multiply there (in Babylonia) and not diminish. Seek the peace of the city whither I have exiled you and pray on its behalf to Yahve, for in its tranquillity will you have peace. [29:5-7]

This counsel contrasts oddly with the despair expressed in the touching Psalm 137:1-6:

By the rivers of Babylon, there we sat and we wept
When we remembered Zion.
On willow trees there we hung our lyres.
For there our captors demanded songs of us,
Our tormentors words of happiness:
"Sing to us one of the songs of Zion."

How shall we sing the song of Yahve on foreign soil?

If I forget you, O Jerusalem,
May my right hand cease to function.[9]
Let my tongue cleave to my palate,
If I do not raise Jerusalem above my own joy.

What is meant by the line, "How can we sing the song of Yahve in a foreign land?" Does it merely mean that in exile the poet could not bring himself to undergo the pain of recollection by singing a melody of his native land? Or, is the significance even greater? Does the verse suggest that Yahve could not be worshipped outside the territory of Palestine? Clearly there is not sufficient information in the verse itself to justify this latter conclusion. We have some other suggestions, however, that point toward it. The first of these is the account about Naaman, the Syrian, who on becoming leprous is reported to have gone to Palestine where he received a cure by dipping himself in the Jordan River seven times. This narrative is told with unusual skill. Naaman is incensed when he is advised to dip in the Jordan.

"Are not Amanah and Pharpar, the rivers around the Damascus, better than all the waters in Israel? Can I not wash in them and become cured?" And he departed in wrath. Then the servants came to him and said: "If the prophet had told you to do some tremendous thing, would you not have done it? How much more than [should you do it] when he has said to you simply to wash and become purified." So Naaman went down and dipped in the Jordan seven times in accordance with the word of the prophet, and his flesh became restored like the flesh of a little

[9] The Hebrew contains a play on words. Literally the verse reads: "If I forget you, O Jerusalem, let my right hand come to be forgotten."

boy and he was purified. He returned to the man of God (Elisha) with his whole encampment, stood before him and said: "Behold, now I know that there is no God in the world except in Israel. Now take the present from your servant."

Elisha said, "As Yahve lives before whom I stood, I shall not take it." Naaman tried to persuade him but he persisted in refusing. Naaman said: "If [your answer] is no, nevertheless let [me] your servant be given a load of earth which a pair of asses can carry; for no longer will your servant offer burnt offerings and sacrifices to false gods but only to Yahve." [II Kings 5:12–17]

It is impossible to determine how much of the story of Naaman is history and how much is legend, but if there is a kernel of truth in the story, we can see that Naaman, in order to worship Yahve, felt the need to transport some Palestinian soil to the land of Syria. The connection of the Deity with the land was an important one in his eyes. In the time of Naaman and Elisha there had not yet arisen the need for clarification of the Deity's relation to the land and to the people.

Jeremiah clarifies, and indeed redefines this relationship. The instruction in the letter to the Babylonian exiles that they should worship Yahve in Babylonia assumes that the connection of the Deity is no longer with the land but is now with the people. From Jeremiah's time on, it became a standard assumption that emigration or expulsion from Palestine did not mean an end ,of the worship of Yahve, for Yahve could be worshipped wherever the Judeans might chance to go. Jeremiah insisted both that Yahve could be worshipped in Babylonia and that the Judeans would be restored to Palestine. Although the primacy of the land was shattered, the affection for it remained.

But, we may ask, how could the worship take place in Babylonia, remote from the Temple and without access to it? And what could be Yahve's justification for providing a continuation of this worship? Again Jeremiah supplies the answer:

"Behold, days are coming," says Yahve, "When I shall make a new covenant with the house of Israel, not like the covenant which I made with their fathers in the days when I took hold of their hand to take them out of Egypt—a covenant which they broke and over which I was master," says Yahve. "But rather this is the covenant which I shall make with the house of Israel after those days," says Yahve. "I shall put My revelation in their innards and I shall write it on their heart, and I shall be their God and they will be My people. No longer will one man teach his neighbor and his brother, saying, 'Come to know Yahve,' but instead all of them will know Me, from the small to the great," says Yahve, "For I shall forgive their sin and their transgression will I no longer remember." [31:31–4]

As Jeremiah speaks of the new covenant only in this passage, we cannot draw too many conclusions, and we certainly must not go beyond the evidence. Some scholars believe that the passage and the mention of the new covenant are not by Jeremiah but are later additions. I do not favor this view. Rather, I find it reasonable that Jeremiah, who abstained from saying "I told you so" and pointed instead a way to preservation, should have spoken about a new kind of covenant. We saw above that he had no affection for or confidence in the Temple. Therefore we can understand that he would now speak of a new worship based not on ceremonial, but on what we might describe as inner conviction.

By the very nature of things, the old covenant had to end in doom. When the people fell short of their obligation, the cumulative tabulation, generation after generation, of their misdeeds was bound to lead to the rupture of the covenant and to defenselessness and destruction. To say this in another way, the old covenant could not possibly continue forever. When the Babylonians had invaded and captured and destroyed the awaited doom had arrived.

Through the new covenant and through the contention that Yahve could be worshipped outside Palestine, Jeremiah provided a completely new connection between Yahve and His people. Jeremiah does not expand upon the laconic statement that Yahve would forgive sins, but later writers do. That the exile was for discipline presupposes that men would improve through experiences on strange soil. When men could worship Yahve outside Palestine, an event such as invasion by the Babylonians or exile was a significant incident, but no longer the climactic catastrophe of Yahve's just displeasure. In Jeremiah's significant contribution we can see a transition from the old Hebrew religion to Judaism. The old Hebrew religion was inexorably bound to end in doom; no other fate could result from cumulative guilt. Judaism, on the contrary, provides a system whereby the people and the individual can be restored to good standing in the eyes of the Deity.

The very important change from the Hebrew religion to Judaism gave rise to difficult theological problems, into which Jeremiah does not enter. We shall consider some of these later, especially when we turn to Ezekiel and the prophets of the period of the exile and the early period of the return. These theological problems can be summarized in a single question: if we grant that Yahve is providing a new covenant, *why* should He deign to do so? The subsidiary questions are, Does He do so because Israel has merited it? Is there some divine plan in which His forgiveness and restoration are necessary? Does He act this way out of pure grace?

Jeremiah expands on the theme, common also to Amos, Isaiah, and Habakkuk, that Yahve controls history. The historian would say, very simply, that the Babylonians conquered Judah and transported the leading citizens to Babylonia. The prophet, however, expresses this differently: because of Israel's sins, Yahve caused the Babylonians to invade in order to punish Judah. Through the Babylonians, Yahve sent Judah into exile. Jeremiah's contribution to the theme was the idea that Yahve did not bring about these events merely to punish, but to effect moral regeneration. The Babylonian incident was not doom, nor, as Jeremiah interpreted matters, would Yahve fix doom as the climax of history. Rather, Yahve was accompanying the means for moral regeneration with a new relationship, that is, with a new covenant. Jeremiah, then, continued the tradition of interpreting the events of history as the revelation of Yahve's will and plan. Prior to the Babylonian conquest, he said that Yahve's doom was inevitable. But once the events had happened, Jeremiah said that this was not doom, but Yahve's plan to refine and purify the Judeans.

One might have expected some vindictive word from Jeremiah as a result of the personal frustrations and the physical dangers and damages he suffered. It is the mark of the greatness of the man that, although he had suffered so much through observing the failings of his fellow men, yet he could point to the future with hope and with confidence.

THE PRE-EXILIC
PROPHETS

A Summary

IT WILL BE useful at this point to draw together certain threads of thinking common to pre-exilic prophets whom we have considered separately. Any effort to characterize pre-exilic prophecy involves overlooking the individuality of each prophet. Yet there are some advantages in such a summary, for pre-exilic prophecy, as we shall see, differed from exilic prophecy, and differed even more markedly from prophecy in the postexilic period.

In the first place, it is a central conviction of pre-exilic prophecy that the way of Yahve is a way that demands rigid standards of ethical conduct. Man is a social being and his relationships with fellow men are of intimate concern to Yahve. To do injustice to one's fellow man is to act in such a way that eventually the covenant with Yahve will be broken.

Secondly, Yahve has no interest in being approached by ritual or ceremony. Not one of the pre-exilic prophets says a single word in favor of ritual sacrifice. When they speak of ritual and ceremony, they speak in opposition to it. We saw this most clearly in the case of Amos; we also saw it in Jeremiah's conviction that the Temple in Jerusalem, for all its vaunted glory, was of no utility whatsoever.

Thirdly, it would follow that if Yahve had no interest in worship by animal sacrifice directed toward Him, He was even more averse to ritual acts directed to the Queen of Heaven or the Phoenician Baal. The worship of these gods was equivalent to apostasy from Yahve. These prophets felt that unethical conduct towards one's fellow man was a concomitant of or a consequence of the worship of pagan deities. Hence, they persistently denounced the worship of gods apart from Yahve. Such denunciation was appropriate at a time when pagan deities were available to be worshipped. Many centuries later, when there were no such pagan deities or pagan temples, the insistence on the solitary worship of Yahve became transformed into a kind of exclusiveness and a rigid demand on the part of Yahve. The later philosophy, though similar in tone to early thought, is quite different in application. Thus, in the Graeco-Roman world, let us say from 250 B.C. to A.D. 150, Jews, and, later, Christians too, evoked the displeasure of Greeks and Romans by what seemed intolerance and fanaticism. The affirmative aspect of the insistence of the exclusive worship of Yahve was the development of the purest possible theological ideas about the Deity. The negative aspect was the emergence in some quarters of a marked and unseemly disparagement of even that which was good in foreign cultures. Jews and Christians not only attacked the idolatry of the Greek or Roman world; they disparaged the whole Greek civilization, including Plato and Aristotle. As a result we have inherited, especially from the early representatives of Christianity, a lack of respect for the Greek and Roman classical tradition that is alien to the homage which we now pay to it.

Fourth, we have remarked that while Isaiah is mentioned in I and II Kings, Amos, Hosea, and Jeremiah are not. The necessary inference, at least for the moment, is that prophecy in the pre-exilic period was a sporadic affair. It was marked by outstanding individuals of striking significance whose messages were written down by their disciples.

In the pre-exilic prophetic literature, we do not get any reflection of a systematic cult or a systematic priesthood. We might conclude that prophet vied with priest, and vied successfully, for the priesthood had not become so stabilized, nor priestly practices so well organized, as to be something formidable to the prophets. Indeed, we see from the Reformation of Josiah, which disqualified the priests and the temples outside Jerusalem, destroyed the outlying temples, and brought certain of the priests of the outlying places to Jerusalem, that only toward the end of the pre-exilic period did priesthood begin to be organized and systematic. The pre-exilic prophet was therefore able to oppose the as yet unauthoritative priest. We shall see in subsequent literature what happened to prophecy when priesthood attained a position of stability and authority.

Fifth, pre-exilic prophecy was largely based on the assumption that Yahve controls the events of history. Events do not just happen; rather, they are an unfolding of the divine plan. Since Yahve controls history, history discloses Yahve, His will, and His purpose.

Sixth, it is useful perhaps to exaggerate a little in order to contrast pre-exilic prophecy with exilic prophecy. Pre-exilic prophecy was concerned with concrete, real life situations, not with theory. The pre-exilic prophet gave his judgment on those incidents that had occurred or that he believed were bound to occur. When he touched on religious convictions, he usually did so by implication or by reference to a tacit common assumption. This was not the case in the exilic period, when abstract theology became important in prophecy. It would, of course, not be correct to describe pre-exilic prophecy as quite concrete, nor exilic prophecy as completely theological and uninfluenced by incident and action. It is in this sense that I speak of exaggerating the nonabstract character of pre-exilic prophecy: when compared with exilic prophecy, it is relatively practical, a spontaneous reaction rather than a meditative consideration. The pre-exilic prophets did not ask the question "why"; they only made assertions that began with the word "because." In the period of the exile, stimulated by Jeremiah, Jews had to ask questions that began with the provocative "why."

EZEKIEL

WHEN WE TURN to the Book of Ezekiel we turn to prophecy in the exilic period. In the previous chapter we intimated that the experience of the exile was of far-reaching significance in the development of the religion of Israel; the exile marks the dividing line between the ancient Hebrew religion and that which we call Judaism. The new experience provided a conviction of the continuous relationship between the Deity and Israel. There still remained the need to inquire why such a relationship existed. More specifically, if we start with the assumption that God is just, then we are apt to conclude that justice demands both the reward of the righteous and the punishment of the wicked. If Israel was wicked enough to have merited the Babylonian invasion of Judea and the destruction of the Temple, then why would the Deity continue His relationship with her? We know that such a question was asked in the exilic period, for we find statements that appear to answer it. We shall see that the prophet Ezekiel gives us certain answers.

It must be confessed that the Book of Ezekiel is very difficult. Most of us know about it primarily from an American spiritual, "Ezekiel Saw de Wheels," or from the celebrated vision of the valley of dry bones in the 37th chapter. It is such a difficult book that I can think of nothing less rewarding for the untrained person than to try to read it in the King James Version without explanatory help. The book consists of forty-eight chapters. Chapters 40–8, at the end of the book, are a description of a vision of what the restored Temple in Jerusalem was to look like. We can set aside this section for later consideration, as well as Chapters 25–32, which consist of denunciations of foreign nations. The remainder, Chapters 1–24, presents a series of visions and predictions, which announce that the ruin of Jerusalem is going to take place, as it did in 586. Chapters 33–9 deal with the future restoration of Israel. One can say, then, that the total book consists of the prophetic call and commission, predictions of the destruction, denunciations of foreign nations, visions of restoration, and, finally, a plan for religious restoration.

But if the book can be so conveniently catalogued, what is the nature of the difficulties? First, the text is not well preserved. Many verses are unintelligible simply because we cannot discern the author's intent. In other verses, there are repetitions of words and phrases, so that the intent is very blurred, unless one is prepared to strike out the seemingly unnecessary particles.[1] We need to correct this or that verse because, after the prophet had dictated or written his message, the manuscript suffered in the process of being copied. Some words were omitted, some were misspelled, and some were added by copyists. The ancient Greek and Syriac often assist us in recovering a more intelligible text.

Another problem is that, unlike ordinary prose, which is easier to understand than poetry, Ezekiel's prose is more difficult than the poetry of the earlier prophets; we miss in it the simple parallelism which, in the poetic prophecies, gives clarity to the writer's intention, even in obscure verses. If Ezekiel was a poet at all, he was one in a minor way only. There is a certain grandeur in some of the visions, but it is grandeur of content and not of style or expression.

The modern age is so unattuned to the style of writing found in this book that the interpretive literature of the nineteenth century considered Ezekiel to be an epileptic. I regard this view as nonsense. In Ezekiel we see the flowering of what in earlier prophets was only a tendency—a tendency seen in Isaiah's use of parable and symbolic incident, and in the visions of Amos. In Ezekiel, symbolic expression is carried so far that even if we restore an intelligible text we are in danger of distorting or misinterpreting the import of the details of the symbolism.[2]

[1] See, as examples, 1:4, 11, and 24.
[2] The chief danger is that of isolating each detail and assuming that it connotes something specific. This is not the case; it is the total effect of the symbolism that

The book begins with a statement of the divine call to the prophet.[3] It is not expressed with the simplicity of Amos, who said: "Yahve took me from the sheep and said to me, 'Go, prophesy'" (Amos 7:15); rather, it plunges us immediately into symbolism. Ezekiel was by the River Chebar in Babylonia, among exiles from Judah. He saw a storm wind coming out of the north, with fire flashing about it, and with some shining substance emanating from the fire. Four creatures were to be seen, each with four faces; one face was that of a lion, one that of an ox, one that of an eagle, and the fourth that of a man. The two pairs of wings of each creature were separated from each other, one pair being on the upper part and the other on the body below. When the creatures moved, they went in the chosen direction without veering. In the midst of the four creatures was a bright fire from which lightning was coming out. Near each creature there was a wheel, and a wheel (possibly a hub) within each wheel. When a creature moved, the wheel moved; when a creature was lifted off the ground, the wheel was lifted too. The prophet was seeing a chariot throne.[4]

Above the creatures was a firmament which looked like crystal, and above the firmament a throne. On the throne there was something with a human appearance, above whose loins was something like gleaming bronze, and below the loins a great brightness. This was a vision of the radiance of Yahve; at the sight, Ezekiel fell on his face and heard a voice speaking (Ch. 1). The chapter would be more forceful if it were brief and unadorned, but the function of the symbolism is to add color and mystery to the message. Moreover, the symbolism, far from being artificial, is, rather, a remarkably full assortment of ancient conceptions preserved by folklore. If we contrast Ezekiel's elaborateness with Amos' simplicity, it is the latter that should be judged unusual and surprising.

After the divine call in Chapter 1, the prophet describes, in 2–3, the divine commission to him; it consists of four parts. First, the children of Israel have been rebellious against Yahve. Ezekiel is to speak to them, whether they listen or not, so that at least they will know that a prophet has been among them. Ezekiel is told that he is not to be afraid of them, however unfavorably they may receive his message. Next Yahve unrolls before Ezekiel a scroll inscribed on both sides with lamentations and moanings and woes. Ezekiel is

---

is important. A preoccupation with details distorts the meaning, for it distracts attention from the content to the style.

[3] It is not possible to advert here to all the textual difficulties in Chapter 1.

[4] In Daniel 8:9 there is a comparable description of the chariot throne. In the remote background, it was the chariot of the sun-god.

commanded to eat the scroll and then to go to speak to the house of Israel; when he eats it, he finds its taste as sweet as honey. He is told that if he were sent to people who did not understand his language, they would hearken to him, while Israel understands his language but will not hearken because she is wayward. Ezekiel is also told to speak to the "captivity" (2:1–3:11).

When the Deity finishes this part of the commission to Ezekiel, there is a loud roar as the radiance of Yahve rises from the place where it was and departs from him.[5] The creatures fly away and a wind takes Ezekiel, bitter and wrathful in mood, to the exile, to a place called Tel-abib, where Jews are dwelling. He sits there for seven days in utter silence (3:12–15). The third part of the commission is as follows:

> Son of man, I have made you a watchman for the house of Israel.
> When you hear a word from My mouth then you shall warn
> them as though from Me. When I say about a wicked person:
> "You shall surely die," if you have not spoken to deter him from
> his evil way that he may live, then he remains evil and dies in
> his sinfulness, but I will require his blood from your hands.
> [3:17–18]

That is to say, if Ezekiel does not warn the wicked so that they may change their conduct, he will be responsible for the divine judgment on them, and God will punish him.

> But you, if you have warned the wicked man, if he does not re-
> turn from his evil and from his wicked way, then he dies for
> his sin, but you have saved yourself. Again, if a righteous per-
> son turns from his righteousness and does wrong, [that is,] if I
> lay a stumbling block before him, he shall die. Because you will
> not have warned him, he dies in his iniquity, and the righteous
> deeds which he did will not be remembered. And I will require
> his blood of your hand. But if you have indeed warned the right-
> eous man that he should not sin, so that he does not sin, the
> righteous man will surely live, and you will thereby have saved
> yourself.[6] [3:19–21]

Although we now expect some account of what happened when Ezekiel carried out the divine mandate, we find that the following section fails to provide it. A fourth commission comes instead: Ezekiel is commanded to go into a valley where the radiance of Yahve

[5] In the Jewish ritual an error in the text properly goes unnoticed. Where the prayer book reads "*Praised* be the glory of God in His place" we ought to read in Ezekiel "*in the rise* of the radiance of Yahve from the place where it was."
[6] This message is found again in 33:7–9.

again appears to him. He is enjoined to be silent and not to reprove the people, for they are rebellious. He is to maintain this silence until he gets a specific injunction to speak (3:22–7).

What is the relationship of these last two passages to each other? We do not know. Perhaps one of them is misplaced, and they should not be read in sequence. Some suppose that the second passage, enjoining silence, comes from a period long after the first. I confess that I do not know. Ezekiel is addressed throughout the commission by the phrase "son of man." In the centuries long after Ezekiel's time the phrase "son of man" acquired many overtones and special connotations; here it is simply a form of address by which the Deity would normally speak to a human being.

In the long fourth chapter and most of the fifth chapter, we read what amounts to a series of prophecies of the destruction that occurred in 586.[7] These prophecies are couched in symbolism, not in straightforward prose. Ezekiel is commanded to spread upon a clay tablet a representation of Jerusalem under siege, with a siege wall and all the other implements of attack. Moreover, he is to place an iron plate as a wall of iron between himself and the represented city, as though he also were laying siege to the city. Then he is to lie on his left side so as to be symbolically bearing the sin of Israel, that is, the northern kingdom. He is to remain in this position for a total of three hundred and ninety days, as if the exile, which began for the northern kingdom in 721, was to terminate after 390 years. He is to lie on his right side for forty days as symbolic of the exile of the kingdom of Judah, as if that were to last just forty years. As he lies there, he must consume certain food in token of the scarcity to be suffered by the inhabitants of Jerusalem during the siege. For fuel with which to bake barley cakes, he must use human dung, symbolic of the disgrace to the people who will eat their bread unclean in exile. When Ezekiel protests to Yahve, he is granted the boon of being allowed to use cow's dung instead, so that he shall not become ritually defiled.

Next Ezekiel is enjoined to cut off the hair of his head and his beard and to divide this hair into three parts. One part he is to burn in Jerusalem when the days of the siege are fulfilled; another part he is to chop with a sword; the third part he is to scatter to the wind. He is to reserve a few hairs to represent a pious remnant, and even some of these must be thrown into the fire. These symbolic actions of burning, chopping, and scattering refer, of course, to the fate of the inhabitants of Jerusalem at the moment of the destruction in 586.

[7] It is to be recalled that the initial conquest by the Babylonians was in 597. The destruction of Jerusalem and the Temple came eleven years later.

Only a few would survive, and of the few that survived, an even smaller number would survive further ordeals. The Book of Ezekiel does not give the direct explanation of these symbols, as though the prophet and his audience were in such clear communication that exposition of the symbols was unnecessary.

The remainder of Chapter 5 contains a more straightforward denunciation of Jerusalem and a prediction of an evil fate for it. The nearest thing to an explanation of the preceding symbols is found in 5:12:

> A third part of those in Jerusalem will die by pestilence and perish from famine, a third will fall by the sword, and a third I will scatter to every wind and then pursue with the sword.

The thoughtful reader may ask: If the prophet is in exile in Babylonia, having gone there presumably in 597 with the first deportation, to whom is he addressing this denunciation of Jerusalem? Is it to those in Babylonia, and if so, what is the point of it? On the other hand, if he is addressing the remarks to Jerusalem, is he in Jerusalem, even though the book seems to have made it clear that he is in Babylonia? Scholars do not agree in their answers, and the symbolic nature of the text increases the confusion.

The sixth and seventh chapters denounce the non-Yahvistic worship, on the high places in the land. The prevailing tone indicates that the destruction of Jerusalem is near at hand, not some six or seven years away, and that destruction is deserved, as the punishment for iniquities. Yahve is pouring His wrath upon the people of Israel, punishing them without compassion, according to their deeds. There is no defense against the foe; the conquerors sieze all the wealth of the land. The prophet goes on to describe the confusion:

> Mischief comes upon mischief and rumor upon rumor. They shall ask a vision of the prophet, but revelation will perish from the priest and counsel from the elders. [7:26]

No word of palliation will come from the Deity.

When we come to Chapters 8–11, we are given a date that represents September 592. As if in response to the questions about where Ezekiel is and whether he is speaking to Jews in Babylonia or in Jerusalem, we read:

> He [Yahve] stretched forth the form of a hand and took me by a lock of my hair; a wind lifted me up between earth and heaven and brought me to Jerusalem in the visions of God to Jerusalem, to the portal of the northern gate of the inner court [of the

Temple] where there stood an image of jealousy which provokes jealousy.[8] [8:3]

It is emphasized that the radiance of Yahve, symbolic of the presence
of the Deity, is there in the Temple. At the door of the court, Ezekiel
bends and enters and sees forms of reptiles and idols which the house
of Israel portrayed on the walls around. He sees seventy of the elders
of the land engaged in surreptitious rites; he sees women weeping for
the god Tammuz. This god, worshipped in Phoenicia and Babylonia,
seems to have been identified with the Greek god Adonis. He was the
god of the spring, and the myth was told of his early death and of the
descent into the underworld of his bride Ishtar in search of him. The
myth is an explanation of why the summer heat destroys spring
vegetation. The death of Tammuz was celebrated by seven days of
mourning. Ezekiel is objecting to the introduction of the Tammuz
mourning into the very Temple in Jerusalem.

Next Ezekiel goes into the inner court of the Temple. He sees
twenty-five men facing eastward and worshipping the sun. Six men
descend from the upper gate with weapons of destruction in their
hand; one of these men is clothed in linen and has a writer's inkhorn
in his belt. The radiance of Yahve, which is now high above the men,
enjoins the man in linen to go through the city marking the foreheads
of those who have disapproved of the abominations. Ezekiel himself
is told to go through the city and to smite without pity all but those
who have the mark on their foreheads. In the midst of the smiting
Ezekiel falls on his face and calls out to Yahve:

"Do you intend to destroy all the remnant of Israel in pouring
out your wrath on Jerusalem?" And Yahve said to me: "The sin
of the house of Israel and Judah is very very great; the land is
full of blood and the city is full of strife. They say that Yahve has
abandoned the land and therefore Yahve does not see. Therefore
I will not pity nor have compassion. I will visit their way on their
head." [9:8–10]

Meanwhile the man in linen returns, saying that he has done all that
he was commanded to do. Next, the same man is commanded to take

[8] The Temple had two courts, a large outer one and an inner court of the priests;
see I Ki. 6:36 and II Chron. 4:9. As to the arrangement of the gates, very little is
known.

The image of jealousy is an idol and is so named because it provoked divine
jealousy. The reference may be to an image set up by King Manasseh (reigned
687–642), the story of which is found in II Ki. 21:7; it is likely that this was the
image which King Josiah removed, II Ki. 23:6. If it is correct that the reference
is to this idol set up by King Manasseh then this chapter seems to be giving a review of the non-Yahvistic rites indulged in over a period of decades by the people
of the southern kingdom.

fire from between the cherubim (over whom the radiance of Yahve has ascended) and to burn the city. These cherubim, the same creatures Ezekiel saw beside the River Chebar, have the wheels with them (9:11–10:22).

In the account that follows, the leaders are promised that they will receive their punishment of death, not in Jerusalem but in places to which they are to be exiled (11:1–12). Ezekiel falls down on his face and cries out: "O Lord Yahve, do you mean to make an end of the remnant of Israel?" (11:13). In reply, Yahve enjoins Ezekiel to speak a hopeful message. Though Yahve has moved those already exiled to far-off places, He has prepared a sanctuary for them in those lands. In the future He will gather them back to the land of Israel from among the nations. "And I will give them a different heart, and put a new spirit in their innards. And I will remove the heart of stone from their flesh and I will give them a heart of flesh." (11:19) With this promise, the wind lifts Ezekiel up again and brings him to Babylonia, where he tells the exiles all that he has heard (11:22–5).

Considerations of space prohibit a detailed review of such parts of the Book of Ezekiel as the denunciations of the foreign nations in Chapters 25–32. These bear dates indicating that some precede and some follow the destructive events of 586. If enough of the message of Ezekiel has been portrayed for the reader to have some sense of its mood and color, surely he can see why it provokes so many questions. When, as Ezekiel says, a wind (or, as some translate, "spirit") lifted him up and bore him to Palestine, was he in a trance? Was he in Babylonia, imagining what was going on in Jerusalem? Did he make trips from Babylonia to Jerusalem, trips he described as divinely enjoined by portraying the wind as his means of transportation? Was he describing present events, predicting the future, or recalling the past? Was he describing what had already occurred, asserting that it had been revealed to him in advance?

There is a strange paradox in the Book of Ezekiel. The whole of it reads as if it came from a single hand. Fifty years ago scholars seemed to agree that the Book of Ezekiel, unlike the Book of Isaiah, represented a literary unity, except for certain minor interpolations. Yet problems of the kind we have noticed have caused scholars of our day to produce ingenious and amazing solutions to what they regard as the great puzzle of the Book of Ezekiel. One scholar has asserted that only those passages that are clearly poetry (about one seventh of the book) belong to Ezekiel, and that the remainder was added a century after Ezekiel's time. Similarly, other scholars have declared that only certain passages are Ezekiel's, but without agreeing as to which ones they are. Theories have proliferated. According to a recent viewpoint, the true Ezekiel lived in Palestine in the time of Manasseh, and a century later an editor rewrote his message, providing the Babylonian setting. Another scholar supposes that there never was an Ezekiel; the person who created the book lived in the third century of the pre-Christian era, and the book was revised at some later time. Still another scholar would put Ezekiel back in the eighth century, supposing that the events deal with the exile of the northern kingdom, not the kingdom of Judah. There have been lengthy debates as to whether Ezekiel lived in Palestine or Babylonia, and some scholars, preferring not to choose between Babylonia and Palestine, ascribe to Ezekiel a career in both countries.

Granted that the problems that stimulate the theories are real, it seems much better to me and to many others to be burdened with the problems the book itself provides, than with inconclusive scholarly theories. No biography of Ezekiel can be written, and the location of his ministry cannot be ascertained. My own inclination is to believe that he was in Palestine before 586 and in Babylonia after 586. I find his exact knowledge of non-Yahvistic religious practices and of the political events within the city explainable only on the basis of his having been in Palestine before that time.

Whether Ezekiel was in Babylonia or Palestine after the destruction of 586, he, like Jeremiah, turned from denunciation to words of comfort. In Chapter 33 he sets forth his expectation of a rebirth of the nation from those who have gone into captivity into Babylonia. Ezekiel is depicted as addressing those exiles who say to him that iniquity and sin are upon them, and who therefore ask how they can survive. Here is Ezekiel's reply:

"As I live," says the Lord Yahve, "I do not desire the death of the wicked person, but rather that the wicked person should turn aside from his way and live. Return from your evil deed! Why should you die, house of Israel! Now you, son of man, just say to your people, the righteousness of the righteous will not save him on the day of his transgression, nor will the wicked stumble in his wickedness on the day when he turns aside from his evil. The righteous will not be able to live because of his past righteousness on the day when he sins. When I say about the righteous that he shall surely live, if it is one who has relied upon his previous righteousness but has done evil, all his righteous deeds will not be remembered, and in the iniquity which he has done, will he die. When I say about the wicked that he will surely die, if it is one who turns aside from his sin and does justice and righteousness and returns the pledge taken unjustly, or that which he has seized in robbery, and walks in statutes of life without committing iniquity, then he shall surely live and will not die. All the sin which he sinned will not be remembered against him. If he has done justice and righteousness he will surely live.

"Now your kinsmen will say that the way of Yahve is not right, but it is they whose way is not right. When the righteous turns from his righteousness and does evil, then he shall die thereby. And when the wicked turns from his wickedness and does justice and righteousness he shall live because of these things, and as for your saying 'The way of Yahve is not right,' I shall judge each man according to his ways, O house of Israel." [33:11–20]

The same subject is discussed in Chapter 18. Ezekiel begins by quoting the following proverb for the purpose of repudiating it: "The fathers have eaten sour grapes and the children's teeth are set on edge." The proverb means that children suffer for the iniquities of their parents.

Behold, all souls are Mine—the soul of the father as well as the soul of the son is Mine. The person that sins, he [alone] shall die. [18:4]

Ezekiel goes on to describe a righteous man. He is one who avoids idolatry, who does not defile his neighbor's wife, nor approach a woman in her impurity (her menstrual period). He wrongs no one, does not keep garments taken in pledge, does not rob; he gives bread to the hungry and clothes the naked; he does not lend at interest and follows the statutes of Yahve. Now, if there is a person who is the opposite of this, that person has done abominable things and will die. But if a son sees his father doing wicked things, and the son abstains from them, then it must be clearly understood that the son will not bear his father's iniquity.

This section and the passage [9] in Chapter 33 contain two doctrines of the utmost importance in the development of religious ideas. The first of these is called "individualism." This idea can best be understood by noticing that in the old covenant, prior to the time of Jeremiah, the Deity was concerned with the collective people rather than with individuals. When the cumulative guilt had reached the

[9] The end of Chapter 18 is repeated in 33.

point of saturation, the Deity broke his covenant with all the people, the righteous as well as the wicked. Ezekiel is asserting that this collective guilt is no longer the case, because the Deity deals with individuals. In the second place, Ezekiel makes specific what the prophet Hosea had only implied when he spoke in general terms about the desirability of repentance. Ezekiel states plainly that sincere and full repentance is accepted by the Deity. It is not the past of a person that is important, but rather his present. The man who was once righteous but has become wicked is regarded as a wicked person; the man who was once wicked but has become righteous is regarded now as a righteous person.

Nowhere in Scripture is there as clear an exposition of individualism as that which appears in Ezekiel 18 and 33. But one must not assume that these clear statements of individualism amount to a pure invention on the part of Ezekiel. The roots of individualism were sunk earlier; moreover, no religious system is intelligible unless it has some place for the individual. Ezekiel has applied to his own time what was always implied when individual people's actions were described as righteous or unrighteous. Ezekiel answers the implied question of how Yahve can continue His relationship with the Israel which forfeited His benign providence and underwent the terrible destruction at the hands of the Babylonians. The old covenant was collective; the new covenant is individual. In later times the symbol of this individual covenant was the circumcision of the young. Genesis 17:9–14, a late narrative about early times, depicts the Deity as saying to Abraham:

> You shall observe my covenant, you and your seed after you for the generations. This is my covenant which you shall observe between me and you, and your seed after you, the circumcision of every male child. You shall circumcise the flesh of the foreskin; this shall be a sign of the covenant between Me and you. . . . If a male child will not be circumcised then that soul shall be cut off from his people for that will be a rupture of my covenant.

The emphatic assertion of individualism and the possibility of repentance are Ezekiel's answer to the question of how the Deity continues His relationship with Israel. Jeremiah spoke of a new covenant; Ezekiel specifies that a people with a heart of flesh rather than a heart of stone can live justly rather than unjustly, and that the Deity can have a continuing bond with them.

Ezekiel's individualism can be overstated, and has been by some scholars. Similarly, insufficient attention can be paid to what Ezekiel declares is the Deity's abiding concern for the collective people. True, the covenant with the collective people has been superseded, yet Ezekiel firmly believes that from among the exiles in Babylonia will emerge a new community, or perhaps even a new nation, which Yahve will restore to Palestine and to whom He will give back the land. Why should Yahve do so? Ezekiel gives an answer in several places. It can be summed up in the phrase *"For the sake of My name"*:

> Son of man, when the house of Israel dwelt in their own land, they defiled it by their ways and their deeds. Their way was unto Me like the impurity of a menstruous woman, so that I poured my wrath upon them and I scattered them among the nations and they wandered in the land, for I judged them in accordance with their way and their deed. When they came unto the nations, they profaned My holy name, in that people said of them, "These are the people of Yahve but they have gone forth out of the land."
>
> But I had regard for My holy name. . . . Therefore say unto the house of Israel, thus says Yahve: "Not for your sake do I act, O house of Israel, but rather for the sake of My holy name which you have profaned among the peoples where you have come. I shall sanctify My great name. . . . The nations will know that I am Yahve when through you I sanctify Myself in their eyes. For I shall take you from the nations and gather you from all the lands and bring you to your land. I shall pour upon you clean waters and you will be pure of all your impurities and from all of your abominations will I purify you. . . . The nations that are left around shall know that I, Yahve, have rebuilt the ruined places and replanted that which had become desolate. I, Yahve, have spoken and I will do it. . . ." [36:*17–36*]

In effect Yahve declares that He cannot permit Israel to dissolve into nothingness, for thereby His reputation would suffer among the nations. Yahve does not act as the restorer for Israel's sake, since she has not deserved it, but rather for His own sake. Somewhat similarly, we read in Numbers 14:*11–16* that when Yahve became dissatisfied with the children of Israel in the Wilderness, He proposed to destroy them and to build a new nation from Moses. Moses replied that if Yahve did that, then "the nations who have heard your reputation will say, it is because of the inability of Yahve to bring this people to the land which He has promised them; therefore He slew them in the wilderness." [1]

---

[1] See also Exodus 32:*12*.

That the Deity must so guard His reputation that He must change His desired course of action to demonstrate His greatness is by no means an exalted doctrine. Yet this is precisely what Ezekiel sets forth. A more edifying explanation of why Yahve should continue to have relations with collective Israel comes somewhat later, from another prophet of the exile whom we refer to as Second Isaiah. Ezekiel does not reach the high eminence of his successor.

The famous Chapter 37 of Ezekiel relates that the hand of Yahve was on Ezekiel and brought him to a valley full of bones, strewn about and very dry. Yahve informs Ezekiel that spirit can enter these bones so that they will live, and that sinews and flesh will be put upon them; they will be covered with skin and be alive. There is a noise and a commotion, and then the bones come together, with sinews upon them. Flesh comes up and skin covers them. But as yet there is no breath in them. Then Ezekiel, in conformity with divine injunctions, speaks to the four winds so that the proper spirit or wind enters these slain and gives them life. The meaning is made clear:

> Son of man, these bones are all the house of Israel. Notice that they say: "Our bones are lost and our hope is perished, and we are completely cut off." [37:11]

That is to say, the chapter does not deal with personal resurrection (a doctrine mostly unknown in the Tanak) but with group resurrection. The resurrected Israel is promised that she will be placed back on her own soil in Palestine. This promise includes not only the Judean exiles of 586, but also the northern exiles of 722/721:

> Behold, I will take the children of Israel from among the nations whither they have gone and I will gather them around about and bring them to their soil. I will make them into one single nation (not as in the past when there were two kingdoms). [A descendant of] my servant David will be king over them, and one single shepherd will they both have. They will walk according to My statutes and they will observe My ordinances to execute them . . . I shall make a covenant of peace with them, a perpetual covenant will there be with them . . . My dwelling place will be with them and I shall be their God and they will be My people. All the nations will know that I, Yahve, sanctify Israel through My sanctuary's being in their midst forever. [37:21–8]

These promises for a glorious future are not limited by any specification as to when the events are to occur. Ezekiel gives a general assurance rather than a particular one. The pattern of hope, including the ingathering of the exiles and a Davidic king on the throne, was to play an important part in subsequent Jewish, and therefore Christian, thought. Though Ezekiel speaks of the new covenant as a perpetual one, he does not specify what this means. If we can infer his meaning, it is that the old covenant terminated in 722/721 for the northern kingdom and in 586 for the southern kingdom; moreover, since Yahve's relations are now primarily with individuals, the covenant is perpetual, for there will always be individuals (even if they are a minority) who will remain firm and loyal in their devotion to Yahve.

The promises to a collective Israel do not contradict the high individualism Ezekiel has articulated. Indeed, we must always be wary of imposing our western logic upon biblical matters, for it is misplaced there. According to western logic, individualism carried to the extreme would imply that the group has disappeared, while the insistence on the group, as in the period before Ezekiel, would imply that there was no individualism whatsoever. This would be carrying logic to an absurdity, for the oriental mind was capable of harboring unresolved items that are contradictory in theory but compatible in practice. Ezekiel, then, emphasizes individualism but also has room in his thought for the collectivity.

In Chapters 40–8 we are given a vision of a Temple to be restored.[2] Scholars debate about these chapters. There are those who doubt that the chapters are the work of one man, while some admit that they might be the work of one man, but doubt that they are the work of Ezekiel.

Two objections have been raised against accepting these chapters as the work of Ezekiel. The first of these has some validity. An understanding of the growth and development of the Sacred Calendar and the use of sacred vessels requires this section to be later than the period of the exile. The other objection does not seem valid. We have

[2] Chapter 40 discusses first the outer aspects, and then the inner court and its gates, Chapter 41 discusses the inner structure, including the room which is to be the "Holy of Holies." 42 contains a description of the priests' chambers and then the dimensions of the whole area. 43 describes the restoration of the Temple worship and the measurements of the altar on which the burnt offerings are to be placed. In 44 and 45, the obligations and emoluments of the priests and the Levites are set forth; part of 45 lists the function of the *nasi* which we usually translate "prince." Chapters 45 and 46 present aspects of the Sacred Calendar and then the specifications for the worship. Chapter 47 describes a stream of water which comes from underneath the threshold south of the entrance of the Temple. The remainder of the chapter, giving us the boundary of the land, and the last chapter, discussing the division of the land and the plan of the city, are even later appendices.

noticed that the pre-exilic prophets were either unconcerned with or opposed to the Temple in Jerusalem. If these chapters are by Ezekiel, they are a complete reversal of prophetic tendency. It is argued that because Ezekiel is a prophet, he could not have been so loyal to the idea of a sanctuary as to have set forth a vision of how it would be built. This argument seems erroneous to me.

Ezekiel differs from his predecessors in his attitude towards ritual. To him, ceremony is not offensive but has a high significance. This can be seen in chapter after chapter of his book, even before we reach Chapter 40. Ezekiel was himself of a priestly family (1:3). When he deals with the Temple before the destruction of 586, he expresses a feeling of outrage that the Temple is being contaminated by improper conduct. An Isaiah or a Jeremiah might have said that the conduct at the Temple is of no significance since Yahve is not favorably inclined to the Temple. Ezekiel, on the other hand, is distressed that the Temple, a worthy institution to him, is not being treated worthily. To deny that Ezekiel is interested in the Temple is to miss one of the most significant elements in the transition from the pre-exilic to the exilic prophets. In short, while Chapters 40–48 seem to me not to be by Ezekiel himself, they are consistent with Ezekiel's viewpoint.[3]

A significant matter appears in Chapter 43. The radiance of the God of Israel comes into the Temple through the eastern gate, filling the whole Temple. Ezekiel is told that this is to be the place of Yahve's throne where he will dwell forever. Then, at the beginning of Chapter 44, Ezekiel is brought back to the eastern gate, only to find that it is shut. The Deity says to him:

> "This gate shall be shut and shall not be opened; no man shall come into it, for now Yahve, the Lord of Hosts, has come into it and it is to be shut." [44:1–2]

As we have seen above (page 65) and shall see in more detail when we look at the Sacred Calendar, the Temple was built on an east-west alignment, so that on the days of the equinox (in our calendar, March 21 and September 21) the first rays of the rising sun (that is, the radiance) entered the sanctuary. This radiance was the equivalent of the Deity Himself. The verses we are considering tell us that Yahve

[3] A reasonable suggestion has been made that a later hand greatly amplified Ezekiel's nucleus. Certainly the "prince" who appears so prominently in these chapters is not a figure whom we can recognize from any history of the exile or of subsequent times. Ezekiel or whoever wrote these chapters seems to have no place for a king, yet Chapter 37 has promised specifically that a descendant of David would reign as king.

no longer dwells in the sky from which in the past He made a visit into the Temple on equinoctial days; rather Yahve "is in His holy Temple," as the well-known hymn expresses it.

The permanent closing of the eastern gate was unquestionably designed to do away with the non-Yahvistic worship, depicted in Chapter 8, of the twenty-five men who were facing eastward worshipping the sun. The fact that Yahve was conceived of as having a radiance which entered the Temple on the equinoctial day made His worship perilously close to solar worship. Part of the change in the calendars, which we shall examine later, was an effort to get away from solar aspects and from rites too akin to those of the pagans. Many passages show that the Book of Ezekiel conceived of Yahve as having taken up His permanent dwelling in the Temple in Jerusalem. Accordingly, far from being opposed to the Temple, Ezekiel considered it the key institution in religious life, and the dwelling of the Deity.

In Chapter 44 access to the Temple is forbidden to foreigners and uncircumcised people. We are told that the Levites, because they went astray, are to be servants in the Temple but may not serve as priests. The only legitimate priests, according to 44:15, are those who are "Levites, the sons of Zadok." Who were these sons of Zadok, and what is the significance of this limitation of priesthood, and of the division of duties and responsibilities between Levites and priests?

Scripture relates that King David had two priests, Abiathar and Zadok ben Ahitub. In the upheavals after the death of David, both priests became partisans. Abiathar was a partisan of Adonijah, the legitimate heir; Zadok was a partisan of Solomon, who came to the throne in place of Adonijah. Zadok anointed Solomon; Abiathar was banished to the little town of Anathoth.[4] From the account of the banishment of Abiathar we conclude that subsequently there were two priestly families. One was regarded as legitimate, namely that of Zadok, while the other, that of Abiathar, was considered to be disqualified. When we couple this information with what we know about the great Reformation of Josiah, which disfranchised all priests outside Jerusalem, we begin to see a progressive limiting of those who can legitimately be priests.

There are many puzzles about the Levite. The word seems to have meant almost the equivalent of priest without regard to ancestry, and it seems also to have meant someone who was supposedly a

---

[4] II Ki. 2:26–27. See II Sam. 20:25 and II Sam. 8:17. Some confusion exists in this last passage, but the text when corrected would read: "and Zadok . . . and Abiathar ben Ahitub ben Ahimelech were the priests."

descendant of Levi, the second son of Jacob. In these chapters priests are distinguished as a select group within the larger group of Levites. We are at a way station in the evolution of priesthood in Israel.[5]

To resume where we began, the Book of Ezekiel presents us with many problems. In only a few chapters is the literary flavor immediately rewarding for the modern reader. Yet, for a knowledge of the development of religion in Israel, Ezekiel has an importance equal to any of his predecessors or successors. This importance does not lie in the personal eminence of Ezekiel, who seems to lack the stature of Isaiah and Jeremiah, but rather in the book's reflection of the great transitions that followed the Babylonian captivity. Ezekiel's stress on individualism was of permanent influence; his conviction that Yahve would restore a purified Israel to Palestine under a Davidic monarchy was of tremendous consequence in later times. A dreamer rather than an incisive thinker, Ezekiel's dreams became the wishes and ambitions of succeeding generations, especially in eras of disaster.

[5] See pages 524ff. That "Levite" was once the equivalent of priest is to be discerned in Judges 16. In that chapter in Judges we read of a lad of Bethlehem in Judea, of the tribe or family of Judah "who was a Levite." This young man, described as the Levite, becomes a *kohen*, priest, to Micaiah. From this narrative two things can be concluded, that priesthood in the early days was not limited to the tribe of Levi, and that the early priesthood was not a hereditary matter.

SECOND ISAIAH

WE SAW in Chapter 5 that the Book of Isaiah is an anthology of prophecies from several hands and several ages. That man whom we call First Isaiah appears in only the first thirty-nine of the sixty-six chapters in the book, and even those thirty-nine are not entirely his. Biblical scholars customarily speak of a Second Isaiah. This is so standard as to be virtually axiomatic, especially since even in medieval times Jewish interpreters recognized that Chapters 40–66 reflected times and conditions different from those reflected in the preceding chapters. But scholars are not agreed as to whether Isaiah 40–66 is the work of one person and age or of more than one. Some scholars, perhaps the majority, consider all the twenty-seven chapters to be the work of one man. I cannot share this opinion, for I believe that many different hands and different periods are represented in these chapters. I shall assume that the anonymous prophet whom I shall speak of as Second Isaiah is to be found primarily in 40–55, and that 35 is to be joined to these chapters. As we saw above (p. 8), 36–9 are an excerpt from II Kings 18–20, and therefore 35 belongs in juxtaposition with 40–55.

In 586 the Babylonians had conquered Palestine as part of their world conquest, but they were threatened, first by the Medes, and later by the conqueror of the Medes, Cyrus the Persian. Cyrus conquered the city of Babylon in 539 and put himself upon the imperial throne. The world empire, now no longer Babylonian, was to become Persian. The Persian rule was to spread rapidly and proudly, even penetrating into Europe.

Second Isaiah deals with the significance of the Babylonian exile and of Cyrus' conquest. What do these incidents mean in the light of the axiom that Yahve controls the events of history? As a result of going into exile, Israel had been propelled into the very center of a world empire. Before, the concern of prophets was, "What do the tremendous upheavals mean to Israel?" Now the concern is, "What do the upheavals mean to the world? And in what way is tiny Israel a vital part in the world?"

The focus of the prophet's attention remains on Israel. Cyrus' assent made it possible for the Jewish community to leave its exile in Babylonia and return to Judah. In my interpretation of Second Isaiah, I assume that 41–8 represent the prophet's thought at the moment when Cyrus, newly victorious, has given the Jews in Babylonia permission to return to Palestine, and that 35, 40, and 49–55 portray a period from fifteen to twenty years later, when the Jews have nearly completed the long journey home.

It must be understood that the text is not quite as conveniently simple as this two-part division suggests. Thus, a most important poem, 50:4–11 and 52:13–53:12, is not to be regarded as by Second Isaiah, but as a fragment surviving from some longer work, the "Suffering Servant," by another poet. Again, certain passages are separated from each other, probably as a result of accident in the scribal transmission; for example, a satire on the making of idols, found in 40:19–20; 41:6–7; 44:9–20; 46:6–7 (and possibly 45:16), may once have been part of a connected section. A consequence of such phenomena is that scholars often justly feel called upon to rearrange the text. The succeeding pages, however, deliberately abstain from drastic rearrangement, although I do suggest a different sequence for entire chapters. This plan is much more restrained than some proposals that involve the transfer of verses and half-verses.

In some passages, often given as 41:8–10; 42:1–4; 44:21–3; 49:1–6; and 50:4–9 (and possibly 52:13–53:12), the subject is a "servant of Yahve." Are these "servant" passages by Second Isaiah or are they also scattered fragments from a different author? And does the "servant" represent the Jewish people collectively, or some individual, such as the hoped for Davidic king? It is not easy to come to a decision. I interpret the servant passages as integral to Second Isaiah, and I identify the servant usually as Israel, but occasionally as the prophet himself.

To divide the material into the two periods is to ignore some real difficulties, but I shall divide it here in order to enable the reader to assimilate the material itself. At some advanced stage he can go on to modify the simplified division I present.

Let us conceive of Second Isaiah as a poet-playwright, rather than only as a prophet. If we consider the poetry we will find passages of great beauty, as well as a distillation of profound thought. As a playwright, the prophet provides the dialogue of a variety of characters, though he does not identify them. The content of their speeches is the sometimes uncertain clue to who they are. The cast of characters consists of at least the following:

> The Deity
> The prophet
> Israel, that is, the Jews in exile in Babylonia
> Israel, that is, the Jews who remained in Jerusalem and Judah
> Cyrus
> The Babylonians
> The nations of the world (the Gentiles)
> A voice, so listed since no better identification exists

Act One, as we see it, is laid in Babylonia shortly after 539. Cyrus has made great progress in his world conquests and has given his consent for the Jews in Babylonia to return to Judah. One scholar has noticed that the sequence of thought in Chapters 40–8 becomes clearer when the chapters are read in reverse order, beginning with 48; it is as if pieces of parchment had been reversed and were unintentionally sewn together in the wrong sequence. Act I consists of 48–41; Act II of 35, 40, and 49–55.

In Chapter 48, the prophet, on behalf of the Deity, addresses the Jews in Babylonia, calling them the House of Jacob and asserting that they are named Israel. Although their place of origin was the sacred city of Jerusalem, they have not [1] depended upon the God of Israel:

I have declared the first things from of old;
They went out from My mouth and I caused them to be
        heard;
Suddenly I have done them and they have come about!
Out of My knowledge that you are obstinate
And your neck is a sinew of iron and your forehead of
        brass,
Therefore I told you these things from of old,
And before they came about I let you hear them,

---

[1] The word "not" has dropped out of the last part of 48:2.

Lest you should say, "My idol has done them,"
Or "My graven image or molten statue has brought them
    about." [48:3–5]

The prophet first asserts that startling and spectacular events have
occurred and that Israel had been told in advance, indeed, long ago,
that these events would occur.

But if Israel has been so deaf and so stubborn, why does the
Deity maintain His relations with them?

For My own sake, for My own sake, I do this.
For why should My name be profaned?
My glory I will not give to anyone else. [48:11]

That is to say, Israel has not merited that the Deity should persist in
His relations with her. His persistence is due to His graciousness, and
not to His desire to maintain His reputation, as Ezekiel maintained.

Hearken unto Me, Jacob, and Israel, whom I have called
    upon:
I am God. I am the first and I am also the last.
It is My hand which laid the foundation of the earth,
And My right hand which spread out the heavens . . .
    [48:12–13]

Now He turns from Israel to the nations of the world.

Gather together and hearken.
Who among you has declared such things?

He whom Yahve loves will carry out His wish against Baby-
    lon
And [execute] His strength against the Chaldeans. [48:14]

That is to say, Yahve has elected Cyrus to do His will against the
Babylonians, who had come in these later times to be called the Chaldeans. The nations do not understand that this is what is happening,
for divine revelation has never come to them.

I Myself spoke and I Myself called him;
I brought him forward and I made his way to prosper.
Come near to Me, O nations, and hear this:
From the very beginning I did not speak in secret,
From the moment that [the purpose] came into existence
    I was there. [48:15–16A] [2]

²**48:16B is untranslatable.**

The result of Yahve's choice of Cyrus becomes clear in the last verses of the chapter. Yahve speaks to the Jews in Babylonia:

> *Go forth out of Babylonia, flee from the Chaldeans.*
> *Tell with a sound of singing, make it be heard,*
> *Proclaim it to the end of the earth—*
> *Say that Yahve has redeemed His servant Jacob.* [48:20]

We hear still another motif—the exodus of Israel from Babylonia is to be a recollection of the Exodus from Egypt. Now it is the prophet speaking:

> *They will not thirst when He leads them through dry*
>   *places.*
> *He will make water flow for them from a rock,*
> *He will split the rock and the waters will gush out.*[3] [48:21]

In Chapters 47 and 46, the prophet turns to speak a word of taunt against Babylonia and its deities. We need notice only one small portion of Chapter 47, a verse that explains why Yahve permitted Israel to be conquered:

> *I became wroth with My people,*
> *So I profaned My inheritance and gave them in your hand.*
> *You showed them no mercy—even on the old you made*
>   *your yoke exceedingly heavy.* [47:6]

In Chapter 46, the attention is at first directed to the Babylonian gods. The prophet is speaking not to the Babylonians, but about them and their gods.

> *Bel is bowed down, Nebo is prostrate.*
> *Their idols have been put on beasts and animals,*
> *On carriages heavy laden, to carry [for the sacred proces-*
>   *sion] a burden which fatigues.*
> *They are prostrate, they are bowed down together.*
> *They (the people) are not able to rescue [their] burden,*
> *And these themselves go into captivity.* [46:1–2]

Probably the capture of the Babylonian deities and their deportation by the Persians is being alluded to. The irony in the assertion that the worshipers cannot save their gods is especially noteworthy. The Deity's treatment of Israel is exactly the opposite. He supports Israel,

---

[3] Most translators take the verbs as descriptive of the past. The context seems to me to rule this out. A "doxology" ends the chapter: "There is no peace, says Yahve, for the wicked." This line, designed to give glory to the Deity, was possibly added when this section was read at later times in the precursor of the synagogue.

as it were, from infancy until old age, and throughout this time He does not change:

> *I have borne you and I shall bear;*
> *I shall carry you and I will deliver you.* [46:3–4]

Such a deity cannot be compared to any idol:

> *To whom will you liken Me and compare Me?*
> *To whom will you assess Me as though we can be alike?*
> *[Am I like an idol] for which people lavish gold out of the*
> *pocket, and weigh silver in a balance,*
> *[And] who hire a goldsmith who makes these into a deity*
> *To which they bow down and prostrate themselves?*
> *Then they carry it on the shoulders and they bear it around,*
> *They set it down and it stands still, without moving from its*
> *place.*
> *They call to it, but it does not answer.*
> *From distress it does not help.* [46:4–7 Heb., 46:5–7 Eng.]

The allusion is again to the Babylonian New Year procession, known to us from inscriptions. Israel is cautioned against any such idolatry, for their deity is different.

> *Remember the former things as of old,*
> *For I am God and there is none else.*
> *I am God and besides Me there is no one.* [46:9]

Here we have a clear and unmistakable statement of monotheism, emphasized by the denial of the existence of any other deities. From this moment on it would be appropriate in studying the prophetic literature to replace the word Yahve with the word God.

The prophet now reverts to the theme that the prediction of events to come had always preceded the events:

> *I declare the end of things from their beginning,*
> *And from the ancient times [even] those things which as*
> *yet have not occurred.*
> *I say that My plan will stand and all that I desire will I do.*
> *I call from the east a ravenous bird [Cyrus];*
> *From a distant land [I call] the man who executes My plan.*
> *I have spoken and I bring it about,*
> *I have planned things, and will do them.*
>
> *Hearken unto Me, you faint of heart,*
> *For whom deliverance seems distant.*

I have brought My victory near and it is no longer far off,
And My salvation will not tarry
And I will bring salvation in Zion
And restore to Israel My splendor. [46:10–13]

Is the emergence of Cyrus an accident in history or part of the unfolding of the plan designed by the One God of the world? Second Isaiah strongly affirms that all is deliberately ordained and all has been told in advance:

Thus says Yahve concerning His anointed one,
Concerning Cyrus, whose right hand He has taken hold of
To subdue nations before Him,
To loosen the girdles of kings: [4]
"I will open gates before him,
Gates that will never again be shut . . ." [45:1]

Cyrus will achieve this conquest because Yahve intended it. The conquest is on behalf, not of Cyrus, but of Israel:

For the sake of My servant Jacob and My chosen one, Israel
        [I do this];
I called you, [O Cyrus,] by your name, I spoke it, even
        though you do not know Me.
I am God and there is no other;
Besides Me there is no God.
I have girded you with strength, though you have not
        known Me
In order that from the east and from the west people will
        know that nothing takes place except through Me.
I am God and there is no other,
I fashion light and create darkness,
I create peace and I create evil,
I am God Who does all these things. [45:4–7]

The point here is that there is not a separate god who is responsible for evil; God controls both good and evil. The Persians conceived of a dual deity, a god of good and light on the one hand, and a god of evil and darkness on the other hand. Perhaps the prophet has this in mind, but more probably he is only stressing the unlimited uniqueness of God, without reference to the dualism of the Persians. The prophet goes on to declare that no one should question or challenge God, Who made earth and created man upon it, for God's

[4] That is, to disarm them.

achievement is to be discerned in the working out of history, especially in the task assigned to Cyrus.

> *I have raised him up for victory and all his ways will I make*
>   *straight.*
> *He will rebuild My city and send away My people from exile,*
> *Yet not for price or reward, says the God of hosts.* [45:13]

Accidents, according to Second Isaiah, do not happen; everything is part of God's providence:

> *He fashions the earth and makes it; He has established it.*
> *He created it not for chaos. He fashioned it to be inhabited.*

The prophet then speaks for the Deity:

> *I am God, there is none else.*
> *I did not speak in secret, in some dark place on the earth,*
> *I did not say to the seed of Jacob "Seek Me in the [remote]*
>   *chaos."*
> *I am God who speaks things that are right.* [45:18–19]

> *Turn to Me and be safe, O all the ends of the earth,*
> *For I am God and there is no other.*
> *I have sworn, a word has gone out of My mouth in right-*
>   *eousness,*
> *It shall not return [unfulfilled]:*
> *"Unto Me every knee must bend*
> *And [by Me] every tongue must swear."* [45:22–3]

In Chapter 44 Yahve promises Israel renewal and growth:

> *I shall pour My spirit on your seed,*
> *My blessing on your offspring.*
> *They shall spring up as though among the grass,*
> *Like willows on water courses.* [44:3B–4]

Not Jews alone will have prosperity, but also Gentiles who are proselytes. This is the earliest prophetic mention of proselytes. It would appear to follow logically that when a deity was attached to a particular
land, a person who moved from one land to another moved from one
deity, to another. In a limited sense such a person might be called a
proselyte. But when, under the impact of the teaching of Jeremiah,
the Deity was connected with a people, the people constituted an entity to which outsiders might attach themselves, even without moving
from land to land. In Second Isaiah a proselyte is a Gentile who joins
the Jewish people, not someone who moves to Palestine. We shall see

that in a very short time after Second Isaiah the idea of proselytism becomes expanded. Here we are given only a hint of it:

> *This one will say, I belong to God*
> *And that one will call himself by the name of Jacob.*
> *This one will enroll himself to God*
> *And surname himself by the name Israel.* [44:5] [5]

The prophet portrays God's attitude to Israel's past sinfulness:

> *I have blotted out, as a thick cloud, your transgressions,*
> *And, as a cloud, your sins.*
> *Return to Me, for I have redeemed you.* [44:22]

Now it is the prophet who speaks:

> *Sing for joy, O heavens, for God acted.*
> *Shout, O lower parts, O earth!*
> *Break forth into singing, O hills, O forest and every tree*
>   *in it!*
> *For God has redeemed Jacob,*
> *He has shown His splendor on behalf of Israel.* [44:23]

This is God, the Redeemer of Israel:

> *He who says to Jerusalem, "You shall be inhabited";*
> *And to the cities of Judah, "You will be rebuilt,*
> *And the destroyed places I will raise up". . .*
> *He says concerning Cyrus, "He is My friend**
> *And all My purpose will he bring to completeness."*
>   [44:26B–28A]

With such assurance of deliverance, Israel is not to be fearful of the future. God speaks to them:

> *When you pass through waters I will be with you,*
> *And through rivers, they shall not overflow you.*
> *When you walk through fire you will not be burned,*
> *Nor shall the flame singe you,*
> *For I am the Lord your God, the Holy One of Israel, your*
>   *savior . . .* [43:2–3A]

---

[5] A long prose section, a satire on the folly of idolatry, is found in 44:9–20. This section is probably an interpolation and not by Second Isaiah, though not contrary to his attitude. It describes how various workmen, the smith and the carpenter and the goldsmith, proceed to make an idol.

After the events of 597 and 586, in addition to the exile to Babylonia, some Judeans fled to Egypt and other countries. Now follows a
promise of the ingathering of all exiles:

From the east will I bring your seed,
And from the west will I gather you.
I will say to the north, "Give up [My people],"
And to the south, "Do not keep them back.
Bring My sons from the distance,
And My daughters from the ends of the earth." [43:5B–6]

Yahve continues to address Israel:

"You are My witnesses," says God,
"My servants whom I have chosen,
In order that you may know and believe Me and understand
*   that I am God.*
Before Me there was no God formed, and after Me there will
*   be no God.*
I, only I, am God, and besides Me there is no redeemer.
I have declared and I have made it known . . .
You are My witnesses," says God, "And I am God." [43:10–
*   12]*

The prophet turns his attention to Israel's return to Palestine. Yahve
is speaking:

Behold, I do a new thing;
Now it springs forth—do you not recognize it?
I make a road in the wilderness,
Streams of water in the desert.
The beasts of the field honor Me, the jackals and ostriches,
For having given water in the wilderness, streams in the
*   desert,*
In order to give drink to My people, My chosen ones,
This people I have formed for Myself, to speak forth My
*   praise. [43:19–21]*

Though Israel has wearied God with her sins He will be forgiving:

It is I who blot out your sins for My own sake,
And your transgressions I will not remember . . .
Your first ancestor [6] *sinned*
And your representatives transgressed against me,

[6] Probably Jacob. See Hosea 12:3, and page 75.

So that I profaned the holy cities,[7]
And made Jacob to be a curse and Israel for reproaches.
   [43:25–8]

In the mind of the poet, the forgiveness of Israel and its restoration to favor are not simply matters of caprice nor ends in themselves. At the beginning of 42 there appears a passage which explains why God has forgiven Israel, and indeed, why Israel had gone into exile. Yahve is speaking about Israel, and a mission to the nations:

Behold My servant Jacob [8] whom I uphold,
Israel My chosen one in whom My soul takes delight,
I have put My spirit upon him, so that he can bring forth
   justice to the nations. [42:1–2]

Israel is to work quietly, unobtrusively:

He will not shout nor raise his voice,
He will not have his voice heard in the street.
He will not break even a bruised reed,
Nor extinguish a smoking wick of wax,
But rather he will bring forth justice with full truth.
He shall not fail nor shall he be discouraged
Until he brings forth justice on the earth
And the isles [9] wait for his revelation. [42:3–4]

Now Yahve speaks to Israel:

I, God, have called you with righteousness and taken hold of
   your hand,
I will watch over you and I will make you a covenant of the
   people,
A light to the nations, to open the eyes of those who are
   blind,
To bring the prisoner out of his bondage, and those who sit
   in darkness out of the dungeon. [42:6–7]

The meaning here is not literal; physical blindness and imprisonment are meant to symbolize the condition of those who have not yet discerned the difference between idolatry and the worship of the true God.[1]

   The prophet goes on to say that God did not forgive Israel on an

---

[7] This translation is based on an emendation of the Hebrew text.
[8] This is added from the Greek translation because it seems to me to belong here.
[9] It is likely that by "isles," a figure to be found frequently in Second Isaiah, the prophet means the civilized world.
[1] However, some interpreters do take the passage as literal.

impulse, but only after He had gone through considerable anguish over her infidelity and the necessity to punish her; now, however, the great moment of forgiveness has arrived. Yahve is speaking:

> I have kept quiet for a long time.
> I have kept still and restrained Myself.
> Now I cry out like a woman in travail,
> I gasp and pant at the same time.
> I shall destroy hills and high places
> And dry up all their foliage;
> I shall make rivers into dry places
> And pools of water will I dry up,[2]
> And I will lead the blind in the way,
> In paths they have not known I will direct them.
> The darkness I will make light before them,
> Crooked places I will make straight.
> These things I will do for them and I will not forsake them.
>   [42:14–16]

The prophet digresses to comment on certain Jews in Babylonia:

> Those who rely upon an idol will turn back and be put
>   greatly to shame,
> Those who say to a graven image, "You are our God!"
>   [42:17B]

These Jews are then addressed directly:

> You who are deaf, hear!
> You who are blind, look and see!
> Who is blind but My servant,
> And deaf but the messenger I want to send? [3]
> You have seen many things but you do not observe,
> Your ears are open but you do not hear. [42:18–20]

The prophet now explains God's forgiveness:

> God has the desire for the sake of His righteousness
> To increase revelation and make it more glorious.
> But this is a people that has been despoiled and oppressed,
> And all of them have been hidden in prison-houses,
> All of them have been snared in holes.
> They were as a prey to people with no one to rescue them,
> A spoil and there was no one to say, "Restore them."

---

[2] He is talking of the miracles to accompany the second exodus.
[3] The last part of 42:19 is untranslatable.

Is there anyone among you who will pay attention and lis-
ten for that which is to come?
Who was it that made Jacob a spoil and turned Israel over
to the despoilers?
Was it not God against Whom we sinned,
And in Whose ways we did not want to go, and to Whose
revelation we did not hearken?
He poured wrath upon us and a heavy military attack.
He set fire around us all around, yet we did not know,
And it burned us, yet we did not lay it to heart. [42:21–5] [4]

Still pursuing the theme that God Himself had acted to punish Israel,
the prophet turns in Chapter 41 to taunt the nations of the world.
Yahve speaks:

*Behold, you are less than nothing ***
And your work is less than nil.
Whoever chooses you chooses an abomination! [41:24]

The following section gives promises of what will happen on the
journey back to Palestine from the east. Yahve speaks to Israel in
Babylonia:

I will open rivers on the bare high places
And fountains in the midst of the valleys,
I shall make the wilderness into pools of water
And the arid land into springs of water.
I will plant the cedar tree in the wilderness,
The acacia tree and the myrtle and the olive tree;
I will put the fir tree in the desert,
The pine and the box tree all together. [41:18–19]

This joyful prediction can be regarded as the climax and the
end of Act One. The heart of its message is that there is only one
God in the world. The tremendous events taking place are not blind
fate, but serve a divine purpose, of which Cyrus is an instrument.
The conqueror unifies mankind through the victory God gives him,
and Israel, now forgiven, takes its place as the "covenant people"
through whom the revelation of God is to become the property of all
society. Proselytes from the Gentiles can join the covenant people.
The insistence that there is only one God is accompanied, as we saw,
by the taunt that idolatry is futile and vain. The proof of monotheism
does not rest on dialectic or demonstration, but rather on the con-

---

[4] I have deliberately read "we" and "us" throughout this passage although in
many places the text reads "they" or "he."

tention that what has happened is the result of providence. Moreover, everything that has happened conforms to a pattern that was preconceived and even told about in advance, though the prophet does not say when or where.

By all logic, if there is one God and one humanity, then all humanity should be the same in His eyes, and the moment of this recognition should be the occasion for the dissolution of Israel. Second Isaiah taught the exact opposite: that Israel was the necessary vehicle through which the revelation of God would be known throughout the world. According to Second Isaiah, Israel is God's servant, or better, God's agent. In the prophet's mind, the agent remains as important as his mission. He asserts that Israel will retain its identity and march triumphantly in a new exodus from Babylonia into Palestine. It will be an easy journey, for all the obstacles on the long road of nearly a thousand miles will be removed.

In what we have called Act Two, the attention turns from Cyrus to Israel. Now that the benevolent Persian power has replaced the hated Babylonian sovereignty, Israel in exile can hope and plan to return to its own land. The keynote of Act Two is contained in the opening words of Chapter 40:

> *"Comfort, comfort My people," says your God,*
> *"Speak to the heart of Jerusalem and call out to her*
> *That her term of toil is [now] fulfilled,*
> *That her penalty is acceptably paid,*
> *For she received from God double for all her sins." [40:1–2]*

The text does not tell who is being enjoined in the first line to speak these consoling words. The addressee is plural and hence cannot be the prophet. It may be the heavenly host or a band of prophets. To the exiles who are about to return a voice cries out:

> *In the wilderness prepare a way for God;* [5]
> *Make straight in the desert a highway for our God.*
> *Every valley will be raised up,*
> *Every hill and high place will be lowered.*
> *The crooked will become straight and the rough places will*
> *be made flat,*

---

[5] The verse as quoted in the New Testament appears as "A voice cries out in the wilderness." This is in defiance of the natural punctuation; but it was common for Jewish and Christian exegetes to disregard punctuation when they used the Tanak as a proof text.

And the glory of God will be revealed and all flesh will see it
    together
For the mouth of God has spoken. [40:3–5]

Jerusalem and the cities of Judah can now expect the return of the exiles, led by the Deity over a beautifully easy road. Indeed, the road and the way stations themselves feel joyful:

The wilderness and the arid places rejoice,
The Araba[6] *is happy and bursts into flower,*
Like the rose, it bursts into flower,
It is happy, joyous and singing. . . . [35:1–2A]

The feeble and the fatigued are to find renewed strength:

The eyes of the blind will open,
And the ears of the deaf will be unstopped,
The lame will jump like a ram,
The tongue of the dumb will sing.
For water will spring forth in the wilderness,
And streams in the Araba. [35:5–6]

There will be a road there;
It will be called the Highway of Holiness. . . .
The redeemed of Yahve will return,
They will come to Zion with song,
And eternal joy will be on their heads. . . . [35:8A–10A]

Then comes a discouraged retort from some anonymous voice:

All flesh is grass
And all its goodliness is like the flower of the field.
The grass has withered,
The flower has faded,
For the spirit of God blew against it—
Indeed the people is grass. [40:6B–7]

The first voice replies, now addressing someone described as "she who brings good tidings to Zion":

O you who bring good tidings to Zion,
Raise your voice with strength,
O you who bring tidings to Jerusalem,
Raise it, do not be afraid,
Say to the cities of Judah: "Here is your God.

---

[6] *Araba* usually means the wilderness area near the Dead Sea, but possibly its sense here is more general.

Here is your God coming in strength.
An arm that can rule does He have;
See, His compensation [7] *is with Him,*
And His reward is before Him.
He leads His flock like a shepherd,
In His arm He picks up lambs,
He carries them in his bosom, and leads the young gently."
     [40:9–11]

There follows a section exalting God's omnipotence:

Who can contain the spirit of God
And who is the counsellor that is able to give Him advice?
     [40:13]

He sitteth upon the circle of the earth,
Yet its inhabitants are like grasshoppers. [40:22A].

Finally the prophet speaks a word to the faint of heart and the discouraged:

Why do you speak, O Jacob, and say, O Israel,
"My way is undisclosed to God
And the justice due me passes God unnoticed"?
Do you not know or have you not heard:
The God of the world, God who created the ends of the
     earth,
Does not grow weary nor does He grow faint,
And there is no limit to His perception.
To the faint He gives courage,
To him of no strength He increases power.
Young men can grow weary, and grow faint,
Youths can stumble to the ground,
But those who trust in God renew their strength;
They rise with wings like the eagles,
They run and do not faint,
They move forward and do not become weary. [40:27–31]

Now a voice is heard, perhaps that of the anonymous prophet describing his call:

Hear me, O coastlands, hearken, O nations afar off.
Yahve called me from the womb,

---

[7] The meaning here is that Jerusalem, having paid double for its sins, will now receive compensation for its sinfulness which has been eradicated.

When I was still in my mother's body, He spoke to me by
name.
He gave me a tongue like a sharp sword, hiding me in His
hand,
He made me a pointed arrow, concealing me in his quiver.
He said to me, "You are My servant, O Israel, through
whom I will be glorified." [49:1–3]

The meaning of concealment is that the world had to wait until the
scheduled time for God's message through Israel to be spoken. The
sword and arrow are figures which, when applied to a tongue, connote
an effective, eloquent spokesman. The voice continues to speak:

I had thought that I have become weary in vain,
For nought have I spent my strength . . .
But now Yahve has said to me—Yahve who fashioned me
His servant from the womb,
So as to restore Jacob to Him, and have Israel gathered to
Him,
(Therefore I am important in Yahve's eyes,
And God is my strength.) He has said,
"That you should be My servant
To raise up the tribes of Jacob, and the scattered of Israel
Is too little!
I am making you a light to the nations,
So that My salvation will extend to the end of the earth."
[49:4–6]

Yahve is indeed planning for Israel to return from exile to Palestine,
and the "servant" is to be instrumental in that plan. Yet a larger
purpose is intended, a purpose inclusive of all mankind.

Attention turns to Jerusalem, which has been destroyed since
586.

Zion says, "Yahve has abandoned me, the Lord has for-
gotten me."
[No!] Does a woman forget her suckling baby,
Does she cease to love the son of her womb?
Even if these might forget,
I [Yahve] do not forget you.
I have inscribed you on the palms of My hand,[8]
Your walls [9] are always before me.

[8] A figure of speech. Just as a lover may tattoo the name of his beloved on his
palm, so Yahve has inscribed Israel.
[9] That is, of Jerusalem.

Your builders [1] are faster than those who destroy you,
Those who laid you waste are leaving you. [49:14–17]

Not only the exiles from Babylonia but also those who have fled
to other lands will return:

Thus says my Lord Yahve.
"Behold, I raise My hand to the nations,
To the peoples I lift high My ensign.
They bring your sons in their bosom,
And your daughters are borne on shoulders.
Kings are your guardians,
And queens your nurses;
They will bow to the ground to you,
They will lick the dust of your feet,
So that you, O Jerusalem, will know that I am God,
Whose faithful ones will not be put to shame." [49:22–3]

Yet it would seem that, although Yahve had never conceived of a
permanent separation, some Jews in Babylonia could not credit the
tidings of redemption:

Thus says Yahve,
"What sort of writ of divorce was given your mother when I
*   sent her away?*
And who are the creditors to whom I have sold you?
See! It was for your sins that you were sold,
And for her [2] transgressions that your mother was sent
*   away.*
But why when I come now, does no man [greet Me]?
Why do I call and there is no answer?
Is My arm too short to redeem?
Do I lack the strength with which to save?" [3] [50:1–2A]

Yahve's address to the unresponding exiles continues:

Hear me, you who essay righteousness, who seek Yahve!
Look to the rock from which you were hewn,
To the cistern from which you stem,
Look to Abraham your father and to Sarah your mother.
I called him though he was solitary,[4]

---

[1] In 49:17 a vocalization is changed and an additional slight emendation made.
[2] The text says "your," evidently an error.
[3] There intrudes (50:4–11) a "Suffering Servant" passage to which we shall turn
presently.
[4] See Genesis 12:1ff.

And I blessed him and made him numerous [in offspring].
    [51:1–2]

Be not afraid of shame coming from man,
Nor be fearful of their taunts.
The moth will eat them as if they are clothing
And the worm as if they are wool,
But My redemption will last forever,
And My salvation for all ages. [51:7B–8]

Now the Deity is portrayed as speaking to Jerusalem:

Waken, waken, rise, O Jerusalem,
You have drunk from Yahve's hand the cup of His wrath,
    [51:17A]

There is an aside, describing Jerusalem's pitiable situation:

She has no one to be her leader
Of all the sons whom she bore.
No one of the sons she raised
Takes hold of her hand. [51:18]

The address to Jerusalem continues:

Wake, wake, put on your ornaments, O Zion
Don your beauteous clothes, O Jerusalem, sacred city.
The alien and the impure [5] *will not continue to enter you.*
Shake off the dust,
Stand up, O captive * *Jerusalem,*
The chains about your neck are broken,
O captive daughter of Zion. [52:1–2]

To this greatly cheering word, there is now added a sense of the immediacy of the great restoration, as if the exiles' return over the splendid highway were completed:

When the announcer of good tidings is [at his station] on
        the mountains,
How beautiful are his feet!
He proclaims peace,
He announces that all is well,
He proclaims salvation,
He says to Zion, "Your God [again] reigns!"

Your watchers have raised their voice,
They sing together joyously,

[5] Literally, the "uncircumcised."

For in their own eyes they see
That Yahve is returning to Zion.
O wasted places in Jerusalem,
Open your mouths and sing together,
For Yahve is comforting His people,
Yahve has redeemed Jerusalem.
Yahve has bared His holy arm in the sight of all the nations
And all the ends of the earth have seen the salvation
        [wrought by] our God. [52:7–10]

Now the exiles lagging behind in Babylonia are urged to leave:

Go out, go out, leave there,
Do not be in contact with the impure.
Come out of her, become pure,
O bearers of sacred vessels! [52:11] [6]

When the Hebrews had come out of Egypt, they had fled in haste (Exod. 12:33, 38). Now, however, their exodus will be different:

You will not come out in haste,
Nor go as if in flight,
For Yahve goes before you,
The God of Israel brings up the rear. [52:12] [7]

The poem continues with words of assurance to Jerusalem:

"For a brief moment I abandoned you,
But in great love I gather you.

In an outpouring of momentary anger, * *I hid My face from*
        you,
But with everlasting reliability I love you,"
Says Yahve, your redeemer. [54:7–8]

Just as Yahve swore in the days of Noah never again to destroy mankind in wrath (Gen. 8:21), He now swears never again to be angry with Israel:

"For the hills may move and the mountains shake,
But My reliability will never move from you,
Nor will My peaceful covenant be broken,"
Says Yahve Who loves you. [54:10]

A great rebuilding is to take place:

[6] The Temple implements had been carried off to Babylonia, according to Ezra 5:14. See II Kings 25:13ff. and Jer. 52:17ff. The sacred vessels would be needed for the Temple when it was rebuilt.
[7] Again, the Suffering Servant poem interrupts, 52:13–53:12.

*All your builders * will be taught by Yahve,*
*And your sons * will have great peace.* [54:13]

In Act One, the focus is on the meaning of Cyrus in Yahve's plan; in Act Two, it is on Israel. Act One declares that Yahve united humanity through Cyrus, and that Israel will teach mankind Yahve's way; Act Two asserts that the meaning to Israel of these events is that her past sins are pardoned. Jews will return to Palestine, led there by the Deity; a glorious new revelation of God will take place, and Israel will be so fully revived that even the recollection of the past disaster will fade.

The central theme of the two acts of the drama can be summarized briefly. The God of Israel is the only God; He is the universal God, Whose universal character is manifest in Cyrus, but taught, indeed explained, by Israel. Israel is not only a means in the working out of God's plan, but also an end.

This summary contains what might seem to western minds an inner contradiction. If God is universal, and if all peoples are the same to Him, it might seem illogical that a particular people should occupy a special place in His plan. But to the Hebrew mind there was no contradiction. The either-or choice is more characteristic of the west than of the east. An ability to maintain seemingly contradictory ideas side by side is also illustrated by the role of Palestine in Hebrew thought. When Jeremiah conceived of Yahve's connection with the people, rather than the land, he nevertheless looked forward to a return to the land. Second Isaiah goes far beyond Jeremiah in describing Yahve as universal and independent of a particular land, yet he moves directly from his assertion of Yahve's universal sway and the role of Israel as a people in it, to the glories that will attend Israel on its miraculous return to Palestine. Hebrew thought after Second Isaiah never completely lost either its conviction of God's universalism or its sense of the unique role assigned to the Jewish people and to Palestine. In subsequent ages a preoccupation with either universalism or particularism would dominate at different times. Nehemiah, for example, represents extreme particularism, and Jonah extreme universalism. To take another example, in the Greek period Jews spread throughout the Mediterranean world and deemed themselves fully at home where they were, but they continued to find some special role for Palestine.

Through following western logic, some interpreters have distorted Second Isaiah by exaggerating either his universalism or his particularism. A more prudent assessment would be that Second Isaiah excels all other prophets in his universalism, while at the same time particularism is not only present but central to his thinking; he is interested in all lands, but he must have Israel restored to Palestine.

The Suffering Servant poems (50:4–11 and 52:13–53:12) are two rather brief fragments preserved from a lost larger work. They are discussed here only because they are found in Second Isaiah and not because they bear any relationship to it in either time or content. We do not know where or when they were written.

The second of the two fragments, containing all of Chapter 53, served early Christianity as a series of predictions about Jesus. It is because of this chapter that Jesus is regarded as the "lamb led to slaughter." Despite its influence, however, the poem in its own right neither predicted nor anticipated Christianity. It has been suggested that the Suffering Servant may have been a character akin to those known from certain Syrian practices which apparently entered even into the Roman Saturnalia. The rites of the New Year, especially when observed in the spring, focused on the thought that a god was annually resurrected. The human king, who was the god's representative on earth, therefore needed an annual resurrection. Since it was not practical to kill him in order to have him resurrected, a substitute king was appointed for the week preceding the festival. The substitute was treated royally as to dress and food, but he was mocked and crowned with thorns, and then was put to death. The true king could then conveniently return to his throne "resurrected." Perhaps the Suffering Servant derives from such a background. In any case, the poems reflect a unique thought—that the death of the "servant" enables the total community to live. He bears their guilt; hence, they become guiltless. Such human "vicarious atonement" appears only here in Jewish literature and tradition; it is, of course, central to Christianity.

We encounter the Servant in the first fragment, speaking as though he were delivering a monologue in a play.

> *My Lord Yahve has given me an instructed tongue*
> *
> *To know how to speak a word with the weary.*
> *In the morning He awakens my ear to hear like stu-*
> *   dents . . .*[8]

> *I have not rebelled, I have not turned back.*
> *I have given my back to smiters*

[8] This verse implies the perfect obedience the next verse goes on to specify.

And my cheeks to be pulled.
I have not hidden my face from shame and spit.

My Lord Yahve will help me;
Therefore I do not feel abashed.
That is why I have made my face like flint,
And I have known that I shall not be put to shame.
He Who will justify me is near.
Would someone litigate with me?
Then let us stand together,
Let him who strives in judgment with me approach me.

If Lord Yahve helps me, who can convict me? [50:4–9A]

In this same fragment the Suffering Servant is next spoken of in the third person:

You who worship Yahve, hearken to the voice of His
      servant!
He walked in darkness,
He had no light.
He trusted in Yahve's name,
He relied on his God. [50:10]

A considerable gap seems to separate the first fragment from the second, for the servant is now dead:

Behold, Yahve's servant was [9] ----
He was lofty, raised up, exalted.
After the mob worked destruction on him
His face was marred from that of a man,
His form from that of a human.

But let the many nations be astonished [1] *at him!*
Let kings shut their mouths,
For they have seen a thing never told before,
They have witnessed something they never heard [before].
    [52:13–15]

The narrator pauses for an aside:

Who would believe this report of ours?
To whom was God's power revealed? [53:1]

[9] There is an error in the text. The word there is "wise" or "prosperous," but I have preferred to leave the doubtful word untranslated.
[1] This translation is a conjecture.

He continues with his eulogy:

> He grew up like a shoot before us,*
> Like a root come out of dry ground.
> He had no form and no beauty,
> His appearance was not pleasing to us.
> He was despised, deprived of human traits,
> A man of agonies, familiar with disease.
> And like one who hid his face from us,
> He was an object of scorn, and we gave him no considera-
>   tion. [53:2–3]

> The fact is, it was our diseases which he bore,
> And our agonies which he endured.
> We thought of him as one with a plague,
> Smitten, afflicted by God.
> He was wounded, for our transgressions,
> He was brought low, for our sins.
> The punishment [necessary] for our well being was on him.
> Out of the wound to him there came healing to us.

> All of us strayed like sheep,
> Each of us turned his own way.
> But Yahve put upon him the sin of all of us.
> He was tortured, he was oppressed, but he did not open his
>   mouth.
> He was brought to slaughter like a lamb,
> Like a ewe dumb before her shearers,
> Silent, he did not open his mouth.
> He was taken against right [2] and justice—
> What can one say of his fate?
> For he was cut off from the land of the living;
> The blow to him was that deserved by his people.
> They set his grave with the wicked.
> At his death, he was placed with evildoers,*
> Though he had done nothing wrong
> And there was no deception in his mouth.

> But Yahve had to crush him with illness [3] ----
> --
> Therefore I shall give him due honor in public [4]

[2] Another conjecture; the meaning of the Hebrew is unknown.
[3] The latter part of 53:10 and almost all of 11 are unintelligible. Only the last phrase of verse 11 is completely clear: "He bears their iniquities."
[4] Literally, "I divide [a portion] for him among the great."

He will take his place with the powerful.[5]
Inasmuch as he gave himself to death
And came to be counted with sinners.
Yet he bore the iniquity of the many,
For sinners he was an intercession. [52:4–53:12] [6]

No clue to any historical event exists in the poem, nor does the time of the composition of these touching lines disclose itself. The suggestion has been made, accordingly, that we deal with an artificial literary composition, perhaps akin to an Athenian drama. It need not follow, even if this is the case, that any direct influence by or derivation from Athens would be discernible. The theological idea contained in the poem found no acceptance in subsequent Judaism; the "Suffering Servant" is a stray poem, which in some unaccountable way came to be included in the Book of Isaiah. But its importance to Christianity as well as its unequalled pathos commands our attention.[7]

[5] Literally, ". . . he will divide spoil with the powerful." I am by no means sure of the sense of the Hebrew.
[6] The meaning is not clear. Some translate, "he made intercession," that is, he prayed. This seems to me unlikely. The poem seems to describe what the servant did, not what he said.
[7] Other passages in the Book of Isaiah, especially in 56–66, will be touched on below. The reader may consult the Index of Scriptural Citations.

CHAPTER

14

Exilic and Postexilic

PROPHECY

IN THE pre-exilic period, the covenant was thought to be between
Yahve and the collective people. When transgressions accumulated
over the generations and reached a point the Deity could no longer
tolerate, the people had broken the covenant. At that stage, doom was
inescapable. Such a fate had overtaken the northern kingdom in 721.
Yet once the evil fate had broken upon the southern kingdom in
597, Jeremiah declared that Yahve, who controls history, intended
the catastrophe only as a chastisement. A new covenant, destined
to endure, had replaced the old. Israel, even in exile, could continue to worship Yahve, for the primary connection was between
the Deity and His people wherever they were scattered, and not between the Deity and the land.

   To this principle Ezekiel added his contribution with his clear
expression of individualism. Yahve dealt with each man in accordance with his actions. Guilt, therefore, could not be collectively
cumulative, and the covenant, in its new form, could not be broken.
Ezekiel provided a justification, though not an exalted one, for
Yahve's continued relation with Israel: Yahve forgave Israel in order

to guard His reputation. This was an answer to the question of why a just God should have abstained from exterminating Israel as Israel might be thought to have deserved. Ezekiel, like Jeremiah, believed that Israel would be restored to Palestine.

Second Isaiah went further than Ezekiel in saying that Yahve forgave Israel, not for the sake of His reputation, but as an act of pure grace. Moreover, according to Second Isaiah, Yahve is in full control of history. Not only does He control events, but He has announced in advance what they will be. Cyrus is an agent of Yahve, who is unifying the world through conquest. Israel went into exile in order to serve as the vehicle through which the world, united by Cyrus, would come to recognize the rule of the one and sole God of the universe. Israel's task was to teach the way of Yahve to the world, and the exile was not so much a disaster as a step necessary in Yahve's plan for mankind. Israel was not destined to stay in Babylonia, but would return to its own. Jerusalem's "sin" had been atoned for. The one true God was going to manifest His sole sovereignty to all the nations by the restoration to Palestine of the exiles from Babylonia and the other lands. The great act of gathering the scattered Jews would impress the nations with Yahve's power as the only God. Exilic prophecy begins with a desperate note of hope barely heard in the night of great despair; yet it rises to a remarkable glow of confidence and assurance of divine favor and guidance.

In the postexilic period there was no king; priests ruled the restored community.

In the view of modern scholars, several layers of legislation are discernible in the Pentateuch, each layer representing a given age. The legislation found in Deuteronomy 12–26 is in some way associated with the Reformation of Josiah of 621; that is to say, it arose in the days of the monarchy. At least two layers of legislation, one in Exodus 20–4 and the other in Exodus 32–4, are deemed to be from even earlier periods in the monarchy. The greatest part of the legislation, however, is "priestly"; within the priestly legislation there are further layers, some of it seemingly from late exilic or early postexilic times and the bulk of it from a later postexilic age. There was, accordingly, a transition from legislation by the kings to legislation by the priests. Significantly, this priestly legislation was not limited to what we would today call "religious" matters, but encompassed every aspect of life. Perhaps the kingly legislation in pre-exilic times distinguished between the civil and the religious, though we cannot be certain. It is evident, however, that the priestly absorbed the kingly, and the demarcation, if any, between the civil and the religious disappeared in postexilic times.

Various terms for laws are found in the codes that come from monarchic times. The *hoq* ("statute") may represent a royal decree, its Hebrew meaning implying that it was "etched" on stone or clay. The *mishpat* ("judgment") may have originated as the decision in a law case; *mitzvah* ("commandment") seems a generic term without any indication of a precise origin. But even the early layers of Pentateuchal law were so relatively advanced that the terms had already lost their original sense and had come to be synonymous. The priestly writings added another word, *torah*, connoting not revelation but simply a law. Yet the emergence of the term in this sense is unquestionably a reflection of the transition from monarchic to priestly rule.

While there are indications that in the ancient Near East the king was conceived of as in some sense a representative of deity, this is not clearly the case in the Hebrew writings. If a king such as David were the divine representative on earth, it seems strange that two priests, Abiathar and Zadok, are brought into close relation with him, for he should not have needed them, or the prophets Gad and Nathan. Although the relation of king to priest in pre-exilic times is not clearly defined, it seems reasonable to conclude that the king was the ultimate source of civil law, and the priest the spokesman for religious law. (King and priest could, of course, co-operate, as in the case of the Reformation of Josiah.) But when the monarchy came to an end, legislation from the past remained to be administered by the priests, who also, as the spokesmen for and the surrogates of the Deity, promulgated new legislation. Priestly legislation was presumed to be not human but divine in origin. Indeed, this divine origin could be ascribed, in the period of Priestly ascendancy, even to the legislation from monarchic times which the priests were administering and thereby reaffirming. We call that state of affairs in which the rule and the power resides in priests a theocracy ("rule of God"). Since the priest is God's representative and the intermediary between Him and the people, God is the ultimate source of authority. We deal with a monarchy in pre-exilic times, with a theocracy in postexilic times.

The transition from a monarchy to a theocracy was accompanied by a change in the conception of the source of laws as emanating from man as the source to God as the source. It is a change from law as *mitzvah* to law as *Torah*. A divine origin was now ascribed even to the man-made laws of earlier times. The effect of the emergence of theocracy was to alter the conception and the scope of *Torah,* revelation. We do not know how early *mitzvah* and *Torah* came to be identified. The process started at least as early as the Reformation of Josiah in 621 and was completed in early postexilic times with the emergence of theocracy.

This identification rested on the assumption that all aspects of living were under God's watchful care. Whether the subject was religious ritual, the rules of real estate inheritance, or the distinction between theft and burglary, all legislation was *Torah,* the product of revelation. The Hebrew law was to be regarded as divine, not man-made. This was a natural development of the prophetic contention that man's social conduct is of concern to the Deity. The end result of the identification of *mitzvah* with *Torah* was that *Torah* was conceived of as encompassing every phase of man's existence. *Torah* was not limited to legislation; it came to be identified with *hochma* ("wisdom"). The inclusion in Scripture of Proverbs, Ecclesiastes, and Job is the end result of this second and complementary identification.

Pre-exilic prophecy, and indeed all the Hebrew literature composed or preserved in the postexilic period, was to share in being *Torah.* A pre-exilic prophet like Amos might have been uninterested in legislation, and concerned only or primarily with the ethics of conduct. The postexilic prophets, however, were concerned with fidelity to law as well as with ethics. Pre-exilic prophecy opposed priesthood and the Temple; postexilic prophecy was their stay and support, as we shall now see.

CHAPTER

15

HAGGAI AND FIRST ZECHARIAH

WE SAW an exhilarating picture in Second Isaiah of the impending restoration of the Jews to Palestine; in Haggai and Zechariah we read of the reality, and the exhilaration is mostly absent. Instead, we find reflections of poverty and want, and even indifference to the religious life. Haggai and Zechariah give us mere glimpses, not a consecutive or full account. There are some especially acute problems in interpreting Zechariah because we find hints and clues rather than direct statements. By way of introduction we shall mention four matters which are central in these two books.

First of all, the two prophets took the leadership in rebuilding the Temple, which the Babylonians had destroyed in 586. Since portions of the two prophets' messages are dated, we know that the period involved was 520–519. Zechariah's first message precedes the last two of Haggai by a month. Second, those who returned to Jerusalem were displeased that some Jews preferred to remain where they were. The former were apparently a small community. Their political status was fixed by the Persians; a descendant of David named Zerubbabel was the *peha*, "governor," and he shared the hegemony with a priest named Joshua. The third matter is not so clear. Apparently Zerubbabel led an abortive rebellion in an effort to change his governorship under the Persians into independent kingship. His downfall caused a radical change in the way in which he was portrayed: he is a hero in Haggai and in parts of Zechariah, but elsewhere in Zechariah he is regarded less favorably, or else the references to him have been edited or suppressed. We shall not see him distinctly.

Fourth, the failure of Zerubbabel did not obliterate the hopes, as expressed in Ezekiel, of a restored monarchy under a descendant of David. The immediate hope changed to a remote expectation; it became an idealized vision of what would happen when a Davidic king ultimately came to the throne. Peace would be universal. God's sway would be so completely recognized by all the world that proselytes in great number would be attracted to Judaism. The concept of the "Messiah" and messianic days is of great importance in the development of the religion.

The literary merits of the books of Haggai and Zechariah are less than their religious and historical significance, and this is especially true in the case of Haggai, a summary of whose brief book follows.

The five "messages" in Haggai can be dated fairly certainly; the first (1:1–12, 14) comes in August or September of 520. The new Persian king, who has succeeded Cyrus, is Darius, and the Jewish community has returned in some numbers from Babylonia. The passage reflects a totally different attitude toward ritual from that of the pre-exilic prophets. Although the pre-exilic prophets were indifferent or opposed to ritual (we saw Jeremiah's conviction that the Temple was of no great importance), Haggai takes the lead in urging the populace to rebuild the Temple. Prosperity, he says, is being delayed by the Deity until the rebuilding is accomplished. Haggai tells us about two leaders, Zerubbabel the *peha* and Joshua ben Yehozadak the "high priest." This is the first mention in prophetic literature of the office of high priest. These two men will be discussed later in the chapter when we deal with Zechariah.

The second message (1:15, 13 and 2:15–19), twenty-three days later, repeats the contention that poverty is caused by neglecting the Temple; when it is rebuilt, prosperity will ensue.

The third message (2:1–9), delivered in October, contains an admission that the new Temple seems unlikely to rival the old; but the Deity, Who owns all the wealth in the world, gives assurance that the new one will be even more splendid than the old. Two months later, in a fourth message, Haggai objects to the participation by people who are ritually unclean in the construction of the New Temple (2:*10–14*). On the same day, Haggai is bidden to speak to Zerubbabel. It is the Deity's intention to destroy the kingdoms of the earth and to make Zerubbabel His "signet," [1] that is, His representative.

The first message of Zechariah [2] (*1:1–6*) comes a month before the last two messages of Haggai. It is a rebuke to the restored community for not repenting. The date of Zechariah's second message (*1:8–17*) is February, 519. In a nocturnal vision, Zechariah sees a man riding on a red horse, and behind him are horses of various hues; he is told by an angel [3] of the Lord that there is ease and quiet among the nations. The likely meaning is that certain disorders in the Persian empire have been quelled and that therefore the moment is not propitious for a local rebellion. Nevertheless it is predicted that God's house, the Temple, will be rebuilt. In the second vision (*2:1–4* Heb., *1:18–21* Eng.) Zechariah sees four horns and four artisans. The horns are the world powers who had scattered Judah—perhaps Assyria, Babylonia, the Medes, and Persia. The artisans are the agents—are they human or divine?—who will overthrow the four "horns." Next (*2:5–9* Heb., *2:1–5* Eng.) Zechariah sees a man with a measuring line, a symbol that Jerusalem will be so populous that no city walls can confine it.

The visions are interrupted by three random messages. One of these appeals to the Jews still in Babylonia to return (*2:10–11* Heb., *2:6–7* Eng.). The second declares that the nations who had despoiled Judah would become its booty (*2:12–13* Heb., *2:8–9* Eng.). The third message, which is more significant, tells that Yahve is coming to dwell in the midst of Zion. Moreover it promises explicitly—and here a new note is struck in prophetic thought—that many nations will join themselves to Yahve through conversion. We saw this idea intimated in Second Isaiah. The motif is repeated here only briefly (*2:14–17* Heb., *2:10–13* Eng.); we shall see presently how it comes to be expanded.

The next vision (*3:1–10*) also discloses something new in prophetic thought. Joshua, the high priest, and the angel of the first

[1] See Gen. 41:42; Esther 3:10; and Jeremiah 22:24 for the ring or the seal as symbolic of the transfer of authority.
[2] It is customary to speak of 1–8 as First Zechariah and of the remainder, 9–14, as Second Zechariah.
[3] For the first time in prophetic literature we meet an angel; previously, the revelation of the Deity to prophets was direct.

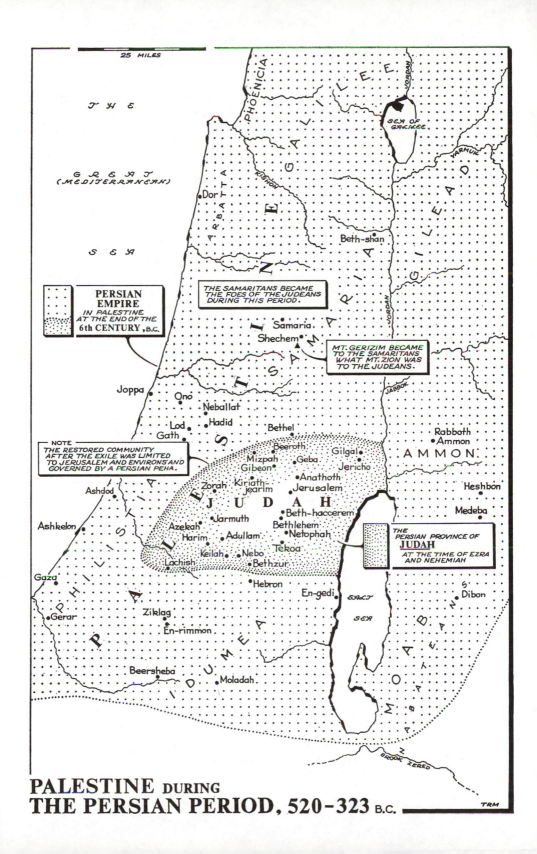

25 MILES

THE

GREAT
(MEDITERRANEAN)

SEA

PHOENICIA

GALILEE

JORDAN

SEA OF
GALILEE

YARMUK

GILEAD

Dor

Beth-shan

ARBATTA

KISHON

SAMARIA

THE SAMARITANS BECAME
THE FOES OF THE JUDEANS
DURING THIS PERIOD.

PERSIAN
EMPIRE
IN PALESTINE
AT THE END OF THE
6th CENTURY, B.C.

Samaria
Shechem

MT. GERIZIM BECAME
TO THE SAMARITANS
WHAT MT. ZION WAS
TO THE JUDEANS.

JORDAN

JABBOK

Joppa

Ono

Neballat

Hadid

Bethel

Rabboth
Ammon

Lod
Gath

Beeroth

Gilgal

AMMON

NOTE
THE RESTORED COMMUNITY
AFTER THE EXILE WAS LIMITED
TO JERUSALEM AND ENVIRONS AND
GOVERNED BY A PERSIAN PEHA.

Mizpah
Gibeon

Geba

Jericho

Heshbon

PHILISTIA

Zorah

Kiriath-
jearim

Anathoth
Jerusalem

Ashdod

J U D A H

Medeba

Ashkelon

Azekah

Harim

Jarmuth

Adullam

Beth-haccerem

Bethlehem
Netophah

THE
PERSIAN PROVINCE OF
JUDAH
AT THE TIME OF EZRA
AND NEHEMIAH

Keilah

Lachish

Nebo
Bethzur

Tekoa

Gaza

Hebron

En-gedi

SALT
SEA

Dibon

Gerar

Ziklag

En-rimmon

I D U M E A

MOAB

NABATANS

Beersheba

Moladah

BROOK ZERED

PALESTINE DURING
THE PERSIAN PERIOD, 520–323 B.C.

TRM

vision are confronted by Satan.[4] This vision is symbolic of the fear that the priesthood may have been disqualified, through some impurity, from serving in the Temple. Joshua dons new clothes and is put in charge of the Temple. He is then told that "The Sprout"— we infer that this means a descendant of David—is to emerge.

The vision in Chapter 4 raises a problem that is best handled by assuming that verses 6B–10A are an insertion which we can consider later. The angel (4:1–6A, 10B–14) shows Zechariah a candlestick with seven "lamps," and on its sides, two olive trees. The seven lamps, at the end of seven branches, are the eyes of Yahve, scrutinizing the world. The olive trees are the two "sons of oil," or the anointed ones, who are to share the reign—Joshua, the religious leader, and Zerubbabel, the political leader. The joint leadership needs to be emphasized here, for later we shall see that ideas on this subject changed.

The insertion itself represents, in all likelihood, two different parts, the second of which (4:7–10A) is an assertion that despite mountains (that is, obstacles), Zerubbabel will succeed in completing the Temple. The first part is the well-known verse (4:6): This is the word of Yahve to Zerubbabel, "Not by power, nor by might, but by My spirit . . ." What can this verse mean? Can it be anything other than a rebuke to Zerubbabel for resorting to military power? We shall return to this question later.

Two visions are found in Chapter 5. In the first (5:1–4), Zechariah sees a flying scroll, full of curses, which is able to enter the house of a thief or one who swears falsely, and there to work its dire effects on the house. The second (5:5–11) shows a woman in a large container, known as an *ephah*. The *ephah*, symbol of wickedness, is borne toward Shinar, probably a cryptic name for Babylonia. That is, wickedness dwells in Babylonia, as righteousness dwells in Jerusalem.

In the next vision (6:1–8, 15) four chariots emerge from between two bronze mountains and head in the four directions. This vision seems to mean that the chariot going northward to Babylonia will stir Jews there to come complete the building of the Temple. Im-

---

[4] This is the earliest mention of Satan in the Tanak. His function here seems to be to accuse Joshua of not being ritually proper. Satan is found also in the prologue to Job, where he is again an accuser, charging Job with being pious only because he has been prosperous, but there Satan has the additional function of testing Job. In even later passages, such as I Chron. 21, Satan is the title of some being who causes evil. We see this from the circumstance that the passage in Chronicles recasts II Sam. 24; in the latter, Yahve provokes David to sin, but in I Chron. 21 the provocation comes from Satan. For further data, one should consult an encyclopedia under "Satan" or "Devil."

bedded in this vision is a message (6:*9–14*) in which Zechariah is told to make crowns (note the plural) and set *them* on the head of Joshua. Zechariah is to say (6:*12*): "Here is a man, Sprout is his name. . . ." The rest of the verse is corrupt. This man, whose name is not mentioned, is (6:*13*) "to build the Temple and sit on the throne." The verse then becomes difficult, not to translate but to interpret: "He shall be a priest on his throne and the counsel of peace shall be between them." Why is there the variation from singular to plural, and why should one man be regarded in part of the text as both the king and the high priest? The explanation is, in all likelihood, that the text originally spoke of two crowns, one for Zerubbabel and one for Joshua. It was apparently expected that Zerubbabel, a descendant of David,[5] would cease to be merely the *peha* (governor) and would become the king. We saw that the Book of Haggai ended with the statement that Zerubbabel would be God's signet ring; in Zech. 4 we saw Zerubbabel anointed and also rebuked. In the present chapter, the material about him appears to be partly suppressed. It is principally on the basis of this passage that Zerubbabel is assumed to have led a movement that tried by the use of military power to reconstitute the Jewish monarchy. The movement failed. In the postexilic period there is no Jewish king; the high priest is the ruler. The phrase, "not by power, nor by might" (4:6), is a rebuke to Zerubbabel for his failure, ascribed by the prophet to the wrong methods, for he should have acted by "Yahve's spirit."

There is another passage possibly related to the crushed hopes centered in Zerubbabel. In Isaiah 11:*10* we find the expectation that a "shoot from the stock of Jesse," David's father, will arise to become an ideal king. So perfect will society be that the wolf and the lamb will dwell together:

> *No one will do evil or destroy in all My sacred mountain.*
>   [Isaiah 11:9]

The anticipation of a restored monarchy would indicate a time when no monarchy existed. The last king of Judah, Jehoiachin, was taken into Babylonia after 586 and survived there at least until 549. Isaiah 11, usually regarded as a late addition to the Book of Isaiah, may possibly come from the period just before Zerubbabel, or possibly from the period just after him. The idealization of the king into the monarch of a perfect regime reflected a distant hope, not an immediate expectation. Indeed, the more the expectation was idealized, the more it needed to be allocated to the remote future.

[5] See I Chron. 3:*17*.

It was conceived less as a genuine future and more as something eschatological.

The ceremony that proclaimed a king involved anointing the person with oil. An anointed person was a *Mashiah*, "messiah." The word itself has no connotation of the remote future; it gained such a connotation when it became an expression of hopes and desires. Once the Messiah, who was to be David's descendant, was conceived of eschatologically, some connection arose between him and the awaited Day of Yahve.[6] The eschatological picture therefore combines disparate elements—on the one hand, Yahve bringing final judgment to the world through Israel's conquest over the foreign nations, and on the other, universal peace under a perfect king.

An inquiry is made of Zechariah in 7:1–8:23 whether a fast day, apparently instituted during the exile, is to continue to be observed. Zechariah replies that Yahve desires ethical conduct rather than ritual; he therefore eliminates this fast day and three others. When people behave as Yahve wants them to, the fasts can be turned to days of joy, and other nations will follow Israel:

> Thus says Yahve of hosts: "It will be yet that peoples, inhabitants of many cities will come—[indeed] they will go one to another and say, 'Let us go to worship Yahve; we too are [among those] going.' Many peoples and mighty nations will come to seek Yahve of Hosts in Jerusalem, to worship Yahve. . . . In those days ten men of all the nations of different languages shall take hold of the garment of a Jew, saying, 'Let us go with you, for we have heard that God is with you.'" [8:20–3]

We find in Isaiah 2:2–4 a similar passage that also occurs in Micah 4:1–3:

> *In the end of days the mount of Yahve's Temple will be*
>   *firmly above all hills*
> *And higher than the hills.*
> *Nations will stream to it.*
> *Many nations will go, saying,*
> *"Come, let us ascend Yahve's mount to the Temple of*
>   *Jacob's God*
> *And let Him teach us of His ways*
> *And we shall walk in His paths."*
> *For it is from Zion that revelation goes out,*
> *And from Jerusalem that Yahve's word [comes.]*

[6] See pages 109–110.

> *He shall judge between the nations and rebuke many*
>   *people.*
> *They will beat their swords into plows*
> *And their spears into pruning hooks.*
> *No nation will raise the sword against another,*
> *And they will no longer resort to war.*

To this Micah 4:4 adds:

> *Every man will sit under his vineyard and his date tree,*
> *There will be no one who causes fighting,*
> *For Yahve's mouth has spoken.*

Zechariah, then, envisages proselytes to Judaism on a broad scale. A clear reference to them is found in a late passage in Isaiah:

> *Let not an alien, a proselyte to Yahve say,*
> *"Yahve has set me distinctly apart from His people. . . ."*
>
> *The aliens, proselytes to Yahve to serve Him,*
> *To love His name, and to be His servants, [and]*
> *All those who prefer to keep the Sabbath rather than to pro-*
>   *fane it,*
> *And those who hold fast to My covenant—*
> *These I shall bring to My sacred mount,*
> *And give them joy in My house of prayer,*
> *Their offerings and sacrifices will be acceptable on My al-*
>   *tar,*
> *For My Temple will be called a House of Prayer for all na-*
>   *tions.* [Isaiah 56:3A, 6–7]

We do not know whether those proselytes were people who acted completely on their own initiative, or whether they were converted by a missionary movement in the time of Zerubbabel. But when Yahve was finally thought of as the universal Deity, it followed that people of all kinds could seek Him out and join themselves to His people.

Everyone did not share the view found in Ezekiel 44:2 that Yahve was to take up His permanent residency within the Temple. The first words of Isaiah 66 are:

> *Thus says Yahve*
> *"The heavens are My throne,*
> *And the earth is My footstool.*
> *What sort of house can you build for Me,*
> *And what sort of place for Me to rest?"*

For some, the Temple [7] was the place of Yahve's dwelling. For others, probably including Zechariah, it was His special place, His special symbol, but He dwelled in heaven.

The climax of First Zechariah is the prediction of a great wave of converts to Judaism. Whatever may have been the vicissitudes caused by Zerubbabel, Haggai and Zechariah terminate in the great optimism of Judaism as a universal religion, about to be adopted widely or even universally.

The importance of the two prophets, as we have said, lies in the information they provide about the early postexilic period, even if this information consists of mere glimpses. The obscurity of Zerubbabel's role is an example. Moreover, Ezra 3:1–4:5, and 4:24–6:22 contain a consecutive account that mentions Haggai and Zechariah by name. The subject of most of the narrative in Ezra goes unnoticed in the two prophets, namely the hostility between the newly returned community in Jerusalem and the northerners who did not go into exile. These latter are called the Samaritans.[8] Between them and the Jews great hostility persisted through at least seven centuries.

The final universalism of Zechariah 8:20–3 is in startling contrast to the anti-Samaritan feeling. When religious animosities exist, the nearness of a hatred group tends to increase, not diminish, the conflict. We do not know what Zechariah thought of Samaritans eager to become proselytes. Indeed, we know far less about the postexilic period than we know about the exilic and pre-exilic periods.

[7] See page 27.
[8] Perhaps the Book of Ezra is in error in ascribing the Samaritan schism to these early postexilic days, for otherwise we should expect some allusion to it in Haggai and Zechariah.

CHAPTER

16

Between

ZECHARIAH AND
EZRA

THE PROPHETS Haggai and Zechariah do not tell of the completion
of the new Temple. From their writings we know only that it was
begun. The completion and the dedication (516) are spoken of in the
Book of Ezra, 6:6–18. Neither is any mention made in Haggai and
Zechariah of the rebuilding of the city of Jerusalem. However, the
tone of Zechariah, especially Chapter 7 with its great optimism about
the growth and the expansion of the population, would lead one to
suppose that there was a constant improvement in the situation in
Jerusalem. Yet some decades later, Nehemiah, a Jewish official at
Shushan (Susa), the capital of Persia, reported that a certain Hanani
had brought him the report that the inhabitants of Jerusalem were in
"great difficulty and disgrace; the wall of Jerusalem is breached, and
its gates have been destroyed by fire" (Nehemiah 1:3).

Did Jerusalem come to some stage of security immediately after

516? If so, what could have happened between the optimism of 516 and the despair of the later time? Since no consecutive account of events for the postexilic period appears in Scripture, we do not know the answers. It is a curious state of affairs that for the pre-exilic and exilic periods we have the Books of Samuel and Kings and Chronicles; but for the later period of Jewish history—indeed for the Jewish people's most formative period—there is no such account. Why not? Possibly because whatever was written somehow failed to survive, or possibly because no account was written, owing to the absence, in the postexilic period, of a monarchy and a dynasty to provide the frame of reference so essential to a consecutive account. Our lack of historical information for the postexilic period is underscored by a major archaeological discovery made in 1907–8—that of the Elephantine Papyri. These are a large number of Aramaic documents (primarily letters) from Elephantine in Egypt, written in the early postexilic period by a colony of Jewish soldiers in the employ of the Persian government. Nothing in the Tanak would have led us to suspect that such a colony existed.

Since we are in the dark about the postexilic period, it is almost impossible to set the prophecies of the period in any clear historical perspective. Yet we should take our cue from the curious circumstance that in the days of Nehemiah, Jerusalem presented a picture of forlorn destruction, the effect of some event subsequent to the days of Zechariah.

On the supposition that Jerusalem was sacked and the Temple destroyed sometime between 516 and 450, certain passages usually taken to allude to the destruction by the Babylonians in 586 probably allude to the later disaster. Thus, for example, the Book of Lamentations, which deals with a terrible destruction, has traditionally been placed shortly after the disaster of 586. Indeed, the opinion was held many, many centuries ago that Jeremiah himself had written Lamentations; in the Christian Bible Lamentations is to be found immediately next to Jeremiah. The view offered here is not only that Lamentations is not by Jeremiah, but also that it deals with some postexilic destruction, and not with that of 586.

We shall see that Malachi and Obadiah have some sharp things to say against the Edomites, who are accused of taking the lead in bringing some disaster to Jerusalem, and of rejoicing at the misfortune. There is evidence to show that such actions by the Edomites cannot fit in with the disaster of 586. Jeremiah 27:2–22 shows that the Edomites were conquered by the Babylonians, in about 586, just as Judea was. Jeremiah 40:11–12 depicts Edom as one of the hospitable countries to which Jews fled in 586. On this basis, we might conclude that Edom's hostility, which awakened that of the Jews, must be allocated to some other time.

One passage more than any other fixed the erroneous connection between 586 and Edom in the minds of interpreters. This is the famous Psalm 137, the first six verses of which depict the gloom of the exiles in Babylonia, where they hung their "harps on willow trees." The next three verses read:

> *Remember, O Yahve, the day of Jerusalem against the*
> *Edomites*
> *Who said, "Raze it, raze it, to its very foundations!"*
> *O offspring of destructive Babylon, happy is he who repays*
> *you for what you have done to us,*
> *Happy is he who takes hold of your infants and crushes*
> *them on the rock!* [1] [Psalm 137:7–9]

Only in the late middle ages was the Tanak divided into chapters. The fact that our present Bible gives us Psalm 137 as a single chapter in the one hundred and fifty chapters of the Book of Psalms must not mislead us into regarding Psalm 137 as a unit; it consists, rather, of fragments from two distinct works. The first verses are a product of the Babylonian exile, while the last three verses are from a later time.

A series of passages from Psalms and from the prophetic writings round out the evidence for the theory that there was probably a destruction later than that inflicted by the Babylonians. A passage in Isaiah 63–4, for example, strengthens this conclusion, for it laments a destruction the Deity permitted:

> *Look from heaven, from Your holy and glorious dwelling,*
> *and see!*
> *Where is Your zeal and strength, Your supply of mercy?*
> *Do not withhold * Your solicitude!* [Isaiah 63:15]
> *For a brief interval Your holy people held possession;*
> *Our foes have trampled down Your sanctuary*
> *We have been [Yours] from eternity!*
> *Them You did not rule, nor was Your name put on them.*
> *Would that You would tear the heavens and descend! . . .*
>   [Isaiah 63:18–19A Heb., 63:18–64:1A Eng.]
> *For You have hidden Your eyes from us,*
> *And crushed us because of our sins.*
> *Yet, O Yahve, You are our father;*
> *We are the clay, and You the one Who fashioned us,*

---

[1] This word is a pun. The Hebrew for rock, *sela'*, is the name of Edom's capital. The city is known in Greek as Petra which also means "rock."

And all of us are the work of Your hands.
Do not be limitlessly angry, O Yahve,
And do not recollect [our] sins forever.
But, see, that we are Your people.

Your holy cities have become a wilderness.
Zion has become a wilderness, Jerusalem a waste place.
Our Temple, our pride,
Where our fathers praised You,
Was consigned to a burning fire.
The place in which we delighted became a shambles.
             [Isaiah 64:6B–10 Heb., 64:7B–11 Eng.]

Even more explicitly, Psalm 79 laments:

Nations have entered Your inheritance,
They have desecrated Your holy Temple,
They made Jerusalem heaps of rubble . . .
They spilled blood like water around Jerusalem,
There was no burier.
We became despised by our neighbors,
Scorned and taunted by all around us . . .
Pour Your wrath on the nations who do not know You,
And on the kings who have not worshiped You,
For they consumed Jacob, and destroyed his dwelling place.
             [Psalm 79:1, 3–4, 6–7]

Psalm 83 specifically describes the league of surrounding nations that joined together to assault Jerusalem.[2] Like Isaiah 63–4, it laments that the Deity impassively has permitted the destruction. Psalm 74 tells of the destruction in detail:

They put Your temple to the flames,
They profaned to the ground the sanctuary named for You.
             [Psalm 74:7]

Psalm 44 is a prayer to the Deity to waken and succor His people who despite hardships remain faithful to Him:

You made us like sheep to be eaten
And scattered us among the nations. [Psalm 44:12 Heb., 11
             Eng.]

The destructive siege would appear to have been carried out by some seven nations, chief among whom was Edom. Postexilic litera-

---

[2] "Assyria" in Ps. 83:9 is to be regarded as Persia.

ture reflects a responsive hatred of the despoilers, concentrated in an animosity towards Edom.[3] The hopes expressed in Zech. 8 that nations would be converted to Judaism were transformed by the cruel event into vindictiveness and exclusiveness.

Can the conjectured event be dated? A bare and laconic verse in Ezra 4, a chapter that reviews the relations of Jews and Persians, is perhaps the clue:

> In the reign of Xerxes [of Persia], in the beginning
> of his reign, they penned a hostile letter
> against Judea and Jerusalem. [Ezra 4:6]

In what precedes and follows the brief review in Ezra 4 of relations with the Persian overlords there is nothing that might be connected with the ordeal undergone by Jerusalem. The verse itself is far from clear. "Penned a hostility" is a literal rendering of the words. We do not know who did the writing nor what the nature of the penned hostility was. The only clear portion of the verse is the date given, the beginning of the reign of Xerxes. Since Xerxes' dates are 485–465, the beginning is 485.

In ensuing chapters when I refer to the events of 485, I shall mean a destruction of Jerusalem and its Temple by an alliance of surrounding nations, led by Edom. In no sense can the destruction of 485 be regarded as unshakably proven, but without such a hypothesis, there is much in the postexilic literature that we cannot account for. It is a reasonable hypothesis, and I am persuaded that it is correct. Nevertheless, the reader must be sure to remember that it is a hypothesis and not a fact.

---

[3] The passage interpolated in Amos 1:*11–12*, would come from this same period; so too would Ezekiel 35.

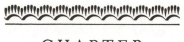

CHAPTER

17

Other Postexilic

PROPHETS

MALACHI

THE AUTHOR of the Book of Malachi must be regarded as anonymous. We do not know when in the early postexilic period the book was written. Malachi is not a proper name, but a word meaning "my messenger." The opening section (1 : 2–5) asks if the Deity loves Israel. It is affirmed that He does, and the proof given is the disasters that have overtaken the Edomites. Genesis relates that Jacob, one of Israel's forefathers, and Esau, the forefather of Edom, were brothers; hence the two nations are brothers. God, the text asserts, has hated Edom [1] and loved Israel, and His ability to destroy the Edomites

---

[1] The history of Edom, and its geographical location in the Biblical period, present some puzzles. Perhaps in the earliest age the Edomites lived in southern Judea or the Negeb, and then pushed southward, establishing themselves in the vicinity of Sela, known in Greek as Petra. They were apparently pushed northward by an Arab people known as the Nabataeans; in the 5th pre-Christian century, the Nabataeans came out of the wilderness to become a power of some significance. A Greek historian, Diodorus Siculus, *Hist.* XIX, 94ff., is our source of knowledge that the Nabataeans had occupied Petra by the year 312. In early post-Biblical

is convincing proof that His power extends beyond the borders of Judah.

The second section (1:6–2:9) laments that while Yahve's name is great among the nations, His own priests in Jerusalem dishonor Him by carelessness and indifference toward their ritual obligations. Though they are descended from Levi, a son of Jacob, they do not maintain the high standard of their ancestor with whom Yahve made the covenant of priesthood.

In a third section (2:10–16) three charges are brought. The first is that treachery exists among the people. This is a shameful thing, for if they regard God as their father, are they not all brothers? "Have we not one Father? Has not one God created us?" (2:10A). Second, intermarriage with Gentiles is occurring, and this is displeasing to the Deity.[2] Third, divorce is taking place, in violation of the covenant between groom and bride to which Yahve was a witness. The text does not state whether the objection is only to unjustified divorce or to divorce in general.

In the succeeding section (2:17–3:12) it is promised that God will punish and thereby purify those guilty of such transgressions, as well as those guilty of social injustices. At that time He will suddenly come into the Temple, though not until He has sent "My messenger" (*Malachi*) to prepare the way. The offerings of the people will then be acceptable, just as they were in earlier days. Purification, not destruction, will take place, for "I am God; I do not change; therefore you, O sons of Jacob, are not consumed" (3:6). Similarly (3:13–18) God will punish, though not destroy, those who consider it vain to serve Him and to heed His requirements. Those who remain recalcitrant are wicked, and must be distinguished from the righteous. On a coming day (that is, the Day of Yahve) the wicked will be burnt up in fire, like stubble. For the righteous, however, the sun will bring healing on its wings[3] (3:19–20 Heb., 4:1–2 Eng.).

To the foregoing, a later hand added an appendix, which identifies the "messenger" who will precede the sudden appearance of God as Elijah. It will be recalled that Elijah, instead of dying, went up to heaven in a chariot in a storm (II Kings 2:11). He was therefore

---

times the Edomites who pushed northward but still south of Judea were known in Greek as Idumeans. King Herod (reigned 37–34 B.C.) was of Idumean extraction. The Idumeans had been forcibly converted to Judaism.

[2] Intermarriage appears to have been tolerated in the pre-exilic period, but discountenanced after 485. This late disapproval was then attributed to the age of the patriarchs, even though presumably there were no Jews at that time extant for intramarriage. See Gen. 24:3 and 26:46. The Book of Ruth implies that intermarriage is not necessarily evil.

[3] The winged sun is found on many monuments from Egypt, Assyria, and Persia.

assumed to be still alive. The Book of Malachi caused Elijah to become the forerunner of the Messiah in both Jewish and Christian tradition. In the Christian view, Jesus was the long-awaited Messiah. John the Baptist was identified with Elijah as the appropriate forerunner of Jesus.

In Malachi equal attention is given to ritual and ethical transgressions. Postexilic prophecy did not neglect the ethical; rather, it blended it with the ritual.

OBADIAH

Nothing is known of Obadiah the man, and only an approximate date can be inferred from the text. Like Malachi, Obadiah contains a denunciation of Edom, but while Malachi seems to regard its destruction as an event already in the past, Obadiah seems to look forward to the destruction of Edom. Accordingly, Obadiah can be dated before Malachi. Obadiah has the distinction, if it is indeed a distinction, of being the shortest book in the Tanak. When the books of the Bible were arranged into chapters in the Middle Ages, Obadiah emerged as too short for subdivision; it is therefore only one chapter. In content, however, it falls into at least two sections, which probably represent two different authors.

The first section, *1–15*, is concerned with Edom.[4] An emissary appears to be travelling among the nations, summoning them to join in an attack on Edom. The Edomites, who dwell in a rocky, craggy region (we have mentioned above, p. 209, that their capital, *Sela'*, means rock) are sure that they are out of reach just as is an eagle's nest. But a concert of nations, once united in a pact with Edom, will lay siege to her. Their motive is not simply to recover what Edom has stolen from them, but to plunder Edom completely. Even the proverbially wise men of Edom are to perish. This united action is the result of God's plan and desire, a divine repayment for Edom's joining with other nations in a siege of Jerusalem. This Edom should not have done, for Jacob (the Patriarch) was the brother of Esau, Edom's patriarchal ancestor; the Edomites should have regarded the Jews as their brothers and not acted as viciously and as pitilessly as the other foreign nations.[5] A large part of this material also appears in Jeremiah 49:*7–16*, sometimes in identical verses. At one time scholars argued that Obadiah was quoting Jeremiah, but it is more often concluded now that the passage is largely secondary in Jeremiah, and that the two versions are chance duplicates of each other.

[4] It is likely that *15A* should follow *15B*, and be grouped with the second section.
[5] The events alluded to are those of 485; see above, pp. 208–209.

The second section, *17–21*, is still another Day of Yahve passage. The nations of the world have come to the sacred mountain, Zion, to "drink" where formerly the Jews drank; that is, the nations have come to seize Zion. Yet a sacred remnant of Jews will arise on Mount Zion and, saved from Edom's onslaught, will besiege, conquer, and rule Edom,[6] but the kingship will in reality be God's.

The Book of Obadiah is a curiosity, a period piece. It might have had the fate of being incorporated in the Book of Isaiah; in that event it would have lacked the attention it has attracted as a separate and distinct book in the Tanak. It has neither literary nor religious importance; its sole significance, and that a limited one, is the pale light it throws on Edom.

J O E L

Although we know nothing about Joel the man, we can perhaps glean from the contents of his book some vague and general information about his times. Scholars debate whether the entire book is from one hand; at least one scholar maintains that it is a rather old pre-exilic book, rewritten in postexilic times. There is, however, nothing of great importance at stake in these questions of authorship, and the student can start by accepting the book as a unit.[7]

The first section, *1:2–12*, describes an unusually severe plague of locusts. These locusts are called a "nation" in *1:6*, and some commentators have felt (mistakenly in my judgment) that the locusts are a cryptic or allegorical allusion to some foreign nation. In any case, the author has fashioned a colorful and impressive poem out of the unpromising material of a locust plague.

In the second section,[8] *1:13–20*, the priests are told to proclaim a fast, as a petition for the end of a famine that has spread over the land. The poetry is of a high order, especially in the following prayer:

> *To You, O Yahve, I call out,*
> *For heat has devoured the pastures of the wilderness*
> *And flame has burned up all the trees of the field.*
> *Even the wild beasts bring their longing to You,*
> *For the watercourses have dried up,*
> *For heat has devoured the pastures of the wilderness.*
> [*1:19–20*]

---

[6] An even later hand in verses *19–20* extends the conquest to include virtually all the territory that was once part of David's possessions.

[7] The chapter division is different in the Hebrew and the English versions. Heb. 3:1–5 are 2:28–32; and Heb. 4:1–21 are 3:1–21, respectively, in the English

[8] Omit verse *15*; it is an interpolation.

In the third section, 2:1–14, there are three interpolated portions (1B, 2A, and 11B), which reflect a copyist's desire to transform the section into a Day of Yahve message. But these portions so clearly break the sense and the rhythm in the Hebrew that they are easy to recognize as additions. When they are removed, the section has a close unity. A plague of locusts is described as if it were an invasion of horsemen and chariots. In the previous section, the plague was described as having already come; in this section, it is expected in the near future, or else is already at hand. The people are addressed by the Deity:

> *Turn to Me with all your hearts,*
> *With fast, and weeping, and mourning.*
> *Tear your hearts, and not your clothes.*[9]
> *Return to Yahve your God*
> *For He is gracious and merciful,*
> *Slow to anger and fully reliable*
> *And disinclined to impose evil.*
> *Perhaps He will turn and relent,*
> *And leave unconsumed, as a blessing,*
> *[Sufficient] for a meal and drink offering unto Him.* [2:12–
> *14*]

There follows (2:15–17) a staccato proclamation for an assembly and a fast. All the populace, including suckling child and new bride, are to attend the gathering in the Temple. The substance of their prayer is to be that if Yahve does not save His people, the heathen nations will mock Him, using Israel as a byword for an abandoned people. There is a favorable divine response (2:18–27). Yahve promises corn, wine, and oil; the locusts (conceived of as a "northern army") are to be driven out. The land is to rejoice, and hearts are to cease to fear, for the pasture lands have become grassy again; fruit trees bear their yield. Moreover, an even greater plenty will come:

> *You shall eat, and be sated*
> *And praise the name of Yahve your God.* [2:26A]

All this good is to be exceeded by still another blessing:

> *Afterwards, I will pour My spirit on all flesh;*
> *Your sons and daughters will prophesy,*
> *Your old men will dream dreams,*
> *Your young men will see visions.*
> *Even on slaves, men and women, will I pour My spirit.*
> [3:1–2 Heb., 2:28–9 Eng.]

[9] The tearing of one's clothes still today represents a sign of mourning.

This latter blessing is the final prelude to the arrival of the Day of Yahve (3:3–5 Heb., 2:30–2 Eng.). Heavenly portents of blood, fire, and smoke will usher it in; the sun will be darkened and the moon will be the color of blood. A general destruction is to take place; escape will be available only for

> . . . *Those who call in Yahve's name,*
> *For on Mount Zion and in Jerusalem there will be a de-*
> *livered group.* . . . [3:5 Heb., 2:32 Eng.]

At that time, when the fortunes of Judah and Jerusalem will have changed,[1] Yahve will gather all the nations of the world into the valley of Jehoshaphat.[2] He will execute judgment on them for scattering the Judeans, that is, the Jews, among the nations and dividing the land by lot, for turning boys into male harlots and girls into drunks. More specifically, the two Phoenician cities, Tyre and Sidon,[3] are denounced for pillage and for selling Judeans to the Greeks. In retaliation Yahve will cause the Tyrians to be sold to the distant Sabaeans, a people of southwest Arabia (4:1–8 Heb., 3:1–8 Eng.) The section about Tyre and Sidon is probably an interpolation, for it is in prose, not poetry, and it interrupts the statement of what is to happen in the universal judgment.

The nations are urged to gird themselves for war. The well-known words of Isaiah and Micah undergo a startling reversal:

> *Beat your plows into swords,*
> *And your pruning hooks into spears.* [4:10 Heb., 3:10 Eng.]

God's host is to descend (from heaven?) and to be arrayed against the nations. It is the time of the full harvest. Then Yahve will roar out of Zion and speak forth from Jerusalem.[4] All the nations will recognize that Yahve dwells on Mount Zion, and foreigners will no longer pass through it. Vivid as this picture is, it does not conclude with a climax or definite statement. The doom on other nations is not expressed in such specific terms as was the evil fate predicted for the Tyrians. Either something has been lost from the text or the author considered it wiser, and adequately climactic, to assert that Yahve would gather the nations to execute judgment on them. The final verses (4:18–21 Heb., 3:18–21 Eng.) predict great prosperity.

[1] This is the meaning of the phrase, frequent in the Tanak, "return the captivity of Judah."

[2] The name means "Yahve judges." Later tradition identified this unknown place as the valley of the stream Kishon.

[3] See also Amos 1:9–10, a postexilic passage. Information about Tyre and Sidon is to be found in Diodorus Siculus, *Hist.* XVI, 40, 44 and XVII, 46.

[4] Joel 4:16 (Eng. 3:16) is repeated in Amos 1:2, probably through a scribal error.

Egypt and Edom, Judah's constant foes, are to be destroyed, but Judah will abide forever.

We do not know when Joel was written. It has been suggested that the two passages dealing with the locusts reflect some occasion of public worship when the plague was a dire threat and incantation was resorted to. This suggestion is very reasonable, but it goes beyond the direct evidence.

The contents outlined above lack direct and striking religious significance, even in those places where the literary merit is high. Although the Day of Yahve passage is of some note in itself, it is more significant as a step in the development of the later and more extensive visions. The Book of Daniel, in its more extended sections, and the New Testament's Revelation of John (which was in all probability originally a Jewish book) show to what extent the motif was capable of development.

An understanding of certain commonly used terms will enable the student to orient himself to this whole genre of passages or books. When the subject is the remote future, the descriptive word *eschatological* applies. In interpretive literature the word *apocalyptic* is also used. These two terms are often confused and misapplied.

Prophecy in the Tanak and apocalypse are closely akin; both are revelations. Yet prophecy in general is expressed in clear prose and deals with recognizable notions and events. The word *apocalyptic* is reserved by careful scholars for that class of prophetic writings in which symbolism replaces direct expression. Apocalyptic writings also predict future events, but often the events predicted seem to be quite outside the ordinary course of history. Isaiah's foretelling of the doom to descend upon Assyria is prophecy, while Joel's prediction of a judgment that is to befall a vague group of nations at a vague time is an apocalypse. Indeed, if Joel had spoken of "beasts of the world," for example, rather than of nations, his symbolic language would have made him even more apocalyptic.

The passage we have just considered about the Day of Yahve is eschatological. *A passage can be apocalyptic if its manner of expression is symbolic and vague; it is eschatological if it deals with the end of time.* Because much of the apocalyptic literature is simultaneously eschatological, a regrettable and confusing tendency has arisen to use the two words interchangeably.

Still another pitfall lies in the air of unreality of the apocalyptic-eschatological writings. I have said that in apocalyptic writings the events predicted seem to be quite outside the course of history. But we may properly ask whether the writers really envisage these happenings as outside history or whether only the modern western reader rushes to such a conclusion. The question of whether the future events are conceived as being within history or outside it arises out of New Testament problems. In Matt. 4:17 Jesus predicts the early arrival of the Day of Yahve in these words, "Repent, for the Kingdom of God is at hand." Almost two thousand years have passed; in any usual sense, that kingdom has not arrived, and Jesus would appear to have been mistaken. It is understandable that some devout people have found it distasteful to infer that Jesus was mistaken. The passage "My kingdom is not of this world" (John 18:36) serves as a proof text for those who declare that Jesus was not wrong, but that the events predicted are "suprahistorical" rather than historical.

To complicate this problem even further, the age immediately after Jesus interpreted him not so much as predicting the events as being central to them. In such reinterpretation it is not the man Jesus but the divine Christ who is of primary concern. It became quite natural to distinguish between "the Jesus of history" and the Christ who, according to this reinterpretation, in some way transcends history. That is to say, the early documents are read—so far correctly—so as to suggest that when conceptions of the Christ replaced Jesus, then the "Day of the Lord" ceased to be awaited as a historical event of the near future.

But it is incorrect to conclude that the historical became suprahistorical. Rather, eschatology receded to a minor role in Christianity. As a result, the emergent church came to conceive of itself as God's representative, mentor, and guide in a world destined to endure. The Day of the Lord did not become something suprahistorical; it only receded to a vague doctrine, which either elicited lip service or else failed to attract any notice or excitement.

This was the situation in nineteenth-century New Testament scholarship, especially in that numerous sequence of books reviewed by Albert Schweitzer in his *The Quest for the Historical Jesus*. These books, which often conceived of Jesus as a nineteenth-century man, so thoroughly ignored eschatology that a scholar, Johannes Weiss, rather startled the academic world in 1892 when he suggested that a Jesus studied without reference to the prediction of the early end of the world made no sense. After Weiss's valuable contribution, eschatology attracted new attention from New Testament scholars, an interest that was increased by Schweitzer himself. If one reads the books surveyed by Schweitzer, one sees that the "quest" for the "historical" Jesus was an effort to disentangle supposedly reliable material from the legends and the theology of the Gospels. The scholars, after carefully sifting the Gospels, declared that much, indeed most, of what the Gospels relate about Jesus was the product of meditative piety. Incident after incident was denied historical validity, to the point where virtually nothing was left. The main lines of scholarship did not follow those eccentrics who declared that Jesus never lived; scholarship said, in effect, that he lived but that we know nothing of substance about him.

Schweitzer himself has subscribed to this judgment, but, following the lead of Weiss, he came to the conclusion that despite the large quantity of unhistorical material in the Gospels, the eschatology attributed to Jesus can hardly be legendary. Legend, says Schweitzer, would not have attributed to Jesus a prediction of the early arrival of the Kingdom of God, for the age that would have produced the legend must have known already that the prediction was mistaken. Therefore, however much in the Gospels must be denied historical validity, the historical validity of the eschatology attributed to Jesus must be affirmed. Schweitzer's contribution resulted in the paradox that New Testament scholarship since that time has emphasized as authentic teachings of Jesus those predictions about the end of the world that did not come true. The escape from this paradox has been a resort to the alleged distinction between the historical and the suprahistorical. If there is some genuine distinction (that is, if "suprahistorical" connotes more than just theological jargon), then this much must be said plainly: the Tanak knows of no such thing as the suprahistorical. Nor does the New Testament. The word is useful to describe a twentieth-century theological concern, but it is wrong to read the twentieth century back into the Tanak.

The apocalyptic-eschatological message in no way implied that God was acting outside of history. Apocalyptic and eschatology said that God is acting now, but the effect will be seen in the remote future, when He will still be acting.

The sense of God as the controller of history and as revealed in history is never lost in the eschatological writings. Rather, they reflect an effort to answer the problem of "theodicy." They state that since God is just, He will be discerned, not now but in the future, to be doing the just thing. The Day of Yahve passage in Joel is to be understood as Joel's view of what will happen *within history* in the most remote future.

Joel's concept of God's spirit being poured on all mankind is found in a different form in Numbers 11:16–30. There the text relates that Moses, sorely tried through having no meat to give the Israelites, was to assemble seventy men outside the Tent of Meeting, where Yahve appeared. Yahve informed Moses that meat would be supplied, but Moses was skeptical. Thereupon Yahve reminded Moses of His omnipotence, and told Moses that he would soon witness it. After the seventy men were placed in a circle aroung the Tent, Yahve, snatching some of His spirit which had been on Moses, gave that portion to the seventy men. Meanwhile, Eldad and Medad, two men in the encampment, were "prophesying," and a boy rushed from the encampment to the Tent of Meeting to report this to Moses. Joshua, Moses' right-hand man, then advised Moses to exterminate the two, whereupon Moses asked Joshua if jealousy animated him. He, Moses, had no such jealousy: "Would that all of Yahve's people were prophets, if only Yahve would put His spirit on them."

Whereas Moses expresses his wish for Yahve's people, Joel speaks of "all flesh." Did Joel really mean "all flesh" or only Jews? There are interpreters who conclude that since Numbers refers to Jews, Joel really meant only Jews; and it is often added that Judaism is marked and marred by a narrow particularism, in sharp contrast with the alleged universalism of Christianity. A passage in Acts 2:1–4, which relates that the Holy Spirit was poured on the whole Christian community in Jerusalem on Pentecost, is cited in support of the supposed contrast. A more prudent judgment is that Judaism and Christianity are both marked by motifs of universalism and particularism. The contrast of a particularistic Judaism with a universalistic Christianity has been greatly overdrawn by particularistic Christians. There are many particularistic passages in the Tanak, as there would be in any national literature, but there are also counterbalancing universalistic passages. The nineteenth or twentieth centuries should not be read into the Tanak. It would be ridiculous to think poorly of Lincoln's Gettysburg address for its failure to envisage the United Nations; it would be equally ridiculous to criticize a national literature of the ancient world for its particularistic motifs. What is amazing about the Tanak is how frequently universalism breaks through the particularism. This seems to me to be the case of the passage in Joel. "All flesh" means all flesh—humanity, not just Jews.

SECOND AND THIRD ZECHARIAH

Scholars conventionally divide the contents of Zechariah 9–14 into five sections. Three of these appear to come from one author, or one tradition, school, or age; the other two represent a different authorship, whether one or more is uncertain. Sometimes the group of

three is spoken of as Second Zechariah and the group of two as Third
Zechariah. Chapters 9–14 could just as easily have been appended to
the long Book of Isaiah. They are random pages which by some
chance—unknown to us—were sewn together with Zechariah.

The poor condition of some of the text reduces the clarity of the
first section (9:1–7). It seems to express a hope that a king, possibly
a messianic king, will enjoy a victory over neighboring nations and
even over Greece. In all probability, the author expected that soon
all the nations bordering Israel would be conquered, though the text
does not state how or by whom this would be accomplished. A king,
foreign to the Philistines (called a bastard in the text), is to reign in
Ashdod, a city that is to become a portion [5] of Judea; the inhabitants
will become as Jewish as did the Jebusites, the people who inhabited
Jerusalem in ancient Canaanite times. After this conquest and conversion, Judea's king (the conqueror?) is to come to Jerusalem. He is
victorious and a deliverer; [6] he is humble, riding upon an ass [7] instead
of in a chariot. Indeed, neither chariot nor horse will be needed, for
the king will reign in peace [8] from sea to sea—from the Mediterranean in the west to the sea conceived of as far to the east, and from
the Euphrates River to the "ends of the earth."

The mention of Greece helps in dating the prophecy. Alexander
the Great conquered Palestine about 332 B.C. This section is later
than that date, though we do not know how much later.

The second section, 10:1–11:3, which is less straightforward
and more symbolic, is more difficult. It appears to emphasize that
God is the true ruler, and that He assesses and evaluates, appoints
and removes "shepherds." The passage supposes that new shepherds
will achieve a victory, and that the scattered Jews will return from
the lands to which they have fled. New leadership is needed to replace
the old leaders who have turned to idols and diviners, away from
Yahve, from Whom the beneficial rains come (10:1–2). The old
leaders having been displaced, Judea is now a fine military machine
("A horse who is one's pride in battle"); Yahve is to fight on their side

[5] The text says, incorrectly, a "governor."
[6] "Just and having salvation" is the King James translation. This is beautiful,
perhaps, but both meaningless and not entirely true to the text.
[7] The text says "on an ass, even on a colt, the foal of an ass." In the Hebrew such
parallelism is so usual that one animal is obviously being referred to, not two.
Mark and Luke allude to this verse (9:9) in describing the entry of Jesus into
Jerusalem; Matthew, quoting the verse in 21:1–5, misunderstands the parallelism, and portrays Jesus as riding two animals. Manuscripts of Matthew exhibit
efforts of copyists to correct Matthew's error.
[8] The "just king" is the addressee of Psalm 72, which ought to be read in connection with this section.

(10:3–7). Now Yahve will whistle, and His sons, scattered to Egypt or Syria (Ashur in the text), will come home (10:8–12). The section ends (11:1–3) with a poem of satisfaction that the old leaders have been removed. Nothing in the section gives any clue to its time. The events alluded to are totally unknown.

The third section (11:4–14, 13:7–9, and 11:15–17) is obscure. Not only is the text in bad shape, but the content, where the text is clear, is couched in symbolic language. The following summary is quite uncertain: A prophet is apparently being instructed to save the "slaughtered," since Israel is a flock whose owners slay their sheep; the owners hypocritically invoke Yahve's name, as though He had made them wealthy (11:4–6). The prophet takes two staves—one he calls Noam ("pleasantness") and the other Hoblim ("bonds"?)—and he tends the flock. Three leaders—what office they occupied is not told—are removed within one month. Becoming impatient, the prophet now breaks the staff called Noam, thereby nullifying the covenant with the peoples (we do not know what covenant). The merchants (a corrected reading for "so the poor") recognize that this is God's will; the prophet asks for his salary and they give him thirty pieces of silver,[9] which he throws into the Temple treasury. He burns the second staff, Hoblim, thus breaking the covenant between Judah and Jerusalem[1] (11:7–14).

Now Yahve speaks to His sword to waken and smite the leader. Once the shepherd is smitten, the sheep are to be scattered. Two thirds of the people are to be smitten, but one third will survive. This third, once it has been refined, will be Yahve's special people (13:7–9).

Next, the prophet is to take the tools of a foolish shepherd and, presumably, give them to a tyrannical, cruel shepherd (11:15–17). Since this third section is so obscure, we cannot be certain of its meaning. It is impossible to know what and who are being spoken of, although some guesses are on record.

The first section (12:1–13:6) of Third Zechariah has both clarity and confusion. It begins with a prediction that great frustration will attend certain nations who lay siege to Jerusalem. The loyal chieftains, with God's favor, will destroy the nations, so that Jerusalem will dwell in peace[2] (12:1–9). There will be a lamentation (over

---

[9] See Matt. 26:15; Judas is said to have received the same amount for betraying Jesus.
[1] A few Greek manuscripts give this reading.
[2] I have corrected the text, which says "Jerusalem. . . . will dwell in Jerusalem."

whom we do not know [3]) as great as the lamentation over the dying
Canaanite god Hadad-Rimmon. The mourning will proceed according
to families, which we can identify only as of the houses of David
and of Levi (12:10–14). Then a fountain for ritual purification will be
opened in Jerusalem and idolatry will cease. Prophecy, which has
degenerated into false prophecy, will disappear (13:1–6).

The second section (14:1–21) is an apocalypse, dealing with the
Day of Yahve. All the nations will gather against Jerusalem and will
capture it, through God's action. God will then go out to do battle on
the nations. When He stands on the Mount of Olives, the hill will
split into two, with half the mountain moving north and half moving
south. People will flee to the valley—here the text is most uncertain.
Their flight will be like the flight "during the earthquake in the days
of Uzziah." [4] Then Yahve will enter Jerusalem with all his "holy
ones," [5] or angels. On this day there will be neither cold nor frost, [6]
and neither light nor dark. Waters will go out of Jerusalem, flowing
eastward and westward, both winter and summer (that is, the
streams will cease to dry up, as do Palestinian *wadis*). Perfect monotheism will exist over all the earth. "On that day Yahve will be
[acknowledged] the only God, and His name the only one." The land
will be turned into a plain and Jerusalem, with its borders extended,
will be safely and abundantly inhabited (14:1–11). Yahve will then
put a plague on all who have fought against Jerusalem [7] (14:12–15).

Those who survive from among the nations will go to Jerusalem
once a year on the festival of Tabernacles (*Sukkoth*) to worship God.
There will be enormous pots (in which to seethe sacrifices in the
Temple), for the pilgrims will be many. On that day there will be no
more merchants in the Temple (called money changers in the New
Testament), a token that the Temple has been purified.

The lack of clarity and the heterogeneity make it difficult for us
to form a concise judgment on either the meaning or the significance
of the latter half of the Book of Zechariah. One can, of course, note
that passages such as 9:9 and 14:21 are cited in the New Testament
as though they allude long in advance to Jesus. But this only tells us
that in the age when the Gospels were written men were accustomed
to search Scripture for proof-texts, and fails to clarify the content of

[3] The text reads, "They shall look at me whom they stabbed." Some scholars
emend the *me* to *him;* this seems right, but the verse remains obscure.
[4] See above, p. 69.
[5] See Ps. 89:6 and 8; and Daniel 8:13 for other mentions of the "holy ones."
[6] Verse 14:6 has been emended; the Hebrew word for "light" has been altered to
"cold."
[7] Verses *13* and *14* are either out of place, or are tiny fragments from other writings which perished.

the passages themselves. The themes are only touched on and not elaborated. Jews are scattered throughout the world; they are to be gathered home. Nations besiege them; with God's help the nations will be defeated. Jewish leaders are corrupt; they will be replaced. Prophecy is deceptive; it will disappear. The Temple is impure; it will be purified.

Our inability to relate the sections to specific historic events shows that those who preserved the five fragments for ultimate inclusion as the latter part of Zechariah were more interested in the themes than in the historic settings. Unrest and chaos are the most we can piece together of the history of the Jews in the latter part of the postexilic period. The fragments reflect the anxieties and the hopes of that time. Vindication by God, restoration, national sovereignty, worthy leadership, and a truly sacred Temple are earnestly desired. In part, the realization of these desires is expected in the near future; in part, especially in the last fragment, it is thought that only the Day of Yahve can bring it.

While there is no relationship between Zechariah and Daniel, and in Daniel we are fortunately not plagued with such unclarity, Second and Third Zechariah help us to understand the great transition from the crystal clarity of Amos to the cryptic style of Daniel. The manner of Daniel is no surprise after Second and Third Zechariah, for they underline the transformation of prophecy into the apocalyptic.

DANIEL

WHEN THE ancient Jews collected their writings into a Scripture, the Book of Daniel found its place in the third division, the Hagiographa, rather than in the second division, the Prophets. It may well be that by the time the Book of Daniel was cast into its present form, the prophetic collection had already been made, for Daniel is the latest book in Scripture. I discuss it with the Prophets because the book is more nearly related to them than to the Hagiographa, which are a heterogeneous collection. In the Greek and Latin, and therefore the English Bible of the Christians, the Book of Daniel is ordinarily found in the section of the Prophets. (I discuss Jonah, which is found in the prophets in the Hebrew Bible, with the narrative books, see pp. 494ff.)

A large section (2:4–7:28) of Daniel is in the Aramaic language, rather than in Hebrew. Aramaic is a near relative of Hebrew, which around the sixth pre-Christian century began to supplant Hebrew as the spoken language of Jews even in Palestine. The first six chapters are exclusively narrative, while the last six chapters contain a series of four visions. In the Greek version[1] there are materials added to

1 The usual Greek version of the Tanak is called the Septuagint. There were, however, additional Greek versions. In the ordinary manuscripts of the Septuagint the translation of Daniel is not that of the Septuagint but of a version known as Theodotion.

what is found in the Hebrew. These include a so-called "Song of the Three Children," the "Story of Susannah," and two additional stories about Daniel, relating his mastery over the god Bel and a dragon.

The opening verses of Daniel assert that the events described occurred in the third year of the reign of King Jehoiakim, whom Nebuchadnezzar, King of Babylonia, attacked. The third year of Jehoiakim would be the year 606. Nebuchadnezzar, however, did not become king of Babylonia until a year later. But the author of Daniel was not a precise historian. Moreover, a host of considerations lead to the conclusion that Nebuchadnezzar and his Babylonians are merely cryptic references to Antiochus Epiphanes and his Syrian Greeks. After the death of Alexander the Great (323 B.C.) his huge empire fell into four kingdoms—Syria, Egypt, Thrace, and Macedonia. Great rivalry developed between Syria under the Seleucidians and Egypt under the Ptolemies. The Seleucidians and the Ptolemies alternated as the conquerors of Palestine. Greek customs, institutions, and language were transplanted into Palestine.

A Seleucid king, Antiochus, established control over Palestine, wresting it from the Ptolemies in the year 198. He was interested in introducing a larger measure of Greek culture than were his Seleucid or Egyptian predecessors. Moreover, in Palestine there were Jewish "hellenizers" who responded affirmatively to this culture, which to other Jews seemed alien and wrong. In 175 Antiochus IV, with the surname Epiphanes, came to the throne. Shortly after his accession, inner difficulties arose in Jerusalem between the so-called "hellenizing" party and their opponents. Moreover, there occurred an ugly rivalry for the High Priesthood between a certain Onias III and his brother Jason. Jason, an ardent hellenizer, paid the Seleucids a bribe for the office and was appointed to it. The displacement of the legitimate priest was distasteful, especially to those Jews who were opposed to hellenizing. Then a third man, named Menelaus, coveted the High Priesthood. Again bribery was effective, and Menelaus received the office. To strengthen his position he assassinated the legitimate Onias III; Jason saved himself by fleeing.

When around 170 Antiochus was again engaged in wars with the Egyptians, as the Seleucids usually were, Jason gathered troops, entered Jerusalem, and drove out Menelaus. At this point Antiochus IV had temporary relief from his external wars and was able to intervene in the affairs in Jerusalem to the extent of reinstating Menelaus.

To Antiochus it seemed that the cure for the repeated disorders in Jerusalem was forcible hellenization, such as he had decreed elsewhere. Such hellenization meant discrediting the local worship, and even attempting to wipe it out. In accordance with this intention, emissaries of the King desecrated the Temple at Jerusalem in 168. The result of this desecration, a climax to a series of provocative acts, was the outbreak of the Maccabean Wars. The revolt itself began at a village known as Modin, and was led by a priest named Mattathias, who had five sons, and the leader was Judah Maccabaeus. Guerilla warfare under the Maccabeans was successful; in 165 the pagan altar set up to desecrate the Temple was removed, and the Temple was cleansed and rededicated. The holiday *Hanukkah,* which means "dedication," celebrates the purification of the Temple.

The Book of Daniel appears to come from the period when the Maccabean revolt had just succeeded and when people faced problems as to what the future could bring. The book's purpose is to suggest that the contemporary situation is not new but is similar to what existed in the days of Nebuchadnezzar. At that time, so the book suggests, a celebrated wise man, Daniel, set forth certain answers to the questions of the time, which are applicable to the present period. It is likely that there were in existence stories about an ancient Daniel, mentioned with Noah and Job in Ezekiel 14:14. Indeed, the Ras Shamra tablets [2] disclose that Daniel is a hero of even greater antiquity than was thought before their discovery.

The first six chapters are devoted to telling stories about the wise man Daniel. Just how ancient these stories are we cannot be sure. It is more reasonable to suppose that the author of the Book of Daniel retold ancient stories than to suggest that he created them. Only after the author completes the narration of the stories do we come to the real point and purpose of the book, which is to make certain predictions about the future.

These predictions are in the form of a series of revelations. Since pre-exilic times there had developed a tendency to resort to symbol and to secret or cryptic speech. Normally (and here I repeat) we use the word "prophetic" to describe the early type of straightforward utterance, and the word "apocalyptic" to describe the cryptic and symbolic utterance of later times. The apocalyptic message in the Book of Daniel is connected with eschatology; this is also the case in such similar books as Revelation in the New Testament and a number of books received into neither the Hebrew nor the Greek Tanak.

The difficulty of interpreting an apocalyptic message is that the ancient author, intent on a cryptic mode of expression, in many places conceals from the modern student what he has in mind.

[2] See page 513.

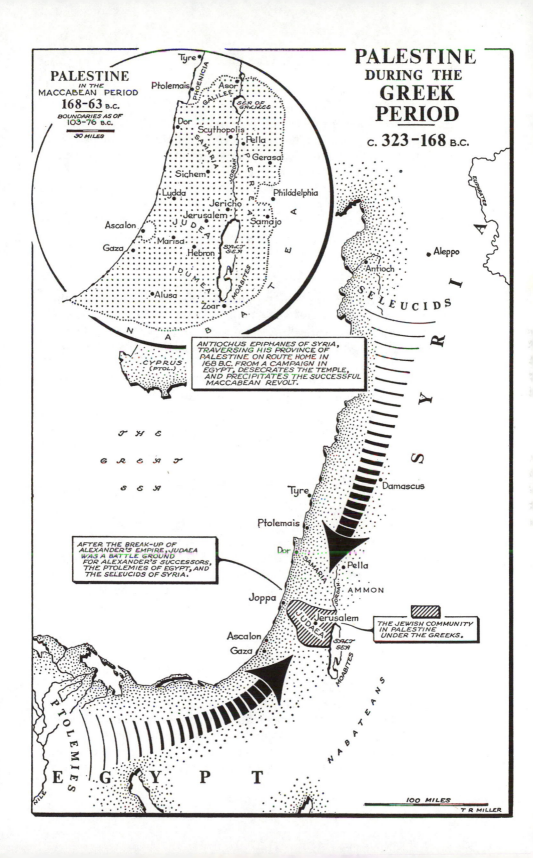

PALESTINE DURING THE GREEK PERIOD

c. 323-168 B.C.

PALESTINE IN THE MACCABEAN PERIOD 168-63 B.C.

BOUNDARIES AS OF 103-76 B.C.

30 MILES

Tyre
Ptolemais
PHOENICIA
Asor
GALILEE
SEA OF GALILEE
Dor
Scythopolis
Pella
SAMARIA
JORDAN
Gerasa
Sichem
PEREA
Lydda
Jericho
Philadelphia
Jerusalem
JUDEA
Samajo
Ascalon
Marisa
SALT SEA
Gaza
Hebron
IDUMEA
MOABITES
Alusa
Zoar
NABATEA

ANTIOCHUS EPIPHANES OF SYRIA, TRAVERSING HIS PROVINCE OF PALESTINE ON ROUTE HOME IN 168 B.C. FROM A CAMPAIGN IN EGYPT, DESECRATES THE TEMPLE, AND PRECIPITATES THE SUCCESSFUL MACCABEAN REVOLT.

CYPRUS (PTOL.)

SELEUCIDS

SYRIA

EUPHRATES

Aleppo

Antioch

THE GREAT SEA

Tyre
Damascus
Ptolemais
Dor
SAMARIA
Pella
JORDAN
AMMON

AFTER THE BREAK-UP OF ALEXANDER'S EMPIRE, JUDAEA WAS A BATTLE GROUND FOR ALEXANDER'S SUCCESSORS, THE PTOLEMIES OF EGYPT, AND THE SELEUCIDS OF SYRIA.

Joppa
Jerusalem
JUDEA
SALT SEA
Ascalon
Gaza
MOABITES

THE JEWISH COMMUNITY IN PALESTINE UNDER THE GREEKS.

PTOLEMIES

NABATEANS

NILE
E G Y P T

100 MILES

T R MILLER

Moreover, the details of an apocalyptic message are often involved; we are able to see the broad outlines but are unable to determine the significance of each of the details. This inability, to which the earnest student must confess, has not always impeded the ultra-pious. The imaginative quality of the Book of Daniel, or of the Book of Revelation, has stimulated the even more fertile imaginations of interpreters of many ages, to the point that passages in the Book of Daniel have been taken to be predictions of our own future. This mode of interpretation is quite foreign to the purpose of the Book of Daniel and equally alien to the usual procedure of a modern scholar in his study of a book.

We can grasp the intent of the four visions only by first reading the preceding narratives. It should be kept in mind that the king Nebuchadnezzar is really Antiochus Epiphanes and that the fidelity to Judaism on the part of Daniel of Babylonian days is the fidelity commended to people of the Maccabean age.

In the first narrative the enemy king commanded that young men, gifted in mind and without blemish in body, be brought to serve in the royal palace, and among these were four Judeans—Daniel, Mishael, Hananiah, and Azariah. These boys, who were commanded to learn Aramaic, were given Babylonian names. Daniel became Belteshazzar, Hananiah became Shadrach, Mishael became Meshach, and Azariah became Abednego. When the young men refused to eat food improper for Jews, their surpervisor was fearful for their health, since he would be blamed if their countenances revealed their ill condition. The four were able to persuade the supervisor to provide a diet of vegetables; within a short time they were as healthy looking as the other young men who worked in the palace. All four were intelligent and wise, unquestionably the most outstanding of all the young men in the service of the king; but Daniel in addition was able to interpret visions and dreams (Chapter 1).

Nebuchadnezzar had a dream that upset him. He summoned all the sages of the court, related the dream to them, and offered great rewards if they would interpret it. When they were not able to do so he ordered them all to be executed. Daniel informed the royal executioner that he could accomplish the king's wish. The four Jews prayed to God to give Daniel the insight to interpret the dream, and, strengthened by this prayer, Daniel had the executioner bring him before the king. Daniel told the king that only one enlightened by the true God could reveal the meaning of what was to happen, especially at the end of time. Daniel did not require the king to reveal the dream, but described it himself. There was a huge statue with a head of gold and chest and arms of silver, a belly and thighs of brass, legs of iron, and feet partly of iron and partly clay. A huge stone destroyed the statue and smote the feet, shattering them, and the stone itself became a great mountain. In Daniel's interpretation Nebuchadnezzar of Babylonia was the head of gold; thereafter there would be a second empire, that of the Medes; the Persian empire would follow, symbolized by the brass; a fourth empire, Alexander's, was symbolized by the iron legs. The mixture of iron and clay represented the divisions after Alexander's death. The huge rock that destroyed the statue was the kingdom of the Judeans, which God had created to endure for all eternity.

In gratitude, Nebuchadnezzar bowed down to Daniel, acknowledging Daniel's God. He appointed Daniel governor of all Babylonia, even putting all the sages of Babylonia in his charge. Daniel appointed his three friends, Shadrach, Meshach, and Abednego to be his assistants (Chapter 2).

Nebuchadnezzar then built a golden image and ordered all his officials to bow down and worship it at the sound of certain musical instruments. Anyone who refused would be thrown into a fiery furnace. Daniel and his three associates refused to bow down. When this was reported, Shadrach, Meshach, and Abednego were brought before Nebuchadnezzar. He again ordered them to bow down, but they again refused. Thereupon the fiery furnace was made seven times as hot as it usually was. Shadrach, Meshach, and Abednego were bound and thrown in. But a spark from the fire killed the men who threw them in, while the three were unhurt. Nebuchadnezzar thereupon acknowledged the God of the three as the one God of the world (Chapter 3).

Next, Nebuchadnezzar related another dream which frightened him and which his sages were unable to interpret. He had seen a great tree, so powerful and tall that it was visible over all the earth. A celestial being came down and gave instructions for the tree to be cut down, with only a stump to be left. When Daniel arrived, he interpreted Nebuchadnezzar as being the tree, and the experience of being cut down as representing seven years of insanity, which Nebuchadnezzar would undergo so that he might know that God was the true king. In response the king began to brag of his greatness, and at that very moment he became insane. After the required time, Nebuchadnezzar was restored to sanity and acknowledged the sovereignty of the true God. The splendor of his kingship was restored to him (3:31–4:34, Heb., Chapter 4 Eng.).

The successor to Nebuchadnezzar was King Belshazzar. At a great feast he brought out the vessels of the Temple in Jerusalem, which Nebuchadnezzar, his father, had brought to Babylon. The king, his officers, and his consort drank toasts in these vessels to the gods of brass, iron, wood, and stone. While they were busy drinking, the hand of a man wrote something in chalk on the wall, terrorizing the king. The wise men of Babylon were called upon to read and interpret the writing, but they were unable to do so. Thereupon the queen suggested that Daniel be brought in.

He read the writing: *Mene, Mene, Tekel, Ufarsin.*[3] The three words are all puns. *Mene*, Daniel said, means "to mete out, or number." God had fixed the number of days that the kingdom was to last. *Tekel* means "to weigh." The king had been weighed in the balance and found wanting. *Farsin* (the *u* is one of the forms of the Hebrew word "and") means "divide" or "separate"; the kingdom, once a unit, was to be divided and given to the Medes and the Persians. Daniel was rewarded with royal clothes and made third in rank in the kingdom. But that night Belshazzar was slain and the kingdom passed to Darius the Mede [4] (5:*1*–6:*1* Heb., Chapter 5 Eng.).

King Darius had subdivided his authority among one hundred and twenty satraps or officials. He had put three supervisors over these, one of whom was Daniel. The other two supervisors and the satraps plotted against Daniel unsuccessfully; they therefore determined to bring charges against him based on his religion alone. They persuaded the king to prohibit prayer to any god for a period of thirty days. The king signed the prohibition, thereby making it irrevocable, for once the king signed something it could not, "according to the law of the Medes and the Persians," be changed. Daniel nevertheless prayed to God. When this was reported to the king, Daniel was thrown into the lions' den to be eaten by the animals. After a sleepless night at the palace, the king returned to the lions' den at dawn; he discovered that an angel had come into the den to close the lions' mouths and that Daniel was still alive. So Daniel was taken out of the den and replaced there by the men who had plotted against him. Thereupon Darius gave orders for all the people in his domain to worship the God of Daniel (6:*2*–*29* Heb., *1*–*28* Eng.).

After relating these stories, the author describes the four visions

---

[3] Literally, these three are different weights. The word *mene* appears in the text twice, but most of the ancient translations give the word once. Therefore many modern editors delete one of the *mene's*.

[4] There is some error here, for it was Cyrus, rather than Darius the son of Cyrus, who conquered the Babylonians. Ingenious efforts have been made to get around the difficulty, but the simplest explanation is that the author of the Book of Daniel had no pretensions to precise history.

of Daniel. In the first of these, Daniel saw four beasts emerge from the sea. The first was a lion with the wings of an eagle; the second was a bear with three bones or ribs in his mouth; the third was like a leopard, with four wings on his back and four heads. The fourth, unlike any other animal, had ten horns,[5] but as Daniel looked a small horn destroyed three of the animal's ten horns. Daniel then saw the "Ancient of Days," or God, sitting as a judge, before Whom the record books were opened. While Daniel was looking, the terrible fourth beast was destroyed and burned up. The other beasts were not destroyed immediately; their lives were prolonged for a limited time.

Next comes a passage of great significance in later times, especially in the Gospels. Daniel saw someone like a "Son of Man"[6] coming with the clouds of heaven; that is to say, he saw someone who looked simply like a human being. This humanlike being came to the "Ancient of Days" and received dominion, power, kingship, and the assurance that all the nations would worship him, for his sovereignty was to endure forever. Daniel asked one of those standing around the "Ancient of Days" for the explanation. He learned that the four beasts were the four kingdoms of the Babylonians, the Medes, the Persians, and the Greeks. The destroying horn (Antiochus Epiphanes) was allowed to do his evil for "a time, times, and half a time," meaning probably a year, two years, and half a year. Three and a half years could correspond to the dates 168–165 (Chapter 7).

The second vision was of a ram with two horns, one of them higher than the other, and a goat, which came from the west. This goat had a conspicuous horn between his eyes. The goat attacked the ram, broke the two horns, and destroyed him. But then the goat became puffed up, so that its great horn was broken, and in its place there came up four horns. Daniel again requested an explanation. This was given to him by someone having the appearance of a man,[7] in the text identified promptly as Gabriel, presumably the angel

5 The ten horns are probably to be interpreted as Alexander and nine Seleucid kings, or else as ten Seleucid kings and their pretenders. The little horn is Antiochus IV Epiphanes, and the three horns which he roots out are identified as various domestic and foreign opponents. But great uncertainty exists here in our interpreting the details.

6 A simple interpretation of this "Son of Man" is that he is the Messiah. Some, however, find a difficulty below in verses 27–8, in which the interpretation is not that of an individual but of the "people of the saints and the Most High." In this passage in Daniel, in my opinion, the phrase "Son of Man" simply means a human being. It does not yet have the force of a technical title that it comes to have in the Gospels.

7 Chapter 8 is in Hebrew, while Chapter 7 is in Aramaic. However, the English "someone like a son of man" can fit the two phrases, the one Aramaic and the other Hebrew.

much better known to us from later times. Gabriel interpreted the vision as follows: the ram represented the king of the Mede-Persian empire, while the goat was the Greek kingdom. The goat's horn was Alexander; the four horns were the four portions of the empire that became the kingdoms mentioned above (p. 227). Out of one of the four goat's horns had sprung a little horn, presumably Antiochus IV Epiphanes. Daniel was enjoined to seal up the vision because it dealt with things in the distant future (Chapter 8).

The third vision takes its point of departure from predictions, described in the text of Jeremiah, that the Babylonian exile was to last for seventy years. It seeks to account for the injunction to Daniel at the conclusion of the preceding section to seal that vision up until the end of time. In the present vision we see what is to happen when the time to unseal the previous vision is near at hand. While Daniel meditated about the seventy years, he prayed to God to forgive the iniquities of the people and to look favorably upon Jerusalem (9:18): "For not on our own merit do we lay our supplication before You, but rather on Your abundant mercy." As Daniel was so praying, Gabriel came to him and explained that the seventy years were not really years, but seventy weeks of years, that is, 490 years. This period of seventy weeks of years was to consist of three segments. The first segment, seven weeks, was the interval between the announcement of the divine word and the coming of an anointed prince who was to rebuild Jerusalem and the commencement of the rebuilding. The second segment, sixty-two weeks of years, was the period in which the rebuilding was to take place, and it was to end with the "cutting off" of the anointed prince. The third segment, one week of years, though divided into two parts, was to be marked in the first part by the cessation of sacrifices in the Temple, and in the second part, if we can trust an uncertain text, by the destruction of the one who caused the cessation (Chapter 9).

How are these strange numbers to be interpreted? Possibly the 490 years begin in 586. The first segment may end in 516 with Joshua, the priest contemporary with Zerubbabel at the time of the return of the Jews from Babylonia. (See above, pp. 198ff.) The sixty-two weeks, or 434 years, may begin in 516, and terminate in 171, when Onias III was slain by Menelaus; but this is scarcely consistent with the arithmetic involved. The arithmetic is an insurmountable problem, especially since we do not know for sure what the author intends as a beginning date, nor can we be sure that his chronology agrees with that accepted by modern scholars. If we ignore the mathematical difficulty, we may possibly explain the intent as follows: the last period of seven years could be the seven years from the death of Onias to the present "favorable" time. During half of this period, an unhappy half, the Temple worship was to cease, as it did under Antiochus IV Epiphanes; at this time an "abomination of desolation" would be in the Temple. The remainder of the time would be the interval of the successful Maccabean uprising.

The fourth and last vision in the book encompasses three chapters (10–12). It is unclear in Scripture, and paraphrase of it is necessarily difficult. Chapter 10 is a kind of prologue, 11 is the vision and its interpretation, and 12 is the epilogue. Daniel, after a fast of twenty-one days, saw a vision, which his companions did not see. He saw a man clothed in linen and girded with gold. The "man" explained to him that the "guardian angel" of the Persians had prevented his coming until Michael, a Jewish "guardian angel," came to his help. On hearing this, Daniel became dumb, but someone in the likeness of a "Son of Man" touched his lips so that he could speak. Daniel complained of his lack of strength; the man touched him, thus giving him strength. The man explained that he was going back to war with the guardian angel of the Persians, and before long he would also war with the guardian angel of the Greeks. Meanwhile he told Daniel the future (Chapter 10). There were to be four more kings after the present Persian king,[8] and the last of these was to be great and rich. It was his kingdom that was to fall to the Greeks, led by a Greek king, Alexander. Then, in turn, Alexander's kingdom was to be divided into four parts, which would be seized by pretenders (11:1–4).

There follows a review of the complicated history of the Seleucids and the Ptolemies (11:5–20). A contemptible man (Antiochus IV Epiphanes) would take over the kingdom; he would slay "the prince of the Covenant" (possibly Onias III), looting some of his provinces, but giving gifts to others. He would attack the king of the South (Egypt) and then return to his own land, but his attention would be fixed on Judea; "and his heart will be on the Holy Covenant." Again, obscurities appear in the text, but there is another reference to the erection of an abomination of desolation (11:31). Antiochus would flatter some hellenizing Jews into treason, but the faithful would stand firm and act bravely, even though many might fall by sword and flame. Antiochus would exalt himself over every god and speak contemptible things to God. There would be a great war between him and a certain king of the South. Finally he would come into the glorious land of Palestine, and though tens of thousands would fall,[9]

[8] The Hebrew (11:1) reads Darius, but the ancient translations, probably correctly, read Cyrus.
[9] The text (11:41) is quite unclear, especially in the mention of Edom and Moab.

he would meet his doom in the land of Palestine with none to help him[1] (Chapter 11).

In an epilogue, the book predicts that Michael, the guardian angel of the Jews, will emerge at the height of the troubled time, so that the Jews will be delivered in accordance with what is written in the Book of Daniel. Thereupon, "Many of those who sleep in the dust of the earth will wake up, some to life eternal, and some to shame or everlasting reproach." This verse, 12:2, is the first and indeed the only clear mention in the Tanak of the resurrection of both the wicked and the righteous.[2] Daniel was commanded to seal up these words until the end of time. When Daniel looked a second time, he saw two other angels, one on each bank of a river. He inquired, "How long will it be until this wonderful end?" One angel replied that it would take "a time, two times, and a half" before all these things would come about. Daniel heard but did not understand. He asked, "What will the outcome of all these things be?" The angel replied that the pure would purify themselves and become better, and the wicked would abide in their wickedness and would not understand[3] (12:4–10). The book ends with the instruction to Daniel to go his way until the very end, when he will "rest," that is, die. He will finally arise again at the end of days (12:13).

The student of the history of religion can note what a profound influence the Book of Daniel had on subsequent writings, especially through its relatively clear statement of resurrection and its use of the phrase "Son of Man," which was subsequently elaborated. Some interpreters today have also tried to show that this kind of literature has permanent value. A typical effort of this kind is made by H. H. Rowley,[4] who contends that the belief in the apocalyptic writings that God is in control of history is of lasting validity.[5] The apocalyptists, however, would seem to defer the action of God until some ultimate climax, as though He did not really control events while they are unfolding; but Rowley seems unbothered by this contradiction. He

---

[1] Antiochus actually died in Persia.

[2] For the resurrection of the righteous individual, see Isa. 24:24–7, and Ezek. 37:11. Dan. 12:2 is greatly debated.

[3] The two next verses, 12:11–12, are believed to be an interpolation. Chapter 8:14 had suggested that 1150 days would elapse from the abolition of the worship of the Temple to the cleansing; apparently that period had passed. Verse 12:11 now tries to correct things by making it 1290 days, and verse 12 prolongs it to 1335 days.

[4] In *The Relevance of Apocalyptic* (London: Lutterworth Press; 1944).

[5] *Op. cit.*, pp. 141–5.

confesses [6] that the apocalyptists have been mistaken in most of the details of what they have expected and that their hopes have been illusory. Yet he finds in their predictions what he describes as "a sound instinct"; that is, they see "more that is fundamentally true than all that is false." He believes the apocalyptists have a sound instinct when they describe the meaning of human tribulation. [7]

Rowley finds that he can also share the apocalyptists' faith that the glorious future, when it comes, "will come only by the power of God, and is only for the saints." [8] The dream of a world "where the will of God would be perfectly done," he considers relevant to our own age. [9] He is troubled by the idea that the decisive victory of the good, which he calls Kingdom of God, should not be established by human means but only by a divine act. [1] Rowley sees that a thorough-going emphasis on divine initiative could well "seem calculated to kill all human initiative." [2] He quotes a poem:

> *Sit down, O men of God,*
> *His kingdom He will bring*
> *Whenever it may please His will;*
> *You cannot do a thing!* [3]

Rowley finds it impossible to gain any satisfaction from the "merely evolutionary view of the advent of the kingdom, in the sense that forces innate in man will gradually lift him to its establishment." [4] Although he tries hard to deny that the apocalyptists leave man no role to play, [5] his effort only emphasizes their picture of man's uselessness and imperfection. In short, it seems to me that Professor Rowley, who is an admirable scholar and gentleman, fights a gallant but losing battle on behalf of the continued relevance of the apocalyptic writings. The affirmative things he says about writings such as Daniel apply more cogently to other types of writings, such as the Prophets.

Indeed, the point of a book like Daniel is not that God controls history, for this, by the time of Daniel, was a truism in Hebrew thought, but rather that the author knows God's plan. The interpolation [6] of two verses (12:11–12) shows that the author, however noble was his heart, was basically wrong on exactly those points where he should have been right if he knew God's plan. The apocalyptists made the mistake of being so specific and precise in their predictions that events were able to prove them wrong.

[6] *Op. cit.*, p. 148.　　[7] *Op. cit.*, pp. 146–52.　　[8] *Op. cit.*, p. 154.
[9] *Op. cit.*, 156.　　[1] *Op. cit.*, p. 157.　　[2] *Op. cit.*, p. 158.
[3] *Op. cit.*, p. 160.　　[4] *Op. cit.*, p. 159.　　[5] *Ibid.*
[6] See note 3, page 236.

There are edifying tales in the first half of the Book of Daniel, even if we cannot share Professor Rowley's enthusiasm about the apocalyptic section. Is it not sufficient that at the time of its composition this book gave hope and comfort and courage to people? Today, however, it can have little more than an antiquarian interest for us.

PSALMS

THE PSALMS are the lyrical masterpiece of the Tanak. This book, numbering one hundred and fifty poems, arranged in five parts, has traditionally been ascribed to King David, even though many of the poems are ascribed to Asaph, Moses, Solomon, and others, and even though the last verse (20) of Psalm 72, concluding Part II, reads "The prayers of David ben Jesse are ended." This verse, which is crystal clear, occurs in a psalm which at its beginning is ascribed to Solomon! To add to the puzzle of the authorship of the Psalms, Psalm 86, fourteen psalms later, bears the unexpected legend that it is by David. The necessary conclusion is that only some, and not all, of the Psalms are by David and that we are dealing with an anthology from many hands. The presence of duplicates is further evidence that the book is an anthology: Psalm 14 is identical with 53; 40:*13–17* with 70; and 108 with 57:*7–11* and 60:*5–12*.

Since it is an anthology, the Book of Psalms contains material both diverse in content and varied in quality. Some poems are liturgical and exalted, and some are secular. This is inevitably the case, for, as we have often said, the Tanak is as much folk literature as religious literature. In view of the diversity, to study the Psalms means to study one hundred and fifty separate poems. The economy of space prohibits such total study here.

. . .

Because the Psalms are often published with the New Testament in a single book, they are well known to Christians. Since the substance of Jewish daily and festival liturgy is the Psalms, Jews likewise have a great familiarity with the book. Psalm 23, beginning "The Lord is my shepherd; I shall not want," is unquestionably the best known, and is frequently read at both Jewish and Christian funerals.

Yet the familiarity of the Psalms has not made them easy to understand and appreciate. One fears that a succession of varying interpretations by scholars has done as much to obscure as to illuminate the Psalms. Sixty years ago many, perhaps most, scholars held the opinion that the Psalms, far from being by David, were the latest writings in the Tanak. Three reasons were usually cited for this judgment. In the first place, thirteen [1] of the Psalms are prefaced by statements that such and such a psalm was composed by David at such and such a moment in his career. For example, Psalm 57 is ascribed to David "on his fleeing into the cave from Saul." Psalm 59 is ascribed to the occasion "of Saul's sending, so that they guarded the house to slay him." The contents of these psalms exhibit no relation to the prefatory statements. It was hence inferred that just as these single psalms lacked connection with David, so too did the entire Psalter. The supposition of his authorship rested on David's fame as a musician (I Sam. 16:18ff.) and on the eulogy of him (II Sam. 23:1) as the "sweet singer of Israel." In the second place, since the Psalms reflected a high literacy, which it was assumed could not exist in early Israel, they must be very late. In the third place, the Psalms often exhibit a close relation to liturgy. Because it was assumed that liturgy was very late in developing, the Psalms, it was concluded, must perforce be late.

Moreover, certain psalms [2] are "alphabetical acrostics"; that is, the first line begins with *aleph*, a, the second with *beth*, b, and so on through the alphabet. Some scholars thought they could also find "nominal acrostics," poems that reveal through the first letters of initial words of the verses the name of the writer, or of the worthy to whom or about whom the poem was written. Thus one poem, Psalm 2, was so tortured as to make it disclose Yannai,[3] Alexander Jannaeus, who reigned from 103 to 76 B.C. This prepossession towards a late date prompted one scholar to declare that the question was not whether any of the Psalms were as late as the Maccabean age (165–37 B.C.), but whether any were earlier.

[1] These are Pss. 3, 7, 18, 34, 51, 52, 54, 56, 57, 59, 60, 63, and 142.
[2] Pss. 9, 10, 34, 37, 112, 119, 140, and 145. At one time 9 and 10 were a single Psalm.
[3] Similarly, Ps. 110:1–4, was regarded as an acrostic of Simon, the high priest in 141 B.C.

At Ugarit, twelve miles north of Latakia in north Syria, at a mound called Ras Shamra, many material remains were uncovered in the late 1920's and early 1930's, revealing remarkably close parallels to the Psalms in content and in a language kindred to the Hebrew. The Ras Shamra tablets come from the sixteenth–fourteenth pre-Christian centuries. Therefore, the view that the Psalms must necessarily be late was proven untenable. The attempt to date the Psalms reverted to the scrutinizing of each psalm, and the "late dating" was properly abandoned or at least used with discretion.

The "late dating" of the Psalms represented an extreme position; there is a present trend in interpretation that in its own way is also extreme, and, to the extent that it is, beclouds the understanding of the Psalms. This is the view that virtually all of the Psalms are ritualistic in character. That is, they were not free compositions of random poets, but rather productions designed for the Temple or temples, and created, presumably, by temple adherents or officiants. The consequence of this view is that a particular psalm depicts a man involved in some ritualistic endeavor rather than a poet spontaneously expressing a heightened emotion. Thus, Psalm 30 would not be an occasional poem written by a man grateful for having escaped some great danger or desperate illness, but rather a more or less conventional recitation, designed to be used by a worshiper who had escaped from danger on his appearance at a sanctuary. Is this fine poem one man's personal emotion, or many men's mechanical recitation? If it is suggested that the poem of one man can in time be the ritual recitation of many, then the extreme contention that the Psalms were created deliberately for ritualistic purposes is rejected.

Moreover, the chief ritualistic usage of the Psalms is alleged to be on the New Year day, bound up with the Semitic, and therefore Hebrew, custom of assuming that on every New Year the Deity ascended His divine throne, to be recrowned as the sole king of the universe. Any mention in the Psalms of Yahve as *king* would be an echo of the supposed "Ascension Day" ceremonies. As this view was elaborated, the human king was conceived of as annually reascending his throne, thus symbolizing or dramatizing the divine ascension. The human king descended from his throne, and for the period of seven days preceding the New Year a substitute king was selected from among the poor and unfortunate. This substitute was treated both royally and mockingly—crowned, for example, with a crown of thorns. After the week was over, he was put to death. Thereupon the real king, deposed for a week, was able to reascend the throne.[4]

The difficulties of the "Ascension Day" interpretation are multi-

---

[4] See page 190.

ple. The evidence to support the basic contention, though some does indeed exist, is sparse and scattered. However, the theory is all-embracing and pervasive, and out of proportion to the evidence. More-over, that period in which the king abdicated the throne for his substi-tute would be equivalent to the death of the Deity, with the ascension symbolic of the Deity's resurrection. Although the myth of the dying and rising deity is well attested in many folklores, it is significantly absent respecting Yahve. That is, traces of divine ascension are dis-cernible in the Psalms, but nothing like a conception of Yahve as dy-ing and rising. The crucial set of data needed to confirm the particu-lar theory is lacking in the Tanak; therefore, the theory must be spun from inferences from laconic texts. Finally, one could even concede that the theory is correct; yet the procedure of reading a reflection of it so broadly into so many psalms grossly overstates the case, to the point of negating it.

Neither a theory of late composition, nor a theory of a thorough-going ritualistic liturgy connected with an annual ascension, makes the Psalms intelligible or does justice to them. A more appropriate view is that the Book of Psalms is a heterogeneous anthology, contain-ing poems from many hands and from many ages. Some poems were definitely ritualistic, some were only poems. Some, indeed most, are inspired compositions, but some are pedestrian.

Virtually every psalm has a superscription, which tells its supposed authorship. The three that are most frequent are "of Da-vid," "of Asaph," and "of the sons of Korah." Asaph [5] is not completely known to us. Korah is a character known to us from Numbers 16. A first cousin of Moses, and like him, of the tribe of Levi, he is portrayed as having challenged Moses' leadership and paid the penalty of death. A group of Levites known as Korahites are mentioned in I Chron. 9:19–31 and 12:6 as porters and doorkeepers in the Temple. In the Psalms the "sons of Korah" would presumably be a group of singers or musicians. An attractive theory holds that a superscription such as "of David" or "of Asaph" is designed not to attribute specific author-ship but rather to refer to the repertory, as it were, of different groups or guilds of singers. This opinion has no direct bearing on whether David did or did not write any of the Psalms; it only maintains that the superscription "of David" is to be understood in a sense other than that of authorship.

Many of the Psalms bear titles or certain terms of a technical

[5] A man by that name is mentioned in I Chron. 6:39, and in 15:17 as one of David's chief musicians. An Asaph is mentioned in II Chron. 29:30, as a "seer"; the verse depicts a mandate by King Hezekiah upon the Levites to "praise Yahve in the words of David and Asaph, the seer."

nature. Psalm 24 is called a "song" (*mizmor*); 17 is called a "prayer"
(*tefilla*); 16 is called a *michtam*, whose meaning is unknown; 32 is
called a *maskil*, and may possibly mean "meditation." Some are addressed to a *menatzeah*, "overseer," often translated as "chief musician" or "choir-master." *Amen* is a Hebrew word that means "truly,"
and possibly represents a refrain, or a word of assent, interpolated
into a psalm when it came to be recited or read publicly. *Selah* is unknown; one may regard it either as a point in the public reading when
a pause was made for some benediction to be interpolated, or as an
instruction to repeat the verse just concluded.

Since the Psalms are an anthology, it is quite impossible to summarize their contents or to reproduce them in their entirety. The student
may be assisted, however, by a consideration of certain selected
psalms, which are in a sense typical of others and which will thereby
serve to introduce him to those he will read on his own. Indeed, the
most fruitful scholarship on the Psalms has resulted from studying
together those psalms that could be classified together.[6]

As a first sample, illustrative of many other psalms, we turn to
Psalm 100. Brief though it is, it takes us quickly into an exultant
mood:

> *A song of thanks,*
> *O all the land, shout to Yahve!*
> *Serve Yahve in joy,*
> *Come before Him with song.*
> *Know that Yahve is God.*
> *He made us and we are His,*
> *His people, the sheep of His pasturing.*
> *Come into His [Temple] gate in thanksgiving,*
> *Into His [Temple] courtyards with praise.*
> *Thank Him, bless His name.*
> *For Yahve is good; His reliability is eternal,*
> *His faithfulness [endures] throughout the generations.*

A comparable mood is found in Psalm 19:1–6:

> *For the chief musician. A song of David.*
> *The heavens relate God's glory,*

[6] The scholar alluded to, Hermann Gunkel, found five major types and five minor
ones. Since a single Psalm can fit into more than one "type," it is easy to quarrel
with Gunkel's categories. Nevertheless, his work remains the most perceptive
study. His major categories are Hymns, Communal Laments, Royal Psalms, Individual Thanksgiving, and Individual Laments. His minor types are Pilgrim
Songs, Communal Thanks, Oracular Poems, Prudential Psalms, and Liturgical
Poems.

And the celestial vault declares what His hands have made.
Daily the utterance is poured forth,[7]
Nightly, the knowledge is made known.
(There is really no utterance, and there are no words,
And no sound of these is heard!)

*
Yet their voice penetrates throughout the land,
And their words to the end of the earth.
*He [Yahve] has made a tent for the sun in the ocean; ***
It comes out like a groom from the bridal chamber,
Happy to run its course like a champion.
At one end of the heaven is its place of setting out,
And its circuit is to the [other] ends—
And no one can escape its heat.

This poem describes how the Deity is revealed in and controls nature.

Any representation of this kind takes us inevitably in the direction of mythological language. Such language is indeed present in the Psalms, though English translations often conceal it. The justification for such concealment is that the *matured* view of Yahve in the Tanak is devoid of mythological belief. Moreover, we have become so accustomed to conceive of the Tanak as reflecting a pure monotheism that we automatically interpret mythological elements so that they are consistent with pure monotheism. But mythological statements are scattered throughout the Tanak. A clear vestige is found in Psalm 82:1–7:

A song of Asaph,
God stands in the assembly of gods,
He administers justice in the midst of deities, [Saying to
          them:]
"How long will you judge perversely
And favor the wicked?"
Selah! [82:1–2]

The poet now addresses the assembly:

I had thought you were gods,
The sons, all of you, of the Most High,
The fact is, you must die just like men,
And you must fall like the [divine] princelings.[8] [82:6–7]

---

[7] Literally, "one pours forth the utterance."
[8] The allusion is to a myth, found in various forms and alluded to in the Tanak (Isa. 14:12–14) and in the New Testament (Luke 10:18; Rev. 12:7–9). The myth tells of a revolt against the Deity, led in some versions by Satan, in others by high-ranking princes. As punishment, they are cast out of heaven. See also Gen. 6:1–4.

In Psalm 29, the heavenly beings again are addressed and urged to acknowledge Yahve's power:

A song of David:
O sons of the gods, ascribe to Yahve,
Ascribe to Yahve [alone] glory and might . . .

Next follows an identification of Yahve and thunder, indicative of the Deity's triumph over the waters. Again we are in a mythological framework; the motif that the Deity had been locked in battle with the waters has echoes in several psalms and in Job.[9] The background of this concept is clarified for us by Babylonian accounts of the same myth, or a related one. The Deity represented the principle of law and order, while the water (capable of flood in the case of a river, or of devastating turbulence in the case of the sea) represented disorder and anarchy. The water was depicted as a great sea serpent, eager to conquer and dominate the land. The Deity, as the myth relates, slew the sea creature, symbolizing His control over the deep. The Babylonian account tells of the victory of the god Marduk over Tiamat, the water; echoes in Scripture give the sea creature the name of Rahab. In Psalm 89 we read:

Who in the sky compares with Yahve,
Who among the sons of the gods is like Yahve?
He is God, regarded with terror in the great council of the
         [heavenly] saints,
Awesome over all those about Him.

The poem reverts to the second person:

You [O Yahve] rule over the arrogance of the sea.
When its waves arise, You still them.
You broke Rahab into pieces, as a corpse;
You scattered Your foes with Your strong arm. [89:7–11
         Heb., 6–10 Eng.]

Similarly, we read in Psalm 74:13–14:

By Your strength, You broke the sea into pieces;
You crushed the heads of the sea monsters in the waters.
You shattered the heads of the leviathan;
You made him food for the dwellers in the wilderness.[1]

Reverting now to Psalm 29, it is not so much a mere recounting of the primeval conquest, as a hymn of praise to the Deity who has

[9] See Job 26:12–13.
[1] That is, desert dwellers find springs and oases, for the Deity, having subjected water, can make it available.

long ago done this great deed. The Deity, and not the deed, commands the poet's acclaim, for he is exulting in Yahve's control of nature:

> *The voice of Yahve is on the waters;*
> *There thunders the glorious God;*
> *Yahve [thunders] over great waters.*
> *Yahve's voice [comes] with power.*
> *Yahve's voice [comes] with majesty.*
>
> *Yahve's voice breaks cedars—*
> *Yahve breaks the cedars of Lebanon,*
> *Making them dance like a calf,*
> *Making Lebanon and Sirion*[2] *[dance] like the young of wild*
>   *oxen.*
> *Yahve's voice hews out flames of fire.*
> *Yahve's voice shakes the wilderness,*
> *Yahve shakes the wilderness of Kadesh.*[3]
> *Yahve's voice makes the does drop their calves.*
> *Yahve's voice strips the forest bare.*
>
> *In His Temple, every thing says, "Glory!"*
> *Yahve is seated above the water.*
> *Yahve is seated as the eternal king.*
> *Yahve gives strength to His people,*
> *Yahve blesses His people in peace.* [29:3–11]

Clearly, only the remote background of this psalm is mythological, not the intent of the poet or the age that assented to the incorporation of this psalm in Scripture. The poet, moved to exult in his awesome admiration of the Deity, draws on the ordinary language and the folk motifs that are in his ken.

This glimpse of recurrent "nature" motifs must satisfy us. We turn now to look at a related though different motif. Three psalms (93, 97, and 99), which begin "Yahve reigns," are similar in tone.

> *Yahve reigns; He is clothed in majesty;*
> *Yahve has clothed Himself, girded Himself with strength.*
>
> *
> *You [O Yahve] have established the world so it is immov-*
>   *able.*
> *Your throne was established of old;*

[2] Sirion is Mount Hermon.
[3] Kadesh Barnea symbolizes the extreme south, as Lebanon does the extreme north.

You have existed from eternity.
O Yahve, the waters have raised,
The waters have raised their voice.
The waters raise their roaring,
[Yet] above the voices of the great waters,
Above the mighty breakers of the sea,
You, O Yahve, are exalted on high! [93:1–4]

Another motif, the belief [4] that on the New Year the Deity came into the Temple, is reflected in a poem, Psalm 24, in which various voices are heard. First comes a hymn:

A song of David.
Yahve's is the earth and its fullness,
The world and its inhabitants.

For He established [the world] upon waters,
And made it firm upon floods.

Now the question arises of who is worthy to attend the sacred worship of the Deity:

Who may ascend the mount of [the Temple of] Yahve?
Who may stand in His place of holiness?

The reply:

He whose hands are clean and whose heart is pure;
He who has not raised himself to falsehood,
And has not made deceitful oaths.
[Such a person] will receive blessing from Yahve,
And approval from the God of his salvation.

Then comes the conclusion:

Such is the generation of those who seek Him,
Those who seek Jacob's God.
Selah.

Now the poet turns to the eastern gates, which are open for the Deity to enter:

Raise your heads, O gates!
Be raised high, O everlasting portals,
And let the radiant King enter!

A voice asks:

Who is the radiant King?

[4] See pages 64–65.

The reply:

> *He is Yahve, powerful and mighty,*
> *Yahve, heroic in battle.*

Again:

> *Raise your heads, O gates!*
> *Raise them, O everlasting portals,*
> *And let the radiant King enter.*

Again:

> *Who is the radiant King?*

The answer:

> *He is Yahve of Hosts;*
> *He is the radiant King.*
> *Selah.*

Similarly, Psalm 98:4–9 reads:

> *Shout to Yahve, O all the earth;*
> *Break forth, sing, and be melodious.*
> *Sing to Yahve with the lyre,*
> *With the lyre and the sound of song,*
> *With trumpets and the sound of the ram's horn;*
> *Shout before the King Yahve!*
>
> *Let the sea and all it contains roar,*
> *The world and its inhabitants.*
> *Let the floods clap their hands;*
> *Let the hills sing together,*
> *Before Yahve, for [now] He comes to judge the earth.*
> *He will judge the world righteously*
> *And the peoples fairly.*

Some of the psalms reflect the poet in a mood when, distant from the Temple, he recalls his emotion at having been there, or his joyful expectation of making the pilgrimage.

> *How beloved is Your Temple,*[5] *O Yahve of Hosts;*
> *I yearn, I even perish for the courtyards of Yahve.*
> *My heart and my flesh sing for the living God,*

---

[5] The Hebrew here is in the plural, as it is often, and is correctly translated as "tabernacles." Yet the correct translation belies the Scriptural intent, for the plural is clearly intended to allude to a single place, the Temple, which was a complex building.

[Searching] even as a birdling which has found a home,
Or a swallow a nest where to put his young,
[So have I found] Your altar, O Yahve of Hosts,
My King and my God.

Happy are those who inhabit Your house,
Continually praising You.
Happy is the man for whom You are his strength,

*In whose heart [is the joy] of pilgrimage;**
Such [a man is like] those who traverse the valley of weep-
   ing [6]
*Which He makes into a place of springs;**
*Indeed, by early rains, [He makes it] a place of wells.**
They go [thence] from stronghold to stronghold,
And appear before God at Zion. [7]

Better is one day in Your courts than a thousand in my
   *chambers;**
[Better is it] to lie on the threshold of God's house than to
   dwell inside tents of wickedness. [84:1–7, 10]

Again:

A song of Ascents. [8] *Of David.*
I was happy when people said to me,
"Let us go to Yahve's house!"
Our feet were standing in your gates, O Jerusalem!—
Jerusalem rebuilt like a city altogether united,
To which tribes, the tribes of God, ascend,

*To praise Yahve's name as commanded to Israel.**
There once sat thrones of justice, the thrones of David's
   house.

Pray for peace, O Jerusalem;
*May your dwellings be at ease.**
May there be security in your ramparts,
Prosperity in your mansions.
On behalf of brothers and friends I speak forth,
"Peace be with you."
On behalf of the house of Yahve, our God, I ask,
"May it be well with you." [122]

[6] That would be a bare and cheerless valley.
[7] This is the mount on which the Temple stood.
[8] Since the Temple was on a mount, one reached it by "ascending."

A psalm that seems clearly liturgical reads:

Yahve reigns; the peoples tremble.

He sits over the cherubim; [9] *the earth quivers.*

Yahve is mighty in Zion; He is exalted over all the nations.

Let them praise Your great and awesome name:
"Sacred is He!"

He reigns with might; He loves justice.

Now there is a more direct shift to the second person.

It is You Who have established [standards of] fairness:
You Who have fashioned justice and righteousness. *

The poet now addresses the people:

Exalt Yahve, our God, and prostrate yourselves at His foot-
stool:
"Sacred is He!" [99:1–5]

There are, however, a great many psalms that are the outpour-
ings of an individual, rather than liturgical recitations. Sometimes
the mood is one of lament, but often it is one of thanksgiving.

I extol You, O Yahve, for You have drawn me up,
Thus preventing my adversaries from gloating over me!
O Yahve, my God, I cried to You; You healed me.
O Yahve, You brought me out of Sheol; [1]
You preserved me alive from the grave. [2]

A shift in person takes place:

Out of His wrath comes smiting; [3]
Out of His favor comes life.
Weeping was there at evening to lodge for the night,
But in the morning there was rejoicing!
Therefore I said, in my security,
"Never shall I be moved."

[9] Within the wilderness tabernacle was the room called the Holy of Holies. Above
the Ark were two cherubim. When Yahve entered, He was believed to sit above the
cherubim.
[1] Sheol was the place of the dead. Hence, the verse means, "You saved me from
death."
[2] Literally, "From being one of those who descend into the pit."
[3] An emendation has been made, altering "moment" to "smiting."

There is another shift in person:

> Yahve, in Your favor You had made me stand, a mountain
> stronghold;
> You had hidden Your face; I was in dismay!
> I called to You, O Yahve,
> I made supplication to You, O Yahve, [saying]:
> "What advantage to you is my death,[4]
> My descent into the pit?
> Will the dust render You praises?
> Will it make known Your fidelity?
> Hear, O Yahve, and be gracious to me!
> O Yahve, become my help!"

> For me, You turned mourning into a dance,
> You took off my sackcloth, and girded me with joy! [30:1–
> 12 Heb., 1–11 Eng.]

Much less dramatic, but just as exultant is a psalm described as a "Song for the Sabbath Day":

> It is good to praise Yahve, and to sing to Your name, O most
> High.
> To relate in the morning Your reliability, in the night Your
> fidelity,
> With a ten-string and a flute, with the plucking of a harp.
> For Your deeds have gladdened me;
> I sing of the acts of Your hands.

> How great are Your acts, O Yahve!
> How deeply profound are Your thoughts!
> This a crude man does not know, nor a fool understand.

> When the wicked sprout like grass,
> And evildoers blossom—
> It is for their eternal destruction,
> For You, O Yahve, are eternally exalted.
> Your opponents are now perishing, O Yahve—
> Evildoers are all scattered!

> As for me, You have exalted my horn like that of a wild ox,[5]
> *
> You made me luxuriant in fresh oil. [92:1–11 Heb., 1–10
> Eng.]

[4] Literally, this reads "my blood."
[5] That is, You have made me free and untrammeled by foes.

However, the other mood, that of lament, is much more frequent. The homeless wanderer is eloquently portrayed in an exile's psalm:

> *By the streams of Babylon,*
> *There we sat and wept*
> *When we remembered Zion.*
> *On willows there we hung our lyres,*
> *For there our captors demanded songs of us,*
> *And our oppressors entertainment:*
> *"Sing to us one of the songs of Zion."*
> *How shall we sing Yahve's song on foreign soil!*
>
> *If I forget you, O Jerusalem, let my right hand be forgotten.*
>
> *Let my tongue cleave to my palate*
> *If I fail to remember you,*
> *If I do not raise Jerusalem above my own joy.* [137:1–6]

The difference between thanksgiving and lament can be seen in a psalm in which lament is blended with an emotion closely related to thanksgiving:

> *O Yahve, how abundant are my foes,*
> *How numerous are those who rise against me!*
> *Many say to me, "There is no help from God."*
>   *Selah.*
> *But You, O Yahve, are a shield about me,*
> *My glory, He who raises my head.*
>
> *I lift my voice to Yahve;*
> *He answers me from His sacred mountain.*
>   *Selah.*
>
> *I lay down and I could sleep; I woke [alive]—*
> *For Yahve sustains me.*
>
> *I do not fear myriads of people*
> *Who are arrayed against me on all sides . . .*
> *For You have smitten all my foes on the cheek;*
> *You have broken the teeth of the wicked.* [3:1–8 Heb., 1–7
>   Eng.]

In the psalms of lament there is frequent mention of foes. Can they be identified? Sometimes, and very clearly. Such is the case in the explicit vindictiveness against the kindred people, the Edomites:

> *Remember against the Edomites, O Yahve,*
> *The [disastrous] day of Jerusalem.*

[Remember] how they said, "Raze it, raze it, down to its
    foundations."
Happy is the one who repays you,
O Babylon's daughter,[6] *for the devastations,*
[Repays you] in the way that you treated us.
Happy is the one who seizes your babes
And dashes them on the rocks. [137:7–9]

But usually the "foe" cannot be identified precisely. The superscriptions that attribute certain psalms to David would imply that these foes are in some cases Saul and his cohorts and in other cases foreign peoples such as the Philistines. But if we assert that a superscription is not truly related to the psalm to which it is joined, then we lose that basis for identifying the foes.

In the laments, the adverse circumstances that move the Psalmist to complain are seldom the ordinary vicissitudes of life such as sickness, death, or the disasters of flood and earthquake. With rather high consistency, the plaintive utterance is due to unidentified adversaries. A recent trend in scholarship has identified these "foes" with sorcerers who used their magic powers against the lamenter. This view asserts that those reassuring lines in a psalm of lament are spoken by temple priests in response to the worshiper's prayer to have the magic spell broken. In the field of Tanak there have been many surprising theories advanced, but none has been quite as unlikely as this one.

The foes are, rather, the ordinary opponents who exist in any social situation. A variety of sources have acquainted us with the imaginative character of the oriental mind, and its capacity to exaggerate. A rival becomes an adversary, an adversary a foe, and a foe the enemy. Moreover, the standards of our own genteel age—genteel in personal relations, rather than national ones—ought not to be applied to ancient times. The age of the Psalms did not know suppression and subterfuge. One hated—and expressed his hatred. Yet it should be said that the laments, insofar as they deal with foes, are not the fruits of meditation but spontaneous utterances. They disclose a man in a situation that to him is real. The animosity in the Psalms is uncharitable, but it is authentic and undisguised.

The pathos of a lament seems always genuine, as one sample can show:

O Yahve, do not rebuke me in Your anger,
And do not chastise me in Your wrath.

---

[6] A figure of speech, likening the Edomites to the ferocious people who conquered Jerusalem in 597.

Be kindly to me, for I am weak;
Heal me, for my bones tremble.
I tremble very much—
But You—O Yahve—how long?

Turn, O Yahve, save me,
Deliver me in accord with Your reliability.
In death [I] can make no mention of You;
Who in Sheol can give You praises?

I am wearying of my groaning;
Each night I make my bed swim; I drench my couch with
        my tears.
My eye has wasted away from grief;
It has faded because of my foes.

O evildoers, go away from me,
For Yahve has heard the sound of my weeping.
He has heard my supplication;
He has accepted my prayer.

All my foes are ashamed and greatly dismayed—
They are rejected, ashamed all at once. [6:2–11 Heb., 1–10
        Eng.]

The best-known of the Psalms (23) is one of assurance:

Yahve is my shepherd; I lack nothing.
He pastures me in grassy meadows,
He leads me to still waters,
He brings me back.
He guides me in right paths——.
Even when I go through a gloomy valley, I do not fear evil
For You are with me;
Your rod and staff—these direct [7] *me.*

You set a table before me, despite my foes;
You anoint my head with oil.
My cup [8] *is filled to overflowing.*

Nothing but God's good and reliability attend me all my
        life,

[7] This emendation is in the Hebrew a slight one, that of dropping a letter. Unemended, the meaning is "comfort."
[8] The meaning is "my portion."

And I shall live in my house [9] *a great length of days.*

Scattered here and there in the Psalms are poems that are didactic and moralistic; in these the teacher has possibly conquered the poet. An example is Psalm 133:

See, how fine and pleasant it is
For brothers to dwell in unity.
This is like precious oil on the head
Coming down on the beard . . .
It is like the dew of [Mount] Hermon,
Descending on Zion's hills.

There [on such unity] Yahve has commanded His blessing:
Life until eternity.

In even less exalted poetry, we read:

Praise God!
Happy is the man who reveres Yahve,
And delights in His commandments.
His seed will be mighty in the land,
A blessed generation of the upright.
Wealth and riches are in his house.
And his success endures. [112:1–3]

In a similar vein is the portrait of what a good king should be like:

O God, give Your ability to judge to the king,
And Your sense of right to the prince.
Let him judge Your people justly
And Your poor with equity. [72:1–2]

Similarly, another psalm first outlines the responsibilities of the king, and then turns to the royal consort:

A king's daughter [1] *[O King] is by you,*
The consort stands at your right hand bejeweled with the
gold of Ophir.

A word now to the consort-queen:

Hear, young woman, and observe, and incline your ear:
Forget your [own] people and your father's house;
Then the king will desire your beauty.

[9] This is a correction for "House of Yahve."
[1] An emendation has been made; the text, unemended, says "daughters."

Now, he is your master; be subservient to him.
You come * with a bundle [2] *and a gift,*
For the wealthy of the people entreat your favor,
They honor you with pearls;
Your gowns have threads of gold.

[45:*10–1* Heb., *9–13* Eng.]

This is colorful, perhaps, but it is not great poetry, either in the confused Hebrew or in my guesses as to how the original might be restored.

But poetry, no matter how great, could be included in the Tanak, and therefore in the Psalter, only if it contained, or was thought to contain, some religious or moral aspect. Esthetics was not the basic or ultimate concern of the compilers of the individual books of the Tanak. There existed no objection to beauty in literature, but the essential element was instructive. Indeed, there exists among Jews a Yiddish phrase, difficult to render in English, that speaks of the "beauty of a teaching" (*a shane bissel Torah*). That which was beautiful was expected simultaneously to edify. The quest in certain "Wisdom" Psalms seems to have been for a form in which edification could be phrased in beautiful language.

The Psalter could not have properly reflected a basic concern of the Tanak unless it contained a preface indicating that the poems to follow are designated to be edifying. This preface is Psalm 1. Its poetry is not so exalted in the Hebrew as it is in the King James translation. If the author attempted to blend edification with beauty of expression, he did not succeed. But the preface is necessary, for it transforms the book from a collection of great lyrics into a more wonderful vehicle of religious expression, thus providing a high eloquence in prayer for the inarticulate of later days. The poems rise higher than the preface, but the preface, in a sense, gives the poems their highest elevation:

Happy is the man who has not walked in the way [3] *of the*
        wicked,
Nor stood in the council of sinners,
Nor sat in the parlor of the scorners.
His delight, rather, is in God's worship,*
And he meditates day and night on His teaching.
He becomes like a tree by water-courses
Which [is able to] give fruit in the due season,

---

[2] The text reads literally: "and the daughter of Tyre with a gift"; the translation given rests on emendations.
[3] I transpose "way" and "council," as does an ancient version.

And the leaves of which do not wither [from dryness]. . . .
Such is not the case with the wicked,
For they are, rather, like the chaff which the wind drives
   away. [1:1–4]

All the Psalms, then, are not of the same quality; some are not products of the highest poetical inspiration. Psalm 119 is notable primarily because it forms an alphabetical acrostic, with eight verses for each letter of the alphabet; all too many of the verses are uninspired. Psalms 135 and 136, which are in part reviews of history, are less than impressive blends of ancient events and poetry. Yet what is notable about the Psalms is not that some of them are poetry of only indifferent value, but, rather, that so few of them fall into this category, and that the eloquence of most of the Psalms is unmatched.

Certain Christian versions, such as the King James, carry notations before each psalm or at the top of each page which relate the contents to the Christ or the church, as though the Psalms were written to foreshadow later Christian theological views. Two psalms, 22 and 69, were influential in the accounts of the passion ("suffering") of Jesus. It is debated whether the contents of these psalms led to ascribing these events to Jesus' career, or whether the events reminded the Gospel authors of these psalms.

The authenticity of the Psalms should be apparent to the reader; he should perceive that they arise from flesh-and-blood people. The lament, or the thanksgiving, or the eloquent acknowledgment that Yahve is the creator and ruler of all things including man—all such themes reflect real human situations, even though the frame of reference has changed radically since then. The modern man is more apt to explain lightning, thunder, and rain as aspects of a discipline called meteorology than to ascribe them to the Deity; yet even the most ultramechanistic plays and novels of the twentieth century frequently utilize the theme of man's helplessness before a neutral and hence unfriendly nature. The times, the geography, and, of course, the intellectual climate change, but man remains essentially the same. The reader of the Psalms who devotes undue attention to the incorrect meteorology or the vestiges of exceedingly primitive mythology to be found in them is guilty of distortion. It is the human voice, with the echo of the human heart, that should claim our attention.

Therein, for students of college age, lies the true difficulty in appreciating the Psalms. At this age physical strength is still growing; horizons expand and persuade the young person of his increasing mastery of the universe; ambition often blinds him to the variety of vicissitudes that lie ahead for him. Most young people still have both their parents, and hence few of them are personally and intimately acquainted with death. Because the Psalms reflect human experience they themselves have not undergone, the very reality of them strikes young people as unrealistic. I have found many students mystified at the hold the Psalms have had on the hearts and minds of men throughout the generations. Perhaps, when one is young, it is sufficient to know the Psalms, rather than to try completely to appreciate them. That appreciation will come as the years unroll with their inevitable events.

Indeed, not only the young, who have not yet plumbed deep emotional experiences, but even the mature, if they crush their emotions, can fail to respond to the Psalms. The Psalmist wept, or laughed, or was angry, or was fearful, and he made no effort to restrain his feelings. To share the Psalmist's emotions, the reader must be willing to admit that these emotions exist within him too. The admission can often lead him to respond fully to the Psalms and to realize, then, how eloquently the Psalms express his own emotions. Such can be the case with one of the finest verses in the whole Psalter:

> *As the hart longs for streams of water,*
> *So my soul longs for You, O God.* [42:2 Heb., 1 Eng.]

Here, at their best, religion and poetry are combined.

CHAPTER

20

PROVERBS

THREE BOOKS of the Tanak are called Wisdom Literature, a title that is both apt and inept. These books are Proverbs, Ecclesiastes, and Job. The books do not deal with prophecy or with law; they deal with those matters that are considered in folklore or meditated upon by the thoughtful.

The Book of Proverbs is a collection of collections. Some of the component collections still retain titles; Chapter 10 is called "The Proverbs of Solomon"; Chapter 25 is headed "Proverbs of Solomon which Associates of King Hezekiah Copied"; Chapter 30 is "The Words of Agur ben Jake"; and Chapter 31 is entitled "The Words of Lemuel."

In ordinary usage, a proverb is a short, pithy statement. Such brief statements are found in abundance in the Book of Proverbs, but they by no means comprise the totality of the book. The reader must be prepared for passages in the nature of essays as well. Moreover, large portions of the Book of Proverbs are exhortations rather than pithy sayings. Indeed, the first nine chapters[1] are really an

[1] The following is some of the detail to be found in the first nine chapters. There is a warning against the temptation to commit crime, 1:7–19. Wisdom, personified, cries aloud, denouncing those who are not true to her, 1:20–33. Chapter 2 deals with wisdom and understanding as the avenues leading to true reverence and true righteousness: Chapter 3 tells of the advantages that come from wisdom

introduction to the proverbs that follow, rather than a series of proverbs in themselves.

In this first chapter we are dealing with the advice of a mentor to his student or of a father to his son. The theme of these first nine chapters may be paraphrased in this way: wisdom is wonderful and therefore the young should cultivate it. The advantage of pursuing wisdom is clearly indicated:

> *My son, listen to the instruction of your father*
> *And do not forsake the teaching of your mother*
> *For they are a wreath of grace for your head*
> *And a necklace about your neck.*
> *My son, if sinners entice you, do not succumb.** *
> *My son, do not go on the way with them,*
> *But withhold your foot from their path*
> *For their feet run to evil*
> *And they hasten to spill blood.* [1:8–10, 15–16]

This is possibly sufficient to indicate the nature of the exhortation. There is no great unity in the first nine chapters, but rather a series of passages related to each other only by their common theme of wisdom.

In Chapter 10, we come to the short and pithy sayings. It is quite impossible to reproduce them all, but certain individual passages merit citation because they show the clear nature of the proverb. We should notice the following characteristics: brevity, parallelism, the regularity of the form, the cheerfulness of the tone, and lastly but importantly, the secular rather than religious character.

> *The memory of the righteous is a blessing,*
>   *But the name of the wicked rots.* [10:7]

> *Hatred stirs up strife,*
>   *But love covers all transgressions.* [10:12]

> *In the multiplication of words sin is not absent,*
>   *But he who restrains his lip is prudent.* [10:19]

---

and from true piety. Chapters 4 and 5:1–6 are a father's advice to his son or sons; the remainder of the chapter, 5:7–23, commends marital fidelity. 6:1–5 advise against being surety for someone, 6:6–11 caution against laziness, and 6:12–35 warn against a variety of sins, including adultery. Chapter 7 is both a warning against adultery and a description of how a streetwalker operates. In Chapter 8 Wisdom is again personified, giving us a description of the benefits she can bestow upon men. In Chapter 9 Wisdom and Foolishness, both personified, are contrasted with each other.

The slanderer discloses a secret,
  But one of faithful spirit conceals a matter. [11:13]

Like a ring of gold in a pig's nose
  Is a beautiful woman devoid of taste. [11:22]

A righteous woman is a crown to her husband,
  But a shameful one is rottenness in his bones. [12:4]

He who withholds the rod hates his son;
  He who loves him gives him abundant chastisement.
    [13:24]

Righteousness exalts a nation,
  But its absence is a sin to the people. [14:34]

A soft answer turns away wrath,
  But a harsh word provokes anger. [15:1]

These examples, especially in contrast to some of the extended passages of the first chapter, give us a clue to the growth of the book. Apparently the individual proverbs were gathered from Solomon and his time or from the other worthies; these collections existed either in oral or in written form. The present Book of Proverbs is the result of compiling the collections. Though the heading ascribes the book to Solomon, the ascriptions within the book to other worthies prevent our ascribing the whole book to him. The Book of Proverbs contains 935 verses; I Kings 5:12 (4:32 in English versions) speaks of Solomon's having spoken 3000 proverbs, but that number is not to be taken seriously. Some scholars want to deny that Solomon wrote any of the proverbs. They note that the Book of Proverbs seems to lack what we might speak of as a royal viewpoint. But even if none of the proverbs goes back to Solomon, by the time the Book of Proverbs was assembled into the total collection, his figure represented wisdom. It would have been strange, therefore, for the book not to have been attributed to him. While I see no urgent reason to ascribe any of Proverbs to Solomon, I see no reason to doubt absolutely some possible connection between him and some of the contents.

Proverbial sayings are so universal and so ancient that to speculate on the date of their origin is futile. Speculation, if it is justified at all, must be limited to the restricted question of when this book could have been compiled. If we assume that the compilation was made in postexilic times, it should be understood that the materials compiled are of much earlier ages. The high antiquity of individual proverbs is known better from Egyptian records than from the Assyrian and Babylonian, for the latter give us only a chaotic conception. There is reason to suppose that one section of the Book of Proverbs, namely 22:17–23:4, exhibits what may be a direct literary dependency on an Egyptian work, "The Wisdom of Amenenopes."

The last section of the Book of Proverbs is an alphabetical acrostic. The passage has been greatly influential in determining the role of Jewish wives and mothers. If the artificiality of the form conquers the poetry of some of the verses, it does not quite succeed in overshadowing the idealism. One could almost regard the conclusion as advice to a daughter, thus counterbalancing the many sections in the Book of Proverbs that are advice to a son:

> *When one finds a worthy wife,*
> *Her value is far beyond that of pearls.*
> *The heart of her husband is confident about her*
> *And he does not lack gain.*
> *She does good and not evil for him*
> *All the days of her life.*
> *She seeks and works gladly with her hands,*
> *She becomes like a merchant ship bringing her food from*
> *far off.*
> *She rises while it is still night,*
> *Giving food to her household and a portion to her*
> *maidens.*
> *She estimates the worth of a field and buys it,*
> *And with the fruit of her hands she plants a vineyard.*
> *She girds her loins with strength,*
> *She gives vigor to her arms.*
> *She makes sure that her merchandise is good;*
> *Her light does not go out at night.*
> *She puts her hands upon the distaff,*
> *And her hands take hold of the spindle.*
> *She stretches out her hand to the poor*
> *And extends her hand to the needy.*
> *She does not fear what snow can do to her household,*
> *For all her house is dressed in warm clothing.*
> *She makes coverings for herself*
> *And she is dressed in fine linen and in purple.*
> *Her husband is well known in public life* [2]
> *When he sits with the elders of the land. . . .*

[2] **This is, literally translated, "the gates."**

Her children rise up and declare her blessed,
   Her husband also, and he praises her:
"Many daughters have done virtuously,
   But you have excelled them all."
Mere grace is delusive and beauty is empty;
   The woman who is reverent toward God is worthy of
     praise.
Give her the fruit of her hands
   And let her works render praise to her openly. [31:10–23,
     28–31]

Such counsel to a bride or such pithy sayings as we have seen could be considered representative of an aspect of a national literature. The essential characteristic of the Tanak, of course, is that it is religious literature; however, much of the wisdom of Proverbs, even when they praise religious piety, has a predominantly secular tone. Moreover, whatever values inhere in the book are scarcely those of literary quality or of profound or daring thought. While I shall seek to show that there is a certain excitement connected with the significance of Proverbs in intellectual history, that excitement is scarcely due to the contents of the book. The advice offered in the book is sound and good; it is also safe and prudential, without the slightest element of risk. One who follows the advice of the Book of Proverbs ought to be quite capable, either in ancient Israel or today, of winning friends and influencing people. Since such prudential wisdom can be found among all peoples, the student may question in what sense the Book of Proverbs differs from the proverbs or the wise sayings of ancient sages of other lands. Probably there is no essential difference, but Proverbs, by virtue of being part of the Tanak, became more than secular wisdom—they became Torah, that is, Revelation.

When it became evident in the early postexilic period that, in place of a kingship, a priestly hierarchy would control the religious and political life, the theoretical separation between civil life and religious life came to an end. In the theocracy everything that previously had been secular tended to become sacred. We saw above (pages 195–197) that the legal requirements, previously secular, now became Torah.

The Hebrew word for wisdom is *ḥochma*. When one says that the effect of the Book of Proverbs, especially in its reception into Sacred Scripture, was to equate *ḥochma* with Torah, one is accurately distinguishing between wisdom as it was conceived of in Israel, and as it was conceived of by other ancient peoples. In the postexilic period, wisdom came to be regarded as a product of God's revelation. With the incorporation of the Book of Proverbs in Scripture, that revelation came to occupy the same high place as the revelation in the Five Books of Moses. We cannot say precisely when *hochma* came to be identified with Torah, but surely the identification was made before the acceptance of Proverbs into the sacred list, for only on the basis that Proverbs was Torah could it have been received into Scripture.

We must suppose that there was a relatively long period of development from the initial equation of *hochma* with Torah until the ultimate acceptance of the identification. The beginning of the identification was very much later than the recording of the very ancient individual aphorisms that constitute the bulk of the book. But once men began to discuss Torah and *hochma* as interchangeable, *hochma* was regarded as an entity different from other entities encountered in human existence. The technical scholars distinguish two stages in the development of the unique place of *hochma*. Whereas there is little reflection of abstract thinking in the Book of Proverbs, abstract wisdom is *personified*. Personification is the first stage we shall want to distinguish from a subsequent one.

In personification, an abstract quality is given human characteristics. It can move about, it can walk, it can talk, it can call. In the first chapter of Proverbs there is a section in which Wisdom is personified:

Wisdom cries aloud in the streets;
In the open squares she puts forth her voice.
At the head of the noisy thoroughfare she calls out;
She speaks her pieces at the gates of the city:
"How long, O foolish ones, will you love foolishness,
And scorners will delight yourselves in scorning and
fools hate knowledge?
Turn about at my rebuke; see I shall put my spirit on you
And I will make my words known to you.

Because I have called and you refuse,
Because I have stretched out my hand and no man listens
But you set aside my advice and did not desire my guid-
ance,
I, in turn, will laugh at your calamity,
And I will mock when what you dread comes upon you.
When your dread comes like a storm

And when disaster comes like a whirlwind
And when trouble and distress come upon you—
At that time they will call upon me but I will not answer;
And they will seek me diligently, but they will not find me.
In return for their hatred of knowledge and their failure to
   choose reverence for God,
They did not want my counsel and they rejected my guid-
ance.
They will eat the fruit of their way,
   And they will become sated from their own suggestions.
For the backsliding of fools will ultimately kill them
   And the complacency of fools will bring them to perish.
But he who listens to me will dwell in security and at ease
   without fearing any evil." [1:20–33]

In a similar vein there is another monologue by Wisdom, the first portion of which (8:1–21) is similar in tone to that which we have just examined. The latter part takes an additional step which is of some note:

God made me as the beginning of His ways,[3]
   The earliest of His works of olden times.
Aeons ago I was fashioned, at the beginning,
   Even before earth,
Before there was the sea I was brought forth,
   Before there were fountains full of water.
Before the mountains were settled in their foundations
   And before the hills, I was brought forth.

Before God had made earth and the fields
   Or the first dust of the world,
When He set up the heavens there was I;
   When He set a circle over the face of the deep;
When He made firm the skies above
   And when He made fountains of the deep.
He gave the sea its limit,
   That the water should not transgress its domain.
When He laid the foundations of the earth,
   Then I was with Him as an instrument.[4]

I was His delight every day,
   Playing always before Him,

[3] That is to say, His first creation.
[4] This is an uncertain word which is sometimes translated, "nestling."

Playing on His inhabited earth,
  And my delights are with human beings.

And now, my children, hear me,
  Hear my instruction and be wise and do not reject it.
Happy is the man who hears me;
  Happy are they who follow my way.[5]
They watch daily at my gates,
  Waiting at the posts of my door,
For whoever finds me finds life
  And wins favor from God,
And whoever misses me wrongs himself;
  Those who hate me love death. [8:22–36]

The view that wisdom was an entity that existed before the world and was available for the Deity as an instrument in creation takes us, as we have said, a step beyond the personification of wisdom which we noticed in the citation from Proverbs 1. Personification was the first of a two-step development; it consisted in speaking of Wisdom figuratively, as though Wisdom were a person. The second step in the progression was to speak of Wisdom, and regard it as though it were an entity of actual, rather than abstract existence. This second step is known as hypostatization; when Wisdom is conceived of as having real existence, and as something distinct from everything else, in the way that one man is distinct from all other men, it is called a hypostasis. It is an open question whether in the passage we have just considered wisdom is actually hypostatized or is only personified.

When Jews spread throughout the Greek world, after the time of Alexander the Great in the last quarter of the fourth pre-Christian century, they encountered, especially among the Stoics, doctrines about wisdom and a universal mind. The Stoics often spoke of universal mind or wisdom (*sophia*) as if it had a separate and distinct existence. As a result, Greek Jews began to equate Stoic *sophia* with Hebrew *hochma*. The further equation then arose (just as *hochma* equalled Torah and the Stoic universal mind equalled *hochma,* by the rule that things equal to the same thing are equal to each other) of *sophia* with Torah. That is to say, Greek Jews extended revelation from the wisdom of the Jews to include those facets of Greek wisdom they found congenial.

Tradition among the Greeks, even before the Stoics, dealt with a

---

[5] A slight rearrangement of the verses in accordance with the Greek translation has been followed.

conception summarized by the word *logos*. When the Greeks used the word, they meant the ideal form of logical thinking; it is an ideal to strive for, normally beyond the individual man. *Logos* means both "reason" and "the power to reason." The power to reason without human error would represent some superhuman capacity; it could represent the power of divine reason. Wisdom would represent accumulated knowledge, and reason the process of attaining wisdom. If ideal reason or *logos* is beyond the individual man, he can nevertheless often get glimpses of it; this occurs when man's reason is for an interval free from human error.

To continue with our equations, Greek Jews inherited from their Judaism an identification of *hochma* and *Torah*, wisdom and revelation. They encountered in their Greek environment *sophia*, to be equaled with *hochma*, and *logos*, which they took to be equated with Torah. They ascribed to Logos-Torah the separate, distinct existence akin to that of hypostatized *hochma*. To a Greek Jew, true philosophy was a vehicle by which one acquired wisdom and, thereafter, a glimpse of divine revelation. Wisdom, reason, and revelation were terms that revolved about a complex of closely intertwined correlations. We find this in the Book of Wisdom (also known as the Wisdom of Solomon), which is in the Greek Bible, and in the writings of Philo of Alexandria (20 B.C.–A.D. 40).

There was another aspect, and possibly the most important one in this complex of ideas. If man and God are separated from each other in different worlds, what is to bridge this gap? Greek Jews found the bridge in the *logos*, which was divine but available to man. Such thinking led naturally to the conclusion that *logos* was both a bridge and an intermediary between God and the world. Philo often describes the *logos*, to him a "hypostasis," as the first-born son of God, or the chief of the divine messengers. In Philo, *logos* is the image of the remote God, which acts on behalf of God in this world.

In the New Testament, Jesus, conceived of as both human and divine, was termed Christ from the standpoint of the divinity ascribed to him. *The Christ* was conceived of by Paul along the lines similar to those of Philo's *logos* (though Paul never uses the term *logos* itself). The identification of *Christ* and *logos*, implicit in Paul, becomes explicit in the Gospel According to John. This Gospel begins:

In the beginning was the *logos* and the *logos* was with God and the *logos* was divine. He was in the beginning with God. All things came into being through him. Apart from him nothing which has come into being came into being. . . . And the *logos* became flesh and dwelt among us. [John 1:*1–3, 14*]

Without the intervening Greco-Jewish blend of wisdom and Torah and *logos*, there could not have emerged that type of thinking reflected in Paul and explicit in the Gospel According to John. The Greco-Jewish thinkers and writers have not played an important role in the history of Judaism, and they did not become part of the later heritage of Jews and Judaism. But wisdom-*logos* as a "hypostasis," developed from ideas in Proverbs, is found in this literature for the few who occasionally penetrate it.

There is an important connection in the history of the development of Christian thought to be found in the study of Proverbs. When we see how *ḥochma* acquired from the Book of Proverbs a separate existence, which became identified with *Torah,* and how *ḥochma* became identified in the Greco-Jewish world with *logos,* we can begin to see the long line that leads from the Book of Proverbs to the Gospel According to John. It is this aspect of the Book of Proverbs that gives it some excitement. The book itself never strays from that which is right, socially acceptable, and useful. It is an edifying and sound book, but unimaginative righteousness may, for some, become tedious.

ECCLESIASTES

ECCLESIASTES, which together with Proverbs and Job is classified as Wisdom Literature, is said to be by Koheleth, the son of King David. Tradition early identified Koheleth as Solomon. It is possibly this identification that brought this interesting and amusing book into Scripture.

The book may call to mind a country store with men sitting around a cracker barrel, while one of them, wise, sagacious, and full of human experience, regales the others with his sharp tongue and acid comments on affairs, uttering bold and heretical statements. He keeps his hearers fascinated, for what everyone else calls black, he calls white, and what everyone else calls good, he calls bad. Just as they are about to conclude that he is a heretic par excellence, he suddenly arises, says good night, and announces that he must go home to get a good night's sleep in order to be in church bright and early the next morning.

The Book of Ecclesiastes consists of twelve chapters. Eleven chapters contain skepticism, cynicism, and pessimism, but the twelfth chapter seems to repudiate and deprecate the seriousness of the intent of the eleven chapters. Some scholars believe that the twelfth chaper is not by the same hand that wrote the preceding eleven. This may be the case, but the theory is quite unnecessary, for the same author might easily have lost the courage of his lack of convictions.

It has been denied that "Koheleth" is a name, but if it is not a name, it is hard to know what else it might possibly be. Koheleth begins with the startling and striking statement:

> *Vanity of vanities, vanity of vanities,*
> *Everything is vanity.* [1:2]

We must understand the word "vanity" not in the sense of conceit, but in the sense of emptiness. A pedestrian but more accurate translation has been offered: "Futility of futilities, all is futility."

Koheleth proceeds to ask the question:

> *What advantage is there for man in all his exertions,*
> *In all the things that he exerts himself for under the sun?*
> *A generation comes and a generation goes,*
> *But only the land remains forever.*
> *The sun rises and the sun sets,*
> *And hurries to its rising place.*
> *The wind blows to the south*
> *And then circles back to the north.*
> *Circling, circling goes the wind,*
> *And on the circuit the wind returns.* [1:3–6]

That is to say, what final aim is there to all this movement? There is none. The forces of nature simply repeat their cycles over and over again:

> *All the rivers flow into the sea,*
> *Yet the sea is never filled up.*
> *They flow back to whence all streams flow,*
> *So as to flow again.*
> *All things weary [a man]*
> *And a man is not able to describe it,*
> *[For] the eye is not satisfied with what it sees,*
> *Nor is the ear adequately filled with what it hears.*
> *What has been is what will be,*
> *And what has been done is what will be done,*
> *For there is nothing new under the sun.*
> *Is there anything about which it may be said,*
> *"See, this is a new thing"?*
> *It already existed from eternity,*
> *From the time before the present!*
> *There is no recollection of the men who were earlier,*

And as for those who will be later,
There will be no recollection of them
On the part of those who will be even later. [*1 : 7–11*]

Such is the keynote to the first eleven chapters of Ecclesiastes.
Next the author presents us to Koheleth who says:

> I, Koheleth, was a king over Israel in Jerusalem. I set my mind
> to investigate and to explore by wisdom every thing that has
> been made under the sun. It is a bad business that God has
> given man to be concerned with. I saw everything that was
> being done under the sun and the whole matter is emptiness
> and a striving after wind. That which is crooked can never be
> made straight and that which is lacking can never be counted.
> . . . More wisdom brings more trouble and whoever increases
> his knowledge increases his pain. [*1 : 12–15, 18*]

As the account continues, Koheleth implies that having tried
wisdom and found it useless, he now turns to pleasure. He will try
mirth and enjoy pleasure—and see that this is also empty.

> I made great works and built houses and planted vineyards . . .
> I gathered silver and gold and treasures from all over. I brought
> together singers and entertainers. . . . Whatever my eyes de-
> sired, I supplied them. I did not deny my heart any joy. . . .
> And I looked at all that my hands had done, and the exertion
> that I had made, and behold, all was vanity and a striving
> after wind—there is nothing lasting under the sun. . . . In-
> deed, I observed that though wisdom is as superior to folly as
> light is to darkness, the same fate overtakes the wise man as
> overtakes the fool. . . . There is nothing better for a man than
> to eat and drink and make himself enjoy pleasure in this world,
> and this also is emptiness and a striving after wind. [Chapter 2]

Moreover, everything seems to be fixed in its proper time:

> *There is a time to be born and a time to die.*
> *There is a time to plant and a time to pluck up what is*
> *   planted.*
> *There is a time to kill and a time to heal.* [*3 : 1–3A*]

Since things are so allotted to time, what plus is there for a person
in the labor that he pursues? There is none (*3 : 1–15*).

Next, Koheleth turns his attention to justice. In the place of it,
there is wickedness. He must conclude that God judges both the
righteous and the wicked; but then he comes to the conclusion that

the same fate awaits man as awaits beasts. They both have the same breath; they both die. Man has no pre-eminence over the beasts, for everything is vanity. All go to the same place; all are from the dust and all return to the dust (3:16–22). Moreover, there is oppression in the world, so that "I praised the dead who already died more than the living who are still alive; but better than both of them is the one who has not yet been born" (4:1–3). He dilates on the uselessness of working hard (4:4–16). Yet despite this negativism, he advocates a proper attitude to God, especially if one comes into the house of God (4:17–5:6 Heb., 5:1–7 Eng.).

Riches, he tells us, are not only unsatisfactory, but are really a curse. If a man has good things, he should enjoy them, for life is short, and God approves of his being happy (5:7–19 Heb., 8–20 Eng.). Yet he has seen that man's desire is so insatiable that even those who get wealth and treasure do not enjoy any of it (6:1–9). He concludes with the statement that there is no advantage in fruitless efforts to penetrate the meaning of existence (6:10–12).

In the next section (7:1–9) we find verses that are really an assembly of proverbs. In view of his experience the author can give advice: "Do not be too righteous and do not make yourself too wise— why should you destroy yourself" (7:16). Thinking is futile and one must avoid the guile of a woman (7:15–29).

Chapter 8 begins with maxims for the prudent conduct with kings (8:1–5), but the author resumes his observation of man's limitations (6–9) and of the vanities of life (10–15). He concludes, next, that the ways of God are beyond fathoming (16–17). Again he asserts that the same fate awaits the good and the bad, and that hope exists only while there is life. A living dog is better than a dead lion, for the living know that they will die but the dead know nothing. Men should seize their opportunities for enjoyment, for the outcome of a man's efforts is determined as much by chance as by merit. Man does not know his fate. Like fish caught in an evil net or birds caught in a snare, so men are caught in an evil time, which suddenly falls upon them (9:1–12).

Moreover, although wisdom may provide a service, it is never really rewarded. This is illustrated by a statement about a small city besieged by a great king. In the city there was a poor man who was able to save the city—yet nobody remembers that poor man (9:13–16). This skepticism about the high place of wisdom is the point of departure for two verses that speak in great praise of wisdom (17–18). Koheleth concludes that just as dead flies can make the perfumes of a druggist putrid and stinking, so a little folly can destroy precious wisdom (10:1). Next follows a series of random proverbs

(10:2–11:4), which is probably an interpolation from another hand.

Since skepticism is justified on the part of man respecting what life offers, what is man to do? Is he to give way to despair or resign himself to an evil fate? The answer (11:5ff.) is to enjoy life. Indeed, Koheleth proceeds to give some prudent advice: "Remember your creator in the days of your youth, before the evil days come and the years draw near of which you have to say, 'I have no pleasure in them'" (12:1).

This reverse into piety, in contradiction of all that has gone before, gives the last chapter of Ecclesiastes a sufficiently orthodox tone to rescue it from being mere heresy.[1] At the very end of the book (12:9–10) some later editor has noted:

> Koheleth was wise, he taught many people knowledge. He was a speculating man and he looked into things. He tried to find agreeable things and to write them pleasantly as words of truth.

This editor tells us that the words of the wise are goads and that these wise words are found in "collections made by one shepherd" (12:11); some scholars believe, as I do, that the shepherd is Solomon, but others believe that he is God.

The passage continues (12:12) with the statement that there is a limit to the advantage of study: "Of making books there is no end, and too much study is mere weariness of the flesh." It concludes with this observation:

> The sum of the matter, when everything has been heard, is this: Revere God and observe His commandments, for this is the whole [duty of] man. For God brings every work into judgment concerning even the hidden thing, whether it is good or whether it is evil. [12:13–14]

It is not enough to say of Ecclesiastes that it only circulated and was brought into the Tanak because it was supposed to have been written by Solomon. There is so much truth in Ecclesiastes that one cannot close his eyes or ears to these statements. If it is countered that the literal meaning of much of Ecclesiastes is hostile to religious faith, one must reply that all too often religious faith is misconceived of as a sombre gloomy matter, never lightened by the spice of wit or made tolerable by a little malicious but healthy doubt. The genu-

---

[1] There is a contrary view, which regards the lines "Remember your creator in the days of your youth" as a later interpolation. Supporters of this view maintain that what we have in 11:9–10 and in the first part of 12, is skepticism to match the cynicism of the earlier chapters; hence 12:1 is supposedly added. But we must deal with the text as it stands; and such a drastic revision is a little difficult to accept.

inely religious do not blot out the doubts that are to be found in Ecclesiastes by pretending that they do not exist. They tolerate them as part of the normal expression of perceptive and thoughtful people. These words of doubt do not defeat genuine religious faith, but form that counterbalance that keeps religious faith effective and suitable for human beings.

On the more pedantic side, some scholars insist that Ecclesiastes was influenced by Greek thought, and that it is this influence that has created pessimism. It is not necessary, however, in the case of two parallel thought patterns, to assume without specific evidence that one was derived from the other; and there is not enough evidence to prove that passages in Ecclesiastes are taken bodily from Greek writers. In its present form Ecclesiastes is unquestionably a post-exilic book, a compilation of many earlier strands.

CHAPTER
22

JOB

THE BOOK OF JOB is the literary masterpiece of the Tanak. In its profundity, it is not surpassed; in its poetic beauty, it scarcely has a peer; in its boldness and daring, it is not approached by any other book. It is a challenge both to the Deity, and to the nimble, superficial, and platitudinous things which were, and are, said in His name. One can wonder, first, how Job came to be written, and second, how a book with its untraditional content came to be included in the Tanak, for in tone, emphasis, and content it stands in direct opposition to themes basic in other Scriptural writings.

In brief, Job has fallen abruptly from extreme prosperity to poverty, from health to abject and loathsome illness, and from the possession of the supreme joy of the Semite—many children—into childlessness. After his disaster, Job is visited by three men who come ostensibly to comfort him. They and Job agree that the disaster which has befallen him has come from God, but differ as to whether Job has merited what God has done to him. The three assert that Job's disaster proves that he had previously committed some sins. Job asserts that he had not sinned, or that his sins, if any, were not such as to prompt a disaster of the magnitude he has experienced; accordingly, he argues that one's fate is not determined by one's conduct. In this latter contention Job is contradicting a motif that is both frequent and axiomatic in the Deuteronomic writings.[1]

The profundity of the Book of Job emerges from the formidable issue raised, its poetic beauty from the manner in which deep emotion is expressed in stirring phrases and sentences, and its courage from the resoluteness with which the great issue is pursued unflinchingly to the ultimate. Students of comparative literature have found some alleged parallels to the book in Indian, Babylonian, and Egyptian literature; these are either superficial, as in the case of the Indian, or oblique, as in the case of the Babylonian and Egyptian, and serve only to underline the uniqueness of the Scriptural book.

In its external form, the Book of Job consists of a prologue (Chapters 1–2), the body of the poem (3–42:6), and an epilogue (42:7–17). In each of these three parts certain problems intrude, but we can consider them as we review the content. The prologue and epilogue are in prose, the body of the book is in poetry.

In its own way, the prose prologue has admirable literary qualities. It is a narrative with the attractive simplicity and clarity of the folk tale. Job, it tells us, was a man of Uz, southeast of Judea and bordering on a desert; he was decent, upright, reverent, and completely free from evil deeds. Seven sons and three daughters and great flocks of animals were the blessings that marked him as the foremost resident of the east. Solicitous for his children, he piously offered animal sacrifices, lest they forgot to offer them.

But in heaven, on an occasion we identify as New Year's Day, when the heavenly beings assembled with Yahve, Satan,[2] too, was present. To Yahve's question as to how the noble Job was faring, for Satan had been visiting the earth, Satan replied that naturally anyone whom God has treated so generously was bound to be pious. In disagreement with Satan, Yahve gave him permission to hurt Job, though he was not allowed to hurt Job's person.

In turn, a series of catastrophes befell Job. These included raids by desert brigands, heavenly fire, Chaldean invaders, and a mighty windstorm—the last killing his children. Thereupon Job said:

> *Naked came I from my mother's womb,*
> *And naked do I return [3] there.*

---

[1] See below, pp. 407ff.

[2] In later times, Satan became even more satanic, as the devil, than he is in Job. His appearance is a sign that the prologue was written after Persian influence was felt, that is, after 530, for it was from Persian thought that the idea of a "satan" was adopted.

[3] He does not literally mean "return," but rather, that he is now bereft as when he possessed nothing at his birth.

Yahve gave, but Yahve took away;
May Yahve's name be blessed. [1:21]

In all this, the narrative continues, Job did not sin, nor did he ascribe any blemish to God.

Accordingly, when on the next New Year the heavenly host reassembled with Satan again present, God inquired about Job, again lauding him and charging Satan with vainly having enticed Him to injure Job. Satan's reply was that in the disasters Job himself had remained untouched. Thereupon Yahve, confident that Job would pass the test, permitted Satan to injure Job himself. Satan inflicted on Job evil *sheḥin* ("boils"?) from head to sole. To relieve the debilitating itch, Job used a broken piece of potsherd for scratching himself, and he sat on an ash heap (that is, no longer in his mansion) outside the city. His wife upbraided him: " 'Do you still hold on to your piety? Curse God and die.' Job replied, 'Do you, too, talk as do foolish women? Shall we receive good from God, but not evil?' " So Job abided in his piety (2:1–10).

The three friends, Eliphas, Bildad, and Zophar arrived to comfort Job. They wept and tore their clothes and poured dirt on their heads. They sat on the ground by him for seven days and seven nights, but from sympathy for his great pain they remained silent. Then Job said:

May that day on which I was born perish!
May the night [perish] when my mother conceived a male child.* [3:3]

With these words, we have left the prologue, and have entered the poem itself.

Since the poem presupposes that something has preceded it to set the stage for the speeches of the characters, it is logical to assume that there must have been a preamble of some kind. But the body of the book at no point hearkens back to the details of the prologue, and hence there arises the frequent opinion that the present prologue does not completely fit the subsequent poem. In the first place, by attributing Job's misfortunes to Satan, the prologue diminishes God's responsibility. Secondly, by making Job, though a worshiper of Yahve, a resident of Uz and not a Jew, the prologue is implying that the unorthodox questioning, which would be inappropriate to a pious Jew, is now intelligible if Job was a Gentile. In the third place, Job is declared in the prologue merely to be undergoing a test, the product of a momentary divine caprice. Is human suffering the exceptional lot of those whom God decides to test? The poem will say no, for evils are assumed in the poem to be quite other than capriciously exceptional.

Rather, the poem deals with what is set forth as frequent human experience. If it is true that disasters test a human being, then the poem carefully abstains from equating Job's experience with a test. It is only coincidentally that Job is tested in the poem; in the prologue, the test is the direct purpose. Job in the poem seems a real person; in the prologue he is a puppet, though a lifelike puppet. One effect of the prologue is to compromise the earnestness of the poetic discussion.

An explanation for these discrepancies between poem and prologue is the suggestion that whereas the dialogues have a fixed poetic form, the prose prologue went through several stages of recounting common to folk tales. The prologue in its present form is to be regarded as younger than the poem, but as containing bits of folklore much more ancient than the poem.

The poem's dialogue form has suggested that it is in reality a drama; and there are those who have seen in the Book of Job the influence of Greek tragedy. This attractive theory must be rejected. We do not find dramatic progression in Job, but only a static situation. The dialogue is a series of three cycles [4] of discussion; in each cycle, Job and each of the friends alternate in speaking at length. Each speaker terminates his discourse without interruption; there is no crisp, curt, back-and-forth dialogue. The discourses are comments on the static situation; there is no plot complication, nor is there any genuine ascent to climax and resolution. The deep emotion in the dialogue is that which emerges out of meditation, not out of spontaneous response to unfolding incident. Job was not written to be acted.

The poem begins with Job's words cursing the day of his birth. He goes on to lament that he was born, or, that he was born and survived.

> *Why did I not die at the womb,*
> *Perish when I came out of the belly?*
> *Why did knees greet me,*
> *And breasts which I could suckle?*
> *[If I had died] then now I would be inert and be quiet,*
> *I would sleep in tranquillity. . . .*

---

[4] The first cycle comprises Job's lament (3); the comment of Eliphaz (4–5); Job's reply to Eliphaz (6–7); the comment of Bildad (8–9); Job's reply (10); Zophar's comment (11); and Job's reply (12–14). The second cycle is Eliphaz's second comment (15); Job's reply (16–17); Bildad's comment (18); Job's reply (19); Zophar's comment (20); and Job's reply (21). The third cycle is in disarray; see pages 293–4. It encompasses 22–7.

Or, like an aborted embryo, I would have never existed,
Like babies which never saw the light. [3:11–13, 16]

But instead, he is like

Those who wait for death, but it evades them;
They dig for it more than for hidden treasures . . .
My anguish displaces solid food,
And my cries of distress are poured out like liquid.
That which I dreaded has come upon me,
That which I feared has overtaken me.
I have no peace and no tranquillity, and no rest—
Only anger comes upon me. [3:21, 24–6]

To these pitiable words Eliphaz the Yemenite replies:

If some one tried to speak to you, would you bear it?
For who can restrain himself from replying?
You used to counsel many, you strengthened weak hands.
Your words lifted up those who had stumbled,
And you stiffened wobbly knees.
But now when [disaster] comes on you, you go into panic;
When it touches you, you become confused.
Is not your reverence your source of stability?
Is not the piety of your ways your source of hope?
Really now! Who was there ever who, innocent, perished?
Where have the upright been destroyed?
In my experience, those who plough iniquity,
Indeed those who sow evil, harvest it! [4:2–8]

Eliphaz goes on to declare that God finds frailties even in heavenly beings. Does Job expect man to appear, as it were, more just than God, or purer than his Maker (4:17–19)? No, for evildoers reap evil. Temporary prosperity is delusive, for disaster strikes abruptly (4:20–1). Accordingly, man must rely totally upon God:

He causes wounds, but He binds up;
His arrows hit, but His hands heal. [5:18]

God, Eliphaz avers, saves from disaster. Indeed, those who turn to Him can be assured of tranquillity and a ripe and healthy old age (5:19–26). All this, concludes Eliphaz, is a question he has looked into, and Job should adopt his viewpoint (5:27).

Job's reply to Eliphaz begins with a description of the deep weight of his grief and the calamity God has caused:

> *The arrows of the Almighty have pierced me;*
> *Their poison consumes my spirit.*
> *The terrors of God are arrayed upon me.* [6:4]

He wishes, therefore, that God would grant his request for death:

> *Let God proceed to crush me,*
> *Loose His hand and cut me off . . .*
> *What strength have I, that I should hope?*
> *And what is my ultimate fate, that I should prolong my life?*
>   [6:9, 11]

He pauses to lament that his comforting friends betray him, in the same way that a water course betrays a caravan by being dried up (6:14–20). Job has not asked them for any of their substance, nor for rescue from a foe, but only for a reasonable and persuasive explanation of what has happened and why (6:24–30). He resumes his consideration of man's plight:

> *Is there not a burden for men on earth?*
> *Are not his days like those of a hired man? . . .*
> *The legacy of months of emptiness has been forced on me,*
> *And nights of toil have been designated for me.*
> *If I lie down, then I say, "When will I arise?"*
> *Every night, and until dawn, I become sated with tossing*
>   *about.* [7:1, 3–4]

He turns to describe his illness briefly:

> *My flesh is clothed in worms and dirt,*
> *My skin has broken out and become loathsome.* [7:5]

Then his mood changes:

> *I shall not restrain my mouth*
> *But shall speak in the bitterness of my spirit,*
> *I will murmur in the bitterness of my soul.* [7:11]

It is to the Deity that he now speaks, charging God directly with being the author of his disasters and suffering.

> *Am I the sea, or a sea serpent,*[5]
> *That You put a restraint upon me?*
> *When I say, "My bed will comfort me,*
> *My couch will bear my complaint,"*
> *Then You frighten me with dreams,*
> *And You terrify me with visions,*

[5] See page 245.

So that I should choose to be strangled,
[Choose] death, rather than my sorrow.[6] *. . .*
What is a man that You raise him to the importance of
          Your notice,
That You should set Your attention on him,
That You visit him every morning,
And try him constantly? . . .
Very well, I have sinned.
What do I [thereby] do to You, O guardian of man?
Why do You make me Your target? . . .
And why do You not forgive my transgression, and remove
          my guilt?
For now I shall [soon] lie in the dust;
You will seek me some morning—
I shall not be there. [7:12–15, 17–18, 20–1]

From the above it is clear that Job has two levels of complaint. He takes it amiss that in his distress he hears from his friends words he regards either as misdirected or as nonsense. But his profound complaint is that he, a mere man, has been fixed upon by the Deity for a hostile attention inconsistent with the grandeur of the Deity. The friends do little more than annoy Job. The true profundity of Job's lament is in that which he has addressed to the Deity.

In the absence of "stage directions" it is only from the words of the second friend, Bildad, that we realize how shocked he is. Bildad seems genuinely outraged by Job's bold address to the Deity. He rebukes Job:

How long will you go on saying such things?
[How long] will your words be a powerful wind?
Does God pervert justice?
Does the Almighty distort what is right?
If [even] your sons sinned against Him,
Then [of course] He put them into the consequence of their
          transgression.

But you—[just] seek God constantly,
And be a suppliant to the Almighty,
If you are pure and upright,
He will answer your prayer.
He will prosper your righteous habitation. [8:2–6]

Bildad is apparently not an old man, for, unlike Eliphaz, he does not point to his own experience, but to that of mankind.

---

[6] A slight emendation alters "bones" into "sorrow."

Ask of the former generation,
Give attention to the quest of our fathers:
We are of yesterday and know nothing,
Our days on earth are a shadow. . . .

Can a rush grow up without mire?
Can a weed grow tall without water?
While still in its greenness, and still uncut,
These wither before every other plant.
Such is the fate of all who forget God,
And the hope of the blasphemer perishes! . . .

But understand! God does not despise the perfect man,
Nor does He grasp the hand of evildoers. [8:8–9, 11–13,
         20]

The force of Bildad's argument is that since God does not distort
justice, that which has happened to Job must be just. By implication, what Job has received, he has deserved. Bildad speaks what can
be called the opinion of most people.

In reply, Job begins by conceding (9:2–11) that in view of God's
grandeur, His power to create, His dominion over sun, moon, and
stars, no mere man can address Him: Who can say to Him, "What
are You doing?" (9:12).

There is, moreover, a futility in man's speaking to God:

Even if I speak, and choose my words with Him,
If I am in the right, I will not be answered * . . .*
[Or] if I call and He answers, I cannot believe He has heard
         my voice,
For He looks at me stormingly,
And gratuitously increases His wounds on me. . . .
                                        *
If I am in the right, yet His mouth can convict me;
I can be perfect—yet He can distort me.
I am guiltless. Do I not know myself?
I despise my life!

As I have said, it is all one:
He destroys the guiltless and the sinner. . . .

If indeed I am guilty, why do I suffer so unnecessarily?
If I washed in snow and cleansed my hands entirely, *
You would still plunge me into a pit

And make me, and my clothes, abhorrent! [9:14–15A, 16–
17, 20–2, 29–31]

For He is not a man like me, for me to speak to Him,
Or for us to come together for a trial.
Would that there was a referee between us,
To put a hand upon us both,
And to take His rod away from me,
And stop His terror from overwhelming me!
Then I would speak, and I would not fear Him.
But such is not the case for me. [9:32–5]

Instead, Job must speak in bitterness as well as in fear:

I say to God, Do not [merely] condemn me,
But show me the basis of Your quarrel.
Does it benefit You to oppress,
To hate what You created? . . .
Have You eyes of flesh?
Can You see like a man?
Are Your days like a man's,
Your years like a human's?
Why must You inquire into my sin
And search into my transgression? . . .
Remember that You made me like clay,
And You will return me to the dust . . .

If I sin, You observe me,
And You will not acquit me of my transgression!
If I were truly guilty, woe unto me;
But if I am innocent, I still cannot raise my head . . .
For You renew Your toil against me!
Why did You bring me out of the womb?
I should have perished, and no eye seen me,
I would have been as though I never existed,
Had I been brought from the womb to the grave.
Are not my days on earth few?
        *
Turn away from me, so that I may have a little surcease
Before I go, not to return, to the land of utter darkness!
        [10:2–6, 9, 14A–15A, 16B, 17B–21]

It is now the turn of Zophar to speak. He begins not politely, as
Eliphaz had, but bluntly and with some scorn. He asks whether a
man as loquacious as Job is to go unanswered; therefore he proceeds

to give the answer. Not that Zophar meets the issue raised by Job directly—quite the contrary! The gist of what he argues is that Job, a mere man, is unable to comprehend the Deity:

> *Would that God would speak and enter into conversation*
> > *with you*
> *And declare to you the things, obscure to wisdom, which are*
> > *
> > *wondrous.*
> *Can you find the dimension of God, or reach to the limits of*
> > *the Almighty?*
> *They are higher than heaven; what can you do?*
> *Deeper than Sheol, what can you know?*
> *They are longer in measure than the earth and wider than*
> > *the sea.* [11:5–6A, 7–11]

Therefore, man must be resigned and penitent:

> *If you direct your heart properly*
> *And stretch your hands [in plea] towards Him*
> *And put away whatever evil is in your hand,*
> *And prohibit unrighteousness from dwelling in your tent,*
> *Then you can lift up your face without blemish,*
> *And you will be firmly established and will not need to fear.*
> *Then you will be secure, for there is hope;*
> *You will search and will find a safe resting place . . .* [11:
> > *13–15, 18*]

Zophar has not replied at all to Job. He has said only that Job, instead of challenging the Deity, should mend his allegedly wicked ways and appeal to God's graciousness.

Job's reply, a long one, falls into two parts. The first is addressed to the three men who have come to comfort him.

> *You, indeed, are the knowing ones*
> *And when you pass away, so will wisdom!*
> *I have understanding as good as yours*
> *And I do not fall short of you in any way. . . .*
>
> *Is wisdom a matter of old age*
> *And is length of days the equivalent of understanding?*
> *[No!] With Him is wisdom and understanding,*
> *It is He who possesses counsel and understanding.*
> *When He tears something down, it cannot be rebuilt,*
> *When He closes over a man then there is no way out.*
> > [12:2–3, 12–14]

Such banalities as the comforters speak are the common possession of all people, says Job:

> *This my eye has seen,*
> *My ear has heard and understands.*
> *For I am in no way inferior to you. What you know I also*
> *   know.*
> *[You answer me;] but it is with the Almighty that I would*
> *   speak,*
> *And it is to argue with God that I desire.*
> *You people are all whitewashers of falsehood,*
> *Physicians of no value.*
> *I wish that you would keep quiet—*
> *For that would be for you a genuine wisdom.*
>
> *Would you speak falsehood on behalf of God,*
> *Or for His sake talk deceitfully?*
> *Will you show partiality to Him?*
> *Must it be on God's side that you argue?*
> *Would it turn out well if He should search you out?*
> *To see whether you would delude Him*
> *As you would delude a fellow man?*
> *He would surely rebuke you*
> *If He found you secretly showing some partiality.*
> *Be quiet and let me alone, and let me speak,*
> *No matter what happens to me.*
>
> *I take my flesh in my teeth [7] and I put my life in my hand.*
> *Behold, He will slay me; I have no [8] hope.*
> *Yet I will defend my ways to His face.*
> *Behold now, I will set forth my case,*
> *For I know that I am right.* [13: 1–5, 7–10, 13–15, 18]

Now Job turns to address the Deity:

> *I ask You not to do two things,*
> *And if so, I will not hide from You.*
> *Do not keep Your hand upon me,*
> *And do not let terror of You frighten me.*
>
> *Either You call out, and I will answer*
> *Or else let me speak and You answer me.*

[7] The meaning is uncertain but in the context it seems to be, "I run a great risk."
[8] The traditional interpretation of this verse is surely wrong. It runs: "Though He slay me, yet will I trust in Him."

How many sins and transgressions are charged to me?
Let me know exactly what my transgression and sin are.
Why do You rather hide Your face from me
And treat me as though I am Your enemy?
Would You stoop to scare a driven leaf
And would You pursue dry stubble?
Why do You loose upon me such bitter things?
Is it the sins of my youth that You are making me answer
      for now? . . .

Man, born of a woman, allotted only a few days,
And these full of trouble,
Comes out like a flower and is cut down,
And has no permanent place as though he is a shadow.

On such a being do You fix Your stare
And bring him into judgment with You? [13:20–6; 14:1–3]

Job pursues the theme of man's helplessness in view of man's short span on earth (14:4–13). Then he continues:

When a man dies, does he live again? [9]
[If so,] I would wait all the days of my agony
Until my renewal came.
You could call and I would answer,
You could be greatly concerned for the work of Your hand.

But [instead] You number my footsteps
And You will not pass over my transgression.
My misdeeds are sealed up;
In a bag You have fastened up my iniquity.

A hill can be eroded
And a rock be moved from its place
And waters wear away stones;
Floods wash away the dust of the earth.
So You [too] destroy the hope of man;
Inevitably You prevail against him and he passes away;
He changes his countenance and You send him away.
His sons rise to honor, but he does not know it;

[9] The author of Job is not repudiating resurrection, a doctrine that is later than the Book of Job and came to be widely accepted. The author is merely denying that man lives a second time.

Or they are brought low, and he knows nothing about it. [14:
    14–21]

With these despairing words we have reached the end of the first
cycle. The thread of Job's arguments can be summarized in this way:
he is weak, God is strong; he is transient, God is eternal. He has not
deserved the misfortunes God has sent upon him. Why has God sent
them? Let God enumerate for Job the list of his supposed sins, if
there are any. Yet even if there were such sins, why has God brought
on Job disasters out of proportion to any possible misdeeds? Why
does God visit on a mere man punishments and terrors beyond man's
capacity to endure? And why are these visited on a man who has not
deserved them?

We turn to the second cycle. Whereas previously Eliphaz has
been somewhat gentle, he is in his second speech much more severe:

Does a wise person speak with such inflated knowledge
And fill his belly [1] *with such storm,*
So as to argue without profit and with words of no util-
    ity? . . .
Are you the first person to be born a man,
And were you brought forth before the hills?
Were you privileged to listen in on the councils of God,
And did wisdom withdraw from others and come to you?
What do you know that we do not know,
Or understand that we have not already understood? . . .
Is God's comfort too little for you,
And the gentle word insufficient?
Why is your heart carrying you away,
And why are your eyes flaming,
That you direct your anger against God
And pour such words out of your mouth?

What is a man that he should claim merit?
Or a human being that he should pretend to righteous-
    ness? . . .

A wicked man is in trouble all the days of his life,
The given number of years set aside for the haughty.
The sound of terrors is in his ears,
And the spoiler comes upon him in the midst of prosperity.
    [*15:2–3, 7–9, 11–14, 20–1*]

[1] The belly was regarded as the seat of understanding. He is charging Job with
saying violent but empty things.

Eliphaz continues in this vein, always with the lot of Job in his mind:

> *The company of the godless is sterile,*
> *And fire consumes the tents of bribery.*
> *They conceive mischief, and they bring forth misfortune,*
> *And their belly prepares their disappointment.* [15:34–5]

Job replies, addressing himself first to Eliphaz's severity:

> *I have heard many such things,*
> *For you are comforters who bring trouble, all of you.*
> *Is there no end to empty words?*
> *What provokes you that you speak this way?*
> *I could also speak like you if you were in my place.*
> *I could join words together against you,*
> *And shake my head at you.*
> *But, I rather would strengthen you with my mouth*
> *
> *And would not withhold the solace of my lips.* [16:2–5]

Job continues with a restatement of what God has done to him, summarized in these words:

> *I was at ease, and He split me into pieces.*
> *He took hold of the back of my neck*
> *And dashed me into pieces. . . .*
> *My face is red from weeping,*
> *And my eyelids have become darkened,*
> *Even though there is no guilt on my hands*
> *And my prayer is pure.* [16:12, 16–17]

Yet though it is God Who has caused this, Job believes that, paradoxically, God knows his righteousness and will vindicate him.

> *Even now I have a witness* [2] *in heaven,*
> *An attester on high . . .*
> *He should argue for a man with God*
> *As one does between a man and his neighbor.*
> *For a few years will pass by,*
> *Then I will go the way from which I will not return.* [16:19,
> 21–2]

But that witness remains inactive, and Job now describes his sense of the nearness of death:

[2] Disputes center on the identity of this unidentified witness. I take him to be God. Others take him to be simply an anonymous intermediary, although 9:33 denies that there is such an intermediary. It seems to me, therefore, that Job is appealing, as it were, from God—to God. Surely this is a unique poetic declaration.

My days are past; my plans are broken off,
Yet those were the desire of my heart . . .
But I must look forward to Sheol as my house,
And spread out my couch in darkness,
And call the grave my father
And call the worm mother and sister.
Then where is my hope?
And who will ever see any good come to me?
Will these [hope and the good] go down into Sheol with
*   me?*
Will I and these things descend together into the dust?
*   [17:11, 13–16]*

To Job's despair Bildad replies sharply in his second speech. Job has talked enough. Bildad goes on to suggest that what is happening to Job is merited, for such is the dire fate of the wicked.

Nothing that is his remains in his tent,
For brimstone is scattered upon his habitation.
His roots dry up beneath and his branch is cut off above.
The memory of him perishes from the earth
And he has no name in public.
He is pushed from the light into darkness
And is chased out of the world.
He has neither son nor grandson among the people,
There is no survivor where he has dwelt. [18:15–19]

To this climax in Bildad's speech, Job replies:

How long will you vex me and crush me with words?
This is ten times that you have reproached me!
But you are not ashamed that you deal so wrongly with me.
*   [19:2–3]*

To the question asked above (8:3), "Does God pervert justice?", Job now gives his reply:

You must understand that God has dealt unjustly with me
And thrown His net around me.
I call out for help,[3] but I am not answered;
I call out, but there is no justice . . .
He has stripped my glory from off me,
And taken away the crown from off my head . . .
He has let His wrath burn against me;
He has reckoned me as His enemy . . . [19:6–7, 9, 11]

[3] Literally, "violence!"

He enumerates some of the consequences of this injustice:

> *My brothers are remote from me,*
> *And my acquaintances are estranged.*
> *My relatives and my friends have vanished,*
> *And those who have dwelled in my house have forgotten me.*
> *The servants count me as a stranger*
> *And I am an alien in their sight.*
> *I call to my slave, but he does not answer;*
> *I am constrained to entreat him.*
> *My breath is offensive to my wife*
> *And I am loathsome to those*
> *Who have issued forth from the same womb.* [19:13–17]

He turns to the three in despair:

> *Have pity on me, have pity on me,*
> *For you are my friends!*
> *The hand of God has touched me!*
> *Why do you persecute me as does God?*
> *And are not satisfied with calumnies?* [4]
> *Would that my words were written down,* [5]
> *Would that they were inscribed [indelibly] in a book,*
> *As though with an iron pen they were engraved on a rock!*
> [19:21–4]

Quickly he makes a transition to his righteousness and his assurance that it will at some time be demonstrated:

> *But I know that my vindicator lives,*
> *And will rise in the future over the dust* [6] *[of my grave].*
> [19:25]

That is, some time after Job's death, his righteousness will come to be proved and acknowledged—by God.

Now Zophar makes his second speech. Again he does not confront the problem raised by Job, but only restates the sad fate of the wicked man and his children. The language is often colorful, though

---

[4] Literally, "satisfied with my flesh."
[5] That is, since acquaintances do not respond, the written appeal can be made to those who do not know him.
[6] Probably no verse in Scripture has had so many translations as this one. If its meaning were not uncertain there would not be so many differences of opinion about it. The text conveys Job's assurance, but abstains from describing the vindicator. The verses following are impossible to translate, for the text is in bad order. They read literally: "After my skin is destroyed this, and from my flesh I shall see God Whom I see for myself, and my eyes have seen, and not a stranger; my reins fail within me."

the ideas only repeat what Zophar has already said (Chap. 20). In reply Job asks, "Is it really true that the wicked prosper for only a moment?"

> Why is it that the wicked live,
> And become old and increase in power?
> Their seed is well established before them,
> And their offspring before their eyes.
> Their houses are safe from fear
> And the rod of God is not put upon them . . .
>
> They end their days in prosperity
> And go to Sheol in tranquillity.[7]
> Yet these had said to God, "Go away from us,
> For we do not want the knowledge of Your ways.
> What is the Almighty that we should serve Him?
> And what profit is there if we pray to Him?". . .
>
> How often is it that the lamp of the wicked is put out
> And calamity comes upon them? . . .
> [You say:] "God lays up the iniquity for the children."
> Let Him pay it, that the wicked one may know it,
> Let his own eyes see his calamity,
> Let him drink the wrath of the Almighty.
> For the wicked [dying peacefully] has no interest in his
>   house after him,
> When the number of his months is finished. [21:7–9, 13–
>   15, 17, 19–21]

Job now turns to comment that the inequality of life turns to equality in death:

> One man dies in full strength, wholly at ease and quiet . . .
> Another dies in bitterness of soul, and has never tasted the
>   good.
> But they lie down together in the dust and the worm covers
>   them. [21:23, 25–6]

Job concludes by asserting that world travelers can attest to the magnificent funerals received by the unpunished wicked:

> Who declares to his face his way?
> And who repays him for what he has done?
> He is brought to the grave and watch is kept over his tomb;

[7] Literally, "instantly," which is to say, not, like Job, lingeringly and in great pain.

> *The clods of the valley are sweet to him,*
> *And all men draw after him,*[8]
> *And they come numerous beyond counting.* [21:31–3]

Since this is the case, he rebukes the three:

> *Then how can you comfort me with empty words?*
> *Of your answers nothing abides but falsehood.* [21:34]

It is now the turn of Eliphaz to speak for the third time. Convinced as he is that Job would not be suffering if he had not been unrighteous, Eliphaz is now moved to add some charges of specific sins to the general accusations made earlier. We are given the feeling that Eliphaz is improvising, concocting a list of accusations so as to buttress his claim that an evil fate arises from past sinfulness:

> *Is not your wickedness great?*
> *Are not your iniquities without end?*
> *You have taken pledges from your brother for nothing,*
> *And have stripped the naked of their clothing.*
> *You have not given water to the weary to drink,*
> *And you withheld bread from the hungry.*
> *A mighty man, possessing land, dwelling in it,*
> *As a man of great repute,*
> *You sent away widows empty-handed,*
> *And let the arms of orphans be crushed.*
> *That is why there are snares around you*
> *And sudden fright terrifies you,*
> *Why there is darkness that you cannot see and abundance*
>   *of water* [9] *covers you.* [22:5–11]

Moreover, Job is wrong if he thinks his sins have escaped God:

> *Is not God aloft in His heaven?*
> *And are not the stars exceedingly high?*
> *Therefore you conclude, "What does God know?*
> *Can He judge through the thick darkness?*
> *The clouds are covering Him so that He does not see*
> *But simply walks about the circuit of the heaven."* [22:12–
>   *14*]

Then, what recourse has Job?

> *If you return to God and humble yourself*
> *And remove unrighteousness from your tent . . .*

---

[8] That is to say, a very large funeral.
[9] "Abundance of water" is a figure of speech for calamity.

You will pray to Him and He will hear you
And you will make vows and pay them.
You will make a decision and it will come about
And light will shine on your way. [22:23, 27–8]

In Job's next speech there is no direct reply to Eliphaz's accusations or proposals. Job asserts again his wish to find God so that he can enter into judgment with Him:

Would that I knew how to find Him! . . .
I would fill my mouth with arguments.
I would grasp what He answered me,
Understand what He said to me. [23:4B–5]

Yet he cannot find God for this trial:

I go forward but He is not there,
And backward, but I do not discern Him.
I look for Him on the left but do not see Him,
I turn to the right but I cannot observe Him. [23:8–9]

Job moves on now to comment that what has happened to him is not exceptional. The wicked do evil and yet prosper; the righteous are oppressed and exploited. He who expects the wicked to have an untimely fate will be disappointed:

*
God makes the mighty man survive His power
So that he survives [illness] not believing that he really is
        alive.
[God] gives him assurance and He sends supporters
And His eyes are on his ways . . .
If this is not so, then let someone prove me a liar,
And make my speech worthless. [24:22–3, 25]

At this point (Chapter 24) in the third cycle of speeches, a series of difficulties arises to confuse the reader and plague the student. First, Chapter 24 presents difficulties in translation and comprehension which are insurmountable. Second, the speech of Bildad as found in the Hebrew is only the six verses of Chapter 25, and these read like an introduction to a longer speech. Third, there is no speech allotted to Zophar in this third cycle. Fourth, Chapter 28, a great poem on the elusiveness of wisdom, is scarcely germane, and must be regarded as accidentally inserted here; it is an independent composition and not truly a part of Job.

Scholars have often confronted these difficulties by rearranging the materials in 25–7 and by ascribing portions to speakers in a manner different from that of Scripture. Thus 26:*5–14* are ascribed to Bildad instead of to Job, and made to ensue on 25:*1–6;* and 24:*18–24* are ascribed to Zophar. Such suggestions would clarify the text, but they are guesses, not certainties. It is preferable, accordingly, for the beginner to skirt these solutions, provided he recognizes the problems.

Job's speech in 24 asserts that God is unresponsive to prayer of the righteous, even in their suffering (24:*1–12*); he laments that God knowingly permits the wicked to triumph (24:*13–25*). Bildad's short speech (25:*1–6*) contrasts man's puniness and God's majesty. In reply, Job charges Bildad with a lack of concern for his fellow man (26:*2–4*), and laments that man knows little of God. Those things that Job has related about creation and the killing of Rahab are scarcely the essence of God:

> *These are only the outskirts of His ways.*
> *What whisper of a word do we ever really hear of Him?*
> *Who can comprehend the thunder of His mighty deeds?*
>   [26:*14*]

As the text stands (27:*1*) Job speaks again.[1] He reaffirms his innocence and will continue to maintain it, come what may (27:*2–6*). Job scorns the way of the wicked (27:*7–10*) and proceeds to introduce a daring subject whose sequel is lost, namely, that it should be clear to man that God does not always act in a seemly way (*11–12*). In place of the expected sequel, the next verses (which truly belong to one of the three visitors rather than to Job[2]) describe the evil fate of the wicked (*13–23*). The continuation[3] of the poem is in a long speech by Job (29:*1*–31:*40*). In the first part (29:*1–25*) he reviews, in most piteous fashion, the days of his happiness and prosperity when God was still with him and his children were round about him. He tells

[1] If there was once a speech intervening between Chapters 26 and 27, it is either totally lost or else displaced to some other portion and beyond ready recovery.
[2] A typical rearrangement is to ascribe 27:*1–6* to Job himself; *7–10* to Zophar; *11–12* to Job; *13–23* to Zophar.
[3] Ch. 28 is an interpolation; the chapter has undergone some disarrangement. An attractive, though not necessarily correct, arrangement would divide it into four portions, as follows: (a) Verses *12, 13, 5, 6, 1* and *2*; (b) *12, 3, 4, 9, 10, 11*; (c) *20, 21, 7, 8, 14, 22*; (d) *12, 15, 16, 17, 18, 19*. It is to be noted that *12* has the appearance of a refrain and hence it can stand to be repeated. Following such an arrangement, there are four themes in the chapter. The first is that ore deposits are buried in the earth. Second, miners are able to reach them. Third, wisdom, however, is not found in the world either in the air or in the deep or anywhere else. Therefore, four, wisdom cannot be acquired.

of the respect with which he was treated, and how he helped the poor
and succored the unfortunate:

Eyes I was to the blind,
And legs to the lame was I.
A father was I to the needy,
And I looked into the cause of people whom I did not know.
I broke the fangs of the unrighteous,
And made him drop his prey from his teeth. [29:15–17]

In those days men gave ear to him and waited, silent, for his counsel
(29:21–5). Yet now his lot has changed. The aged and the nobles
who used to do him reverence are replaced by youngsters who mock
at him; indeed, those who mock at him are the outcasts of society
(30:1–8). Job has been brought low (9–15) and in his lowliness he
complains to God:

I call for You to help but You do not answer me,
I stand in prayer, but You do not look at me.
You are turned into one cruel to me,
And with the might of Your hand You oppose me. . . . .

I looked for good, but evil came upon me,
I waited for light, but darkness came.
My bowels have been made to boil, they are not silent;
Days of deep affliction have come to meet me. . . . .

My harp has turned into mourning,
And my pipe into the sound of weepers. [30:20–1, 26–7, 31]

He now returns to his insistence on his righteousness (31:1–34). For
example, he never looked upon a virgin in lust; he was never dis-
honest or covetous; he never treated his slaves with cruelty, for had
not God, the God Who made Job in the womb, also made the slave?
Job did not withhold anything from the poor or let the widow go un-
aided. He never let the naked go unclothed. He never smote anyone
who was not deserving of punishment. He never committed the idolatry of worshiping the sun or the moon. He never rejoiced at the ruin
of those who hated him. He never denied anyone the hospitality of his
tent. He never was guilty of hypocrisy.

The ending of the chapter (35–40) is textually uncertain, but the
total effect of the chapter is clear. Job, having heard all the accusations and all the arguments against him, repeats vigorously his affir-

mation that he has been just and righteous and that the punishment
that has come upon him is completely unmerited. The proper sequel [4]
to this last speech of Job is to be found in Chapter 38.

Job and his friends lapse into silence, a silence broken by the
Deity's speaking out of the whirlwind (38:1). What whirlwind is not
specified. God is speaking to Job, not the friends. His speech reproves
Job not for the evil which the three comforters have ascribed to him,
but rather for the evil of maintaining his own integrity at the expense
of aspersing God's, in the sense that if the three comforters were
guilty of ignorance of the true ways of God, then Job has himself been
misrepresenting God through his own ignorance. Accordingly, God's
speech sets forth in sharp contrast the limited nature of Job's knowledge and the greatness of His knowledge and His divine use of it.

> *Who are you who are obscuring [God's] counsel by words*
> *devoid of knowledge?*
> *Gird your loins like a mighty man and let Me ask you and*
> *you reply to Me.*
> *Where were you when I made the foundations of the earth?*

[4] There intervenes a long speech (32–7) by one Elihu, who is not identified for
us. The Elihu section is an interpolation. Job has spoken and the friends have
been silent; thereupon Elihu intrudes. He has kept silent so far, he says—implying that he has been present—because he is young and his companions are old.
He asserts that Job is wrong to suppose that God does not answer him. In fact,
God does answer, only Job does not understand how. God has many modes of
speaking to men, sometimes by visions and sometimes through suffering. When
suffering is rightly interpreted, not wrongly as by Job, it leads a good man to say,
I have sinned. Thereupon God redeems the sinner. In Chapter 34 Elihu takes up
Job's claim to righteousness and his contention that God has subverted the right;
Elihu insists that Job is wicked. God never subverts the right; He cannot, since He
is beyond question. Moreover, God observes the actions of the wicked and is un-
failing in His punishment of them. The text of the third speech of Elihu in
Chapter 35 is in bad order; as far as we can make it out, Elihu is contending that
God is too exalted to derive any profit from Job's righteousness or wickedness.
Men who suffer at the hands of their fellow men may call upon God and not be
heard; this is not because God is unjust but rather because those who call are not
truly righteous and pious. It would follow therefore that Job did not appeal to God
in the proper way. The next speech of Elihu, found in Chapters 36 and 37, says
that God treats men either with favor or with cruelty, depending on their conduct;
beyond that, God looks to see how men receive the punishment designed as
discipline, and Job, he contends, has the wrong attitude. He should rather be
grateful to God, Whose greatness is beyond searching out or sharing. God is not
available to men; men should simply revere God.

This interpolation enters in because in the original poem the three friends
were not able to satisfy or convince Job; this latter is clear from 32:5. The
unorthodoxy of the book called this exceedingly orthodox section into being. That
the Elihu speeches are an interpolation is much more clearly evident in the Hebrew than in the English, for the stylistic differences are so great that even the
beginning Hebrew student can see them. While the Elihu poems are inferior to
the Job poems, they have their own quality.

If you have true understanding, then tell Me.
Who fixed its measurements so that you seem to know
*   them,*
Or who stretched the [measuring] line over it?
On what were the bases sunk?
Or who laid the cornerstone of it? . . .
Have you in any of your days commanded the morning,
Or have you let the dawn know its place? . . .
What is the way to where light dwells,
And where is the place of darkness? . . . [38:2–6, *12, 19*]

A sarcastic line follows:

Do you know, because you were born then,
And the number of your days is great? [38:*21*]

The speech goes through the various phenomena of nature, over which God rules (38:22–38); there are allusions to the sea, to Sheol, to rain from heaven and stars. Similarly, the speech goes on to emphasize (39) the Deity's rule over wild animals—lions, wild goats, wild asses and oxen, ostriches, hawks, and eagles. The question is persistently addressed to Job, Is it he who rules over the animals or is it the Deity? Is it Job who gives strength to the horse? Is it he who commands the vulture to mount up?

Let Job therefore answer the question implied in the total speech: Is it Job or God who rules? If it is God, on what basis can Job set his knowledge against that of the Deity? The conclusion of the speech is this:

Will the would-be reprover contend with the Almighty?
Let him who argues with God answer! [40:2]

Job's reply is briefer:

Behold, I am of small account; what shall I answer You?
I will put my hands over my mouth.
One time have I spoken, but I will not do so again;
Yes, twice [I have spoken] but I will not do so further.
*   [40:4–5]*

In God's second speech (40:6–42:6 Heb., 40:6–41:34 Eng.), Job is challenged to prove himself the equal of God and to save himself.

Do you deny Me justice,
And condemn Me in order to be justified?
Do you have an arm like God?

And can you make thunder in a voice like His?
Do you deck yourself out with majesty and loftiness,
And dress yourself with glory and splendor?

Scatter about the wrath of your rage;
Look at everyone lofty and bring him low. . . .
I too will acknowledge you,
If your own right hand can save you. [40:8–11, 14]

There follows in the Deity's speech a section (40:15–24) that is probably an interpolation. The first part of it deals with the Behemoth, which in form is the plural of a common Hebrew term for a beast. The detailed description of this animal leads scholars to identify him with the hippopotamus. The point of the Behemoth section is that God has created this animal, which is so strong and which is exceedingly difficult to capture; can Job, with his pretensions to God's knowledge, capture the Behemoth?

The second section of the speech (40:25–41:26 Heb., 41:1–34 Eng.) has to do with the Leviathan, possibly the crocodile, a symbol, like Rahab, of primordial chaos. Can the crocodile be captured with an ordinary hook and line? The implication is that he cannot. This simple theme is expanded into a very realistic picture of the horrible creature, which does not end, as one might expect, with the restatement of the original question to Job, Can you capture the crocodile? The Deity's second speech never really comes to a specific point and certainly never to a climax; therefore many scholars declare that the passages dealing with the Behemoth and the crocodile are both interpolations. It is most unfortunate that at this crucial point in the Book of Job we are forced to confess that obscurity and vagueness exist, and baffle us.

The reply of Job to the Deity's second speech is as follows:

I know that Your power is unlimited
And no plan is impossible to You. . . .
Therefore I spoke, but really did not understand,
Things too wonderful for me, which I did not compre-
*   hend. . . .*
By the report of the ear, [previously] I heard of You,
But now my eye has seen You.
Therefore I reject my words
And I repent, sitting on dust and ashes. [42:2, 3B, 5–6]

This brief reply of Job is obviously much less than what we might reasonably expect as a conclusion to the long and profoundly exploratory speeches and to that portion of the Deity's speech which is authentically part of the original poem. We feel a double letdown at the speech of Job, first, because of its brevity, and, second, because we seem to feel the need for him to say something of such substance and weight that it will be a climax and conclusion to what has gone before.

We cannot know whether it is a mangled text that disappoints us or whether the author of Job has in these short words said all that there was in his mind to say. Job has challenged God to meet with him and dispute. Contrary to Job's spoken expectation, the Deity appears to him. The Deity speaks, and thereupon, as the text now stands, Job is rebutted and convinced, and in a few halting words expresses his regret at having raised the issue. Perhaps it is inherent in the essential problem of evil and theodicy that there is not much more to say than Job is reported to have said. There have been many who have written at great length on the matter, yet when an analysis is made of what is said, one wonders whether it is simply a multiplication of words, or whether new and convincing ideas are being expressed.

What is missing at this point in the Book of Job is a further explanation, not of ideas, but of Job's state of mind at this juncture. Not that the text of the Book of Job ends here. An epilogue runs another ten verses. This epilogue is, in all probability, itself made up of different parts. In the first verses (42:7–9) the Deity rebukes the three comforters for having offered wrong and misleading arguments on His behalf. They are enjoined to offer up animals and to have Job pray for them, for Job has spoken what is right. This is lame, but the remainder of the epilogue (10–17) is even more so. It relates that after Job had prayed on behalf of the friends, the Deity granted him twice as much as he had previously had. All of Job's brothers and sisters and acquaintances came to visit him with gifts. The text enumerates how many sheep and cattle and oxen and asses Job now came to possess. It tells us that he was now blessed with seven sons and three daughters and assures us that in all the land there were no women as beautiful as these. This is indeed a bathetic conclusion.

The prologue and, especially, the composite epilogue reduce the force of the poem. Whereas the poem seems to make the normal, or at least the common, human experience its subject of discussion, the prologue has suggested that we are dealing with an unusual circumstance—the trial of a particular person. The viewpoint of the poem is also contradicted by the conclusion. The epilogue makes it appear that Job, having passed the test, is now rewarded for what he has endured. The author of the poem might reasonably raise the question,

"Does a man who has gone through disaster emerge triumphant with a double portion of that which he had before disaster?"

The figure of Satan in the prologue tends, as we have said, to shield the Deity from the responsibility of what happened to Job. Indeed, Satan and all the developments out of Satan, as these expand and proliferate in later literature, have as their objective a wish to protect the Deity from being considered the source of evil. The most extreme form of such protection is reflected in the forms of Persian religion in which there are really two deities, one of good and one of evil; a less extreme form is found in the myth of the fallen angels (see p. 244), in which evil is explained by a rebellion of certain superhuman or divine creatures against the ruling God. Such proposals solve the problem of theodicy by saying that there is no true problem, since evil comes from a source other than God. Contrary to the prologue, the poem itself at no time tries to shield the Deity from responsibility for what has happened to Job. What Job and his three friends are debating is not whether or not evil comes from God, but why God, Who supposedly is just, causes good people to undergo evil. The prologue and the epilogue combine to rob the thesis of the poem of its very substance.

The author of the Book of Job, that is, of the poem, remains within the framework of Hebrew thought in attributing to the Deity a control of history. It is the Deity who presides over events, and it is through these events that the Deity is disclosed. If this were not the case, then the poem would have no reason for existence. Job is not a poem on the subject of why the Deity permits a Satan to exist and flourish. Truly and forthrightly, both Job and his opponents insist that the events have come from God and that the mind and heart of man must try to reconcile God's rule of the universe with the inescapable fact that evil exists.

We saw that Ecclesiastes is a gentle or even whimsical comment on the prevailing and traditional view found in many passages, especially in the Book of Deuteronomy. If man observes the divine commandments, then he receives the reward of long life, of wealth, and of children. Ecclesiastes says that though this may be so, it is not alway the case; but Ecclesiastes does not say this profoundly, nor with full seriousness. The poem in the Book of Job, however, makes a straightforward and courageous denial that the Deuteronomic pattern is real and authentic. It is in this clash with the Deuteronomic view that its greatness lies.

There are residual questions that have their own piquancy. So real at many points does Job seem that it is natural that the view should have emerged that Job was a historical person and that the substance of the book narrates actual history. Twice in Ezekiel (14:14 and 20) Job's name is coupled with those of Noah and Daniel as men of great righteousness and wisdom, so that we must conclude that in the ancient mind there was a recollection of some individual by that name renowned for his sagacity. Nothing in the Book of Ezekiel, however, bears any relationship to the contents of the Book of Job. There is much to be said for the view of an ancient rabbi, Samuel ben Nachmani, that Job never existed and that the whole story is a parable.[5] Neither in the prologue nor in the poem are we given any indications of the time in which Job is supposed to have lived, or any direct statements of when the poem was written. A cumulative series of observations leads to the conclusion that somewhere around the year 400 B.C. is a reasonable date for the composition. In the first place, there are references to some observances distinctive to the religion of Israel, such as pledges, vows, landmarks, and the judicial procedure against people guilty of adultery and of worshiping the sun and moon. A knowledge of the contents of the Five Books of Moses seems to be indicated. In the second place, a constant wish on the part of Job to enter into litigation with the Deity implies a developed legal system rather than a primitive Bedouin nomadic life, and hence we appear to deal with a rather advanced state of society. In the third place, the essence of the book is the questioning of a view that is old enough to have become traditional. Therefore, we must allow for a date late enough for the traditional view to have become deeply ingrained.

Next, and more to the point, the technical student of Semitic languages notices the strong influence of the Aramaic language on the Hebrew of Job. This phenomenon would incline one to regard the book as coming from the postexilic period, for during the exile Hebrew began to be replaced by Aramaic as the spoken language of the Jews.

Moreover, the book deals with the fate of individuals. Indeed, it is so individualistic that quite possibly, as scholars have argued, it could not have been written before the forthright statement of individualism found in Ezekiel. I mention this argument, but to my mind it has only limited force, for, as indicated in our discussion of Ezekiel (pp. 160–163), I have not found it possible to accept the view that individualism was unknown until Ezekiel.

If we accept a date as late as 400 for Job, then it is theoretically possible that Job is a drama that owes some debt to the Greek drama, a view we said must be rejected. There is no harm in ascribing some Greek influence to the Book of Job; on the other hand, there

---

[5] The opinion is found in the Talmud, Baba Batra 15A.

is no great gain from it, for this is only an unimportant external item which in no way determines the content of the book.

It is not possible to know whether the acceptance of Job into the canon rested in small or great measure on the prologue and epilogue. Perhaps the orthodox character of the beginning and the end made the admission of Job easier. It is likely, however, that it was the essentially high quality of the Book of Job that made it well known to thoughtful Jews, and that any collection of books deemed especially sacred would have been incomplete without this masterpiece. It must be stated candidly that one can be surprised that Job was admitted into the canon. But for one who has read and studied the book it would be even more surprising had this writing, rarely equaled and never surpassed in world literature, failed of inclusion.

CHAPTER

23

LAMENTATIONS

THE FIRST FOUR of the five poems in the Book of Lamentations are alphabetical acrostics, yet all five are fine examples of elegiac "mourning" poetry. A metrical form, the *qinah,* which is clear and distinct in the Hebrew, was usually employed for the elegy. Specimens are found in the Tanak outside Lamentations; for example, Amos 5:1 introduces the *qinah* found in 5:2–3.

But two questions about these poems transcend the merely formal element. They are: Who is lamenting? and, What is he lamenting? Ancient tradition [1] thought that the lamenter was Jeremiah and that the event lamented was Jerusalem's destruction in 586 B.C. In the Septuagint translation of Lamentations, Jeremiah's authorship is directly stated; in Christian versions of Scripture, Lamentations is therefore found adjacent to Jeremiah. In the Jewish version it is found in the Hagiographa.

There can be no doubt, as a reading will confirm, that what is lamented is Jerusalem's destruction. But if such a destruction occurred in 485 B.C. (see above, Chapter 16) as well as in 586 B.C., the later destruction may well be the subject of the touching poems. But in either case, modern scholarship is agreed that Jeremiah is not

[1] See II Chronicles 35:25.

the author. This conclusion rests on three observations. First, a difference in the Hebrew style and vocabulary between Lamentations and Jeremiah is noticeable; second, Jeremiah is unconcerned about monarchy, the priests, and the Temple, while Lamentations is very much concerned; and third, the five poems represent more than one author.

Poems 2 and 4 are probably by a single author, Poem 1 by another, Poem 5 by still another, and Poem 3 by a fourth author. The latter, which, indeed, is the poem of some "eyewitness," begins with the words: "I am the man who has seen misery from the rod of His wrath." In the other poems, however, Jerusalem, personified as a woman, is the protagonist. This personification, coupled with the acrostic form, has led some interpreters to the conclusion that Lamentations is artificial. This judgment seems superficial and mistaken, for the poems are genuine and touching. Were they written merely to express sorrow? That would have been purpose enough. But we shall see, I believe, a second purpose in the poems.

Poems 2 and 4 seem to stand in closest relation to the catastrophic event:

How [greatly] has God put the daughter of Zion to shame!
He has cast from heaven to earth Israel's splendid [temple];
He has not, on the day of His wrath, remembered His footstool [2]. . .
God has become truly an enemy; He has swallowed up Israel,
He has swallowed its palaces, destroyed its strongholds;
He has multiplied mourning and lamentation for the daughter of Judah . . .
God has scorned His altar, disclaimed His sanctuary;

He delivered the walls of its palaces to the foe.*
They emitted a shout as though it were a festival day.
God has deliberately laid the wall of Zion's daughter in ruins;
He has stretched a line and has not withheld His hand from destroying;
Rampart and wall together lament [and] are miserable.
Her gates are sunk into the ground; He destroyed * their base.

[2] See Ps. 132:7 and, especially, Isaiah 66:1 for the possibility that the footstool is either the Temple or Jerusalem.

*Her king and princes are among the Gentiles; there is no
revelation;*
Even the prophets have found no vision from God . . .

My eyes are consumed from weeping, my emotions [3] *are in
turmoil,*
My heart is poured onto the ground,
At the destruction of my people's daughter,
*At the sight of infants and suckling babies lying faint in the
city streets . . .* [2:1, 5, 7–9, 11]

The poet now turns to the personified Jerusalem:

*What shall I say, to what compare you, O daughter of Jeru-
salem?*
*What shall I speak to comfort you, O virgin daughter of
Zion?*
Your ruin is as extensive as the sea—who can repair you?
[2:13]

The poem continues with a denunciation of prophets for failing to reveal those sins which might have led to repentance; passers-by, that
is, other nations, mock the daughter of Zion. All this has come because

God has [finally] done what He purposed;
He has fulfilled His word [of threat]
Which He ordained as of old.
Without pity, He has torn down. [2:17A]

The theme of the preceding verses is not strictly one of lament at
destruction; rather, the attitude is that the catastrophe is a merited
punishment devised and executed by God. Faithful to the conviction
that God controls events, the poet surveys the disaster primarily to
say that God has punished Israel.

Poem 4 again reviews the details of the calamity, especially the
suffering of those who before were at ease. The following reason is
given for the catastrophe: "The sin of the daughter of my people has
exceeded Sodom's transgression" (4:6A). The catastrophe was a surprise:

The kings of the land, indeed the world's inhabitants,
*Had not believed that a foe or enemy could enter Jerusa-
lem's gate.* [4:12]

[3] Literally, bowels.

The poem terminates with a denunciation of Edom, whose own destruction is destined to come some day:

> *Rejoice and make merry, O daughter of Edom . . .*
> *The cup will pass to you too; you will be drunk and be*
> *stripped naked.*
> *O daughter of Israel, the punishment of your iniquity is*
> *over;*
> *He [God] will not again exile you.*
> *But, O daughter of Edom, God will surely visit your guilt on*
> *you,*
> *He will uncover your sins. [4:21–2]*

Poem 1, we have said, seems to come from a period a little removed from the catastrophe. The poet in most of the poem speaks of Jerusalem in the third person; in some half-verses (1:9 and *11*) and in two short sequences (1:12–16 and *18–22*) Jerusalem herself speaks. The poem begins with a set of contrasts:

> *How lonely she sits! The city, once populous, has become*
> *like a widow.*
> *She had been chief among the nations,*
> *A princess among the provinces;*
> *She has become a tribute-payer.*
>
> *Bitterly she weeps at night, her tears on her cheeks.*
> *She has no comfort from among her [former] lovers.*
> *Her neighbors have all been treacherous,*
> *They became foes to her.*
>
> *Judah is in affliction in exile,*
> *She is in severe servitude;*
> *She dwells among the nations, but finds no rest;*
> *Her pursuers have overtaken her in the midst of her dis-*
> *tress.*
>
> *Zion's roads are desolate*
> *From the lack of travelers who once came to the feasts.*
> *Her gates are destroyed;*
> *Her priests are useless,*
> *Her young women have been afflicted.*
> *As for her—what she has is bitterness! [1:1–4]*

As in the other poems, sinfulness has brought about the catastrophe (1:8–9). But, artfully, the poet interrupts the indictment to let Jerusalem speak:

O God, see my affliction.
How the foe has conquered! [1:9B]

The ultimate in disgrace has occurred:

She has seen Gentiles come into her Temple—
Those whom You, O God, have forbidden to come into Your
  congregation. [1:10B]

Many interpreters cite in this connection Ezekiel 44:9, which prohibits the uncircumcised from entering the Temple. More precisely, however, the verse is lamenting that certain peoples, *excluded from the congregation,* have entered the Temple. A list appears in Deuteronomy 23 of those who may and may not be admitted to the collective people. Deuteronomy customarily uses the word *qahal,* "congregation," rather than *edah,* "assembly," or *am,* "nation." We read there:

A bastard[4] may not enter Yahve's congregation; even the tenth generation may not enter Yahve's congregation. An Ammonite and a Moabite may not enter Yahve's congregation . . . You may not exclude an Edomite . . . You may not exclude an Egyptian . . . sons of their third generation may enter Yahve's congregation. [Deut. 23:3–9 Heb., 2–8 Eng.]

Curiously, not one line in Lamentations directly identifies the Babylonians as the foe and destroyer. This omission seems most surprising. Yet we cannot readily assume that the catastrophe is that of 485 because of the reference to the "kingship" in 2:2 and 9. We have no knowledge of *any king* in the postexilic period. But, on the other hand, the shadowy figure of Zerubbabel (see pp. 198ff.) can give rise to the speculation that there was some pretender to the shaky throne in the early postexilic period. But, to remain within the confines of demonstrable evidence, Lamentations gives no clue that the Babylonians are meant. The supposition that the event is a different one, however, is hypothetical, even though it is likely.

The lament continues in the spirit of Poems 2 and 4. It concludes with a prayer about the enemies:

Let all their evil come before You;
Deal with them as You have dealt with me for all my sins;

---

[4] Probably the offspring of an incestuous union, rather than an illegitimate person.

> *For my groaning is multiplied*
> *And my heart is faint.* [1:22]

Poem 5 is not an elegy or a dirge, but rather a plea to God:

> *Remember, O God, what has happened to us;*
> *Look and see our shame.*
> *Our possession is turned over to foreigners,*
> *Our homes to aliens.*
> *Our mothers are truly widows . . .*
>
> *You, O God, reign forever;*
> *Your throne endures to all generations.*
> *Why do You forget us completely,*
> *Abandon us for so long a time?*
> *Restore us to You, O God, and we shall return!*
> *Renew our days as of old.*
> *For if You have indeed rejected us,*
> *You have been too angry with us.* [5:1–3, 19–22]

The word artificial, though inappropriate for the other four poems, can be applied to Poem 3. Not only is it an acrostic, but three lines are allotted to each of the twenty-two letters of the Hebrew alphabet.[5] The beginning, as we have seen, is quite stirring:

> *I am the man who has seen misery at the rod of His wrath.*
> *He has led me, and brought me into darkness, and not light.*
> *Moreover, He returns to me to turn His hand [against me]*
>   *all the day.*
> *He has wasted my flesh and skin and broken my bones.*
> *He has laid siege and surrounded me with gall and tribula-*
>   *tion;*
> *He has set me into darkness like the dead of ages past.*
> *He has fenced me in beyond escape; He has put heavy*
>   *chains [on me].*
> *Even when I call and cry for help, He ignores my prayer.*
>   [3:1–8]

The poem continues in the same vein. Though there is some measure of self-searching, the poem is never as profound as the Book of Job.

While the general assertion is that God only punishes, one sequence (3:31–3) declares that He does not cast off forever. Moreover, there is justice in the punishment. Clearly Lamentations bewails not

---

[5] In Poem 3 the order of the alphabet is reversed at one point; the *ayin* follows *pe*, instead of preceding it, as normally, and as in Poems 1, 2, and 4.

the destruction of Jerusalem, but the fact that God had ample reason for destroying it. In all five poems the suffering and the vindictive hatred of the conquering nations are secondary to the sense of shame that Jerusalem has merited the punishment God has sent. The poems say: "See, O God, how much suffering You have caused by having the nations conquer us. You are right, we deserve this. See the depths of our agony, and help us. Punish those who injured us, even though they were Your tools, because of the evil in them." God's just wrath, not Jerusalem's fall, is the subject of Lamentations.

SONG OF SONGS

LOVE POETRY should certainly have the right of existence for its own sake. In the case of Song of Songs it is not difficult to understand that this warm and admirable pledge of affection between a man and a maiden should have been admitted, for the Tanak is both the literature of a people and a religious literature.

There is nothing particularly religious in Song of Songs. One must hasten to add that neither is there anything irreligious or antireligious, except to those prurient minds who identify sensual love with impiety. But in the same way that the secular wisdom of Proverbs became identified with Torah, so the presence of Song of Songs in Scripture caused the love poetry to be invested with a deeper significance. In Judaism, there are echoes of opposition to the inclusion of Song of Songs in Scripture, that is, until it was interpreted as God's love for Israel. In Christianity, similarly, Song of Songs was considered an allegory expressing Christ's love for the Church.

There is, generally speaking, some justification for regarding passages in the Tanak as symbolic. It is universally acknowledged that the prophets used symbols; the Book of Daniel transmits its message almost entirely in symbols. However, to make Song of Songs symbolic is far-fetched. Those who have tried to find the symbols of God's love for Israel, or Christ's love for the Church, have had to compete with others who have gone further and have seen in Song of Songs, preposterously, a cryptic description of the history of Israel from the Exodus to the Messiah. Symbolic interpretation tends to lack restraint and limit.[1] It is wiser, therefore, to take Song of Songs for exactly what it is, namely a collection of love poems.

Since it is a collection, indeed a small anthology, the contents are not all of a piece. Some passages indicate clearly that we are dealing with a bride and a groom and with events prior to and during their marriage. Other passages do not seem so clearly related to the nuptials.

The ordinary reader who first encounters Song of Songs cannot help feeling bewildered when he notices that although the lines represent words spoken by different characters, there is no indication of who these characters are. Accordingly, reading Song of Songs can be equivalent to reading a play in which the dialogue is run together in paragraph form without any indication of who is speaking. Sometimes the contents of the lines indicate whether the speaker is the young man, the young woman, or their attendants. But often this clarity is lacking. Any introduction to Song of Songs requires the teacher to indicate to the student who the speaker is in any given passage. I try to do so, although it is not always possible to be sure. The reader, forewarned of this uncertainty, is free, of course, to make his own judgment.

One more introductory word is needed. Not only is the collection romantically attributed to Solomon (the best date for Song of Songs in its present form is no earlier than 300 B.C.), but Solomon is referred to in the third person (1:5; 3:7–10; 8:11). Therefore, some scholars assert that the marriage which is central in the poem is one of Solomon's many marriages, this time, so it is argued, to the Egyptian princess. A more reasonable interpretation is that the bridegroom, indeed every bridegroom, is regarded as figuratively a king in his own right, and then compared with Solomon. This conforms to the colorful character of oriental imagery.

I shall assume that the first poem depicts a bride and her attendants. The groom is of course not present, but the bride longs for him, even speaking to him as if he were there.

The bride speaks first, initially speaking of the groom in the third person and then changing to the second person:

Would that he would kiss me with the kisses of his mouth—
Your love is better than wine.

[1] The symbolic interpretations can have their own admirable insights. What is wrong, though, is that they are read into Scripture as though they are truly there, when in fact they are not.

The fragrance of your cosmetics excels all spices,*
But your name itself is a cosmetic poured out;
Therefore young women have loved you.
Take me along with you and let us run;
Bring me, O king,* to your rooms.

The bride's attendants now speak:

We are glad and rejoice in you;
We regard your love as better than wine . . .[2]

The bride speaks again:

Dark am I but pleasant looking, O daughters of Jerusalem.

The attendants reply:

Like the tents of the desert,[3]
Like the draperies of ——.[4]

The bride speaks again:

Do not look askance at me because I am darkened,
That the sun has browned me;
My brothers were angry at me;
They made me the keeper of the vineyards—
But my own vineyard[5] *I have not kept.*

She now turns to address her absent groom:

Tell me, O you whom I love,
Where you are at this moment,[6]
Where at noontime you let your flock rest.
For why should I be like a lost person *
Among the flocks of your comrades?

Now the attendants speak to her:

If you do not know, O fairest of women,
Follow in the footsteps of the flocks
And feed your goats by the shepherd's tents.[7] [1:2–8]

[2] The next words "sincerely have they loved you," do not make sense. Some regard these as either a corruption for something else or possibly a misplaced phrase.
[3] The text gives *Kedar*, which was a region in the Arabian desert. Travelers have recorded that the tents there were made of black goatskins.
[4] The text says *Solomon*. This is probably a mistake for some place such as Kedar where dark hangings or curtains were used.
[5] That is, beauty.
[6] Literally, "where you are pasturing." The groom is presumably a shepherd.
[7] "Until you find him" is to be understood.

The preceding, if my interpretation is correct, is a picture of the bride in her chambers some days before the wedding. She speaks of her love for her shepherd groom and wonders where he may be at the moment when she is speaking.

In the second poem, the bride and the groom are together, and we hear a dialogue between them. The groom speaks first:

> *I compare you, my beloved,*
> *To a mare in Pharaoh's chariots.*
> *Your cheeks are pleasant with spangles,*
> *Your neck with jewels.*
> *We will make for you spangles of gold,*
> *With studs of silver.*

The bride replies:

> *While his Majesty is on his couch,*
> *My nard* [8] *sends forth its fragrance.*
> *My beloved is a bundle of myrrh for me,*
> *Lying between my breasts;*
> *My beloved is for me a bouquet of flowers*
> *From the vineyards of the En Gedi.* [9]

The groom speaks:

> *Behold, you are beautiful, my beloved,*
> *Behold, you are beautiful;*
> *Your eyes are like doves.*

The bride:

> *You are handsome, my beloved, you are comely.*
> *Our wedding couch is green.*

The groom:

> *The beams of our house are cedars.*
> *The rafters are cyprus.*

The bride:

> *I am a rose of Sharon,* [1]
> *A blossom of the valleys.*

[8] Nard is regarded as a perfume produced in India.
[9] The flowers are probably white ones which grow in clusters like grapes; En Gedi is on the west shore of the Dead Sea.
[1] A coastal region in north-west Palestine.

The groom:

> Like a rose among thorns,
> So is my beloved among women.

The bride:

> My beloved is among men like an apple tree
> Among the trees of a forest.
> I love to sit in his shadow;
> His fruit is sweet to my palate. [1:9–2:3]

She continues to speak as though now addressing her attendants.

> O, bring * me to a wine house
> And put over me a banner of love.
> Strengthen me with raisin cakes,
> Revive me with apples,
> For I am sick because of love.
> Let his left hand be under my head,
> And let his right hand embrace me.
> I importune you, O daughters of Jerusalem,
> To swear by the gazelles and the hinds of the field
> That you will not awaken or stir up love
> Until the proper moment. [2:4–7]

In the next poem we hear the girl speaking:

> My beloved is coming—hear his voice.
> He leaps upon the mountains, he skips on the hills.
> My beloved is like a stag or a young deer.
> Now he is standing beyond our wall;
> He is looking through the window;
> He is peering through the lattice;
> He speaks and says to me:
> "Get up, my beloved,
> My beautiful one, and come away,
> For the winter is over;
> The rainy season is over and gone.
> The flowers appear in the land,
> The time of bird songs is here,
> And the voice of the turtledove is heard in the land.
> The fig tree puts forth its green figs
> And the grapevines in blossom
> Send forth their fragrance.
> Get up, my beloved, my fair one,

My beautiful one, and come away.
O my dove, in the clefts of the rock,
In the hidden place of the cliff
Let me see your form and let me hear your voice,
For your voice is pleasant and your form is beautiful."

At this point a commentator adds a line regretting that the beauty of a bride sometimes fades after marriage. This figure of speech is drawn from the farm:

Catch for us the foxes,
The little foxes that spoil our vineyards,
For our vineyards are in bloom.

The bride continues:

My beloved is mine and I am his.
He pastures among the lilies
Until the day becomes cool
And the shadows flee away.
Turn and become like a hart, O my beloved,
Or like a gazelle on mountains of spices. [2:8-17]

There is still another short poem. It depicts the bride lying on her bed at night and in her loneliness yearning for her beloved. This is a dream:

On my bed at night I searched for him whom I loved;
I searched for him but did not find him.
Let me rise and circle about the city
In the markets and in the broad places.
I seek for him whom I love;
I look for him but I do not find him.
O watchmen who go about the city, find me!
[I say:]
"Have you seen him whom I love?"

I had barely passed from them
When I found my beloved.
I hold him and do not let him go
Until I bring him to my mother's house,
Into the chamber of my parent. [3:1-4]

The next poem describes the approach of the groom bearing his possessions. He is exaggeratedly compared not only to royalty but to Solomon himself. The groom's men are portrayed as sixty heroes:

What is it that is coming from the wilderness
Like a column of smoke?
Fragrant with myrrh and with incense,
Indeed, with all a merchant's cosmetics?
Why, it is the litter of Solomon—
Round about it sixty heroes, heroes of Israel.
All are wearing swords,
[All] skilled in warfare,
Each with his sword at his hip
Against the danger of nighttime.

Now one maiden speaks forth, enlarging on the comparison of the group with ancient Solomon:

Solomon made himself a palanquin of wood from Lebanon.
Its uprights he made of silver,
Its back of gold,
Its bench of purple.
It was wrought inside with leather.²
O daughters of Jerusalem, go out and see King Solomon
With a crown his mother made him for his wedding day,
For the day of the gladness of his heart. [3:6–11]

We come next to a poem in praise of a young woman. It is difficult to determine whether it is connected with the marriage poems we have just looked at. The poem can stand by itself and is paralleled later in the book by somewhat similar poems. In these love poems the young man describes the physical beauty of the maiden:

Behold, you are beautiful, my love!
Behold, you are beautiful.
Your eyes behind your veil are doves.
Your hair is a flock of goats
Trailing from Gilead.³
Your teeth are a flock of sheep ready for shearing,
Emerging from their washing,
All of them fertile,
Not a sterile one among them.
Your lips are like a thread of scarlet
And your mouth is pretty.
Your cheek behind its veil is red

² In error the text adds "from the daughters of Jerusalem.
³ The northern region east of the Jordan.

Like a piece of pomegranate;
Your neck is like one of David's towers,
Built for a fortress
Hung about with a thousand shields [4]
All of them bucklers of mighty men.
Your breasts are like two fawns,
Twins of a gazelle.[5]
Until the day breaks and the darkness departs
I will betake me to the mountain of myrrh
And the hill of incense.[6]
You are altogether beautiful, my love;
There is no flaw in you. [4:1–7]

There is a similar poem by the maiden about her young man in 5:10–16; there is another poem in praise of the maiden in 6:4–10. The young maiden is addressed in 6:13 as "O Shulammite," but we do not know whether this is her name. Many explanations have been proposed, but it is better to confess our ignorance.[7]

In Chapter 7:2–10 (in the English versions 7:1–9), there is another sensuous poem, even more outspoken than the one in Chapter 4. It is quite capable of startling some modern readers by its plain speech. Certain nineteenth-century scholars found the book immoral, thereby demonstrating that they could judge an ancient writing only by the standards of their own era.

In recent years there has arisen a tendency to regard Song of Songs not as a collection of secular love poems, but as survivals of ancient New Year liturgies.[8] It is said that the poems emerge from an ancient fertility cult; the male lover is the Deity, and the beloved is the cult prostitute, symbolic of the Deity's divine consort. The proponents of this theory, who by their own admission lack convincing proof, rely on what they term cumulative evidence. The strongest argument, however, for judging the poems to be simply secular love songs is the fact that God never appears in the book. In pristine origin some (though by no means all) of the poems may have had a cultic background, before they became secular poems.

---

[4] That is, jewels.

[5] The text has been abridged.

[6] These metaphors are unquestionably allusions to the physical form of the maiden.

[7] Some want to change the word from Shulammite to Shunammite. This change enables them to identify the girl with Abishag, who was described as a Shunammite, that is from the town of Shunam. This young woman, very beautiful, was brought to warm David when his clothes did not supply sufficient heat; see I Ki. 1:1–4. This seems to me a bad guess.

[8] So Meek, in *The Interpreter's Bible*, V, especially pp. 94–6.

If this is so, then Song of Songs has the history of being partly sacred in origin, having then become secular, and finally, as we saw, having been restored to sanctity, though of a kind quite different from that of the primitive fertility cult.

An early rabbinic work called the Mishna (Yadaim 3:5), records that differences of judgment existed about the inclusion of Song of Songs in Sacred Scripture. Ecclesiastes was similarly disputed. Perhaps it is of some significance that there was a more sturdy defense of the right of Song of Songs to be admitted in the canon than there was of the right of Ecclesiastes, though we know that ultimately both were included. To the famous Rabbi Akiba (who lived in the second Christian century) is attributed the statement, "The entire world, from the beginning to the end, does not outweigh the day on which Song of Songs was given to Israel; all Scripture is holy, but Song of Songs is the Holy of Holies." Some scholars infer from the extreme nature of Akiba's defense that Song of Songs was under heavy attack. I have not seen evidence that this is so. It was perhaps attacked, but not heavily so.

In Judaism and especially in Christianity the allegorical interpretation undoubtedly gave the book its full credentials for entrance into Scripture, especially in the light of its having been ascribed to Solomon. But what kept the book alive, and therefore available to be considered for inclusion, is its content, well summarized in the phrase "Song of Songs." A better way of expressing the same meaning in English would be "The Best of All Songs." The book was written and read and appreciated long before the dualism of the Greek world was incorporated into aspects of Christianity to distort the significance of physical love and to bequeath this distortion to the modern world. The ancient Hebrews not only considered physical love beautiful, but, as their inclusion of Song of Songs in Scripture testifies, believed that it could be holy as well.

Introduction to the
NARRATIVE BOOKS

CERTAIN BOOKS of the Tanak, including some of the most important ones, are akin to historical writing. Genesis narrates the events from the creation of the world through the career of Joseph, Abraham's great-grandson. Exodus, Leviticus, and Numbers portray the career and the achievements of Moses, from the death of Joseph until the traversal of the Wilderness. Deuteronomy repeats, in the first person, some of the contents of Exodus, Leviticus, and Numbers. Joshua carries on after Moses' death, concentrating on the Conquest of Canaan. Judges relates the events of the Settlement subsequent to the Conquest. I and II Samuel and I and II Kings (called in the Greek the four books of *Kingdoms*) trace the events that led to the origin of monarchy under Saul, the passing of the kingship to David, and the long series of reigns of his successors. I and II Chronicles repeat most of the contents of Samuel and Kings. Ezra and Nehemiah were detached from Chronicles, of which they were once part; they carry the account beyond the terminal point of Kings, relating events of the postexilic period when Ezra and Nehemiah returned from Babylonia.

In addition, Ruth and Esther are two short narratives of individual significance. Jonah, which is found among the prophets, is a didactic narrative.

Before we consider the narrative books in detail, we must look at some general considerations that justify speaking of them as akin to history, rather than as pure history. Biblical historians did not approach history in the way that modern historians do. With us today history tends to be regarded, in the university tradition, as a discipline involving objectivity and scientific detachment. Indeed, in some universities history is classed with the so-called social *sciences* or the humanistic *sciences*. While most modern historians would grant that objectivity is an impossible ideal, it is nevertheless the continuing goal of modern historians. Indeed, the discipline of history has been described as the task of setting down "exactly what happened."

Pure objectivity was not the goal of the biblical authors, however. Indeed, the very first thing the student must learn is that biblical narrative is not so much history as philosophy of history. Biblical writers were more concerned, for example, with inferring what it signified that a great flood (in Noah's day) had taken place than they were in investigating the date, extent, and damage done by that flood. Because their writings were preoccupied with the significance of events rather than with the events themselves, biblical narrative is properly described as theological and not historical. Biblical historiography is the product of religious faith, and not an exercise in accuracy and precision.

But if biblical history is not pure history, how reliable is it? It has been observed that when we move from the age of the Patriarchs to the periods of the Conquest, the Settlement, and the Monarchy, we move from what may be called prehistory into history. For these later periods, records were more numerous and longer, and the events nearer to the time of the writers. Therefore, the historical data are more reliable in Joshua through Nehemiah than they are in Genesis through Deuteronomy. However, although there is a higher proportion of reliable history in the books of Joshua, Judges, Samuel, and Kings than in the Pentateuch, there is just as much theology in Joshua through Kings as there is in the Pentateuch. All biblical history is theological.

Scholars of the Bible are accustomed to inquire closely into the process by which a biblical book attained its form and shape and outlook. Such an inquiry is usually called the "literary history" of a particular book. Let us use a fictitious example, for clarity, before we try to see what the "literary history" means respecting biblical books. Suppose that there existed an anonymous work entitled "George Washington as President." Suppose that we did not know who wrote it or when it was written. Suppose that we made the most acute analysis that we could, from several viewpoints. First, did the author, as far as we can tell, have a firsthand acquaintance with the events, or did he, rather, at a later time, use written sources? How could we tell? Perhaps some external written sources survive to our own day—as, for example, newspaper accounts preserved in the National Archives, which appear verbatim as portions of the book. If this were the case, it would be relatively easy to pick out some of the sources used. But if no separate written sources survive, then any opinion we might have about written sources could be based only on our consideration of such matters as style and consistency of viewpoint. If, for example, after three pages of terse sentences with monosyllabic words, the style changed to long periodic sentences replete with polysyllables, then we might infer that the author used some written source or sources without acknowledgement. But this would be only an inference.

Suppose, further, that midway in the book on Washington we came across a mention of Abraham Lincoln. This would fix for us the earliest date at which the Washington book could have come into its surviving form. If, furthermore, the mention of Lincoln included the fact that Fort Sumter had already been fired on, then our earliest date becomes more precisely fixed, for it is not just in Lincoln's time, but in a restricted period in Lincoln's time. If, in addition, Lincoln is spoken of either as a great hero or as a hated foe, we could possibly infer whether the author was a northerner or a southerner. And, proceeding further with our assumptions, if the terse sentences reflected the northern point of view, and the periodic sentences the southern one, then our book on Washington would cease to be a simple piece of writing by one man at one time, and emerge instead as a compilation. Furthermore, suppose that we were able to discover several different layers, and not simply northern and southern viewpoints, but midwestern viewpoints, New England viewpoints, and a Texan viewpoint. Our book would be something truly complicated!

Most of the narrative books in the Bible have very complicated literary histories. The analysis of them discloses the existence of sources diverse in age and length, in locality and viewpoint.[1]

Reverting to the fictitious book on Washington, let us assume that we find in it seven old sources as well as three viewpoints—

[1] In the case of Chronicles we can be no less than fully certain that Samuel-Kings was one of the many sources used.

a New England, a Texan, and a midwestern. In the material of a New England viewpoint, suppose there are indications that it was composed about 1850; in the Texan, about 1862; and in the midwestern, about 1875. (Biblical sources or viewpoints seldom lend themselves to such precise dating!)

Then comes the question of who collected the seven sources and supplied the connective material which transformed the sources into a book, and secondly, the question of what we shall call the person, or persons, who gathered the sources and provided the connective material. Shall we speak of an author or of a compiler? Shall we call the Texan and the midwesterner authors? Or shall we call them editors—or, to use a similar term, redactors?

It is a general rule that biblical books were compiled; it is a general rule that there were successive redactions. This rule has been formulated from those elements that comprise the text—sentences, paragraphs, or sections. It is not the fantasy of hypercritical scholars. The history of biblical scholarship is the record of efforts to explain the actual phenomena in the text. Some explanations have turned out to be inadequate or even wrong. But the phenomena that lead to the explanations are present in the text of Scripture.

If one asks, what is the importance of the literary history of a biblical book, a just reply is that the study of the literary history illumines the book. It clarifies portions otherwise unclear; it puts aspects of the book into perspective, and it gives bolder relief to the emphases in the book.

While this is true for all the narrative books, the literary history of the Pentateuch is of especial significance. According to both Jewish and Christian tradition, Moses wrote the Pentateuch. Modern scholarship challenges this. If modern scholarship is right to challenge the Mosaic authorship, then perhaps it can clarify for us the process by which the Pentateuch came into existence. Chapter 26 is a brief survey of the literary history of the Pentateuch as scholars have tried to reconstruct it.

It is beyond the scope of this volume to relate in detail the literary histories of the books outside the Pentateuch. However, certain considerations can be enumerated here that apply to all the narrative books. These are:

1) The nature of the Hebrew language is such that sources utilized by a compiler are not too difficult to discern.
2) Hence, a biblical book consists of a source, or of sources, used by a compiler-author.
3) Problems of consistency in viewpoint, together with those of style, lead to the conclusion that it is more appropriate to

conceive of a succession of later editors than of just one compiler-author.

4) It is a noticeable phenomenon that erasures or omissions were relatively infrequent. Reverting to our example of the Washington book, it is as though a Texan in his rewriting had not expunged distasteful portions written by a New Englander but rather added his own opinions, as if the mere addition successfully obliterated what was distasteful. The abstinence from erasure, and the addition of a new viewpoint, explain why Scriptural books, using multiple sources, abound in inconsistencies and contradictions.

5) Sources were diverse in extent and reliability; the succession of compilers or editors are not represented in equal quantity or significance.

Presently we shall turn to specific books or groups of related books. We shall want to have some idea of their literary history. But how much? For the technical scholar, the more the better, but there is a diminishing return for the beginning student in too detailed a study of literary history, particularly of its refinements. There are manuals that present such material in full and even petty detail.[2] We shall consider the literary history of the narrative books only in broad outline, except for the Pentateuch. The Pentateuch merits close attention. Hence, in the following chapter, a brief description of the Pentateuch is followed by an account of its literary history.

[2] An older such book is Driver; a newer one is Pfeiffer. These books, described in the bibliography, are indispensable to the scholar but a plague and confusion to the beginner.

THE PENTATEUCH

THE FIVE BOOKS OF MOSES are the religious masterpiece of the
Tanak. They were compiled and written deliberately and consciously
to answer the two most fundamental questions that can be asked
of religion: what should a man think, and how should a man live?

Since the books were written a long, long time ago, and reflect a
world view that is no longer valid, the answers given in the Five
Books of Moses can satisfy modern man only in a limited sense.
Much in the Five Books of Moses was antiquated even two thousand
years ago when Rabbinic Judaism arose to transmute their character
and content, and when Pauline Christianity emerged to propose as
the alternative to Moses' law inspiration by the Holy Spirit (see
pp. 529–531 and 539–540). Neither these ancient developments nor
today's straightforward acknowledgement of the irrelevancy of much
of the Five Books of Moses should be allowed to prevent the student
from recognizing the sublime conception and achievement which the
Five Books represent.

The individual books are known in Jewish tradition by the first
important word appearing in each, and in the Greek by titles assigned to them: Genesis ("origin") is known in Hebrew as Breshith
(in the beginning); Exodus ("the way out," that is, from Egypt)
as Shemoth ("the names"); Leviticus ("pertaining to Levites") as

Va-yiqro—("[God] called"); Numbers, from a census taken, as Ba-midbar ("in the wilderness"); and Deuteronomy ("repetition of the Law") as Devarim.

Did Moses indeed write these books? If not, how and when and why did they come to be written? The literary history of the Pentateuch presents questions of appealing puzzlement; the attempts at solving its problems have justly attracted fine and ingenious minds. Yet it must be understood that this literary history is of relatively minor significance, except in one important regard, namely, the necessary conclusion that Moses did not write the Five Books of Moses. If such a statement appears to be startling or upsetting to one's personal religion, then this is the only way in which the literary history is important. The determination to see Moses as the author is an unhappy substitution of a secondary consideration for a primary one. Who wrote the books is scarcely as important as what they say.

The fact is that nothing in the first four books would have ever disposed anyone to regard Moses as the author. In the first place, nowhere in these four is it stated or implied that Moses wrote them; secondly Moses is always spoken of in the third person, and often glowingly, surely a strange procedure had he been the author. It is only the fifth book, Deuteronomy, which seems to have been written by Moses. In this book, we move from the third to the first person, except for the last twelve verses, which describe Moses' death. Since in Deuteronomy Moses is presumably writing his memoirs, the supposition that he wrote the fifth book was easily extended to the first four. Moreover, in a number of passages in Samuel, Kings, Chronicles, and Ezra-Nehemiah, mention is made of "The Book of Revelation of Moses." Thus, we read:

> On the second day the heads of patriarchies of all the people, the priests and the Levites, gathered before Ezra the Scribe to give attention to the words of the Revelation. They found a passage in the Revelation, which Yahve had commanded at the hand of Moses, that the Sons of Israel should dwell in booths on the festival in the seventh month. [Nehemiah 8:*13–14*]

This passage and many others similar to it reflect the conviction that the Pentateuch, presumably already in existence, had been written by Moses. Certainly in the age of Jesus that conviction had become virtually an unchallenged axiom, as we can see in the literature of the period, namely, the New Testament, rabbinic literature, and Greco-Jewish writing. Indeed, while an opinion is recorded in a rabbinic book, *Baba Batra* 14B, that Joshua wrote the last

verses of Deuteronomy, this opinion was merely calculated to underscore Moses' authorship by attempting to explain away the third
person account of his death. But another opinion, still occasionally
to be found among Fundamentalist Christian groups, was that Moses
prophetically described his death in advance.

As we shall see, the initial Jewish doubts about Moses' authorship were not expressed, even in cautious form, until the twelfth
century. On the one hand, rabbinic literature, which grew out of the
closest possible scrutiny of the Pentateuch, noticed almost every
problem in the Pentateuch that concerns modern scholarship. But
the ancient rabbis started with Moses' authorship as an axiom and
ingeniously handled the problems by explaining away even those
contradictions and inconsistencies which they themselves brought
into sharp focus.

On the other hand, certain obscure tendencies in Christianity
which were known collectively as Gnosticism occasionally denied
Moses' authorship, but this was the result of the peculiar idiosyn-
cracies of Gnostic theology rather than of any thorough study of
the text. In simplified form, Gnosticism extended Paul's argument,
as expressed in Galatians and Romans, that the Laws were an in-
efficient vehicle for achieving salvation, and that inspiration by the
Holy Spirit was a better and more effective way. But Paul still held
to Moses' authorship while Gnosticism moved on from denying the
efficiency of the Laws into an occasional repudiation of the Mosaic
authorship, in order to add "historical" doubts to theological objection.[1] Apostates from Christianity, such as the Emperor Julian
(A.D. 331–63), joined with these peripheral Christian voices to deny
Moses' authorship. Yet the overwhelming Jewish and Christian view
that Moses was the author went unassailed and even unchallenged.
And in the twelfth century, when expressions of doubt did appear,
they were guarded and elliptical.

A Spanish Jewish scholar, Abraham ibn Ezra, wrote an excellent
commentary on the Pentateuch about 1152 or 1153. His reservations
are primarily based on matters of chronology. He speaks of the
"secret of the twelve," but exactly what he has in mind is not certain.
Perhaps he means the last twelve verses of Deuteronomy, which
describe Moses' death and burial. Perhaps, though, he means that
there are twelve scattered passages, each of which contains a
chronological problem. We find him thus "puzzled" in places in his
commentary, but these places do not total twelve.

Among the passages that caused Ibn Ezra anxiety was the

[1] See pages 539ff.

beginning of Deuteronomy, presumably written by Moses. Its first verses describe Moses as delivering a speech east of the Jordan river, "trans-Jordan," as the text has it. But trans-Jordan would mean some place west of the Jordan; Moses died east of the Jordan without ever crossing westward. Whether out of fear of offending, or fear of reprisal, Ibn Ezra speaks, cryptically, of "the Secret of the Twelve." If you know this secret, the difficulties here and in other passages, so he intimates, will vanish. In Deut. 31:9 we find the words, "Moses wrote this Revelation." *This* implies, Ibn Ezra suggests, that Moses wrote only certain portions, and not the whole five books. To imply total authorship the quotation would have come near the beginning of the Pentateuch and not virtually at its end.[2]

Again, still following Ibn Ezra, Gen. 12:6 and 13:7, in speaking of Abraham's time, state that *then* the Canaanite nations were in the land of Canaan. To Ibn Ezra the word *then* was crucial; he understood it as "then but not now." From the standpoint of the author of these passages, these nations were in his time *no longer* in the land. But Moses never entered Canaan; in his day the Canaanites were still undestroyed; and so under no circumstances could Moses have said that the Canaanite was "then but not now" in the land, for obviously the Canaanite was still in the land. Also, Gen. 22:14 speaks of Mount Moriah as the mount "where Yahve will appear." This Mount Moriah is identified, moreover, as Mount Zion [3] on which Solomon built the Temple, many generations after Moses. The passage, then, would appear to have been written after Solomon, not during the time of Moses.

Ibn Ezra, we have said, was most cautious in making these observations. Only the nature of his personality and the character of Spanish Jewish biblical scholarship enabled him to make them at all. Contact with the Arabs had increased and broadened the knowledge of the Hebrew language; a rational impulse existed among both Jews and Mohammedans. Hence, biblical commentaries of the age began to distinguish between the respected fancifulness of tradition and scientific explanation. The word scientific is not misused here, for the groundwork that was later to serve modern scholars, especially Protestants, was laid in admirable and thorough fashion by the Spanish Jewish exegetes.

After Ibn Ezra's time there were others—Jews and even Christians like Luther—who in the same cautious way questioned Moses'

---

[2] He suggests that Moses himself wrote some passages such as the denunciation of Amalek, Exod. 17:14; the "Book of the Covenant," Exod. 24:4ff.; the decalogue in Exod. 34; the itinerary in Numbers 33:2ff., and the song in Deut. 32.
[3] The identification is found in II Chron. 3:1.

authorship. Among Christian humanists or philosophers (for example, Masius in Belgium, died 1573; Thomas Hobbes in *Leviathan*, 1651), such questioning or even rejection was expressed from time to time. Indeed a Protestant, Isaac de la Peyrère, in 1655, not only expressed doubt that Moses had written the Pentateuch, but suggested further that the authorship represented not one man but several. Hence, to the question of Moses' authorship was added the possibility of more than one author.

As a result of Ibn Ezra and possibly his successors, the renowned Dutch Jewish philosopher Benedict Spinoza was moved to set forth (in Chapters VII to X of *Tractatus Theologico-Politicus*) a number of contentions of far-reaching significance. These were stated with such clarity that modern biblical criticism can be said to begin with him.

Respecting the Pentateuch, Spinoza not only pointed to the long-known difficulties centered in chronology, contradictions, and repetitions, but also departed from the ancient harmonizers by declaring that the Pentateuch was not homogeneous. Moses was not the author of the totality, but only of certain portions.[4] Moreover, the true author was Ezra (about 450 B.C.; not to be confused with Ibn Ezra, twelfth century A.D.), but Ezra, according to Spinoza, was a compiler rather than an author. As to the time of composition, Spinoza regarded the Pentateuch as merely a portion of the longer sequence of books from Genesis through Kings. At the close of Kings, we read of the release of King Jehoiachin from prison in the thirty-seventh year of the Exile (which had taken place in 586). Therefore, Spinoza maintained, the whole sequence of books could not have been written until after Jehoiachin's time.[5]

The selection of Ezra as the compiler-author was not capricious. The Books of Ezra and Nehemiah describe a certain chaotic condition in Jerusalem about 450, which was remedied by Ezra's assembling the people and reading Moses' Torah to them. The ancient rabbinic tradition had paid Ezra the compliment of declaring that when the Torah was forgotten in Israel, Ezra came from Babylonia to bring it back to mind. Moreover, a somewhat similar legend in a book (IV Ezra[6]) goes a step further. According to this work, after the Babylonians had burnt the Torah in 586, Ezra dictated it from

---

[4] This is reminiscent of Ibn Ezra; see note 2 above.

[5] Spinoza also ably set forth a program and method for biblical research.

[6] Chapter 14:21–6. The book has survived in translations, such as the Latin, made from a Greek version of the original Hebrew or Aramaic. It was composed about A.D. 85–100.

memory. It was, therefore, only a short step from that additional legend to a sober (if misguided) theory that Ezra was the true author-compiler.

A curious retort to Spinoza came in 1678 from a French priest, Richard Simon. Indeed, Spinoza was not the only target, as Simon was also attacking Protestants. Protestants had declared, to justify the Reformation, that salvation lay in Scripture, not in the Church. Simon, the French priest, wished to emphasize the high importance of the Church. His procedure was to present Scripture as so laden with difficulties of consistency, order and chronology, and stylistic difference, as to make it impossible for Moses to have been the only author. Hence, he argued, Catholic tradition was a better and more secure basis for faith than Scripture with all its defects. Simon's book was seized by the police and its first edition banned, but too late to prevent its ultimate reissue.

A Protestant, Leclerc, wrote a reply to Simon in 1685. He conceded that some portions of the Pentateuch were by Moses, but said that a study of the social aspects of the Pentateuch suggested that most of it was later than Moses.[7] The debate was on in full force, carried on by both traditionalists and the early deists. The question of whether one person wrote the Pentateuch had been raised, but had not yet come to the fore. Most people were still concerned about whether Moses or some later person was the author of the Pentateuch.

The next important writer on the subject, not abler but only more influential than others, was a French physician, Jean Astruc. In 1753 he published a book whose title can be translated as "Conjectures about the original memoirs which Moses used in composing Genesis." Astruc's principal contribution was his analysis of a usage long recognized in Scripture, namely, that the Deity is normally known by two different names, Yahve and Elohim.[8] The ancient Rabbis, who had also noticed this, had asserted that Elohim emphasized God's mercy, while Yahve (which they pronounced Adonoi) emphasized His strict justice. Astruc maintained that passages which use the same divine name are coherent and complete in themselves. Therefore, the repetitions, contradictions, and chronological problems are the result of interweaving two different ancient sources.

---

[7] Specifically, he thought that the Pentateuch was compiled shortly after 721, by a priest restored to the Northern Kingdom from the eastern exile imposed by the Assyrians. He drew this priest from II Kings 17:27-8. Leclerc a little later responded to pressure by a retraction in a subsequent book.

[8] There are additional divine names: El, Shaddai, Pahad, Elyon, and others.

These sources, according to Astruc, were more ancient than Moses, but Moses had brought them together.[9]

In effect, Astruc was denying the essential unity of Genesis (he dealt only with Genesis and two chapters of Exodus), while still asserting Moses' authorship. But, as we shall see, his contention that the divine names indicated different sources would lead other scholars to attribute the compilation to someone later than Moses.

In 1779, Eichhorn, a German scholar of oriental languages, published views borrowed from Astruc, but carried through with greater learning and skill. Another German, Ilgen, made an observation in 1798 about the relationship of sources to the use of Yahve and Elohim, but his book went unnoticed. We shall return to him.

In a study published in 1806-7 De Wette dealt not only with Genesis but with the elements he considered unique to the Book of Deuteronomy, namely, the requirement of a single central sanctuary and the recurrent expression that the priests were to be of the tribe of Levi. De Wette then declared that there was a conformity between what Deuteronomy sets forth and what the Reformation of Josiah in 621 had accomplished, as described in II Kings 22-3. To put this in a different way, the program of Josiah was contained in Deuteronomy, and Deuteronomy was in some way to be associated with the date 621. If this were the case, then there was a source additional to the Yahve and Elohim sources, which could be called the Deuteronomic code.

Moreover, up to this time even those who believed that the terms Elohim and Yahve were clues to different ancient sources had been unable to date the sources and thus root them in history, for the sources gave no clear internal indication of their age or occasion. When De Wette associated Deuteronomy with 621, he was fixing a date and an occasion for the book as well as implying an authorship later than Moses. Furthermore, when he identified Deuteronomy with a definite date, he was setting the stage for future comparisons of material on similar subjects. Thus the material found in the Yahvist and Elohist codes was soon compared with the Deuteronomic. A typical question was, "What do E (Elohist) and J (*Jahweh*, the German spelling of Yahve) say about priests and about sanctuaries?" We shall see how these questions came to be answered.

But with three sources under consideration, various other observations were made between 1807 and 1853. One scholar set forth the view that the three principal codes represented a collection of relatively small fragments; this is called the "fragmentary hypothesis." Opposed to this arose the "supplementary hypothesis"; it differed from

[9] He adds that copyists after Moses' time made errors which increased the problems already inherent in the use of sources.

the fragmentary principally in supposing that the Pentateuch consisted of a large basic writing, to which fragments were added at a later time. Specifically, the Elohist was thought to be the major source and J a collection of additional fragments.

For some eighteen to twenty years the supplementary hypothesis held the center of the stage. In 1853, Hupfield set forth the view, independently, that Ilgen had previously expressed. Although Ilgen had gone unnoticed, Hupfield's work attracted universal attention among Tanak scholars. His theory was that the portions of Genesis that used the name Elohim actually consisted of not one source but two quite different sources. One of these (Hupfield called it the first Elohist) was marked by a constant, deep interest in priestly matters; the other was similar in interest and manner to the J source. (Indeed, it was this kinship with J that had led to the earlier view that J was a supplement to the other source.) The sources had thus increased in number from Astruc's two to four: First Elohist, Second Elohist, J, and D. After Hupfield's time the first Elohist, because of its emphasis on the priesthood, was given the name "the Priestly Code."

By and large Tanak scholarship has accepted the hypothesis that the Pentateuch is the end result of the blending of J, E, D, and P. We may consider this the usual scholarly conclusion, although there have been dissenters, of course. But the identification of the four sources was only the first step; there still remained the tasks of rooting each of the sources in history, of arranging them chronologically, and of discovering the reasons or purposes that led to their composition.

Even before Hupfield's time studies had been made of institutions such as the single sanctuary and the priesthood. Thus, the view had already been expressed that there were probably three religious ages in Israel's history. The first was the primitive age of the Ten Commandments (found in Exodus 20 and Deuteronomy 5). The second age was that of poets and prophets, until the time of Josiah. The third age was that of the priestly hierarchy after the time of Josiah.

But what was the relationship of the four sources to the three ages? And when several sources narrated the same incident, but with striking differences, which version was the most historical? An Englishman, Bishop Colenso, startled England by asserting that the P code was the least historical. He maintained that the P code contained not folk legends but newly created fictions fashioned for P's purposes.

Was this P code an early or a late writing? In 1865–6, Graf, an Alsatian, presented an answer to the question of the history and the relative dates of the sources. Graf refuted the prevailing view that P was the oldest source; P was the youngest and, in fact, was written after the Babylonian exile. More precisely, Graf now distinguished between the E and P narratives. Although he had formerly believed that these two documents, in a combined form, represented the oldest source, he now supported the following sequence for the four documents: (1) J: (2) E; (3) D; (4) P.

Various expositions were made of the significance of Graf's view, for in some way the alleged *three ages*, primitive, poetic-prophetic, and priestly, were connected with it. In 1878 appeared a work of major importance by Julius Wellhausen. The work was called *Prolegomena to the History of the Religion of Israel*, and in it Wellhausen drew together the implications for the religion of Israel of Graf's view. Since that time it has been customary to allude to the analysis of the documents in the Pentateuch (Graf's contribution) and the synthesizing account of the history of Israel's religion (Wellhausen's contribution) as the Graf-Wellhausen hypothesis. This hypothesis is still the point of departure for the scientific study of the Pentateuch and is therefore the initial milestone in a student's approach to scientific biblical criticism. Yet a point of departure scarcely deserves its name unless it is departed from. For a student in the 1960's to remain glued to the Graf-Wellhausen hypothesis is evidence of nearsightedness.

That which is notable and still broadly adhered to in the Graf-Wellhausen hypothesis is the amazing correspondence between the sequence of the documents (with D associated with Josiah, and P with the postexilic period) and the contents of the prophetic literature. Moreover, as we shall see, this correspondence extends to the reflections of pre-exilic religion preserved in the books of Judges, Samuel, and Kings.

If we should start, as Wellhausen did, with the latest literature and work backwards, then the following picture would emerge. The P writings, in their great concern for the Temple at Jerusalem, are related to such postexilic prophets as Haggai, Zechariah, Malachi, and late portions of the Book of Isaiah. These writings take it for granted that there should be one central sanctuary. Moreover, still moving backward, Ezekiel not only endorsed the Temple, but prescribed for it; in Chapters 40–8, he limited priesthood to the "sons of Zadok." The P code limits priesthood to Aaron and his descendants, a family of the tribe of Levi. Continuing backward, the Book of Deuteronomy does not yet know of a limitation on priesthood as extreme as Ezekiel or that of P. D restricted priesthood to the "Levitical priests"; it made provisions for "Levites of outlying places" to come to Jerusalem (Deut. 18:6–7) to take high place there with other "Levites." The Reformation of Josiah made the same provision for the priests (II Kings 23:8–9).

But in the age antecedent to Josiah, pre-exilic prophecy as well as J and E did not limit those eligible for the priesthood or the location of a sanctuary. Priestly functions were performed by people not even descended from Aaron, and not even of the tribe of Levi, for example by Gideon, Manoah, Saul, Samuel, and Elijah. Temples were found throughout the land: Gilgal, Bethel, and Beer-Sheba are a few of them. A passage, usually called E, reads:

> You shall make Me an earthen altar and sacrifice on it your holocausts, your peace offerings, your sheep, and your cattle; in every place where I cause My name to be mentioned, I will come to you and bless you. [Exod. 20:21]

Again, if one uses the Sacred Calendar as the basis for comparing and contrasting the documents, one finds that in J and E the names of the festivals and the times when they fall differ from P. In J and E we deal with rather vaguely described festival seasons, rather than calendar dates; in D, the calendar is becoming fixed, though Yom Kippur does not appear in J, E, and D.[1] But the P document (Lev. 23) is definite, even precise; Yom Kippur now exists. There would appear to be a parallel between the growth of a priestly caste and the development of a precise Sacred Calendar and its observances.

If the Graf-Wellhausen view is correct, then the view expressed in the Pentateuch cannot be taken literally. The Pentateuch, in its present form, supposes that in the Wilderness Moses prescribed a priestly system and a Sacred Calendar, and enjoined a single central sanctuary. If this were the case, then the pre-exilic period of Israel's religion represents a tremendous deviation from Moses' prescription. The Graf-Wellhausen hypothesis denies, however, that what truly happened was a deviation from Moses. Rather, it holds, a fictional account was composed in the postexilic period, which read back into the times of Moses the origin and justification of those things which had developed in the postexilic period. The pre-exilic period had known no high priests; that institution had not developed until after the exile. Then it was romantically, and falsely, traced back to Moses' brother Aaron.

To repeat, the pre-exilic prophets are in agreement with Graf-Wellhausen. Amos 5:25 denies that there had been the kind of animal sacrifices in the Wilderness period which reflect P's interest in the early chapters of Leviticus; Jeremiah 7:21–4 reads: ". . . I did not

[1] It seems missing, also, from Nehemiah 8; see below, p. 482, note 4.

speak with your fathers and did not command them, on the day I brought them out of Egypt, concerning holocaust and sacrifice." Jeremiah is saying, in effect, that requirements such as Leviticus and Deuteronomy attribute to the Wilderness were never made. Any disinclination to accept the Graf-Wellhausen hypothesis as a point of departure stems from a theological reluctance. The evidence supports it.

There are two reasons why the Graf-Wellhausen hypothesis should be considered as a point of departure rather than as a final explanation. In the first place, in the ninety odd years since Graf, Pentateuch scholarship, far from standing still, has moved on (though not always forward!). Archaeology has yielded new knowledge, not only of history and religion, but also of the Hebrew language. In the second place, there have always been three major deficiencies in the Graf-Wellhausen hypothesis.

The first difficulty was a result of the thoroughness with which the Wellhausenites went through the Pentateuch and assigned its contents to the various sources. Their analysis was too acute. In their own view, there had been a J, written perhaps about 850, which had been combined with E, written about 750. These had been combined by a redactor, RJE. Then came D, about 621, followed by P. P wrote a major document (*Grundschrift*) into which he inserted the work of RJE and D. Hence, analysis had to separate and redistribute these component parts. For the convenience of the eye, editions were published in which each document appeared in a different size or face of type (boldface or italics), or in which colors differentiated one document from the others. The end result carried analysis beyond logic into absurdity, for a Hebrew sentence with four words could appear in a scientific edition in four kinds of type. Source analysis became excessively subjective and even fantastic.

The second difficulty was an assumption of rectilinear (straight-line) development. Anthropology was called upon to support the view that religion always moves from the free and spontaneous into the organized and the systematized. Accordingly, systematic religion, as represented by Priestly religion, was seen as a development from, and therefore later than, spontaneous prophetic religion. In rectilinear development, there is little or no room for diverse impulses to exist side by side, and surely no room for steps backward. The Wellhausen view was too often excessively mechanical.

The third difficulty was that what purported to be objective description was unconsciously subjective evaluation. The nineteenth-century German scholarship, which was pre-eminently Protestant, was largely conducted by exponents of individualism in religion. Hence there was little or no sympathy for institutional religion in general, and since Roman Catholicism is priestly, little for the biblical priestly system. As a result, many Wellhausenites described the P code as if they were describing the Catholic Church, to which they felt superior and condescending.[2] They felt a warm sympathy, therefore, for the pre-exilic period and, as a result, they wrote eloquently about the Hebrew religion. The Hebrew religion, they asserted, had degenerated into that mumbo-jumbo of priestly religion called Judaism. These scholars, except for a few, were not so much consciously anti-Jewish as simply limited in their outlook. But in the final analysis, their evaluation of the P code was not only wrong-hearted but also wrong-headed.

These three difficulties do not negate the Graf-Wellhausen hypothesis, but rather point to notable flaws in it. From the time that the hypothesis was put forward until it gained an almost complete acceptance among scholars, some major refinements were made.

First, there arose, even in Wellhausen's own refined view, a more fluid view of the documents. As a result, a document, whether it is J, E, D, or P, came to represent not one single composition or date of composition, but various stages of composition—for example, J 1, J 2, E 1, and E 2. Stages are envisaged especially in the P document; Leviticus 17–26, which is marked by frequent use of the word holiness, represents an early stage of P; hence it has been called P_H or simply H. Random bits of Priestly materials, later than or different from H, but earlier than the P major writing, are called P_T, meaning Priestly *toroth* or Priestly "regulations." The major writing is called P_G, meaning Priestly *Grundschrift*, a German word for "basic writing." Moreover, some bits and pieces are later than P_G; they are know as P_s or Priestly supplements. This theory brings us fairly near to the old "fragmentary hypothesis," yet with the difference that symbols such as D 1, D 2, and D 3 point to a more or less continuous chain of traditional writing, as if from a school or sequence of directly related generations. The fragmentary hypothesis implied scattered and haphazard fragments.

The second type of refinement of the Graf-Wellhausen hypothesis made use of the knowledge that certain events are found in various forms in different documents, while certain types of similar traditions

---

[2] An acquaintance with the attitude of Protestant scholars can be gained from reading Harnack, *What is Christianity?* (translated from his *Das Wesen des Christentums*). But the Catholic reply, Loisy, *The Gospel and the Church,* ought also to be read.

are associated with quite different people. Respecting the former, we are told twice that Sarah, Abraham's wife, was abducted to a harem, first by Pharaoh of Egypt (Gen. 12) and next by Abimelech of Philistia (Gen. 20). Moreover, a third version of the same type of story is related about Isaac and Rebekah with Abimelech (Gen. 26). There are many stories of the wife long sterile who finally bears a child, and of a preference of a younger son over an older brother or brothers. Often a laconic allusion is made to an incident or person. Of Rebekah's nurse, Deborah, we are told only that she died (Gen. 35:8). Reuben, Jacob's son, had an affair with his father's concubine Bilhah. The beginning of the story is related in one passage, while the remainder seems to be suppressed (Gen. 35:22). Another allusion to the incident (Gen. 49:4) reveals that the details are known by the author of this second passage.

Brief allusions to individuals or events suggest that the written documents are based on an oral tradition; unquestionably, in the oral stage, a story such as that of Reuben and Bilhah circulated in full form. The double or triple narratives also can be interpreted as pointing to oral tradition. It is reasonable to suppose that because they circulated orally in many forms they came to be recorded in more than one written form. The analysis of similar or parallel accounts has yielded a good insight into aspects of oral tradition and the manner in which traditions tended to change and develop. If oral tradition lies behind a given document, then the material is more ancient than the document itself.

Some modern scholars who are partisans of oral tradition seem to assume that the writing stage is quite unimportant. The older scholars had assumed that the written document represented a clear and unmistakable viewpoint; the present emphasis, especially among Scandinavian scholars, would suppose that those who began to write had no viewpoint at all, but were merely recorders. Perhaps oral tradition has now been overemphasized. The significance of written documents must not be forgotten. On the ground that folk memory is retentive and dependable, supporters of oral tradition are prone to attribute a historical reliability to this tradition which exponents of written tradition would not attribute to documents. Oral traditionalists acknowledge that there are no documents in the Tanak which come from the age of the Patriarchs, Abraham, Isaac, and Jacob, but they often consider the narratives about these figures historical, even though they were recorded centuries later. In recent decades, some archaeologists have joined hands with the oral traditionalists "confirming" the general picture of the Patriarchal age. Yet, as at least one archaeologist[3] has conceded, archaeological statements have often represented enthusiasm rather than evidence. If the literary critics have been too prone to use such terms as myth and legend, some archaeologists have been too prone to speak of historical verification. Thus, although the traditions about Abraham may accurately reflect the Patriarchal age, archaeology has not recovered one single memento of or about Abraham, Isaac, and Jacob.

Still another significant result of the emphasis on oral tradition has been its refutation of the rectilinear view. Before this emphasis, the older theory implied that when P appeared, D disappeared. But suppose that P and D represent schools or viewpoints that long existed side by side. D need not disappear simply because P appeared. Accordingly, scholars at the turn of the century held that the four major documents extended beyond the Pentateuch and into the sixth book, Joshua; scholars customarily spoke of the Hexateuch ("six books"), rather than the Pentateuch, as the basic unified compilation. Today, there is a tendency to speak of the Tetrateuch, "four books" (Genesis through Numbers), as the Priestly writing, and of Deuteronomy through Kings as the Deuteronomic collection.

Lastly, an approach has arisen which is a complex of several impulses. There have been a tendency to credit the Tanak with far-reaching historical reliability, a disposition to declare the Tanak theologically relevant today, and a use of the existentialist approach. Since this attitude is not to my taste, I may do it an injustice. It seems to me that the exponents extract from existentialism an unrestrained subjectivity, which they combine with an exaggeration of the historical reliability of the Tanak. They parrot a limited selection or range of Tanak items which they invest with their own meaning, not that of Scripture. Such "biblical theologians" at their best pay some lip service to the historical study of the Tanak; at their worst they do little studying at all. The old-fashioned orthodoxy can and should command the respect of those who must disagree; this self-styled "neo-Orthodoxy" scarcely commands a similar high regard. To state that the Pentateuch, especially Genesis, contains some or much valid history, is quite different from saying that the Pentateuch is historical. Indeed, not a single document in the Pentateuch was written simply to narrate history.

Yet, can the theological interpretation be logical, acceptable, and persuasive if the factual basis is questionable? The candid answer must be a forthright no. But we should notice that while an assembly

[3] See G. Ernest Wright in *Biblical Archeologist*, XXII, 102-3.

of facts or pseudo facts existed for the biblical writer to draw upon, he started with the theological conclusions and supported them with facts, rather than the reverse. He did not say, "Here are the facts; see how they reveal God." Rather, he said, "God reveals Himself in history; here is the set of facts which demonstrate this." It is the biblical theology which should challenge modern debates and not the bare facts of biblical history.

The acceptance of four major documents by scholars is so universal that a student should know something about how scholars characterize them. While theoretically it might be reasonable to suppose that a document as late as P is much more theological than J, the documents themselves, rather than theory, should bring us to such a conclusion. Scholars believe that they do. Indeed, the J document, consisting of several layers, ranges from an early stage which is deeply rooted in folklore to a later stage which is markedly theological. In general, E is more theological than J, D than E, and P than D.

The J Code, and here I oversimplify the scholarly view, was a written saga which used a much older oral tradition and one older written source. The code (J 1) can be dated conveniently about 800, and the older written source about 850. Later developments in the code (J 2) were recorded about 500. While older commentators associated J with Judea, the southern kingdom, more recent ones do not consider it markedly southern in its early stages; similarly, older scholars consider E markedly northern and later ones do not. (Indeed, there is a minority of scholars who do not consider E a written saga, such as J, but rather a conglomerate mass; E to them consists of theological and literary recastings of portions of J, containing some items which are as ancient as, or even more ancient than, J.)

J and E are both sagas, or else ancient versions of the same saga. At places, E virtually contradicts J (J calls the sacred mountain Sinai, while E calls it Horeb). When J and E were combined, the redactor (RJE) made little or no effort to expunge the contradictions or to harmonize them. He seldom used the ancient equivalent of the modern eraser or blue pencil. In Exodus 3:16, the name Yahve is identified with Elohim. Thereafter, we encounter certain double accounts, one of which is reasonably J and the other E, but it is almost impossible to decide which is J and which E.

D is virtually absent from Genesis through Numbers, and J, E, and P are virtually absent from Deuteronomy through Kings. Where D touches on legislation also found in J, E, and P, D's tendency to ethical exhortation causes it to be usually regarded as reflecting prophetic influence. D's major interests are in a single central sanctuary, and in the purity and fidelity to Yahve of the corporate group.

The P writer composed rather than compiled his major work. It was a brief history of the events from creation until the entrance of Israel into Palestine. He began on the largest canvas, the world, and progressively narrowed the focus to Israel. After P had completed this work, he revised it by inserting such material as J, E, RJE, or H. Like RJE, he was not disturbed by the presence of contradictory elements. Therefore, he can allow the proximity of two conflicting genealogies of the generations from Adam to Noah; he can allow two divergent stories of creation to appear side by side. Possibly, especially in view of the elasticity of the religious mind, he regarded divergencies as identities. Or perhaps he was not sufficiently concerned, not reckoning that subsequent generations, especially modern scholars, would examine his work minutely.

I have reservations about the generally accepted explanation of the literary history of the Pentateuch.[4] The manner in which I would personally differ from it will emerge in the subsequent discussion. Also, since the contents of this chapter may be a burden for the student to retain, I shall deliberately repeat relevant portions of it, especially those dealing with the work of the P author or authors, in the ensuing discussion of the individual books of the Pentateuch.

[4] See my "The Haggada Within Scripture," *Journal of Biblical Literature*, LXXX (June 1961), 105–22.

GENESIS

A SERIES of story cycles and of short episodes make up the book of Genesis. The cycles are Creation, Noah, Abraham, Isaac, Jacob, and Joseph. Individual episodes are those about Dinah, and Judah and Tamar. The framework of Genesis was provided by a late author (or authors) who was a priest. After he (or they) had completed the framework, he interspersed it with older material which was at hand. The P writing is marked by precision and by regularity of style. Its tone is solemn, its mood austere. In P, God is unseen and formless. P has an interest in chronology. He tells us the ages of characters, relating the age of a new character to the age already given of an earlier character.

J, the oldest source interspersed in P, is the born storyteller. He is simple and brief. He uses adjectives only when they provide a characterization necessary to the plot. Thus, in the tale of Eve's temptation by the serpent, he tells us that the serpent is wily; thereby we are led to understand why the serpent does what he does. J, moreover, is a teller of folk tales. He will relate stark tragedy, such as Cain's murder of his brother Abel in a fit of jealousy. But like any teller of folk tales, J has a very rich sense of humor. (It is unfortunate that the Tanak is often approached so lugubriously that its humor and wit are neither noticed nor appreciated.) Sometimes J's humor is broad and almost coarse; he portrays Rachel as sitting on the gods of her father, and unable to rise at her father's entrance with the excuse that she is in her menstrual period. At other times his humor is more delicate, as when Ephron the Hittite discloses the price of the cave Abraham wants to buy with the words, "What are four hundred pieces of silver between you and me?" J has a fondness for puns (these are known technically as *paronomasia,* a term calculated to obscure the fun in them); he tells us that the wily (*'arum*) serpent disclosed to Adam that Adam was naked (*'arom*).

P's characters are high-minded protagonists, completely above reproach. J's characterization of these same protagonists makes them completely human and fallible: Rebekah favors her son Jacob over her son Esau, while Isaac favors Esau over Jacob. Sarah gives her maid Hagar to Abraham as a second wife, whereupon Hagar ceases to regard Sarah with proper deference. When Sarah wants Abraham to drive Hagar from their household, he is deeply troubled, but he complies.

J almost invariably reveals character through incident rather than by adjectives. It is the biblical way to state that a character *said;* it is seldom that a character *shouts* or *groans* or *chuckles.* What the character says provides the clue to the manner in which the words have been spoken: Isaac "trembles a great trembling" when he recognizes that Jacob has taken Esau's blessing, yet he neither cries nor weeps but simply "says." Esau, in turn, "shouts a very great and bitter shout," but simply "says." Deft characterization by incident combines with dramatic situation to create a direct emotional impact on the reader, even while J is sparing in words.

J has a bent for sentiment and romance. Abraham's servant, who has gone eastward for a wife for Isaac, encounters Rebekah at a well. She meets the test which has previously been foreshadowed, in that she volunteers to draw water both for the servant and for the camels; surely she is the ideal bride. And when the servant brings her westward, it is her intended fiancé Isaac whom she first spies.

J, moreover, has a great interest in explanations of why things are as they are. He tells us why a serpent crawls on its belly (instead of walking on feet); why man must sweat and toil for a living; why childbirth is painful. Similarly, he tells us how certain places received their names (usually they represent a Hebrew pun). He is aware of the relationships of kindred peoples, and he accounts for the kinship by telling of the ancestor and the ancestor's genealogy, carrying this out extensively. The Canaanites are descended from Canaan, Noah's grandson; the Ammonites and Moabites have as ancestors Ammon and Moab, the offspring of the incestuous relation of Lot and each of his daughters.

In the J narratives, Yahve, though He is the Deity, is nevertheless a folk character. He fashions man out of dust and breathes life
into him; He plants a garden eastward in Eden. He ponders that it is
not good for man to be alone, so He has man fall asleep, and He ex-
tracts a rib which He builds into a woman. Then Yahve regrets that
He created man. He causes a flood from which He permits Noah and
his family to be saved. Yahve obligingly closes the door on the ark
after the family has entered it. When the flood is over He remembers
Noah.

He scatters humanity over the earth, to speak different languages.
He descends at the tower of Babel and confuses (*Babel* and *balal*,
"confused," are a pun) man's tongues.

J was unaware of any unseemliness or disrespect in his familiar
portrayal of Yahve.

Between J's folk level and P's austerity there lay centuries of
development, how many we do not know. Reflections of these developments are shown in scholarly analyses by symbols such as E, E 1, and
J 2. The method I shall follow will not use these symbols, for they are
cumbersome, and to me not fully persuasive. I shall revert to this
question presently.

The P code is the climax in the Tanak of a constant refinement
of incident, character, and conception. This refinement did not
cease with P. Rather, it continued after the Pentateuch was completed, and even after it was canonized and became a fixed text. We
can understand most clearly the development that occurred between
the assembly of the J folk tales, and the thoughtful, sober P code, by
looking at some of the refinements that arose after the Pentateuch
was canonized. For example, the J account of Abraham's acquisition
of wealth (12:10–20) relates that the patriarch had gone to Egypt
because of a famine. Aware that Sarah his wife was beautiful and
fearful that the Egyptians might slay him in order to possess her,
Abraham represented her as his sister. She was taken to Pharaoh's
harem. Yahve smote Pharaoh and his household because of the abduc-
tion of Sarah, with the result that the Egyptian king restored her to
Abraham and gave Abraham a great many possessions.

On the one hand, the folk tale does not hesitate to exalt the wiles
of its heroes; on the other hand, a religious story necessarily has regard for moral and ethical values. From this latter standpoint, at
least three blemishes mar the short episode of Abraham in Egypt.
He seems to have told a lie; Sarah seems to have been possessed by

the Pharaoh; and Abraham's acquisition of wealth seems to have resulted from conduct that was not quite straightforward.

The P editor did not expunge or rewrite this particular story, but elsewhere in his portrayal the characters of Abraham and Sarah are completely above reproach. In J (18), which P does rewrite, Sarah laughs in disbelief when the divine visitors predict that her sterility is about to end and that she will have a child, and then she denies that she has laughed. As P rewrites this story (17), it is Abraham and not Sarah who laughs; the laughter is for joy, not from disbelief; no mention is made of Sarah's having passed the menopause; and there is no denial of the laughter. In the same manner, P rewrites the account of the announcement that a son will be born. He does not rewrite the story of Abraham in Egypt, but in the context of the affirmative character he has given Abraham, the bare details of incident take on a different tone.

The person who read the total J and P versions necessarily started with the axiom that Abraham and Sarah were worthy. They could do no wrong, and hence they did no wrong. Thus, the ancient rabbis embellished and refined the episode of Abraham in Egypt on exactly this basis. They tell us that Sarah was so virtuous that when Abraham and Sarah came to Egypt and she had to disrobe to cross the Nile, this was the first time that Abraham ever saw her naked. They tell us that Sarah was never alone in Pharaoh's bedchamber, but that an invisible angel was present, whip in hand, to lash Pharaoh every time he made an unseemly advance. Thus Pharaoh was wondrously frustrated on that night of lust. The rich gifts to Abraham were motivated by Pharaoh's wish to have Abraham intercede with God to end the plague.

Josephus, a Jewish writer who flourished in the first Christian century and who wrote for Greeks, tells us that the purpose of Abraham's journey to Egypt was to discuss religion with the Egyptian priests, with the objective of persuading them or being persuaded by them. In the course of their discussions Abraham taught them mathematics, which he had learned in his native Ur, and in turn, the Egyptians taught the Greeks mathematics; thus Abraham was the source of the discipline in which the Greeks excelled. As to Sarah's sojourn in Pharaoh's harem, Josephus reproduces not a word.

Another writer in Greek, Philo of Alexandria (20 B.C.–A.D. 40) relates the episode without mentioning Abraham's lie or his acquisition of wealth. He makes it plain that Sarah's virtue was untarnished. In his narration, Pharaoh is a despicable example of a man without any sense of true hospitality and the high standards it requires. To

Philo, Sarah represents virtue and Pharaoh hypocrisy; Pharaoh has pretensions to virtue but never attains it.

The post-biblical refinements go under the name of *midrash,* a Hebrew term that calls for explanation. In its root meaning, it could be translated as "inquiry," inquiry into what a Scriptural verse means or implies. But the term has a derived meaning that might be rendered as "embellishment." Scripture introduces us to Abraham when he is already seventy-five. Midrash tells us about the period that Scripture omits. It makes Abraham's father Terah an idol worshiper, the owner of a shop where idols are sold. When one day he left the youthful Abraham in charge, Abraham chopped to pieces all but the biggest idol. Into the idol's hand he put the axe, and when Terah returned to find his shop in a shambles Abraham explained that the large idol had gone about chopping the others into pieces. Indignantly Terah replied that idols cannot move. "Let your ears hear what your lips are saying," said Abraham.

Midrash, as embellishment, takes on the connotation of the romantic, or the fanciful, or the bizarre, for imagination was often creative and unrestrained. The ancient rabbis were gifted at midrash,[1] as was Paul; the various accounts of Jesus in the New Testament Gospels and in those gospels that were not included in the New Testament reveal a comparable Christian gift for midrash. In the post-biblical period, then, midrash had a rich and robust existence.

But midrash did not wait until the canonization of the Pentateuch to emerge. Between the J code and the P code the midrashic impulse was already at work. As a result, there appears in Genesis a sizable variety of anecdotes that illumine the developments in the period between J and P.

There is in Scripture (Gen. 20) a rewriting of the episode of Abraham in Egypt (Gen. 12:10–20). This midrashic rewriting, occasioned by a transition from the simplicity of a folk tale to an awareness of moral and ethical standards, transfers the incident from Egypt to Philistia, and replaces the Pharaoh with King Abimelech. As the story is now related, Sarah's virtue is explicitly kept intact, and Abraham, in representing Sarah as his sister, is not lying, for she is described as his half-sister.

Similarly, the midrashic tendency is disclosed in the tales of the marriages of Isaac and Jacob. It was unthinkable that either patri-

---

[1] Midrash in this sense is a process or approach. When *The Midrash* is spoken of, it refers to the collection of embellishments recorded and preserved into our day. Thus, there is *The Great Midrash* to Genesis, Exodus, and so forth. Where midrash deals with regulations, it is described as *halacha;* midrashic narrative is called *haggada.*

arch should have married outside the fold, yet at that time in the supposed history, there were no Jewesses whom they could have married. Midrash found solutions to the dilemmas: Abraham's chief servant journeyed eastward to Abraham's kinfolk to find a bride for Isaac, since Sarah could not abide the Hittite wives of Isaac's half-brother, Ishmael; Rebekah sent Jacob eastward for a wife, again to kinfolk, because she could not stand the Canaanite wives of her first born son, Esau.

So fully does J present the unmoral folk tale about folk heroes that the midrashic tendency inevitably developed when these folk heroes were turned into ancestors and thereby symbols of the collective people. The Abraham of the episode of Egypt is not the same as the Abraham who earlier in the same chapter is majestically told by Yahve to leave his native land, because Yahve plans to make him into a great nation. When Rebekah, after a period of sterility, has become pregnant and undergoes discomfort, she is told by an oracle that the twins she has in her womb are two nations. Indeed, the more the J account portrayed the folk character as unmoral, the more urgent it was for midrash to rehabilitate him, if he was to be suitable as an ancestor. We shall see that this was especially the case with Jacob. An identification, then, of a folk character as a national ancestor represents one of the developments between J and P. A second midrashic tendency between J and P is illustrated by two episodes in the cycle of Abraham stories. It may be recalled that the cities of proverbial wickedness, Sodom and Gomorrah, were destroyed; the Tanak refers several times to Yahve's destruction of them. Yet as we now read the account, two angels arrived in Sodom as the instruments of destruction, rather than Yahve Himself. These angels were two of three who had appeared to Abraham (Gen. 18) to inform him of Sarah's impending pregnancy. But this chapter is unclear about whether it was Yahve who appeared and spoke to Abraham, or three men. In some verses Abraham's visitors are one, in some they are plural. The first verse begins the confusion: "Yahve appeared to Abraham at Elone Mamre; he was sitting before his tent at the heat of the day, and he raised his eyes and saw three men . . ." Why is there this confusion? We shall see the explanation presently.

The other episode is the well-known story (Gen. 22) of the test of Abraham. God (Elohim) tested Abraham by enjoining him to offer Isaac as a sacrifice on a mountain named Moriah. Abraham met the test to the point of journeying to the mountain, of building an altar, and of binding Isaac on it. Yet when he raised his hand to slaughter Isaac he was ordered to desist by Yahve's angel—not by Elohim. The clue to the shift from Elohim to Yahve's angel and from Yahve to the three men is to be discovered in a significant but subtle aspect of the Hebrew conception of God. The Hebrews would have denied that there existed any ultimate power but Yahve, but they shrank from depicting Him boldly and directly doing something evil or unseemly. They would have held that He was the ultimate source of the destruction of Sodom, but He had no direct connection with this evil and instead sent His angels. He could agree to put Abraham to a test, but the actual testing was done by an angel. In the case of the binding of Isaac, the substitution of Yahve's angel for Elohim is not carried through consistently, appearing only in the latter part of the episode. Comparably, when Hagar is driven into the Wilderness (Gen. 16), it is Yahve's angel who finds her, but the chapter is unclear as to whether it is Yahve or His angel whom Hagar encounters.

These substitutions, imperfectly carried out, represent a self-conscious inquiry into what could legitimately be ascribed to Yahve and what could not. Angels appear in recastings in the period between J and P, because in J, Yahve, as we have said, is something of a folk character, and the Hebrews were exalting Him increasingly. In P, the concept of Yahve as an invisible yet omnipotent spirit has become so stabilized that while he reproduces sources that mention angels, P never resorts to them himself.

The moralistic recastings and rewritings are not everywhere they could be, nor are they thoroughgoing where we find them. They are frequent enough, however, and full enough for us to be able to see, when they are set alongside P's exalted approach, why it was that postbiblical midrash attributed to folkish J the high attributes of P. The traditional midrash in the postbiblical period is quite blind to the folk character of extensive sections of Genesis, which has only been recognized by modern scholarship.

A third type of midrashic development between J and P is illustrated by an aspect of Abraham's character as it is portrayed in the story of Sodom and Gomorrah. The story depicts two men proceeding to Sodom to destroy it, but the narrative is interrupted, and Yahve is portrayed as raising the question of whether it is right for Him to conceal from Abraham His intention to destroy these wicked cities. When He discloses to Abraham what He plans to do, Abraham intercedes on behalf of the cities, bargaining with Yahve, and delicately suggesting that Yahve must do justice. This is scarcely the same Abraham as the one in the episode in Egypt.

This incident reflects the great growth in biblical materials. Ancient tradition long before J had told of an earthquake which destroyed Sodom and Gomorrah; for the Hebrews, Yahve had caused the earthquake because of Sodom's wickedness. Thereafter, developing legend brought Abraham into connection with Sodom, in that his nephew Lot had come to reside there. As the tale grew, Yahve appeared to Abraham to announce that he would have a son Isaac; here we have entered the period of J. In the development after J the three men tend to replace Yahve, and two of them go from Abraham to Sodom. Even later there arose the story of Abraham's intercession.

In a comparable way, Jacob, an extremely wily folk character, came to be conceived of as an ancestor. J had portrayed him as fleeing in fear from Esau; a later hand altered his flight to a journey to find a proper wife. To the ancestor (as distinct from the wily folk character) Yahve appeared in the incident of angels ascending and descending a ladder that reached up into heaven. The episode bound Yahve and Jacob to each other, as if in a covenant. Such a relationship, even though the covenant is not explicit, fits in with Jacob as symbolic of the nation. A covenant with Abraham was to be expected. Genesis provides two accounts. In the P account, the covenant is associated with its symbol, circumcision, for P is consistently interested in observances. Yet between J and P there was an account of God's making the Covenant of the Pieces (Gen. 15) with Abraham.

This third type of midrashic tendency, then, accounts for the various elements in Genesis that are younger than J but already formed and recorded so as to be available to P. While these elements emerged primarily from imagination and meditative piety, it is quite possible and even probable that some of them incorporate echoes of folk materials derived from some source other than J, and just as ancient. In the present state of our knowledge, however, such derivation is at best hypothetical.

In the light of the foregoing, I shall mean by J a level of artistic narration which is that of the folk tale. I shall allude to "nationalizing" and other forms of recasting the folkish tone of the tales. I shall speak of a P author (or authors) who wrote a framework into which they inserted both J and the embellishments that arose between J and P.

In recent decades there has developed, as I have said, a rather strong insistence on the historical reliability of the materials in Genesis. This insistence comes especially from some archaeologists. They point to the correspondence which they assert exists between what Genesis relates and what is known as a result of deciphering certain tablets and inscriptions and of the excavation of ancient sites.

What is overlooked in this misguided emphasis is that it is not the correspondence of the general backgrounds that would establish historical reliability, but rather the confirmation of the particular. I have already noted that no mementos of Abraham, Isaac, and Jacob have been found. Perhaps the issue can be further clarified by asking some pointed questions. Can the archaeologists confirm for us that creation took place in six days? Can they confirm that the serpent spoke to Eve? Can they confirm that Noah brought two (or seven!) living creatures of each species into his ark? Can they confirm that Abraham bargained with Yahve to save Sodom? Can they confirm that with trimmed poplar rods Jacob controlled the kinds of animals born to the flocks? Can they confirm that Moses' rod became a snake? Can they confirm that Joshua made the sun stand still? There is, therefore, a limit to what archaeology can prove.

What archaeology has confirmed, however, is that the general picture of early Palestinian life as depicted in the Tanak is reliable. This confirmation has been desirable, or even necessary, to refute a skepticism found in some nineteenth-century scholars who found absolutely nothing in Scripture credible. But we should not move from excessive skepticism to excessive credulity. The traditions in Genesis are folk tales modified and embellished by religious belief. To seek to authenticate these as historically valid in the form in which Genesis relates them is to misapply a useful science.

The literary history of Genesis, indeed of Genesis through Numbers, culminates in the P writing. Yahve in P is no longer Israel's national god, He is the God of the universe. The patriarchs are no longer folk characters but the worthy ancestors from whom Israel is descended and whose meritorious deeds can stand Israel in good stead.

When we fragmentize Genesis into J and P and the intervening layers, we are not reading what P intended us to read. We are contravening his purpose, and we are thereby missing his intention. To ignore the literary history of Genesis leads to a failure to appreciate P's great achievement. To look at Genesis without seeing P's synthesis, as even some scholars have done, is to be bogged down in source analysis, as though the raw material which Shakespeare used were the equivalent of Shakespeare himself. Our task is therefore to look at Genesis, and not just at its analysis. For Genesis is greater than its component parts.

The intention of P, which will gain in clarity as we see more and more of his handiwork, was to provide a handbook for religious living. In Exodus, Leviticus, and Numbers he provides us with a broad range of instructions in answer to the question we noted earlier, "What shall a man do?" In Genesis he is giving the answer to the other question, "What shall a man think?" In answer to this second question, Genesis tells us how the world came to exist, and how man came to be created. In solemn and majestic tones, the writer begins with what for him is the most primitive of events, the creation of the world by an omnipotent, invisible Deity. Creation results from a divine decree, for the one God needs merely to speak, and that which He has spoken comes about. Since His power is without limit, His creative acts are effective, and therefore He looks on each act and pronounces it good.

It is the religious poet and not the geologist or astronomer who is reflected in this story of creation. Poetic license is evident, for light is created on the first day, but it is not until the fourth that the sun, moon, and stars are created. Only after birds, worms, fish, and animals, is man created. In Hebrew man is *adam;* Genesis calls him *the* man, and keeps him nameless, but tradition came to call him Adam. This story of creation is simple and dignified. The author knew no science; he gave an interpretation based not on knowledge but on his meditative piety. And he concluded that as early as creation the Sabbath existed, implying that man should observe the Sabbath, for God, upon completing His work of creation, had observed it.

As yet there were, of course, no Hebrews. Only when there were to be many peoples could the Hebrews arise. An account was necessary, accordingly, of human events prior to the emergence of the Hebrews. P did not himself write this account; rather, he incorporated a J version of the first man and of early mankind. Since P was dealing with man, not with the Hebrews, he was constrained to set forth universal aspects of man. The old legends he quoted were not inconsistent to his mind as they are to ours. He first told us (1:26-8) of the creation of man and woman. What looks to us like a repetition (2:4ff.) was to him only a filling in of details. And while in this repetition we moderns can see a view of God discordant with P's first presentation, no such discordancy troubled the author.

Yahve, the amplifying repetition tells us, made man out of dust and breathed life into him. (How else could it have come about that a physical being like man was so unlike a stone or a clod of clay?) Hebrew has a word for man besides *adam.* This word is *ish,* and related to it is the word for woman, *isha.* Yahve took a rib from the sleeping *ish* and built the rib into an *isha.* This relatedness of woman to man accounts for the universal practice of a man's leaving his parents and cleaving to a woman.

Unaware that aborigines in remote areas even today go naked, the author raises the question, "Why do people universally wear clothes?" It is out of a sense of shame, he tells us; he gives no hint that the origin is for protection from cold or sun. How did man come to have this sense of shame at nakedness? Yahve had put him in a luxurious garden in which there were many trees whose fruit he might eat. Two trees were forbidden. One conferred immortality, the other conferred knowledge. The serpent persuaded the woman to eat of the tree of knowledge. She took some fruit, gave some to her man, and they both ate. Thereupon they knew that they were naked, for the *'arum* serpent did that which made them aware they were *'arom*, naked. Man can learn, for he ate of the tree of knowledge; man dies, for he did not eat of the tree of eternal life. As for the serpent, he lost his arms and legs, and crawled on his belly.

Did the P author believe that the serpent could talk? Of course not! He had at hand a good story, and an old one, so he told it. Besides, the story had a good twist in it; when Yahve scolded the man for eating the fruit in disobedience, the man blamed the woman, and the woman in turn blamed the serpent. It is the universal which these legends set forth. It is universal that women travail at childbirth; it is universal (or it was, in the biblical world) for woman to be subservient to man. It is universal that man must labor in pain and sweat to produce food to sustain himself.

In the era before there were Hebrews, there were already shepherds like Abel and farmers like Cain. Jealousy is universal, and murder is ubiquitous. Cain killed Abel, rudely asserting that he was not his brother's keeper. Murder needed to be punished; Cain must wander about the face of the earth (for peoples did wander about), wearing a sign (for tribes did carry identifying symbols).

Are there not cities all over the world? It was Cain who first built one, for his son Enoch. (Where did Cain get his wife, if only Adam and Eve existed? The old legends were unconcerned with such details.) Cain had a descendant, Lamech, who had two sons, by one wife; one son was the ancestor of cattle keepers, the other of musicians. By a second wife Lamech had a son who worked in clay and metals. Diverse trades and occupations are universally found among men. But all mankind is not descended from Cain, a murderer. Adam and Eve had a third son, Seth, who had a son Enos. Old legend had it that in Enos' time the worship of Yahve began.[2]

P wrote a genealogy (5), from Adam through Lamech, different from the implied J genealogy (4). He omitted Cain the murderer and attributed to Seth the descendants whom his J source had attributed

---

[2] P quotes this legend because it is in his source, but in Exod. 6 he will reject the legend, for he does not wish to ascribe Yahve worship to the period before there were Hebrews.

to Cain. The P genealogy clashes with that of J; P was unconcerned, for his genealogy, with its precise (though exaggerated) longevities, was for him the right list, and his source, J, scarcely in need of correction.[3] Of the worthies whom P names in the ten generations from Adam to Noah, only Enoch merits more than a summary of years. "Enoch walked with God, and was no more, for God took him." We do not know what this means. P probably had further information about Enoch but did not relate it, possibly because some legend about Enoch was so well known among people that it was enough to allude to it.[4]

The longevities ascribed to the generations imply that a great length of time has elapsed between the days of Adam and those of Noah. It is presumed that man has multiplied and is now numerous. But in Noah's time God must reassess His handiwork, man. The assessment bodes ill for man, for there were women who were very fair to behold, and wickedness was rife. What was it that had gone wrong? The P writer, who has been at pains to depict God as pure spirit, now surprisingly quotes an old source which told that the "sons of the gods" saw the fair women and took as wives "whomever they chose" (6:1–8). This passage is the sole vestige clearly reproduced in Genesis of an elaborate available mythology. Indeed, one can say that what is striking about Genesis is that there is practically no mythology in it.

In the usual ancient accounts of creation, the sequel runs that first the world was created, and next the gods came into existence. In Genesis, however, first the one and only God exists, and then He creates. It is the structure of the whole that prompts the P author to utilize the ancient myth of the divine beings who came to earth and mingled with men. He is about to relate the story of the great flood. He might have ascribed the flood, as does a Babylonian myth which he shows some knowledge of, to discord among the gods. Instead, the flood comes, according to him, because of mankind's evil. The extremity of this evil could not be ascribed to mere humans, such as the generations he has enumerated; therefore it came from an unusual circumstance, the marriage of divine beings with women.[5] This same age of long ago was one when giants, enormous men of great notoriety, lived on earth.

[3] The two genealogies are these: J: Adam, Cain, Enoch, Irad, Mehujael, Methusael, Lamech, Jabal/Jubal/Tubal-Cain; P: Adam, Seth, Enosh, Kenan, Mahalalel, Jared, Enoch, Methusaleh, Lamech, Noah.
[4] In post-Tanak times, Enoch was regarded as having been taken to heaven where he received revelations. Enoch was a prominent character in apocalyptic writings.
[5] See Ps. 82 for another mention of sons of the gods. Semitic mythology told of a rebellion in heaven by lesser gods, and these were cast out from heaven to earth. Perhaps the psalm reflects this rebellion.

The flood story was universal among peoples, and P, in addressing himself to universal man, feels the need to narrate it. A J legend
was available to him, but he is not content to use it unannotated. He
alters the number of animals from J's account of seven pairs of pure
and one pair of impure to one pair each of both pure and impure.
(Both J and P assume that the reader knows which are the pure and
impure animals.) J has the flood last forty days and forty nights; in P,
the water rises for one hundred and fifty days and recedes until the
ark rests on Ararat for one hundred and fifty days, and another sixty-
four days are required for the earth to dry up. The precise dates of
Noah and his sons and the flood are the work of P; so, too, are the
precise dimensions of the ark. J's account is robust, vivid, and spontaneous; the P portions are systematized, stolid, and studied.

There can be no question that the Genesis flood narrative is derived from Babylonia. This has long been known, for portions are
quoted by the fourth-century A.D. church historian Eusebius from a
Babylonian priest Berosus. In 1872 an archaeologist, George Smith,
found an extensive Babylonian text, part of what is known as the Gilgamesh epic. Therein it is related that the gods had decided to destroy
a certain city, Shurapah. One of the gods, Ea, determined to save a
man, Utnapishtim; Ea appeared to him in a dream and instructed him
to build a vessel. When the flood came, the gods themselves were in
dire danger from it. The rainstorm lasted six days and nights and then
the vessel rested on a Mount Nisir for six days. Utnapishtim sent out a
swallow, which returned, and then a raven, which did not. He disem-
barked with his family and the various animals; he offered sacrifices
the scent of which the gods savored. The chief god, Enlil, was persuaded by Ea to limit punishment of man in the future to ordinary
floods, wild animals, famine, and pestilence. Utnapishtim and his
wife were then made gods.

Not only are the similarities striking, but the supposition that
Noah's ark rested to the east on Ararat, rather than on a Palestinian
mountain, indicates the alien origin of the flood story. Even the J
account, though relatively old and in some ways naive, illustrates the
Hebraic method of adapting ancient and alien matters. In the Babylonian myth the flood comes because gods quarrel, in J because man
has become corrupt. In the myth there is a pantheon of gods who are
themselves threatened by the flood; in J, Yahve is the universal God,
sovereign over all the earth. In the myth the flood is the result of
caprice; in J it is an act of divine justice. P merely refines further
what J has already refined.

P rounds off the story of the flood with two significant details.

He is aware that some laws are universal among men, for example, those concerning the spilling of blood. The universality of such laws came about, P tells us, because the universal God enjoined them. They are not the specific Hebrew regulations; there are as yet no Hebrews in the world. Rather, these are the laws that all men obey and should obey.

Moreover, in P's time there were no longer "sons of the gods" around to recontaminate society. Also, the Persian conquest, just before P's time, had revealed that the world extended far to the east; not only were there the western islands in the Mediterranean, but the Persians had broadened horizons by penetrating into Europe, to be repelled at Marathon and Thermopylae (485 B.C.). Floods, if they came, were now only local, and destruction could no longer be universal. That this was so was not an accident, according to P, but the result of God's determination. He made a covenant with Noah to that effect, and periodically He could remind man of the covenant by exhibiting a rainbow in the midst of a downpour. The rainbow was the sign of God's covenant with Noah.

The flood had wiped out a populous world. Now that the flood was over, the world was to be repopulated; men were to be so abundant that the individual man could no longer be the focus of P's attention. P now turns to tell us, therefore, how different peoples came into the world. First he quotes an old J legend. Noah planted a vineyard, made wine, and rolled about his tent drunk and naked. His second son, Ham, told the brothers, Shem and Japheth. These two would not gaze on their father's nakedness as Ham had done; they covered up their father, averting their eyes as they did so.

The mention of Ham at the beginning of the account includes the statement that he is the father of Canaan. This is our first encounter of names of individuals representing peoples. When Noah awoke from his stupor, he uttered a curse against his son Ham. This curse, however, does not mention Ham. It runs as follows:

> *Cursed is Canaan; an abject slave he will be to his brothers;*
> *Bless, O Yahve, the tents of Shem, and let Canaan be his*
>   *slave!* [9:25]

This old legend tells why the Canaanites sank into slavery. The Hebrews were descended, according to Scripture, from Shem. (Shem's descendants are *Semites*.) The tale of Noah's sons marks the transition from individuals to peoples. The legend is followed by the account of the many descendants of the three sons (10).

Genesis 10 tells which were the peoples of the world and where they lived. In Genesis 11, a J legend relates how the peoples came to be scattered over the face of the earth, and why they spoke different languages. This legend supposed that the repopulated world had settled in an eastern region in a valley in Sumeria. They feared they might be scattered, so at Babel (Babylon) they tried to build a tower the top of which would reach to heaven. Yahve came down to look over the work. He considered it a piece of effrontery for men to aspire to reach heaven, and He determined to frustrate their plans by confusing their tongues. Yahve at *Babel* confused (*balal*) man's languages and scattered the people over all the earth to their places of dwelling.

Thus far we have seen creation, individual men, the flood, and the growth of peoples diverse in language and in place of residence. After having brought the reader to the context of a world of many nations, the author was ready to introduce the Hebrew people. Just as in the case of other peoples, there were individuals who were group ancestors. Yet whereas in the case of other nations one person was the ancestor, the Hebrews had a succession of three—a father, Abraham, his son, Isaac, and his grandson, Jacob.

This ancestry was presented as triple rather than single for several reasons. The primary reason was the testimony of tradition. The prophetic literature before the Babylonian exile contains frequent mention of Isaac and Jacob; moreover, the collective people was known as Israel. It would have contradicted the knowledge of tradition for the ancestry to be limited to a single progenitor.

Secondly, the author recognized an unmistakable kinship with certain other peoples. These kindred peoples were not properly Hebrews, yet they were close enough to need to be included in some way even in a focus that had narrowed from the many peoples to the one people. The desert nomads were kindred; hence Abraham had a son Ishmael from whom the nomads were descended. The Edomites were kindred; hence Isaac had a son Esau who was their progenitor. The Ammonites and Moabites were kindred, but a little more distant; hence they had as their progenitors Abraham's nephew, Lot. Accordingly, a recognition that many peoples were kindred to Israel meant the need for the succession of three "fathers."

The third reason is more complicated. The pre-exilic prophets make frequent reference to the Wilderness origin of the Hebrews, but they say not one word about an origin in the east. The Pentateuch, on the other hand, emphasizes and magnifies eastern origin; it conceives of the Wilderness stage as enduring for *only* forty years, and as the transitory period between a long residency in Egypt, lasting four hundred years, and the entry into Canaan. The Pentateuchal emphasis on the east is shown by its being made the birthplace of

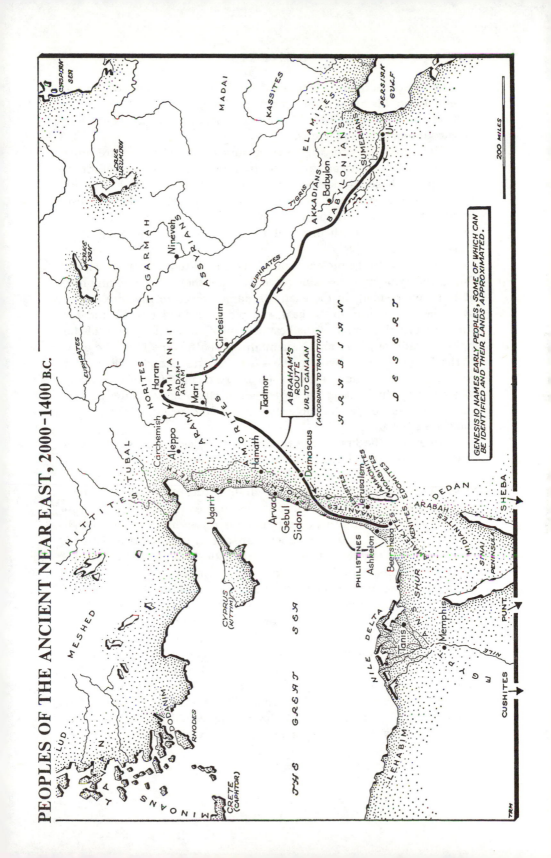

PEOPLES OF THE ANCIENT NEAR EAST, 2000–1400 B.C.

GENESIS 10 NAMES EARLY PEOPLES, SOME OF WHICH CAN BE IDENTIFIED AND THEIR LANDS APPROXIMATED.

ABRAHAM'S ROUTE
UR TO CANAAN
(ACCORDING TO TRADITION)

200 MILES

CASPIAN SEA

MADAI

KASSITES

ELAMITES

PERSIAN GULF

Ur

SUMERIANS

BABYLONIANS

Babylon

AKKADIANS

TIGRIS

LAKE URUMIYAH

TOGARMAH

Nineveh

ASSYRIANS

EUPHRATES

GREAT ZAB

Circesium

MITANNI

HORITES

Haran

PADAM-ARAM

Mari

Tadmor

ARABIAN DESERT

EUPHRATES

TUBAL

Carchemish

Aleppo

ARAM

AMORITES

Hamath

Damascus

HITTITES

Ugarit

Arvad

PHOENICIANS

Gebul

Sidon

Ashkelon

PHILISTINES

Beersheba

CANAANITES

Jerusalem

AMMONITES

MOABITES

EDOM

AMALEKITES

KENITES

ARABAH

MIDIANITES

DEDAN

SHEBA

SHUR

SINAI PENINSULA

PUNT

MESHED

GREAT SEA

CYPRUS (KITTIM)

TYRE

DODANIM

RHODES

CRETE (CAPHTOR)

MINOANS

LUD

NILE DELTA

Tanis

Memphis

NILE

EGYPT

LEHABIM

CUSHITES

Abraham, Rebekah, and Leah and Rachel, the wives of Jacob. In the case of Isaac, his bride is brought from the east to Canaan by Abraham's servant; in the case of Jacob, he journeys eastward and there he encounters Leah and Rachel.

The actual facts of the early history of the Hebrews are quite uncertain. The eastern origin of Abraham may echo a dim recollection that among those tribes who entered Canaan there were some that had moved from the Wilderness to the east and only thereafter westward into Canaan. Perhaps this recollection is contained in the tradition of Abraham's birth in Ur of the Chaldees and his removal to Haran.

Curiously, in the pre-exilic prophets Abraham goes unmentioned. But in the exilic and postexilic periods, when there was a community of Hebrews resident in the east, his name comes to the fore. Moreover, the community to the east was regarded by Jeremiah and his successors as the source of the best and most authentic bearers of the Hebrew tradition; Ezra and Nehemiah had both come from the east. If the P author, who lived in the same general period as Ezra and Nehemiah, was prone to regard the eastern community of his day as in some way duplicating the early age of the origins of the people, then it becomes understandable that he would conceive of the east as the place of origin.

Abraham, the first of the progenitors, is described as an *'ivri*, a "Hebrew." Exactly what the word means is debatable. It is taken by some to mean "he who crosses," that is, he who crossed from east to west. Others take it to mean "the merchant." Ancient Egyptian sources speak of a people the consonants of whose name are similar. This similarity is not transparent when the name is represented in an English transcription of it. It is sometimes transcribed as *khabiri* or *habiru*, and sometimes as *apiru*. Students of linguistics will recognize that the three basic consonants [6] are variants of the same sounds, or, more precisely, the sounds can be represented in writing by related symbols. The suggestion is made, then, that the Hebrews and the *Khabiri* are identical. Perhaps this is so; it is, however, uncertain.

The name Abram (altered to Abraham, according to Genesis 17:5) is partly similar to the word *'ivri*, "Hebrew." What we know about consonants in Semitic languages would lead us to conclude that the first consonant of Abram (an *aleph*) and the first of *'ivri*, an *ayin*, are unrelated. It would be impossible, therefore, to derive *'ivri* from *Abram*. Yet the nature of Hebrew puns would not rule out a reverse possibility, namely that the word Hebrew gave rise to the name

[6] They are: kh or k; p or bh or v; r or l.

Abram.[7] This too cannot be proved, but if it is so, it would mean that Abraham as an ancestor is less a historical figure than he is one imagined and created in late times.

The cycle of Abraham stories lacks that unity which is unmistakable in the Joseph stories and discernible in the Jacob stories. In both these latter cycles there is a connected story line with incident growing out of incident, and complications growing to climaxes. The Abraham cycle, however, is a succession of relatively unrelated events. What unity is present is to be found mostly in the genealogical tables. At the start we are told of Abraham's family relationships; we are told that the family moved from Ur to Haran and that Sarah was childless. Then the focus abruptly turns to Abraham.

Yahve appeared to him (in Ur or Haran?) enjoining him to leave home and go to an undesignated land. He is to become a great nation, and all the families of the earth are to be blessed in Abraham; that is, he is not an individual here but the national symbol. Abraham, accompanied by Sarah and Lot, went to Canaan. Yahve appeared to him to tell him that He was giving the land to Abraham's seed. The implication is clear: since the land is Yahve's, it is His to do with as He pleases; Abraham's descendants are not usurpers. The Canaanites simply chanced to be there when Abraham arrived to hear Yahve's promise.

When famine caused Abraham to go to Egypt, Pharaoh's lust for Sarah resulted in Abraham's acquisition of wealth. So prosperous had Abraham and Lot, his nephew, become that pasture lands were insufficient, and quarrels arose between Abraham's shepherds and Lot's. Magnanimously, Abraham allowed Lot to choose the pasture lands he preferred. (No mention is made of any rights of the Canaanites.) Lot selected the fertile area of Sodom. To Abraham and his seed Yahve was to give in perpetuity whatever land Abraham could see when he looked in all directions. He was enjoined to traverse the land in width and length, for Yahve was giving it to him.[8]

In those ancient days four eastern kings had conquered Sodom and the surrounding towns, and, we are told, even the great "giants." Indeed, they conquered much of the southern part of Palestine. The kings of Sodom and the surrounding towns arose in rebellion but

[7] Thus, Scripture tells that Samuel is derived from "I asked of God"; Cain from "I acquired"; Noah from "he will comfort us." The Tanak gives the supposed meaning of Abraham, but not of Abram.

[8] The traditions about the Patriarchs are often allocated to specific localities. Thus, Abraham sojourns near Hebron, and in the Negeb, and in Beer Sheba; Isaac is at Gerar and at Beer Sheba; Jacob is associated with Bethel and Shechem. Scholars have found the study of the geographical data of Genesis illuminating, but there is no room in this volume to reflect their conclusions.

were decisively beaten, and Lot was captured. Abraham, pursuing with only three hundred and eighteen servants, destroyed the easterners and pursued them beyond Damascus; that is, he drove out of the land promised to him the invaders who should not have been there. At Salem (later known as Jerusalem) there was a priest named Melchizedek to whom Abraham gave a tithe of what he had captured (just as his descendants were to pay tithes at Jerusalem).

Though Abraham was childless, his faith that he and his exceedingly numerous seed would inherit the land did not waver. A covenant between Yahve and Abraham made formal the relationship between them. Yahve disclosed to Abraham the future enslavement (in Egypt) of his descendants, who would thereafter take possession of Canaan. The native Amorites would retain the land until that time, when their sin (which justified their losing their land) would be complete (Gen. 15). This early covenant account is paralleled by a P narrative (Gen. 17). The P covenant has as its symbol the circumcision of all future males at the age of eight days. This covenant is to run through the line of Sarah's unborn child, who is to be named Isaac, and not through Ishmael. Abraham circumcised all the males of his household, including Ishmael and himself. This chapter rewrites both the covenant in Chapter 15 and Sarah's carelessness about her laughter, in Chapter 18.

Still childless, Abraham accepted Sarah's offer of her Egyptian maid Hagar, through whom he might beget a son. As soon as Hagar was pregnant, she became impudent to Sarah. Abraham permitted Sarah to abuse her, so that Hagar fled, but Yahve's angel found her and advised her to return home and submit to Sarah. (This account in Chapter 16 is rewritten in Chapter 21, where Sarah has given birth to Isaac and has come to disapprove of Hagar's son Ishmael. When Sarah asks Abraham to drive Hagar out and Abraham is, properly, distressed, the Deity advises him not to be upset but to do what Sarah wishes. Abraham sends Hagar away in the morning, with a small supply of water. When that gives out Hagar is in great difficulties, until the Deity opens her eyes to the presence nearby of a well. In the rewriting it is the divine plan, and not mere capricious human cruelty, which took Ishmael into the Wilderness where he was to dwell.)

Yahve visited Abraham—an interpolator alters the narrative in Chapter 18 to relate that three men visited the hospitable Abraham—to inform him that a son would be born to him and Sarah. Since she had passed the age of childbearing and Abraham was very old, the news stirred Sarah to skeptical laughter. (This explains why the child was named Isaac, "laughter.") Though she denied that she had laughed, the visitor affirmed that she had. Two of the three visitors went on to Sodom. Yahve, out of consideration for Abraham's future eminence through his children, disclosed his intention to destroy Sodom and Gomorrah. Abraham persuaded Yahve to spare the cities if as few as ten righteous men could be found. When the visitors arrived, Lot extended warm hospitality to them, but the Sodomites gathered about the house, demanding that the visitors be turned over to them for homosexual purposes. The wicked city deserved destruction, so Yahve overturned it. Lot and his two daughters were saved; Lot's wife disobeyed instructions not to look at the destruction, and she became a pillar of salt.[9]

The rewriting of the Egyptian incident (20) protects both Sarah's virtue and Abraham's truthfulness. Indeed, Abraham was now a prophet whose intercession saved the lustful monarch, Abimelech, king of Gerar, and all his kingdom from the sterility which had come upon them. Sarah gave birth to Isaac. His name "laughter" now derived from the surprise that neighbors were to have at Sarah's childbearing and not from her own skepticism. Abraham circumcised Isaac at the age of eight days (21:1–21). Abraham was tested by being told by the Deity to offer Isaac as a sacrifice. When Isaac lay on the altar, Yahve's angel bade Abraham desist.[1]

A description of Abraham's relatives in the east (22:20–4) prepares the way for the marriage of Isaac. Sarah passed away; Abraham purchased a double cave as a burial place (23). Now Abraham sent his servant eastward for a wife for Isaac. The latter met Rebekah at the well, arranged with her parents for her to accompany him home, and she and Isaac loved each other (Gen. 24).

It is then related that Abraham married still another woman, Keturah, by whom he had children. Also, he had concubines who bore children. (Hence there were people[2] kindred to his preferred desendants, i.e., those descended from him through Isaac.) At Abraham's death[3] Isaac and Ishmael buried him beside Sarah.

This résumé may reflect the absence, alluded to above, of an inherent unity in the cycle of Abraham stories. A true life story can well lack a pattern, but the account of Abraham, as the rewritings and

[9] Lot and his daughters took refuge in a cave. His daughters lay with him in turn, after first giving him wine. From these acts of incest were born the ancestors of the Moabites and Ammonites.
[1] The narrative attacks human sacrifice by showing that Yahve did not want it even from faithful Abraham. In the course of retelling there was a shift in emphasis from this didactic purpose to a concentration on Abraham's obedience to God.
[2] Ishmael's descendants, and their geography, are set forth in 25:12–18.
[3] Some scholars have conjectured that there is some disarrangement, and that Abraham's death was originally narrated as preceding rather than following Isaac's marriage.

the "nationalizing" show, is scarcely a true life story. What seems at the beginning to be a theme—"go and be a blessing"—fails to be carried through to the end; and prior to the end it is only alluded to, never brought into sharp focus and accentuated.

What, therefore, may be said in summary about the author's preface? Yahve had elected to give Canaan to Israel. He showed the land to the prime ancestor Abraham, but the time of the gift was deferred for four hundred years. The ancestor had come to Canaan, traversed it, pastured his great flocks in it, shared its fields with his nephew, and kept its borders inviolate. Yahve made a covenant with him, a covenant handed down through only one of his many children. Tested by Yahve, Abraham triumphantly met the test.

These disconnected items are not primitive folk legends such as those of creation and of Eden; on the other hand, they are not well unified like the folk tales about Jacob. (Isaac is a shadowy person who virtually lacks characteristics.) In the case of Jacob, as we shall see, a folk character was transformed into an ancestor. In the case of Abraham, an ancestor was created. This was done in part by borrowing folk tales (the Egyptian episode), in part by retelling stories of heroes (the defeat of the eastern kings), and in part by telling didactic tales (the sacrifice of Isaac, the plea on behalf of Sodom, and the two accounts of the covenant). The character of Abraham was not inherited, as was that of Jacob, but was built up, exalted, and stabilized.

In the three versions of what we have called the Egyptian episode, the end result of the successive rewritings is the heightened moral character attributed to the patriarch, but we should not attribute this merely to a desire to whitewash the Patriarchs. The rewritings reflect the growing awareness of moral and ethical standards. In the nature of folk and national literature it is more to be wondered at that a growing ethical sense caused stories to be recast than that there are clear vestiges of earlier and less ethical versions. Because the Tanak very seldom expunges the primitive and the distasteful we are able to see aspects of the ever-deepening dimensions and refinements of the religious sense of the Hebrews.

As we have said, Scripture tells us very little about Isaac, indeed only one incident, detached from both the Abraham and the Jacob cycles. This incident (26) is a third version of the Egyptian episode. It may have been inserted because an editor was conscious of the absence of Isaac material and wanted to fill in the gap. It has been suggested, however, that the Isaac version is the oldest [4] and that the two

---

[4] It is considered the oldest because in some aspects it seems more primitive than the other two. In my judgment, it is the youngest of the three versions.

Abraham versions derive from it. Whatever may be the reason, that this incident is one of three accounts of the same story underlines a notable fact, the relative scarcity in Scripture of data about Isaac.

In the case of the cycle of Jacob stories we are given more than a mere glimpse of the process of refinement. The basic stories of Jacob are very, very old. His name means "cheater"; Esau, whom he has deceived, cries out (27:36), "Did they call him Jacob (*ya'aqob*, "cheater") because he would cheat me (*ya'aqbeni*) twice?"

The basic tale is an amusing one. Twin brothers were in their mother's womb, and even at that very early stage the younger tried to supplant the older. Indeed, they caused the mother so much distress that she felt the need to consult an oracle.[5]

There is a second pun on "Jacob"; at birth he is holding on to the ankle (*'aqeb*) of Esau; hence the name Jacob (25:26). The impossibility of a newborn baby's holding on to anything, much less his brother's ankle, did not bother the punster; unquestionably the original hearers found the gross exaggeration very funny. Moreover, the episode reflects the naïveté of the parents, who did not seem to recognize the true import of the name they gave the baby.

Genesis characterizes the twins briefly but adequately. Esau was a hunter, an outdoors man, and from birth hairy; Jacob was a shrewd man, who stayed close to home. It is the classic contrast between the sharpster of the city and the trusting simpleton of the country.

The needs of the story require that Isaac prefer Esau and Rebekah Jacob; this is all we are told of the growing up of the boys, for Genesis is as usual quite laconic. The narrative then moves forward. Jacob had prepared a soup (of red lentils?); Esau came from the outdoors worn out and hungry. The two made a trade: the valuable rights of primogeniture ("first-born") were exchanged for a paltry serving of soup. And after having made the exchange, Esau scorned the primogeniture rights, as if to say, what were they worth anyway? A simpleton!

The second episode requires the circumstance of Isaac's having become virtually blind and being close to death. He informed Esau of his intention to bless him, but first Esau had to go hunting and prepare some delicacies for his father. (The delicacies were required more for the plot than for Isaac, for if the father had given the blessing forthwith, the second deception could not have taken place.) The mother, Rebekah, sided with Jacob. Not only did she tell him about Isaac's intention to give Esau his blessing, but she advised Jacob just how to proceed and she even helped him. So Jacob appeared before his

[5] The oracle's answer to Rebekah (25:*13*) is nationalized, a token of a late stage of rewriting.

blind father; since he did not imitate Esau's voice, Isaac spoke a line, the irony of which was not lost on the early generations (as it was on later ones[6]): "The voice is the voice of Jacob, but the [hairy] hands are the hands of Esau." So Isaac blessed Jacob—the blessing has been nationalized, for it deals with Jacob's descendants, not Jacob himself —and once again, it cannot be taken away. Esau the simpleton entered, having hunted and prepared the favorite delicacies. He learned of the deception—this time of the *beraka*, "blessing," whereas before it had been the *bekora*, "primogeniture," an admirable pun. There was no blessing left for him—the nationalizer puts into Isaac's mouth a description of the remote dwelling place of Esau's descendants, the Edomites. Esau vowed revenge, so that Jacob fled from home.[7]

At this point is is well to note that there are three distinct stages in the character of Jacob in Scripture. In the folk tale, he is the sharpster whose immoralities were of no concern to an audience that liked a robust tale. In the second stage, he is nationalized, and hence an ancestor. But there is a third stage, in which he is not only the forebear but indeed the *respected* ancestor, destined later in the account to bear a name different from Jacob and to be called instead Israel.

An old folk tale of how Bethel ("God's house") got its name is adapted to the respected ancestor. Jacob, on his trip eastward, dreamed that he saw a ladder (some would translate it a "ramp") with angels ascending and descending. Yahve appeared to him, renewing the promise of an abundance of offspring, to whom He would give the land. Moreover, He would go with Jacob wherever he went, and He would restore Jacob to this land, Canaan. Jacob awoke, and he changed the name of the place from Luz to Bethel.

Jacob went to Haran. He met Rachel at a well (Abraham's servant had met Rebekah at a well, also) which was covered by a rock that was so heavy that all the shepherds had to gather and use their collective strength to move it. Yet as soon as Jacob saw Rachel, he, like a character in a good folk tale, moved the rock himself. Rachel took him home to her father Laban ("white" or "smooth"). Laban would not allow Jacob to work for him without compensation—or so

---

[6] Generations of midrashic embellishment led to an interpretation of the verse as a contrast between spiritual force (Jacob's voice) and brute physical power (Esau's hands).

[7] A late recasting (27:46–28:9) gives a different motive for Jacob's trip. Esau had married two Hittite girls (26:34) who had vexed Rebekah and Isaac. Hence, Jacob was going eastward so as to find a bride who would not be an accursed local girl. Indeed, Esau himself took another wife, *Mahlath*, the daughter of Ishmael, the son of Abraham. However, a summary (36:2–3) names Esau's wives as Adah and Aholebama, Canaanites, and *Basmath*, the daughter of Ishmael.

he said. Jacob proposed to work for seven years, in return for which he would have the hand of Rachel. But Rachel had an older sister, whose homeliness is described by Scripture as "soft eyes"—that is, not sparkling bright ones. After Jacob worked for seven years, Laban gave a great wedding banquet, and Jacob retired with his bride. He saw in the morning that it was Leah whom he had slept with. The deceiver had been deceived. Laban explained that a younger sister must not marry before an older one, so Jacob undertook to work for seven more years, and then he married Rachel too.

The nationalizing editor, aware of tribal distinctions among the Hebrews, proceeds to relate the succession of births of the sons of Jacob, who are conceived of as the progenitors of the twelve tribes. Since Jacob preferred Rachel to Leah, Yahve equalized matters by making Leah fruitful and Rachel barren. In quick succession, Leah bore Reuben, Simeon, Levi, and Judah. Rachel gave to Jacob her maid Bilhah, who bore Dan and Naphtali. Leah, temporarily sterile, gave her maid Zilpah to Jacob, and Zilpah bore Gad and Asher. Yet even in the midst of the "nationalizing," there is preserved a tale (30:14–18) of mandrake roots—thought to be certain to cause pregnancy. Reuben had the roots and gave them to Leah; Rachel wanted them. The price of the roots was to be Leah's right to have Jacob that night. So Leah became pregnant and bore Issachar; next she bore Zebulun. Rachel—either through mandrake roots or through Yahve's help (30:22)—became pregnant and bore Joseph.

Now Jacob felt it time to return home to Canaan. Prosperous Laban asked him what he wanted as a gift. The smooth one had met his master, for Jacob wanted practically nothing—only the spotted and speckled animals that would be born to the flocks. Laban agreed, but he removed all these from the flocks and let Jacob tend the rest. But Jacob contrived for the flocks to produce speckled and spotted animals—the text is not entirely clear as to the devious method by which this was achieved. But Jacob, the folk character, became very rich, and Laban's sons were jealous.

Yahve now told the respected ancestor Jacob that he should return home. Jacob related to his wives that the Deity Whom he had encountered at Bethel had appeared to him—an appearance Scripture does not describe, nor does Scripture relate all the maneuverings of Laban that Jacob reported to his wives. It seems clear that the ancestor has replaced the folk character in the last phases of the cycle, but there are just enough vestiges of the latter to show that at one time the account dealt at greater length with the shenanigans of Laban and Jacob. There survives the incident (meant to be hilarious) of Rachel's theft of her father's gods, and Laban's magniloquent assertion that

Jacob's flight with his wives deprived him of the opportunity to give a farewell party! The retort to Laban is couched in words of the respected ancestor. Had it not been for the intervention of the Deity of Abraham and of Isaac, Laban would have sent Jacob away empty-handed.[8]

Thereafter in the cycle Jacob is always the respected ancestor. He sent a message and a gift to his estranged brother Esau, hoping to appease him. Fearful of Esau, he divided his entourage into two camps, so that one might escape if Esau should attack. Then, humbly, he prayed to Yahve, declaring himself unworthy of all the good Yahve had done for him. To explain the change of his name, an old tale was adapted of a wrestling match (*he-abeq*) between a man and a divine being at the river Jabok, *yaboq* (a pun, of course). The story, now told of Jacob, culminates in a blessing by the Divine Being, who tells Jacob that his name is henceforth to be Israel.[9]

Jacob and Esau met and were reconciled. Esau had become so rich that he refused Jacob's gift. So the brothers became friends.[1] Jacob went on to Bethel to build an altar to the Deity Whom he had encountered there. P gives a second account (Gen. 35) of the change of Jacob's name to Israel, completely without allusion to the primitive incident of the wrestling; indeed, the account repeats the naming of the place as Bethel.

The same chapter relates that Rachel died in childbirth in bearing Benjamin while the entourage was on its way (35:16–20). When they settle down, there occurs the ugly incident of Reuben's consorting with Bilhah which is not pursued. A summary of Jacob's children follows; then an editor remembered the death of Isaac, imminent twenty years earlier, for this is now recorded; the brief note that Jacob and Esau buried Isaac concludes the cycle (35:21–9).

From the nationalizing passages in the Jacob cycle it becomes possible to follow some of the process by which the folk character became the respected ancestor. The oracle which Rebekah consulted brought her Yahve's words:

> *Two nations are in your belly*
> *And two peoples will separate from your bowels.*
> *One people will be greater than the other,*

---

[8] A tale (31:45–32:2) of how *Galed* (Gilead) and Mahanaim got their names concludes the Laban episode.

[9] The place of the wrestling was Penuel ("God's face"), and Jacob limped as a result of the combat.

[1] There intrudes the extraneous account of Dinah (Chapter 34) on which see below; and the list of the descendants of Esau (Chapter 36). Edom is widely regarded in Scripture as the nation most kindred to Israel; this may be the reason for the inclusion of the latter material.

And the older [the Edomites] will serve the younger
[the Israelites]. [25:23]

Isaac's blessing of Jacob reads:

Behold, the scent of my son is like the scent of a field which
    Yahve has blessed.
Let God give you of the dew of heaven, and of the fertility of
    the earth,
And abundance of corn and wine.
Let nations serve you,
And peoples be prostrate before you.
Be the master to your brothers,[2]
And let your mother's sons be prostrate before you.
Cursed are they who curse you,
Blessed are they who bless you. [27:27B–9]

So completely is the cheater [3] transformed into the respected ancestor
that not one vestige of the folk character is found in the role Jacob
plays in the Joseph novelette, which we shall turn to presently.

The incident of Jacob's daughter Dinah (Gen. 34) is, briefly, as follows: a local Canaanite, Shechem, became enamoured of her. The
negotiations for the marriage were made; all the local inhabitants
had to be circumcised. While they were in pain the sons of Jacob
exterminated them. This is not an edifying story, and its presence in
Scripture is to be accounted for in the following way. Isaac and Jacob,
it is related, had both obtained eastern wives, disdaining the local
Canaanite women. The Dinah story illustrates an aspect of this disdain, though disdain is too mild a term. Scripture gives no clue to the
origin of the wives of Reuben, Simeon, Levi, Judah—indeed, we are
told only of Joseph's wife, the Egyptian woman Asenath (41:45). The
Dinah episode is inserted to suggest to us that her brothers did not
marry local women.

Two layers are found in the story, for the author of the later version was horrified at the implications of the basic story. The earlier
account told that Shechem fell in love with Dinah and asked his father Hamor to arrange a marriage; Hamor proposed that this should
be the first of a sequence of marriages between his people and Jacob's

[2] No brothers or sisters are spoken of in Scripture, as if Esau and Jacob are the
only offspring. The allusion here, accordingly, is to be taken in a nationalized
sense, as referring to kindred peoples and not to siblings.
[3] A summary of Jacob in this role is found in Hosea 12:4–5.

offspring. Dinah's brothers proposed the circumcision of the whole community, and then they annihilated it.

Some significant alterations occurred in the rewriting, according to which Shechem raped Dinah; the brothers figured in the arrangements because it was rape, rather than a simple marriage proposal made to the father Jacob. Rape, according to the story, could not be tolerated. The act of annihilation was done, in the second version, by only two of the brothers, Simeon and Levi, and it called forth Jacob's denunciation and made him afraid of reprisals. The retort of the brothers to Jacob was that their sister should not be treated like a whore.

The first version, then, told of the craftiness by which a whole town was exterminated. The second version both justified the annihilation and condemned it. The incident is alluded to in 49:5–7, a strong denunciation of Simeon and Levi. The second layer of the narrative stands between a barbaric account told with relish, and the passage in Chapter 49 which replaces relish with utter disgust.

An incident, similarly unrelated to the immediate context, is told of Judah and Tamar (38). Judah had begotten three sons, Er, Onan, and Shelah, by a Canaanite woman. Er had married Tamar, but Yahve slew Er because of his wickedness. Judah therefore wanted Onan to enter into a "levirate marriage" [4] with childless Tamar, but Onan "spilled his seed" on the ground,[5] and therefore Yahve killed him, too. The third son, Shelah, was very young,[6] so Judah advised Tamar to return to her home. The levirate marriage was not concluded.

When Judah's wife died—her name is not given—he went to visit his sheep shearers with a certain friend. Tamar, learning of this, removed her widow's clothes, and put on other garments. (Shelah, now grown, had not become Tamar's husband, so the levirate marriage was still unconcluded.) Judah saw Tamar and, failing to recognize her, thought her a prostitute. He made a proposition to her, and the price was fixed at a kid. Tamar asked for a pledge until the kid should be brought, namely the seal on his ring, his chain, and his staff. Tamar became pregnant by Judah, and reverted to her widow's garb. Judah sent the kid, so as to recover his pledge, but the "prostitute" could not be found.

---

[4] Levirate means "brother-in-law." Deut. 25:5–6 provides that on the death of a childless man, his brother should marry the widow; the child thereby born is to be regarded as that of the first husband. See also Ruth 4:9–10.
[5] That is, he began, but did not complete, sexual intercourse with her.
[6] Perhaps, also, Tamar seemed to be a woman contact with whom brought death, and, hence, Judah feared for Shelah's life.

Three months later, it was commonly reported that Tamar, in view of her pregnancy, had gone wrong. Judah gave instructions that she was to be taken out and burned, but Tamar sent the three parts of the pledge—the seal, chain, and staff—to Judah, with the message that their owner was her partner in sin. Judah thereupon recognized his own responsibility, especially in having withheld Shelah from her. He did not again have sexual relations with her. Tamar had twins. At birth, the hand of one babe emerged, and a red ribbon was tied on it. But the hand was withdrawn, and the other babe was born first. The midwife said to him, "Why did you tear out?" He was named *Perez*, "tear." When the other came out, with the red ribbon on his hand, he was named *Zerah*, "red".

The story of a woman on her way to execution on false charges who is abruptly saved [7] is common in folklore. Tamar is a heroine to the narrator, and worthy of admiration (as she is in Ruth 4:*11–12*). The role of Judah is unadmirable; yet it is noticeable, especially in the Hebrew, that the beginning portions and the final verses of the chapter are terse and laconic, while the central incident is told in rounded form. It is likely, therefore, that an old folk tale, originally not connected with Judah, was taken over from Canaanite circles and made Israelite by being told about Judah. The point of the folk tale is to commend Tamar for her tenacity in demanding levirate marriage. The incident of Onan adds pathos and depth to this tenacity. Perez, according to Ruth 4:*18–22*, was an ancestor of David; so, too, I Chron. 2:*3–15*.

The Joseph novelette is the product of a skilled writer who had a moral to teach. So well unified [8] is it that twice-told incidents are at a minimum. Indeed, these are virtually limited to the occasional substitution of Judah for Reuben, Jacob's oldest son.[9] Otherwise, the novelette has fine unity. The narrative skill of Hebrew writers, usually brilliantly exemplified in short pieces, is here exemplified in a long and somewhat complicated story. The narrator, indeed, has op-

[7] Such, too, is the story of Susanna in the Apocrypha.
[8] The Tamar incident, 38, is not part of the Joseph novelette but an independent item inserted by an editor. So, too, the Blessing of Jacob, 49, is a separate poem inserted into the narrative.
[9] Reuben is Joseph's protector in 37:21–2, Judah in 37:26–7. Reuben finds the pit into which Joseph was thrown empty, 37:29–30. In the Judah verses, Joseph is sold to Ishmaelites, but in other verses to Midianites. In 42:22, Reuben is the leader, as he is in 42:37; but in 43 Judah becomes it and Reuben fades into anonymity. Perhaps the substitution is the result of late moral censure of Reuben for the incident with Jacob's concubine Bilhah (35:22), which is denounced in 49:4.

portunity here for character development, so that incidental situations illuminate the personalities. We follow Joseph from priggish adolescence, through misadventure, temptation, and ordeal, into triumph and magnanimity.

The story is well known to modern readers and can be summarized briefly. Joseph, the favorite of his father Jacob, so alienated his brothers that they sold him into slavery in Egypt, though they reported to Jacob that Joseph had died. In Egypt Joseph became the trusted servant of one Potiphar and was to become the supervisor of his master's estate and possessions. Unhappily, Potiphar's wife tried in vain to seduce Joseph, and, being rebuffed, charged Joseph with having attempted to rape her. Potiphar had Joseph thrown into jail. Quickly Joseph became the chief trusty and confidant of the jailer.

When two fellow prisoners had dreams Joseph was able to interpret them, and events bore out the correctness of his interpretations. Accordingly, when Pharaoh dreamed two similar dreams, whose meaning eluded his Egyptian advisers, he was led to consult Joseph. The interpretations that Joseph gave spoke of seven years of plenty, to be followed by seven years of famine. To Joseph was entrusted the responsibility of organizing and administering the marshalling of resources in the years of plenty, so that there would be no want in the evil times. Joseph rose to be second in command in Egypt.

When famine made it necessary for Jacob and his sons to look for food, ten of the sons were sent to Egypt to make purchases. Joseph recognized them, but they did not recognize him. He accused them of spying, and even had them detained under guard for three days, releasing them with the word that should they ever return for a further purchase of food, they must bring with them Benjamin, their youngest, and Joseph's only full, brother; the others were his half brothers. When the continuing famine impelled Jacob to send his sons back to Egypt, the requirement that Benjamin must accompany them brought anguish to Jacob, but he reluctantly consented. In Egypt, the brothers were brought before Joseph; briefly, but movingly, Joseph asked if their old father was still alive. He was deeply touched at the sight of his brother Benjamin. Nevertheless, he continued to toy with the brothers, this time by having his wine goblet discovered in the possession of Benjamin. The brothers stood before Joseph in their great fear, and Judah in eloquent words offered himself in place of Benjamin. Now Joseph revealed himself to his brothers.

Jacob was brought to Egypt to be reunited with Joseph. The family was assigned the fertile land of Goshen to dwell in. Before his death, Jacob blessed the sons of Joseph, Ephraim, and Manasseh. He was buried by Joseph in the cave of Machpelah in Canaan, beside Abraham and Isaac.

The brothers were fearful that now that Jacob was dead Joseph would repay them for the evil they had done to him. Joseph said to them: "Am I in God's stead? You devised evil against me; God intended it for good, so as to bring about things as they are today, the nourishment of many people" (50:*19*). This moral hearkens back to the recurrent theme in Hebrew history, that events do not simply happen, but God guides them, turning apparent evil into good.

Nothing quite like the Joseph novelette is to be found in ancient literature. Occasionally it is suggested that aspects of the plot are derived from an Egyptian folk story, "The Tale of the Shipwrecked Sailor." The Hebraic character of the story, however, is manifest in every aspect. It is all too seldom that didactic stories carry the appeal and the artistry of the Joseph novelette. It is noteworthy, as we have said, that Jacob in the Joseph novelette is completely the respected patriarch, dignified and righteous, almost as if unrelated to the Jacob who acquired Esau's blessing and birthright.

In no instance is it related of Joseph that Yahve appeared to him as He did to Abraham, Isaac, and Jacob. Joseph is a man who is faithful to God and unceasingly under divine guidance. The only direct revelation of Yahve in the Joseph novelette (46:2–4) occurs to Jacob/Israel. It takes place, we are told, in a night vision, and its substance is the divine promise to accompany Jacob to Egypt. In the patriarchal stories the Deity had been an active participant; in the Joseph novelette, He is conceived of as a pervasive influence. Accordingly, the Joseph novelette is not composed out of the unsophisticated folk materials that mark the patriarchal cycles. In the latter, authorship was secondary to compilation; in the Joseph novelette we encounter a gifted and reflective author.

Certain clues in the Joseph novelette have indicated an origin quite independent of the Jacob cycle. We have noticed already the profound difference in Jacob's character. In addition, some interpreters have argued that the novelette is unaware of the previous death of Rachel; this unawareness they infer from the verse (37:*10*), in which Jacob asks Joseph, "Will I, your mother, and your brothers come to prostrate ourselves to the ground before you?" Yet such details are scarcely of great significance, for pure and unassailable history is not a characteristic of Pentateuchal narratives. The Scriptural supposition that Israel was composed of twelve tribes descended from twelve sons of Jacob is a romantic conclusion rather than pure history. Indeed, the full list of tribes, as compiled from the Pentateuch, would total fourteen rather than twelve, for Machir and Gilead (Num. 26:29–30) should be added to the normal list of twelve. That is to say, it is historically true that the Hebrews were composed of closely related tribes who settled Canaan, and among whom there existed a sense of confederation.[1] But that these tribes were descended from a set of brothers is not history so much as a mode of expressing the sense of relatedness the historic tribes felt for each other.

The Priestly compiler of the Pentateuch interrupts the Joseph cycle at a number of points, for example, when he gives a list (46:8–27) of the names of those who came into Egypt. But these interruptions are too few to impede the flow of the narrative, while just numerous enough to reflect the overall Priestly control of the material at his hand. For the Priestly editor, the Joseph novelette serves a purpose beyond its own worthy substance; by means of it P bridges the gap between the tradition of eastern origin and the tradition of Wilderness origin. The Joseph novelette tells of those events that account for the presence of the Hebrews in Egypt, before their entrance into the Wilderness under Moses. The traditions of an Egyptian sojourn, frequently alluded to in the prophets, are brilliantly accommodated to the Joseph novelette. Thereby the two items, the slavery in Egypt and the Wilderness wandering, fall into place in the body of theological history, to which the Priestly editor feels so strongly bound.

With the Joseph cycle, the tracing of Israel's history moves from the account of individuals to the emergence of a collective people. The immigrants into Egypt are said (46:27) to total seventy; four generations later (for that is the extent of the supposed interval from Joseph's time to Moses') their number is presumed to have grown to more than 600,000 (Exod. 12:37). This last number is quite impossible, and the first number is equally fanciful. The purpose, however, is to tell us that the age of the individuals is past and we are now in a time when there was a Hebrew people.

Genesis exists as a separate book because it contains sufficient material for a scroll, rather than because it was planned as a unit. The division was strictly a matter of convenience. One should read on into the beginning of Exodus without a pause.

[1] Recent writers use the word *amphyctyony* as a synonym for the confederation of the tribes.

CHAPTER

28

EXODUS

THIS SECOND BOOK of the Pentateuch falls naturally into two parts, 1–19 and 20–40. The latter portion consists primarily, though not exclusively, of legislation portrayed as revealed to or through Moses. The first part, preponderantly narrative, might well be regarded as a prolongation of Genesis. The same literary problems that confronted us in Genesis continue into Exodus, and they become even more complex.

The narratives in the early chapters of Exodus are very well known and may be reviewed briefly. After the death of Joseph, the Hebrews increased in number. There arose a new Pharaoh, uninterested in Joseph and his achievements. Fearful of the populous Hebrews, he enslaved them (*1:8–14*). Moses might have met death as a result of the cruel policy of killing all the Hebrew children at birth, but he had the good fortune to be found and adopted by the Egyptian princess (*1:15–2:10*). At maturity his fidelity to his people asserted itself. His slaying of an Egyptian taskmaster forced him to flee to Midian (a region south of the Dead Sea, extending southwestward into what is called today the Sinai peninsula). He was welcomed into the home of Reuel, also known as Jethro, the priest of Midian, whose daughters Moses saved from harassing shepherds at a well. Moses married one of the daughters, Zipporah.

While Moses was pasturing sheep near the sacred mountain in the Wilderness, Yahve appeared to him at the Burning Bush, enjoining him to return to Egypt and to obtain the release of the Hebrews from slavery (3:1–22). To arm Moses against the disbelief in him that might arise among the Hebrews, two miraculous signs were wrought. Moses' staff became a snake (he restored it to a staff by taking hold of the snake's tail); and his hand underwent *zora‘ath* ("leprosy") when he put it into his bosom; it was cured when he put it into his bosom a second time (4:1–8). Because Moses was "heavy of tongue," his brother Aaron, described as the Levite, was to be his spokesman (4:10–16).[1]

Then Moses and Aaron went to Egypt to effect the release of the Hebrews. The lot of the slaves immediately grew worse (5:1–23). In a contest of magic deeds (turning a staff into a crocodile), the Egyptian magicians equalled Moses and Aaron (7:8–13). Thereupon there followed a series of ten plagues, calculated to persuade Pharaoh to release the Hebrews. The Egyptian magicians were able to duplicate to some extent even the first plagues (7:14–8:15) though not to stop the disasters; at the fourth plague Pharaoh expressed a limited willingness to release the Hebrews, but only for three days. As soon as Moses had Yahve call off the plague, Pharaoh changed his mind (8:16–28). This occurred for five more plagues (9:1–10:29). Finally came a tenth plague (11:1–12:51) in which all the first-born males of the Egyptians died, and this time Pharaoh sent the Hebrews out (13:17–22). They left with all their own possessions, and some newly acquired from the Egyptians (11:2–3).

This last plague of the first-born males involved Yahve's passing throughout Egypt for the smiting. The Hebrews were able to escape this plague by having made the advance preparation of slaughtering a lamb and smearing blood on the door posts. Yahve, on seeing this sign, was led to *pass over* the Hebrew homes; therefore a holy day, *Pesah*, "Passover," was instituted as a memorial of Yahve's action (12:1–13:16).

---

[1] On the way to Egypt a curious, and unintelligible, incident (4:24–6) occurred. Yahve encountered Moses, wishing to slay him (Moses, or the baby son Gershom?). Zipporah picked up a flint, cut off her son's foreskin, and touched it to his (whose?) leg, saying—something which we cannot translate; and the Deity desisted.

Countless explanations have been offered. For example, it is suggested that since Moses was reared by Egyptians, he had not been circumcised; hence Zipporah, following Midian custom, circumcised her son. Again, it is "explained" that the story is really about Moses and his wedding night, but a late scribe rewrote it about Moses' son. In my opinion, this is an old etiological legend about the origin of circumcision, a legend rewritten by P in Gen. 17, there ascribing the origin to Abraham.

Yet once the Hebrews had departed, Pharaoh changed his mind again (14:5–25). He and his Egyptian hordes pursued the fleeing Hebrews. Ahead lay the waters, the shallow sea of reeds and the deep Red Sea; behind were the Egyptians in hot pursuit. Miraculously the sea of reeds split, enabling the Hebrews to cross on dry land. The Egyptians pursued but when the Hebrews had completed their crossing, the waters came together, drowning the Egyptians (14:26–31). Thereupon Moses and the Israelites sang a song of triumph.[2]

Then commenced the journey, not by the short coastal route, but across the Sinai peninsula.[3] The trip was hard, the water was bitter (15:22ff.), and food was scarce (16:1ff.). In their distress, they once received a supply of quail (16:11ff.). "Manna"—it means, says the text, "what is it?"—came down for them (16:14–36); on Friday they collected a double portion for the Sabbath. (Manna is often explained as a sweet discharge from a tamarisk tree.) Thirst prompted complaints about the lack of water. Moses smote a rock, and water flowed from it (17:6ff.).

Amalek, a hostile people, attacked them (17:8–13). Moses observed the battle from a hilltop. When his arms were raised, the battle went for Israel; when he rested them, it went for Amalek. Therefore, when he was weary, Moses sat on a rock while two trusted helpers, Aaron and Hur, held up his arms. Moses' father-in-law came to visit (18:1–27). Observing that Moses was harried by too many tasks, Jethro suggested that an officialdom be created to assist him. This was done. Finally the Hebrews arrived at the sacred mountain (19:1–2).

Of the many intriguing aspects of the foregoing story, we shall be forced to limit ourselves to remarking on only a limited number. In the first place, we deal with an account full of miracles, and not with a political account. Curiously, the name of neither the hostile Pharaoh[4] nor of his daughter who rescued Moses is given; yet we are told the names of the two Egyptian midwives, Shifrah and Puah. (Did just two midwives suffice for an Israelite population that included 600,000 men [12:37]?) Though Moses has been reared in Pharaoh's palace and remained there until manhood, no allusion is made to this period, in the subsequent dealing with Pharaoh, nor is it at all implied that Moses and Pharaoh know each other. Moreover, the motives of the

[2] Exod. 15:1–18. Though the poem celebrates the Exodus, it was written much later. Its latter part (13–17) reflects the entry into and settlement in Canaan.
[3] It is not possible to trace the precise route, either from the sporadic details given in Exodus or from the idealized journey, a product of late romance, in Numbers 33, principally because the location of Sinai-Horeb is unknown.
[4] Pharaoh is a title, "king," and not a name. It is related in 2:23–4 that the hostile Pharaoh has died, but the subsequent account makes no mention of the accession of a new one.

Egyptians seem mixed. On the one hand, the midwives were to slay the male children. If the motive was to be freed of the Hebrews by preventing them from propagating, why retain them in slavery— why not simply kill them or send them away? On the other hand, if they made good slaves, why seek to keep them from propagating and increasing?

Whatever history may lie behind our account, in the form in which we now find it, it has grown into folk legend. That this is so can be discerned from the story of Moses' youth. The story of the great leader, who in babyhood almost perishes at the hands of those who in later years become his foes, has many parallels in folklore.[5] Moses not only was saved from the Nile by the daughter of his archenemy, but his own mother was engaged to nurse him for pay! The arm of coincidence is never too long for folk legend about a hero.

Secondly, Moses is represented as humble about his capacities. Such a humility we saw in Isaiah's describing himself as "impure of lip" (Isa. 6:5), though Isaiah did not, according to the account, reject the appointment. Jeremiah (1:6) also disclosed a prophetic unwillingness to receive a divine appointment. Yet in the case of Moses the unwillingness was both stubborn and effective. There are two main aspects of this unwillingness. The first of these derives from an assumption found in several passages in Genesis, and culminating in Exodus, that Yahve's name had never been disclosed to the patriarchs or to the Hebrews prior to the time of Moses. Hence, Moses is portrayed as raising the question of how the Hebrews would know that it was their ancestors' God Whom he was representing (3:13ff.).[6]

The second aspect is different. Moses' amazing stubbornness, in which his humility extends almost to disobedience, provokes the Deity's justified anger. Therefore, He replies that Moses' brother Aaron will be his spokesman, but Aaron has not been mentioned at all up to this point (4:14) in Exodus. This is all the more surprising in that a later passage, 6:20, represents Aaron as older than Moses. The

[5] A strikingly similar account exists about Sargon, king of the Assyrians. The babyhood of Jesus in the Gospel According to Matthew is derived from Moses' babyhood.

[6] In the usual source-analyses, it is asserted respecting both E (Exod. 3:13ff.) and P (6:3ff.) that before Moses' time there was no knowledge of the Deity's name. In J, Gen. 4:26, however, Enos, a grandson of Adam, already knows the name; hence, here in J the question before Moses is not what the Deity's name is, but by what miraculous means the Hebrews can be prompted to *believe* Moses. The convincing proof is the twofold wonder of the staff that becomes a serpent and a staff again and of the hand that becomes leprous and is healed. The usual analyses suppose that two ancient written sources were blended; in my judgment, however, there is midrash at work here, altering the issue from the relatively primitive one of convincing through miracles to the theological question of how the Hebrews came to know the intimate personal name of the universal God.

abrupt introduction of Aaron into the narrative, and at this point, is significant. In some of the subsequent incidents (e.g., Exod. 7:14–18; 7:26–9 Heb., 8:1–4 Eng.; 8:16–20 Heb., 20–4 Eng.; 9:1–7). Moses serves as his own mouthpiece, much as though the editor who interpolated the introduction of Aaron failed to carry it through. But in several P summaries (7:19ff., 8:5ff., 8:16ff.), Yahve commands Moses to have Aaron do some particular thing. That is to say, in P Aaron is fully the spokesman and agent for Moses. This is set forth most clearly in 6:28–7:7.

The necessary inference is that Moses' reluctant humility and the association of Aaron with him is a late afterthought of the Priestly editor. This editor, as we shall see, had the notion that all Israelite traditions of any worth are as ancient as the Wilderness period; moreover, in his view, legitimate priests are those, and those only, who can trace their genealogy back to a single priestly ancestor, Aaron. Whereas the Priestly passages in Genesis have only a restricted importance, they come to the foreground in Exodus where Aaron the priest is fully as important as Moses. And whereas hitherto P sections have been scattered and brief, we shall arrive, in the latter third of Exodus and throughout Leviticus and Numbers, at a reversal of the proportions, for there P is the preponderant source.

Thirdly, a recurrent motif is worthy of notice. Yahve wished to have Israel released from Egypt. In His ominipotence, why did He not accomplish this in one single miraculous act? He could well have done so; yet there were piquant and colorful traditions of ten plagues, of which the last was only the climax. To have eliminated the plagues would have been to run counter to traditions in wide circulation, and this the successive editors seemed reluctant to do. The dilemma appeared to have arisen, accordingly, of insisting on Yahve's omnipotence and yet of preserving the ten plagues. The way out of the dilemma was to portray Pharaoh as stubborn, "hard of heart"— though not by his own choice. Yahve made him hard of heart (7:3–5) so that His recourse to the plagues would bring Egypt to recognize Him. Pharaoh's magicians recognized "the finger of God" (8:15 Heb., 19 Eng.), but Yahve hardened Pharaoh's heart again. (See also 9:13–21.) Pharaoh admitted that he had sinned against Yahve (9:27–8); but Yahve hardened his heart so that the Hebrews could relate to children and grandchildren what Yahve had done in Egypt (10:1–3).

As we saw in the teaching of Isaiah (p. 86), there is ascribed to the Deity the control of all events—even those events which seem on the surface to be against His will.

In the fourth place, we need to raise some questions about Passover. In 5:1–3 it is stated that the Hebrews wished release to celebrate some occasion in the Wilderness, a journey of three days. The celebration is essential, for unless it takes place, Yahve may fall upon the Hebrews with pestilence or sword. In 11:4–5, it is set forth that Yahve would go through Egypt in the middle of the night, slaying all the first-born males. In 12:12–27, Yahve, curiously described in the Hebrew (verses 13 and 23) as "The Destroyer," [7] would pass over the Hebrew houses if the lintel and doorposts were smeared with the blood of a *paschal* ("pertaining to Passover") lamb. Yet there is joined to the injunction to smear the blood on the lintel another injunction (12:15) that in memory of this divine action, the Hebrews in subsequent times are to eat unleavened bread (*Matzoth* in Hebrew) for seven days. (A subsequent verse, 12:39, tells that in the haste of the departure from Egypt, there was no time to wait for the dough to rise.)

One can properly wonder about the relationship between the Passover lamb and the matzoth. In Exodus 12 they are tied together, as if they were unified in a single observance of a single historical occasion. But Leviticus 23:5–6 tells us that Passover (*Pesaḥ*) occurs in the calendar one day earlier than the festival of Matzoth.[8] The answer is that the two, Pesaḥ and Matzoth, were once separate and distinct occasions, Pesaḥ emerging from a pastoral background, and Matzoth from an agricultural one. They were blended together because they came near each other,[9] and for no other reason.

Moreover, the connection of Passover/Matzoth with the Exodus is quite artificial, the result of a process consistent in Scripture. There was a heritage from early times of festivals and observances, some originating in the Wilderness and some adapted from Canaanite practice. To each preserved festival or observance some historical antecedent was given. The Sabbath had begun at creation; circumcision began with Abraham; Tabernacles (Sukkoth) commemorated that Israel "sat in tabernacles" (lean-to shelters) when Yahve brought them out of Egypt (Lev. 23:43). The development of Passover and Matzoth can be tentatively reconstructed. Pesaḥ, a spring nocturnal observance at full moon, was inherited from nomadic pastoral times. At the heart of this observance was the belief that the night was a baleful one, a "watch night" on which one needed to be on guard, for to the Deity belonged a sacrifice of the first-born of the males in the flock. If He failed to receive the sacrifice, He would pass through the

---

[7] The Destroyer (II Kings 23:13) had a sacred mount, that of Olives, in Jerusalem.

[8] Pesaḥ is on the 14th day of the First Month. Matzoth is on the 15th day.

[9] See Appendix II, "The Sacred Calendar" and p. 31, above.

encampment, and in His anger at man's ingratitude would slay human first-born. The sign to the Deity that the appropriate sacrifice had been made was the smearing of blood on lintel and doorposts.

Matzoth, on the other hand, was a Canaanite harvest festival of early grain. It was one of the three harvest festivals (the other two were *Shabuoth,* "weeks," also known as Pentecost, from a Greek word meaning fifty, a later spring harvest of fruit; and *Sukkoth,* "tabernacles," an early fall harvest.) The Matzoth festival was observed by burning up the residue of the previous year's grain and then quickly making unleavened cakes out of the new grain.

The historicizing factor, which associated Pesaḥ and Matzoth with the release from enslavement in Egypt, caused the many anomalies in the account. Thus, Moses is portrayed as wanting to lead the Hebrews into the Wilderness to commemorate an event which had not yet occurred. Chapters 11–13 become less confusing once the reader recognizes that successive editors have shifted the emphasis from an event for later observance to an observance prior to the event. Moreover, the more appropriate position for the detailed legislation of the observance might well have come after the Ten Commandments, where other legislation is offered; instead, the narrative is here interrupted for the legislation to be detailed.

The net result of these editorial developments is that although there must be a kernel of history in the account of the enslavement in Egypt, we are dealing with legend here and not with reliable history. The release from Egypt, in the Prophets and in the Psalms, is consistently ascribed to Yahve; events did not happen blindly; Yahve was their author. The tendency to historicize observances and festivals in the Pentateuch is the end result of that conviction.

Moreover, the narrative of the Exodus is told in such a way that the later reader is persuaded, no matter how many generations may have elapsed, to regard himself as a participant in the Exodus from Egypt.

> You shall observe this matter for an eternal statute for you and your sons. When you come to the land which Yahve is giving you, as He has said, you shall observe this service. If your sons say to you, what is this service to you, you shall say, "It is the Passover sacrifice to Yahve, for He passed over the houses of the Israelites in Egypt when He smote Egypt, but our houses He saved." [12:24–7] [1]

---

[1] See also Exod. 13:8. Certain recent commentators, mistakenly in my judgment, tend to see the first fifteen chapters as a cult legend, acted out at some sanctuary. This view goes beyond the evidence, both biblical and extra-biblical. It

The event of the Exodus is the beginning, according to the Pentateuch, of Israel's existence as a nation.

> I shall take you unto Me as a nation, and I shall be God unto you. [6:7]

Thereafter, in countless passages, but especially in the Ten Commandments, the identification of Yahve takes the form of recalling the Exodus.

> I am Yahve your God, who brought you out of Egypt. [20:2; Deut. 5:6]

Accordingly, the close connection between Yahve and His people, as distinct from individuals, begins with the Egyptian enslavement. The "people" are not only the generation that was in Egypt, but also all subsequent generations.

We saw in Genesis that Yahve had made a covenant with Abraham (Gen. 15 and 17), renewed it with Isaac (26:24), and again with Jacob (28:13–22; 35:11–12). The Egyptian incident bound Yahve and His chosen people to each other, but a formal recognition of this relationship was needed. This is the significance of the incident at Sinai. The theme is announced in 19:5; Moses has ascended the sacred mountain.[2] He is told that the people are to purify themselves in anticipation of a divine appearance (technically called a "theophany").

The account of the Sinai episode brings together three elements which are more or less to be expected, and one which is less so. Tradition, as we saw above (page 27), had conceived of a sacred mountain, so that one element was inevitably to be included. Secondly, the historicizing factor led naturally to ascribing a host of customs and laws to the one single episode. These laws are referred to by Hebrew words which indicate a diversity of origins. *Huqqim* ("inscriptions"), appear to be royal decrees; the usual translation is "statutes." *Mishpatim* ("judgments") are in all likelihood judicial decisions. *Mitzvoth* ("commandments"), a relatively late word, gives no clue as to its precise origin. *Toroth* ("revelations"), an even later word, appears to refer to injunctions from priestly oracles. Even though the etymologies are probably correct, the Scriptural material represents an age so

---

fails to assess the historiographic method, and, indeed, the historiographic necessity.

[2] The Hebrew reads: "Moses ascended to God"; the Greek, "Moses ascended the mountain of God."

relatively advanced that the various terms were already synonymous.

Students of comparative legal systems have noted that much of Scriptural legislation owes a debt to civilizations which flourished long before the supposed time of Moses. The Code of Hammurabi (modern scholars now incline to date him 1728–1686) is frequently taken to be the source of much of Mosaic law. The extent of such borrowing, when it is made specific, seems to me to be exaggerated; but it seems nevertheless true that borrowing did take place.

In much of the Pentateuch we are confronted with late narrative materials read back to the early time of Moses. Yet in the case of a large portion of the legislation, its attribution to Moses involves an artificial late dating of it, rather than a predating. Moses is scarcely the author of all the legislation. The denial of Mosaic authorship does not rest on the time factors, for conceivably Moses might have legislated, or relegislated, the commandments, most of which are very ancient. But the denial of Mosaic authorship rests on observing the tendency of historicizing in Scripture. As a result of this tendency a vast accumulation of legislation, of exceedingly early and also of very late date, is depicted as emerging almost in codified form as the product of the episode at Sinai.

A third expected element is the literary skill with which the character of Moses is depicted. Good storytelling involves portraying character through incident, and the character of Moses is shown in scenes of great emotional force. His ascent of the sacred mountain, his anger at the stupidity of those who became impatient in their waiting, his staunch refusal to accede to Yahve's suggestion that Israel be destroyed and a new people emerge from him—all combine to disclose appealing and impressive facets of Moses' character. He rises to the heights of heroic dimensions. The storyteller has not allowed the legislation to engulf and overwhelm the epic hero. Heinrich Heine says it best in these words: "How tiny the mountain seems when Moses stands upon it!"

Yet there is a surprising element in various parts of Exodus, which amounts to a reversal of a prophetic motif. The prophets looked back to Wilderness period as though it had been golden, the ideal age. The words of God in Jeremiah 2:2, "I recollect the reliability of your girlhood, the love of your bridal days, your going with Me in the Wilderness . . . ," are in strange contrast to the Pentateuchal accounts of rebellious murmuring, of outright rebellion, and, in the midst of the Sinai episode, of apostasy in the well-known incident of the Golden Calf (32). If, on the one hand, Jeremiah overidealized the Wilderness period, the Pentateuchal authors, on the other hand, probably ascribed to it a cumulative series of transgressions culled from much later periods. This may be the case with the Golden Calf, for example. Jeroboam (I Kings 12:28–30) set up two such calves, one at Bethel and one at Dan.[3] One wonders just how a golden calf could, realistically, have been made in the Wilderness by a people who left Egypt in such great haste!

It is to be noted that the Pentateuchal writers regard the Wilderness generation as a virtually worthless one. Only two of its members, Joshua bin Nun and Caleb ben Jephuneh, were worthy; the Wilderness wanderings had to last for forty years, so the account goes, so that all the other mature people (those over twenty) could die out without entering the Promised Land (Numbers 14:26–30). That the climax at Sinai indirectly gave birth to a supreme act of apostasy by the Hebrews is a product of the storyteller's art, rather than an act of recorded history. For the Sinai episode is a legend, supplying the origin of Israel's divine laws.

We can only conjecture what it was that prompted the Pentateuchal authors to depict the Wilderness generation in an unfavorable light. The most likely explanation is that their inheritance of prophetic denunciations of apostasy (such as we saw in Hosea and Jeremiah) led them to attribute to the ancient generation the sins and consequent punishment of later generations. Indeed, the authors could caution the readers of their own day by depicting the awful retribution on sinners of ancient days.

Four elements, then, comprise the material out of which a succession of Pentateuchal authors related the episode of Sinai: the tradition of a sacred mountain, the codification of the law, the sublime character of Moses, and the unworthiness of the Wilderness generation. A succession of authors is involved in the account, so that there are minor contradictions and disparities.[4] It is likely that the oldest account, prior to the countless reworkings, is that found in Chapters 33–4. That account, in its present form, deals with a supposed second set of Tablets of the Covenant, for Moses, in his wrath at the Golden Calf, had broken the first set. If we eliminate the allusions to a second set of tablets and also some "corrective" interpolations, the oldest account would read as follows:

Moses said to Yahve, "See here, You say to me, bring up this people. But You have not told me whom You will send with me."

---

[3] See also Hos. 10:5; Jeroboam's calves are alluded to in II Kings 10:29, though some scholars question the authenticity of their mention in that verse.
[4] Source analysis is conceded even by its most devoted practitioners to be difficult to the point of impossibility, for when the supposed strata are isolated, the result in each is fragmentary and incomplete sections.

[Yahve] said, "My face⁵ [presence] will go, and I will relieve you."

Moses said, "If Your face does not go, do not bring us up from here."

Yahve said, "Even this I will do, because you have found favor in My eyes, and I have known you by name."

Moses said, "Show me Your face." ⁶

[Yahve] said, ". . . You cannot see My face, for no man can see Me and survive . . .⁷ I shall put you in a cleft of a rock, and cover you with the palm of My hand until I have passed. Then I will remove My palm, and you will see My back, but My face will not be seen."

We expect such a narration but we do not find it. As this old narrative continues (assuming that we are reconstructing it correctly), Yahve speaks to Moses:

"Hew out two tablets of stone . . . Be ready in the morning, and ascend Mount Sinai. Stand there for Me at the top of the Mount . . ."

[Moses] hewed two tablets of stone. He arose in the morning, and ascended Mount Sinai as Yahve had commanded him, taking the two tablets of stone in his hand.

Yahve descended in a cloud and stood with him . . . Moses quickly bowed to the ground and prostrated himself . . . [Yahve] said, "Now I make a covenant . . . Observe what I command you today . . .

[1] You shall not worship another god . . .

[2] You shall not make a molten god.⁸

[3] You shall observe the festival of Matzoth . . .

[4] Every first-born belongs to Me . . .

[5] Six days shall you work; on the seventh day you shall rest . . .

[6] The Feast of Weeks you shall observe, and the Feast of Harvest at the year's turn.⁹

[7] Three times in the year each male shall appear before the Master, Yahve the God of Israel . . .

[8] You shall not offer the blood as a sacrifice to Me with leaven . . .

⁵ *Face* means here Yahve Himself. That is, "I will go, and I will relieve you."
⁶ In 33:*18* and 22 "glory" has supplanted "face." 33:*19* is a late insertion.
⁷ 33:*21* is an explanatory insertion, tending to clarify the next verse.
⁸ That is, make a metal statue as though it is a god.
⁹ That is, at the end of the year. The new year came at the equinox. Harvest [Ingathering] thus came just prior to the fall equinox.

[9] The first of the early fruits of your land you shall bring to Yahve's temple.

[10] You shall not seethe a kid in its mother's milk.

Then Yahve said to Moses: "Write these words, for in accordance with these words have I made a covenant with you and with Israel." He was there with Yahve forty days and forty nights neither eating bread nor drinking water. He wrote on the tablets the words of the covenant, the ten words.[1] [33:12–34:18]

If this conjectural reconstruction is correct, and if this is the oldest literary version of the Sinai incident, then the three basic ingredients are these: Moses ascends the mountain; he concludes a covenant with Yahve; and Israel's obligation in the covenant is spelled out in ten "words"—phrases in reality—which are inscribed on tablets of stone.

The successive recastings—recastings in which only portions of the early account are rewritten—tend to replace certain primitive aspects with more sophisticated details. For example, in Chapter 19 there is no trace of Moses' wish to see Yahve's "face." Also, this same chapter sets forth the following confusion: the people are to stay clear of the mountain lest they die; yet on the third day, when a horn sounds, the people are enjoined to ascend the mountain (19:13); then, verses 23–4 state that the people must not ascend the mountain. Thus there are traces of one account of the Sinai episode in which the people ascended the mountain along with Moses. The earliest account did not contain this; the latest account does not in its total effect assert this. The traces, then, would come between the early account in 33–4 and a late chapter such as 19.

Moreover, the account in Chapter 34 tells of a decalogue, reproduced above, primarily ritual in character, which was the substance of the covenant, and this covenant was recorded on two stone tablets. A similar "decalogue"[2] is found within Exodus 20:18–24:8. This decalogue is imbedded in an extensive legal section (21:1–

---

[1] The P writer adds (34:29–33) that when Moses descended he did not know that his face was a "ray of light." Ray is the same word in Hebrew as horn; it is because of a confusion of ray and horn that Michelangelo's celebrated statue of Moses depicts him horned.

[2] These are the provisions (Exod. 20:20–6 and 23:10–19):

[1] You shall make no gods of silver and gold (20:20).

[2] An altar of earth you shall make for Me (20:21).

[3] You shall observe the Festival of Matzoth (23:15).

[4] The first born of your sons you shall give to Me (22:28).

[5] Six days shall you do your work, and on the seventh day you shall rest (23:12).

23:*19*) which scholars call the "*Book* of the Covenant"; it is not now found in ready, consecutive form. The extensive legal section is introduced as the *mishpatim,* "laws," which Moses put before Israel. When this section ends, Moses returns to the people and reports what has occurred; the people ratify the covenant (24:*3–8*). Then Moses records "all the words of Yahve" and builds an altar, and there begins a series of sacrifices. The covenant is depicted as being contained in a *book* (24:*7*), rather than on tablets. Therefore we have in "The Book of the Covenant" a tradition quite at variance with both the early account of two tablets, and the latest accounts, which revert to the supposition that there were two tablets.

Furthermore, 24:*1, 9–11* is a fragment of still another and quite diverse account. Yahve tells Moses to ascend:

> ". . . You, and Aaron, and Nadab and Abihu[3] and seventy of the elders of Israel . . ."[4] Moses, Aaron, Nadab, Abihu, and seventy of the elders of Israel ascended. They saw the God of Israel; under His feet was something like a pavement of sapphire, clear as the sky. Against the representatives of Israel, He did not stretch forth His hand. They saw God and ate and drank.

Some scholars believe this fragment to be a variant tradition of the ratification of the covenant, rather than the giving of the covenant on the mountain; but this explanation fails to notice that the representatives are bidden to ascend the mountain. The ratification by the total people would come at the bottom of the mountain, rather than on it.

Perhaps the selected and limited details so far cited have confused the reader. A summary at this point may, therefore, prove helpful. So far, we have observed that there was, first of all, a very old and primitive account of Sinai; it is used by the later editors as a second narrative, for it is separated from what we might call the first narrative by the incident of the Golden Calf. Secondly, we have seen

---

[6] You shall observe the Feast of the Cutting and the Feast of the Ingathering at the close of the year (23:*16*).

[7] Three times a year each male shall see the face of the Master, Yahve (23:*17*).

[8] You shall not sacrifice the blood of a sacrifice to Me with leavened bread (23:*18*).

[9] The first of the early fruits of your land you shall bring to Yahve's Temple (23:*19A*).

[10] You shall not seethe a kid in its mother's milk (23:*19B*).

The great similarity to Exod. 34:*14–26* is noticeable.

[3] Nadab and Abihu are Aaron's sons.

[4] 24:*2* is an interpolation which contends that Aaron, Nadab, and Abihu in reality remained at a distance.

a long legal section, which implies that the covenant was recorded in a book, not on tablets of stone. In both of these, there was a ritual decalogue. And, thirdly, we have noted a fragment, and it is only a fragment, which supposed that Moses, Aaron, and Aaron's sons ascended the mountain.

Finally, therefore, we can look at what in Exodus is now the emphasized account, the celebrated Decalogue:

I am the Lord your God Who brought you out of the land of Egypt out of a household of slavery.

You shall have no other gods before Me.

You shall make yourself no image or picture of anything in the heaven above or on earth below, or in the water under the earth. You shall not prostrate yourself to them, nor serve them, for I, Yahve your God, am a jealous Deity, visiting the iniquity of fathers on sons, grandsons, and the fourth generation of My foes, but preserving reliability to thousands of My friends and observers of My commandments.

You shall not use Yahve's name in false oaths, for Yahve will not exculpate him who uses His name in falsehood.

Remember the Sabbath to sanctify it; six days you shall labor and do all your work, but the seventh day is the Sabbath of Yahve your God. You shall not do any work—you, your son, your daughter, your male slave, your maid slave, your beasts, the aliens in your cities. For Yahve made the heavens, the earth, the sea and its contents in six days, but rested on the seventh. That is why Yahve blessed and sanctified the Sabbath.

Respect your father and mother, so that your days may be long on the land which Yahve your God is giving you.

You shall not murder.

You shall not commit adultery.

You shall not steal.

You shall not testify falsely against your neighbor.

You shall not covet your neighbor's house, your neighbor's wife, his man slave, his maid slave, his ox, his ass nor anything which is his. [20:2–17]

This decalogue[5] is often called the "ethical" or the "prophetic" decalogue, in contrast to the ritual emphasis in the earlier versions. Ritual in this decalogue is at a bare minimum, and aspects of social living replace the requirements of the earlier versions. The key position of the ethical decalogue, coming as it does so early in the long

[5] It is repeated in Deut. 5 with only minor alterations.

and complicated account of the Sinai episode, reflects the maturity of the developed account. The primitive version is left to the very end of the account. At the beginning of the account we get the clear and forthright statement of man's obligation to his fellow man.

In the case of the two so-called ritual decalogues, the context makes clear that they are the covenant documents. The context of this more ethical decalogue neither states nor suggests this, though this is obviously what is meant. Though the covenant at Sinai is legend and not history, it expresses through the ethical decalogue that which is basic in Hebrew religion, and which bears repetition: the essence of religion is man's relation to God; the substance of it is man's relation to his fellow man.

The long "mishpatim" section (21:1–24:8) is not the only legal section in the Sinai episode. Chapters 25–31, an even longer section, are the work of P. The point of this section is that it sets forth a need for certain equipment for the worship of Yahve. In the first place, raw materials, such as gold, were needed. Thereafter, an Ark, in which the Tablets of the Covenant were to be carried about, had to be built. The Ark, moreover, was to be part of a portable [6] sanctuary—"tabernacle" is its usual name, and it is described in great detail. In the tabernacle there was to be an elegant table, with dishes on it, and a candelabrum. Also, there was to be a curtain separating the antechamber from the holy of holies. Both an altar of wood and "gates" of the court around the portable sanctuary are described, the altar in vivid detail. Finally, we are told that Aaron was to be invested as the high priest.

These provisions are set forth in the text in a regular, indeed,

[6] Why a portable tabernacle? It is the answer to the implied question, How will the Hebrews commune with Yahve when they have moved away from the Sacred Mountain? The forerunner of the Priestly "tabernacle" was the "Tent of Meeting," spoken of in Exod. 33:7–11. This tent, probably conceived of as a replica of the cave on the Sacred Mountain, was outside the Hebrew encampment. Moses was wont to enter the tent to meet Yahve for: "Yahve spoke to Moses face to face, as a man would speak to his neighbor."

The tabernacle was conceived in P not so much as the place where Yahve could be met, as that where Yahve had taken up His residency (Exod. 25:8). It was the result of retrojecting a temple—portable, of course—into the Wilderness period.

The P writer is not concerned to tell us the source of the rich and elaborate materials used. So persuaded is he of portability, that he does not pause to consider that the dimensions that he gives of the wood alone would have required modern bulldozers and trailers. P's "tabernacle" in the Wilderness is a product of P's tendency to make the Wilderness period the origin both of the Temple and of a hereditary priesthood. The latter is an exilic or postexilic development; the former began with Solomon.

unvarying style. We have noticed this regularity before in the first
chapter of Genesis. It is a methodical, precise, and majestic manner.
But as applied to the tabernacle and its appurtenances the style is
dull. The prescription for how these objects are to be made (25:1–
31:17) is balanced by a narration (35:1–40:38) of the actual making of them. The two passages are virtually identical. They are separated by the Golden Calf incident and the "second set" of Tablets of
the Covenant.

The latter half of Exodus, Chapters 20–40, may be outlined,
then, as follows:

a. 20:1–17   the prophetic Decalogue
b. 20:18–24:8   the "Book of the Covenant"
c. 24:1, 9–11   the Nadab-Abihu fragment
d. 24:12–31:18   instructions for making the tabernacle
e. 32:1–35   the Golden Calf
f. 33:1–34:35   the "second" Decalogue
g. 35:1–40:38   the carrying out of the instructions in d.

This table reveals how legislation has come to vie for space with narration. In fact, when we have reached Chapter 20, we have virtually
come to the end of narration in the Pentateuch. The few incidents
that remain are scattered, and for the most part they are narrated
with such brevity as to appear to be summaries rather than actual
narration.

The narration in Genesis and the first half of Exodus is designed
only as a prologue to the legislation which begins in Exodus 20 and
extends through Numbers. It is the legislation that commands the
central interest of the compilers of the Pentateuch, and it is for the
sake of setting it forth that the narration has been arranged as a long
preamble.

Some people may be deterred by the dullness of the material,
which seems irrelevant both to Jews and Christians; interest is more
easily maintained when one reads this legal material with a specific
aim.

However, the serious student must not allow his preconceptions
as to the relevancy of the material to blind him to the fact that it is
largely because of the legislation that the Pentateuch is a religious
masterpiece. The question, What shall I do? was as important to the
Hebrew mind as the question, What shall I think? Indeed, in post-
biblical Judaism, the former became even more important than the
latter, because Jews conceived of belief as implicit in conduct, and
generally abstained from making it explicit. When conduct was the
norm, the prescription for it was sought for every avenue of life.

Scripture, beginning in the latter part of Exodus and continuing in the subsequent book, set the pattern for specifying what conduct should be. The latter chapters of Exodus tell in detail how the ritual worship should be observed, what equipment was needed, and how this equipment was made. It is only the detail that is dull; the conceptions are exciting. As we shall see, Pentateuchal religion was a milestone,[7] but not the final stage of Judaism. Properly to understand both post-biblical Judaism and Christianity requires the prior understanding of Pentateuchal religion. Herein lies the relevancy of this legislation for the serious student.

[7] See below, pp. 418 and 531ff.

LEVITICUS

LEVITICUS is a segment of a writing that begins in Exodus and extends into Numbers. It came to be a separate scroll, probably because of the accumulated length of the two preceding ones. It has little individuality as a separate book, except that by coincidence it concentrates primarily on sacrifice and priests. It is this emphasis that provides the name Leviticus, "relating to priests."

The absence of narrative and the monotony of the Priestly style combine with our present attitudes about the contents to make the book heavy and dull for the present-day reader. Ancient rabbis and modern scholars have found a fascination in it—the rabbis because of their devotion to the intricate details of the cult practice, and the scholars because of the light shed on religious developments. Yet the general reader has only an antiquarian interest in animal sacrifice or in rites of purification. Pre-eminently among the five books of the Pentateuch, Leviticus exhibits the character of a manual of instruction in the cult. Its precise instructions make it a guidebook, rather than only a reference book. The Priestly portions of Exodus and Numbers deal with paraphernalia of the cult, but Leviticus deals with the obligations of people to it. The opening words, after the routine formula, are: "When a man among you offers a sacrifice to Yahve. . . ." The accentuation on the man making the offering rather than on the offering itself gives Leviticus a human quality it might otherwise not have.

That the book begins with the laws of the sacrifices is a little surprising in view of where Exodus ended. It indicates either an accidental disarrangement of the material, or that the P writing consisted of blocks rather than one single, consecutive composition.

Thus, in Exodus, after the mandate was given (24:12–27) for the tabernacle and its appurtenances to be prepared, the following section (28–9) had prescribed that Aaron should be invested as the High Priest. Exodus concludes (35–40) with the carrying out of the mandate for the tabernacle and the appurtenances, so that reasonably Leviticus might have been expected to begin with Aaron's investiture. This, however, is deferred until Chapter 8. The first seven chapters, which may by accident occur where they do, distinguish among types of sacrifices. Some are holocausts, that is, burnt up entirely; others have only portions burnt up, with the remainder to be eaten by the priest or the offerer, or both. The type of sacrifice, holocaust or not, depended on the motive, whether it was offered because of a sin or guilt, or for an affirmative reason such as to give thanks.[1] The systematic exposition in Chapters 1–7 tells in detail what kind of animal or bird or cereal was appropriate to each purpose.[2]

The account of the investiture of Aaron (8–9) describes Aaron's elevation as the first high priest. Instructions for priests are continued in Chapter 10, which begins with the incident of Aaron's sons, Nadab and Abihu, being slain for bringing "strange fire" to the altar.[3]

[1] What was the intent in animal sacrifice? In part, the worshiper restored to the Deity a portion of what he had acquired, thus entitling himself to keep the remainder. In the actual burning, when it was not a holocaust, the odor was believed to rise to the Deity as a "sweet savor"; the Deity, as it were, partook of the offering in this form, while the worshiper ate of the meat. With worshiper and Deity partaking together, they were brought into communion.

[2] Chapter 1 describes the holocaust, brought to achieve forgiveness for sins. In Chapter 2 the subject is cereal offering, rather than animal sacrifice. Chapter 3 deals with the "peace" offering, not a holocaust, probably in thanksgiving. Offerings for specific sins (involuntary, communal, the prince, etc.) encompass 4:1–6:7. From 6:8–7:38 the focus is primarily on the role of the priests in the sacrifices.

[3] "Strange fire" is probably to be explained as follows. There is clear evidence of a belief that on the day of the equinox, whether spring or fall, fire descended from the heavens and kindled the altar. "Strange fire" might be coals brought from some ordinary place, rather than fire descending from on high. See II Chron. 7:1; "glory" is really "fiery radiance."

To combat the solar worship involved in the equinox and the descent of the sacred fire, legislation is found in Leviticus 6:5–6 Heb., 12–13 Eng., that the fire must never go out, but must burn perpetually. A relic of the descending sacred fire is found in Lev. 9:24, a verse which is the real beginning of the Nadab-Abihu episode. See also pages 64–65.

From 11:1–15:32 various laws relating to ritual purity are given. First is an exposition of what animals men may eat. (The prohibitions extend beyond pork, though this is not generally known.) Next comes the purification of a woman after menstruation. Then we are instructed in purification after the occurrence of a disease usually miscalled leprosy; 13:47–59 deals with this disease when it is attached to clothing, 14:33–57 with its contamination of a house.[4] Next, there are regulations dealing with secretions of the sexual organs (15).

Chapter 16 describes the establishment of Yom Kippur, the Day of Atonement, and prescribes its annual observance. What is today probably the most sacred of the Jewish holy days is the youngest of the Pentateuchal holy days. It is not found in the sources older than P, and seems to have been unknown even as late as Ezra and Nehemiah.[5] While the institution of the day as an annual observance is late, the ritual prescribed in 16:7–10, that of the scapegoat, is probably a very ancient bit of folklore carried over into the sacred day. The scapegoat is one of two animals used. The one was offered as a sacrifice by the high priest; the other, called in the text "the goat for Azazel," was sent into the Wilderness. The meaning of Azazel is uncertain; possibly it is the name of some evil spirit.[6] What is more certain is that the goat for Azazel was believed to have had the guilt of the people transferred to him; hence the translation "scapegoat" in older English versions.

The Yom Kippur legislation is marked by a change from previous procedure. In earlier writings the Tabernacle or Tent of Meeting in the Wilderness would appear to have been open for use at any time. We are now told (16:2) that Aaron could enter into the inner part (that which was known as the "Holy of Holies," and separated by a curtain or veil[7] from the antechamber) only on the Day of Atonement. Fasting, perhaps the most notable aspect of the observance today, is not specifically enjoined, but developed from the implication of the words, "you shall afflict your souls" (16:31). In this chapter the part of the high priest is the center of attention. The obligation of the lay individual is set forth in 23:27–32.

Chapters 17–26, except for some portions such as 23, represent

---

[4] In this form it was possibly a mold.
[5] In Nehemiah 8–9 an account of the seventh month, beginning with the first day and continuing to the twenty-fourth, makes no mention of Yom Kippur.
[6] See Ps. 106:37 and Deut. 32:17.
[7] In several passages in the New Testament, the continuous availability of atonement through the Christ is contrasted with the limitation in Leviticus 16 of entrance by the high priest beyond the veil to the Day of Atonement. See Hebrews 6:19–20, 9:3 and 10:19–20. The meaning of the rending of the veil at the death of Jesus is similar (Mark 15:38, Matthew 27:51, and Luke 23:45).

a Priestly source older than the other Priestly material in Leviticus. A refrain in this material insists that Israel must be holy, as Yahve is holy. Accordingly, the section is known as the Holiness Code.[8] Insofar as it is possible to assign some date to H, it is likely to have been recorded later than Ezekiel 40–48, but earlier than P. Some clues point to a possible origin in the later period of the Babylonian exile, possibly around 530.[9] While the legislation in H is decidedly ritualistic, there is an explicit ethical interest which may well be present in P also, but only implicitly. In H, the ethical legislation is most articulate, especially in Chapter 19. In this chapter a version of the Golden Rule is found: you shall love your neighbor as yourself (19:18). This verse is quoted in Matthew 19:19. There is a common misconception that the Golden Rule (Matthew 7:12) originated with Jesus; it is found broadly in ancient literatures.

Moreover, a religious attitude often encountered in our day draws a distinction between ritual religion, presumably bad, and the Golden Rule, presumably good. It is necessary, therefore, to point out that the Golden Rule is imbedded in the most highly ritualistic book of Scripture. The P authors never considered that ritual conflicted with ethics. It is likely that they would have denied that ethical living is humanly attainable without a ritual substratum. In their minds and in their writings ethics were inextricably bound up with ritual. Since they were writing a manual of detailed ritual observance, they often composed an elaborate ritualistic passage without expounding its ethical basis; the superficial reader may therefore forget the high importance to the P writers of the ethics both of conduct and of motivation. This misunderstanding of P's ritual can be corrected by remembering that it was priests who taught the Golden Rule.

Chapter 23 is a P summary of the Sacred Calendar. (Appendix II discusses the development of the calendar.) Here it may be noted that the P statement systematically sets the holy occasions on precise and definite days, in contradistinction to earlier calendars in which the sacred occasions are not precisely dated or described.

Chapter 25 sets forth instructions, premised on a view found elsewhere though not explicit here, that the Promised Land is really the property of the Deity, not of men. The land must have a sabbatical, just as God and men have; in the seventh year the land is not to be planted. Moreover, after seven sabbatical years, that is, on every fiftieth year, all property reverts to its original owner.[1]

[8] It is represented, therefore, by the symbol H. Older scholarly literature used the symbol P$_H$, a usage which has virtually disappeared.
[9] Ezekiel 40–48 would come from about 540, H about 530, and P about 400.
[1] The verse on the Liberty Bell is part of 25:10: "You shall hallow the fiftieth year, and *proclaim liberty throughout all the land unto all the inhabitants thereof.*"

Chapter 27 (P, not H) concludes the book. It sets forth certain arrangements whereby money payments may be substituted for vows of gifts or possessions offered as dedications to Yahve. More significant for our purposes is the conclusion of H in 26. It serves well for a brief consideration of Leviticus.

That the legislation in the Tanak is conceived of as divine in origin results in the consideration given in 26 to the alternate possibilities of fidelity or infidelity to it. The result of obedience is portrayed as rain in due season with attendant fertility and satiety; the land would be secure both from foe and from wild beasts, and enemies would be easily routed. Yahve would show favor in that He would multiply Israel and establish (that is, retain as before) His covenant with her. Moreover, He would dwell in her midst and be her God and Israel would be His people.

Yet if disobedience took place, and the covenant was broken, fear and disease would come, and the enemy would succeed in harassing Israel. If even after these misfortunes Israel persisted in disobedience, then dire famine would come, and plagues seven times as numerous as Israel's sins. If after all this Israel was still sinful, then Yahve Himself would bring a vengeance for the rupture of the covenant and there would be great scarcity and hunger. And if Israel was still wicked, then Yahve in His fury would cause parents (in hunger) to eat their children. Cities would be waste, the sanctuaries destroyed, the people exiled, and the land ruined. Terror would overcome the survivors. But if they confessed their sins, then Yahve would recall His covenant with the patriarchs. Even if Israel was on foreign soil, Yahve would not utterly terminate His covenant, but continue as her God.[2]

A system of rewards and punishments is usually regarded by sophisticated people as a token of an unexalted religious system,

---

[2] There is a somewhat similar section to be found in Deut. 27–8, where the respective possibilities are spoken of as blessing and curse. In Lev. 26, these two words do not occur, yet the ideas contained in them are present. But for all the similarity, there is a significant difference between Leviticus and Deuteronomy. There the alternatives of fidelity and infidelity are neatly balanced, especially in Deut. 28, as are the consequences. In Leviticus, however, infidelity to Yahve is clearly conceived of as able to get worse and worse, but even at the worst there is still a residual opportunity for the covenant to be re-established. In Deuteronomy, after a long oration, provision is ultimately made (30:1–6) for repentance and the renewal of relationship. That is to say, the conciseness of Leviticus creates an impression different from the wordiness of Deuteronomy. In Deuteronomy, Israel *may* ultimately return to Yahve, and then Yahve will be disposed to accept her; in Leviticus, Israel cannot ever so completely alienate herself from Yahve as to cut away the possibility of reconciliation. Leviticus supplies a motivation for Yahve to persist in relation with Israel in the form of the Merit of the Patriarchs (26:42); Deuteronomy says nothing of the Merit of the Patriarchs.

since the motivation to proper conduct is mere self-interest. It must be conceded that Leviticus 26 reflects aspects of such a system. Yet although the chapter is built on the supposition that a succession of punishments has not yet succeeded in ending Israel's wickedness, the surprising climax is that a final severance of relations between Yahve and Israel is not to take place. This climax destroys completely a conception alleged by some to be characteristic of Leviticus (and hence of Judaism)—a merely mechanical *quid pro quo* relationship between Deity and people. While it is true that the mechanical aspect is there, it is in no sense the whole conception of Leviticus any more than of the rest of the Tanak. Just as we saw divine forgiveness and divine grace reflected in the literary prophets, so too Leviticus carries many overtones of relationships and motivations transcending the mechanical. The Tanak, indeed, is never simply mechanical; on the other hand, it never completely repudiates rewards and punishments.

This brief survey of the contents of Leviticus can scarcely indicate either its many details or the flavor of the book. The name Leviticus—"pertaining to Levites"—is scarcely apt. A better name is that which rabbinic literature gives the book, "The Regulations of the Priests." Jewish tradition saw in Leviticus the key to the life of purity, and it was therefore customary for children's instruction in Scripture to begin with Leviticus: "Let it be the pure which the pure begin to study."

NUMBERS

THE TITLE "Numbers" of the fourth book is misleading. It arises from the narration of a census. The Hebrew title, *Ba-Midbar*, "in the Wilderness," is more apt, for the book presumably encompasses thirty-five of the forty years of Wilderness wandering. The census occupies most of the first four of the thirty-six chapters. But great attention is given even in the opening chapters to the duties and privileges of the Levites. These regulations are too numerous and various to be reproduced or paraphrased here. Some attention, however, might be given to the Levites who (1:48–53; 3:5–51; 8:5–26) are set apart from the rest of Israel, purified and established as a special order of holy workers. They are the substitutes for the first-born of all tribes who by right should have been consecrated as holy workers (8:16–18).

In the P writings, as we have noted several times, priesthood is conceived of as a hereditary privilege granted to a single family of the tribe of Levi, the family of Aaron. We have seen already that in Deuteronomy the priests are called "the priests, the Levites"; in Ezekiel 40–8 the proper priests are a family, that of Zadok. Levi as an ancient tribe and Levi as the collective name for the second rank of holy workers present something of a problem and a puzzle. The puzzle becomes more acute when we notice, as in Judges 17, that "Levite" is a title equivalent to priest, and borne by a man expressly identified as of the tribe of Judah. To add to the puzzle, Genesis 49 contains a strong rebuke to Levi.

It is likely, though by no means certain, that there was a progression from a sporadic and unrecognized priesthood in pre-exilic days without tribal membership as a prerequisite for eligibility, towards a centralized and organized priesthood after the Reformation of Josiah and after the exile, with gradations ensuing in which the priests of Jerusalem assumed the first rank, and those of the outlying regions, on being brought to Jerusalem, the second. Priest (*kohen*) and Levite (*levi*) became the respective titles. As a result of the historicizing tendency, such late distinctions were read back into Wilderness times. Levites were, accordingly, believed descended from Levi, and priests were a special family of the Levites. Thus, every *kohen*, priest, was a Levite, but only one family of the Levites could be priests.

The rest of these early chapters of Numbers can only be summarized here in a list of the principal topics: the census (1); the manner of the Wilderness encampment (2); Aaron's family (3:1-4); the Levite families and their duties (3:5-51); Aaron's family, spoken of as the Kehathites, from Kehath, Aaron's grandfather and Levi's son (4:1-20); the Levite families of Gershon and Merari (4:21-33); the tabulation of these Levite families (4:34-49).

A brief passage (5:1-4) on isolating certain people (lepers, those with a flux, or those unclean because of contact with a corpse) strikes a discordant note to modern readers; so, too, a section (5:5-10) which obligates a person making restitution for a trespass to add a fifth to the sum being restored. Most strange of all to modern readers is the section on the woman suspected by her husband of having committed adultery. The man brings her to a priest, who puts dust of the floor into holy water and has the woman swear to her innocence. She then drinks the water. If she has been guilty of adultery her belly swells; if her belly does not swell she is innocent (5:11-31). The regulations for the man who consecrates himself to Yahve are set forth (6:1-21) Such a "Nazirite" abstains from strong drink, does not cut his hair, and avoids touching a corpse.

The well-known blessing for use by priests is prescribed in 6:24-6:

May Yahve bless and preserve you,
May Yahve let His face shine on you and be gracious to you.
May Yahve favor you and give you peace.

Chapter 7 refers back to the construction and setting up of the tabernacle described in Exodus 35-40. We are now told of its dedication, of the assignments of Levites, and of the gifts to it by the various tribes. The reference serves to re-establish the narrative movement, which has all but disappeared in the mass of legislative details. The regulations about the Levites (8:5–26) momentarily obstruct the narration, but in 9 we are told that a year has elapsed since the Exodus, and hence the Passover must be observed.[1] In 9:15–22, the sense of travel is again revived, as the action of the guiding pillar of fire at night or cloud of smoke by day is described. In preparation for journeying, alarm trumpets are needed, and silver ones are made (10:1–10).

Now the sojourn at Sinai was over and the encampment moved on (10:11–28) with Moses' father-in-law[2] acting as a guide. There was more complaining (11:1–3), even about the manna (11:4–10). Moses appointed seventy men elders to assist him without begrudging them access to the divine spirit (11:11–30). The Hebrews set up a clamor for meat; quail was provided, but then divine destruction came upon the complainers (11:31–5).

Moses now encountered family trouble. His sister Miriam and his brother Aaron disliked his wife.[3] Miriam, for her unseemly conduct, was struck with leprosy, but on Moses' prayer she was healed (12:1–15). Then the encampment arrived at the Wilderness of Paran, by way of Hazeroth.[4] The stay at Paran encompasses Chapters 13–19. Twelve spies were sent into Canaan. On their return to Paran, ten of them advised against trying to invade Canaan. The people were ready to depose Moses and, under a new leader, return to Egypt. Yahve wanted to destroy the Hebrews and create His new people out of Moses' descendants (14:2–25), but He determined instead to keep out of Canaan all the Hebrews but the two favorable spies, Caleb and Joshua. Therefore, the Wilderness period had to endure for as long as forty years, to give time to the men and women

---

[1] A passage (9:9–14), usually regarded as very late, makes provision for a deferred observance of Passover by those unable to observe it in its proper time.
[2] He is known by three names, Jethro, Reuel, and Hobab. His tribe is sometimes the Kenite, sometimes, as here, the Midianite. In Exod. 18:27 Jethro has apparently departed from Moses after a helpful visit. Numbers 11:29 seems to imply that he is still with Moses.
[3] Moses had earlier married Zipporah, a Midianite. Here the wife is unnamed and is described as a Cushite. Therefore we do not know whether it was Zipporah, or some new wife.
[4] Hazeroth is on the Sinai peninsula, on the west shore of the Gulf of Aqaba. The Wilderness of Paran is perhaps fifty miles north, a bit to the west of modern Elath; Kadesh Barnea is a settlement in Paran. The presumption is that the Israelites have journeyed from the Sacred Mountain in a northerly direction but have not yet left the peninsula.

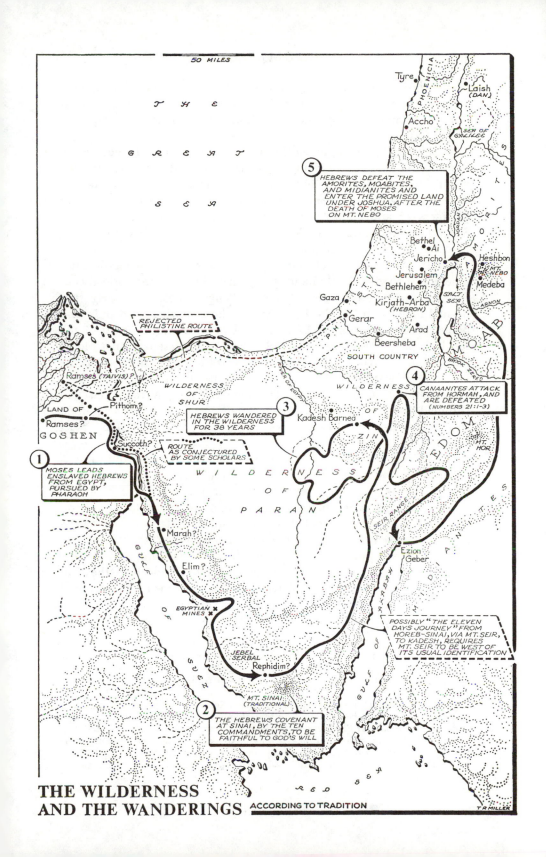

50 MILES

THE GREAT SEA

Tyre
PHOENICIA
Laish (DAN)
Accho
SEA OF GALILEE

⑤ HEBREWS DEFEAT THE
AMORITES, MOABITES,
AND MIDIANITES AND
ENTER THE PROMISED LAND
UNDER JOSHUA, AFTER THE
DEATH OF MOSES
ON MT. NEBO

JORDAN RIVER

Bethel
Ai
Jericho
Heshbon
MT. NEBO
Jerusalem
Bethlehem
Medeba
Gaza
Kirjath-Arba (HEBRON)
SALT SEA
Gerar
Arad
ARNON
Beersheba
SOUTH COUNTRY
MOAB

REJECTED
PHILISTINE ROUTE

RIVER OF EGYPT

Ramses (TAINIS)?
WILDERNESS OF SHUR
WILDERNESS OF ZIN
Kadesh Barnea
④ CANAANITES ATTACK
FROM HORMAH, AND
ARE DEFEATED
(NUMBERS 21:1-3)

Pithom?
③ HEBREWS WANDERED
IN THE WILDERNESS
FOR 38 YEARS
EDOM
MT. HOR.

LAND OF
Ramses?
GOSHEN
Succoth?
ROUTE
AS CONJECTURED
BY SOME SCHOLARS
WILDERNESS OF PARAN

① MOSES LEADS
ENSLAVED HEBREWS
FROM EGYPT,
PURSUED BY
PHARAOH

SEIR RANGE

Marah?
GULF OF SUEZ
Ezion Geber

Elim?
GULF OF AKABAH
MIDIANITES

EGYPTIAN
MINES
POSSIBLY "THE ELEVEN
DAYS JOURNEY" FROM
HOREB-SINAI, VIA MT. SEIR,
TO KADESH, REQUIRES
MT. SEIR TO BE WEST OF
ITS USUAL IDENTIFICATION

JEBEL
SERBAL
Rephidim?

MT. SINAI
(TRADITIONAL)

② THE HEBREWS COVENANT
AT SINAI, BY THE TEN
COMMANDMENTS, TO BE
FAITHFUL TO GOD'S WILL

RED SEA

THE WILDERNESS
AND THE WANDERINGS ACCORDING TO TRADITION

T R MILLER

over twenty to die (14:26–38). The Hebrews, remorseful at having
rejected the favorable report of the two and thereby sinning against
Yahve, attempted an invasion of Canaan at Hormah,[5] but were defeated (14:39–45).

Chapter 15 reverts to legislation, containing miscellaneous laws.
It discusses offerings of flour, oil, wine, and meal; offerings for un-
witting transgressions; Sabbath severity; and the wearing of tassels
as reminders of God's commandments. The narrative is resumed in
Chapters 16 and 17 with an account of a rebellion against Moses.
Several accounts are here blended into one. An old account told of
rebellion by two men, Dathan and Abiram; a later account told of a
rebellion by a relative of Moses named Korah, a Levite.[6] Korah's
rebellion (16:3–11) challenged Aaron's right to the priesthood;
Dathan and Abiram (16:12–15) challenged Moses, alleging that
he had failed to bring the Hebrews to a land flowing with milk and
honey.[7] When resentment arose in mob form over the death of the
rebels, a plague destroyed the mob who had gathered against Moses
and Aaron (16:16–17:13 Heb., 16:16–50 Eng.). So as to settle the
issue of the legitimate priest, Aaron and other Levites deposited their
rods in the Tent of Meeting. The next morning Aaron's rod had
sprouted and put forth buds. Accordingly, Aaron's rod was retained
in the Tent as symbol of Aaron's legitimacy (17:14–28 Heb., 1–13
Eng.).

Numbers reverts to legislation in Chapter 18, specifying the different tasks and remuneration of priests and Levites. Chapter 19 describes how purification from contact with the dead, which defiles,
can be achieved. A red heifer must be slain and burnt to ashes, and
the ashes gathered; the defiled person sprinkles water with which the
ashes are mixed over both things or persons defiled, thus achieving
the first steps to purity, the next being to wash his clothes and bathe.

Now, again, the encampment moved, from Kadesh in the Wilderness of Zin to Moab, east of the Dead Sea. It seems to be presumed
that most of the necessary forty years of sojourn in the Wilderness
have by now passed. Miriam died at Kadesh (20:1). When lack of

---

[5] The Hormah incident here, and its sequel, 21:1–3, is interpreted by some scholars as the vestige of a reminiscence of a Hebrew invasion of Canaan from the
south. Scripture, according to this opinion, is giving a romantic summary in its
almost single-minded view that the invasion was from the east and across the
Jordan at Jericho.
[6] Korah and Moses have a common grandfather, Kehath. In 16:1, the present text
speaks also of one *On* ben Peleth. The text should be corrected to read: "Dathan
and Abiram the sons of Eliab, *the son* of Peleth, the son of Reuben."
[7] The stories become somewhat inextricably mixed, as in 16:24 and 25. But nevertheless it is clear that Korah and his followers were consumed by fire (16:16–24),
while Dathan and Abiram were swallowed up by the earth (16:25–34).

water made the Hebrews complain, Moses brought water from a rock; but although Yahve had enjoined him and Aaron to speak to the rock, Moses struck it with his rod. For this disobedience, Moses and Aaron were not to be permitted to enter Canaan (20:2–13).

The route towards Moab led through Edom (south-southeast of the Dead Sea). Permission to pass through was denied, in a most unbrotherly way, by the Edomites (20:14–21). At Mount Hor—a place that has not yet been identified—Aaron surrendered his high priestly regalia to his son and successor, Eleazar, and died (20:22–9).

Then they were attacked by the Canaanites of the south; the Hebrews were victorious and so great was the destruction that the battle place came to be called Hormah ("destruction")[8] (21:1–3). While circling around Edom south of the Red Sea, the people again complained; fiery serpents bit them and many died. Moses, at Yahve's suggestion, made a bronze serpent[9] and set it on a pale; a person who had been bitten could look at the serpent and avoid death (21:4–9).

The march continued northward into Moab territory east of the Dead Sea (21:10–20). The Israelites requested permission from Sihon, King of Heshbon, to pass through his territory; however, Sihon not only refused but he attacked Israel, and was beaten. The Israelites seized his territory to settle in. So, too, when Og of Bashan, northeast of Sihon's territory, attacked, he was killed and his people wiped out (21:21–35). The Hebrews were now encamped in Moabite territory east of the Jordan, opposite Jericho (22:1), and the end of their wandering had come.

An intriguing episode (22:2–24:25) took place. The Moabite king, Balak, hired a prophet named Balaam, presumably a Midianite, to curse Israel. Two main layers are present, though blended together, in the account. In one layer Balaam is an admirable prophet, devoted to Yahve; in the other he is a rogue, whose services are available to the highest bidder. As the prophet, he is treated with seriousness. As the rogue, he is treated with broad humor, as in the incident of his ass, who, seeing Yahve's angel blocking their way, a sight withheld from Balaam, chided Balaam. But in either role, whether willingly as the prophet, or unwillingly as the rogue,[1] Balaam uttered on Israel not a curse but a blessing, this to the discomfiture of Balak. Indeed, the curse Balaam uttered was on the foes of Israel. The Balaam episode is one of the comic highlights of the Tanak.

[8] We encountered Hormah, as though it had *already* acquired its name, above, 14:45, p. 398.

[9] This brazen serpent is mentioned again, but on the occasion of its destruction by King Hezekiah, II Kings 18:4.

[1] A P summary in Numbers 31 includes the statement, verse 8, that the Israelites slew Balaam, who was (verse 16) the cause of the apostasy described in 25.

In Chapter 25, we are told of a crowning transgression on the part of the Hebrews. Hitherto they had only murmured about their supposed bad lot; now, having arrived near Canaan, many of them forsook Yahve and joined themselves to Baal Peor, the Moabite deity. Plague broke out and destroyed many. Aaron's grandson Phineas [2] slew an Israelite and his Midianite woman. (The text varies in identifying the foe; sometimes they are Moabite, sometimes Midianite.) An unedifying story, its place is important, for it implies that only the Wilderness isolation kept the Israelites from extreme infidelity to Yahve; as soon as they had the opportunity to succumb to Baal, they did so. The blessing of Balaam and the account of infidelity in the plains of Moab are juxtaposed. The biblical author tended to express black and white contrasts.

In Chapter 26, since Israel was on the threshold of entering Canaan, a new census was taken, and the genealogies of the tribal families given. [3] The Wilderness generation had now died out; only Joshua and Caleb were still alive.

Moses was now enjoined to ascend a mountain, Abarim, so as to look at the Promised Land, and then to die. Joshua bin Nun was designated his successor, with Eleazar ben Aaron to be closely associated with him [4] (27:12–23). By all logic, the Book of Numbers should have included the account of Moses' death, but the editors apparently had leftover material which they wanted to include, and, infelicitously, they inserted that material at the end of Numbers.

The Book of Numbers does not narrate the death of Moses. This is deferred to the end of the Book of Deuteronomy. As we shall see presently, the sequence of writings encompassing Deuteronomy, Joshua,

---

[2] The continuity of priesthood through Aaron's descendants is confirmed (25:10–19) because of Phineas' deed.

[3] There intrudes, 27:1–11, the question, exemplified in the daughters of one Zelophehad, of whether daughters may inherit from a father, if there are no sons. The answer is that they may. Then follows a statement on the order of inheritance when there are no children.

[4] Chapters 28–9 are additional laws of sacrifice, especially the sacrifices for Sabbath and the sacred days. Chapter 30 deals with oaths; 31 is narrative, a successful war of revenge against the Midianites, referring back to 25:16–18. Chapter 32 describes the settlement east of the Jordan of the tribes of Gad and Reuben, and half of the tribe of Manasseh. In 33, the route traversed from Egypt through the Wilderness to the plains of Moab is recapitulated. Chapter 34 proposes the boundaries of the lands of the tribes that were to settle west of the Jordan. Since no provision of land is made in 34 for Levites, 35 provides for certain cities for them; it also sets forth certain cities in which those guilty of manslaughter could enjoy the right of asylum. Chapter 36 contains instructions to supplement the question of women as heiresses, touched on in 27:1–11.

Judges, Samuel, and Kings has a literary history quite different from that of the Genesis-Exodus-Leviticus-Numbers sequence. When the Deuteronomy sequence was set into relationship with the Genesis-Numbers sequence and it was observed that Deuteronomy is about— indeed, presumably by—Moses, one consequence was the need to move the account of Moses' death from the climactic moment at the end of Numbers, its original place, to the end of Deuteronomy. With the account of Moses' death so moved, Deuteronomy became separated from the Deuteronomic sequence and joined to the Genesis-Numbers sequence. The four books, Genesis through Numbers, constituted an organic unity; the Pentateuch, *five* books, arose through the detachment of Deuteronomy from its natural grouping and its being joined to the four preceding books.

Genesis through Numbers, as we have been saying, is basically a Priestly creation. The narratives, especially the older ones, were mostly assembled by P rather than originally written by him. Most of the legislation, however, was written by P—or, rather, rewritten, for much of it is inherited from ancient times. P's accomplishment was to set the complex, almost codified legislation into the framework of a reconstruction of Hebrew history. Without the history, the legislation would hang in mid-air. The question, "What shall a man do?" would not have been merged with the question, "What shall a man think?"

So compelling to the Hebrews was their belief that history reveals God that no record of the revelation of God's will and laws could possibly have been written without an account of God's action in history. Though P adapted rather than wrote history, the history was not merely incidental to P. Quite the contrary, P's legislation derived its authority from the history he put together.

The legislation must be regarded as comprising two related though different aspects. In the first place, the material in Exodus and the early chapters of Leviticus prescribed how a public, communal institution arose and was to operate. When P wrote, the Temple in Jerusalem was presided over by a hereditary priestly family; hence the P authors told that this Temple had had its forerunner in the tabernacle in the Wilderness, and the presiding priestly family had been installed at that time. Hence, sanctuary and priesthood and their form of practice were fully authorized, for history and divine legislation combined to authorize them.

In the second place, the history and the legislation instructed the individual Israelite as to what he was to do in the most varied situations. The regulation did not separate religion from "secular" requirements, for with hierarchy replacing monarchy in the early postexilic period, there could be no viable distinction between sacred and secular law. Hence the history and the legislation combined to provide the instructions by which the individual could organize and regulate his daily living.

The Tetrateuch ("four books") was designed as a manual for practical life. It was not, as some scholars have misinterpreted it, utopian; rather, it was meant to be utilitarian, useful. The significance in the history of Judaism of the existence of such a manual can be properly assessed only after we look at the fifth book, Deuteronomy, for it was the Pentateuch, not just the Tetrateuch, which rose to centrality in Judaism.

DEUTERONOMY

THE FIFTH BOOK of the Tanak calls for a double approach. It is the first volume, as we have said, of a long sequence which extends through Kings. Yet it was detached from this sequence and joined to the Tetrateuch to form the Pentateuch. First we shall view Deuteronomy as the concluding book of the Pentateuch; thereafter we shall look at it as the first part of the long sequence of Deuteronomy through Kings.

Deuteronomy consists of three long addresses purportedly made by Moses east of the Jordan[1] immediately prior to his death and the westward crossing of Israel to conquer the land. The first address (1:6–4:40) is introduced by the statement that Moses is *explaining* the divine revelation; that is to say, we are not hearing an initial formulation but rather an exposition of matters already known. Since Moses is speaking of his part in the past events, Deuteronomy is written almost entirely in the first person.

At Sinai—Deuteronomy calls the Mountain, Horeb[2]—Yahve

[1] The geographic data in Deut. 1:1 include some sites not identified by modern scholars, and where sites are identified there are still certain confusions.
[2] All manner of theories attempt to reconcile the divergence in the two names as we have said (p. 27). Thus, the explanation is offered that one name was that of a mountain range and the other that of a single peak in the same range.

declared that the encampment at the Sacred Mountain had lasted long enough, and that it was time for the Israelites to move on, in order to take possession of the land that Yahve had promised to their ancestors (1:6–8). Because the people of Israel had become so numerous, Moses needed to organize them for what we should call administrative purposes (1:9–18). But he now turned to remind them of their lack of faith in Yahve, as shown by their fear of the Canaanites when their spies made the report to them.[3] Therefore, all that Wilderness generation, including Moses,[4] was denied the privilege of entering Canaan. He reminded them, too, of their remorse which had led to an ill-advised attack on the Canaanites and defeat at Hormah[5] (1:20–46).

Then Moses reviewed the march from Kadesh towards the Gulf of Aqaba, and northward. (This route is initially more southerly than, and in frequent conflict with, the one given in Numbers.) He summarized the friendly overtures made to Edom, Ammon, and Moab, and the conquest of Sihon and Og[6] (2:1–3:11). Once the land east of the Jordan was conquered, it was given to Reuben, Gad, and to half the tribe of Manasseh[7] (3:12–22).

When Israel was near the Promised Land, Moses had made a special entreaty to be allowed to enter, but Yahve was too angry at him, because of Israel's infidelities,[8] to grant the permission. Instead He directed Moses to ascend Pisgah[9] and to look at the land he was

---

Others have seen in the word Sinai an etymology involving a semitic root meaning moon, and infer that originally some moon worship was associated with Sinai; and since a root meaning "to dry up" or "scorch," as by the sun, can be associated with Horeb, it is explained that Horeb is a name substituted for Sinai when solar worship replaced moon worship.

[3] See Num. 13–14 and 21:1–3.

[4] No reference seems to be intended to Num. 20:11–12, as if Deuteronomy here ascribes to Moses merely a part of the general insufficient faith in Yahve rather than the specific act of disobedience. See also Deut. 32:50–2.

[5] Num. 14:39–45 and pp. 398–399.

[6] See Num. 21:21–5 and 31–5. I have not adhered to the Scriptural order. Deut. 2:10–12 and 20–3 give data about the aboriginal residents, prior to conquest of Edomites and Moabites. The reference to Og's bed—some call it a sarcophagus—is not amplified by any archaeological data.

[7] Num. 32 relates this.

[8] Again, no reference is made to Moses' disobedience, Num. 20:11–12. On the other hand, Numbers makes no mention of this entreaty by Moses.

[9] The word seems to mean "cleft," a pass between mountain peaks. The injunction appears to be for Moses to ascend to the "head of the pass." Translations have uniformly taken Pisgah as the *name* of a mountain. In Deut. 32:19 Mount Abarim is identified with Mount Nebo, and in 34:1, Pisgah appears to be a peak of Nebo; some, however, take it to be a peak near Nebo. Possibly a way out of a confusion is to regard Abarim as a range, Nebo as a peak, and the *pisgah* as a lookout station at the peak of Nebo. The latter is identified as Jebal Nebo, a 2600 ft. peak in the Transjordan area.

not to enter (3:*13–29*). In view of this decision, Moses drew the lesson that a wise people, to whom God had been so close, must be undeviatingly loyal and faithful. He reminded Israel of the revelation at Horeb, and of the covenant, and of the ten Words which Yahve had inscribed on the two Tablets of stone, and that he, Moses, had instructed Israel concerning regulations to be observed on entering into Palestine. Since at Horeb they had only heard a divine voice and had not seen anything, they were especially to be on guard against making an image of any kind. Moreover, they were not to worship sun, moon, or stars. If they should make any image, then the covenant would be broken and misfortunes would ensue (4:*1–24*).

Moreover, if their descendants, on becoming old settlers in the Promised Land, were to make an image, Yahve would punish them by scattering them among the nations. But if, from exile, they were to call penitently to Him, He would recall His covenant with their ancestors, and redeem the descendants just as He had freed those enslaved in Egypt; this latter event was a proof that He was the only God[1] (4:*25–40*). The first address, then, is a brief historical summary, culminating in an interpretation of that history. Not only does it review the events of the past, but it hints broadly at such late events as the Babylonian exile and the return.

The second address (5:*1*–28:*14*) is a presentation of the revealed regulations. It begins with the Decalogue, substantially the same as in Exodus 20, but here followed by some lengthy exhortations. There is a significant prologue to the Decalogue:

> Not [alone] with our fathers did Yahve make this covenant, but with us, here, alive this day. [5:*3*]

While the Decalogue in Deuteronomy is only a little changed from that in Exodus 20, some of these minor differences[2] are worth noting. In the Sabbath legislation,[3] Exodus 20:*11* reads:

> For Yahve made the heaven and the earth, and all they contain, and rested on the seventh day; accordingly, Yahve blessed and sanctified the Sabbath Day.

---

[1] A section (4:*41–3*) dealing with "cities of refuge," to which one guilty of manslaughter could flee for safety from avengers, is out of place here. It is related in the third person, whereas elsewhere the first person predominates. Verses *44–9*, also in the third person, are a geographical note telling where Moses is speaking.

[2] Exod. 20:*8* reads, "*Remember* the Sabbath to sanctify it"; Deut. 5:*12*: "*Observe* the Sabbath to sanctify it, as Yahve your God has commanded you."

[3] *Ox and ass* are also listed among those who are to rest in Deut. 5:*14*, but not in Exod. 20:*10*.

Deuteronomy has an additional statement: that the rest is required for the following reason:

> . . . In order that your male slave and maid slave may rest as you do. You shall recall that you were a slave in the land of Egypt, but Yahve your God took you out from there with a mighty hand and an outstretched arm. Accordingly, Yahve commanded you to observe the Sabbath Day.

In the commandment to honor father and mother, Deuteronomy 5:*16* has three additional Hebrew words that require a phrase in English:

> Honor your father and mother so that your days may be prolonged, *and things go well* with you, in the land which Yahve your God gives you.

The last commandment (Exod. 20:*17*) reads:

> You shall not covet your neighbor's house; you shall not covet the wife of your neighbor, or his male slave, or maid slave, or ox, or ass, or anything that is his.

Deut. 5:*18* Heb., *21* Eng. reads:

> You shall not covet your neighbor's wife, and you shall not *desire* your neighbor's house. . . ."

There are interpreters who consider such minor changes indicative of an increased humanitarianism in the Deuteronomy Decalogue over that in Exodus. Perhaps this is true, but it is scarcely so clear as to merit undue emphasis.

The exhortation that ensues after the Decalogue supposes that the Hebrews had been willing, through fright, for Moses alone to encounter Yahve at Horeb. Moses had lingered on, after the Decalogue had been given, to receive additional laws, the performance of which would bring long life and prosperity when once the Promised Land had been entered (5:*19–30* Heb., *22–33* Eng.). Though we are apparently led to expect these laws immediately, they do not appear for some interval. Instead, it is asserted that Yahve, in however many forms and places He may have been worshiped, is one single Yahve.[4] Man's attitude to Him should be that of total and unreserved love. Hence, He alone is worthy of Israel's allegiance (6:*1–15*). Later generations should avoid the bad example of the Wilderness genera-

---

[4] This is the meaning of "Hear, O Israel, Yahve our God is one Yahve." Centuries later, when gnosticism and Christianity divided the godhead, the verse became for Jews an assertion of the unbroken unity of God, and as such became and has remained the most noted and characteristic utterance of Judaism. The customary rendering is: "Hear, O Israel, the Lord our God, the Lord is one."

tion with its provocations (6:16–19), and understand that the commandments were from Him who had brought even them out of slavery in Egypt (6:20–4). Deuteronomy consistently credits late generations with the beneficial providence given the early ones.

The Canaanite residents are to be completely exterminated. Intermarriage with them is unthinkable; it could only lead to apostasy from Yahve and move Him to wrath. Israel was sacred to Yahve; He had chosen Israel from among all nations to be His treasured people (7:1–6), not because of Israel's size, for Israel was the least among nations, but because of His love for Israel and because of His oath to the patriarchs (7:7–11).

Obedience to Yahve's requirements would bring love, and blessing, and great progeny, and neither sterility nor any diseases would be found among men or animals. Israel would absorb her neighbors but not their gods (7:12–16). In the light of Yahve's past deeds in Egypt, the foreign nations should not be feared because of their size. Indeed, Yahve would send the hornet to complete their extermination (7:12–26). Fidelity on Israel's part, in recollection of Yahve's past benefits, would yield future prosperity in a land of fertility and abundance (8:1–10). But prosperity must not lead to haughtiness and a forgetting of Yahve, as, for example, through the false view that men, and not Yahve, had brought about the prosperity (8:11–18). Such apostasy would bring upon Israel a destruction akin to that suffered by other peoples (8:19–20). Yahve Himself would lead Israel in her effort to conquer Canaan, not so much because of Israel's righteousness as because of the wickedness of the Canaanites (9:1–6). Israel must recall her acts which had displeased Yahve in the Wilderness, such as the Golden Calf (9:7–21) and other misdeeds (9:22–4). Moses reminds them of his petitions, which he made on their behalf and which lasted forty days and nights (9:25–9), in order that the second set of Tablets would be provided to replace the broken set (10:1–7 [5] and 10–11).

Yahve's demand on Israel was for reverence, obedience, and love. These attitudes were to be exhibited in justice to orphan and widow and in consideration for strangers [6] (10:12–22). Future generations of Israel should know the record of Yahve's beneficent deeds and also His punishment of the past misdeeds, for future generations were as much a part of the covenant as those who stood at Horeb.[7]

---

[5] 10:8–9, a P interpolation, recalls that the Levites were changed from a tribe, like others, into those functionaries who were to carry the Ark.
[6] 10:19 reads: "You shall love the foreigner, for you were foreigners in Egypt."
[7] 11:2, an elliptical verse, should be amplified to read: "You must know this day that not *alone* with you, but with your children . . . *have* I made this covenant"

Unlike Egypt, where land was watered by the feet[8] (in irrigation from the Nile), the Promised Land "drinks water from the rain from the heavens," and Yahve always cares for it (11:1–12). Obedience to Yahve, hence, would bring proper rainfall; disobedience, drought (11:13–17).

If the love of Yahve prevailed, then He would lead a successful conquest (11:22–5). If obedience obtained, blessing was available; if disobedience, then a curse. Indeed, the two, blessing and curse,[9] were to be placed respectively on Mount Gerizim and Mount Ebal (11:26–32). Here ends the direct exhortation.

The legislation, Chapters 12–26, treats of many themes and hence cannot easily be paraphrased. Yet a brief summary is necessary in order to assess the character of Deuteronomy's legislation. As a preliminary it should be noted that some chapters are terse, while others are discursive.

Chapter 12 is discursive. Its tone is that of the orator rather than the lawgiver, despite the legislation presented. The pagan altars are to be destroyed; the Hebrews may bring sacrifices only to the one place, among all the tribal areas, which Yahve will choose (5–6), and they must be on guard against capriciously offering sacrifices just anywhere (13–14). Offerings of harvest crops are also to be brought to the place of Yahve's choice (18). When conquest beyond Canaan's borders increases distances, certain animals may be slaughtered at home, but "sacred offerings" and "vow offerings" must be brought to the place of Yahve's choice (26).

Discursiveness continues in Chapter 13. One must beware of a prophet, despite his ability to work miracles, if he attempts to entice people away from Yahve, for Yahve is only testing Israel through him (2–6 Heb., 1–5 Eng.). If a blood relative, no matter how close, or one's wife or friend tries to entice one away from Yahve, the enticer shall be put to death by stoning (7–12 Heb., 6–11 Eng.). If a city is enticed away from Yahve, it and its people are to be destroyed utterly (13–19 Heb., 12–18 Eng.).

In Chapter 14 the style becomes terse. There are injunctions against pagan mourning rites (1–2); against eating improper ani-

---

[8] No exact explanation of the use of the feet in mechanical irrigation is available. Perhaps it simply means that buckets of water had to be carried from the river to the gardens.

[9] A fuller explanation comes in Deut. 27. Six tribes are to be stationed on Mount Gerizim for the blessing, and six on Mount Ebal for the curses; the passage contains the curses uttered by the Levites, but no blessings. In Josh. 8:33ff., there is a brief account, but reproducing neither blessings nor curses, of Joshua's carrying out what is enjoined here in Deut. 11.

mals, fish, and birds, and anything that dies of itself, i.e., that is not slaughtered. A kid is not to be seethed in its mother's milk[1] (*14–21*). Prohibitions give way now to affirmative injunctions. First there is the tithe (*14:22–8*). Then, in Chapter 15, there is provision for a "year of release,"[2] when all creditors are to cancel debts owed by fellow Israelites (*1–6*). The approach of the "release" year must not deter one from lending to his poor neighbor (*7–11*). A Hebrew slave may serve six years but must be released in the seventh year (*12–18*). Firstlings born to the flocks and herds belong to Yahve (*19–23*).

In Chapter 16:*1–17*, three festivals—Passover, Shabuoth ("Weeks"), and Sukkoth ("Booths")—are briefly described.[3] The remainder of the chapter (*18–22*) prescribes the appointment of judges and the need of pure justice, and prohibits the non-Yahvistic *asherah*[4] and pillar. In 17:*2–7*, the procedure for punishing an individual guilty of infidelity to Yahve is set forth at length. Verses *8–13* prescribe that when a local court is in doubt, the matter is to be brought to "the Priests—the Levites," at the place Yahve chooses. Next (*14–20*), if there is a desire for a king, one may be selected, provided he is not a foreigner or prone to multiply horses (to maintain his power) or to accumulate many wives and much precious metal. The king must, indeed, copy out this passage.

The rights of the Priests-Levites are set forth in 18:*1–8*. Soothsayers, sorcerers, charmers, and necromancers are not to be tolerated (*9–14*) for Yahve will raise up a prophet like Moses (*15–22*). As to whether a prophet is true or false, the outcome of events will tell whether he has predicted correctly. Chapter 19 tersely covers criminal law; first manslaughter and cities of refuge (*1–10*), and then murder (*11–13*). Theft through moving landmarks that serve as boundaries is prohibited (*14*). An accused is not to be convicted on the testimony of a single witness (*15*); false witnesses are to be punished (*16–21*).

Discursiveness returns in Chapter 20, which discusses the conduct of a war. With Yahve leading her into battle, Israel need not

---

[1] In Canaanite and other Semitic practice a sacrifice was prepared by boiling it in milk. The prohibition is found also in Exod. 23:*19* and 29:*26*. The ancient rabbis in the early Christian centuries did not know the folklore behind the prohibition. They interpreted the verse as an injunction to separate milk and meat foods from simultaneous consumption; the separation is still observed today, particularly by orthodox Jews.

[2] Exod. 23:*10–11* and Lev. 25:*1–7* provide for a "sabbatical" year, in which planting should not take place.

[3] Neither Yom Kippur nor the "New Year" is mentioned. See Appendix II, "The Sacred Calendar."

[4] See above, p. 39.

fear. Those who have built houses but have not dedicated them are to be exempted from the military draft; also those who have planted vineyards, but have not enjoyed the fruit; also those who have become betrothed but have not consummated the marriage; and those who are fainthearted and fearful (*1–9*). A city that surrenders to Israel is to pay tribute and its inhabitants are to be enslaved. Where resistance is offered on the capture of the city, if it is distant, all the males are to be executed and the women and children taken as booty; if it is nearby, belonging to one of the pre-Israelite tribes inhabiting Canaan, all the residents are to be put to death (*10–18*). In a protracted siege, fruit trees must be preserved, not be cut down for use as lumber (*19–20*).

Next, in Chapter 21, a discursive chapter, when the victim of an unsolved murder is found in the countryside, the city nearest by actual measurement to the spot where the corpse is found must go through rites of purification (*1–9*). A woman taken prisoner of war who attracts a man through her beauty must undergo disfiguration and be allowed a month to lament her father and mother before she can become the man's wife. If thereafter his taste changes and he does not want her, he must set her free (*10–14*). In the case of a man with two wives, he may not give partisan treatment in primogeniture to the child of the favored wife (*15–17*). A worthless son may have charges brought against him by his parents, so that the elders of the city may decree death by stoning (*18–21*). The body of a man executed in a capital case is to be hung on a tree (*22–3*).

In Chapter 22 the legislation is terse, and encompasses a variety of subjects: the restoration to the owner of found property (*1–4*), a prohibition against a man wearing women's garb, and vice versa (*5*); a prohibition against taking from a nest both egg or fledgling and mother bird (*6–7*); the requirement for a roof [5] to have a parapet to prevent falls (*8*); prohibitions against sowing two kinds of seed in a vineyard, plowing with an ox and ass together, and wearing cloth woven of wool and linen (*9–11*); and the law of tassels [6] (*12*).

Next come six laws of sexual conduct. The first deals with a husband who, on coming to dislike his wife, charges that she was not a virgin when they were married (*13–21*); the penalty for adultery is death for both the man and the woman (*22*); the penalty for fornication with a betrothed young woman in a city is death for both the man and the woman (*23–4*); the penalty for such fornication in the

[5] Which was flat.
[6] This is found also in Num. 15:37–41, and there explained as a reminder of Yahve's commandments.

countryside is death for the man as though it were rape, and the penalty for the rape of an unbetrothed woman is the payment of fifty shekels to the father, and compulsory marriage without permission to divorce (25–7).

In the terse Chapter 23, sex relations with a stepmother are prohibited (*1* Heb., 22:30 Eng.). Next there is a list of those to be excluded from the people of Israel: eunuchs and bastards (*2–3* Heb., *1–2* Eng.); and Ammonites and Moabites (*4–7* Heb., *3–6* Eng.). On the other hand, Edomites and Egyptians may not be permanently excluded (*8–9* Heb., *7–8* Eng.). Next there come the rules for personal hygiene in a military camp (*10–15* Heb., *9–14* Eng.). An escaped slave must not be returned to his master (*16–17* Heb., *15–16* Eng.). Israelites may not be cult prostitutes, male or female (*18–19* Heb., *17–18* Eng.). Interest on loans may be charged a foreigner but not a fellow Israelite (*20–1* Heb., *19–20* Eng.). Vows to God should be made prudently, but once made must be lived up to (*22–4* Heb., *21–3* Eng.). One may enter a neighbor's domain to pluck and eat fruit or grain, but not to carry any away (*25–6* Heb., *24–5* Eng.).

Similarly, Chapter 24 is both terse and miscellaneous. A man may not remarry a woman he has divorced if in the interval she has married another man who likewise has divorced her (*1–4*). A newly wed man is draft-exempt (*5*); millstones (used by the poor in grinding grain) may not be taken in pledge (*6*); kidnapping and selling a person into slavery is to be punished by death (*7*); "lepers" must act in conformity with the instructions of Levitical priests (*8–9*); consideration of the poor must be shown in taking from them pledges on loans (*10–13*); a hired servant must be dealt with considerately (*14–15*); neither parents nor children are to be punished for the others' crimes (*16*); justice must be done to the weak (*17–18*); the right of gleaning by the poor is to be maintained (*19–22*).

In Chapter 25 also we encounter a terse miscellany. A person sentenced to whipping is to be lashed in the presence of the court, but more than forty lashes may not be imposed (*1–3*); an ox may not be muzzled while treading grain (*4*); the law of the levirate [7] ("brother-in-law") marriage is enjoined (*5–10*); a wife may not grasp the private parts of someone fighting with her husband (*11–12*); strict honesty is required in business dealings (*13–16*); the deserved animosity against Amalek is to be remembered (*17–19*).

In Chapter 26 a procedure is outlined for a person bringing a basket of first-fruits to the Temple (*1–11*), and for his paying the

[7] See above, p. 366.

tithe (*12–15*). An exhortation (*16–19*) concludes both the chapter and the legislation.[8] The substance of Chapter 28 is a statement of the blessings (*1–14*) or curses (*15–68*) which are to attend either obedience or disobedience of the laws. With this statement the second of the three addresses is complete.

This long second section can be conceived of as an address only with great difficulty. Those chapters in which the style is terse scarcely conform to the view that we are hearing an explanation of legislation previously delivered; rather, it is as if the legislation were being presented for the first time. On the other hand, the discursive chapters, as has been intimated, are more hortatory than legislative.

Moreover, the sheer length of this discourse, as contrasted with the brevity of the first discourse and of the third (encompassing two chapters, 29 and 30), makes it unlikely that this second section is a single discourse. The detail, especially in the terse chapters, is for the eye and for reference, rather than for the ear and quick absorption.

The supposition of a relationship between Deuteronomy and the Reformation of Josiah in 621 is almost an axiom in biblical scholarship. Nevertheless, a host of problems cluster about the relationship, even when it is accepted. In II Kings 22:*5–13* the account of the discovery of a "Book of the Torah" in the Temple fails to suggest the size of that book. Also, the question of age arises: was it an old book, newly discovered, or was it a new book, conveniently found? If it was indeed Deuteronomy, was it what is today Deuteronomy, or was it only some portion, such as the legislation? Does Deuteronomy exhibit such unity as to lead to the conclusion that it was written by one hand and at a single time? Or are there indications of layers of growth and development, as though the present book represented a succession of writers—what might be called a school of "Deuteronomists"?

All these questions elude definitive answers, yet the indications are that Deuteronomy attained its present form long after Josiah's time, and no earlier than the postexilic period. Yet the earmarks of antiquity attach to enough of the terse legislation to point to an origin well before Josiah.

If we are to accept as valid a connection of Josiah with Deu-

---

[8] We have mentioned Chapter 27 above, p. 392, in connection with its curses, *11–26*. Chapter 28 is usually regarded as the direct continuation of 26, and 27 as an interpolation. It is prescribed in 27:*1–10* that on crossing the Jordan the Hebrews are to plaster great stones and inscribe the laws on them, and, after sacrifice on an altar, hear the blessings and the curses. Chapter 27 contains no blessings.

teronomy, then it is not with all of Deuteronomy but only some portion of it. The terse legislation in general is older, though some of the discursive part may be a product of Josiah's time. Perhaps older legislation was rewritten in Josiah's time so as to emphasize a single central sanctuary and the sole legitimacy of the Jerusalem priests. But the rewritten portion itself must have been added to and expanded long after Josiah's time. Any such explanation is mere hypothesis, however, for the facts can never be truly known.

But what should stand out above all is the boldness of the midrash of which Deuteronomy consists. Meditation on the great role of Moses led to the conception that just before he died he delivered three discourses, and that these discourses were in some way recorded and available. This was midrash at its height of vigorous creativity, for it not only boldly imagined Moses in the most vivid personal self-revelation but went on to include an abundance of laws supposedly emanating from him.

The Deuteronomic laws are without any perceptible system, in marked contrast with P's systematic procedure from the tabernacle and its paraphernalia, through the investiture of Aaron and a priesthood, to the various types of sacrifices. As we saw, especially at the end of Numbers, the pattern disappeared as miscellaneous laws were incorporated. In Deuteronomy, however, no pattern is discernible; there are only motifs and refrains. For, despite the abundance of laws in 12–26, Deuteronomy is not pre-eminently legislative. D is probably *quoting* when the chapters are terse; he is writing his own exhortation when they are discursive. D is, accordingly, not a legislator but an exhorter, a preacher.

The third address (29:1–30:20 Heb., 29:2–30:20 Eng.) supposes that the covenant, made on Horeb with a past generation, must now be renewed. The key words are these:

> But not alone with you do I make this sworn covenant, but both with him who is here standing today before Yahve, and with him who is not here today (that is, later generations). [29:13–14 Heb., 14–15 Eng.]

The covenant is not with mere representatives, but with everybody:

> Your children, your wives, and the stranger in your camp, the hewers of wood, and the drawers of water. [29:10 Heb., 11 Eng.]

The penalties for disobedience are set forth (29:15–28 Heb., 16–29 Eng.); so, too, is the benefit (30:1–10) which may ensue from earnest repentance. That obligation which is being imposed on people is not beyond successful obedience or easy understanding (30:*11–14*). Involved in the covenant is a choice between life and the good, on the one hand, and, on the other hand, death and evil. Israel should love Yahve and cleave to Him (30:*15–20*). The covenant is then renewed.

With the third address, we have reached the logical end of Deuteronomy.[9] We will look presently at the P passages, 32:*48–52* and 34:*1–12* transposed from the Book of Numbers. But first we must grasp the significance of Deuteronomy in its own light.

The Greek name Deuteronomy ("repetition of the Law") is not a good name, for only a few individual laws are here repeated. As we have seen, exhortation precedes and follows the laws, and, furthermore, in most of the legal chapters, especially the discursive ones, we are not dealing with a legislator. We are not being given bare law so much as the significance believed to exist in the laws, or in obedience to them. The emphasis is not so much on bare requirement as on the motive, or reward, for fidelity.

Accordingly, the purpose of Deuteronomy in its present form is scarcely that of providing legislation, and it is an error of interpretation to seek to find a particular and single age or epoch which the legislation represents. Some exhortations are postexilic, reflecting the experience in Babylonia and the return from there. However ancient some of the legislation may be, the present book of Deuteronomy is a postexilic compilation.

The signs of the postexilic period are unmistakable. Israel is spoken of not as usual as an *'am,* a nation, a people, but rather as a *qahal,* a congregation. The entity is a reduced community, no longer extending from Dan in the north to Beer Sheba in the south. Ammonite and Moabite may not join it, but Edomites and Egyptians may; we are past the time of the first missionary movement.[1] The religious purity of the congregation is to be maintained; over and

[9] A series of appendices is present. Chapter 31 is mostly concerned with the transition of authority from Moses to Joshua. In Chapter 32:*1–47* there is found a psalm called the Song of Moses, which declares that Yahve had faithfully guided an only partially faithful Israel in the past; Israel's lapses from fidelity represented sheer stupidity, for their God was unique, indeed the only God. Chapter 33 contains a series of benedictions of the various tribes. The blessings are in context ascribed to Moses, but they are of unknown authorship and date, though presumably from a very early time. Chapter 34, which should be appended to 32:*48–52*, was originally at the end of Numbers (see Num. 27:*12–14*). It narrates the death of Moses in the third person.
[1] See above, pp. 204–205.

over again there occurs the formula, "You shall cleanse the evil from the midst of your people." Evil things, "abominations," are not to be tolerated; indeed, to abominate (Hebrew *ta'ab*) takes on the meaning, "to exclude from the congregation." The attitude towards heathens is most severe, and the worst of all transgressions is apostasy from Yahve. Yet on the other hand, an extensive humanitarianism is to be found in many of the laws and much of the exhortation.

That we are not dealing with genuine legislation—it is to be recalled that the legislation is found in the midst of an address—is proved both by the non-legal language of many of the requirements, and by the presence of material that tends to make a farce of law. The absurd legislation for the conduct of a war (20), or that for recognizing a false prophet from a true one (18:18–22) are cases in point.

Deuteronomy is friendly to the priesthood, but in no sense a Priestly writing. It is ritual purity which commands the recurrent interest of the writers, and not priestly purity. Indeed, in Deuteronomy the priests exist as a "them" who can be discussed and valued highly; in P the priests are "us." It is this observation which has prompted generations of modern scholars to regard the Deuteronomic authors as representatives of prophecy. If we mean by this the recurrent humanitarianism of Deuteronomy, then the term *prophetic* is possibly apt. Yet Deuteronomy is not a reflection of active, contemporaneous prophecy, but rather a harvest of the prophecy of a bygone age.

It is more to the point to regard the author or authors not as prophets but as sages. They are not the coiners of proverbs and aphorisms, but rather teachers with a bent for theology. They are men who write from a particular theological viewpoint: God works in history; obey His laws, lovingly, and He will work good for you; but disobey, and He will work ill for you. The teacher-sages who wrote Deuteronomy were part of a process which has not yet ended today, that of presenting a contemporary message as though it emerged from authoritative figures in the past. The teacher-sages had great regard for other personalities—Joshua, Samuel, David, and Solomon—as well as for Moses. Of their long work, the portion which is now the Book of Deuteronomy is the part that is centered on Moses.

The material on the priests (which calls them Priests—Levites) represents a stage of development earlier than, or different from, the writing of P, in whose conception the priests are a family within the Levites. Also, the calendar of Deuteronomy is both shorter and less precise than P's specific calendar. Deuteronomy comes to us via P; and P edited D.

But it is not to be presumed that P is simply a late and direct successor to D as did the scholarship of two generations ago. Rather, we must conceive of the teacher-sages as constituting a class, perhaps something akin to a guild, which flourished even into the time of the Priestly ascendancy and literary activity. Though in postexilic times the priests ultimately became dominant, and it was they who created the Pentateuch, the teacher-sages and the priests were contemporaries.

The Pentateuch came into existence when the conclusion of the P writing was moved from its original position at the end of Numbers to the end of Deuteronomy.

> Yahve spoke to Moses on that same day, "Ascend this Mount Abarim, the peak Nebo in the land of Moab opposite Jericho, and look at the land of Canaan which I am giving Israel for a holding . . ." [32:48–9]
>
> So Moses went up from the plains of Moab to Mount Nebo, to the top of Pisgah opposite Jericho. Yahve showed him all the land from Gilead to Dan [in the north], and all of Naphtali and the land of Ephraim and Manasseh, and all of Judah to the outer [Mediterranean] sea; and the Negeb [the southern Wilderness], and the plain of the valley of Jericho, the palm city, as far as Zoar [at the south end of the Dead Sea] . . . Moses, Yahve's servant, died there in the land of Moab, as Yahve had said. He [Yahve?] buried him in the valley in the land of Moab . . . but no one has come to know his burial place even today . . . There never arose another prophet in Israel equal to Moses, whom Yahve knew face to face, respecting all the signs and wonders which Yahve had sent him to do in Egypt to Pharaoh, to his household and all his land, and respecting the great power and the tremendously awesome things which Moses did in the sight of all Israel. [Deut. 34:1–12]

Without Deuteronomy, the Pentateuch might have lacked applicability and stirring appeal. Deuteronomy is the peroration which turns an impersonal lecture into a moving, relevant sermon. The author brilliantly concluded his masterpiece with the most perceptive and admirable of all his inclusions.

The Significance of the

PENTATEUCH

THE PENTATEUCH is a handbook. We have already stated its meaning. The essence of Hebrew religion is man's relation to God; the substance is man's obligation to his fellow man. Since conduct is the touchstone for the religious life, the Pentateuch is a guidebook to conduct. Its raw materials are both ancient ritual practices and the more recent and elevated contentions of the prophets and exhortations of the sages. The Pentateuch is an answer to the question: "How shall I, a loyal Israelite who wishes to live in obedience to God's will, translate that wish into my daily living?" Prophetic teaching was abstract; Pentateuchal legislation sought to translate prophetic ideals into living practice. He who obeyed the Pentateuch, even with its ritual, was living in conformity with the ethical standards of the prophets.

The legislation, running from Exodus 20 through Numbers, is preceded by the quasi-history of Genesis and the first half of Exodus, for without the narrative the legislation would have lacked a context and might have become dry-as-dust laws. Instead, the legislation became the climax to which the careers of the ancestors led logically. Just as each of these had made a covenant, so at Sinai their descendants, now a people, had re-entered into that same covenant and re-newed it just before Moses' death, thereby sharing in the high emi-nence of their ancestors. The hortatory character of Deuteronomy, emphasizing that the covenant made in earlier generations extended unbroken to future generations, provided a stirring appeal to the indi-vidual; he was reading not only about his forefathers, but also about himself. Genesis and half of Exodus stirred pride in the ancestors; Deuteronomy persuasively inducted the descendant into their com-pany. In Exodus-Numbers the motive for the legislation is that God has commanded it; in Deuteronomy, it is the love of God which is to be man's motive in observing the commandments.

The Pentateuch was the creation of priests, who wrought even better than they themselves thought or even dreamed. They fashioned a literary work which enfranchised them and the Temple over which they presided; yet their treatment of this literary work eventually made both their institution and themselves unnecessary. That which they created as a manual came to be used as the source of religious authority, and then as an object of veneration quite as sacred as the Temple itself. Scripture was never intended to be a rival to the Tem-ple, but from the perspective of today we can see that that is exactly what it became.

When Jews, after Alexander the Great, moved into the Greek world, they could not build temples where they were, for Deuter-onomy prohibited it. But they took the Pentateuch along with them and they translated it into Greek. It remained, despite their absence from Palestine, their manual for living, their code of laws. Greek or, in later times, Roman law bound Jews and their Pentateuchal laws, but Greek and Roman law were only a broad framework, for Jews continued in their routine needs to be regulated by the Pentateuch. Hence the Temple was for them a remote, ideological institution which they occasionally visited, but the Pentateuch was with them always.

So also in Palestine, the Temple and its priesthood tended to be the institutionalized form, but the Pentateuch was the living religion. The Temple was the center of the routinized worship; the Pentateuch was the center of the living religion. The Temple was scarcely an apt subject for meditation, day and night, as Deuteronomy 6 describes the contents of the Pentateuch to be. The Temple was where certain aspects of religious requirements could be carried out; the Pentateuch could stimulate and be the object of study, thought, and devotion. Once the Pentateuch was created, a unique phenomenon developed in Judaism, the identification of study and worship as interchange-able aspects of the same process. The synagogue was the place where the Pentateuch was taught and studied; the rabbi ("teacher") was the instructor. The Temple was destroyed in A.D. 70, and with it the Priestly cult also came to an end. But Scripture abided, for it, and not the Temple, had become the true center of Judaism.

The origin of the various laws, in judicial decisions, decrees, or statutes is lost sight of in the Pentateuch, for they are all subsumed under Torah. When law and Torah became identified, law ceased to be the function merely of the lawyer and became the province of every man. Deuteronomy has not one word to say to lawyers. Rather, it insists that every man can know the Torah. Moreover, the Torah is presented (Deut. 6:5–9) as something that should be in the heart; it should be taught to sons, be discussed at home and away from home, late at night and early in the morning. The Pentateuch was Torah, not law.

The
DEUTERONOMIC
HISTORIES

THE LONG SEQUENCE from Deuteronomy through Kings has a literary history in which three elements are blended together. First, there are ancient written sources, both secular history and folk tales. Second, these sources were utilized by the Deuteronomists, a series of writers of similar mind and attitude. Third, all of the Deuteronomists' work was available to P writers. The principal reflection of P in the book of Deuteronomy is the transfer, described above, of the death of Moses from the end of Numbers to the end of Deuteronomy. Much of the latter half of Joshua is P, but P appears only sporadically in Judges, Samuel, and Kings.

The ancient sources, identified tentatively by some scholars as continuations of J and E, are of various kinds. The Deuteronomists make frequent reference to "The Books of the Chronicles of the Kings," either of Israel or of Judah. In II Samuel 9–20, there is an account of the court of David which reads as though it were actually written by an eyewitness; the cycle of Samson stories, on the other hand, appears to be ancient folklore. The Book of the Upright, a poem or collection of poetry, is also quoted. There is a very old piece of secular, anthologized history preserved in Judges 1:1–2:5.

These and other ancient sources were used by successive generations of Deuteronomic writers in the construction of their theological history of Israel. Onto the ancient sources the Deuteronomists superimposed their view of God's action respecting Israel in the past, thereby pointing to what Israel should do in the present and future. So relatively few are the Priestly additions [1] that the import of the Deuteronomists is felt fully throughout the sequence of writings.

One speaks of successive generations of Deuteronomists, for the viewpoint varies. There are different attitudes expressed, for example, towards kingship. So, too, there is an admiring assessment of Saul together with thoroughgoing detestation. Midrashic embellishments created, or recast, legends about the great worthies. As in the Pentateuch, a later writer did not expunge something with which he disagreed but simply added his own viewpoint.

The Deuteronomic writers, then, were a school who used sources of varying antiquity and varying reliability in their theological interpretation of Israel's past. It was said above that the age of the Patriarchs can be regarded as prehistory, while the period beginning with the Conquest by the Hebrews of Canaan is historical. For the latter period accounts are confirmed by both biblical and extra-biblical sources contemporaneous with the events; this is not true of the patriarchal narratives. Yet the contention that we are dealing with more reliable history beginning with the period of the Conquest must be qualified. Our inherited accounts are more reliable, but are by no means completely so. Indeed, theological motifs are so abundant that they counterbalance the purely historical material. And even in the material that is admittedly historical, there are many knotty problems.

The Deuteronomists saw a marked distinction between the period of the Conquest and that of the Settlement. Yet many modern scholars would disagree. Thus, the Deuteronomists set forth (in the portion that became the Book of Joshua) that under a great leader a single and thorough conquest of Canaan took place, and even those tribes that had chosen to dwell in areas east of the Jordan had taken

---

[1] Source analysts often allot to P a great portion, though not all, of Joshua 15–24, along with such short passages as 13:15–33. In Judges they allot to P primarily portions of 20 and 21. In Samuel and Kings, P is usually limited to brief passages, a half-verse, such as I Sam. 2:22B, or a verse and a half, such as 2:35B–6.

part in Joshua's conquest. Furthermore, according to the Deuteronomists, once Canaan was conquered and the tribal lands were appor-
tioned, the unity prevalent under Joshua gave way to a loose confederation of autonomous tribes, the leaders of which were "Judges."

Both of these ideas as presented by the Deuteronomists are open
to question. Joshua 15 describes the apportionment by Joshua of land
to the tribe of Judah; it relates that the Judahites had been unable to
dislodge the Jebusites from Jerusalem—yet Judges 1:21 tells that it
was the Benjaminites who had been unable to do so. But Judges 1:1–7
tells that Judahites and Simeonites smote Adonibezek and brought
him to Jerusalem to die, implying that these tribes had some power
over Jerusalem. Joshua 10:1 ascribes to Joshua a defeat of Adoni-
zedek, King of Jerusalem; in the Greek translation the man is known
as Adonibezek. The problem, then, is whether Joshua, in a presumed
single conquest, took power over Jerusalem too; or whether that city
was conquered by people other than Joshua; and, indeed, whether the
conquest had to await the time of David, as we read elsewhere. The
Deuteronomists, accordingly, give us a writing which attributes a single total conquest to Joshua, attributes to others than Joshua the
conquest of Jerusalem, and then contradicts both by deferring the
conquest to David's time so as to credit it to him.

Again, respecting the Conquest, Joshua 11:1–11 credits Joshua
with the conquest of the city of Hazor, while Judges 4:1–24 allocates
the conquest to the later time of Deborah. In Judges 1:13 the conqueror of Kiriath Sepher is Othniel (so, too, Joshua 15:17); but in
Joshua 10:38–9 it is Joshua himself who is the conqueror. There can
be no question but that there was a tendency to ascribe to Joshua victories won by others. Since the other victors, Deborah for example,
presumably did not live in Joshua's time, it is not possible to harmonize the contradictions merely by saying that the Deuteronomists
attributed to Joshua the conquests of his lieutenants.

A single conquest by Joshua, then, is probably an idealization
of the events. The Deuteronomists, who had said repeatedly in Deuteronomy that Israel need not fear to invade, for Yahve would go before them to fight for them, were not reluctant to depict a very easy
and simple conquest. The P writer who had promised that a hornet
would clear the way for invading Israel (Exod. 23:28; see also
Deut. 7:20 and Josh. 24:12) only increased the supposed ease of conquest. The modern historians who discount a single conquest regard
Joshua as one of several leaders in a gradual infiltration and conquest of Palestine, either by single tribes carving out a place in a
restricted area, or by several tribes doing so in concert. The period of

50 MILES

THE

GREAT

SEA

Sidon

Tyre

Achzib

Beth-anath

MT. CARMEL

Dor

Megiddo

Taanach

Dothan

HILL

COUNTRY

Tirzah

MT. EBAL

Shechem

MT. GERIZIM

Aphek

Joppa

ISRAEL

Beth-
horon

Gezer

Ajalon

Ekron

Ashdod

Ashkelon

Gath

Lachish

Eglon

Gaza

Gerar

Beersheba

Rehoboth

Hormah

Aroer

SOUTH

Ziph

COUNTRY
(NEGEB)

MT. LEBANON

LEONTES

MT. HERMON

Laish
(DAN)

Hazor

Merom

LAKE HULEH

SEA OF GALILEE

YARMUK

PLAIN OF ESDRAELON

MT. TABOR

PLAIN OF JEZREEL

Shunem

JORDAN

Damascus

① THE JORDAN WAS MORE A
BOUNDARY THAN A BARRIER,
AND THE REGION WEST OF
THE SYRIAN DESERT WAS
LARGELY ONE AREA, NOT
TWO. HEBREW TRIBES
SETTLED ON BOTH SIDES
OF THE JORDAN.

Karnaim
Ashtaroth

B A S H A N

Edrei

Ramoth-gilead

G I L E A D

JABBOK

Mahanaim

Rabbah

A M M O N

② CANAAN WAS MOSTLY TINY
KINGDOMS, OFTEN OF ONLY
ONE TOWN, BUT ALSO OF
SEVERAL, LIKE THE
PHILISTINE TOWNS.

Bethel
Ai

HILL

Gibeon

Jericho

Heshbon

Bezer

MT. NEBO

Medeba

COUNTRY

Jerusalem

Bethlehem

OF

Hebron

JUDAH

SALT

SEA

Dibon
Aroer

City of Moab

ARNON

Arad

Ar

M O A B

T H E   S Y R I A N   D E S E R T

Zoar

BROOK ZERED

E D O M

**PRE-ISRAELITE
CANAAN**

TRM

the Judges is, from this viewpoint, not that of Settlement but that of initial conquest and settlement.

The Deuteronomists were, as historiographers, schematizers. They arranged the material available to them to conform to their scheme. They had depicted Moses as renewing with the Israelites, just prior to the conquest, the covenant made at Horeb with the preceding generation. Leadership now passed to Joshua, who was to have an easy conquest and thereafter to renew the covenant again.

How did the Deuteronomists schematize the period presumably after Joshua's time? Traditional material told of other heroes and of the rise of kingship under Saul; it also told of tribal confederations. The Deuteronomists conceived of an interval, extending from Joshua to Saul, marked by leaders but not, as yet, by a king. For these leaders they used, or possibly even created, the title *Judges*.

The actual history of a long period of sporadic settlement and of piecemeal conquest was converted by the Deuteronomists into the two periods, Conquest, under Joshua, and subsequent Settlement, under the Judges. Just as the Deuteronomists conceived of Joshua's conquest theologically (that is, as an easy, divinely led conquest), so too they conceived of this artificial later period of the Judges theologically, namely as a series of cycles, moving from fidelity to Yahve to apostasy from Him, punishment and the need of redemption, fidelity again, apostasy again, and punishment and redemption again. What is remarkable in this schematized history is the good measure of reliable, indeed verifiable, material which shines through the theology.

CHAPTER

34

JOSHUA

THE ACCOUNT of Joshua's entry into and conquest of Canaan is rather brief. The Deuteronomic portion is primarily Chapters 1–12, and 22:1–6 and 23; later, P writers expanded the Book of Joshua into its present twenty-four chapters.

A brief summary reveals the conception of the easy conquest of Canaan. With the death of Moses, Joshua assumed command of the Israelites, 1:1–9; the Jordan was crossed, 10–11; the tribes destined to settle east of the Jordan were to join in the conquest of the region to the west, 12–16. The first city to be attacked was to be Jericho, so spies were now sent there who were helped by a prostitute named Rahab (2). At the crossing of the Jordan, the waters, swollen because it was the wet season, were cut off through Yahve's miraculous intervention so that the Israelites crossed on dry land. The priests preceded the people and they carried the ark containing the Two Tablets (3). Twelve stones (indicating the twelve tribes) from the bed of the Jordan were set up in mid-Jordan in memory of the miraculous crossing (4:1–11), and then the river resumed its flowing (4:15–18). At Gilgal, twelve more stones were set up to memorialize the crossing of the Jordan, so reminiscent of the crossing of the Red Sea [1] (4:19–24).

---

[1] Two etiological legends now follow. The first (5:1–8) accounts for a place name, *Gibeath Ha-'areloth*, "mountain of foreskins," possible a place where in

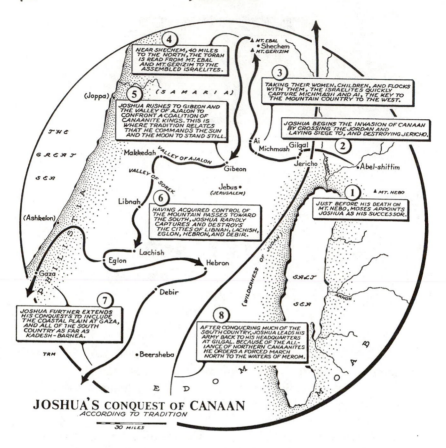

JOSHUA'S CONQUEST OF CANAAN
ACCORDING TO TRADITION

30 MILES

The attack on Jericho followed soon after. There appeared to Joshua the "commander [2] of Yahve's army," presumably to advise but actually to lead the assault on Jericho (5:*13–15*). Miraculously the walls of Jericho fell, enabling its easy capture; the account of this is one of the best-known stories in the Tanak (6).[3] Though Jericho was

---

ancient times circumcisions were held. The second (5:*9*) suggests that the place name *Gilgal* ("circle") derives from a root meaning "roll away." Then Passover is observed 5:*10–13*.

[2] Possibly the miraculous fall of Jericho's walls has blotted out an earlier account of a conquest led by this "commander." He fades quickly from the account.

[3] The account is composite. One layer (6:2, 3, 5B, 7, 10, 12A, 14, 15A, 16B–17) supposes that Israelite soldiers marched about Jericho daily for six days; on the seventh Joshua gave a signal and the soldiers rushed in to destroy the city. In the other, younger account, which seeks to recast the older one, seven priests carrying seven horns encircle the city seven times, apparently on the same day; at the blast of the horns, at which the people set up a great shout, the walls tumble down (6:4, 5A, 6, 8–9, 11, 12B–13, 15B–16A). The recasting of the story of Jericho is motivated by the wish to increase the miraculous and thereby to emphasize Yahve's role in the capture of Jericho.

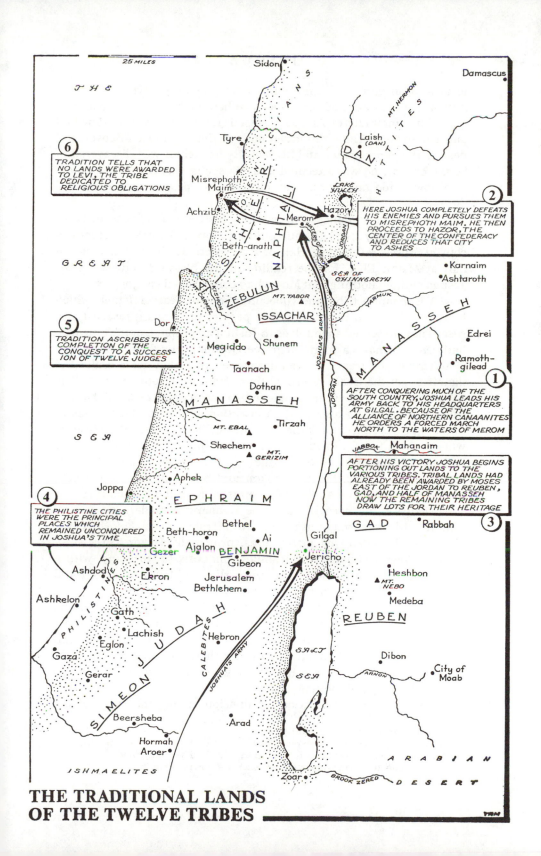

THE TRADITIONAL LANDS
OF THE TWELVE TRIBES

25 MILES

THE
PHOENICIANS

Sidon

Damascus

MT. HERMON

Tyre

Laish
(DAN)

HITTITES

DAN

⑥ TRADITION TELLS THAT
NO LANDS WERE AWARDED
TO LEVI, THE TRIBE
DEDICATED TO
RELIGIOUS OBLIGATIONS

Misrephoth-
Maim

LAKE
HULEH

② HERE JOSHUA COMPLETELY DEFEATS
HIS ENEMIES AND PURSUES THEM
TO MISREPHOTH MAIM. HE THEN
PROCEEDS TO HAZOR, THE
CENTER OF THE CONFEDERACY
AND REDUCES THAT CITY
TO ASHES

Achzib

Hazor

Merom

WATERS OF MEROM

JORDAN

Beth-anath

NAPHTALI

MT. NAPHTALI

GREAT

SEA OF
CHINNERETH

Karnaim

Ashtaroth

⑤ TRADITION ASCRIBES THE
COMPLETION OF THE
CONQUEST TO A SUCCESS-
ION OF TWELVE JUDGES

Dor

ZEBULUN

MT. TABOR

ISSACHAR

MT. CARMEL

KISHON

YARMUK

Edrei

MANASSEH

Ramoth-
gilead

Megiddo

Shunem

JOSHUA'S ARMY

① AFTER CONQUERING MUCH OF THE
SOUTH COUNTRY, JOSHUA LEADS HIS
ARMY BACK TO HIS HEADQUARTERS
AT GILGAL. BECAUSE OF THE
ALLIANCE OF NORTHERN CANAANITES
HE ORDERS A FORCED MARCH
NORTH TO THE WATERS OF MEROM

Taanach

Dothan

SEA

MANASSEH

Tirzah

MT. EBAL

Shechem

MT.
GERIZIM

JORDAN

Mahanaim

JABBOK

③ AFTER HIS VICTORY JOSHUA BEGINS
PORTIONING OUT LANDS TO THE
VARIOUS TRIBES. TRIBAL LANDS HAD
ALREADY BEEN AWARDED BY MOSES
EAST OF THE JORDAN TO REUBEN,
GAD, AND HALF OF MANASSEH.
NOW THE REMAINING TRIBES
DRAW LOTS FOR THEIR HERITAGE

Aphek

Joppa

EPHRAIM

④ THE PHILISTINE CITIES
WERE THE PRINCIPAL
PLACES WHICH
REMAINED UNCONQUERED
IN JOSHUA'S TIME

Bethel

Beth-horon

Ai

GAD

Rabbah

Gezer

Ajalon

BENJAMIN

Gilgal

Gibeon

Jericho

Ashdod

PHILISTINES

Ekron

Jerusalem

Bethlehem

Heshbon

MT.
NEBO

Medeba

Ashkelon

Gath

JUDAH

Hebron

REUBEN

Lachish

CALEBITES

Eglon

Dibon

Gaza

SALT

City of
Moab

Gerar

SEA

ARNON

SIMEON

Beersheba

ARABIAN

Arad

Hormah
Aroer

DESERT

ISHMAELITES

Zoar

BROOK ZERED

to have been destroyed, and none of its properties seized, a certain
Achan had appropriated some spoils. When, next in the order of conquest, the small city of Ai was besieged, the Israelites were defeated
and put to rout. Yahve informed Joshua that he must discover and
destroy the appropriator and his loot. By lot Achan was discovered to
be the culprit; he was executed and his spoils burned. A new attack
was now made on Ai, and the city and its people were destroyed
(7:1–8:29).

Then, in accordance with previous instructions (found in Deut.
11:29–32 and 27:1–8), Joshua built an altar and wrote on stones a
copy of Moses' revelation.[4] Half of Israel were at Mount Gerizim and
half at Mount Ebal, for the reading of the blessing and the curse.
Joshua omitted nothing that Moses had commanded (8:30–5).

A Canaanite tribe, the Gibeonites, out of fear of Israel, which
had now overtaken the other native peoples of Canaan, resorted to a
ruse. They presented themselves to Joshua as people from far off who
had come to make a treaty of peace. Joshua, though initially suspicious, made the treaty. It was discovered that they were really Canaanites; yet the treaty protected them from being put to death. The
Gibeonites were, however, consigned to the menial tasks of hewing
wood and drawing water [5] (9). A coalition of five southern kings of
Canaan proposed to attack the Gibeonites. These appealed to Joshua,
who set forth to help them. Yahve assisted him with a deadly rain of
hailstones. Moreover, on that same day the sun stood still. The five
kings fled to a cave, but were taken and put to death. Joshua conquered southern cities, the hill country, and the Negeb (11).

Then the northern kings of the Canaanites made a confederation. A battle was fought at the stream Merom, in which Joshua was
victorious. He destroyed many cities, principally Hazor (11:1–15).
There follows a summary of Joshua's conquests (11:16–23), with a
list of the kings, first those defeated earlier by Moses (12:1–6) and
then those defeated by Joshua (12:7–24).

It is to be noticed that the account of the conquest of Jericho
takes up five chapters, that of Ai one, and that of the Gibeonites one.
One chapter is devoted to the narrative of the more extensive southern
conquest, and a half-chapter to the northern conquest. Hence, we
must conclude that we are not really given any genuinely rounded
historical account of the conquests.

Chapters 13–21 [6] describe the division among the tribes of the

---

[4] We are left uncertain as to what this was.
[5] The point of this story is to explain how it was that some Canaanites survived
the Conquest, even though their full extermination had been enjoined.
[6] These are mostly P; D resumes either in 22:1–6, or possibly in 23.

country conquered up to this point. Joshua summoned the Reuben-
ites, Gadites, and half of the Manassehites, permitting them to re-
cross the Jordan and to settle there (22:1–6). He then assembled all
Israel, made a farewell address, attributing his great victories to
Yahve, and enjoined an unwavering loyalty to the Deity [7] (23–4).

Those who wrote Deuteronomy through Kings were interested in
great personalities. Joshua is second to Moses in their view, and
hence they devote so much attention to him.

The feeling of the Book of Joshua towards the Canaanites is neither
generous nor, by any respectable standards, admirable. It calls to
mind the attitudes of the American colonists, especially of those who
pressed westward, toward the Indians. The sentiment "there is no
good Injun but a dead Injun" was deeply ingrained in our American
mentality. A recognition of this blemish in ourselves may possibly
give us some perspective towards evaluating the equally bloodthirsty,
and equally deplorable, attitude attributed to the immigrant Israelite
tribes. The attitude cannot be condoned, but the intent of the biblical
authors needs to be understood. They were relating what they believed to be the history of God's people doing God's will. The Canaanites, in their view, had never done anything but oppose God's will. It
was the Canaanites' misdeeds that brought about their downfall, for
Yahve was punishing them and Israel was Yahve's agent. To Yahve
the Canaanites had become justly hateful, and hence Israel must also
hate them.

There is little religious affirmation to be found in this unrelieved
animosity. What religious note there is seems limited to a recognition
on the part even of the biblical writers of the wrongness of the animosity. They did not, however, try to expunge the animosity from
the account, but rather attempted to justify it by developing the view
(found also in Gen. 15:19) that the Canaanites had earned Yahve's
displeasure.

[7] The death of Joshua comes at the end of Chapter 24. Note that Judges 2:7–9
repeats Joshua 24:30–1, while the opening words of Judges 1:1 relate to the
death of Joshua. These repetitions point to a series of editorial actions needed
to blend the parts into a growing whole.

JUDGES

THE SETTLEMENT—which the Deuteronomists artificially separated from the Conquest [1]—is the substance of the Book of Judges. More properly, the English translation of the title should be "The Book of Rulers"; the Hebrew word *shoftim,* "judges," means rulers as well. Indeed, the book focuses persistently on personalities who have in common little more than that they were the heroes of times of distress. The Book of Judges could appropriately be called "The Book of the Great Deliverers." The true beginning [2] of the Book of Judges is 2:6; its true ending is Chapter 16.[3] The beginning is a clear statement of a cyclical view of history (2:6–3:6) to which we now turn.

From the standpoint of those who compiled the book, the Settlement was an era of chaos. Unified leadership had died with Joshua.

---

[1] See above, pages 421–422.

[2] Judges 1:1–2:5 is quite an ancient piece describing tribal conquests; it was interpolated into its present position after Joshua-Judges had already been written. The interpolator preceded this piece by copying Judges 2:8–9 and inserting it into Joshua 24 as verses 29–30. When Joshua was separated from Judges, there was prefixed to this ancient account still another notice of Joshua's death (Judges 1:1), giving us a total of three such notices. Judges 1:1–2:5 is a fragment of a very early chronicle, composed no later than the tenth pre-Christian century.

[3] Chapters 17–21 are joined by some scholars to 1:1–2:5, as if they came from the same ancient document. I doubt that they do, though both sections are quite ancient.

Hence, there is introduced in Judges a theme, significant not only for Judges but also for Samuel and Kings, that the prevalent religious anarchy could be overcome only through a king. The Book of Judges argues that had there been a king the distresses that necessitated the Great Deliverers would not have developed. A king would have been able to prevent the self-willed acts of people. Prosperity, according to the authors, led to license, and license was equivalent to apostasy from Yahve, and Yahve punished the disobedient by having them harassed or conquered. Then a Great Deliverer arose who destroyed the enemy. Ultimately, thereafter, prosperity returned, but since there was no king, prosperity again led to apostasy, apostasy to punishment, and punishment to the need of another Great Deliverer. Since this "cyclical view" of events is schematized writing, its substance consists of materials of different kinds, used and shaped to fit the predetermined scheme.

The first Great Deliverer was Othniel [4] ben Qenaz. Of him no more is here related than that he delivered Israel from the Arameans (3:8–12). We shall note that several other Great Deliverers are mentioned, whose careers are not described. We move on from Othniel to the Great Deliverer, Ehud ben Gera. This time it is the Moabites, under King Eglon, who oppress apostate Israel. The story of Ehud is a rollicking one. Ehud's tribe was Benjamin, which means "son of the right," but Ehud was left-handed. Ehud brought to Eglon the payment of tribute due him. (Presumably, since Ehud is left-handed, the palace guards searched him for arms as though he were right-handed, and thereby overlooked a short dagger.) Ehud asked for a private interview with Eglon, who was very fat. When Ehud then stabbed Eglon, the hilt followed the blade in, and the fat closed in on the weapon! Ehud made his escape, and led Israel to a conquest of the Moabites. Tranquillity followed for eighty years [5] (3:12–30).

The next oppressor was Jabin, king of the Canaanite city, Hazor.[6] Jabin had a general, Sisera. Deborah, a prophetess, summoned a leader, Barak, to gather men to contest with Sisera near the stream Kishon. Barak's men waited on Mount Tabor, near the Kishon, and attacked successfully at a judicious moment. Sisera fled, finding what he thought was a refuge in the tent of a woman named Jael.[7] While

---

[4] Othniel is mentioned in Judges 1:13 as the conqueror of Debir; see also Joshua 15:17.
[5] Judges 3:31 tells briefly—very, very briefly—of one Shamgar ben Anath, who slew 600 Philistines. He is mentioned, passingly again, in Judges 5:6.
[6] See above, p. 422.
[7] Her husband, Heber, was a descendant of Moses' father-in-law, Judges 4:11.

he slept, Jael killed him by driving a tent peg into his head[8] (4–5).
The land now had rest for forty years.

The two preceding accounts are brief. Now comes the story, a
long one (6:1–8:35), of Gideon. The Midianites and Amalekites had
been raiding from the desert, ruining crops. An angel of Yahve appeared to Gideon, a young farmer, with instructions to overthrow the
Midianites. Gideon asked for a miraculous sign to prove that the
commission was indeed a divine one, and he received it.[9] Gideon's
father had an altar to Baal; Gideon destroyed it. The people of the
vicinity wished to kill Gideon, but his father retorted that Baal should
contend against Gideon! Thereupon Gideon was named Jerubbaal
("Baal contender").

The foe, meanwhile, was encamped in a fertile valley (Jezreel,
at the east of the plain of Esdraelon). Gideon needed another sign of
divine assistance and received it[1] (6). Gideon and his troops, encamped, were so numerous that Yahve feared they might attribute a
victory to themselves instead of Him. Therefore the army needed to
be pruned down.[2]

Gideon and his servant entered the foe's camp to spy. They over-
heard a Midianite relate a dream,[3] which a companion interpreted as
Yahve's intention to turn the Midianites over to Gideon. Gideon now
attacked and routed the foe.[4] He pursued them into Ephraimite territory. At Gideon's call, the Ephraimites now joined against the enemy
(7), but were angry at having been called in so late. Gideon, through
his self-effacing modesty, appeased them (8:1–3). He pursued the
foe across the Jordan—the cities of Sukkoth and Penuel refused him
supplies—and captured the Midianite kings. He punished the leaders
of Sukkoth[5] and destroyed the town and the people of Penuel

[8] As we saw above, pp. 34ff., the "Song of Deborah" is the oldest writing in the
Tanak; Chapter 4 is a late prose version which concludes by reproducing the old
poem. The Deuteronomists had both versions, and they used both.
[9] The angel caused fire to consume some food which Gideon had prepared.
[1] He laid fleece on the ground where threshing was done. The ground was dry
and without dew, but the fleece was wet enough that when it was squeezed
the water filled a bowl.
[2] First, the fearful—twenty-two thousand soldiers—were sent home. Next, those
who, at a stream, knelt to drink the water were also sent home; these numbered 9700 out of ten thousand. Only those who lapped water like a dog were
retained; these numbered three hundred.
[3] The dream (7:13) tells that a barley cake rolled into the Midian camp and upset a tent.
[4] He divided his army into three groups. The soldiers carried trumpets and jars;
in the jars were burning torches. At the attack, the trumpets were blown, and
the jars broken, so that the torches could be seen. The foe fled in terror.
[5] Just how is uncertain. The text says, "He took wilderness thorns and briers and
with them taught the men of Sukkoth." Did he torture them to death?

(8:4–17). The Midianite captives, it appears, had previously slain Gideon's brothers.[6] Gideon now slew them.

Then Gideon gathered from his people the golden earrings taken from the Midianites and made an ephod,[7] a source of later disaster. But there was tranquillity for forty years.

Gideon had seventy legitimate sons and also other children, of whom one was Abimelech. After Gideon's death, Israel reverted to Baal worship (8). Abimelech found support for his ambitions in his mother's city, Shechem.[8] He slew the seventy legitimate sons, except for the youngest, Jotham.[9] The Shechemites crowned Abimelech king. Three years later the Shechemites vainly rose against Abimelech, who burned the town and its people. When Abimelech conquered Tebez, twelve miles northeast of Shechem, he approached its tower. A woman threw a millstone which crushed his skull, and he knew that he would die. He asked his slave to kill him, to avoid the disgrace of dying at a woman's hands. This was the retribution for the murder of his seventy brothers (9).

The heterogeneous stories—the amusing story of Ehud, the miracles done for Gideon, the military ardor of Deborah, and the gruesome account of Abimelech—have no real unity; it is only the editorial framework that binds them together. Moreover, the subsequent narratives add to the heterogeneous character of Judges. The individual narratives are told each with great gusto. Indeed, these stories are so colorful that a clear distinction between fact and fancy is often elusive. Yet although much of the material is folklore or legend, it nevertheless provides us with a good and reliable glimpse of conditions and situations, much as a modern novel can illuminate an age and environment. In their use of this material, the Deuteronomists blur the past but do not blot it out, for legend and folk tale reflect times, places, and conditions with real fidelity.

Two more Great Deliverers, Tola and Jair, are only mentioned (10:1–5). Then attention shifts to an unusual man, Jephthah. Again the occasion for the necessity of deliverance is set forth: apostasy

[6] The narrator had forgotten to include this in the early part of the story. Or, better, the adaptor omitted the item, but forgot that he had done so and referred to it later.

[7] Exactly what an ephod was is not known, beyond the fact that it was a cult object. The same name may perhaps have been applied both to a sacred vestment and to a statuette.

[8] Aspersions of Shechem probably reflect the anti-Samaritan sentiment of the postexilic period. See below, page 463.

[9] In a parable Jotham characterized Abimelech as worthless: Worthy trees—olive, fig, and grape-vine—are sheltered under the shade of a bramble, a useless plant.

from Yahve has brought oppression, this time from the Ammonites
(10:6–18). Jephthah, an illegitimate son whose mother was a prostitute, was banished from his home in Gilead by the legitimate sons of
his father. He dwelled in Tob (the location of which is uncertain),
where he gathered worthless people about him. With the Ammonites
threatening, however, he was summoned home, and asked to become
the leader, and told that, if he was victorious, he would be named the
head of the Gileadites (11:1–11).

Jephthah and the king of Ammon exchanged communications
about the proper rights to disputed territory, but the Ammonite was
bent on war. Jephthah swore to Yahve to offer to Him as a holocaust,
if victory were granted, whatever would first come out of his house on
his return. Jephthah was victorious, and when he returned home it
was his daughter—her name is not given—who came out to greet
him. In great emotion he told her of his oath. She recognized that he
could not break it[1] and asked only for a delay while she went to the
mountains with companions to "lament her virginity," that is, that
she was to die childless. Then Jephthah carried out his oath[2]
(11:12–40). The dramatic story is told with moving simplicity. Seldom has such deep emotion and vivid characterization been expressed
in so few words.

Now the Ephraimites, piqued that Jephthah had not summoned
them to assist against the Ammonites, attacked him and were routed.
When Jephthah's men intercepted fugitives who out of fear denied
being Ephraimites, they were put to a test. This consisted of pronouncing the word *shibboleth;* the Ephraimites were accustomed to
pronounce the word *sibboleth.* Those Ephraimites who were betrayed
by their mispronunciation were slain (12:1–7).

Three more Great Deliverers are mentioned briefly: Ibzan of
Bethlehem, Elon the Zebulonite, and Abdon, apparently of Ephraim
(12:8–15). Now attention turns to Samson, and at some length
(13–16). Here, as in the case of Jacob, a tale about a folk hero has
become transformed into a religious story. Accordingly, Samson's
birth and his achievement are given a significance at variance with
some of the bare facts set forth, for midrashic embellishment was at
work. The folk tale told of a man with a strong back and a weak mind;
the religious tale was about another Great Deliverer.

It was the Philistines[3] who now troubled Israel, again because of

[1] See Num. 30:2 and Deut. 23:21–2 on the unbreakability of oaths.
[2] It is added (11:39–40) that it became customary for Israelite girls to lament
for Jephthah's daughter four days each year. No further reference is found in
the Tanak to this strange bit of folklore.
[3] Emigrants from Crete, they settled on the coast of Canaan about the thirteenth pre-Christian century. The name *Palestine* came from the word Philistine.

Israel's apostasy from Yahve. Before Samson was born, Yahve's angel appeared to his mother—she is unnamed—with instructions that when she bore her son, he was to avoid wine and hard liquor, eat nothing prohibited, and never cut his hair.[4] She told this to her husband Manoah, who prayed that the angel might return and instruct the parents how to raise the child. So the babe Samson was born, and Yahve's spirit began to stir him (13). It is so far the tale of the birth of a hero.

But our Samson proves to be the stupid but powerful character of folklore (14). On his way to a city, Timnah, a lion attacked Samson when he was unarmed, but Samson slew it.[5] In Timnah he saw a Philistine girl,[6] whom he asked his parents, when he presumably went home, to acquire for him.[7] Again he returned to Timnah, and, in passing the corpse of the lion, found in it bees and honey. He scraped the honey into his hands, eating as he went; he then gave his parents some of it.

When it was time for the wedding Samson made a feast, and to thirty "companions" present he told a riddle, promising a good reward for whoever could guess it:

> From out the eater came something to be eaten,
> From the strong came out something sweet.

The companions could not guess the riddle. They threatened Samson's bride, who, weeping, enticed the answer from him and related it to them. They gave Samson the riddle's solution, and he said:

> If you had not plowed with my heifer
> You would not have solved my riddle.

To pay the promised reward, Samson went to the Philistine city of Ashkelon, slew thirty men, and gave their clothes to the thirty companions (14).

---

[4] One so set apart is a "Nazirite." There are Nazirite laws in Numbers 6:1–21; another requirement is found there, that the Nazirite must have no contact with a corpse. Samson appears here to be a Nazirite for life; in Numbers a Nazirite appears to have been under an oath for only a restricted period.
[5] The strong man in various folklores (e.g., Hercules) slays a lion with bare hands.
[6] There are difficulties in the text, which says that Samson *and his father and mother* went to Timnah. He had asked them to go and acquire the girl. They are depicted as all going together. Moreover, father and mother do not figure in the episode.
[7] This wish on the part of a Great Deliverer to marry outside the fold troubled the editor; he ascribed it (14:4) to Yahve's wish, for Yahve was looking for an excuse to punish the Philistines!

Next, it appears that Samson and his wife had been separated. He went to visit her to exercise his marital rights, but her father informed him that she had now been taken by somebody else; in her place he offered Samson a younger daughter. Angered, Samson caught three hundred foxes, joined them by the tails, tied some burning brands to each pair of tails, and sent the foxes into the grain fields and vineyards of the Philistines. The Philistines in anger slew Samson's wife and father-in-law. Samson, in turn, slew a great many Philistines (15:*1–8*). Now the Philistines sought retaliation. Samson was in Judean territory. The Judeans, to escape the ravages of war, bound him and handed him over to the Philistines. When Samson was brought to the Philistines, he broke the bonds, found the jawbone of an ass, and with it as a weapon slew a thousand men (15:*9–20*).

In Gaza, another Philistine city, Samson was spending the night with a harlot. The Gazaites awaited him, intending at morning to ambush him and slay him. But Samson left the harlot at midnight and made his escape from the city by pulling up the gate and gateposts, putting these on his shoulders and departing (16:*1–3*).

Samson now came to love a woman named Delilah. Possibly herself a Philistine, she was given the task by the Philistines of discovering the source of Samson's great strength. He told her that he would become weak like any other man if he were bound with seven bowstrings. She bound him with the bowstrings—presumably when he was asleep—but he promptly broke them (16:*4–9*). She tried again to learn his secret. This time he replied that if he were bound with new and unused ropes he would be weak. She used new ropes; he broke them like a thread (16:*10–12*). Next, he told her to weave seven locks of his hair with the web of the spinning loom. This too failed to weaken him (16:*13–14*).

Delilah reproached him for not truly loving her and she nagged him incessantly. Finally he told her that he was a Nazirite, and that his strength lay in his uncut hair. When Samson fell asleep, Delilah had his hair cut off. Now that his strength was gone, the Philistines seized him, gouged out his eyes, and took him to the prison at Gaza. There his hair began to grow back (16:*16–22*). The Philistine nobles gathered for a festival in honor of their god, Dagon. Samson was brought to the temple to be mocked at. He found the moment to dislodge the pillars, causing the temple to crash on the Philistines and on him. In his death he slew more people than he had slain in his lifetime (16:*23–31*).

· · ·

With the conclusion of the story of Samson, we are at the end of the account of Great Deliverers. The Book of Judges, however, goes on, for later Deuteronomic hands appended some additions, which we will turn to presently.

The narratives of the Great Deliverers cannot by any stretch of the meaning of the term be called history. History may lie behind Jephthah, Gideon, and Ehud, but in the case of Samson it is more likely to be myth (without historical basis) than legend (with some remote historical basis). Samson as a name is related to the Hebrew word for sun; his hair is analogous to the rays of the sun, for when there are no rays the sun is without strength.

Seven of the Great Deliverers are merely listed; there are tales about only five. That the total of Deliverers adds up to twelve suggests editorial schematization, as if the seven were listed only so as to achieve a number equivalent to the traditional number of the tribes. In these folk tales, the moral and religious values are found, if at all, in the introductions and summaries and not within the stories themselves. (Samson is deficient by even the most modest of standards, and is even lower if measured by the standards expressed in other parts of Scripture.) The editors who incorporated these tales did not greatly alter them from within; they only introduced and followed them with their moralizing. The result is that Judges presents us with the paradox of religious exhortation buttressed by narratives with little or no religious content. The determination of the Deuteronomic editors to show us that the Settlement period without a king was chaotic led them to string together the five folk tales and to append seven names. In the absence of monarchy, each person "did what was right in his own eyes." In the case of Gideon, he commendably refused to rule (8:22–3). His son Abimelech, a half Canaanite, usurped the kingship of the town of Shechem, but in no sense was he a king over all Israel.

What Judges tells us, in effect, is that the Great Deliverers were necessary because kingship had not as yet arisen in Israel. The sequel to the account of the Great Deliverers is found in Samuel, the next book of the series. The stories about Samuel should come immediately after the tale of Samson.

The intervening chapters between Samson and Samuel (Judges 17–21) break the sequence, for we no longer deal with the cycles and the Great Deliverers. Yet these appendices have a tremendous value for the student interested in religious development. They are ancient materials, reproduced in late times with a minimum of editing. More-over, they are not folk tales or legends but documents much more reliable historically.

The first appendix (17–18) tells how the tribe of Dan relocated itself and built a sanctuary. This came about in the following way: A certain Micah, an Ephraimite, had stolen eleven hundred pieces of silver from his mother. The money, if restored, was to be used for some sacred images. Micah restored the money, the images were made, and one of Micah's sons was installed as priest. But a Judahite wandered in, a Judahite who was a "Levite." [8] He was from Bethle-hem.[9] He was engaged to preside over the sanctuary (17).

The tribe of Dan, looking for a place to settle, sent out spies. These visited Micah's priest, and recognized him—just how they did is not stated. The spies were impressed by a city, Laish, settled by Phoenicians, and the Danites set out to capture it. On the way, the spies suggested that the Danites consult Micah's priest. The army therefore paused at Micah's place. They invited the priest to accom-pany them and to serve as their priest. Micah was powerless to do anything in retaliation. The Danites attacked and captured Laish,

[8] The term creates a problem. See above, pp. 167–168. To repeat here, if Levite is a tribal name, how can a person be simultaneously a Levite and a Judahite? Levite must in this context be a sacred functionary. This particular Levite was indeed a priest. At one time priest and Levite were synonyms. Levite as a term for a subordinate functionary represents a later period when priest (*kohen*) and Le-vite had become differentiated. Our Judahite here apparently lacks the family qualifications elsewhere insisted on as part of the right to be a priest.

[9] The text adds "and he dwelled there." But the Hebrew letters, if divided differ-ently (*vehu gar shom*) can yield the sense, "and he was Gershom" (*vehu gershom*). Gershom is mentioned in 18:30 as the father of the priest. Some schol-ars want to emend "he dwelled there" to read, "and he was Jonathan ben Ger-shom."

As for this Gershom, 18:30, in giving us the name of his father, offers a scribal peculiarity the effect of which I try to reproduce in English consonants (it is to be recalled that ancient Hebrew was a consonantal alphabet, and vowel signs were added at a very late time): GRSHM BN M^{N}SHH. Note that the N is not in alignment; in Jewish biblical notes, the N is called "suspended."

Without the N, the father of Gershom would be MSH, Moses. With the N, the father would be Manasseh. What is the function of "suspending" the N? Is it an afterthought, changing the reading from Moses to Manasseh, and is the correct reading Moses? Or is the N suspended so as to emphasize that the name is Manasseh and must not be misread as Moses? Why would such a misreading take place? Because in Exod. 2:22 and 18:3 Moses had a son named Gershom.

To accept the reading of Moses implies an overthrow of much that is hard and fast in traditional history and chronology. Presumably the Settlement period lasted 410 years, a sum resulting from adding up the periods of "judgeship" given in the book. If Jonathan is Moses' grandson, four hundred and ten years have scarcely elapsed. Moreover, Moses is represented in several passages as the great-grandson of Levi; how could Moses' grandson be a Judahite?

Such are the problems that arise in any open-minded effort to extract solid history from the accounts in the Tanak, such as those in Judges.

giving it the new name Dan (18). This brief chronicle tells us where the Danites settled and how their sanctuary was established. The major trace of the Deuteronomic editor is his comment in 17:6 and 18:1 that there was no king in Israel and each man "did what was right in his own eyes."

The second appendix is a long and bloody tale. A Levite sojourning in Ephraim had a concubine who was from Bethlehem in Judah. Angered at him, she left him and went to Bethlehem for fourteen months. He visited her to become reconciled, and her father provided a series of feasts. The couple finally departed, arriving at nightfall at Jebus, the old name of Jerusalem. The girl would not spend the night there, for Jerusalem had not been conquered and hence was not an Israelite city. Instead they pushed on to Gibeah, in Benjaminite territory (19:1–15). An old man welcomed them into his home (19:16–21). The riffraff surrounded the house (as in the story of Lot, Gen. 19:5) and demanded to have the Levite for homosexual purposes. The old man offered them, instead, his virginal daughters and the concubine, but they did not want them. The old man, however, pushed the concubine out of the house, and the riffraff abused her until morning (19:22–6).

When in the morning the Levite came out of the house he found the concubine lying at the threshold dead. He brought the corpse to his home in Ephraim. Then he cut up her body into twelve pieces and he sent them to the twelve tribes to stir them up against the perpetrators of the disgraceful act (19:27–30). Four hundred thousand men assembled at Mizpah. They heard the Levite's account, and affirmed that they would not go home until they had avenged him (20:1–11). They demanded that the Benjaminites turn the offending riffraff over to them, but the Benjaminites refused. Thereupon they attacked the Benjaminites. The Benjaminites repelled this initial attack, and a later attack was also beaten off. But the third attack, accompanied by a ruse, was successful. The Benjaminites were defeated, pursued, and decimated (20:12–48).

The tribe of Benjamin was on the verge of extermination, for an oath had been taken by the others not to permit their daughters to marry the surviving Benjaminites. To prevent a whole tribe's extermination, women had to be provided for them; it was determined that these were to come from among the Gileadites who had not joined the rest of Israel in the battle against Benjamin. Thereupon, Jabesh-Gilead was attacked. All the inhabitants were slain except for four hundred virgins. These were captured and turned over to the Benjaminites. But four hundred were not enough (21:1–18). Accordingly, it was arranged that when an annual festival at Shiloh was to take place, and the girls of Shiloh came out to the vineyards to dance, the Benjaminites would seize the girls; such seizures would not be the same as arranged marriages, and the oath would therefore not apply. By this device, the tribe of Benjamin was renewed (21:19–23).

There is history behind this legend. The ending is folklore, and the explanation of a confederation against, and an attack upon, Benjamin as due simply to the violation of the Levite's concubine is questionable history. The figures given for the size of the respective forces are not to be taken seriously. But the existence of an actual historical confederation against Benjamin is quite plausible.

The accounts of Dan and Benjamin reveal a primitive state of ethics and religion. The editors of the Book of Judges, however, do not interrupt the accounts to condemn the participants; they do not need to. The events speak for themselves.

Denunciation and not glorification is the editors' purpose in including these accounts. For they return to their theme at the close of the appended materials:

> In those days there was no king in Israel, and each man did what was right in his own eyes.

The stories of disreputable people and shocking events illustrate the theme that kinglessness is anarchy; this is why they are appended to the accounts of the Great Deliverers. These stories gave form and substance to the artificial distinction between Conquest and Settlement.

CHAPTER

36

SAMUEL
AND KINGS

THE EMINENT FIGURE of Samuel serves the Deuteronomic editors as
the key, in their view of history, to the transition from the disorgani-
zation of the Settlement period to the rise of monarchy. The Books of
Samuel and Kings are an account of the significance of monarchy to
the religion of Israel. Today the account is divided into four "books,"
First and Second Samuel, and First and Second Kings; the Greek version names the books better as I–IV Kingdoms.[1]

The nub of the books is kingship, and all else, except for the
personalities involved, is subsidiary. Samuel-Kings was initially written in the days of Josiah (d. 608), who represented to the editors a
great and constructive king. At that time, especially in the light of
Josiah's Reformation in 621, kingship seemed as great a blessing to
Israel as had been the Great Deliverers of earlier times. At one stage
in the literary growth of these books, the achievements of Josiah led
to what might be called a first edition of Samuel-Kings. This edition

[1] The text of Samuel-Kings offers many problems; some of these are being solved
by fragments found in the Dead Sea Scrolls.

traced kingship from its origin under Saul, through the transfer of monarchy to David, to the achievements of Solomon, and, after the division of the kingdom into two (the North, Israel, and the South, Judah), the merits or demerits of the many kings. Two procedures, which seem traceable to this first edition, are worthy of note. First, the figure of Samuel seems to be in part a Great Deliverer, like the other Judges, and possibly the material on Samuel was detached from a previous position within Judges, to be brought now into relationship with monarchy. Since the biblical editors seldom expunged but often added materials, Samuel is presented as a protagonist of prime importance in his own right, but he is also subordinated first to Saul and then to David. Secondly, David was regarded as so pre-eminent that the theme—the significance of kingship to Israel—tends to be obscured by the sheer abundance of material on David, the inclusion of which seemed irresistible to the editors.[2] The David material includes legends (some contradicting each other) and midrashic embellishments, but also some unique ancient sources. Moreover, the partiality for David results in an ambivalence towards Saul, who is portrayed as a man overcome by jealousy to the point of villainy, while he is also eulogized as a great hero.

But the history after Josiah's time was one of disaster, encompassing invasion, subjection, and finally exile. From the vantage point of this later time, kingship was not nearly as appealing as it had earlier seemed. Early in the postexilic period a second edition, as it were, was issued. It carried the narrative beyond Josiah to the days of Jehoiachin, the king in exile. In customary fashion the second editor did not erase what he objected to, but neutralized it by additions. Especially in I Samuel, there are long chapters opposing kingship as an improper institution, and interpreting the desire on the part of the people to have a king as apostasy from God. Kingship, in this altered view, is seen as a curse, not a blessing.

Accordingly, viewpoints in Samuel-Kings clash and contradict each other. The antimonarchy chapters seem oblivious of the theme recurrent in Judges that a king was an urgent necessity. David and Solomon are both idealized and also severely criticized. The great

---

[2] This literary disproportion is discernible even statistically: Samuel-Kings numbers 112 chapters. Samuel is the subject of eight chapters (I Sam. 1–8), Samuel and Saul, eight (9–16); David is introduced in I Sam. 17 and is the protagonist through the remainder of I Samuel (17–31), throughout II Samuel (twenty-four chapters), and into I Kings 2. Saul, of course, is present in I Sam. 17–II Sam. 1, and Samuel appears passingly, but David is unquestionably the center of attention. Solomon is dealt with in I Kings 2–11; II Kings 12–25 reviews the reigns of some thirty-six kings or regents. Thus, of the 112 chapters, David is the subject of approximately forty. These forty chapters cover one man's life; the 112 chapters nearly half a millennium.

Solomon is interpreted as the culprit responsible for the division of the monarchy. The editors seem to find it here recurrently necessary to explain why it was that the privilege of building the Temple was withheld from David and given to Solomon. The abundance of the material on David, with long sections reproduced from ancient sources without Deuteronomic comments, tends to obscure the true character of Samuel-Kings. If, however, one were to skip from the account (the first of two) of David's anointing, in I Samuel 16, to I Samuel 31, the death of Saul; from there to II Samuel 5, David's election as king by the tribes, and the summary of his reign, to the account of his death in II Samuel 2, then the restored perspective will bear out that Samuel-Kings is an interpretation of kingship and not a history of it.

The events of Solomon's reign are glossed over; the primary attention is to his building of the Temple. His wars are rarely mentioned, but the editors found room for legends about his wisdom. The division of the kingdom was ordained, we are told, by Solomon's infidelity to Yahve. We move immediately to thumbnail sketches of the subsequent kings. Curiously, the editors spend time and space on the prophets Elijah and Elisha, but leave the literary prophets, except for Isaiah, unmentioned. Generally, a king is mentioned, his reign is briefly summarized, and judgment is passed on him according to whether or not he was faithful to Yahve. Not one northern king is praised; most southerners do not fare much better, though some, such as Josiah, do.

It is only slightly to be lamented that the elaborate inclusion [3] of the material on David obscures the Deuteronomic philosophy of kingship. It is a small price to pay, for there is a richness in the material about David which makes it more precious even than the rest of Samuel-Kings. On the one hand, as literature it rises to the eminence of the best prose in Scripture; on the other hand, the reliability of the material is high, so that we are in possession of a remarkable insight into the religion, the morals, and the human failings of the time.

In the light of the long interpolations about David, Elijah, and Elisha, it is to be concluded that the literary history of Samuel-Kings (like that of the other Deuternomic writings) presents us with its own variation of the usual pattern of the narrative books: ancient sources, a succession of editors, and some minor interpolations by P.[4]

[3] See note 2 above.
[4] By and large, P did little interpolating. The Book of Chronicles is a Priestly rewriting of the period covered by Samuel and Kings (though extended both into earlier and later times); it is as though the Priestly authors felt that to write a totally fresh account was preferable to editing an account they considered unsatisfactory.

SAMUEL

The editors of the first edition, in their partiality to kingship, considered it to be Yahve's will as revealed through one of His prophets. Tradition had told of a Great Deliverer named Samuel, who had become a leader in the time of a Philistine invasion.[5] But Samuel was, or came to be, conceived of as more than a Judge; he was a prophet. He had been dedicated to Yahve even before his birth. His mother Hannah, when childless, had prayed in the Temple at Shiloh for a son. Eli, the priest (pathetically for Hannah), had misinterpreted her trembling lips, moving in silent prayer, as a sign of drunkenness, and he had rebuked her. But Yahve blessed her with a son, Samuel.[6] When the boy was weaned, she brought him to Eli to serve him.

Prophecy was rare in those days. Hence, when Yahve called to the lad Samuel at night, Samuel was sure it was Eli. Three times Yahve called to Samuel, and Samuel rushed to Eli. Now Eli understood that it was Yahve calling. Indeed, all Israel came to know that Samuel was a reliable prophet.[7]

But some interpolations slow up the momentum of the Deuteronomists' narrative. An old account of how the Israelites improperly brought the Ark of the Covenant into the battle lines, and of the plagues which the Ark caused the Philistines, takes up some three chapters; only at the very beginning (4:1) and the very end (7:3ff.) is the story of the Ark brought into relationship with Samuel.

The story of Samuel continues in Chapter 9. There it is related how Saul's father had lost some asses. Saul set out in search of them. He wondered if perhaps the prophet, now in the vicinity, could tell where the asses were. A day earlier Yahve had disclosed to the prophet—it was Samuel—that He was sending Saul to him to be anointed as a *nagid*, "prince." Accordingly, Samuel anointed him (9–10:16). When the Ammonites attacked Jabesh-Gilead, which lay across the Jordan, Yahve's spirit animated Saul[8] so that he undertook

[5] See I Sam. 7.

[6] In her piety, it was appropriate for her to have thanked Yahve. Chapter 2:1–11 is, accordingly, a psalm attributed to her. However, its content is unrelated to the context.

[7] A P editor found it distasteful that Eli, who was not a descendant of Aaron, should be a priest. He recast portions of Chapters 2 and 3, so that Eli's reputation remains high, but priesthood passes from his family. Eli's sons are wicked (2:12–17); a "man of god" visits Eli to inform him of Eli's lack of a proper ancestry, of the impending death of his sons, and the impending appointment of an eligible person, whom we interpret as Zadok, a priest of David (2:22–36). The P editor appears to have substituted a prediction of the end of Eli's line for some other content in Yahve's first revelation to the lad Samuel (3:11–17). These alterations virtually exhaust P's editing of Samuel-Kings.

[8] As a result of his anointment.

leadership against the Ammonites. He had support from both north and south. A dawn attack routed the foe. Saul thereupon was confirmed as king, both by the people and by Samuel (11).

But we must look at the material not yet summarized: Chapter 8 sets forth that Samuel was old and his sons were worthless. Accordingly, all the elders of Israel gathered around Samuel, and, in their anxiety about the future, proposed that Samuel—he seems more a Judge than a prophet—appoint someone as king to succeed him. Samuel was displeased, but Yahve now spoke to him, telling him that the wish for a human king was equivalent to rejection of Yahve as king. Samuel, therefore, was to explain to the people what kingship would mean. He did so:

> This is the way of the king who will reign over you. Your sons he will take, appoint them for his horsemen,* and they will run before his chariots. He will designate to his benefit officers over thousands, and officers over fifties, to plow his plowing and harvest his harvest, and make his weapons and his chariot parts. Your daughters he will take for spice mixers, butchers, and bakers. He will confiscate your fields, your vineyards, and olive groves, and give them to his [own] servants . . . If you cry out some day against the king whom you have chosen for yourself, Yahve will not answer you on that day. [I Sam. 8:11–18]

Obdurately the people insisted on a king. This insistence Samuel reported to Yahve, and Yahve instructed Samuel to accede to their wishes. This chapter reflects a very late attitude, a time when monarchy was regarded as a catastrophe to Israel.

Similarly, 10:17–27 depicts Samuel as telling the people that it was Yahve who brought them out of Egypt and saved them from the many oppressors. It was Yahve who was their deliverer. It was He Whom they were rejecting in wishing for a king. So, too, in Chapter 12, Samuel sets before the people and their newly anointed king his own unspotted record as their judge. He reviews the history of Israel and Yahve's deliverances. However, the people have demanded and received a king. If henceforth Israel would be obedient to Yahve, she and her king would abide; if, however, she were disobedient, she and her king would come to an end.

These late interpolations, a product of the second edition, reverse the thesis of the first edition and also the explicit attitude in the Book of Judges.

As a byproduct of the present antimonarchy chapters, the reader encounters ambivalent attitudes to Saul. At the end of I Samuel, Saul dies in battle against the Philistines. From an ancient source, the

Book of Yashar,[9] there is quoted David's eulogy over Saul and Jonathan:

> . . . *Saul's sword never returned empty.*
> *Saul and Jonathan were beloved and pleasant in their lives.*
> *In their deaths they were not separated.*
> *They were swifter than eagles,*
> *They were stronger than lions.*
> *O daughters of Israel, weep over Saul* . . . [II Sam. 1:22B–24A]

There is, then, a strand that was favorable to monarchy, one that depicted Saul as Yahve's choice and culminated in David's moving eulogy. But the other strand, which regarded kingship as a misfortune, naturally assessed Saul in an unflattering way.

This shift in attitude becomes emphasized by the adulation accorded to David. It can well be that history lies behind the accounts of Saul's great hostility to David. Yet the compilers of Samuel-Kings have assembled both legends and history, and it is often difficult to disentangle the two. This is especially the case in the description of the beginning of the relationship between Saul and David.

DAVID

The prelude to the introduction of David is a story told of a misdeed of Saul's (I Sam. 13–14). War is being waged with the Philistines. At one juncture (13:7B–15A) Saul was at Gilgal waiting for Samuel, but Samuel was delayed. Saul thereupon offered a burnt sacrifice. The text here does not specify in what way this was a misdeed; we know, however, that the Deuteronomists regarded a single central sanctuary as the only valid place for sacrifice. When Samuel arrived he chided Saul for not having kept Yahve's commandment; accordingly, his dynasty was to pass to someone else whom Yahve would choose.

The narrative into which this account was interpolated runs its course [1] (13–14). Chapter 15 is the sequel to the interpolation (13:7B–15A), mentioned in our preceding paragraph. Saul had been enjoined to smite the Amalekites, but, disobediently, he had preserved the Amalekite king alive (15:1–9). Yahve therefore repented [2]

---

[9] See above, pages 45ff.

[1] A legend, 14:24–46, told of Saul's curse on whoever would eat; Jonathan, unaware, ate honey, but was spared the curse. A summary of Saul's achievements, apparently ancient, is in 14:47–52.

[2] 15:11. That Yahve would repent was theologically offensive to an interpolator who inserted the statement in 15:29, that Yahve was not a man and therefore not subject to such repentance.

that He had made Saul king. Samuel informed Saul of Yahve's decision, ignored Saul's plea for forgiveness, and himself slew the Amalekite king.

Now we are given a first introduction to David, in a legend
(16:*1–13*) which relates that at Yahve's word Samuel went to Bethlehem to visit a certain Jesse who had many sons. These were brought
before Samuel, but he refused to select any of them. Told that the
youngest, David, was away, Samuel sent for him. Yahve instructed
Samuel to anoint David. He did, and Yahve's spirit now animated
David. There ensues immediately a different introduction, a product
of the growth of the legendary. According to 16:14–22, Saul was
subject to fits of melancholy. On being told that a musician might
dispel his moods of depression, Saul ordered that one be brought to
him. This musician was David.

We have now entered into the stories and legends about David.
Chapter 17 is the account of his slaying the Philistine giant, Goliath.
His only weapon was his sling; he wore no armor, for when Saul's
was put on him he was unable to move because of its weight. Also, the
reward offered to the slayer included the hand of Saul's daughter.
The careful reading of I Samuel 17 discloses that it is composite.
Verses *12–31* and *55–8* suppose that David had not yet made Saul's acquaintance; he had not yet come to the court, but was still at home.
Three older brothers were in Saul's army. David was sent by Jesse
with food for them. He went into the trenches and heard the taunts
of Goliath. He inquired what would be the reward for slaying Goliath,
and the fact of his inquiry was brought to Saul, who sent for him.
David volunteered to fight Goliath. Saul as yet did not know who
David was; only when David brought him Goliath's head did Saul
learn. The other account (*1–11* and *32–54*) supposes that David and
Saul already know each other [3] (through David's musicianship at the
court).

We read in II Samuel 21:*19* that the slayer of Goliath was a certain Elkanan. Legend transferred the achievement to David; growing
legend took two forms—the one of making the Goliath incident the
occasion for the meeting of Saul and David; the other, since they have
presumably met, ascribes it to a development in David's life at the
court.

We cannot know how much history lies behind the accounts of
the personal conflicts of Saul and David; we cannot know whether
Saul's melancholy is historical or only legendary. The multitude of

[3] Verse 17:*15* is a gloss designed to unify the two conflicting accounts. It tells
that David went back and forth to feed his father's sheep at Bethlehem.

tales about David, in addition to obscuring the leading motif of Samuel-Kings, also robs us of an impartial assessment of Saul.

As the narrative proceeds, it tells of the friendship of David with Saul's son Jonathan, and of Saul's jealousy, destined to grow even greater. As to the daughter whose hand David presumably had won, Saul's eldest, Merab, was promised to David but withheld from him. Another daughter, Michal, is depicted as loving David; Saul found in Michal a tool for his jealousy of David and gave her to David. How much history is there here? Is Merab the editor's device for portraying Saul as a promise-breaker? Is Michal the compiler's device for disparaging Saul and all his family? We cannot know.

A legend, obscene by our standards, has Saul set as a price for Michal (though he already owed one daughter to David by his previous promise) not a sum of money, but the foreskins of a hundred Philistines. David delivered these (18). Jonathan now intervened with Saul on David's behalf, but Saul soon lapsed into jealousy again. A tale, meant to be hilarious, depicts Saul as sending agents to the home of David and Michal to seize David. With Michal's connivance, David feigned illness and escaped. She gained time for David by putting the *teraphim* [4] in his place in his bed, having told the agents that David was sick (19:1–17).

The derogation of Saul continues. Saul pursued David to Ramah and there joined up with loathsome whirling dervishes and acted like them (19:18–24). His mad jealousy was so unrelieved that on one occasion he threw his javelin at David. Now even Jonathan was convinced of Saul's evil intent towards David (20). The ensuing chapters tell of David's further flights and Saul's pursuits. The priest of Nob fed David; therefore Saul had the priest and all his family slain (20–2). Saul next pursued David near Keilah, where David had defeated some Philistines. David fled to Ziph; there too Saul pursued him. David fled to Maon; again Saul pursued him, desisting only when he needed to return to face the constantly threatening Philistines.

But again Saul pursued him, this time to the Wilderness of En Gedi. A legend, intended to be funny, and again by our standards obscene, relates that Saul went into a cave to defecate; David stealthily cut off part of Saul's skirt. When presently David showed the skirt to him, they were reconciled. Saul's recognition of David's magnanimity in sparing his life led him to acknowledge to David that the monarchy was to pass to him (24). A different version, unmarred by uncouthness, has Saul pursue David to the Wilderness of Ziph; David and a

[4] These may have been the household gods, statuettes. Rachel, as we saw above, pp. 340–341, stole Laban's *teraphim*.

companion stole into Saul's camp and took his spear and canteen. When Saul learned this, the two were reconciled. (The reconciliations in one chapter do not seem to have precluded pursuit in the next; the legends of the pursuit were merely strung together.)

Chapter 25 suggests an answer to the question of how David sustained himself while in flight. A rich man, Nabal, refused David food. Nabal means "fool." Nabal's wife, Abigail, brought David the food prepared for Nabal and his sheep shearers. She told David: "His name is Nabal, and that is what he is!" After Nabal died of a stroke, David married Abigail.[5]

But a note at the beginning of Chapter 25 tells us that Samuel has died. This is skillful preparation for the episode to be told in 28. David had fled to the Philistines, to King Achish (21:11–15), and had been captured by this Achish. He had feigned insanity, and was therefore released by Achish, who demanded of his men, "Don't I have enough lunatics around here already?" (21:11–16 Heb., 10–15 Eng.) Now, as if the editor was oblivious of this account of David's clever escape, David found refuge with Achish, and was even given a city, Ziklag,[6] for headquarters from which to raid in the south (27). But Achish prepared to fight Israel, and David was presumably to accompany him. The lieutenants of Achish objected, so David remained in the land of the Philistines.

The peak of the editorial antagonism to Saul appears in this account. Saul had exterminated all wizards, but his fearful desperation was such that he sought out a witch at En-Dor. She raised Samuel's ghost at his request. Samuel, far from reassuring Saul, rebuked him and foretold that Saul would die the next day (28:3–25). The Philistine invasion led by Achish (27, 28:1–2, 29, and 31) was triumphant. Saul slew himself by falling on his sword. Three sons, including Jonathan, died.

The news of Saul's death came to David at Ziklag. His informant was an Amalekite whose story (at variance with the above account of Saul's suicide; perhaps there is the intention to substitute the derogatory death at the hands of the Amalekite for the "honorable" death by suicide) was that the Amalekite himself had dealt the death blow to Saul. The Amalekite paid for his story (if not for his action) by

[5] He has as wives at this point Abigail and Ahinoam; his wife Michal had been given to one Palti [el] ben Laish.
[6] Chapter 30 is a long account, probably with a strong historical kernel, of David's activities at Ziklag. It is much out of place in its present position, interrupting the account of Saul's death, 27–9 and 31.

death at David's hands (II Sam. 1:1–16). Now the compiler quotes from the Book of Yashar the celebrated eulogy by David (17–27).

David consulted Yahve, with the result that he went, with his wives, to Hebron. There the Judahites anointed him king (II Sam. 2:1–4). Saul's surviving son, Ishbosheth (also called Ishbaal) became king over some northern and Transjordan regions. David remained in Hebron for seven and a half years (5–11). Here and in what follows we seem to have reliable history of a period in which David reigned over the south and Saul's offspring reigned over the north. A skirmish took place between David's troops under Joab and those of Ishbosheth under Abner (6–32) in a war that lasted "a long time" (3:1). A list is given of David's sons; he had, at this stage, six wives, four of whom we meet here for the first time (2–5).

Abner quarreled with Ishbosheth and prepared to defect to David (and David reclaimed his erstwhile wife Michal from her present husband).[7] Joab, however, slew Abner, in revenge for the slaying of Joab's brother in the skirmish mentioned above (3). Ishbosheth was weakened by the defection of Abner, and two of Ishbosheth's captains killed him and brought his head to David. David promptly slew them.[8]

Now the northern tribes came to Hebron, and David was anointed king over both north and south (5:1–3). At this stage we are given, curiously, a summary of David's reign, both at Hebron and in Jerusalem (4–5). Up to this point Jerusalem seems still to have been unconquered; the authors now tell us of that conquest (6–9) and of the greatness David attained (10). More summary notes—notes, not narration—are included (11–16), among them the birth of Solomon, the narrated account of which comes much later.

The text reverts to narration, and again gives an account of war with the Philistines (5:17–25). The Ark of the Covenant (as though forgotten after the events related by an old source in I Sam. 4–5) was brought to Jerusalem (6); again we are in an old source.[9] Next, however, the Deuteronomists of the first edition are reflected. David had built a house of cedar; the Ark was still kept in a tent. A prophet, Nathan, appeared to David with a message from Yahve: Yahve had no need of a Temple of Cedar; He was giving respite from foes and tranquillity to Israel; a son of David would build the Temple; and David's dynasty would last forever (7). We

[7] Above he was called Palti. Here his name is given as Paltiel.
[8] The chapter (verse 4) mentions a surviving son of Jonathan, a cripple named Mephibosheth.
[9] This antiquity is attested by the peculiar narrative of David's naked dance before the Ark, an act which brought about his estrangement from his wife Michal (6:20–3).

shall encounter very little more of the Deuteronomists until after we read of David's death in I Kings 2.

In Chapter 8 an old source is again preserved. It summarizes David's conquests and his officials. Another ancient source, probably by someone of, or close to, David's court, runs from Chapters 9–20. The predilection to quote ancient material about David was a happy one, for a unique and magnificent chronicle is preserved for us. This eyewitness chronicle is a literary document of superlative quality, especially in respect to its understanding of human motives and reactions. Since it is told with simplicity, it has great emotional force, and produces a strong sense of tension.

The first two chapters of this chronicle can be considered as atmospheric. David, in generous recollection of his friendship with Jonathan, invited to his palace Jonathan's surviving son, the crippled Mephibosheth.[1] Though David tried to conciliate the neighboring Ammonites, he was forced into war with them and with their allies, the Arameans (9–10). But in the midst of the campaign, an incident took place in Jerusalem. From the roof of his palace, David saw a beautiful woman bathing herself. Her name was Bathsheba, the wife of Uriah, a soldier away on the campaign. She became David's mistress, and then she became pregnant. David summoned Uriah from the battle-lines[2] and sent him back to the fray with instructions to the general, Joab, to put Uriah into the thick of battle. Uriah, accordingly, was killed. Then David, to Yahve's displeasure, married Bathsheba (11). The prophet Nathan denounced David to his face[3] —here the hand of the Deuteronomist is evident. The child of Bathsheba died. A second son, Solomon, was born to David and Bathsheba. The Ammonites were now conquered, with David participating in the final siege of the Ammonite capital (12).

Next (13–19) there comes the touching and tragic account of Absalom and the grief he brought to his father David. The bare outline cannot do justice to the story. Absalom and Tamar were brother and sister. Another son, Amnon, a half-brother to the two, fell in love with Tamar. Amnon raped Tamar; two years later Absalom slew him in revenge. Then Absalom fled to the neighboring king of Geshur

[1] The name is given in I Chron. 8:34 as Meribaal. *Bosheth* means shame; it is a common biblical substitution for *baal*, as in Ish*bosheth*.
[2] A succession of editors can be discerned. On the one hand, David is regarded critically. On the other hand, Bathsheba did bear Solomon, so that she needed some favorable portrayal. Hence in the summoning home of Uriah by David, the point is made (13) that Uriah had no sex relations with Bathsheba on this furlough.
[3] Nathan tells a parable of a rich man who stole a poor man's lamb. David was righteously furious, demanding that the man be punished. Nathan said, "You are the man."

(13). David, sorely longing for Absalom, was prevailed on by his general Joab to bring Absalom home. Absalom's sole punishment for the murder of his half-brother was the deprivation of contact with David; yet after two years, father and son began to see each other again (14).

Absalom began to conspire against David. He established himself in the hearts of people and went from Jerusalem to Hebron proposing to lead a movement from there to seize the kingship. So great were his forces of rebellion that David was compelled to flee from Jerusalem for fear that Absalom would successfully attack him. Absalom occupied Jerusalem (15) and following the counsel of one Ahithophel, he appropriated David's concubines in order publicly to signify that he had seized the kingship (16). David fled across the Jordan and Absalom and his followers went in pursuit (17). In the battle, David's forces were triumphant. Absalom, who had long hair (14:26), tried to ride past an oak tree and was caught by his hair. Joab hastened to the place and slew Absalom. When the news of his rebellious but deeply beloved son was brought to David, he was filled with profound anguish (18). The chronicle is vibrant and alive, for it concentrates more on David's sorrow than on the complex details of Absalom's rebellion.

Now David was again fully accepted as king over all of Israel, though jealousies between the ten northern and the two southern tribes were smouldering (19). The last incident in the chronicle is that of another rebellion of which a certain Benjaminite, Sheba ben Bichri, was the leader. Joab was sent to put it down. He laid siege to a city named Abel where Sheba was. On the advice of an old woman, the residents cut off Sheba's head and threw it to the besiegers. Joab called off the siege and returned to Jerusalem [4] (20:1–23). This ancient chronicle (II Sam. 9–20) is only the most important of a series of miscellanies about David. The others occupy the remaining chapters in II Samuel.

The Gibeonites (Josh. 9:3–27) had been promised that they would be spared extermination. Saul, however, had tried to exterminate them. To win their loyalty, David acceded to their suggestion that seven of Saul's surviving [5] sons be given to them to hang (21:1–15). Warfare arose again with the Philistines. David was nearly slain in battle, so it was determined that henceforth he should not venture into the fray [6] (21:15–17). Chapter 22 is virtually identical with

---

[4] There follows, 20:24–6, a short list of David's officials.
[5] The impression of II Sam. 9, however, is that Mephibosheth was the only survivor of Saul's family.
[6] Four giants (including Goliath) were slain by David's men after the decision that David should not venture into battle (18–22).

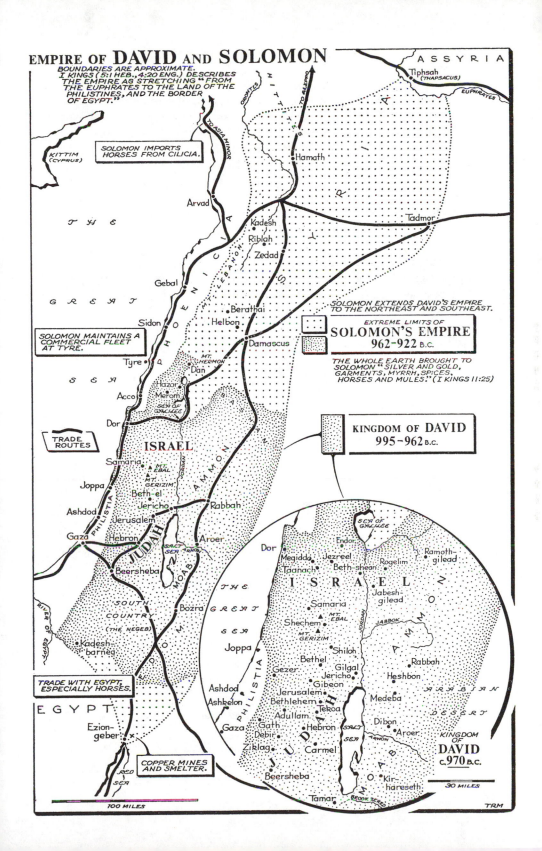

EMPIRE OF **DAVID** AND **SOLOMON**

BOUNDARIES ARE APPROXIMATE.
I KINGS (5:1 HEB., 4:20 ENG.) DESCRIBES
THE EMPIRE AS STRETCHING "FROM
THE EUPHRATES TO THE LAND OF THE
PHILISTINES, AND THE BORDER
OF EGYPT."

ASSYRIA

Tiphsah
(THAPSACUS)

EUPHRATES

KITTIM
(CYPRUS)

SOLOMON IMPORTS
HORSES FROM CILICIA.

ORONTES

TO ASIA MINOR

TO ALEPPO

HITTITES

Hamath

R

Arvad

PHOENICIA

Kadesh

Tadmor

Riblah

LEBANON

Zedad

Y

Gebal

Berathai

SOLOMON EXTENDS DAVID'S EMPIRE
TO THE NORTHEAST AND SOUTHEAST.

THE
GREAT

Helbon

Sidon

EXTREME LIMITS OF
SOLOMON'S EMPIRE
962–922 B.C.

SOLOMON MAINTAINS A
COMMERCIAL FLEET
AT TYRE.

Damascus

Tyre

MT.
HERMON

Dan

THE WHOLE EARTH BROUGHT TO
SOLOMON "SILVER AND GOLD,
GARMENTS, MYRRH, SPICES,
HORSES AND MULES." (I KINGS II:25)

SEA

Acco

Hazor
Merom
SEA OF
GALILEE

Dor

KINGDOM OF **DAVID**
995–962 B.C.

TRADE
ROUTES

ISRAEL

BASHAN

Samaria

MT.
EBAL
MT.
GERIZIM

JORDAN

AMMON

Joppa

Beth-el

Ashdod

Jericho

Rabbah

Jerusalem

PHILISTIA

Aroer

Gaza

Hebron

JUDAH

SALT
SEA
ARNON

Beersheba

MOAB

THE

SEA OF
GALILEE

Endor

Dor

Ramoth-
gilead

GREAT

Megiddo

Jezreel

Beth-shean

Rogelim

SOUTH
COUNTRY
(THE NEGEB)

Bozra

EDOM

Taanach

I S R A E L

Jabesh-
gilead

SEA

Samaria

Z

Shechem

MT.
EBAL
MT.
GERIZIM

JABBOK

A
M
M
O
N

Kadesh-
barnea

RIVER OF EGYPT

Joppa

Shiloh

Y

PHILISTIA

Gezer

Bethel

Gilgal

Jericho

Rabbah

Gibeon

Heshbon

TRADE WITH EGYPT,
ESPECIALLY HORSES.

Ashdod

Ashkelon

Jerusalem

Medeba

ARABIAN

E G Y P T

Bethlehem

J U D A H

Adullam

Tekoa

DESERT

Gaza

Gath

Hebron

Dibon

Ezion-
geber

Debir

Ziklag

Carmel

SALT
SEA

Aroer

ARNON

KINGDOM OF
DAVID
c. 970 B.C.

COPPER MINES
AND SMELTER.

RED
SEA

Beersheba

Kir-
haresth

MOAB

30 MILES

Tamar

BROOK ZERED

TRM

100 MILES

Psalm 18. Still another Psalm (preceded by the note that David was "the sweet singer of Israel") occupies 23:1–7; the remainder of the chapter (8–39) is a catalogue of David's great warriors. A census taken by David (24) evoked Yahve's displeasure.[7] The count was made, but the divine wrath was provoked, lasting until David purchased a field from a Jebusite named Araunah. These appendices interrupt the natural progression in the chronicle to the account of David's death in I Kings 1–2, in the same way that all the interpolations interrupt, and nearly overwhelm, the theme of kingship.

The narrative of David's end naturally turned attention to David's successor.[8] The logical heir was his oldest son Adonijah. However, this son took advantage of David's infirmity to proclaim himself king even before David's death. David was persuaded, principally by the prophet Nathan, to name Solomon instead (I Kings 1:1–40). Adonijah fled to a sanctuary and took hold of the altar horns[9] but finally subjected himself to Solomon (1:41–53). David spoke farewell words to Solomon, and then passed away (2:1–11).

SOLOMON

Solomon, now king, took pains to safeguard his position. When Adonijah wanted Abishag[1] for a wife, Solomon regarded the wish as a threat to his throne and had Adonijah slain. Moreover, he banished one of David's two priests, Abiathar, who had helped Adonijah, retaining the other, Zadok. Solomon also slew Joab, David's general, who had also helped Adonijah. A certain Shimei[2] was confined to Jerusalem; he left to recover some escaped slaves, and for this he was put to death (2). Then Solomon's throne was established.

In Chapter 3 the hand of the Deuteronomist, obscured in the account of David, appears clear and unmistakable. Though Solomon

[7] Why was there divine disapproval of a census? Possibly because of the tradition of the divine promises (as in Gen. 15:5) that the Israelites would be numerous beyond the possibility of counting them. A census, then, amounted to distrust of a divine promise, although the census in Numbers 1–4 was taken by divine command. The census of David may well be historical, though the numbers are not to be taken seriously. The chapter, however historical its kernel, is legend. The field of Araunah comes to be regarded as identical with Moriah where Isaac was offered, and as the site for Solomon's temple (II Chron. 3:1).
[8] A curious narrative tells that just prior to his death, David, being cold, was warmed by lying, chastely, next to a young virgin, Abishag the Shunammite.
[9] From which no one was to be taken if he had fled there for safety.
[1] See note 8 above. Since Abishag was David's concubine, as it were, for Adonijah to have her would imply that he had the status of David.
[2] Shimei, who was of Saul's household, cursed David (II Sam. 16:5–11), but later (II Sam. 19:18–23) joined in allegiance to him. David had sworn not to kill Shimei; evasively, he put this chore on Solomon (I Kings, 2:8–9).

was destined to build the Temple, people were still sacrificing on high places. Solomon himself was faithful to Yahve, yet, on the other hand, he too sacrificed on high places. In Gibeon Yahve appeared to him in a dream and promised him future greatness because of his fidelity. Therefore Solomon returned to Jerusalem and offered sacrifice before the Ark (3:1–15).

No consecutive narrative of Solomon's reign is given. Rather, we find a legend of his wisdom[3] (3:16–28), a summary (4:1–6) of his deputies, lists of his twelve officers who provided the provender for the court, one month a year each (7–19), and the amount of the provender (5:2–3 Heb., 4:22–3 Eng.). The extent of his territory (5:1, 4 Heb., 4:21, 24 Eng.) and of his horses and stables (5:6–8 Heb., 4:26–8 Eng.) is set forth. His great wisdom is acclaimed; he "spoke 3,000 proverbs" (5:9–14 Heb., 4:29–34 Eng.).

The bulk of the material is an account, often very detailed, of Solomon's building of the Temple. Solomon appealed to King Hiram of Tyre for cedar wood (5:15–26 Heb., 5:1–12 Eng.), paid for by taxes (5:27–8 Heb., 5:13–14 Eng.). He had innumerable laborers (5:29–32 Heb., 5:15–18 Eng.). A description of the Temple begins in Chapter 6. An account of his palace interrupts (7:1–12), but the account of the Temple construction, focusing on the artistry of Hiram, is resumed (13–51). The Temple was dedicated (8:1–11). Solomon spoke a blessing (12–21) and then a long prayer (22–53). Again he blessed the people (54–61), and sacrifices were held by the assembled people (62–6).

Yahve appeared to Solomon for a second time, promising, in Deuteronomic fashion, prosperity for fidelity and punishment for infidelity (9:1–9). Attention turns to mundane matters: Hiram had received twenty cities in payment for his work, but he was not pleased (10–14). There follows (15–28) a catalogue of other achievements of Solomon.[4]

The queen of Sheba came both to admire Solomon's wisdom and to bring expensive gifts (10:1–13). His wealth, tabulated in great detail (14–29), was enormous.

Yet the Deuteronomist proceeds to pass a negative judgment on Solomon. He loved many foreign women, even of the proscribed na-

---

[3] His wisdom is illustrated by the well-known story of the infant claimed by two women; Solomon discovered the true mother by the instruction to cut the baby in two and divide it, for the true mother preferred the other woman to have the baby rather than to have the baby slain.

[4] The cities which he built (9:15–19); the levy put on the surviving Canaanites, made bondsmen (20–1); his use of Israelites (22–3); a house built for his Egyptain wife (she is mentioned in 3:1) outside Jerusalem, at Millo (24); his use of the Temple (25); and his navy (26–8).

tions. His wives numbered seven hundred and his concubines three hundred. Influenced by these wives, Solomon built altars to their deities, provoking Yahve's wrath, so that kingship was to be taken away from his descendants[5] (11:1–13). Yahve stirred up two foreign adversaries—Hadad, an Edomite (14–22), and Rezon of Damascus (23–5)—and one domestic one, Jeroboam ben Nebat. A prophet, Ahijah, encountered Jeroboam, who was to usurp the kingship. Ahijah rent Jeroboam's garment into twelve pieces, giving ten of them to Jeroboam as a symbol of his destiny to reign over ten of the tribes of Israel (26–46). Solomon reigned for forty years and then passed away (41–3).

THE MONARCHS

From this point on the interest is in kingship, except for the characters of Elijah and Elisha, about whom the Deuteronomist inherited sources which he incorporates with virtually no comment. His method is usually to mention a king by name, to attempt to correlate him with the king of the other portion, Israel or Judah, to pass a judgment on him, and scarcely ever to go into details of the reign; he does so only in the case of extreme wickedness or merit. He normally ends his brief account by referring the reader either to the "Chronicles of the Kings of Israel" or the "Chronicles of the Kings of Judah."

The prediction that in punishment of Solomon's transgressions kingship would be taken away from his sons came true. Rehoboam, Solomon's successor, faced dissidence in the north and refused to make concessions to an assembly of northerners who came to petition him. The northerners rebelled, and Rehoboam was left as king only of Judah and Benjamin. Jeroboam ben Nebat became the king of the north and he built a capital in Shechem. To deter possible defection to Rehoboam at Jerusalem, where the Temple was, he introduced elaborate non-Yahvistic practices at Shechem (12). A prophet,[6] outraged by these actions, denounced[7] Jeroboam's altar (13).

Nowhere is the hand of the Deuteronomist more vivid than in Chapter 14. Jeroboam's son was sick. His wife disguised herself and

[5] The Deuteronomists depict Yahve (11:11–12) and Ahijah (11:34) as promising that Solomon's punishment, the loss of the kingdom, was to come only after Solomon's time.
[6] Most of the chapter narrates the legend of this unnamed prophet.
[7] In this denunciation he predicted, as the first Deuteronomic editors would have it, that Josiah, some three hundred years later, would rectify Jeroboam's grievous errors (13:2).

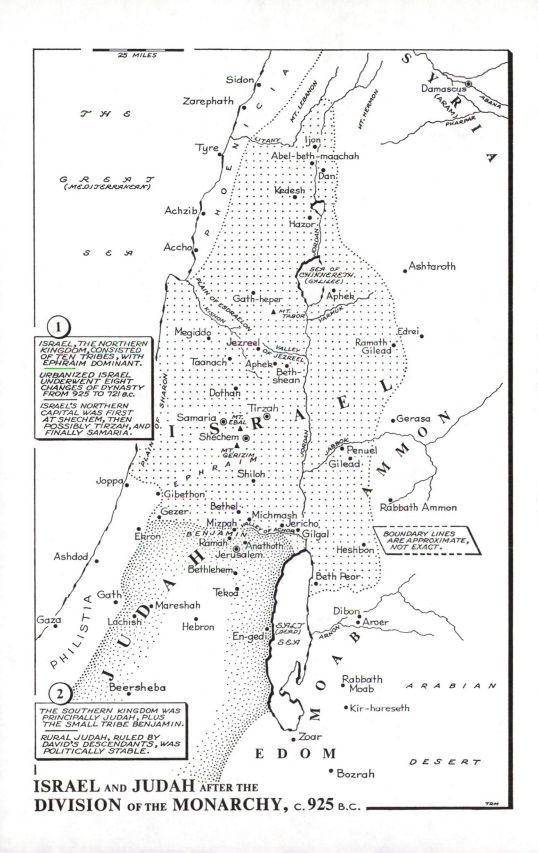

ISRAEL AND JUDAH AFTER THE DIVISION of the MONARCHY, c. 925 B.C.

Map labels:

25 MILES

THE GREAT (MEDITERRANEAN) SEA

SYRIA (ARAM)

Damascus
ABANA
PHARPAR

Sidon
Zarephath
Tyre
Achzib
Accho

PHOENICIA

MT. LEBANON
LITANY
MT. HERMON

Ijon
Abel-beth-maachah
Dan
Kedesh
Hazor

SEA OF CHINNERETH (GALILEE)

JORDAN

Ashtaroth

Gath-heper
Aphek
MT. TABOR
YARMUK
Edrei
Ramath Gilead

PLAIN OF ESDRAELON
KISHON
Megiddo
Jezreel
VALLEY OF JEZREEL
Taanach
Aphek
Beth-shean
Dothan
Tirzah
Samaria
MT. EBAL
Shechem
MT. GERIZIM

I S R A E L

Gerasa

AMMON

JABBOK
Penuel
Gilead

PLAIN OF SHARON

E P H R A I M
Shiloh

Joppa
Gibethon
Gezer
Bethel
Michmash
Mizpah
VALLEY OF ACHOR
Jericho
Gilgal
Ekron
BENJAMIN
Ramah
Anathoth
Jerusalem
Heshbon

Rabbath Ammon

BOUNDARY LINES ARE APPROXIMATE, NOT EXACT.

Ashdod
Bethlehem
Beth Peor

J U D A H

Gath
Tekoa
Mareshah
Lachish
Hebron
En-gedi

PHILISTIA

Gaza

Dibon
Aroer
ARNON

SALT (DEAD) SEA

M O A B

Beersheba

Rabbath Moab
Kir-haresheth

A R A B I A N

Zoar

E D O M

D E S E R T

Bozrah

Legend box 1:

① ISRAEL, THE NORTHERN KINGDOM, CONSISTED OF TEN TRIBES, WITH EPHRAIM DOMINANT.

URBANIZED ISRAEL UNDERWENT EIGHT CHANGES OF DYNASTY FROM 925 TO 721 B.C.

ISRAEL'S NORTHERN CAPITAL WAS FIRST AT SHECHEM, THEN POSSIBLY TIRZAH, AND FINALLY SAMARIA.

Legend box 2:

② THE SOUTHERN KINGDOM WAS PRINCIPALLY JUDAH, PLUS THE SMALL TRIBE BENJAMIN.

RURAL JUDAH, RULED BY DAVID'S DESCENDANTS, WAS POLITICALLY STABLE.

TRM

went to consult Ahijah. The prophet by now was blind, but Yahve told him who the woman was. Ahijah's words to the woman are typically Deuteronomic: Jeroboam will lose his kingdom; the son will die; and Israel will be conquered and go into exile (7–16). Jeroboam reigned twenty-two years; he was succeeded by his son Nadab (14:1–20).

As for Rehoboam, his reign was marked by faithlessness to Yahve: indeed, Shishak, king of Egypt, plundered the Temple in the fifth year of Rehoboam's reign. Rehoboam's son Abijam (also called Abijah) was almost as bad, but Yahve spared him somewhat on account of the merit of David (15:1–8). After three years, Asa succeeded his father Abijam. Asa reigned forty-one years. He eliminated non-Yahvistic practices, including those indulged in by his mother, who apparently was regent for a while. The Deuteronomists regard Asa favorably.[8] His entire reign was marked by war with Israel. His son and successor was Adonijah (15:9–24).

Jeroboam's son, Nadab, reigned only two years. Baasha who overthrew him was quite as bad (25–34). Yahve therefore removed Baasha, whom a prophet, Jehu, was commissioned to denounce. Baasha's son Elah reigned only two years; Zimri, a captain of the chariots, slew him and took the throne. Seven days later, however, a general, Omri, overthrew Zimri (16:1–20). For some time the northern kingdom was divided between Omri and a certain Tibni, but Omri became the sole king of the north at Tibni's death (21–2). Of Omri, we are told that he was worse than all who came before him. After twelve years he was succeeded by Ahab. We are told that Ahab did even more evil than his predecessors. His most glaring transgression was his marriage to a Phoenician, Jezebel, for whom he built a Baal temple at which he himself worshiped (23–34).

We have encountered the prophets Gad and Nathan in David's time, Ahijah in Jeroboam's, and Jehu in Baasha's. In Ahab's time the prophet was Elijah, whose career is considered at some length (I Kings 17–II Kings 2:11). The relevancy of the Elijah material to the motif of Kings is only limited, almost as if the Elijah stories were added as an afterthought.[9]

Few legends in Scripture are as rich in appeal as those of Elijah.

[8] There is confusion in the chapter. We are told in verse *17* that Baasha of Israel attacked Asa. Yet up to this point we have not been told of the successor to Jeroboam. In verse 25 we read that Jeroboam's son Nadab succeeded to the throne. Baasha was a rebel who, 27, slew Nadab and seized the throne, and exterminated all of Jeroboam's household.

[9] The natural continuation of I Kings 16:33 is I Kings 22:39. The Elijah material is not well blended into its context.

The authors introduce him at an advanced stage in his career (17:1), but promptly, as if in flash backs, show us his early career. Commanded by Yahve, Elijah fled (for solitude?) to the brook Cherith; there ravens fed him. Next, a poor widow of Zarephath found in feeding him that her flour and oil never gave out. And, finally, when her son stopped breathing (and died), Elijah by prayer to Yahve returned the child's breath (17).

Before appearing to Ahab, Elijah met pious Obadiah, Ahab's chief steward. There was drought, for Elijah had kept away the rain. Obadiah was fearful of complying with Elijah's wish that he carry a message to Ahab, but he was willing to tell Ahab when Elijah would meet him. Elijah proposed to Ahab that there should be a contest between Elijah and the Baal prophets, who numbered four hundred and fifty.[1] Both sides were to have bullocks cut into pieces and each side was to call on his deity. The victory would belong to the side whose deity answered by fire.

First, the Baal prophets took their turn at invoking fire from their deity, but there was no reply. Elijah began to mock the prophets: perhaps Baal was asleep! Then it was Elijah's turn. He made the altar preparations and prayed. Yahve's fire descended and consumed the bullock, the stones of the altar, and even the water in a trench dug around the altar. Yahve, accordingly, was recognized as the true Deity, and the Baal prophets were slaughtered (18:1–41). Elijah prayed for rain to end the drought and the rain came (42–6).

When Jezebel heard from Ahab about the death of the Baal prophets, she threatened to kill Elijah. He fled southward, entered the Wilderness (where he was miraculously fed), and journeyed to Horeb. He spent the night in the cave there and divine words[2] came to him. One of these was the instruction to recruit Elisha as his servant (19).

Warfare broke out with the Syrians, whom Ahab defeated. The Syrians ascribed their defeat to the hilly country, for Israel's god was a hill god. They would try a second time, but on the plains. Again the Syrians were defeated. When the battles were over, Ahab made a treaty with their king, Ben Hadad, thus sparing his life. For this an unnamed prophet later denounced Ahab (20). But an even sharper denunciation came from Elijah over the matter of a vineyard belonging to Naboth. Ahab wanted it and offered to buy it, but Naboth

[1] The text (19) mentions an additional four hundred *Asherah* prophets, but these do not reappear in the legend.
[2] See above, page 27; this is the story of the "still small voice," which ought to be translated "stillness, and then a small voice."

would not sell. After Jezebel conspired to have Naboth charged and convicted of cursing God and the king, Naboth was executed by stoning and Ahab took possession of his field. Thereupon Elijah predicted that Ahab and Jezebel would be eaten by dogs [3] (21:1–26).

Three years later Ahab joined with Jehoshaphat of Judah against Syria. When the kings consulted a prophet, Micaiah ben Imlah, he predicted death in battle for Ahab. This came about (22:1–41). Jehoshaphat elicits the commendation of the authors (41–50), but they regarded Ahab's son, Ahaziah, as a scoundrel (51–3). When Ahaziah was hurt in an accident (II Kings 1:2) it was to Baal of Ekron, not to Yahve, that he sent messengers to inquire whether he would recover or not.

Elijah (who had virtually vanished from the account) intercepted Ahaziah's messengers at Yahve's behest and gave them a divine rebuke, as well as a prediction that Ahaziah would die. The king sent successions of troops of fifty men to arrest Elijah, but Elijah called down fire to consume his arrestors. When the third group came, Elijah went before the king, made his prediction, and Ahaziah died (II Kings 1).

By then, however, Elijah too had come to the end of his career. At the Jordan in the company of Elisha, he smote the waters with his mantle so that they parted, and the two prophets crossed on dry land. The waters then came together (2:1–9). A chariot of fire and horses of fire came between the two, and Elijah went up to heaven "in the whirlwind." Elisha smote the Jordan with Elijah's mantle, and again the waters parted (10–18). He "cured" [4] the waters of Jericho; he cursed some little children who mockingly called him "bald head" by having two bears destroy forty-two of the children (19–25). The Deuteronomists, we can see, very seldom altered from within the sources they included. At the death of Ahaziah, a brother, Jehoram, came to the throne of Israel. In Judah, the king, only a little later, was also Jehoram, the son of Jehoshaphat (I Kings 1:17). The northern Jehoram was bad, though not as bad as his predecessors. His compact with Jehoshaphat of Judah and the king of Edom brought defeat to the rebellious Moabites (3). Elisha's part in the defeat of the Moabites under Mesha [5] was his trance, induced by music, after which he promised victory to the wavering Jehoram.

The text digresses to tell of legends of Elisha (4). He gave a

[3] It is related that Ahab humbled himself; therefore Elijah's prediction of evil was readjusted and scheduled to fall on Ahab's son (21:27–9). What this means is that the fate of Ahab did not bear out the curse, so that a later editor felt the need to account for the failure.
[4] We do not know what this means.
[5] Archaeology has recovered the "Mesha Stone." See page 514.

widow a miraculous supply of oil (*1–7*). At Shunem he promised a son to his worthy hostess.[6] The boy was born, but one day he became sick and died. The mother put him on the bed that had been Elisha's, and set off for Mount Carmel to have Elisha restore the boy's life. Elisha did so (*8–37*). In a famine, he took food that was inedible and made it palatable (*38–41*). A gift of food which his servant thought small was adequate for the whole populace, and some was even left over (*42–4*).

A Syrian general, Naaman, was a leper. His wife's Israelite maidservant recommended for a cure a trip to the prophet in Israel. Despite the objections of the king of Israel (his name is not given) Naaman arrived in Israel and was sent to Elisha. The prophet's advice was that Naaman bathe in the Jordan seven times; Naaman was cured of his leprosy. He asked for two mule loads of soil, from which he would worship Yahve, the only God in all the earth (*5:1–19*). Elisha's servant, Gehazi, through a lie, received a present from Naaman, and promptly became leprous (*20–7*).

Elisha made an iron axe head float (*6:1–7*). He deterred some of Syria's incursions (*8–23*), but now Syria invaded, and Israel went through great distress because of lack of food (*24–33*). Elisha promised great plenty within a day (*7:1*). The Syrians were fooled[7] into lifting their siege and fleeing (*2–20*). The woman of Shunem went to Philistia during a famine; in returning home she found her house and land usurped. On appeal to the king, an officer was appointed to look out for her (*8:1–6*). Elisha came to Damascus in Syria; the king, Ben Hadad, was sick. He sent a servant, Hazael, to Elisha. (One of the instructions to Elisha, I Kings *19:15*, had been to anoint Hazael king of Syria.) Elisha disclosed to Hazael the harm he, Hazael, would some day do to Israel (*8:7–16*).

Now a bit of history interrupts the Elisha legends. Jehoram came to the throne in Judah (by this time there was also a Jehoram on the throne in Israel). The Judahite Jehoram was quite as bad as the northern kings; indeed, he had married a daughter of Ahab. His reign of eight years was marked by revolts (*17–24*). Next, Ahaziah came to the throne at the age of twenty-two. His mother was Athaliah, a daughter of Omri, king of Israel; it is for this reason, the editors imply, that Ahaziah was as bad as the northern kings (*25–7*). Jehoram of Israel and Ahaziah became allied for war against Syria. Jehoram was wounded, and needed to convalesce (*28–9*).

Elisha, however, started a movement (either of rebellion or of

---

[6] This is reminiscent of Gen. 18.
[7] A great noise prompted them to flee. An Israelite nobleman, who doubted Elisha's prediction, was trodden to death by the people who rushed for the food.

conspiracy) with the professional prophets. He commissioned the anointing of one Jehu to seize Jehoram's throne (9:1–3). Jehu hastened to see Jehoram; Jehoram and Ahaziah came out to meet Jehu; promptly Jehu slew Jehoram, and had him put in Naboth's field for dogs to eat. Jehu also slew Ahaziah (9:4–29). Jezebel was still alive; at Jehu's command she was trampled so thoroughly that those who wanted to bury her could find only the skull, the feet, and the palms[8] (9:30–7).

Jehu had all of Ahab's family, including seventy surviving sons, slain (10:1–11). He slew the brothers of Ahaziah of Judah (12–14). He had the holy man Jehonadab ben Rechab[9] with him when he destroyed the rest of Ahab's family in Samaria (15–17). He craftily proclaimed a solemn assembly in honor of Baal, and Baal worshipers came from all over Israel. Thereupon Jehu had them slain; he ended Baal worship in Israel (18–28).

But Jehu (now the Deuteronomist reappears) was nevertheless imperfect. The golden calves in Bethel and in Dan, put there by Jeroboam,[1] were left untouched. Jehu, the authors tell us, was told by Yahve that he was good enough only for his dynasty to last four generations (10:29–34). His reign lasted twenty-eight years, and his successor was his son Jehoahaz (35–6).

After the death of Ahaziah of Judah, his mother Athaliah killed all of the royal family except Joash, a son of Ahaziah (11:1–3). Joash was crowned king by a priest, and his grandmother, Athaliah, slain (5–21). Joash, who had to pay tribute to Hazael of Syria (12:1–18) was assassinated in the fortieth year of his reign (19–21).

The reigns of Jehu's son Jehoahaz and his grandson Jehoash were bad ones for Israel. Jehoash was succeeded by his son Jeroboam (13:1–13).

Elisha contracted a fatal illness and died (14–21). Jehoash recovered some cities which the Syrians had taken (13:22–5). In Judah, the new king Amaziah, an approved monarch, was conquered by Jehoash of Israel, and later assassinated (14:1–21). He was succeeded by Azariah[2] (21–2). Though Israel merited extinction, Jeroboam delivered them; yet he was a wicked king[3] (23–9). Azariah reigned over Judah fifty-two years; he was a good king, though smitten with leprosy (15:1–7). In Israel Jeroboam's son Zechariah

---

[8] All this was predicted by Elijah, I Kings 21:19.

[9] See Jer. 35, where the "Rechabites" are portrayed as tent-dwellers who drink no wine.

[1] See I Kings 12:28–9.

[2] He is called Uzziah in 15:13, II Chron. 26:1, and Isaiah 6:1.

[3] The favorable aspect of the judgment is likely to be the result of the length of his reign, forty-one years.

reigned for only six months, fulfilling the prophecy to Jehu (15:8–12). His assassin, and successor for a month, was Shallum. In turn, Menahem ben Gadi assassinated Shallum, seized the throne, and reigned ten years (13–18). Menahem was forced to pay tribute to Pul (Tiglath Pileser) of Assyria as the price for not occupying Israel (19–20). (The Assyrians could scarcely have been introduced more routinely!) Menahem's son Pekahiah reigned wickedly for two years; he was assassinated and his throne was seized by the equally wicked Pekah ben Remaliah, who reigned then for twenty years (20–6). The Assyrians now took territory away from Israel, and Hoshea ben Elah slew Pekah and took the throne (27–31).

In Judah, the successor to Azariah-Uzziah was his son, Jotham, a good king (32–8). His son, Ahaz, was wicked like the kings of Israel, even practicing child sacrifice (16:1–4). Syria and Israel made an alliance against Ahaz; the latter appealed to Assyria for help, and received it. Assyria captured Damascus of Syria, and Ahaz journeyed to that place to meet the Assyrian king. Ahaz saw an altar in Syria; he had his priest copy it (5–20) and use it. In the sixth year of Hoshea of Israel, Shalmaneser of Assyria exacted tribute from him. Three years later, suspecting that Hoshea was conspiring with Egypt, Assyria carried Israel into exile. This was Israel's punishment for rejecting Yahve (17:1–23). A long sermon marks the passage; the events are related only briefly. The Deuteronomist was here less interested in events than in his view of their significance.

Into the northern kingdom there were brought emigrés, exiles from the east. At first these people did not worship Yahve; therefore He sent a plague of lions. On the petition of the inhabitants, the Assyrians sent home an Israelite priest to teach the populace how to worship Yahve. The people did not cease worshiping their transported gods; they merely mixed Yahve worship with their own alien and improper worship [4] (17:24–41).

In Judah, Hezekiah succeeded his father Ahaz. A very good king,[5] he reigned twenty-nine years. He defied the Assyrians at first, but then had to pay them tribute. The threats grew, however. Also, Assyria suspected Hezekiah of plotting with Egypt (18). Hezekiah received comfort from the prophet Isaiah; Assyria would not be able to capture Jerusalem, for domestic difficulties would take the Assyrians home

[4] We are being told in this anti-Samaritan passage that these northerners, the Samaritans, are not really Israelites but descendants of transported peoples and that we are not to be misled into thinking that they worship Yahve exclusively or appropriately.

[5] He is praised for destroying the brazen serpent supposedly made by Moses (Num. 21:9).

(19:*1–7*). Hezekiah prayed to Yahve, eliciting Isaiah's approval (*8–34*). An angel of Yahve smote the besieging Assyrians [6] (*35–7*). So good was Hezekiah that his life was extended for fifteen years beyond its allotment (20:*1–7*). The sign for this extension was that the sun retreated ten degrees (*8–11*).

The Babylonians, meanwhile, appeared on the scene; Hezekiah received their emissaries. For this Isaiah rebuked him, and told him that the Babylonians would one day take Judah into exile (*12–21*). The editor of the second edition introduces the Babylonians as casually as the editor of the first had introduced the Assyrians. Interpretation, and not the events themselves, interested the Deuteronomist. Hezekiah's son Manasseh came to the throne at the age of twelve; he reigned for fifty-five years. He was as wicked as his father had been good.[7] He succumbed to all sorts of non-Yahvistic practices, even inside the Temple. Accordingly, Judah was to have a fate of destruction similar to that of Israel (21:*1–18*). Amon succeeded his father Manasseh, and in the two years of his reign was as bad as his father. He was assassinated; his eight-year-old son Josiah came to the throne (*19–26*).

Josiah was a very good king. In the eighteenth year of his reign, when he gave orders to refurbish the Temple, a Book of the Torah was found there. Its words gave alarm to Josiah, for its prescriptions were not being obeyed. A prophetess, Huldah, was consulted. She said that Yahve planned to bring evil punishment, but not until after Josiah's lifetime; he would live out his days in peace (*22*). Josiah convened all the elders, read them the words of the Book of the Covenant [8] found in the Temple, and made a covenant with Yahve. The non-Yahvistic symbols were elaborately destroyed. The priests of the high places were slain (23:*1–20*). A unique Passover was observed (*21–3*). Josiah was an exemplary king,[9] without peer among his predecessors (*24–5*).

Yahve, however, did not swerve from His intention to destroy

[6] The prediction of a recall home is here supplemented by the legend of the mysterious smiting of 185,000 Assyrians. It is said that when the Assyrians awoke in the morning they were all corpses. Some modern scholars, not understanding the humor, have wanted to emend the text! That the Assyrians were compelled by events at home to desist from the siege may well be historical.

[7] Later generations pondered that a man could be a scoundrel and yet be permitted so long a reign. It is asserted in II Chronicles 33:*12–13* that Manasseh repented. In the Greek, there is a fine prayer of penitence attributed to him. This "Prayer of Manasseh" is customarily printed in the Apocrypha.

[8] In 22:*8*, it is called Book of the *Torah*.

[9] This is the point at which the first edition of Kings is believed by scholars to have ended. Signs of editorial revisions are clear. Josiah did not live out his days in peace, a clue that the prediction that he would so do antedated the account of his sudden death in battle.

Judah (26–8). Josiah was slain in battle with the Egyptians (29–30). His successor, Jehoahaz, reigned for three months; the Egyptians replaced him with his brother Eliakim, a bad king (31–7). Nebuchadnezzar of Babylon made a vassal of the king of Judah, who rebelled, so that the Babylonians sent many hostile nations against Israel. Jehoiakim [1] reigned eleven years (24:1–6). His son Jehoiachin came to the throne. In the third month of his reign (597) the Babylonians besieged Jerusalem and captured it. They deported Jehoiachin and the leading citizens to Babylonia (7–16). The new king, Zedekiah, was Jehoiachin's uncle. He reigned eleven years (597–586) and was wicked. Moreover, he rebelled against Babylonia (17–20). Nebuchadnezzar again besieged Jerusalem, a siege lasting about a year and a half. The walls were breached (586) and Zedekiah fled, only to be captured and blinded, and taken in chains to Babylonia (25:1–7).

The Babylonians burned the Temple and destroyed the walls of Jerusalem. Only the poor of the land were left in Palestine; the others were all transported to Babylonia (8–12). The Temple vessels were also carried away into Babylon (13–17). In Judah, a certain Gedaliah was appointed the ruling officer, but he was assassinated; there was a flight of the remaining Judeans to Egypt (18–26). In Babylonia, the exiled Jehoiachin was released from prison and treated royally by his captors (27–30). So ends the accounts of the Kings.

There is a noticeable margin of difference between the primitive religious attitudes, practices, and standards preserved in the old sources, and those of the Deuteronomic editors, whether of the first or of the second edition. The fact is that were it not for the Deuteronomic judgments, Samuel and Kings would appear to be the account of a succession of kings most of whom were scoundrels. Indeed, the searching question could be asked how such unlikely material could ever have been deemed suitable for a religious interpretation of history. It would seem that the bare events are irreligious beyond rehabilitation.

The teacher-sages would have agreed that the history of the kingdom was a sorry one. Yet they would have gone on to say that it was nevertheless the history. They lived in a real world, and hence they were, we may say, realists. They knew, of course, how things should be, having set forth in the Book of Deuteronomy an ideal state of affairs. Then they came to survey Israel's history, measured by

[1] His name was changed from Eliakim.

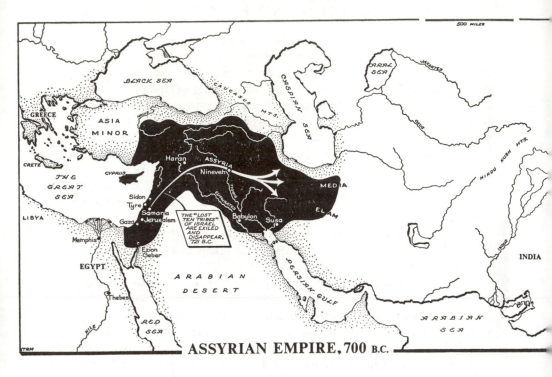

ASSYRIAN EMPIRE, 700 B.C.

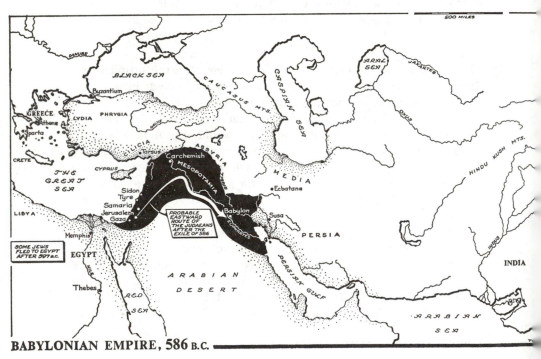

BABYLONIAN EMPIRE, 586 B.C.

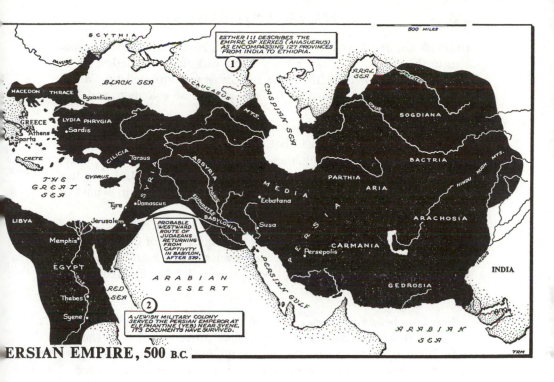

ESTHER 1:1 DESCRIBES THE
EMPIRE OF XERXES (AHASUERUS)
AS ENCOMPASSING 127 PROVINCES
FROM INDIA TO ETHIOPIA.
①

PROBABLE
WESTWARD
ROUTE OF
JUDAEANS
RETURNING
FROM
CAPTIVITY
IN BABYLON,
AFTER 539.

② A JEWISH MILITARY COLONY
SERVED THE PERSIAN EMPEROR AT
ELEPHANTINE (YEB) NEAR SYENE.
ITS DOCUMENTS HAVE SURVIVED.

ERSIAN EMPIRE, 500 B.C.

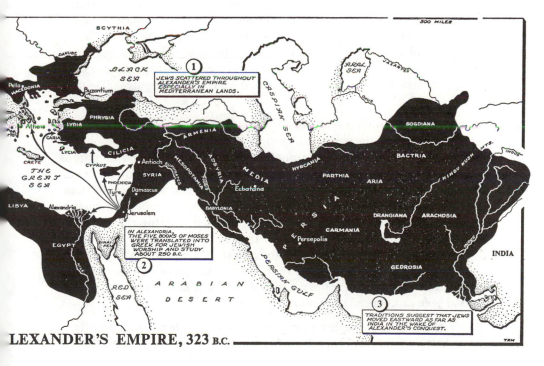

① JEWS SCATTERED THROUGHOUT
ALEXANDER'S EMPIRE,
ESPECIALLY IN
MEDITERRANEAN LANDS.

② IN ALEXANDRIA,
THE FIVE BOOKS OF MOSES
WERE TRANSLATED INTO
GREEK FOR JEWISH
WORSHIP AND STUDY
ABOUT 250 B.C.

③ TRADITIONS SUGGEST THAT JEWS
MOVED EASTWARD AS FAR AS
INDIA IN THE WAKE OF
ALEXANDER'S CONQUEST.

LEXANDER'S EMPIRE, 323 B.C.

those ideals, and found it a deplorable one. However, a greater problem to them even than the history itself was their conviction, common to Hebrew writers, that this history was controlled by Yahve. Was He therefore responsible for the parade of evil men and evil events?

They had reached a dilemma recurrent in religious tradition, that of providence and free choice. If, on the one hand, God controls and foresees everything, then man acts mechanically, as it were, and is hardly liable to moral judgment. On the other hand, if man has the fullest freedom of choice, then God does not enter into events to foresee or control them.

The Deuteronomists did not solve the dilemma. They accepted divine providence, for to them history was the record of God's actions; they also accepted choice, in that they assumed that man could select between alternatives. They expressed this belief in the freedom to choose in unmistakable terms:

> See, I set before you today life and the good, and death and the bad, in that I command you today to love Yahve your God, to walk in His ways, and to observe His commands, statutes and judgments. Then you will live and multiply, and Yahve will bless you in the land where you are going to take possession. But if your heart turns away, and you do not obey, and you are enticed and bow down to alien gods and worship them, I tell you today that you will surely be lost . . . I call to witness to you today heaven and earth: I set life and death before you, blessing and curse. You shall choose life, that you and your seed may live. [Deut. 30:15–19]

In the Deuteronomic view, God indeed controlled events, but man had both the opportunity and the obligation to choose. The Deuteronomic portions of Samuel-Kings assess the various monarchs by the standard of what they chose. Usually the judgment is a summary one: Such and such a king was evil (as bad as, or worse than, Jeroboam ben Nebat). But very often a prophet becomes the spokesman for the Deuteronomists; indeed, were it not for the prophets who appear from time to time in the book, the Deuteronomic viewpoint would not emerge in its fullest clarity. Moreover, it is the important role of the prophets that justifies the place of Samuel-Kings among the "Former Prophets" in the Tanak. The theme of prophecy had been announced in Deuteronomy:

> I shall raise a prophet like you [Moses] for them from among their brothers, and I shall put My word in his mouth, and he shall

speak to them all that which I command him. [Deut. 18:18]

Accordingly, the Deuteronomic writings make provision for prophets to arise again and again. Moses had been the supreme prophet (Deut. 34:10); Yahve spoke directly, and frequently, to Joshua. A prophet appeared in Gideon's time (Judges 6:8–10) to rebuke the generation; Yahve spoke directly to Gideon (7:4Bff.); and, though Jephthah was not a prophet, Yahve's "spirit" was on him (11:29). An angel, also described as a man of God, appeared to Samson's mother (13:2ff.).

In Eli's time (prior to Samuel's emergence) an unnamed man of God appeared (I Sam. 2:27ff.); Samuel was acknowledged as a prophet by all Israel (3:20), and it was he who anointed first Saul and then David. It was Nathan the prophet who disclosed to David that Solomon, not David, would build the Temple (II Sam. 7:12–13), and who denounced David for the Bathsheba incident (II Sam. 12:7). The denunciation of David for the census came from "Gad, David's seer" (II Sam. 24:11ff.). Nathan was instrumental in David's selection of Solomon, and participated in his anointing (I Kings 1:34).

To Solomon Yahve spoke directly (I Kings 3:5ff.; 9:2ff. and 11:11ff.). The selection of Jeroboam ben Nebat was done by the prophet Ahijah of Shiloh (I Kings 11:29ff.). It was the man of God Shemaiah who counseled Rehoboam of Judah not to attempt to regain the northern tribes (I Kings 12:22). A man of God from Judah was active in Jeroboam's time—often he is fancifully conjectured to be Amos. The denunciation of Jeroboam, delivered to his wife, came from Ahijah (I Kings 14:5ff.). The denunciation of Baasha came from the prophet Jehu ben Hanani (I Kings 16:1). It was Elijah who denounced Ahab and Jezebel. An unnamed prophet advised Ahab on his warfare with Aram (20:13ff.). The denunciation of the incident of Naboth's vineyard comes from Elijah (I Kings 21:20ff.). Micaiah ben Imlah was active in the days of Jehoshaphat (I Kings 22:8ff.). Elisha is regarded as active for several reigns. King Jehu had Jehonadab ben Rechab (II Kings 10:15ff.); indeed, Yahve spoke directly to Jehu (10:30ff.). Hezekiah had Isaiah (II Kings 19:2ff.), especially when Hezekiah was spared from what seemed a fatal illness (20:1ff.). In Josiah's time there was Huldah (II Kings 22:14ff.).

Thus we can see that there is quite a large amount of material relating to prophets. This should not be regarded as an accident, but rather as reflecting the deliberate purpose of the compilers. That some of the prophets are unnamed prompts the thought that they were more a convenience to the Deuteronomists than historical characters. The brief résumés of the reigns, which scholars often call epitomes, do not contain the references to the prophets; these come in the Deuteronomic commentaries.

Accordingly, the Deuteronomists depict the monarchs as having had the choice of accepting Yahve's way or of rejecting it, and scarcely any generation appears to have been bereft of the possibility of prophetic guidance. So uniformly do the Deuteronomists tell us this that they are occasionally led into certain absurdities. Thus, they have before them a knowledge of the sweep of history, and they know which dynasties did not last, and they know that Israel was exiled in 722/721 and Judah in 586. In the light of their knowledge they portray prophets as predicting these events in advance. Yet they faced the anomaly of long reigns by wicked kings, and short ones by good kings—in their view a miscarriage of justice. They therefore appended to their disapproval of certain wicked kings a statement to justify the delay of the merited punishment. Solomon's misdeeds caused the division of the kingdom, but it was deferred until his son's time (I Kings 11:11). Jeroboam ben Nebat caused Israel's subjection to Assyria, but an interval of another dynasty was to intervene (I Kings 14:15ff.). The punishment for Ahab's misdeeds was deferred to the days of his son (I Kings 21:28–30). The Babylonian exile was caused by Manasseh (II Kings 21:12ff.), even though it did not take place until the time of Manasseh's great-grandsons.

Accordingly, we read, sometimes in close juxtaposition, that events are determined in advance, and yet monarchs are judged in the light of the good or bad choice they made. The Deuteronomists, as has been mentioned, did not resolve the dilemma of providence and free will. Rather, they found room in their thinking for accepting the implications of both. If it is assumed to be a defect that the Deuteronomists failed to solve this philosophic problem, then the question may be asked in their defense, who has ever solved it?

The Deuteronomists held that God works in history and history reveals His works. They also held that man could choose or reject God's way. They wrote history so as to influence man to choose the good, by enabling him to learn from the choices of his ancestors.

CHAPTER

37

First and Second

CHRONICLES

THE CHIEF ATTRACTION of Chronicles, now divided because of length into two parts, is scarcely its literary flavor. Indeed, the first nine chapters are deadly dull genealogies. But there is a fascination in comparing Chronicles with Samuel and Kings, which it largely overlaps. Chronicles carries the events just a little beyond the last event recorded in Kings, for it tells of the rise of Cyrus of Persia to world power.

One wonders why another account was deemed necessary. The answer is to be seen in the character of Chronicles. It was noted above, page 443, that few Priestly interpolations are to be found in Samuel-Kings, almost as if the priests preferred to compose a new version rather than to make interpolations into the older book. Chronicles is Priestly in the same sense that Samuel-Kings is Deuteronomic. Moreover, the Chronicler used Samuel and Kings as a literary source. He copied, but he also altered and omitted. Besides Samuel and Kings he had other sources,[1] and he blended his selected material into a unified account.

[1] These are to be principally: *The Books of the Kings of Judah and Israel* (II Chron. 16:11; 25:26; 32:32). A similar title, perhaps the same book, is

Samuel-Kings is a history of kingship. Chronicles is a history of the Temple and its institutions. History is, of course, to be understood as interpretive theology, and not as a reliable set of events arranged in their proper sequence. In looking primarily at the differences between Samuel-Kings and Chronicles, differences resulting from omission, additions, and rewritings, the fullness of the character of Chronicles will become clear. The exposition of Chronicles here should be followed by frequent reference to the material given above in Samuel and Kings.

I Chronicles 10 is in a sense the continuation of the P portions of Joshua (see above, pages 425–429). The Chronicler was uninterested in the Conquest and Settlement to the point of completely ignoring the events depicted in Judges and those depicted in I Samuel except for Chapter 31, which told of Saul's death. Indeed, the Chronicler begins his narration, once the genealogies[2] are over, with the Philistine triumph over Saul and Saul's death. For the most part he follows the Books of Samuel, except to add (10:13–14) that Saul's death was deserved, for Saul was faithless to Yahve and consulted wizards (an allusion to the witch of En-Dor); and that all of Saul's sons perished with him (10:6). The significance of this last observation is that Ishbosheth goes unmentioned, as does the period of war between him and David.

Having omitted the war between Ishbosheth and David, the Chronicler next relates the crowning of David by all Israel and Judah at Hebron (II Chron. 11:1–3; II Sam. 1–4 have been omitted), and David's conquest, aided by all Israel, of Jerusalem (11:4–8). Now the Chronicler gives (11:10–41) a list of David's heroes (found in II Sam. 23:8–29), though he presents (11:42–12:40) material not found in Samuel. The moving of the Ark towards Jerusalem is the very next step, according to the Chronicler (13). Samuel-Kings had portrayed David as building a palace and fighting the Philistines

---

known as *The Book of the Kings of Israel and Judah* (II Chron. 27:7; 35:27; 36:8). Another title is *The Book* (or *The Words*) *of the Kings of Israel* (II Chron. 20:34 and 27:24). Next, *The Midrash of the Books of Kings* (II Chron. 24:27).

Works attributed to Samuel (I Chron. 29:29), Nathan (II Chron. 9:29), Gad (I Chron. 29:29), Shemaiah and Iddo (II Chron. 9:29, 12:15, and 13:22), Jehu (II Chron. 20:34), an unnamed seer (II Chron. 33:19), Ahija (II Chron. 9:9), Isaiah (II Chron. 26:22 and 33:32).

Much scholarly debate goes on about these sources, and some doubt that they ever existed at all; they are sometimes regarded as figments of the Chronicler's vivid imagination. Skepticism is justified, but scarcely to the point of assuming that the Chronicler had no sources at all but Samuel-Kings.

[2] The genealogies (1–9) are to be regarded as prefatory to Chronicles, and not integral to the Book. They contain much that is worthy of study.

prior to returning the Ark. In that earlier account, only David and his followers brought the Ark; in Chronicles all Israel joined with David in the event, including the remnants of the ten tribes of Israel and their priests, who were to be assembled from their exile.[3] The Chronicler (14) follows the account of the movement of the Ark with that material which in Samuel-Kings (II Sam. 5:11–25) had preceded it.[4] Samuel-Kings had given some nine verses (II Sam. 6:12–20) to the account of the further movement of the Ark from the home of Obed-Edom to Jerusalem; the Chronicler's account runs for seventy-two verses (I Chron. 15–16). The expanded account has some items of interest. The Ark, though still housed in a tent, had a place provided for it by David; that is, it was not just put anywhere (15:1). David gave orders that only the Levites could carry the Ark. Accordingly, he instructed, by name, the family heads among the Levites in their tasks (15:2). An appropriate preparation of sanctification by priests and Levites preceded the actual carrying (15:3–15). Next, David instructed the chiefs of the Levites to appoint the musicians; we are given their names (15:16–24). Michal's scolding of David (II Sam. 6:20–3) is altered (15:29) to a silent animosity.[5]

In the Chronicler's expanded account he has changed an incident into a high formal pageant. He inserts a psalm[6] suitable for the occasion (16:8–36), and then gives us the names of the various functionaries who were henceforth to minister at the Ark (37–43). The revelation through Nathan that Solomon, not David, was to build the Temple is repeated from II Sam. 7:1–29 with little modification (17:1–27). The only significant alteration is the omission by the Chronicler, in the first verse, of the intimation in Samuel-Kings that David waited for a period of tranquillity before discussing a Temple with Nathan.

In the next three chapters (18–20), the Chronicler appears to be reducing by omission the material he is excerpting from II Samuel 8–21. The Chronicler omits completely the contents of II Samuel 9, the hospitality extended by David to the son of Jonathan. He omits the incident of Uriah (II Sam. 11:2–12:25) entirely. There

---

[3] The Chronicler has been guilty of an anachronism, for the event of exile occurred three hundred years after David. Already in the time of the Chronicler there was a legend in existence that the "lost ten tribes" would some day be found.
[4] That is, Hiram's offer of assistance, and the list of David's sons.
[5] The Chronicler would not portray a woman treating the great David so disrespectfully.
[6] This psalm is apparently a compilation. I Chron. 16:8–22 is the same as Psalm 105:1–15, 23–33 the same as Psalm 96, and 34–6 the same as Psalm 106:1, 47–8.

is not one word about Absalom (II Sam. 13–19) or about the rebellion of Sheba ben Bichri (II Sam. 20). The result of these and other omissions [7] is the idealization of David as a proper king and of Solomon as a legitimate heir.

The account of the disastrous census is repeated by the Chronicler, but with this difference: in II Sam. 24 it was told, as it were, as a self-contained incident, while the Chronicler uses the episode as an introduction to material not found in Samuel-Kings. The ending of the incident of the census was the purchase by David of a field from one Araunah, his building an altar there and offering sacrifices (II Sam. 24:18–25). Chronicles makes some minor changes in the ending (I Chron. 21:25–30), relating that David confirmed the place as the site for the Temple [8] (I Chron. 22:1). Solomon, according to the Chronicler, was young; therefore David summoned him and gave him specific instructions about the Temple,[9] for the construction of which David had already allocated wealth and materials (almost as if there was little left for Solomon to do). David appointed Solomon (23:1ff.) to rule in his stead after assembling all the leaders of Israel, and all the Levites—the Chronicler omits both the attempt at seizure of power of Adonijah and the story of the girl Abishag. He gave those assembled the tasks they were to execute in building the Temple. First he divided the Levites into groups (23:6–26) and instructed them in their obligations.

These specific instructions for Levites and priests and other ministers comprise four chapters [1] (23–6). There is evidence that later writers after the Chronicler embellished and extended the material in these chapters, but to him is to be attributed the basic motif, that David organized everything because the Temple was the matter foremost in his mind. In 28, David convened Israel, spoke about Solomon's mandate to build the Temple, and even gave to Solomon the pattern (we would say blueprints) for everything. In 29, David announced what his own contribution was to be; thereupon those in attendance made their contributions. Then Solomon was confirmed as king, and David died.

The Chronicler rewrites the accession of Solomon, omitting Solomon's vengeance on the supporters of Adonijah (I Kings 2:23–46), for to the Chronicler Solomon was the uncontested, pub-

---

[7] II Sam. 22 and 23 are also omitted.
[8] This after Yahve sent down Sacred Fire, I Chron. 21:26.
[9] David tells Solomon that Yahve has disqualified David because of the blood he had shed in battles (22:8).
[1] A fifth, Chapter 27, gives the list of David's military aids.

licly approved successor to David. As a result of those omissions, virtually the first act of Solomon, according to the Chronicler, was his visit to Gibeah. But by an addition the Chronicler changes the import of the visit. In I Kings 3:1–3, we are told that sacrifices were still being offered on the high places, for there was as yet no Temple, and Solomon himself did such sacrificing; he went to Gibeah because that was the site of the "high place." In Chronicles, however, Gibeah was the place where the Tent of Meeting, made by Moses in the Wilderness, rested; there too was the proper altar made by Bezalel (Exod. 38:1–2). Thus, in Kings, Gibeah represents Solomon in an impropriety; in the same place in Chronicles, Solomon is propriety itself [2] (II Chron. 1:1–13). Solomon now proposed to build the Temple and his palace [3] (II Chron. 1:18 Heb., 2:1 Eng.). He corresponded with Hiram of Tyre (the Chronicler calls him Huram) and the construction was eventually completed (II Chron. 2:1–5:1 Heb., 2:2–5:1 Eng.).

Whereas in I Kings 8 there is only the Ark to bring into the Temple, the Chronicler has available also the Tent of Meeting [4] and the other holy vessels (II Chron. 5:5). The differences between Chronicles and Kings respecting the Dedication of the Temple are rather minor (5:2–7:11). The summary of Solomon's career (8:1–9:31) runs similar to that in I Kings 9:10–11:43, the chief difference being the omission by the Chronicler of the misdeeds of Solomon found in II Kings 11:1–8.

In Kings there is a large measure of attention given to Jeroboam ben Nebat, who was responsible for the division of the kingdom into two. In Chronicles, Jeroboam is mentioned only when to do so is unavoidable, but the narratives about him and the summary of his achievements are not given. This treatment of the northern king becomes the standard, for later ones kings are scarcely mentioned. The ignoring of the northerners is counterbalanced by insertions of material not found in Kings about southerners (such as II Chron. 11:5–12:1).

I Kings 14:2–29 had told briefly of an invasion of Judah by Shishak of Egypt. The account is longer in Chronicles, especially by the addition of a message from the prophet Shemaiah, which

---

[2] The Chronicler reproduces in II Chron. 1:14–17 a summary of Solomon's horses and chariots, II Kings 10:26–9. He omits all reference to Solomon's Gentile wives, I Kings 3:1–2 and 11:1–3.
[3] This is mentioned but disappears from notice.
[4] The Tent of Meeting disappears from further notice; it is replaced by the Temple, and is therefore not equipment to be brought into it.

interpreted Shishak's invasion as Yahve's punishment on Israel for its infidelity (II Chron. 12:5–8). Midrashic embellishment puts into the mouth of Rehoboam's son, Abijah (II Chron. 13:3–4), a statement of why the northern kingdom was able to rebel, and a proclamation of the great piety of the South, especially in its respect for the priests. As the same midrash tells it, the southerners had a glorious victory over the north (II Chron. 13:2–21), something unmentioned in I Kings 15:1–9. With Asa, too, we are given embellishment. A tremendous army of Ethiopians attacked; Asa prayed to Yahve, Who alone could help. Yahve smote the Ethiopians, and sent a prophet, Azariah ben Oded, to preach the need of fidelity to Yahve (II Chron. 14:6–15:15). But when Asa made war on Baasha of Israel, he called on Syria for help rather than on Yahve; the Chronicler has Hanani the seer condemn Asa (16:7–11).

The Chronicler makes quite an eminent man of Jehoshaphat (II Chron. 17:2–19). His alliance with Ahab of Israel against Syria was ill fated. Chronicles adds that the prophet, Jehu ben Hanani, condemned Jehoshaphat for allying himself with Ahab (19:2). Yet Jehoshaphat was repentant in earnest and did good things, especially in using Levites and priests in a judicial capacity. When the Ammonites and Moabites attacked, Jehoshaphat prayed to Yahve. The prophet Yahaziel reminded the king and the people that the war was not theirs, but Yahve's. Indeed, they had no need to go to war at all, for the invaders fought and exterminated each other (II Chron. 19:1–20:20). Yet when Jehoshaphat made an alliance with Ahaziah, he was denounced by one Eliezer ben Dodavah (20:37). The successor, Jehoram, was very wicked, having married a daughter of Ahab of Israel. Elijah[5] sent him a letter which promised that Jehoram's bowels would fall out, so wicked was he (21:10–19).

The Chronicler rewrites the account of the refurbishing of the Temple by Joash. The Levites in the new account are the trustees of the Temple, under the priest Jehoiada (24:5–22); in Kings, they were treated as scarcely better than slaves. But Joash became evil, so that Zechariah ben Jehoiada prophesied against him. Joash then slew Zechariah (24:14–25). When King Amaziah, the son of Joash, hired some mercenaries from Israel, a prophet (left unnamed) advised him that Yahve would have no favorable dealings with the northerners (25:7–9). Amaziah conquered the Edomites but worshiped their deities, prompting still another unnamed prophet to denounce him (25:15–16).

Amaziah's successor, Uzziah, was prosperous only so long as he

[5] This is the only place in which Elijah is mentioned in Chronicles, for the Chronicler omitted the narratives about Ahab, and hence omitted Elijah too.

consulted a prophet, Zechariah. His leprosy (II Kings 15:5) is explained (II Chron. 26:16–21) as coming from his usurpation of the prerogative of the priest Azariah.[6] This is clearly legend rather than history. Indeed, the Chronicler assigns the name Azariah to the priest, as though unaware or careless that Kings had assigned to the king both the names Uzziah and Azariah.

The Chronicler has little love for Ahaz. Having even less love for the northern kingdom, he attributes Ahaz's subjection to it as being the result of his infidelity to Yahve. This he put into the mouth of a prophet named Oded (II Chron. 28:9–11). He omits the conquest of the northern kingdom by Assyria (II Kings 17). He expands the material on Hezekiah greatly, especially in attributing to him a notable celebration of the Passover (29–32). As for Manasseh, who was so wicked in Kings, the Chronicler (33) has him repent his deeds on being captured by the Assyrians (33:12–16).

Josiah did his work with the proper Levites, whom the Chronicler names (II Chron. 34:12–14). The account of Josiah's Passover (II Kings 23:21–3) is expanded (II Chron. 35:1–19), to make everything conform to Priestly and Levite requirements. For the rest, Chronicles follows the account in Kings.

The significant difference between Samuel-Kings and Chronicles is the clear index to the religious viewpoint of the Chronicler. Through his additions, he has depicted David not, as the Deuteronomist had, as wishing to build the Temple, but as having made the Temple the first item of business, accumulating the necessary materials and organizing the Temple personnel. Indeed, he has David do so much for the Temple, that Solomon's building of it becomes a minor mechanical task of completion. Presently we shall inquire into the meaning of this shift of credit from Solomon to David.

The ignoring of the northern monarchs is not unrelated to the centrality of the Temple in Jerusalem. Not only was the Chronicler aware that the northerners had had a Temple at Samaria, but this Temple on Mount Gerizim, illegitimate to the Chronicler, was still functioning in his day; it was the sanctuary of the hated Samaritans. The Chronicler did not denounce the northerners as did the Deuteronomist; instead, he expressed his disapproval by ignoring them. When, with some inconsistency, he does display an interest in the north, it is by the curious statement that David had assembled de-

---

[6] The legend grows; see Josephus, *Antiquities*, IX, 10, 4. The act of usurping is given as the cause of the earthquake mentioned in Amos 1:1 and hearkened back to in Zech. 14:5.

scendants of the ten lost tribes. These were, to the Chronicler, part of the true people of God; the Samaritans, as II Kings 17:24ff. had stated, were the descendants of the aliens whom the Assyrians had moved into the north.[7] To sum up, the Chronicler was so preoccupied with his account of the Temple that he had no room in his narrative for the northerners, who in his view had no part in, or advantage from, the institution.

As a result of this determination to ignore the northern monarchs, Elijah is merely mentioned and Elisha fails even to appear. Like the Deuteronomist, the Chronicler held that Yahve had sent prophets to reveal His will in almost every generation. Having pruned from his account the importance given in Kings to Elijah and Elisha, he was constrained to concoct new prophets, or to extend the significance of the few southern ones mentioned in Kings, so as to restore prophecy to some adequate emphasis. The Chronicler gives us a good many prophets, but not one prophet of any great significance. Furthermore, the Chronicler would not allow the prophets to vie with the Temple.

The transfer of credit for the Temple from Solomon to David is a byproduct of the Chronicler's intention, and not a reflection of his direct purpose. It is true that David has become a singularly attractive figure in popular legend and esteem. Yet the intention of the Chronicler is to be discerned from his great omissions; he leaves out virtually all of II Samuel except the bringing of the Ark to Jerusalem, an incident he greatly expands; he omits David's years as a fugitive from Saul; he omits Saul, except for his death; and he omits Samuel, except for his anointing of David.

Even more significantly, he omits the entire age of the Judges, as though it had never happened. These periods in history, which in the Deuteronomic account extend from Joshua to David, do not figure in his narrative at all; these were the periods when there was no Temple, and when there abounded the irregularities in ritual with which the Book of Judges is replete. The nine chapters of genealogies which begin I Chronicles are a later interpolation; the Priestly account in Chronicles supposes that there was little or no lapse of time between Moses (or possibly Joshua) and David. That is, in the Chronicler's view, Moses transmitted his leadership to Joshua, who conquered Canaan, and promptly David became the king and did everything for the Temple but the brick-laying. The Ark and the Tent of Meeting do not lie unused for generation after generation as in the Deuteronomic account. The emphasis on David, then, is not so much

[7] See above, page 463.

to glorify him as to suggest that there was an unbroken continuity in Levitical practice. In order to emphasize this the Chronicler does not want the Temple to be delayed as much as one generation. That is why he has David assemble the materials and stabilize the function of the Temple ministrants. The Chronicler has read back into David's time the idealization of Temple organization that was prevalent in the Chronicler's day.

Chronicles was at one time joined to Ezra and Nehemiah. All three books, except for interpolations, were completed and written by the same hand. When Ezra and Nehemiah were detached, they (unlike Chronicles) underwent interpolation in a matter of some importance; this scattered interpolation reflects the interest of the Priest as distinct from the Levite. It will be recalled [8] that there was a stage at which the terms *levi* and *kohen* ("priest") were interchangeable; the Levites come to be conceived of as a tribe descended from Levi, a son of Jacob. When Chronicles-Ezra-Nehemiah was written there had not as yet developed fully the view that one family, that of Aaron and of his descendant of David's time, Zadok, constituted an elite within the Levites. The distinction was interpolated into Ezra and Nehemiah; Chronicles, however, remained Levite rather than Priestly.[9] Ezra and Nehemiah were apparently admitted into the canon before Chronicles. A rounded understanding of the religion of the Chronicler must be deferred until we have looked at Ezra and Nehemiah. Chronicles carries events down to the year 539. Ezra and Nehemiah carry them to about 430 or 398. Chronicles-Ezra-Nehemiah was written either between 350 and 250, or else about 350, continuing to be added to as late as 250. Ezra and Nehemiah came into the canon because they contain virtually the only data we have on the postexilic period. Chronicles was accepted as an afterthought. It was the centrality of the Temple in Chronicles that preserved it from disappearing during the interval when Ezra and Nehemiah were canonized and Chronicles was not. Since it did not disappear, it too came into the canon as the last book in the Hebrew list. Chronicles, properly assessed, is a useful book, but not an inspiring one.

[8] See above, page 438.
[9] Indeed, some scholars hold that Ezra and Nehemiah were not written by the same hand because of the fact that Chronicles stresses Levites, and Ezra-Nehemiah priests. They interpret the identity of verses at the conclusion of Chronicles and the beginning of Ezra, not as a sign of the same author's hand, but as an artifice designed to give a misleading impression of identical authorship.

EZRA

AND NEHEMIAH

EZRA AND NEHEMIAH, once separated neither from each other nor from Chronicles, deal with events mostly subsequent to the Babylonian Exile. Whereas the Books of Samuel-Kings are known to us as a source for I and II Chronicles, enabling us to follow the literary method of the Chronicler, we are without such an aid and guide to Ezra and Nehemiah. Accordingly, it is difficult to determine what sources were available, and even more difficult to know just how the Chronicler used them.

Indeed, a number of vexing problems emerge from the Books of Ezra and Nehemiah. Before discussing them, we will give a brief résumé of the contents of the books. Ezra falls into two natural divisions. The first six chapters, except for one short passage,[1] recount the events of the return of Jews to Jerusalem from Babylonia, after Cyrus (538) had permitted the migration. They immediately built an altar, and then, under the leadership of Haggai and Zechariah, in the reign of Darius, began to rebuild the Temple. The rebuilding had

[1] 4:6–23, discussed below, p. 484.

been impeded by the Samaritans, who had made accusations by letter to the Persian capital that the rebuilding was against Persian policy. However, Darius replied in a letter that both authorized the rebuilding and even instructed Persian officials to support it.[2]

Ezra himself is introduced in 7. The time is now the seventh year of the reign of Artaxerxes.[3] Ezra had a royal decree, called a firman (reproduced in 7:11–26), authorizing him and all Jews who wished to, to return to Palestine, and to bring with them whatever generous contributions the Jews of Babylonia had made. In 7:27–8, the account shifts from third to first person and Ezra relates what ensued on the granting of the decree.

In Chapter 8, again in the first person, we have a list of those who returned with Ezra (1–14). These people, who gathered near Ahava, included priests but no Levites, so that Ezra needed to assemble some of the latter (15–20). Divine guidance, rather than Persian troops, brought them safely through the journey; the valuable metals contributed were brought along (21–34). The Jews then offered sacrifices (35–6). The Jewish leaders (9) apprized Ezra of the intermarriages that had taken place with the natives. This sinfulness led Ezra to pray to Yahve for guidance.

Chapter 10 reverts to the third person. The community gathered around Ezra. Most acknowledged the sin of intermarriage and proposed to banish their wives. Ezra adjured each guilty person to do this, on penalty of the loss of his property. These divorces could not all be concluded immediately, but needed to be arranged on a schedule (10:1–17). A list of the priests who had alien wives concludes the book.

The short section mentioned above (4:6–23) summarizes events from the year 485 to the days of Artaxerxes (465 on), and deals with the building of the walls of Jerusalem, and not with the Temple. It is sandwiched into the account of the events of 538–520, and is therefore clearly out of place in its context, probably through accidental misplacement.

The Book of Nehemiah is best seen as consisting of three parts. Nehemiah is portrayed in the first person in 1–7. As cupbearer in Shushan

---

[2] Chapter 1 relates the return of the Jews; 2 is a list of those who returned. Chapter 3 tells of the building of the altar and the start of the rebuilding of the Temple. 4:1–6:12 relates the Samaritan efforts at obstruction, and reproduces epistles sent to and from Jerusalem and Ecbatana, Persia's capital; 6:12–22 narrates the conclusion of the building (516) and an impressive celebration of Passover.

[3] If it is Artaxerxes I (465–425), the date is 458; if Artaxerxes II, the date is 398.

(Susa) to the Persian king, his countenance reflected his grief at hearing the disheartening news from Jerusalem that the walls of the city were in ruins. The king Artaxerxes gave him permission to visit Jerusalem (1:1–2:9). Despite hindrance by the enemies of the ·Jews, and though armed guards were needed, Nehemiah was able to begin the work of rebuilding the walls (2:10–4). He persuaded the rich Jews not to treat other Jews who were financially indebted to them as slaves (5:1–13). He served as Peha ("governor"), but without accepting the governor's emoluments (14–19). With the walls rebuilt, the enemies approached him to ensnare him (6). Nehemiah appointed gatemen and set forth regulations for the time of the opening and closing of the gates (7:1–4). He found the list of those who had returned originally in the time of Zechariah (7:5–73), a duplicate of Ezra 2.

In the second part, 8–10, the narration shifts to the third person, but Ezra rather than Nehemiah is the center of attention. The people gathered near the Water Gate on the first day [4] of the seventh month, eager to hear the Book of the Torah of Moses. Ezra, with the Levites present, read from dawn to noon (8:1–12). The next day there was another assembly; a passage in the Torah of Moses prescribed Sukkoth, a festival not observed since the days of Joshua,[5] which was now observed for the necessary seven days [6] (8:13–18). The festival over, the people were led [7] in a long confession of sin (9). A written statement of covenant obligations was drawn up, and sealed by Nehemiah and others. The document prohibited intermarriage, and specified ritual obligations [8] (10).

The remaining three chapters are a collection of miscellaneous items. Chapter 11:1–24 names the men, one in ten, chosen from the list in Chapter 7, to dwell in Jerusalem. 11:25–36 lists the towns and cities in which the returning Jews dwelled. Chapter 12:1–26 gives the names of the priests and Levites who returned with Zerubbabel (1–9); the series of high priests from Joshua, the contemporary of Zerubbabel (536) through Jaddua,[9] a total of six (10–11); the heads

[4] The New Year now comes on that date and Yom Kippur on the tenth. The name New Year is seldom used in Scripture; possibly 8:10–11 refers to it. Yom Kippur is totally ignored in the passage; it was probably not yet fixed on VII/10.
[5] This is an incredible exaggeration. See the Sacred Calendar, page 520.
[6] So prescribed in Lev. 23:4–42.
[7] In the Hebrew, the Levites lead the confession; in the Greek translation, Ezra leads them.
[8] These include an annual gift for the Temple; the showbread; the various offerings—Sabbath, New Moon, and festivals; sin offerings; first fruits; tithes; etc. That is, they represent various obligations owed the Temple.
[9] A Jaddua is named by Josephus as the high priest at the time of Alexander's conquest in 331. This Jaddua is the great-grandson of Elyashib (Neh. 3:1), the

of the priestly families in the time of Joshua's son Joiakim (*12–21*); the chief families of the Levites until the time of Jonathan ben Eliayashib (*22–6*). The text reverts to the first person at verse *31* in the account of the dedication of the walls of Jerusalem (*27–43*), of the appointment of those who were to receive the gifts contributed for the priests and Levites (*44*), and of the generosity shown to the Temple porters and singers (*45–7*).

Chapter *13* relates, still in the first person, a second trip to Jerusalem by Nehemiah, after an absence of twelve years.[1] Tobiah, an Ammonite—a people proscribed to Jews—had been given a chamber in the Temple precincts.[2] Nehemiah had him ousted (*1–9*). Next, he was dismayed to find that the contributions due to the Temple, and payable to the Levites, were not coming in (*10–13*). He enforced observance of the Sabbath (*14–22*) and took steps to bar intermarriages (*23–31*).

The problems raised in the books are both historical and literary. Is the Persian monarch Artaxerxes I or II? Why does Nehemiah go unmentioned in the Book of Ezra? Why does the Book of Nehemiah suddenly shift its focus from Nehemiah to Ezra, after so long a section (Neh. *1–7*), without even a mention of Ezra? Is the view of Scripture correct, that first Ezra came to Jerusalem, and then Nehemiah, and the two were collaborators for a time? Perhaps the answer is that sections of the books got mixed up, either prior to the Chronicler's use of the documents, or else by the Chronicler himself when he began to use the documents.

These questions are not matters of tremendous importance, but since they arise in Scripture, scholars have sought for a reasonable solution. Two different solutions are frequently offered, both of which tend to make Nehemiah precede rather than follow Ezra. Thus, it is suggested that the king was Artaxerxes I. Ezra came up to Jerusalem, however, not in the seventh year, as Ezra *7:7* reports, but the reading is altered by some scholars to the *thirty*-seventh year, that is 428. Nehemiah's first journey was in 445; he remained there for twelve years (Neh. *5:14*), that is, until 433. This would mean that Nehemiah had gone back to Persia before Ezra arrived.

---

contemporary of Nehemiah. The date when Chronicles-Ezra-Nehemiah was written is guessed at in various ways by scholars, depending on how they treat Jaddua, and whether this verse is a later interpolation or not.

[1] This would have been about 422; the date given is the thirty-second year of Artaxerxes I, who came to the throne in 465.

[2] We are not told the use made by Tobiah of the chamber.

As for the statement in Nehemiah (13:6–7) that Nehemiah came to Jerusalem a second time in Artaxerxes' thirty-second year, perhaps this date too is wrong, for it was apparently the year that Nehemiah returned to Persia. If Nehemiah's second trip was later by a few years, then Ezra could have been in Jerusalem in the interval when Nehemiah was away. If this is the case, it was Ezra who made the initial attempt to have Jews divorce their non-Jewish wives, and Nehemiah who subsequently tried to enforce what Ezra had initiated.

The second solution supposes that the king whom the Book of Nehemiah mentioned was Artaxerxes I, while the Book of Ezra means Artaxerxes II. According to this view, Nehemiah's activity took place around 445–432; while Ezra's return under Artaxerxes II was in 398 or 397. It is supposed that either the Chronicler or some compiler just before him added three verses [3] which incorrectly made Ezra and Nehemiah contemporaries.

Accordingly, one may choose the traditional view, which is a difficult one to support, or one of these untraditional views, which also have their drawbacks.

Once historical problems are raised in this way, there is no end to them. A second problem, for example, is the repetition of Ezra 2:3–70 in Nehemiah 7:6–73. The question arises why this list should come twice. Or there is a third problem: Ezra 4:1–5 relates that when Zerubbabel was rebuilding the Temple (520–516) certain hostile peoples, identified only as foes (they are apparently Samaritans) wished to join in the enterprise, and on being refused managed to frustrate the plans to build from the days of Cyrus (539) to those of Darius I, who ascended the throne in 522. Ezra 4:24 states that the building of the Temple was resumed only in the second year of Darius' reign. The intervening verses (6–23) deal with efforts ascribed to the reigns of Xerxes (485–465) and Artaxerxes (465–425) to impede the rebuilding not of the Temple but of the city walls. That is, the intervening verses are surprising, respecting both chronology and the specific aim of the foes. The effect of this puzzling passage is to raise the question of when it was that the difficulties with the Samaritans became acute, in 520–516 or in 458–445?

The question of sources used by the Chronicler is another problem that these books pose. The Hebrew of Ezra gives way in two places (4:8–6:18, 7:12–26) to Aramaic. The bulk of this Aramaic is a series of documents relating to the legitimacy of the activities of the Jews who returned to Jerusalem. The first of these quoted documents is a letter written by foes (Samaritans) to the Persian king,

---

[3] Neh. 8:9; 12:26 and 34.

warning that if the Jews were to be permitted to complete the building of the walls of Jerusalem, rebellion would ensue, and the king would lose the taxes due him (4:9–16). The king responded (4:17–22) by forbidding the rebuilding of the city. It is to be recalled that the passage (4:6–23) is out of place, as we saw above. Next, a letter (5:6–17) went to King Darius, reporting that Jews were building the Temple, and justifying their doing so on the basis of a decree given earlier by Cyrus to the Jewish leader, Sheshbazzar. Information about this decree of Cyrus was requested. Darius' reply (6:2–12) reported a confirming discovery of Cyrus' decree; moreover, the Persian officials were enjoined to co-operate generously in the rebuilding. Next, when Ezra came to Jerusalem he brought with him a letter from Artaxerxes, giving him unlimited powers (Ezra 7:12–26).

The allegation has been made that these documents are not genuine. It is contended that they are so pro-Jewish as to be unrealistic, and hence they are pious forgeries concocted to justify what the Jews were doing. What those who make the allegation seem to have explained inadequately is for what audience the documents were intended. If for Persians, it would have been risky to forge them, as the facts could readily have been ascertained. If for the Jews, what practical purpose would "forgeries" have served? The reply to these questions, when reply is made, is the suggestion that the documents are midrashic embellishments, consistent with the imagination of the Chronicler. A reasonable view, however, would be that these are authentic documents, which have been retouched.

The first person sections are regarded as "memoirs," either by Ezra and Nehemiah themselves, or else, in Oriental fashion, by admiring disciples. The memoirs and the Aramaic documents, plus some inherited third-person accounts, would constitute the sources utilized by the Chronicler. Since his material does not deal with kings, his manner of writing is naturally different, and his hand is not as obvious as it is in I and II Chronicles. He seems to be evident, however, at least in Ezra I, 3, 6:16–22 and Nehemiah 12:1–26 and 44–7.

In the scholarly discussions of whether Ezra preceded Nehemiah or Nehemiah Ezra, it is set forth that the issue at stake is really which of the two was the "actual founder" of Judaism.

This form of the question requires some explanation. In the schematization that resulted from the Graf-Wellhausen hypothesis,[4] it was presumed that in the postexilic period there took place those

[4] See page 335.

developments that introduced priestly organization and priestly ritual. These developments, we are told, brought to an end free prophecy
with its great spiritual heights. The free prophecy represents the
Hebrew religion; it is the new developments that are to be called
Judaism. The old Hebrew religion, so we are told, was creative, original, and profound; Judaism was mere formalization, mere lip-service
religion. Accordingly, the argument about Ezra and Nehemiah is not
so much whom we should credit as whom we should blame.

Furthermore, the decline of religion, so we are told, continued
from the time of Ezra and Nehemiah, since it became more external-
istic under the subsequent rabbis. When it became bad enough, Jesus
appeared on the scene to restore things to the former high level of
the Hebrew religion. The view is incorrect both for the age of Jesus
and for that of Ezra, Nehemiah, and the Chronicler.

More specifically, this unfortunate trend in scholarship took
out of the Books of Ezra and Nehemiah, as though it completely
characterized Judaism, one single item, namely the dismay attributed
to both worthies at the occurrence of intermarriage, and their efforts
to bar it. When one reads the surveys of Ezra and Nehemiah, one
sees the tendency to summarize what took place in their time in this
single item. Not only are Ezra and Nehemiah characterized as "particularists," but invariably as "narrow" particularists.

It is scarcely possible to argue that Ezra and Nehemiah were
universalists. But it is wrong in methodology to create modern labels
and categories, and to make ancient worthies fit Procrustean beds.
George Washington is scarcely to be condemned for not having provided relief from the dust storms of the Southwest, or Abraham
Lincoln for not having taken steps to create the United Nations.

Any judgment of Ezra and Nehemiah must assess them in the
light of their times and the problems they faced. To distinguish between the Hebrew religion and Judaism simply by assembling a narrow range of modern value judgments is the height of fatuity.

Insofar as Ezra and Nehemiah do represent extreme views dis-
sents are found in two roughly contemporaneous sources. The Book
of Ruth exalts a Moabite girl to the point of declaring her to have
been an ancestress of King David. The Book of Jonah is a rebuke to
the exclusivist mind.

Just as in the age before Ezra and Nehemiah, a missionary[5]
movement was felt, so in later rabbinic times a broad missionary impulse existed. The view of Ezra and Nehemiah was certainly not
without influence in subsequent Judaism, yet it was an extreme one,

[5] See pages 204ff.

which subsequent ages of Jews did not follow. Accordingly, it is a misinterpretation to equate the single item of opposition to intermarriage with Judaism as a whole, or to identify as Judaism that transient epoch in which Ezra and Nehemiah lived and worked.

The Chronicler permits us to learn very little about Ezra and Nehemiah. It is quite valid to say that Nehemiah is the figure used by the Chronicler to explain how Jerusalem became walled in and stabilized and that Ezra is used to explain how the religious tradition was revived in Jerusalem. Since the Chronicler was not a good historian, he abstained from giving any direct account of the time from Zerubbabel to Ezra, except for the laconic verse, Ezra 4:6: "In the kingship of Xerxes (Ahasuerus), at the beginning of his kingship, they wrote an accusation against the dwellers of Judah and Jerusalem." If the Chronicler is right that in 445 Jerusalem was in shambles and the Priestly system not in operation, then some hypothesis such as is outlined in Chapter 16 above is needed to explain how the rebuilding efforts in the days of Haggai and Zechariah were nullified, and how Jerusalem came to be in ruins.

If, however, the Chronicler is simply schematizing, and if the Aramaic documents are forgeries, and if the "memoirs" are frauds, then the view may be correct which denies that there ever was an Ezra, and which asserts that he was a fictitious person invented by the Chronicler as the embodiment of those accomplishments the Chronicler wished to trace. This view, however, seems to me preposterous.[6] It is much more reasonable to suppose that the Chronicler had sources, documents, and traditions about a Nehemiah and an Ezra. We can understand him once we regard him as a schematizer rather than a historian. He was less interested in being accurate about history than he was in completing his chosen task of showing that the Temple and its officials represented an ancient tradition, bent but never broken, and surviving in its authentic form to the Chronicler's own day. In Chronicles, he finds a threat to the authenticity to be the evil toleration by the monarchs, in spite of prophetic warning, of non-Yahvistic practices and peoples. For the postexilic period he has no monarchs to blame. His strictures against intermarriage are only an adaptation of his previous strictures against non-Yahvistic religion.

[6] I recognize the harshness of this judgment. The radical nature of the suggestion does not trouble me. In other areas views even more radical have appealed to me. An Ezra who became legendary would trouble me not at all; an Ezra who never was seems to me silly.

But in his day there was a new complication. Respecting the Samaritans, he was forced to recognize that they were worshipers of Yahve. Therefore he altered the target of his disapproval from that of wrong practices to that of wrong people. And in disapproving of the Samaritans who were worshipers of Yahve, he naturally extended his disapproval to all Gentiles.

We do not know the details of the admission of Chronicles-Ezra-Nehemiah to the canon. Since Ezra-Nehemiah is normally found in Jewish Bibles [7] before rather than after Chronicles, it is assumed that Ezra-Nehemiah was canonized before Chronicles. Certainly, Chronicles occupies no unique place in ancient rabbinic thought; Nehemiah is regarded as a person of much less importance than Ezra. Indeed, Ezra the Scribe (for so he is known) is regarded as the great man who, when the Torah was forgotten in Israel, came up from Babylonia to revive it. It was this affirmative achievement, not his cruel rupture of marriages, that earned him his great eminence in the eyes of the ancient rabbis.

But an alternative explanation is more likely. When Chronicles was written, the distinction—so basic to the P code—between Levite and Priest had not arisen; therefore the Chronicler wrote at a time previous to the composition of the P code. Ezra and Nehemiah underwent editing after the Chronicler wrote them so as to bring them into greater conformity with the P code. But Chronicles, which came into the canon long after Ezra and Nehemiah were accepted, was not thoroughly edited by a Priest. Hence, it retains its Levite character.

[7] In Christian Bibles, the order is Kings, Chronicles, Ezra, and Nehemiah, coming before the Hagiographa and the Prophets.

CHAPTER

39

RUTH

In the Book of Ruth, the first verse tells us that the events described occurred "in the days when the Judges judged," that is to say, in the period of Settlement, before the monarchy had arisen under Saul. Later in the story a quaint ceremony, which we shall look at, is described as though it were something the generation living at the time of the author needed to have explained to it. We have here an old story in a comparatively young version. The events of the story presumably took place about 1200 B.C., but they are narrated from a time eight or nine hundred years later. In its present form, the Book of Ruth comes from the period between 450 and 250 B.C.[1]

Unlike the Book of Esther, wherein is to be found a plot that unfolds with some complexity and provides us with hero, heroine, and villain, the Book of Ruth is a series of subdued but appealing vignettes, deriving its beauty, and its impact, from character rather than from incident. Or, more precisely, in Esther incident is more important than character; in Ruth homely incident, free from melodrama, brilliantly discloses character.

Granted that the story is, as many assert, an ancient one, we must inquire into the particular form of its retelling. The most im-

[1] The basis for this judgment rests on peculiarities of the Hebrew of the Book, namely the presence of Aramaisms and certain words used only in late times.

portant clue is the set of five verses that conclude the book—the genealogy, which, on examination, seems related less to the events of the book than to the purpose of the author. At the time of retelling, long after David's time, David's stature had risen to exalted heights through the idealization that had set in; for in the late times when there was no king, there existed a profound yearning for one of David's descendants to emerge, establish a throne, and ascend it. If in popular fancy David's name did not carry the austere magnitude of Moses', or the awesome uniqueness of Abraham's, nevertheless in general acclaim and ease of identification, David's name led the rest. He was the hero of the populace, and accordingly the purpose of the narrator could not have been realized better than by ending the book with his name.

The genealogical ending, though appended to the book, is germane to it, for the message of the book may be summed up as: "Let me tell you a story of a fine and worthy woman, not born a Jewess, who joined our people, and who merited having no less a person than King David for her great-grandson." The Moabites were a people kindred to Israel, but regarded with such hostility that Deuteronomy 23:3 prohibits one who had a Moabite (or Ammonite) ancestor ten generations previously from entering the congregation.

In short, the Book of Ruth is a response rather than an initial statement. It retorts to the contention that for a Jew to marry outside the circle of Jewish people is wrong by contending that the Gentile Ruth was, as a person, beyond reproach. It proves this by showing how she attached herself to the Jewish people, and, Gentile though she had been, became the ancestor of King David.

To whom—when and under what conditions—is the Book of Ruth responding? The greatest likelihood is that the period represented is the middle of the postexilic. More specifically, in the Book of Nehemiah it is related that Nehemiah (who flourished about 440) observed that there were Jews with Ammonite, Moabite, and Philistine Ashdodite wives; of the children born of such marriages,

> half of them spoke Ashdodite, but were unable to speak Jewish . . . I [Nehemiah] quarreled with them, cursed them, smote some, pulled their hair, and adjured them not to give their [Jewish] daughters to your sons, or marry your sons to their daughters. Is it not in this way that Solomon the King of Israel sinned . . . The Gentile wives made him sin. [Neh. 13:24–6]

The Book of Ruth is a protest against just such attitudes and policies of Ezra and Nehemiah.

The power of the book lies in its surface serenity. Its strength as propaganda lies in its avoidance of the frequent devices of propaganda. It has a heroine but it lacks a villain. It is affirming a conviction, not attacking an ideological foe. The Book of Ruth is an edifying romance, not a work of history. The names of some of the characters disclose the fictional nature of the book. Naomi means "sweetness," her two sons who die young men are Mahlon ("disease") and Chilion ("consumption"). Orpah means "back," for Orpah turned her *back* on Naomi. Ruth means "companion, friend."

The introduction tells us how Naomi chanced to be in Moab. There had been a famine in Israel. Now that the famine was over, Naomi intended to return home; with her husband and her sons dead, she would go back alone. Her daughters-in-law accompanied her on the way, and offered to go to Israel with her. Naomi refused their offer, and the three women wept. Orpah left to return to Moab, but Ruth would not leave:

> Do not entreat me to leave you, or, returning, go away from you. Wherever you go I will go. Where you lodge, I will lodge. Your people are my people; your God is my God. Where you die, I will die and there be buried. May Yahve now, and in the future, so work things out; only death will part us. [*1:16–17*]

On the arrival of mother and daughter-in-law in Naomi's home, Bethlehem, the city was astounded and asked, "Is this really Naomi?" She said, "Do not call me Sweetness, call me Bitterness, for the Almighty has brought evil things upon me."

In Bethlehem there lived a relative of Naomi's husband named Boaz, a man of substance. Ruth went to Boaz's field to glean[2] corn. When she was pointed out to Boaz he invited her to confine her gleaning to his fields alone and to take her meals with his own household. She thanked him for his consideration to an alien. He replied that he knew how she had left her homeland, come to a new people, and taken refuge under Yahve, Israel's God.

Treated with such kindness, she gleaned in his field. When she brought home to Naomi the grain she had beaten out, Naomi told her again that Boaz was a kinsman. Naomi urged Ruth to take that step which would amount to an appeal to Boaz to live up to the requirement of a next-of-kin marriage.[3] Accordingly, Ruth went to the

---

[2] See Lev. 19:9–10 and 24:19 for regulations which required the leaving of produce unharvested so that the poor might glean ("gather") it.

[3] In a levirate ("brother-in-law") marriage, the brother-in-law of a childless widow was obligated to marry the widow so that she could become a mother; see page 366. Only here in Ruth is there biblical evidence for an extension of the requirement to a mere kinsman. It is therefore argued that Ruth was written at a time so late that the author had no exact knowledge of these obligatory mar

threshing floor where Boaz would spend the night. She lay next to him, chastely. When he was asleep, she uncovered his feet; when he awoke in the middle of the night, she asked him to cover her (apparently with that part of the cover which had been on his feet), for he was her kinsman. Boaz was delighted to assent, for the whole city knew Ruth's high quality; however, there was an even closer kinsman who had to be given the first opportunity.

At the city gate Boaz encountered this other (and unnamed) kinsman, in the presence of ten [4] of the elders of the city, and told him of the opportunity of acquiring the land left to Naomi by her husband, and also Ruth, for whom progeny had to be provided. The opportunity was refused by the other kinsman and so passed to Boaz. To confirm the validity of the transfer, an ancient [5] ceremony was performed. The kinsman took off his shoe and Boaz put it on. [6] Thereupon Boaz announced himself publicly as the kinsman. The elders blessed Ruth, wishing her the noble accomplishments of Rachel and Leah (who were the wives of Jacob) and of Tamar. [7] So Boaz and Ruth were married. A child was born, and Naomi became its nurse.

The book concludes with a genealogy, which begins with Perez, [8] runs through six generations from Perez to Boaz, and continues with the son of Boaz and Ruth, named Obed, whose son was Jesse, who was the father of David.

Ancient rabbinic speculations believed Samuel to have been the author of Ruth. A respectable number of modern scholars, though not accepting Samuel as the author, believe that Ruth was written in the pre-exilic period. Such a view tends to regard the book as reliable history. The allusion to the act of confirmation by the ceremony of the shoe as though it were an obsolete practice is only one of several indications that the book is later than this. Another is the fact that Ruth is found in Hebrew Bibles in the Hagiographa.

It is sounder to regard Ruth, at least in the form in which the book survives, as didactic legend rather than history. In such a view, the value of the book, apart from its intrinsic literary beauty, is en-

---

riages; that in actuality the requirement never went beyond a brother-in-law; and that the purpose was to make the widow a mother, and not, as 3:1 suggests, simply to provide the widow with security.

[4] From this passage stems the traditional Jewish practice of setting the minimum quorum (*minyan*) for community worship at ten.

[5] The text (4:7) makes it clear that the ancient ceremony was no longer being performed in the days of the narrator of Ruth.

[6] Something kindred is prescribed in Deut. 25:9.

[7] See pages 366–367.

[8] The son of Judah and Tamar.

hanced, for Ruth reflects a postexilic Jewish attitude at variance with that of Ezra and Nehemiah and thereby serves to restore a balance by expressing the opposite point of view from them on the subject of hospitality to aliens.

Moreover, the tranquillity of the life described in the book is at variance with the violence found in the Book of Judges and would seem to reflect a later attitude. The author gives a picture of how life should be. Vicissitudes arise in life, but reliable friends and neighbors gladly lend a helping hand; to be an alien is not to undergo scorn, for all the city knew of Ruth, and admired and welcomed her. The piety advocated here is not that of fidelity to elaborate ritual—indeed, ritual is startlingly absent from the book—but that of good and worthy people living together helpfully. It is this piety, rather than the bare events depicted, that has made Ruth the most appealing book in the Hebrew Scriptures.

CHAPTER

40

JONAH

WHILE JONAH is found in both Jewish and Christian Scripture among the prophets, it is more appropriate to discuss it among the narrative books, for its story form makes it quite different from all the other prophetic books.

Jonah should not be regarded as history, and the incredible whale should not be a barrier to the understanding of a simple but eloquent moral fable. The Book of Jonah poses the important question of whether, since there is but one God, His concern is only for Israel or for all mankind. The book is not *by* Jonah but about him.

The author of Jonah is a teacher, gifted in the writing of fiction. For the background of his story, he chooses a period some centuries earlier, and a place consistent with that time. Nineveh, the capital of Assyria is the setting, and the time is well before its fall in 612. Jonah receives the divine command to go to Nineveh to proclaim its wickedness to its inhabitants. Jonah does not want to go. He wonders why he or God should be concerned about those heathens miles away. In order to flee from the divine obligation, Jonah embarked on a ship for Tarshish (possibly Tartersa, a Spanish site which the Phoenicians had reached). But God sent a storm which frightened the sailors, although Jonah slept on peacefully. After the sailors appealed vainly to their own gods to abate the storm, the captain awakened Jonah to pray to God. Jonah, who had already told them why he was in flight, advised that the sea would abate if they would throw him into it, for he was the cause of the storm.[1] The sailors prayed, not to their gods, but to God. They cast Jonah into the sea and immediately it became calm.

But God had prepared a great fish, which swallowed Jonah.[2] After three days and three nights, the fish vomited Jonah, at divine behest, on dry ground. Again Jonah was bidden to go to Nineveh and this time he went. After arriving there he predicted that in forty days Nineveh would be overthrown. The Ninevehites believed Jonah, and they complied with his advice to repent. Accordingly, God changed His plan and did not destroy Nineveh. All this did not please Jonah (a perceptive point on the author's part). In fact, it made him very angry, for he would rather have had the Ninevehites destroyed than his prediction proved wrong.

Jonah stationed himself east of the city, in a booth he had built. God made a "gourd" grow overnight to give Jonah some shade, and Jonah was pleased. The next day God had a worm smite the gourd to wither it, and caused a warm east wind to bring uncomfortable heat to the now unprotected Jonah. The loss of the gourd had made Jonah very, very angry. God says to him:

> You are concerned for the gourd. You did not work for it, you did not grow it. It came up one night, and perished before the next night. Look at Niniveh, a large city, with more than 120,-000 persons—unimportant, uninformed people [3]—and much cattle. Should I not be concerned for them? [Jonah 4:10–11]

The intrinsic value of the Book of Jonah is just as high as that of any prophetic doctrine that has been stated abstractly. The contention that God is the universal God, concerned for all humanity as well as for Israel, is prophetic doctrine at its peak.

There was a historical person named Jonah ben Amittai (II Kings 14:25) who lived in the eighth pre-Christian century. Yet students of Aramaic detect in the Hebrew of the Book of Jonah traces of this kindred language, which became the spoken tongue in Palestine (and the diplomatic language of the then known Eastern world) in the sixth century. The Book of Jonah is considered by modern schol-

---

[1] A "Jonah" in modern slang is a person who is regarded as the cause of misfortune or bad luck.

[2] A later hand considered it essential for Jonah, in the body of the fish, to have prayed. He added a prayer (2:2–10 Heb., 2–9 Eng.) of some beauty but scarcely congruous with Jonah's situation. Perhaps this prayer reflects a thanksgiving for an escape from drowning.

[3] Literally "who cannot discern between the right and the left hand."

ars to come from the latter part of the Persian period (about 375, or possibly even later).

The spirit of this book is in sharp contrast to the motif of exclusivism found in Ezra and Nehemiah, and needs to enter into any rounded estimate of postexilic Judaism. Nineteenth-century German scholars tended to omit it from consideration, and thereby to paint postexilic Judaism as a chauvinistic, narrow legalism. That is a one-sided, distorted view. To omit Jonah from consideration is just as wrong as to depict postexilic Judaism only in the light of Jonah.

ESTHER

THERE HAVE BEEN those who have questioned the right of the Scroll of Esther to a place in Scripture. These include Martin Luther and a number of ancient and modern rabbis. There would be some merit in these opinions if the Tanak were simply a book of religion. But since it is a collection of the literature of a people, reflecting their experiences and vicissitudes, Esther is inherently worthy of inclusion.

Major objections can be cited from the religious standpoint of the Pentateuch. First, the story relates that Esther became a concubine to the King of Persia, before becoming the queen; and in becoming the queen, she was married to a Gentile. Secondly, the story contains incidents of bloodthirsty revenge, at variance with the Pentateuchal view that man must not be vengeful. Even more significant is the total absence of any mention of God. The modern commentators who stress this peculiarity are underlining a fact that also occurred to the ancient Greek translators. Esther in the Greek Bible has been expanded by the addition to the Scroll of some prayers which the Greek Jews felt Esther should have prayed.

Emphasizing its defects too strongly, however, can lead to a faulty approach to the Scroll of Esther. It is a light book, a ribald and funny story, and it is not adequately appreciated when its read-

ers or critics are too somber and long-faced. Moreover, Esther discloses a tremendous narrative skill, for it is as comic a story as has
ever been told. Its change of pace from the flighty to the serious is
abrupt, but, as in good farce, the characters are involved in incidents
that to them are real and menacing. The moments of utter seriousness in Esther never completely conceal the high comedy; the author
never allows the recurrent earnestness of his protagonists' plight to
deter him from those little touches of character and incident that
mark the difference between a mere narrator and a storyteller of
genius.

The Scroll begins with the description of a sumptuous royal
party given in Susa, the capital of Persia, by King Ahasuerus (Xerxes). Everybody of importance from all his one hundred and twenty-
seven provinces was there. For a hundred and eighty days the party
had gone on in all luxury; now, however, the affair was being ended
with a smaller celebration of only seven days, limited to those people
who were then in Susa. The queen Vashti also gave for the women a
seven-day party held in the palace. By the seventh day, Ahasuerus
had become a little tipsy. He therefore ordered his eunuchs—they
numbered seven—to bring Vashti into his presence so as to show her
beauty to the crowd assembled.[1] But Vashti refused to come, and the
wrath of the king smouldered at this disobedience.

He consulted his sages and astrologers—they also numbered
seven—as to what to do about the queen's disobedience. One of them
replied that Vashti had offended not only the king, but all those assembled. Moreover, she had set an example which could impel all
women to disobey their husbands. Therefore Vashti must be deposed,
and someone else selected in her place, so that thereafter women
would obey their husbands! Accordingly, a royal decree went out that
every man was to be the ruler in his own household. We are not told
directly of the fate of Vashti; presumably she was executed. But
when the wrath of the king had quieted down, and he recollected
Vashti, he instituted steps to have beautiful virgins brought from all
his provinces to the royal harem in Susa. Out of this group Ahasuerus would select a successor to Vashti.

There dwelled in Susa a Jew, Mordecai, who had raised an orphan niece, Esther, a beautiful young woman. Esther was brought
to the royal harem along with the other virgins; she found quick
favor with Hegai, the custodian of the harem, and was given the best
quarters for herself and her attendant maids—of which there were
seven. Esther had not revealed that she was Jewish, for Mordecai had

[1] Later tradition, embellishing the story, and wishing to account for Vashti's refusal to come, related that Ahasuerus wanted to exhibit her naked.

commanded her not to. Every day Mordecai went for a stroll outside the harem building so as to keep informed about Esther.

The women needed to spend a year in beautifying themselves (six months of applying myrrh, and six of spices). The procedure was that a woman was taken to the king in the evening, and returned to the harem in the morning. She could not go uninvited but had to be summoned. When it came Esther's turn, the king preferred her to the other concubines. He crowned her the new queen and marked the occasion by a great party.

Mordecai learned of a plot by two men, Bigthan and Teresh, to assassinate the king. He told Esther, who told the king. The two men were hanged and the incident was recorded in the official chronicles.

At this time a certain Haman rose to an eminence greater than all other officials. A royal decree obligated all men to bow and prostrate themselves to him. Mordecai, however, refused to do so. When Haman learned that Mordecai was a Jew, his wrath was boundless. Scorning merely to punish Mordecai, he determined to exterminate all the Jews throughout the kingdom. He would do this by lot (for which the Hebrew is *pur,* and the plural *purim*), and set the date for the month of Adar, twelve months away. For this Haman needed royal approval, which he purchased from Ahasuerus, having first said to the king:

> There is a certain people, scattered and dispersed among the peoples in all your kingly provinces. Their laws are different from those of other peoples, they disregard the royal laws, and it is not advantageous to the king to be permissive to them. [3:8]

Ahasuerus gave his consent to Haman, and royal scribes sent out decrees, written in all the diverse languages of the various provinces, that the date of utter extermination of all the Jews was set for the thirteenth day of the coming Adar.

Hearing this, Mordecai's response was to rend his clothes, don sackcloth and ashes,[2] and come to the gate of the palace. When word of this was brought to Esther, who was ignorant of Haman's plan, she sent fresh clothes to Mordecai, which he refused.

A messenger named Hatach, sent by Esther to Mordecai, brought back the account of what was happening and also the royal decree. She was told that she must intercede with Ahasuerus. Through Hatach, Esther replied to Mordecai that the king had not sent for her for thirty days; it was illegal, she reminded him, to enter into the king's presence without being summoned. Indeed, the penalty for

[2] See also Ezekiel 27:30 and Joshua 7:6 for these symbols of mourning.

doing so was death—unless the king should hold out his golden
scepter to signify that the death penalty was not to be imposed. Mordecai replied:

> Do not privately imagine that you will escape in the royal palace
> any more than the other Jews. If you remain silent at this time,
> relief and deliverance will arise for the Jews from some other
> place, but you and your father's family will be destroyed. Who
> knows but that you came to royalty for exactly a time such as
> this. [4:13–14]

Esther therefore instructed Mordecai to gather together all the
Jews of Susa, so that they might fast, as she and her servants would,
for three days. Thereafter she would run the risk of approaching the
king. On the third day Esther attired herself in royal robes and went
into the inner court of the palace so that the king would see her. He
extended the golden sceptre to her; he told her that she might have
anything she asked for—even half of the kingdom.

This episode might well have ended the story, with Esther denouncing Haman and obtaining a nullification of the hostile decree.
The author, however, appears to have sensed intuitively that to end
here would have spoiled the story. Moreover, there was the need—as
certain theorists of the drama in the nineteenth century have asserted—for the protagonist and the antagonist to confront each
other; such a scene, they declare, is obligatory. The author of Esther
prolongs the story, and, in his keen sense of wit and the ridiculous,
proceeds to add complications. Therefore, Esther's reply to the king
was that she wished to give a dinner for the king and Haman on the
following day.

Haman left the palace after receiving the invitation, puffed up
at the queen's recognition of him. He caught a glimpse of Mordecai,
stolidly not bowing, and this put him in a bad temper. At home, he
bragged to his wife Zeresh and his gathered friends about his great
ascendancy. He boasted that only he had been invited to accompany
the king to the queen's dinner; but, he said, it all seemed empty to
him when he glimpsed Mordecai at the king's gate. Zeresh and the
friends, to relieve Haman's gloom, suggested that he erect a high gallows, hang Mordecai, and go to the dinner in good spirits. So Haman
erected the gallows.

That night the king was troubled by insomnia, so he had the
chronicle of his reign read to him, to help him fall asleep. When the
passage was read about the plot of Bigthan and Teresh, the king
asked what had been done in recognition of Mordecai. Nothing, he
was told. Haman was then in the inner court. The king summoned

him, and asked him what should be done for a man whom the king wished to honor. Haman took it for granted that the proposed honor was for him. He therefore suggested that such a man should be dressed in royal clothes, which the king had worn, given a horse on which the king had ridden, and adorned with a crown. A high official should be assigned to dress the man, seat him on a horse in the city square, and proclaim, "This is the way in which the king honors a man." The king replied that Haman was to hasten and execute these things for Mordecai. Haman did so.

Then he hastened to his home in deep melancholy. Zeresh and his friends said to him, "If Mordecai is of Jewish descent, you will not prevail over him, but instead fall before him." While they were talking, the king's eunuchs came to hurry Haman to Esther's party.

After some drinking, the king asked a second time what Esther's wish might be; it would (he repeated) be granted, even to the half of his kingdom. Esther replied:

Let my life be given as my request,
And my people as my petition.
For I and my people are sold
To destruction, death, and extermination.
Were it as slaves we were sold, I would be silent . . .
  [7:3B–4]

The king demanded to know the author of the outrage. Esther replied, "This wicked Haman."

At this point the king had to go into the palace garden, as a result of his drinking. Haman began to plead with Esther for his life. (Presumably she retreated and he kept pressing forward.) The king re-entered to find Haman prostrate on Esther's bed and said, "Are you trying to make a conquest of the queen with me in the house?"

A eunuch then informed the king that the high gallows Haman had prepared for Mordecai was finished. The king ordered that Haman be hanged on it. Ahasuerus gave Esther Haman's house. Mordecai was summoned before the king and queen. Esther threw herself at the king's feet and weepingly begged that the king annul Haman's plan. Ahasuerus replied that having given Esther Haman's house, he was furthermore publishing throughout his provinces a royal decree permitting Jews to destroy, kill, and exterminate their foes, all this to take place on the same day, the thirteenth of Adar. For Jews, the decree brought light and joy throughout the provinces. Many Gentiles were converted to Judaism.

Thus the thirteenth of Adar was turned into a day of gladness. With Mordecai raised to eminence in the palace, the various officials co-operated, and the Jews slaughtered many of their foes that day. They slew also the ten sons of Haman. Esther made the further request that the permission of the thirteenth be extended to the fourteenth day.

Jews celebrate these days of Adar as days of rejoicing, feasting, exchanging presents, and giving gifts to the poor, in celebration of their relief from their foes—this in conformity with a document written by Mordecai and broadcast throughout the provinces. Because the selected day had been chosen by lot, they called the happy days *purim* ("lots"). Jews and converts to Judaism accepted the obligation to celebrate the two days in perpetuity.

What is known of Persian history, which is a great deal, fails to confirm the account, and even bars it from acceptance. No Esther is known as the queen of Xerxes; his queen was a Persian woman. Indeed, Esther is suspiciously like the name of the goddess Astarte, and Mordecai like the god Marduk; it was suggested long ago that these names were chosen by the author because they seemed to him good Persian[3] names for his Jewish heroes (Esther has a Hebrew name, Hadassah).

Therefore the Scroll of Esther should not be regarded as accurate history. Rather, it is a remarkably well-constructed story, artificially bound up with a celebration, Purim, which had come to have great currency among Jews in the lands east of Palestine. Purim is, of course, never mentioned in the Pentateuch; its adoption by Jews was much too late for that. The story itself is in part akin to others, such as Judith in the Apocrypha, in which a heroine saves the people.

Aspects of Esther indicate that we are in a time when Jews were scattered throughout the known world, a situation existing after the time of Alexander the Great. At that time Jews both attracted proselytes and evoked hostility (as witness the charge that Jews lived by their own laws and refused to obey the laws of the king). They underwent dangerous persecution in the Greek period (such as is related in III Maccabees[4]).

Hence, a story of averted persecution and an adopted festival day were combined into a legend of how that festival came to be cele-

[3] They are in reality Babylonian.
[4] This book relates that a Graeco-Egyptian king, Ptolemy Philopator had passed through Jerusalem after a victory over his Seleucidian foes. He had wanted to enter the Temple, but miraculously he was prevented. He determined in vengeance to destroy the Jews of Egypt. He had them brought into an arena to be trampled by elephants, but the elephants instead trampled Ptolemy's soldiers. An annual observance was instituted in memory of the event. A comparable story is told by Josephus (*Against Apion*, II, 5), but about a different Ptolemy, Physcon. Philopator flourished about 220, Physcon about 150.

brated. The precise origin of the festival itself is unknown, and a
range of theories exists to account for it. An eastern origin seems unmistakable, and Jews in the east may have been the first Jews to
adopt it. They Judaized the pagan festival through telling the story
of Esther. Initially the observance of Purim was regional, being confined to the east.

The purpose of the Scroll of Esther may well have been to commend the festival to Jews in the west, in Palestine, and in the Greek
world. Some fluidity in the time of celebration of Purim existed, as is
attested by what we might call "appendices" to the book (9:20–10:3).
In 9:18–19, the Jews in the provinces observed Adar 13 and 14;
those in Susa added the 15th to these days. We are told (9:19) that
Jews in unwalled towns observed the 13th and 14th. The first appendix[5] (9:20–32) supposes that Mordecai wrote up what had happened and recommended that all Jews observe the 14th and 15th. Another appendix (10:1–3) relates that the achievements of Ahasuerus
are found in the Chronicles of Media and Persia, and that Mordecai
the Jew was second in command.

In the Greek translation a note is added to the ending, saying
that in the reign of Ptolemy and Cleopatra a certain Dositheos, a
priest and Levite, and his son Ptolemy had brought the Scroll (to
Egypt?) after it had been translated in Jerusalem by Lysimachus,
son of Ptolemy. Two different Egyptian pairs bore the names of
Ptolemy and Cleopatra; the one pair flourished about 115 B.C., and
the other about 50 B.C. If the note is reliable, the translation into
Greek took place either about 115 or about 50. The point of the note
seems to be to vouch for the reliability of the contents of the Scroll
of Esther, and hence to be urging Greek Jews to adopt the celebration, which had moved west to Palestine from the east. And just as
the Greek translation was designed to encourage the observance of
the festival, so the Scroll itself, composed in the east, was designed
to spread the holiday westward.

It is difficult to say at exactly what period Esther was written.
Unquestionably it was a fairly late one. The absence of any mention
of the Maccabean revolt is taken by some as an indication that that
event was well in the past. Moreover, an apocryphal book, *The Wisdom of Jesus ben Sirach*, written in 192 B.C., gives a review of notable
Jewish heroes (Chapters 44–9), but makes no mention of Mordecai
or Esther. Perhaps a date of 150 B.C. is a reasonable one.

The dates of Purim were variable for several centuries. Today
Adar 13 is memorialized as "Esther's fast" and Purim is observed only

[5] Perhaps 9:29–32 is a separate appendix, attributing to Esther, as well as to
Mordecai, a letter to all Jews to observe the days of Purim.

for the one day, Adar 14. The Jewish celebration of Purim came to be one of carnival hilarity, and even of occasional excess. The ancient rabbis (that is, those who espoused the festival) declared it permissible to drink on Purim to the point of an inability to distinguish between "blessed is Mordecai" and "cursed is Haman." Masquerades and theatricals marked the day; in European and American rabbinic schools revered teachers were burlesqued by their students. Parodies, even of sacred literature (such as *The Tractate of Drunkards*), were written. Mechanical noisemakers (*Haman-greggers*) were brought into the synagogue to swell the chorus of jeers at the mention of Haman's name. How much of the hilarity of the observance goes back to the pre-Jewish ritual is uncertain. Some of it seems still to shine through the vastly changed circumstances. Purim helped keep Judaism from being an austere religion, a danger that its emphasis on intellectual tradition courted.

If a personal word is not out of order, the Scroll of Esther seemed to me at one time to have no place in Scripture, both because of its barbarity and what then seemed to me its unreality. But Hitler was a Haman *redivivus*, and the generation of those who were adults in 1932 discovered that the legends about the age of Xerxes came to be a traumatic modern experience, multiplied in numbers and intensified in severity almost beyond belief.

Esther is by religious standards not a noble book. But perhaps it **is** a knowledgeable book.

APPENDIXES

A SELECTED BIBLIOGRAPHY

INDICES

Appendix I

ARCHAEOLOGY AND THE TANAK

IN THE POPULAR MIND archaeology is as romantic a pursuit as exists, and consequently popular misconceptions about it prevail. But apart from journalistic excesses, some archaeologists have directly or indirectly fostered the view that "archaeology confirms the Bible," yet without specifying exactly what they mean.

The methods of archaeology and the nature of archaeological finds differ from region to region. Thus, the sandy soil of Egypt has preserved papyri that rotted and perished in Palestine. The baked clay tablets of Assyria and Babylonia are nearly indestructible, but on the whole tablets were not used in Palestine. Archaeological discoveries made outside Palestine ofttimes bear on the Bible, and accordingly there is some basis for distinguishing between Palestinian archaeology, which would imply a geographic limitation, and Biblical archaeology, which would not. Palestinian archaeology concerns itself not so much with inscriptions or documents as with the artifacts (pottery, weapons, coins, religious objects) that disclose the nature of Palestinian civilization at its various stages.

In the popular mind, an archaeologist leads an expedition of native diggers somewhere, gets to work, and, if lucky, finds inscriptions or documents. The fact, however, is that documents and inscriptions are relatively minor, and a failure to find them by no means frustrates an archaeologist's purpose. Of far more concern to the archaeologist are revelations about the particular site itself and the artifacts that most vividly disclose its past. Moreover, surface explorations, even by airplane, throw light on important matters like roads, trade routes, and the availability of a water supply.

Palestine is dotted with innumerable mounds (the Arabic word for mound is *tel*). These were settlements, often on a height, around which a rampart of some kind was frequently constructed. The settlement might be destroyed in war or by earthquake, and consequently abandoned for a longer or shorter period; during this time the superstructures (walls and roofs) might wash away in the rains, but the substructures remain. A second settlement could be built over the debris of the first, and then a third over the second, and so on, so that if a mound were to be sliced like a layer cake, it could reveal comparable layers, called strata. Since the strata represent different ages, the architecture and the artifacts may differ from stratum to stratum.

Tels must be excavated by hand labor, for steam shovels would destroy what the archaeologist is looking for. The careful archaeologist uncovers one stratum at a time—walls, and rooms and their contents. Broken pieces of pottery (shards) occur in great abundance; and it has turned out that pottery is a guide of tremendous significance. This is true because archaeological experience has made it possible to co-ordinate pottery with inscriptions and to date the pottery; and since virtually every period has its own peculiar pottery, the pottery, once dated, becomes a means of dating a stratum. Other useful discoveries include jewelry, tools, and weapons. Archaeologists are accustomed to speak of ages, such as Early Bronze or Middle Iron; flint tools reflect an age earlier than that of bronze, and bronze tools an earlier one than that of iron. These divisions of time indicate the developing aspects of civilization, and are useful as general indices of the constantly evolving life in Palestine. This is especially the case when pottery can help to date strata of the same age in two different tels and reveal the difference between two towns of the same period. Thus, if the stratum of one tel exhibits Egyptian artifacts and the other does not, reasonable conclusions can be drawn about the extent of Egyptian conquest. Sacred objects, such as figurines of god-

MODERN PALESTINE AND
ARCHAEOLOGICAL SITES

desses, throw light on religious belief and practice, and illuminate especially such prophets as Hosea and Jeremiah, who denounced the Canaanite worship absorbed by some of the Hebrew tribes. In short, even when its findings are not of the sort to create sensations in the public press, archaeology is remarkably successful in providing a well-rounded understanding of different ages of a civilization.

A knowledge of the *events* that occurred within a specific civilization, however, requires the assistance of inscriptions or documents rather than artifacts. Archaeology can recover for us a general understanding of Hebrew civilization during the reign of David, but it would take inscriptions about the particular events to confirm or deny the bibilical data we have on them. Most of the inscriptions found so far are in themselves unexciting, but even the promissory note of some borrower to his lender can have a double importance. In the first place, such unspectacular inscriptions give us some knowledge of legal and economic life.

In the second place, our understanding of the Hebrew language or of Hebrew custom is enriched even by such inscriptions. Paradoxically, those inscriptions which are least important in themselves are often highly significant for the coincidental information they disclose. An understanding of the Hebrew of the Bible requires the best possible knowledge of Hebrew. To what other Semitic languages is it kindred, and from what proto-Semitic language did it develop?

Scripture abounds in obscurities which have often been explained simply as the results of copyists' errors, errors preserved, under Masoretic influence, when the received text was copied with undeviating fidelity. The increased knowledge of Hebrew and its Semitic relationships derived from inscriptions has shown that supposed errors are really grammatical constructions rare in Scripture but commonplace in kindred languages. To take a specific example, Biblical Hebrew was needed initially for an understanding of Akkadian, a term that refers both to Babylonian of about 2000 B.C., and to that of the biblical period, beginning at the end of the seventh pre-Christian century. So many Akkadian tablets have been found and deciphered that Akkadian has come to be a means for understanding Hebrew better.

The very great antiquity of both Egyptian and Mesopotamian inscriptions has provided scholars with extensive information about Palestine both in the patriarchal period and that just previous to the Settlement and Conquest. Allusions in Genesis, Joshua, and Judges to ancient peoples have come to be better understood. For example, the man who sold Abraham the cave of Machpelah was Ephron the Hittite. Biblical data alone would scarcely identify these people for us, but today we know a very great deal about them. Similarly we are now in possession of information about Palestine before the Conquest and the Settlement, so that peoples formerly obscure are now tolerably good acquaintances, and place names once mystifying are quite clear.

The remarkable development of the science of archaeology in the past one hundred years, and more particularly in the past fifty years, has made it necessary to revise some views of biblical history which had become virtually axiomatic. To give a single example, there was a dominant trend in scholarship at the turn of the century, as we saw above, to regard the Psalms as products of a very late age. To paraphrase one scholar, the issue was not whether some of the Psalms were as late as the Maccabean age (150 B.C.), but whether any at all were earlier. This view was supported by the argument that neither the alphabet nor literacy existed as early as the time of David. Yet a discovery in 1929 at Ras Shamra (also called Ugarit) yielded a veritable harvest of tablets in various scripts—Babylonian, Egyptian hieroglyphics, and others. One set of tablets, often called Proto-Phoenician because of the alphabetic nature of the script, is remarkably close to biblical Hebrew; moreover, psalmlike poems were found which contain phrases and lines found also in Psalms. The pottery at Ras Shamra and other considerations establish a date between 1475 and 1350 B.C. for the Ras Shamra tablets, a good three hundred years before the time of David.

Since we have seen that archaeology informs us both about civilizations in general and, through inscriptions, about particular events, it will be useful to mention briefly some of the more significant archaeological discoveries, before assessing the present relationship of archaeology and biblical studies.

Modern Near Eastern archaeology is often said to begin with Napoleon, one of whose officers found a stone in 1799 at Rosetta in Egypt. The Rosetta Stone was in three languages, ancient Egyptian hieroglyphics, a later Egyptian script and language known as Demotic, and Greek. On the hunch that the same content was common to the three scripts and languages, a Frenchman named Champollion was able, with help, to decipher the Egyptian (1822). Since then the immense abundance of Egyptian hieroglyphics has been read, studied, analyzed, and catalogued. Hieroglyphics are midway between picture and letter/word (alphabet) writing.

The other ancient civilization, that of the Mesopotamian regions, used not hieroglyphics but wedge-shaped (cuneiform) indentations made on soft clay tablets that were subsequently hardened by baking. In 1835 an Englishman, Henry C. Rawlinson, discovered a great rock on a peak near Behistun, in Persia (Behistun is near where ancient Ecbatana lay). The inscription on the almost inaccessible rock was in cuneiform. Rawlinson managed to make the dangerous climb and to copy the inscription. Before that time there had been sporadic efforts, attended by little success, to decipher cuneiform. Rawlinson first managed to decipher that portion which was in ancient Persian, and about ten years later he translated the other two languages in the inscription. One of these was Median; the other was Babylonian. The inscription dealt with a rebellion against Darius I, which was efficiently crushed by the monarch. Subsequent discoveries disclosed that picture-writing was the ancestor of cuneiform; speed in writing was gained by reducing the pictures into lines that were represented by wedges.

As with Egyptian, the key had been found to a progressive decipherment of inscription after inscription, as these came more to light. In 1854 a huge collection of tablets (known as the Library of Asshurbanipal) was discovered. Among them was a story of creation somewhat similar to that in Genesis (though the Babylonian account was polytheistic) deciphered in 1872. In the same year the Gilgamesh Epic was deciphered; it told a story of a great flood, with both striking similarities to and differences from the story of Noah.

In 1901 the discovery of the Code of Hammurabi not only yielded countless parallels to the legal requirements in the Pentateuch, but also led to some extravagant conclusions. Thus, Amraphel, king of Shinar (Genesis 14) was promptly identified with Hammurabi, an identification that subsequently was abandoned. But, going even further, some scholars assumed that everything in Scripture was derived from Babylonia; moreover, the implied absence of any originality in Scripture showed that the Hebrew heritage was inferior to the Babylonian achievements, and that the Tanak was therefore dispensable. This "Pan-Babylonianism" is no longer taken seriously. The Hebrew legal codes are judged to owe a debt to a source common to the Semitic world rather than specifically to the code of Hammurabi.

Two important discoveries emerged from Egypt. First, in 1887 some three hundred clay tablets, in cuneiform and not in hieroglyphics, were found at Tel el Amarna. They were the letters sent by petty kings of Palestinian cities to the capital el Amarna, about one hundred and seventy-seven miles south of where Cairo is today.

In the letters of Abdi-Hiba of Jerusalem, mention is made of the *Ḥabiru* who are ravaging the area; these *Ḥabiru* are also mentioned in inscriptions found in 1927–9 at Nuzi in Iraq. The word *Habiru* [1] is phonetically akin to the word '*Ibri* (Hebrew), and many, though not all, scholars identify the two.[2] Hence the mention of the *Ḥabiru* may be the oldest mention of the Hebrews.

Second, there were discovered in 1903 the papyri of a Jewish military colony, or more precisely, a mercenary colony in the service of the Persians, at Elephantine in Egypt. These Aramaic papyri come from the end of the fifth pre-Christian century. The complete silence of Scripture about this colony underlines how little we know of the history of the postexilic period. The Elephantine papyri throw virtually no light at all on biblical literature, or on the historical events in Palestine in the Persian period. Their value lies in the introduction they give us to the existence of deviant aspects of Judaism, a subject of great importance in the early Christian period. There was a temple at Elephantine where animal sacrifices were performed; the usual assumption was that after the time of Josiah's Reformation (621) sacrifices were offered only in Jerusalem.

Reverting to Palestinian finds, the Ras Shamra discovery, like that at Elephantine, was a result of finds made by neighborhood farmers rather than of direct excavations. After a farmer had discovered some tablets, the excavations at Ras Shamra were made. The Ras Shamra tablets are possibly the most important of all archaeological discoveries for Tanak studies. They are more important for purely biblical studies than the major discoveries at Boghaz-Koi, Turkey, in 1906, of an immense library of Hittite tablets, through which Hittite was deciphered.

The Ras Shamra tablets are also more important than the Dead Sea Scrolls, found in a cave in 1946. These Scrolls constitute the great exaggeration in the history of archaeology, and the responsibility for the distortion of their worth rests not only on journalists but on the uncontrolled enthusiasm of some archaeologists. Several previous discoveries had been greeted by exaggerated statements of their importance to biblical studies; hence the fantastic claims prematurely made for the Scrolls brought to the surface certain latent reservations about and hostility to archaeology on the part of some biblical scholars. Even more remarkable than the Scrolls themselves was the "Battle of the Scrolls" which scholars waged. Indeed some

[1] See above, page 356.
[2] See Nelson Glueck, "The Bible and Archaeology," in *Five Essays on the Bible*, New York, 1960. All the essays are worth reading.

scholars, on both sides, crawled out so far on a limb that they have not yet had time to crawl back. Some opinions adopted too quickly are still being held too tenaciously. Certain documents found among the Scrolls (The Manual of Discipline, The War of the Sons of Light) reflected a "sectarian group"; these documents received the greatest notoriety, for it was believed, on preposterous evidence, that this sect (supposedly the Essenes) had some *direct* connection with the origins of Christianity. Sobriety, however, is gradually being achieved about the significance of the sectarian documents.

Objectively, the Scrolls are a very important find, especially a full scroll and a partial one of Isaiah, and the countless fragments, recovered from many caves, of verses from almost every book of the Tanak. Previous to the discovery of the Scrolls, the oldest extant Hebrew manuscript of the Tanak came from about A.D. 900; the Isaiah scrolls and the fragments give us manuscript portions about a thousand years older. Some nineteenth-century scholars believed that the Hebrew text had undergone drastic and deliberate alteration at the hands of Jews, and that the Greek translation was a more reliable text than the traditional Hebrew one. The Scrolls refute this opinion and vindicate the relatively high reliability of the traditional Hebrew. Moreover, the Scrolls, especially the fragments, help us to understand the reasons for some of the differences between the Hebrew and the Greek. The Scrolls must therefore be regarded as a find of utmost importance, despite the lamentable, extreme statements made about them.

To this very brief summary two items should be added, selected from countless others, as the immediate prelude to an assessment of archaeology and the Bible. The Mesha Stone, discovered in 1868, relates the victory of King Mesha of Moab over Omri of Israel, and bears some relationship to II Kings 3:4-27. Though there are minor problems connected with it, one might say that the Mesha Stone confirms the account in Kings.

II Kings 20:20 and II Chronicles 32:30 relate that King Hezekiah made a pool and a conduit to bring water into Jerusalem. The second discovery is the so-called Siloam inscription, found in 1880 in a tunnel in Jerusalem. The inscription describes the way in which the tunnel had been bored. In 1909-11, archaeologists cleared through the various tunnels on the west and southwest side of Jerusalem. Though the Siloam inscription does not mention Hezekiah, the clearing of the tunnels makes it clearly credible that Scripture is right in attributing some project connected with the water supply to Hezekiah. In the one case, we have an unmistakable mention of King Omri; in the other, we have a sufficiently great likelihood that the inscription deals with Hezekiah to silence suspicion.

Nineteenth-century biblical scholars, especially those influenced by the Graf-Wellhausen hypothesis, tended to be suspicious of the direct statements of Scripture; to oversimplify, they considered most documents late, and all of them extravagantly and falsely glorifying the past. Archaeology has refuted such skeptical scholars.

The Graf-Wellhausenites were interested in the analysis of the literature of Scripture, and we may call them "literary critics." The literary critics and the archaeologists have often clashed in modern times in their interpretation of some passage in Scripture. This may best be illustrated by an example. Genesis 14 relates that five kings of the Sodom area rebelled against four eastern kings. In the ensuing battle, Lot, the nephew of Abraham, was captured. Thereupon Abraham mustered three hundred and eighteen men of his own household, defeated the eastern kings, and released Lot. Most literary critics have considered Genesis 14 to be a late midrash. Archaeologists, on the other hand, have stressed the surprisingly accurate knowledge of early Babylonian history. The four eastern kings have as yet not been identified, nor has any knowledge of them been recovered, but since conquests or else invasions of this type are known to have taken place, some archaeologists have concluded that Genesis 14 is based on historical facts.

A moment's thought discloses here a failure of minds to meet. Granted that the events of invasion and war conform to historical realities, the issue is whether the account of Abraham's decisive defeat of these great kings with so small a force is historical or legendary. It is the general picture alone that archaeology bears out, and not the specific victory by Abraham. A late writer might well have used an ancient historical account as the basis for a legend glorifying Abraham.

The failure of minds to meet is further illustrated by the so-called documentary theory of J, E, D, and P, which the literary critics have espoused. (My own reservations about the validity of such source analysis are found above, pages 36off.) Now both literary critics and even the most conservative of those archeologists who use the resources of the historical approach agree that many documents, such as the P code, were compiled at a relatively late time. Three generations ago, literary critics may have been, and often were, guilty of attributing the total content of a document to its late moment of recording; today literary critics and archaeologists unite in regarding the content of late documents as including very ancient material.

If one stresses the lateness of the compilation of a document to the point of ignoring the antiquity of much of the content, as did the early literary critics, then one may inadvertently distort what is in Scripture. If one stresses the antiquity of the content to the point of ignoring the implication of the editorial process, as some archaeologists have done, this can be a distortion, too. Much of the continuing debate is the result of diverse emphases. Differences of judgment, of course, are inevitable, both within the group of literary analysts and within the assembly of archaeologists. But it should become evident that the mature Bible scholar must combine a knowledge of both archaeology and literary criticism.

What does archaeology confirm in the Bible? It never confirms the faith in the Bible, nor that distillation of convictions which in the aggregate represents *to biblical authors* the truth of the Bible. Their contention that God is disclosed in the events of history is beyond confirmation or denial either by archaeologists or by literary critics.

The archaeologist has not yet found proof of the enslavement of the Hebrews in Egypt. Suppose he were to find confirming inscriptions. Would these prove, as the Bible contends, that it was God Who brought the Hebrews out of Egypt? Archaeology can recover civilizations; it can find the traces of natural events, such as the Exodus, or the Conquest, or the establishment of the Temple, or the Babylonian exile. It can confirm or contradict historical statements in the Bible, but it scarcely touches on that which is most important in the Bible, that is, the faith in God possessed by the biblical writers.

Appendix II

THE SACRED CALENDAR
AND THE PRIESTHOOD

IN VIRTUALLY all religions the ritual ceremonies and the conceptions underlying them are derived from natural phenomena; seasonal growth and death of vegetation inevitably come to be used, and as the sun and the moon help man reckon when these occasions occur, they too enter into primitive man's religious outlook. Since year after year the growth and death of vegetation and the movements of sun and moon are repeated, it is understandable that the practice of annual observances has developed.

In an agricultural civilization (and without respect to Scripture) there could be various devices by which to fix the time for some particular observance. Today, for example, we use months (a word derived from moon), so that Independence Day comes on July 4. Also, we have the four seasons, spring, summer, fall, and winter, dependent on the sun. However, Labor Day is the first Monday in September, Election Day the first Tuesday after the first Monday in November, and Thanksgiving the fourth Thursday in the same month. Moreover, leap year once in every four years so adjusts our calendar that July 4 always comes in summer, and Christmas in winter.

In light of the various ways of dating recurrent observances today, we should not be surprised at the variety in the Bible, and that at different times different types of calendars existed. A given festival may appear in one biblical calendar but not in another, or a festival may appear under two different names in two calendars. As the change in the name would indicate, the festivals underwent development and reinterpretation. Certain ancient festivals became obsolete, while certain other ones seem to have been established in relatively recent times. The clue to the existence of different calendars in Scripture comes primarily from I Kings 6:*1*, *37–8*, and 8:*2*. In these passages an ancient mode of dating Solomon's acts in dedicating the Temple is equated with dating methods prevalent in the later time of the compiler of Kings. "In the month of *Ziv*, which is the fourth month . . . In the month of *Bul* which is the eighth month . . . In the month of *Ethanim*, which is the seventh month." We can see from this that the ancient months of Solomon's time bore names, while the newer practice was to number them. With this evidence as introduction we turn now to examine the results of scholarly investigation of the Sacred Calendars.

The most ancient calendar used in Israel was a solar one, that is, the reckoning was done exclusively by the sun. The divisions were seasons, not months. The apparent movements of the sun (for it is the earth, of course, which revolves around the sun) fix the beginning and end of each season. On December 21 the sun, at dawn in the east, is at the furthermost southern part of its apparent north-south-north motion. After December 21, the sun moves northward, as it would be plotted on a map at dawn in the east, until June 21. At this latter date the sun has reached its furthermost northern position. From June 21 to December 21 it moves southward again as plotted at dawn in the east. On June 21 and December 21 the sun seems to stop and "*stand*"; the summer solstice ("standing of the sun") is June 21, the winter solstice December 21.

In its northward movement after December 21, the sun reaches the due east point (thereby being directly on the equator) about March 21. In its southward movement it reaches due east on September 21. When the sun is due east, day and night are of the same length, and hence we speak of the "equinox." That is to say, the year can be divided into four equal parts by the apparent movements of the sun. Solstice and equinox were natural occasions for festivals. The winter solstice festival is recalled today by two relatively new holidays, the Jewish Hanukkah and Christmas.

Both spring and fall equinoxes were festival dates more important than the solstices. Since vegetation came to life in the spring, the spring equinox naturally became the time of the festival that ushered in the new year. The festival of Matzoth ("unleavened cakes") was originally a seven-day observance, which culminated in the New Year. The revival of vegetation signalized the revival (ressurrection) of the god. The grain of the previous year had to be burnt up and some of the new grain quickly harvested, ground, and baked into cakes. The haste involved meant that the dough could not leaven. One greeted the resurrected god by eating the grain which was ripe upon his revival, after one had previously destroyed the remnants of the old year's crop. The seven days prior to the "equinox-new year" were spent in lamenting the death of the old god. Temples were built with an east-west orientation so that at dawn on the equinoctial day, with the eastern gates of the temple opened, the sun shone directly through the temple without casting a shadow. The first ray of the rising sun symbolized the resurrection of the deity, supposedly brought about by the lamentations and rites of mourning of the days preceding the equinox. At this equinoctial sunrise, sacred fire was believed to descend and to kindle the fire on the altar of the temple. The festival of the fall equinox was a harvest thanksgiving, signalized by crops being brought to propitiate the god. The oldest scriptural name is *asif,* the festival of the "in-gathering."

But even while this primitive solar calendar was still in use, there existed a different way of dividing the year, one vestige of which is found in Scripture. The solar year of three hundred and sixty-five days was divided into seven periods of fifty days, with a seven-day "Matzoth" and an eight-day spring harvest festival both added to the three hundred and fifty days. The latter festival is called Pentecost[1] because it comes fifty days after Matzoth. It was a harvest of first-fruits. Scripture gives us only vestiges of these two ancient calendars. They were superseded for the simple reason that they were bound up with solar worship and thus with a conception, repugnant to the Hebrews, of the death and resurrection of the god. The Hebrew Yahve was conceived of as eternal.

The Pentateuchal evidence for the solar calendar shows it as already radically modified from the most primitive form. Passover in this modified calendar is found already moved from the equinox day to the full moon in the season of *aviv* ("spring"). (This use of the moon was to be the key to a significant development touched on below.) With Matzoth moved from equinox to full moon, Pentecost was likewise moved, but it retained the same interval of time after Matzoth. Along with the shift of Matzoth from the equinox to a

[1] The term is derived from the Greek word for fifty; as we shall see, the Tanak calls the festival *Shabuoth,* "weeks," dating it as seven weeks after the second day of Matzoth.

spring full moon, the New Year day was shifted from spring to fall. The result of the shift was to de-emphasize the folk belief in a resurrected god. The New Year now fell on the eighth day of the late harvest festival, for the eighth day was the equinox day. We read of the harvest (*asif*) festival as coming at "the turning" of the year (Exod. 24:22) or at the "going out" of the year (Exod. 23:16).

This shift of the New Year to the fall equinox did not completely eliminate the vestiges of solar worship.[2] A more drastic change was needed. Accordingly, a shift was made from the solar calendar to a lunar-solar calendar. What is the difference? In a strictly solar calendar, the year runs three hundred and sixty-five and a quarter days, divided into equal parts, the four seasons. In a lunar-solar calendar, the year runs three hundred and sixty-five and a quarter days, but is divided by the moon. From new moon to new moon is either twenty-nine or thirty days, rather than a completely fixed period. Twelve moons add up to three hundred and fifty-four days. A lunar-solar year has twelve months, but eleven and a quarter days must be taken into account. In a lunar-solar calendar, the retention, as it were, of a July 4 in summer is achieved by a "leap year" device, though not necessarily that of adding a twenty-ninth of February every four years to account for the extra quarter day of each year. Indeed, the Hebrew adjustment for the eleven and a quarter days was made by arranging for seven leap years in a cycle of nineteen years, the leap year consisting of thirteen months instead of twelve.[3]

Since the lunar-solar calendar measured years by the sun, but portions of the year by the moon, "new moon" was an occasion to be observed.

The transition from the solar to the lunar-solar calendar provided a new way to date the festivals. Thus, Matzoth now fell on a particular day of a month rather than at the spring equinox; the New Year fell on the first day of the first fall month rather than on the fall equinox. Initially, the months of the lunar-solar calendar were not named but only numbered one through twelve. The vivid recollection of New Year as a spring occasion prompted the beginning of the numbering with the spring month; the result is the anomaly that the New Year comes on the first day of the *seventh* month in the Jewish lunar-solar calendar.

The next step in the development of the calendar was the sub-

---

[2] The ancient rabbis preserve in a book called the Mishna, Sukkah V, 4, a recollection of solar worship by their ancestors on Sukkoth, as the *asif* came to be known.

[3] Rabbinic literature rather than Scripture is the source of our information about the thirteen-month leap year, still observed in the Jewish calendar.

stitution of names, borrowed from the Babylonians, for numbers. The table that follows begins in the spring:

I	BECAME	Nisan
II		Iyyar
III		Sivan
IV		Tammuz
V		Ab
VI		Elul
VII		Tishri
VIII		Heshvan
IX		Kislev
X		Tebeth
XI		Shebat
XII		Adar

In a leap year, Adar was followed by Adar II. The substitution of names for numbers was part of a slow process; the numbering of months continued side by side with the use of names. Indeed, the introduction of the lunar-solar calendar did not by any means completely blot out the solar calendar, for people continued to use it as late as the first century of the Christian era.[4] In general, the solar calendar dominated virtually to the end of the pre-exilic period. In the late pre-exilic period the lunar-solar calendar, with numbered months, was introduced. In the late postexilic period the practice of naming the months began to supplant numbering.

Today Jews regard Pesaḥ and Matzoth as one and the same observance, commemorating the release from enslavement in Egypt. In the first place, the two were different in origin and significance. Pesaḥ (Passover) was an Israelite pastoral observance, held at full moon; Matzoth was an agricultural festival of Canaanite origin. Because the two occasions came near each other they became blended into one. In the second place, there was a tendency in the Tanak to detach the festivals from their connection with idolatrous practices by attributing to them an origin in some event of Israel's history. Thus, Pesaḥ-Matzoth became the observance of the release from Egypt, and Sukkoth ("booths") a commemoration of the rude lean-to used for encampment by the Hebrews in their flight from Egypt. Though Sukkoth (originally known as *Asif*) preceded the New Year in the solar calendar, it now follows it by two weeks in the lunar-solar calendar.

---

[4] This was long known to us from two quasi-biblical books which were not incorporated into Scripture. See Jubilees 6:23–38 and Enoch 72–5. The Dead Sea community likewise used the old solar calendar.

Though I have spoken of the New Year, this name is rare in the Tanak; the occasion is known rather, as in Lev. 23:24, as "the memorial of the blowing [of the trumpets]." It is only in the third of the three calendars that the Day of Atonement is mentioned. Its origin is obscure.

Although it is undoubtedly ancient, it enters the Hebrew calendar by its present name relatively late. There is evidence to show that there were shifts within the third calendar insofar as it concerned the Day of Atonement. Apparently at one stage the observance practiced on the primitive New Year was shifted to the newly conceived Day of Atonement, but such details need not detain us here.

Rather, we can get some sense of the developments by looking at various calendar formulations. The following list of festivals shows traces of the solar calendar:

	NAME	TIME OBSERVED
1.	Sabbath	Every seventh day
2.	Matzoth	Abib (no date specified), but for seven days
3.	Shabuoth	No date specified; the occasion is the first grain harvest
4.	Asif	At the *cycle* of the year
		[Exod. 34: 18–22]

In the other version of this solar calendar (Exod. 23:14–17) the occasion remains the same, though supplementary information is given. Abib is called a *mo'ed*, "season," as distinct from a month. The name Shabuoth is replaced by *qatzir*, "harvest," but without a specified date. *Asif* comes at the *outgoing* of the year.

Deuteronomy 16:1–8, which departs from the solar calendar, enumerates the festivals more fully, and accompanies the list with more exhortation. The *month* Abib is enjoined to be observed, for in it Yahve brought Israel out of Egypt. No date within the Abib is prescribed for the Pesaḥ; Matzoth is mentioned without a date, as if it were no more than an afterthought to the Pesaḥ. Shabuoth is to be observed seven weeks "after the first putting of the sickle to the grain." That is to say, no exact date for the festival is given, as though the state of the crop determined the occasion (Deut. 16:9–12). Sukkoth is to come at the time of the ingathering of produce from the threshing floor and the wine press (Deut. 16:13–15). Again, no date is specified. The New Year and the Day of Atonement are not mentioned in either the solar calendars or the Deuteronomic formulation.

It is in the Priestly calendar in Leviticus 23:1–8 that the exact prescriptions, absent from the calendars we have just considered, appear. First comes the Sabbath. Next, Pesaḥ is to come on I/14 at twilight, and Matzoth on I/15. Between Passover and Shabuoth there is a period of the "counting of the sheaves" for fifty days (Lev. 23:9–21). This period is to begin, we are told, "on the day after the sabbath." Rabbinic Jews took this phrase to mean that they should begin the counting on the second day of Passover, for they reckoned its first day as an obligatory rest and thus the equivalent of a Sabbath; other Jews began the counting on the Sunday that fell in Passover week. For rabbinic Jews, Shabuoth always falls on Sivan VI; for the ancient dissenters, as well as for their modern spiritual descendants, the "Karaites," Shabuoth always occurs on a Sunday, with its date fortuitously determined by when Pesaḥ begins.[5] The list in this chapter is imprecise only in the case of Shabuoth. Next comes the prescription for the New Year, the "memorial proclaimed with the blowing," specified for VII/1 (Lev. 23:23–5). The Day of Atonement is set on VII/10, in conformity here (Lev. 23:26–32) with the narrative of its supposed inception in the time of Aaron as told in Leviticus 16. Finally, Sukkoth is to occur from VII/15 through VII/22, but with an eighth day added on VII/23 (Lev. 23:33–43).

The Tanak does not provide any comparable calendar of the named months. It is rather from some passages in Zechariah (such as 1:7 and 7:7), Nehemiah (2:1; 6:15), and Esther (2:16; 3:7; 8:9; 9:1) that we learn of the equation of month names with month numbers. This partial information is supplemented in rabbinic literature.[6]

The significance of the calendar development should command our interest, rather than the details. First, we can see a transition from a vague or fluid calendar of festivals to a precise and fixed one. Second, the hortatory material that accompanies the fixed calendar blends together historical antecedent (or the *supposed* historical antecedent) with a prescribed manner of worship from which pagan elements are either removed or, if retained, so adapted as to remove the orgiastic and sexual elements. Third, the introduction of aspects of a new calendar did not completely obliterate the existing calendars.

[5] Until 325 Easter was observed by Christians as the Sunday in Passover week. A new formula freed Christians of dependency on the Jewish Passover for the date of Easter. That formula sets Easter as the first Sunday after the first full moon after the spring equinox. Since Passover begins at full moon, and normally comes after the spring equinox, Easter by coincidence is usually within Passover week. But in some years it is quite far removed from Passover.
[6] Iyyar, Tammuz, Ab, Tishri, and Heshvan are not mentioned in the Tanak; the other seven names do occur.

Fourth, calendar reform was only one aspect of broader religious change and reformation.

The priesthood, somewhat comparably, underwent development and regularization. Judges and Samuel present us with priests (Jonathan ben Gershom in Judges 17–18 and Samuel himself, for example) who did not possess what in later times was the important qualification, namely, proper descent. Leviticus 8 describes the origin of priesthood and assigns it as the prerogative of a single family within the tribe of the Levites, that of Aaron and his descendants.

A dilemma exists for the modern student. Either Judges, Samuel, and Kings present, and even seem to sanction, gross deviations from the Pentateuchal prescription, or the Pentateuchal prescription was a rather late development, anachronistically read back into the Wilderness period. This latter alternative commends itself to scholars. In support of the contention that priesthood became a matter of family descent very late, they show that in the time of Deuteronomy, presumably around 621, priesthood is no longer available to just anybody; but the limitation here is only partial, for according to Deuteronomy, priesthood is the prerogative of the men of the tribe of Levi. Furthermore, the Reformation of Josiah had disqualified the priests of outlying districts and limited the priesthood to Jerusalem priests.

An even sharper limitation than that of Deuteronomy is prescribed in Ezekiel 44:15, to be dated, perhaps, about 540. Here, only the descendants of Zadok are legitimate priests.

This scattered evidence of a progressive limitation on who might be a priest is taken as indicative of the emergence of a regularized priesthood only in the postexilic period. Just as the festivals, even those adapted from the Canaanites, were described as having been enjoined in the Wilderness, so the historicizing tendency read the regularized priesthood back into the Wilderness period.

The term Levite would seem to have had different connotations at different times. In very early days Levi was the name of a tribe that later became extinct. In that period or shortly thereafter the word also meant the same thing as *kohen*, priest.[7] But in postexilic times Levite and Kohen had become distinct; the Kohen was the elite among the Levites, the officiating priest among the temple workers, a distinction

---

[7] See Judges 17:9–10.

found in Chronicles, Ezra, and Nehemiah. The Tanak tells that the ancient tribe of Levi was on a different plane from that of other tribes and therefore not allotted tribal lands, having been set aside for sacred duties (see, especially, Num. 3:3–13 and 40–4; Josh. 13:14, 33). A development took place by which Levi was first the name of a tribe, next a synonym for priest, and thereafter an office subordinate to the priest, recruited from a fictitious tribe of such subordinates.

But a word of caution is necessary. The student must be on guard against attributing deliberate falsehood to those people who, without historical training, felt prompted to read the origins of their living tradition into the remote period which in their eyes was formative. They were guilty only of being incorrect. Moreover, it is the regularized calendar and regularized priesthood that were late in developing. Priesthood itself was very ancient and, to repeat, though the Priestly documents are the youngest to have received their present form, their contents include some of the most ancient materials in Scripture. Yom Kippur is the youngest of the pentateuchal additions to the calendar, but its origin is ancient beyond recovery. The changes and developments in calendar and priesthood occurred for one and only one reason: the religion of Israel was a living religion. Only a dead religion never changes.

Appendix III

THE TANAK IN JUDAISM

THE MOST SIGNIFICANT overlapping of Judaism and Christianity lies in their common possession of the Tanak. Jews have uniformly accepted the sanctity of that body of literature. Many modern students are surprised to learn that there has not been a comparable and unbroken acceptance by Christianity. Indeed, before the literature was finally found acceptable, large and important segments of second-century Christianity debated the validity of the Tanak for Christians. Again in the nineteenth century, there was a renewed insistence that the Old Testament had no significance for Christians. In the next chapter we shall examine this ambivalent attitude of Christianity. For the moment, we must understand only that the Jewish and Christian approach to this same collection of literature is not and has not been the same.

In the history of Judaism, the Tanak was continuously accepted as divinely revealed sacred literature. Moreover, for Jews it represented not only a sacred literature, but also a national, indeed a folk, literature. Without a doubt the affection of the Jews for the Tanak allowed them to overlook the bare quality of portions of the writings. Their attitude has been: the Tanak is ours; it is wonderful, and we love it.

Furthermore, until very recent times, Jews chanted or sang the

Tanak; they did not simply read or recite it. The intonations in the human voice gave a constantly living character to the words. When a Jew sang Lamentations on the feast of Tisha be-Ab (the ninth day of Ab) to commemorate the destruction of the Temple, the tearfulness of the melody underscored the lament of the lines. When on the holiday of "The Rejoicing in the Torah," he marched around the synagogue proudly carrying the scrolls, pausing to let those in the pews kiss the Torah cover, he was expressing a genuine joy.

Specific injunctions in the Tanak, echoed in post-biblical literature, effected an almost complete identification on the part of the Jew of later times with his ancestor of biblical times. The Book of Deuteronomy had portrayed the Deity as saying at Horeb/Sinai, "It is not only with you who stand before me this day that I make this covenant, . . . but also with the [unborn] who is as yet not before me." And when the book stated, "The words of the scroll of Torah must never disappear from your mouth," the Jew of later times took this injunction to apply as strongly to him as to the fortunate generation to whom the words were spoken. Those Psalms that recite the history of Israel made the reader feel that he too had had a share in the details of that history. The Jew applied to himself the statement, "God brought *us* out of Egypt with a mighty hand and an outstretched arm." The Jew experienced the journey of Abraham from Ur into Canaan and of Joseph into Egypt; he groaned in the slavery endured there, and exulted in the release into freedom. With Moses he stood on Sinai, with David he conquered Goliath, and with Solomon he built the Temple. Assyria's assault on the northern kingdom was an assault on him. When persecution embittered his life in Europe, he felt most keenly that he was undergoing the pangs of the Babylonian exile.

A phrase from Psalms summarized the Jew's relationship to the Tanak: "It is a tree of life to those who grasp it, and happy are they who rely upon it." That which is a privilege to carry is never a burden to bear. To be a Jew meant the welcome responsibility of *noblesse oblige*. In all of the innumerable pieces of post-biblical Jewish literature, there is not one single echo of Paul's negative attitude (see below, pp. 538ff). For the Torah, the Jew endured a frequent and bloody martyrdom without complaint.

The principle—axiomatic to the Jew—that the Torah was God's word which he loved, gave rise to certain indirect or even direct conflicts. The Torah obliged him to visit Jerusalem three times a year; but if he had joined the far-flung dispersion of the Jews in Athens or in Rome, such frequent pilgrimages were difficult. He was obliged to pay a half-shekel to maintain the Temple in Jerusalem; he was also under mandate to bring animal sacrifices to be offered there. But what could he do when the Romans destroyed the Temple in 70? In short, the very fact that there was a Scripture created an array of anomalies.

In the first place, the legal sections of Scripture are not entirely specific about matters that, in normal human experience, require the specific. To illustrate by an example, Scripture prohibits labor on the Sabbath. Jews naturally assented that men should not labor on the Sabbath. But what are the human activities that may be reasonably classed as labor? Scripture does not specify. The task of defining just what constituted labor was undertaken by rabbinic Judaism. Is carrying a burden labor? We would all admit that there are times when it is. Therefore, a clarification of what Scripture means in prohibiting labor on the Sabbath could include the specification that one must not carry a burden. But then the next question could be, what constitutes a burden? Four heavy suitcases? Two big boxes of books? A package weighing six ounces? Is the weight the deciding element, or is the prohibition a general and all-inclusive one against carrying any burden, no matter how light or how heavy?

Clarification of Scripture by the rabbis led to the need for the clarification of the clarification, and in turn to the clarification of the further clarification. Does the third stage of clarification retain an overt connection with Scripture, or did the connection tend to disappear? Could not one say, I will obey what is in Scripture, but unless a requirement is explicit, I will not obey it? But such a line of reasoning is, in effect, an argument against the principle of clarification itself.

That is to say, if it could be agreed that clarification of legal requirements was necessary, such clarification led to the growth and observance of nonbiblical laws. However, even in the post-biblical period, there were accepters and rejecters of such clarification. There was no true final authority in Judaism to decide whether legislation could or could not be added to Scripture.

The proponents of adding particulars developed a kind of philosophical justification for their additions. They began by recognizing that their added particulars were not literally in Scripture. But they came to feel that an experience such as the written revelation to Moses must necessarily have been complemented by an oral revelation. In fact, Jews developed the idea that there had been two simultaneous revelations at Sinai; one was the written Torah and the other was the oral Torah. This oral Torah had been transmitted verbally from generation to generation, so that when a person of a late age set forth some clarification of a Scriptural law, he was not giving his own opinion, but only retelling what had been revealed to Moses at Sinai.

Clarification by authoritative interpretation is characteristic of every religious community which has a bible. In post-biblical Judaism, the literalists, or the opponents of clarification, were the Sadducees; the proponents were the Pharisees.

Especially prior to the debacle of A.D. 70, when both the Temple and the kingship came to an end, the Sadducees represented the court, the priesthood, and the upper classes. Previously, Palestine had been subjected to strong Greek influence. (331 B.C. was the year of the Greek conquest.) Greek words, schools, and temples had dotted the land. In 63 B.C., when Rome extended its sway over Palestine, there was no decline in Greek culture in favor of Roman, for the Romans in the east had thoroughly Hellenized themselves. The Judean rulers, to whom Rome granted only a limited measure of independence, were the foremost in conforming themselves to Greek culture. They carried the court and the nobility along with them in a headlong dash to out-Greek the Greeks. The royal dynasty from 165 to 37 B.C. was the Hasmonean family, who rose to the throne after the forebears had successfully led a revolt, in 168, against the Antiochene Greeks. The rebels had fought in protest against the wish of the Antiochenes to coerce Jews into Greek ways; the offspring, having come to wear royal garb, voluntarily embraced what their fathers had gone to war to oppose.

The Greek influence, especially appealing to the upper classes, became a kind of rival of the Jewish environment. A Jew from such an upper stratum found that Greek culture was pulling at him; against this pull was the Jewish religion, with its continuing capacity to elicit good measures of loyalty. The upper-class Jew could remain loyal, to the Temple at Jerusalem in particular. As Greeks too had temples, it was not outlandish for Jews to have them; moreover, the Temple was presided over and operated by members of the upper classes.

The Temple was an ongoing, functioning institution. Its authority, of course, lay in the Scripture which had prescribed it. But the Temple could function without a need for the people constantly to refer to Scripture. An analogy might be drawn with Roman Catholicism. Here is a functioning Church, staffed with officials, possessed of a ritual, and basing its claims on a Scripture— but the Church need not utilize that Scripture in the day to day life of its lay communicants. A Roman Catholic is under many obligations, but to be proficient in Scripture has never been one of these. The

Church as an institution is in theory quite enough. Perhaps the analogy clarifies my intent; a Jew of the upper classes could find the Temple adequate for his religious needs, yet feel no urgency to steep himself in Scripture. The Sadducees were Temple-centered, not Scripture-centered.

The cultural levels in the population added to the differences between the two groups. Among the middle and lower classes, Greek civilization penetrated the native Semitic culture only superficially. Folk culture included the imported folkways (and superstitions) of the Babylonians, Phoenicians, Persians, and others. Thus there arose, out of Persian influence, the conception that a person, after death, could or would be restored to life by being raised from the grave. "Resurrection," in a word, was a motif frequent among Jews of the middle and lower classes.

Greek thought never countenanced resurrection. Even when Christianity spread into the Greek world, with its central contention that the Christ Jesus had been "resurrected," the Greeks defined "resurrection" in such a way as to divest it of its meaning. Resurrection means that after death has occurred the individual is restored to life.

To cultured Greeks, a belief in resurrection was nonsense. To Grecianized Jews, resurrection was similarly nonsense and the Sadducees rejected it. The Pharisees affirmed it.

To settle the issue, an appeal was made to Scripture. As our survey of the biblical writings has disclosed, resurrection is never expressed in the Pentateuch, and very seldom outside it. Indeed, the few passages that express resurrection are outnumbered by passages that plainly deny it. The affirming Pharisees were unable to cite from the Pentateuch a single clear statement of resurrection, but their skill in interpretation satisfied at least them. They "proved" resurrection by contending that a verse in Scripture did express it. This proof rests on a subtlety of Hebrew syntax, and though I give it here, I have little hope of its transference into English. According to a peculiarity of Hebrew grammar, two conjunctions, *az* ("then") and *terem* ("before"), use the imperfect tense to express past action. Normally the imperfect has an affinity to the future. Exodus 15:1 relates that the Egyptians were drowned in the Red Sea. *Then* (here is our conjunction *az*) Moses and the children of Israel will sing this song. The *will sing* alludes to the age of the resurrection, say the rabbis. They conclude that thereby resurrection is proved from Scripture.

I am sure that many an intelligent reader will find himself mystified rather than edified by the proof. An equally bizarre "proof" occurs in the Gospels. There it is related[1] that Sadducees ask Jesus to "prove" resurrection to them. Jesus responds by citing Scripture, in which the phrase "God of Abraham, Isaac and Jacob" occurs. Jesus is portrayed as arguing that as God is the God of the living, not of the dead, therefore, Abraham, Isaac, and Jacob cannot really be dead. *Ergo,* resurrection is "proved." In both these proofs, we have a double contention. It is asserted that resurrection is a reasonable belief, and it is asserted that Scripture proves it. The quarrel[2] between the Sadducees and the Pharisees involved the second assertion as much as the first. This difficult material on resurrection is relevant to our discussion because the basic issue between the Pharisees and the Sadducees concerned the larger topic of whether or not Scripture could be interpreted. If it can, resurrection is not too hard to find; if it cannot, resurrection will scarcely appear. To the Sadducees, the "oral Torah" was an illegitimate addition to a Scripture which they regarded as sufficient. To the Pharisees, Scripture begged for expounding; the "oral Torah" was the indispensable and legitimate exposition.

The destruction in 70 meant that the Temple which Scripture prescribed was no longer functioning. Moreover, royalty and the priests, the guardians of the Temple, no longer had anything to cling to. The year 70 marks the end of Sadduceeism, and of their particular literalism. With the eradication of the Temple and its priesthood, Judaism turned to Scripture as if to the sole primacy. Fortunately for the survival of Judaism, there had been decades and even centuries of unconscious preparation for the catastrophe.

The historic significance of Pharisaism in Judaism lies in the preparatory steps which it fostered, not because of some glimpse of future necessity, but by its very nature. Pharisaism began and developed as that segment of Judaism which more than any other apotheosized Scripture. As the Tanak was in Hebrew, Hebrew had to be studied, much as a Roman Catholic priest has to study Latin. (In the sixth century, as we have said, Aramaic, a cousin of Hebrew, began to replace Hebrew as the spoken language.) Comprehension rested

---

[1] See note 2 below for the references.

[2] I use the word deliberately. The Gospels (Mark 12:18–27; Matthew 22:23–33; Luke 20:27–38) present a controversy on resurrection between the Sadducees and Jesus which illumines the content and tone of the exchanges. The question from the Sadducean side concerns a woman who married a succession of seven brothers when one died right after the other. Let Jesus tell them, they say, to which of the seven she is to belong at resurrection time. In retort Jesus avoids the question, asserting that at resurrection time there is no marriage. Many commentators have noted the affinity here of Jesus with the Pharisees.

on the ability to translate; reliable translation necessitated reliable scholarship. That person who in early Pharisaic times (100 B.C.) was expert and reliable in Scripture was known as a "scribe"; in late Pharisaic times (A.D. 70), he bore the title "rabbi." The best attestation to the vigor and creativity of the Pharisees is the partisanship in the Gospel denunciations of them. The student who wants to assess the reliability of what Christian Scripture says about the Pharisees should begin by reading what Catholics and Protestants said about each other in the comparably controversial sixteenth century (and too often still say today).

The rabbi was the Scriptural expert. Authority lay not in him, but in Scripture. He possessed authority only insofar as his competent learning in Scripture was recognized. This competency he displayed in his exposition of Scripture in the synagogue.

The practice among many Jews in our day of speaking of their synagogue as a temple, as though the terms were interchangeable, tends to conceal the striking, even decisive differences between the Temple and the ancient synagogue. The Temple was the scene of animal sacrifices, presided over by priests, in conformity with specific Scriptural requirements. There is no mention in Scripture of the synagogue, for the synagogue emerged into importance in the period after the Bible. Although the time and occasion of the emergence of the synagogue is obscure, it is a universally acknowledged fact that synagogue and rabbi were at hand to perpetuate Judaism when Temple and priest ceased to function.

Originally the word synagogue did not mean an edifice, but only an "act of gathering." Hence, one could hold a synagogue in one's house. The gathering was not designed as a period of prayer. Rather, it was a gathering for study. The subject was Scripture; the instructor was the rabbi. The lowest level of instruction was that of mere translation, of understanding in Aramaic what Scripture said in Hebrew. Thereafter, one could probe for the intention of the text, and, in pursuit of clarification, expound it. The Hebrew term for "expounding" is *midrash;* literally, it means "seeking out" the intention. The post-biblical period has bequeathed to the modern age an abundance of expositions, known as The Midrash.

When in the synagogue, the rabbi expounded what Scripture meant by the prohibition of labor on the Sabbath, his act of exposition was almost equivalent to the act of legislating. (Similarly, in our day, our Supreme Court issues clarifications of law which are in effect legislation. Integration, as segregationists correctly point out, stems from the judicial, not the legislative branch of the government.) Rabbinic exposition amounted to rabbinic law, and rabbinic law was declared to have been revealed orally to Moses at Sinai.

When the early rabbi became a local judge as well as a synagogue expositor, judiciary legislation made its added contribution to the growing body of law. The impulse of clarifying Scripture, first felt among the Pharisees, developed into rabbinic law. When, in 70, Sadducees and other groups disappeared, the term Pharisees likewise disappeared, for Pharisaism alone of the various groupings survived as the equivalent of Judaism. We can define rabbinic Judaism as that stage of Pharisaism which developed when no other version of Judaism existed.

The clarification and consequent extension of Scriptural law is the process that characterizes and identifies rabbinic Judaism. The axiom was that Scripture needed to be obeyed; the corollary was that derived and secondary laws were the means of obeying Scripture. Jews were aware of the difference between Scriptural law and rabbinic law. While they insisted that both needed equally scrupulous observance, they classified Scriptural law as essentially more important. Indeed, they created a device that led to the development of even more rabbinic law.

They called this important device the *siyyag la-torah*, the fence around the Torah. It amounted to legislating on a secondary level to insure that the primary level would not be violated. Families with children do this all the time. The mother who wants her child not to play in the street will forbid him to play on the sidewalk and confine him to the yard. The fence around the Torah alludes to rabbinic laws which were created to insure that Scriptural laws would not be transgressed. Thus, an apple that has fallen to the ground may not be eaten on the Sabbath, lest the person who picks it up proceed to pluck another from the tree; plucking is prohibited because it is labor and Scripture prohibits labor. The fence around the Torah emphasizes the Jewish conviction that Scripture is divine law and divine law must be obeyed.

Christian critics of Judaism often assess this "legalistic" tendency in Judaism not on its merits or its context, but in terms of the attitude and doctrine of Paul. The great apostle was convinced that religious righteousness was a matter of communion with God, not of observing legal requirements. Having noted that laws are first introduced in Exodus, the second book of Scripture, he chose Abraham who figures in Genesis, the first book, as his example of the righteous man. Paul went on to declare that laws which had first entered Judaism through Moses, now could leave Judaism through the coming of the Christ. In Paul's mind, legalism was the wrong way to attain religious righteousness.

One who is conditioned by Paul is apt to approach Judaism with condescension. He will thus be blind to affirmative aspects of legalism, and totally blind to the existence of a comparable legalism which inevitably arises in all Christian sects of any size and age. There are two widespread errors concerning Jewish legalism. The first is the supposition by Christians that Jews assess the laws much as Paul did, yet observe them anyway. The fact is that while Paul attributed the laws to Moses, Jews attribute them to God. There is a formula which Jews have recited while performing the injunctions. It states: Praised are You, O Lord our God, king of the universe, Who has sanctified us by His commandments and decreed upon us to --------. The blank is filled in with the words describing the action of the occasion: to wash the hands, to eat unleavened bread, or to kindle Sabbath candles. Jews saw in the commandments evidence of God's will and sanctification. Paul saw sin and death in them. In order to understand the Jewish attitude to Jewish laws, the Christian must divest himself of Paul's bias (and the extensions of that bias after Paul's time).

The second error is one of perspective. Imagine someone writing the cultural history of the United States, who restricts his sources to the constitution, codes, and statutes of the federal government. In failing to use non-legal literature, he would know about Mark Twain only if legal literature mentioned him, about Eugene O'Neill only if O'Neill figured in some lawsuit, and about folk tunes only if they entered into some litigation. There are on record alleged descriptions of Judaism which have shunned using the devotional, exhortatory, and philosophic literature of Judaism. Out of such reckless procedures have emerged fantastic conclusions such as these: Judaism is a dry, arid legalism, devoid of warmth and heart; Judaism stresses the mechanical aspects of religion, not the promptings of the heart; Judaism has no room for mysticism and has produced no mystics.

Such accusations are partisan arrogance, not accurate scholarship. Jews historically have used a thick prayer book, in which the Book of Psalms—hardly an arid and dry collection of verse—has figured prominently. The point is, of course, that although Judaism has had its legislation, it has never been only a legalism! (And, as indicated, Christianity has had its legal systems too.)

Our topic is the Tanak in Judaism; hence, we have seen how Pentateuchal law developed into that religion called Rabbinic Judaism.

The eminence of Torah in the synagogue is the natural eminence of the core of a curriculum in a school. Down to our own day, Jews have called the synagogue by the Yiddish [3] word *shul;* in German the word appears as *Schule;* in English it is *school.* In Judaism it was a short step from study to prayer.

The Tanak was read in the synagogue worship. The Pentateuch was divided into weekly readings. Some Jews used an arrangement enabling the whole Pentateuch to be read in a cycle of three years; the custom which triumphed enables the reading to be accomplished in one year. As was mentioned previously, the worship period includes a reading from the Prophets or Hagiographa, selected on the basis of some community of content with the Pentateuchal portion. The use of the Tanak in the worship services simply meant that that which was studied in the class room was used devotionally in prayers.

The Pentateuch in the synagogue is preserved in parchment scrolls and kept in a shrine (called the "sacred ark") on the pulpit. A synagogue is so constructed that the Torah shrine occupies the central place in the sight and attention of the worshiper.

As we saw, Pentateuchal law does not distinguish, as we do, between secular law (we say civil law) and sacred law (we say church law). Rabbinic Judaism likewise made no distinction. As a result, the ancient rabbi was obligated to be as much of an authority on real estate law, inheritance law, and the formation and dissolution of partnerships as on what constitutes a proper fast, and what is piety toward parents!

Only when the ghetto walls fell, at the time of the American and French revolutions, did Jews make the transition from life under rabbinic law to life under civil law. Then, the large segments of Jewish law which had been superseded began to fall into disuse. Disuse became the equivalent of abrogation. Today many Jews are unaware that Pentateuchal and Rabbinic law comprise a constitution and set of statutes which once pervaded all of Jewish life.

The modern rabbi, unlike his forerunner of two thousand years ago, is the honored functionary in a synagogue, rather than the expert in Torah and its exposition. The ancient rabbis could not offer animal sacrifices, but they studied how to do so in preparation for the time when the Temple might be rebuilt. They saw impracticability, but never irrelevancy in much of Scripture's requirements. On the other hand, modern Jews, except for the extraordinarily Orthodox, often see irrelevance as well as impracticability in Scriptural requirements. Yet Torah is still central to Jewish worship, however modified

---

[3] A dialect primarily German, though written in the Hebrew alphabet.

Judaism has become, and however much of the literal has become a whisper rather than the full voice.

Rabbinic Judaism, characterized by synagogue, rabbi, Scripture, and prayer, is a type of religion notably different from Pentateuch religion, marked by Temple, priest, prayer, and animal sacrifices. Midrash clarified Scripture, but it also added to it, and, especially it produced changes in it. Midrash used the Tanak as the text, but often its meaning became wondrously altered. Until the disruptive modern times, the Tanak, as interpreted by the rabbis, was Judaism. Until modern times, they clung to it in unbroken love and unbroken fidelity. The Tanak produced Rabbinic Judaism; Judaism, in turn, apotheosized the Tanak.

Appendix IV

THE TANAK
IN CHRISTIANITY

CHRISTIANITY was born in Judaism, as a movement by and for Jews. By the year 60 it welcomed so many Gentiles that it ceased to be entirely Jewish. After the year 70 the Jewish portion of the faith gradually withered away so that by 150 Christianity became completely Gentile.

Early Christianity set forth certain contentions about the character of Jesus the Christ and about the significance of events in his career. These contentions were buttressed by an appeal to the Tanak and by citations from it. Respecting the death (an atoning death) and resurrection, Paul says that the Christ died *according to the Scriptures* and rose *according to the Scriptures*. In the Gospel According to Matthew, there are many, many passages which assert that verses from the Tanak have been fulfilled by incidents from the career of Jesus. The virgin birth (1:22–3) fulfills Isaiah 7:14 (see above, pp. 87ff.); the summoning of Jesus from Egypt (2:15) fulfills Hosea 11:1, and so on with great frequency. When Luke (4:24–30) presents the incident of Jesus in the synagogue at Nazareth, he portrays Jesus as saying, "This day Scripture is fulfilled in me."

For the first hundred years of Christianity, Scripture for Christians was the Tanak. There was as yet no Christian Scripture. Christian *writings* already existed (several Gospels and the Epistles, especially of Paul), but by definition Sacred Scripture represents a special selection gathered out of a larger literature. We read in II Peter, written about 150, that certain irresponsible people distort the Epistles of Paul *as they do all Scripture*. The Epistles of Paul were written about 50; thus, a hundred years later they appear to have begun to achieve the status of Scripture. Shortly after 150, the canon of the Christian Scripture began to emerge.

During the century from 50 to 150, Christian contentions could appeal to the teachings which, rightly or wrongly, had been attributed to Jesus. But when Scripture was to be cited, that Scripture was Tanak, for until the Christian canon was formed, early Christianity's only Scripture was the Tanak. This was the Greek rather than the Hebrew version but still the Tanak.

Why did Christianity gather its own Scripture? In part, because the issue, what is Scripture, agitates any group which achieves a sense of its own individuality within an older tradition. Thus, the Church of Jesus Christ of the Latter Day Saints, popularly known as Mormons, has added to Old and New Testament the Book of Mormon. Thus, too, Protestants in the sixteenth century declared that the correct and approved list of sacred books in the Tanak was that found in the Hebrew Bible, not the larger list found in the Greek version. Martin Luther did not consider Esther, James, and Revelation worthy of being canonical. Accordingly, the issue of canon tends to arise universally when a new and challenging movement emerges in a historic tradition.[1] Yet, in the case of Christianity's emergence out of Judaism, the prevailing circumstances produced divergent attitudes.

The influence of Paul largely accounts for these divergences. Even though Paul's attitude is well known, it seems to produce both confusion and misunderstanding. Hence it needs to be clarified, even to the point of explaining the obvious. As Paul was a Jew, the Tanak was, of course, his possession and pride. But Paul found, as all students must, a puzzling problem in the Pentateuch. Beginning in Exodus 12, in the period of Moses, long and elaborate legal prescriptions appear. In Genesis and in Exodus 1–11, there are virtually no legal requirements; narrative about the patriarchs, Abraham, Isaac,

---

[1] In the history of later Judaism, the canon of the Tanak was not questioned. The rabbinic literature (principally the Talmud) achieved a position of what might be called secondary canonization. This high eminence of the rabbinic literature was repudiated by the Karaites ("Scripturists") in the eighth century and challenged, on different bases, by Reform Judaism in the nineteenth century.

Jacob and Joseph, is the substance of Genesis. The student could well question the relationship of the early patriarchs who lived before Moses to those laws introduced, as Scripture relates, only in the relatively late time of Moses. In rabbinic literature, the sages "solved" the problem by declaring that the patriarchs had observed the Mosaic laws even prior to their promulgation.

Paul's solution was a totally different one. He contended that the patriarchs achieved the objectives of religious obligation without the need of laws. The recent coming of the Christ, he contended again, provided the opportunity, as in Abraham's time, to achieve the religious objective without recourse to the laws of Moses. Therefore Moses' laws were to be understood as having been introduced after the age of the patriarchs, and to have been abrogated, as unnecessary, in the new age of the Christ. The Mosaic laws, then, were valid only for the interval stretching from the time of Moses until the time of Paul.

From Paul's standpoint, the "interval" nature of the laws made them deficient in some respects; on the other hand, their presence in the Tanak gave them certain assets. They did, for example, have a utility for the immature. In one passage Paul speaks of them as a tutor, that is, as a restraint to the young; in another he likens them to a jailer. In some of his Epistles, however, as for example in Romans, Paul in one paragraph asserts the usefulness of the laws and in the next their deficiency. This type of argument sometimes loses the modern reader.

Moreover, Paul complicates his argument of the "pros" and "cons" by his ultimate contention. Properly understood, Paul does not ask whether the laws are worthy or unworthy. (He would have answered stoutly and resoundingly, "they are worthy.") Rather, the question for Paul is this: which is the better means for attaining the religious objective? Are laws the better way? Or is personal commitment, personal illumination by the Holy Spirit the better way? More specifically, will a man abstain from murder more readily because of a personal commitment to total righteousness than because of a piece of legislation against murder specifically? Will he refrain more easily from stealing because he adheres to a general set of principles than because he is required specifically not to steal?

Paul believed that if the basic attitude of men were correct, then their conduct would be proper. He never questioned that righteous living was desirable for and incumbent upon men, but he believed that righteousness was to be achieved not by laws, but by spiritual conviction. In Paul's view, the laws of Moses were a faulty way to bring men to righteousness. Specific legislation, by the mere mention of the prohibited deeds, actually prompted men to do them; men might not have sinned if the sins had not been mentioned.

Therefore, Paul could declare that the Mosaic laws were abrogated, and still hold as tenaciously as ever to his belief that the Tanak was a divine book. He had turned his back not on Scripture but on the laws contained in Scripture.

It is worthwhile to pause here to notice that the programs of Paul and the rabbis were directly antithetical. The rabbis, persuaded that the laws of Moses were divine and eternal, spun out refinements of and additions to the laws; Paul, persuaded that the validity of the laws was transitory, declared that the time had come when the laws were not needed, and hence they were abrogated.

Many modern students misunderstand Paul's attitude toward Scripture in the same way that some segments of the early Church misunderstood him. In the first place, the largest part of the initial part of Scripture, the Pentateuch, is legal. His turning away from this initial part was misunderstood as his rejection of the whole Tanak. In the second place, Greek Jews, including Paul, called the Pentateuch by the Greek word, *Nomos,* Law. (Jews call it either Torah, Revelation, or Humash, Five Books.) Paul turned away from laws, not from The Law. Yet his doing so was an invitation to misunderstand. There are those today, as there was a segment in the early Church, who have believed that the Tanak has been set aside.

Although in his own lifetime, or, more probably, afterwards, Paul overwhelmingly influenced the early Church, it did not, and could not, follow Paul in everything. It did not follow him in his opposition to marriage. It could not follow him completely in the matter of the abrogation of the laws. Too many people could, and did, infer from Paul's argument that men's conduct was of no concern. Despite Paul's intent, his annulment of the laws against murder, or adultery, or rape, was an invitation to men to commit these crimes. Such misinterpreters are spoken of in the New Testament as "the licentious."

In the second century, through interpreters accepted as authoritative, the Church presented an emendation of Paul's attitude. It was declared that only the ceremonial laws of Moses were abrogated; the moral laws were still valid. Ceremonial laws included those of the Sacred Calendar, food laws, animal sacrifice, and ritual acts. Moral laws, such as the Ten Commandments, were deemed still applicable, and an integral part of Christianity. Had the Church followed Paul slavishly, it could not have apotheosized the Ten Commandments.

Though Paul was undeviatingly attached to the Tanak, his attack on the laws of Moses bequeathed to the Church an ambivalence toward the work. One and the same person could have both an attachment to the Tanak and reservations about it. One community in the Church could be loyal to it; another community, prone to cast it off.

Moreover, when the Church had matured sufficiently to recognize its individuality as an entity different from Judaism, the Church faced the problem of defining its relationship to the Judaism from which it had emerged. This problem was rendered even more acute by the Church's need to relate itself both to its maternal ancestor Judaism and to the Jews of the period.

Jews and Christians alike proclaimed themselves to be the heir to the ancient Judaism. Jews could and did contend that they were the descendants of Abraham, Isaac, and Jacob. Christians, by now predominantly Gentile, asserted that the true descent was not the physical one ("God can raise descendants of Abraham out of these stones"; Matt. 3:9; Luke 3:8), but the spiritual descent. The Jews, so Christians argued, had been rejected by God, so that now Christians were His elect. Second-century Christians despised the Jews of their day, but at the same time considered themselves to be the legatees of the promises divinely made to the ancient Jews.

We may perhaps ascribe to Christendom in the second century three different attitudes toward the ancient Judaism. The first of these is summarized in the expression *Verus Israel*, that is to say, "Christianity is the *true* Israel." No longer Jews but Christians represent the unbroken continuation of that community with its succession of great teachers such as Abraham, Solomon, Amos, and Jeremiah. In this view there was direct continuity from ancient Judaism into Christendom; the Torah had simply changed into the Gospel. (This view is found in the New Testament in Luke-Acts, two works by the same hand.) There were two main peoples in the world—Gentiles on the one hand—and Israel on the other.

The second view is not greatly at variance with the first. However, it divided mankind into three divisions, or "races": Gentiles, Jews, and the "third race" (*tertium genus*). The primary intent of the second view was to distinguish Christians from Jews, a distinction which is not difficult to understand if one will read the devastating attacks on Jews in the polemical ("warlike") literature of the time.[2]

The third view was quite different, and needs a more lengthy

[2] A good many such tracts have survived. A typical title was *Adversus Judaeos* (*Against the Jews*). This partisan literature is devoid of charity or generosity. It can be downright ugly, as in the case of Chrysostom (fourth century) or it can be genteel (Justin's *Dialogue with Trypho the Jew*). That Jews retorted in kind is to be inferred; however, no Jewish anti-Christian tracts have survived except a mocking "gospel," *Toledoth Yeshu* ("The History of Jesus"). Some pagan attacks, preserved by the Church Fathers who quote portions in order to refute them, may have utilized Jewish arguments.

exposition. This view is typified by a man, either of eminence or notoriety, named Marcion. This man emerged to importance in the middle of the second century. The movement which he led came near to capturing the entire Church. When opposition to him arose in Christendom, he was repudiated by the majority of the Church, though his movement lasted on for at least two hundred years.

Marcion is known to us only through quotations which were used by his opponents, principally Tertullian, to refute him. (In an age in which the tone of literature was seldom generous,[3] we cannot be sure how fairly and accurately Tertullian reflects Marcion.) In brief, there are three charges laid against Marcion. The first attributes to him a belief in wrong and false doctrines. Marcion is classified as a "Gnostic," a term of reproach used by the Church Fathers for a heterogeneous sequence of "heretics." A gnostic was "one who knew." What did he know? Presumably, he knew the way to God, through personal illumination, or philosophy, or revelation. A characteristic common to those denounced as gnostics was an extreme "dualism." This view attributed evil to anything material, or physical, and good only to immaterial things. In dualism, the Christ, as a spirit, was immaterial. If, as Christianity held, the spirit Christ had become incarnate as the man Jesus, was not the man Jesus material? Gnostics denied that the Christ had become Jesus, and that Jesus had been truly a man. Within the framework of Gnostic views, there was the opinion that Jesus was only an "apparition"; he only seemed to be human. We call this unorthodox view by the Greek word for *seem*, or Docetism.

The danger to Church contentions in dualism in general and docetism in particular is that these concepts tended to assert that the birth, death, and resurrection of Jesus were not real occurrences, rooted in history. Instead, these events were only mythical representations, accommodated to the way in which men were accustomed to speak, but describing a spirit which never altered from being a spirit. When in the creeds, we find the statement that Christ "was crucified under Pontius Pilate," we are told that this is part of the central and necessary belief that the events truly happened. "Doubting Thomas," in John 20:26–9, must touch Jesus physically.[4] This anecdote appears in a passage designed to deny the assertions of the Gnostics.

---

[3] One can best assess the anti-Jewish writings by seeing how equally uncharitable are the Christian apologists in their attitudes toward pagans, towards the "classical culture" of Greece, and in the tone used in intra-Christian disputations. Pagans used the same tone towards Christians.

[4] Modern Christians often dispute about whether or not Jesus was *divine*, trinitarians affirming that he was, and unitarians that he was not. The ancient dispute, however, was whether or not Jesus was *human*.

Marcion, then, was a Gnostic and an extreme dualist. Now if a Gnostic "knew," he needed neither Church regulation and practice to guide him, nor authorized Church leaders to direct him. Hence, Gnostics were a disruptive force. Moreover, if personal illumination guided them, their conduct would appear to others to be licentious and wicked. Also, since only the spirit (or the soul) was important, the action of the body was of no consequence to them. Marcion and his followers were accused of immorality.

The second charge against Marcion grows out of his Gnosticism, and relates directly to the Tanak. In the Gnostic scheme of things God, in order to be God, must have no contact with anything material. The world is material. God Himself then could not have been in contact with it to create it. Instead, He must have created a creator (the Gnostics called him the "demiurge") who did the work of creation. When one recollects that Genesis 1 relates, in the first place, that God (and not some demiurge) had created the world, and in the second place, that the refrain "God saw, and it was good" occurs repeatedly, one sees the double basis on which a Marcion could charge that Genesis was a pack of lies which should be discarded.

In proposing that Christianity should jettison this false Scripture, Marcion was, in effect, proposing that Christianity should cut itself off from its Jewish antecedents. This application of his attitude marks it as the antithesis of the previous two views we have considered, especially that of *Verus Israel.*

The third charge against Marcion involved an intra-Christian concern. It was averred that the improper views and improper conduct which characterized his movement were being justified by an appeal to certain writings by Christians which Marcion had assembled. Again the charge is a double one. Marcion was accused, in the first place, of having assembled a small collection of writings (only four of the dozen or so Epistles of Paul, and only one Gospel, presumably that According to Luke) and, in the second place, of having tampered with these works so as to provide the Marcionites with confirming quotations from relatively well-known writings.

The Church reply to Marcion took several forms. He and his followers were denounced as heretics. Marcion's act of assembling four Epistles and one Gospel can be considered the earliest selective collection of Christian writings. In response, the central Church embarked on what it considered a more judicious selection. The result was that the Church recognized four Gospels, not just one, and twelve Epistles, not just four, by, or attributed to Paul. The Church acknowledged other early Christian leaders by extending recognition to two Epistles attributed to Peter, one to James, and three to John. In effect, the response to Marcion was no less than the creation of the canon of what came to be called the New Testament.

The central Church rejected Marcion's effort to cut Christianity off from its Jewish antecedents. It set the newly assembled collection of Christian writings alongside the Tanak. It gave the latter the name of Old Covenant, since it dealt with the Jews—until the eighteenth-century "Testament" was a synonym for "covenant"—and called the younger collection New Covenant. *It regarded the two as being continuous and as constituting one single Bible.* 175 can be given as a convenient date for this development.

In accepting Tanak as an integral part of its Sacred Scripture, Christianity was in the paradoxical position of ascribing canonical importance to the Pentateuch, the ceremonial laws which it no longer considered binding. While the Church generally clung tenaciously to the conviction that Tanak was Scripture, the emphasis was naturally on the New Covenant. Certain marginal groups were to appear, especially after the rise of Protestantism, which so emphasized the New at the expense of the Old that for such groups the Tanak virtually ceased to exist. Moreover, in New Testament scholarship a certain tendency arose which devoted itself to interpreting the origin of Christianity so as to see in the movement something totally at variance with Judaism. This was a Marcion-like attitude, though it appeared in the nineteenth century. It rested on the premise—at which the Church Fathers would have been aghast—that there was no bond of continuity between Judaism and Christianity. This unsound "scholarship" contrasted, for example, an alleged God of awe and terror in the Tanak, with a kindly and loving God in the New Testament. By extending the contrast so that the God of the Tanak became one of total negative qualities (no aspect of these, of course, appearing in the New Testament), a travesty on the contents of the Tanak resulted. Similarly, the rabbinic literature was used *selectively,* and out of excerpts inexactly translated, to demonstrate the spiritual impoverishment of Judaism, as against the spiritual abundance of Christianity.[5]

This irresponsible New Testament scholarship was unexpectedly bolstered about 1890 by a curious development. Archaeological discoveries had yielded countless cuneiform inscriptions, and the language having been deciphered, the contents of the inscriptions became available to Tanak scholars. As we have seen passingly (pp. 512ff.), there are many, many points of contact between Baby-

[5] For a full bill of particulars, written by a Christian, see George Foote Moore: "Christian Writers on Judaism," *Harvard Theological Review,* 1921, pp. 197–254.

lonian literature and culture and the Old Testament. A knowledge of the Babylonian language, which like Hebrew is a Semitic tongue, clarifies many Tanak passages which would otherwise remain obscure. Babylonian religious practices often throw great light on practices described in the Tanak.

For one scholar,[6] and for his followers, anything good in the Tanak was derivative from the Babylonians; the Tanak was in reality, so they contended, a quite useless collection of writings which Christians would do well to cast aside. The battle lines were promptly drawn, and the "pan-Babylonians" found themselves confronted by both Bible scholars (perhaps limited in their knowledge of Babylonian) and cuneiform scholars fully as eminent as the pan-Babylonians. The end was a Christian reaffirmation of the Tanak as part of the Christian Sacred Scripture. The pan-Babylonian matter turned out to be a tempest in a teapot, so that it is by now of scarcely any significance.

The random American Pentecostal sects which seem unaware that Tanak is part of Christian Scripture are neither numerous nor widely influential. They are worthy of notice only in order to underscore the contention that there is latent in Christianity, because of its paradoxical attitude to the Five Books of Moses, an opposition to or disdain for the Old Testament. Therefore, this marginal attitude can be expected to appear from time to time.[7]

It is countered by the overwhelmingly affirmative attitude of most of Christendom. The Puritan Fathers, for example, looked to the Pentateuch as containing a constitution to govern them; at such times interest in the Tanak has been revived.

Such is the case today, especially in theological circles; Old and New Testament are deemed so bound together as to constitute an unbreakable unity. Hitler's assault on the Jews was infinitely more noticeable, but not less vigorous than his assault on Christianity—on Christianity, not on Christians. Nazi writings described Christianity, correctly, as a Judaism; curiously, other Nazis came to the remarkable conclusion that Jesus was not a Jew, but an acceptable Aryan. In the Christian response to Nazism, the Jewish origin of Christianity was not only admitted, but was affirmatively proclaimed,

[6] The chief exponent of this view was Friedrich Delitzsch, in his *Bibel und Babel*. A good account of the pan-Babylonian school is found in Emil Kraeling, *The Old Testament since the Reformation*, pp. 149–63.

[7] See G. Ernest Wright: *God Who Acts: Biblical Theology as Recital* (Chicago: Alec R. Allenson, Inc.; 1952) "The Church's Need of the Old Testament, p. 29: ". . . The misuse and disuse of the Old Testament have deprived the Church of its Bible. The New Testament is not itself a Bible."

as by Cardinal Faulhaber, the well-known Catholic prelate.[8] As a by-product, the unbroken unity of Old and New Testaments as the Christian Bible was reasserted.

In the theological efforts to describe the character of the "un-broken" unity, a certain misguided zeal has led all too frequently to untenable generalizations, and, indeed, to assertions of unity which ignore some crucial facts. Among the facts ignored is the diversity of viewpoint unmistakable both within the Old Testament and within the New. The accumulated scholarship of the past century and a half is too often willfully pushed aside as either unnecessary or incon-venient. Sober study has often given way to capricious "proof-texting," this in the process of making the Old Testament into a direct and deliberate precursor of the New—as though the Torah were in no way a possession of Jews.

Lamentable as it is for its disregard of sober scholarship, this theological tendency does emphasize that the main lines of Christian thought continue to regard the Tanak as a permanent portion of Christian Scripture. It is, of course, quite as legitimate for Christians to view the Tanak through the prism of the New Testament as for Jews to view it through that of rabbinic literature. But it is necessary to distinguish between the pristine sense of the Tanak, and what the Tanak came to mean in either rabbinic or New Testament literature.

Although Christianity reflects a sporadic ambivalence towards the Tanak, in its main-streams it has accorded it and still accords it a rightful place within its Scripture. The contrast between the Jewish view of the Tanak can be oversimplified in the following way: Chris-tianity regards the Tanak as superseded but sacred, while Judaism regards it as sacred and unsuperseded.

[8] Courageous Christians in Nazi Germany quoted John 4:22: "Salvation is from the Jews."

A Selected Bibliography

THE LIST given below is very incomplete. The scholarly monograph and the essay in the professional journal go unmentioned; so, too, the materials, indeed sometimes the basic studies, in foreign languages. This list, then, is for the beginning student.

Certain tools are basic: the encyclopedia, the commentary, and the atlas. Respecting encyclopedias, two major ones in English are now over a half-century old, and hence must be used with caution. *Dictionary of the Bible,* edited by James Hastings (New York: Charles Scribner's Sons; 1903–4), is marked by a greater degree of religious conservatism than is *Encyclopedia Biblica,* edited by T. K. Cheyne and J. S. Black (New York: The Macmillan Co.; 1899–1903). The index volume to the former makes it somewhat more usable than the latter. Both seem designed more for the professional scholar than for the usual reader, so that there may be more immediate benefit in certain one-volume encyclopedias, such as *Harper's Bible Dictionary,* edited by M. S. and J. L. Miller (New York: Harper & Brothers; 1952).

The *Interpreter's Bible Dictionary* is at this time (1962) in its final stages of preparation. The first major Bible encyclopedia in English in over a half-century, it may well replace the two mentioned in the preceding paragraph. Judging from the instructions given to those of us who are contributors, the *Interpreter's Bible Dictionary* will be able to satisfy both the usual reader and also the scholar. This encyclopedia has developed from the *Interpreter's Bible* (12 vols.; New York: Abingdon Press; 1956), an admirable enterprise. The text of Scripture is given in both the King James and the Revised Standard Version in parallel columns. The text is accompanied both by an exposition and by suggestions for the use of the material in preaching. Since each book is treated in detail in *Interpreter's Bible,* it is unnecessary to refer to these except to say that the treatment is always good and reliable and occasionally rises to great heights of achievement. Especially in the case of the minor prophets, the *Interpreter's Bible* is either superior to anything else in English, or else is the only reference that would merit listing here. Hence the whole series is mentioned here, as well as in connection with the individual books. While the quality varies from Scriptural book to book, since the authorship varies, in general the exposition is reliable and clear. Volume I contains some broad introductory summaries of fine clarity.

A series of commentaries, usually allocating a full volume to each Biblical book, has become a standard reference in English: *The International Critical Commentary*, known among scholars as *ICC* (New York: Charles Scribner's Sons). The series is not yet completed, even though some of the individual volumes were published before the turn of the century. The *ICC* is much more detailed than the *Interpreter's Bible* and contains many more technicalities. The passing of time has made many of the volumes out of date. A good plan for the serious student who can handle the foreign languages found in *ICC* is to use the *ICC* as a basic work, but to supplement it with the *Interpreter's Bible*. The new *Oxford Annotated Bible* (New York: Oxford University Press; 1962) is the most usable Bible I know; its text is the Revised Standard Version, and its notes are brief but generally excellent.

An uncompleted series, begun in 1945, *Soncino Books of the Bible*, edited by Abraham Cohen (14 vols.; London: Soncino Press; 1945–52) reflects well both the great strengths and also the weaknesses, unperceived by the editors, in undeviating fidelity to tradition.

There are one-volume commentaries available, such as *Commentary on the Holy Bible* by J. R. Dummelow (New York: The Macmillan Co.; 1909) and the *Abingdon Bible Commentary* by Frederick Carl Eiselen *et al.* (New York: Abingdon Press; 1911), but these are of limited utility. The student is advised to use the *Interpreter's Bible*, rather than such series as the *Expositor's Bible*, edited by W. Robertson Nicoll (28 vols.; New York: A. C. Armstrong & Son; 1887–97), or the *Cambridge Bible for Schools and Colleges* (Cambridge: Cambridge University Press), each represented by a series of volumes.

As for an atlas, I have found Herbert G. May, *The Oxford Bible Atlas* (New York: Oxford University Press; 1962) more useful than G. Ernest Wright and Floyd V. Filson, *The Westminster Historical Atlas to the Bible* (Philadelphia: Westminster Press; 1956).

Samuel R. Driver, *An Introduction to the Literature of the Old Testament* (New York: Charles Scribner's Sons; 1891) and countless other editions, including paperback, is highly useful, especially for the analysis of the contents of Scriptural books. Robert H. Pfeiffer,

Introduction to the Old Testament (New York: Harper & Brothers; 1948), also in paperback, is much newer and contains chapters on the text and canon. But his book is distinctly a handbook for the advanced student, and by no means fluent reading for the beginner. To the professional scholar these books are indispensable; to the beginner they may well be useless.

James A. Muilenberg, "The History of the Religion of Israel," *Interpreter's Bible,* I, pp. 292–348, is an essay of high merit and superior, though briefer, to W. O. E. Oesterley, *The Hebrew Religion* (New York: The Macmillan Co.; 1937); G. Ernest Wright, "The Faith of Israel," *Interpreter's Bible,* I, pp. 349–89, is, in Wright's own words (p. 388), "partial and unsatisfactory."

The best book on text, canon, and the ancient translations is Bleddyn J. Roberts, *The Old Testament Text and Versions* (Cardiff: University of Wales Press; 1951), but the book is scarcely for the beginner. He might use two little books by Max L. Margolis, *The Hebrew Scriptures in the Making* (Philadelphia: Jewish Publication Society of America; 1922) and *The Story of the Bible Translations* (Philadelphia: Jewish Publication Society of America; 1917).

Two fine books, and one of indifferent value, can apprise the student of present-day approaches in the scientific study. *Record and Revelation,* edited by H. Wheeler Robinson (Oxford: Oxford University Press; 1938) and *The Old Testament and Modern Study,* edited by H. H. Rowley (Oxford: Oxford University Press; 1952) contain fine summaries arranged in topical categories by outstanding scholars on the state of research. Herbert F. Hahn, *Old Testament in Modern Research* (Philadelphia: Muhlenberg Press; 1954) is better suited to the beginner.

Books on archaeology are mentioned below. Here attention can be drawn to James B. Pritchard's fine *The Ancient Near East in Pictures* (Princeton: Princeton University Press; 1955) and *Ancient Near Eastern Texts Relating to the Old Testament,* rev. ed. (Princeton: Princeton University Press; 1955). The two titles have been abridged and published as one volume, *The Ancient Near East: An Anthology of Text and Pictures* (Princeton: Princeton University Press; 1958).

What has been for many years the standard history of the Biblical period in English is W. O. E. Oesterley and Theodore H. Robinson's *A History of Israel* (2 vols.; Oxford: Oxford University Press; 1932). Fortunately, Martin Noth's book has been translated from German, under the title, *The History of Israel* (New York: Harper & Brothers; 1958). A much more conservative book, considerably less to my liking, is John Bright, *A History of Israel* (Philadelphia: Westminster Press; 1959). Bright's treatment of the patriarchal age seems to be unduly weighted on the side of tradition and to reflect no discernible methodology.

James George Frazer, *The Folk-Lore in the Old Testament* (3 vols.; New York: The Macmillan Co.; 1919), often regarded as a classic, is as apt to mislead as to guide a student, for parallels are piled up and uncritically applied.

The question of Hebrew poetry is too complex for simple treatment, so that relevant bibliography for the beginner is elusive. An older book, the Schweich Lectures of 1910, may perhaps be used. It is George Adam Smith, *The Early Poetry of Israel* (London: British Academy; 1912).

The prophets present us with an embarrassment of riches. My own conviction is that the origins and early history of prophecy—from the beginnings to Amos—cannot be recovered. Two efforts are worth looking into: W. Robertson Smith, *The Prophets of Israel* (New York: The Macmillan Co.; 1882) and a fine, sober study, R. B. Y. Scott, *The Relevance of the Prophets* (New York: The Macmillan Co.; 1944). A very good exposition is James Philip Hyatt, *Prophetic Religion* (New York: Abingdon Press; 1947).

Rolland E. Wolfe, *Meet Amos and Hosea* (New York: Harper & Brothers; 1945), is good for beginners. Nothing else in English is as fine as Julian Morgenstern, *Amos Studies* (Cincinnati: Union of American Hebrew Congregations; 1941), but it is scarcely for beginners. No work in English on Hosea compares with the work of the Swede, H. S. Nyberg, *Studien zum Hoseabuche* (Uppsala: Lundequistka; 1935).

There are many studies on First Isaiah. The beginner may find Sheldon Blank, *Prophetic Faith in Isaiah* (New York: Harper & Brothers; 1958), rough going, but it is rewarding. George Adam Smith, *The Book of Isaiah*, rev. ed. (New York: Harper & Brothers; 1928) has many virtues.

With Jeremiah, again, we face the availability of an enormous amount of literature. Adam C. Welch, *Jeremiah: His Time and Work* (Oxford: Oxford University Press; 1928), is a good book for the student to begin with. He might then proceed to George Adam Smith, *Jeremiah* (New York: George H. Doran Company; 1923). James Philip Hyatt is the author of "Jeremiah" in *Interpreter's Bible*, V, pp. 776–1142; this is the best treatment of any prophet in the *Interpreter's Bible*. Of this fine treatment Hyatt has fortunately provided a much less technical version in *Jeremiah: Prophet of Courage and Hope* (New York: Abingdon Press; 1958).

For Ezekiel, one should rather warn the student which books to avoid than suggest which to consult. Only after he has mastered Ezekiel should he consult C. C. Torrey, *Pseudo–Ezekiel and the Original Prophecy* (New Haven: Yale University Press; 1930), for Torrey's theory is an extreme one (holding that the book comes from the Greek period). So, too, the beginner should defer (though not avoid) William A. Irwin, *The Problem of Ezekiel* (Chicago: University of Chicago Press; 1943).

The view presented above on Second Isaiah is derived, with changes, from Julian Morgenstern, *The Message of Deutero–Isaiah in its Sequential Unfolding* (Cincinnati: University Publishers, Inc.; 1961), a book beyond the beginner. Nowhere else in Scripture are viewpoints quite as sharply varied and mutually contradictory as in Second Isaiah. Many, perhaps most, scholars distinguish (as I see no reason to) between Second Isaiah and the Servant and also (here I agree) the Suffering Servant. There is no short cut to mastering Isaiah 40–66; the student should never let the text become subordinate to the scholarly theories; yet the text has those phenomena which breed the theories. I find a great deal with which to differ in the treatment by James A. Muilenberg in *Interpreter's Bible*, V, pp. 381–773, yet there is a fairmindedness that commends the treatment to the progressing student.

A summary of scholarship on Psalms is reflected in Elmer A. Leslie, *The Psalms* (New York: Abingdon Press; 1949); here the student restricted to English can discover the results of European research. A book useful to the beginner is W. O. E. Oesterley, *A Fresh Approach to the Psalms* (New York: The Macmillan Co.; 1937).

Emil G. Kraeling, *The Book of the Ways of God* (New York: Charles Scribner's Sons; 1939) can be commended to the beginner. Samuel L. Terrien, *Job: Poet of Existence* (Indianapolis: The Bobbs–Merrill Company, Inc.; 1957) may perhaps be too elementary; however, his work on Job in *Interpreter's Bible* is excellent. S. R. Driver in *ICC* puts his technical notes in one volume and the expository in another; the latter could be used to tremendous advantage by a serious student.

For Ecclesiastes, the recent work of Robert Gordis, *Koheleth: The Man and His World* (New York: Jewish Theological Seminary of America; 1951), is a good treatment. In *Interpreter's Bible* the exegesis is by Oliver S. Rankin, who has written a fine volume originating as the Kerr Lectures, *Israel's Wisdom Literature* (London: T. and T. Clark; 1936).

I am not enthusiastic about Theophile J. Meek's exegesis of Song of Songs in *Interpreter's Bible*, V, pp. 89–148, but I am about

Robert Gordis, *The Song of Songs* (New York: Jewish Theological Seminary of America; 1954).

For Daniel, I have seen nothing in English to vie for a student's attention with the exegesis by Arthur Jeffery in *Interpreter's Bible*, VI, pp. 341–549; but I fear that it may be a bit too technical for the usual beginner.

On the historical and narrative books there is a scarcity of treatment in English, especially on historiography. The books cited above by Noth and Bright are to be noted. The history of the Higher Criticism of the Pentateuch is found in Pfeiffer, *op. cit.*, and in *Interpreter's Bible*, I, pp. 127–41, where Samuel Terrien provides an admirable outline. A thin but readable volume is Ernest Trattner, *Unraveling the Book of Books* (New York: Charles Scribner's Sons; 1929); it is outdated, however. The standard work of a half-century ago reflecting technique of source analysis is J. Estlin Carpenter and G. Harford, *The Composition of the Hexateuch* (London and New York: Longmans, Green & Co., Inc.; 1902).

In the field of archaeology I list here first three general works arranged in the order, according to my opinion, of their utility to students: Jack Finegan, *Light from the Ancient Past* (Princeton: Princeton University Press; 1959); Millar Burrows, *What Mean These Stones?* (New Haven: American Schools of Oriental Research; 1941); George A. Barton, *Archaeology and the Bible* (Philadelphia: American Sunday School Union; 1925). Special works are William Foxwell Albright, *The Archaeology of Palestine* (London: Penguin Books Inc.; 1954); and Nelson Glueck, *The River Jordan* (Philadelphia: Westminster Press; 1946) and *Rivers in the Desert; A History of the Negev* (Philadelphia: Farrar, Straus & Cudahy, Inc.; 1959). Special attention is invited to a series, *Views of the Biblical World* (New York and Jerusalem: McGraw–Hill Book Co.; 1959–60). Though the series is as yet incomplete, two volumes have appeared, *The Law* and *The Former Prophets*. The text is accompanied by pictures of the areas mentioned, or of archaeological finds related to the text—these in photographs as beautiful as any I have ever seen.

Index of Scriptural Citations

MATTHEW

1:22–23; pp. 88, 537
2:15; p. 537
3:9; p. 541
4:17; p. 219
7:12; p. 391
19:19; p. 391
21:1–5; p. 222
22:23–33; p. 531
26:15; p. 223
27:51; p. 390

MARK

12:18–27; p. 531
15:38; p. 390

LUKE

3:8; p. 541
4:24–30; p. 537
10:18; p. 244
20:27–38; p. 531
23:45; p. 390

JOHN

1:1–3, 14; p. 267
4:22; p. 546
18:36; p. 219
20:26–29; p. 542

ACTS

2:1–4; p. 221

HEBREWS

6:19–20; p. 390
9:3; p. 390
10:19; p. 390

PETER

II; p. 538

REVELATION

12:7–9; p. 244

Subject Index